in pursuit of justice

in pursuit of justice
collected writings 2000–2003

Ralph Nader

SEVEN STORIES PRESS
New York • London • Melbourne • Toronto

A Seven Stories Press First Edition

Seven Stories Press
140 Watts Street
New York, NY 10013
www.sevenstories.com

In Canada: Publishers Group Canada, 250A Carlton Street, Toronto, ON M5A-2L1

In the U.K.: Turnaround Publisher Services Ltd., Unit 3, Olympia Trading Estate, Coburg Road, Wood Green, London N22 6TZ

In Australia: Palgrave Macmillan, 627 Chapel Street, South Yarra VIC 3141

LIBRARY OF CONGRESS CATALOGING-IN-PUBLICATION DATA
Nader, Ralph.
  In pursuit of justice : collected writings 2000-2003 / Ralph Nader. —A seven stories press 1st ed.
  p. cm.
  Includes index.
  ISBN 1-58322-650-8 (hardcover : alk. paper)—ISBN 1-58322-629-X (pbk. : alk. paper)
1. United States—Social policy—1993-2. Social justice—United States. 3. United States—Social conditions-—1980-4. United States—Economic policy—1993-2001. 5. United States—Economic policy—2001- 6. United States—Politics and govern-ment—1993-2001. 7. United States—Politics and government—2001- 8. Corporate power—United States. I. Title.
HN65.N29 2004
361.6'1'0973--dc22
                                            2004013759

College professors may order examination copies of Seven Stories Press titles for a free six-month trial period. To order, visit www.sevenstories.com/textbook/, or fax on school letterhead to (212) 226-1411.

Book design by Jon Gilbert

9 8 7 6 5 4 3 2 1

Printed in Canada

Contents

Introduction

Justice refers to what is fair, equitable, or morally right. *In Pursuit of Justice* consists of more than two hundred of my columns dealing with various aspects of American and international politics, law, economics, and culture. Many of the columns involve a call for justice for consumers, laborers, taxpayers, injured persons, and others who are all too often denied their rights. But these and the other columns are united by a larger theme: America today lacks the quotient of justice it is capable of providing. People and institutions do not occupy the place or perform the function envisioned by our Declaration of Independence or our Constitution, or dictated by the basic principles of democracy and justice.

Our forebears established the government, and chose to delegate its daily operation to our representatives. We are the masters, they are our servants. Their job is to do our bidding and, if they fail to do so adequately, we can and should replace them. As Abraham Lincoln proudly proclaimed at Gettysburg, American government is of the people, by the people, and for the people.

Our nation's founders did not contemplate enormous, artificial entities called corporations awarded by the courts all kinds of constitutional protections. They anticipated a narrower role for business in society: to provide goods and services to consumers.

Unfortunately, the modern corporation has come to infiltrate, and dominate, spheres of society once considered off-limits to commerce: elections, schools, health-care systems, media, prisons, and much more. Corporations subordinate public values to commercial priorities. This subordination is often costly and debilitating—for the environment, communities, workers, consumers, and democracy itself.

The federal and state governments have unfortunately aided and abetted corporate overreach and malfeasance. Campaign cash is a major problem. After they make their contributions, corporations expect their money to buy access, and it does. They expect this access to yield influence, and it does.

In addition, the revolving door between business and government (placing corporate executives in high governmental positions) weakens government's oversight role; a swarm of lobbyists meet privately with politicians and their minions to present public officials with corporate wish-lists; and a corporate-dominated media narrowly defines public debate. The result of all this is a government that does the bidding of corporate America—a government of Texaco, by Enron, and for General Motors.

There's a vicious cycle at work. Corporations dominate our political process. Because of that dominance, legislators enact pro-corporate laws which ensure continued growth of corporations' mega-wealth. The rich then pour dollars into their legislators' campaigns. The rich get richer and richer and the politicians they rent or own get routinely reelected in more and more one-party dominated districts. And the public pays the price.

If we are the masters, and government officials our servants, why do we tolerate them kowtowing to corporations at the expense of the public interest? The answer is, too few know the details and too few believe they have the power to matter. Many don't know the name of their own congressional representative or senator. Half of those eligible to vote don't show up at the polls. Only a small percentage of people become involved in campaigns, petition their officials, attend rallies, or otherwise exercise their civic rights and responsibilities.

Remember, every instance of injustice is tragic because, in Martin Luther King, Jr.,'s apt words, injustice anywhere is a threat to justice everywhere. We should speak up whenever a conscientious whistleblower loses a job, an injured person is excluded from his or her day in court because he or she lacks the resources to challenge the powerful, or a candidate is blocked by tyrannical ballot access laws. But we must also keep sight of the big picture, the fact that these abuses reflect and feed into the larger structural injustices. This book summons us to stand against this broader injustice, to remedy a situation in which major societal institutions fail to perform their proper roles.

The columns in this book include much more than a vigorous protest against corporate abuse and government complicity. Problems must be identified before we can craft solutions. The pages that follow include a good sampling of proposed solutions as well.

This book has no shortage of villains—greedy corporations and self-serving politicians whose private agendas sabotage the public interest. But the book showcases heroes as well. The heroes appear primarily in Section IX, but are also described throughout. They include ordinary people who put a high premium on active citizenship, as well as leaders of the labor, consumer, and other public interest movements; assorted authors; innovators; business people; and a few uncharacteristically brave and visionary public officials.

They all have found a way to do what I urge each of you to do: pursue justice.

I

Corporate Power

I am often asked why corporate abuse is so rampant. After all, corporations are run by human beings. In their lives outside of their powerful executive positions, these people rarely have a history of criminality or antisocial behavior. Why would they make unsafe and unhealthy products, wantonly harm the environment, and even target children in order to create destructive addictions?

There's a relatively simple two-part answer. First, businesses in a capitalist economy seek to maximize profits. In the case of large corporations, these profits can be in the billions, and their quest produces a disciplined, martial concentration. Second, businesses incorporate to avoid personal risk and accountability. As a result of American corporate law, officers of a corporation can engage in the worst kind of misconduct and rarely pay a personal price.

This combination of the prospect of extraordinary profits, and lack of accountability, can bring out the worst in people. It leads otherwise moral people to stretch and break rules and harm innocent persons and behave in ways they would never contemplate if they weren't hiding behind the corporate veil.

But corporations don't make or enforce the public laws. Government officials, supposedly accountable to all the people, the weak as well as the wealthy, should guard against corporate abuse. Unfortunately, corporations control America's political process as much as they control America's economy.

It's no surprise that corporations, with their mega-profits at stake, press government officials to adopt policies that bolster or protect those profits and expand privileges and immunities. It's no surprise that, with their fat checkbooks to dangle before the politicians, these corporations achieve a near stranglehold on government. The obvious solution is political reform to level the playing field and make certain our representatives represent everyone rather than rewarding the highest bidders for their favors.

Columns in this section catalog the rotten fruit of our diseased political process, including the gigantic growth in corporate welfare even as smaller key social welfare programs are cut; the consolidation of monopoly power while antitrust laws are not enforced; and successive waves of corporate crime while Congress looks the other way. We will also see corporate profiteers respond to 9/11 with a disgraceful demand for special treatment and subsidies.

This last phenomenon carries with it bitter irony. The Bush Administration is quick to question the patriotism of anyone who challenges its foreign adventures and war on terror. Yet this is the same administration that coddles corporations, and it is corporations which have been stunningly lacking in patriotic behavior since 9/11. Of course, such behavior is nothing new. Giant corporations have never hesitated to take jobs overseas, exploit tax loopholes, or demand contracts and guarantees without worrying about the effects on the nation.

The columns in this section are not all about deterioration. Corporate malfeasance has produced a backlash. Readers will learn about Fortune *magazine's cover story on white-collar crime, and other improbable sources of outrage. Leading politicians, including a few conservative Republicans, have said enough is enough to corporate tax evaders.*

"War is a Racket"

Perusing a history book as a college student, I came across a jolting declaration in a footnote by one of the most highly decorated soldiers of the twentieth century. He said: "I spent 33 years in the Marines, most of my time being a high-class muscle man for big business, for Wall Street, and the bankers. In short, I was a racketeer for Capitalism."

Those words and more were written by Brigadier General Smedley D. Butler. At the time I wondered why more was not made of this in the historical accounts of the early decades of the twentieth century.

Well, maybe because General Butler's was too much of an eyewitness account. And he named names. Here is more of what he said:

"I helped make Mexico, especially Tampico, safe for American oil interests in 1914. I helped make Haiti and Cuba a decent place for the National City Bank boys to collect revenues in. I helped in the raping of half a dozen Central American republics for the benefit of Wall Street. The record of racketeering is long. I helped purify Nicaragua for the international banking house of Brown Brothers in 1909–1912. I brought light to the Dominican Republic for American sugar interests in 1916. In China I helped to see to it that Standard Oil went its way unmolested."

The famous journalist, Lowell Thomas, saw fit to introduce General Butler's book *War is a Racket* for a Reader's Digest condensation. The general was no pacifist when it came to defending the U.S.A. He just didn't like bullies and corporate greed sending American soldiers abroad to slaughter or be slaughtered.

"War is a racket," Butler wrote, adding: "It always has been. It is possibly the oldest, easily the most profitable, surely the most vicious. It is the only one in which the profits are reckoned in dollars and the losses in lives.

"A racket," he continues, "is best described, I believe, as something that is not what it seems to the majority of people. Only a small "inside" group knows what it is about. It is conducted for the benefit of the very few, at the expense of the very many. Out of war a few people make huge fortunes."

Butler's language was concrete and gripping; it emanated from his personal warring experience, as follows. "How many of these war millionaires shoulder a rifle? How many of them dug a trench? How many of them knew what it meant to go hungry in a rat-infested dugout? How many of them spent sleepless, frightened nights, ducking shells and shrapnel and machine-gun bullets? How many of them were wounded or killed in battle?"

More from Butler. "The general public shoulders the bill. This bill renders a horrible accounting. Newly placed gravestones. Mangled bodies. Shattered minds. Broken hearts and homes. Economic instability. Backbreaking taxation for generations and generations."

Butler devoted a chapter to naming the corporate profiteers. He wrote about the propaganda to make young men "feel ashamed if they didn't join the Army" and how war propaganda was vicious enough that "even God was brought into it."

The decorated marine general recommended a unique way to "smash this racket." Draft the Big Boys first! "Let the officers and the directors and the high-powered executives of our armament factories and our steel companies and our munitions makers and our shipbuilders and the manufacturers of all the other things that provide profit in wartime as well as the banners and the speculators, be conscripted—to get $30 a month, the same wage as the lads in the trenches get." That will take the "profit out of war," he wrote, and render the remaining wars for the defense of country only, when presumably most everyone would be willing to sacrifice together.

General Butler passed away shortly before Pearl Harbor. This year, with the cooperation of the Butler family, *War is a Racket* has been reissued in paperback by the publisher Feral House (P.O. Box 39910, Los Angeles, CA 90039, www.FeralHouse.com), together with photographs of lasting impressions from the 1932 camera records of "war's gruesome glories" in the book *The Horror of It*. For $9.95 per copy, it gives today's reader more than just a sense of deja vu.

Times have changed and so has the technology of war. But the chicken hawks in Washington, led by Bush and Cheney, are disregarding the advice of many battle-tested officers, retired generals and admirals, diplomats and intelligence officials. Instead, they are enlarging their imperial designs, with the oil and other corporate moguls alongside, that Smedley Butler highlighted decades ago.

In 1937, Butler asked, "Why don't those damned oil companies fly their own flags on their personal property—maybe a flag with a gas pump on it." Today's reply might say, why should they when they can continue to use the American flag.

December 27, 2003

American Enterprise Institute (AEI)—Out of Touch

The American Enterprise Institute (AEI) has a problem. It is loaded with corporate money, full of rich fellowships for Washington, D.C. influence peddlers, masquerading as conservatives, who wallow in plush offices figuring out how to assure that big corporations rule the United States and the rest of the world.

During the past twenty-two years, the AEI, their nearby corporate patrons, their allied trade associations and corporate "think tanks," have, in effect, taken over the executive branch, the Congress, and promoted the judgeships of right-wing corporate lawyers demanding another salary increase.

The Clinton administration hardly slowed their stride. In fact one high official of the U.S. Chamber of Commerce told me that they loved the Clinton government. Why not? Under Clinton they got corporate-managed trade called NAFTA and WTO, laws furthering media, telecommunications, agribusiness, banking, brokerage and insurance industry concentration, weak-to-nonexistent regulation, a chronic softness on corporate crimes against pensioners and small investors, and a pathetically indifferent consumer and labor policy—to name a few surrenders.

What's left to do? How does the AEI keep its corporate supremacists writing those big checks? How do they avoid institutional ennui? Why, go after the liberal or progressive nongovernmental organizations (NGOs). Describe them as a collage of Goliaths running an all-points wrecking machine over government and business. Open a theater of the absurd.

On Wednesday, June 11, 2003, the AEI held such a forum on what to do about this burgeoning civic menace, as they contrive it. Speaker after speaker weighed in with their strained fulminations.

The room was full, of course, with AEI partisans nodding in agreement. These are the affluent ones who cavil against living wages for janitors who clean their offices, farmworkers who harvest their food, and hospital workers who care for their parents. These are the fully health-insured comforted ones who assail pleas for universal health insurance for over forty-five million American children and adults and those who have contempt for the environmental groups that care about stopping toxic polluters in poorer areas of the country, while living in shrubby suburbs far from the incinerators and waste dumps.

Here was speaker Jon Entine of Miami University describing "capitalism's Trojan horse: reasonable people should be concerned about the growing influence of the social investment community, and its emerging partnership with NGOs, most of which share a knee jerk demonization of corporations and free markets. Its leaders are products of the activist community, yet they are different and more dangerous."

Whoa! Trying to persuade shareholders to press for more corporate responsibility, in the midst of a corporate crime wave by the managers, is somehow subversive in his mind. How dare the social investment community advise its clients about corporate misbehavior and urge the owners (shareholders) to exercise more control over their own companies.

Nothing quite captures AEI's intent better than the official AEI statement announcing the conference. Some of its words bear quoting:

"NGOs have created their own rules and regulations and demanded that governments and corporations abide by those rules. Many nations' legal systems encourage NGOs to use the courts—or the specter of the courts—to compel compliance.

"Politicians and corporate ledgers are often forced to respond to the NGO media machine, and the resources of taxpayers and shareholders are used in support of ends they did not intend to sanction. The extraordinary growth of advocacy NGOs in liberal democracies has the potential to undermine the sovereignty of constitutional democracies, as well as the effectiveness of credible NGOs."

Has AEI lost contact with reality? This is what democracy is all about—advocating, petitioning, suing, lobbying, and urging power centers like government and business to do better. AEI has its own positions, together with its corporate allies doing all this and much more with corporate campaign cash and economic power ultimatums. Somehow, citizen groups that have no governmental power—either in fact or by purchase—have become a threat to "constitutional democracies." Has the AEI read our nation's Bill of Rights? What they are condemning, with vague, ironic, regulatory nostrums proposed against dissenting citizen groups, is democracy itself. What the AEIstas prefer is plutocracy.

These corporate think tanks have spent too much time talking to themselves in too comfortable sinecures. They are afflicted by what George Will called "pitiless abstractions" (in a column against anti-air-bag interests). They need to visit factories, foundries, mines, hospitals, prisons, slums, trailer parks, and small farms for some sensitivity training.

Maybe alleviating their chronic empirical starvation will tap some residual humanity that places people before corporations. They might remember that two hundred years ago, the early corporations in New England were chartered by state legislatures to be our servants, not our masters.

For more elaboration by the dreaded NGOs, see www.actagainstwar.org/dc and www.citizenworks.org.

June 13, 2003

Wall Street Accountability

Responding to criticism that he and other regulators had gone lightly in fining ten large Wall Street firms $1.4 billion for alleged conflicts of interests, New York Attorney General Eliot L. Spitzer contended that harsher penalties would have done more harm than good for the economy.

"We made a decision not to destroy these financial institutions," he told reporters.

Never mind that some of the small investors who lost hundreds of billions of dollars were themselves nearly destroyed because of the misleading information they received from these bank and brokerage analysts, who, for their own profits, continued to issue "buy" recommendations even as companies' shares plummeted. Never mind that even *New York Times* columnist Paul Krugman calls the fines a "slap on the wrist." Never mind that after the settlement was announced Morgan Stanley's chairman said: "I don't see anything in the settlement that will concern the retail investor about Morgan Stanley. Not one thing."

Spitzer deserves his due. He filled a regulatory vacuum left by an understaffed and weakly led SEC. He went after the biggest names on Wall Street, exposing a culture soaked through with greed and corruption. But Spitzer should also know that deterrence is an important aspect of crime prevention. And the kid-glove penalties that Spitzer and other regulators meted out last week are hardly the stuff of deterrence.

Criminal enforcement actions are infrequent. The Wall Street firms, like almost all corporate defendants, know that corporate crime prosecution budgets are so inadequate that state and federal agencies are hard-pressed to enforce criminal laws for blatantly defrauding small investors. With no credible threat and no credible deterrent, corporate criminals, and then big corporate law firms, need not be worried.

For Citigroup, $300 million in fines and disgorgement is less than 1 percent of last year's revenues, which topped $92 billion. Likewise, Credit Suisse First Boston's penalty of $150 million is barely pennies on the dollar of the $56 billion in revenues it took in last year. These fines come nowhere near the $7 trillion that investors lost since it became apparent that the corruption on Wall Street is endemic.

Truly shocking is that the majority of the settlements may yet be tax deductible and/or covered under insurance—everything except $487 million in civil penalties, according to Senator Charles Grassley (R-Iowa), head of the Senate Finance Committee.

On Monday, Grassley wrote: "The material made available to me so far indicates that limitations on tax deductibility and insurance reimbursement do not apply to the $387 million in disgorgement, the $432 million in independent research, and the $80 million in investor education." He plans to introduce legislation to guarantee that the costs of all future government-imposed settlements regarding any alleged violations are not shifted onto taxpayers.

Even more astonishing, however, is that these financial institutions and banks got off the hook without a single admission of wrongdoing. What this means is that defrauded small investors, who already have had the decks stacked against them by years of lawmakers rolling back investor rights to seek restitution in the courts (most notably the Private Securities Litigation Reform Act of 1995), will now have an even more difficult time getting their day in court.

Spitzer notably made public a thick collection of Wall Street communications that reveal just how callous many of these high-flyers were. One e-mail from a Lehman Brothers analyst stated: "Well, ratings and price targets are fairly meaningless anyway, but yes, the 'little guy' who isn't smart about the nuances may get misled, such is the nature of my business." Spitzer said he released these documents for the use of defrauded investors.

It is time for some old-fashioned reforms. Federal and state governments must increase resources devoted to corporate crime enforcement. Congress should also repeal the Private Securities Litigation Reform Act of 1995, which made it more difficult for defrauded investors to sue. The only way to end the corruption on Wall Street is to send a message that securities firms engaged in defrauding small investors will be punished to the full extent of the law and their culpable top executives will be convicted and sent to jail.

It is also time to break up the behemoth Wall Street financial powerhouses. The Republicans and Democrats spent the last decade repealing Depression-era protections for investors and allowing financial institutions to combine in unprecedented ways. Firms should never be allowed to combine stock research, investment banking (selling shares to the public) and brokerage (buying shares for customers). Firms now have an ongoing incentive to provide rosy research and have their brokerage firm push stocks on individuals that benefit not the individuals, but the Wall Street firms' corporate clients.

Congress and state regulators need to bring back the Glass-Steagal Act, which separated banking from investing, and even extend it. Until the research function is separated from the brokerage and investment banking function completely, Main Street will not believe Wall Street and certainly will not entrust it with their now plundered retirement savings. (For more information on corporate accountability, visit www.citizenworks.org).

May 2, 2003

The SEC

As the Enron, WorldCom and related corporate crime scandals of 2001 near their second anniversary, most of the promised reforms are still on the drawing board or awaiting full implementation.

Last year, the Securities and Exchange Commission botched the birth of the Public Company Accounting Oversight Board—the centerpiece of the congressionally enacted reforms. The first chairman of the Oversight Board, William Webster, resigned after questions erupted about his own conduct on a corporate audit committee and the manner in which he was selected for the chairmanship. Before the episode was over, SEC Chairman Harvey Pitt, who had handpicked Webster and bulldogged his selection forward in a hamhanded secretive manner, was forced to resign.

Now, SEC has a new chairman, William Donaldson, and the commission has at long last returned to its responsibility to get the vastly overpaid Oversight Board fully up and running as the chief cop over the accounting industry.

As a first step, the Donaldson-led SEC has named William McDonough, a longtime banker and more recently a Federal Reserve official as chairman of the Oversight Board. The Oversight Board's job description calls for a chairman who can be an aggressive regulator who will set tough rules for auditors, enforce them vigorously, and discipline those who ignore the standards. It is a critical role in assuring the public's confidence in the governance and integrity of corporations and the handling of its money. A headline in the *Wall Street Journal* labeled McDonough a "tough cop" and the *New York Times* followed the next day with editorial approval of the appointment. Similarly, news stories carried favorable mention from a bipartisan scattering of commentators.

But there was little in-depth analysis of McDonough's background or regulatory philosophy. Most of McDonough's career has been in the rarified air of the top executive suites of a big bank holding company, First Chicago Corporation (now merged with Banc One) and more recently as president of the New York Federal Reserve Bank.

Essentially, McDonough has been a "financial insider." His twenty-two years in banking was with a multibillion dollar corporation—one of those "too big to fail" corporations whose federal regulators operate more as friendly consultants than as tough objective enforcers. First Chicago, like most commercial banks, has enjoyed free taxpayer-backed deposit insurance in recent years and some of its riskier loans are guaranteed in whole or part by government. Banking, at least big banking, exists in a largely government guaranteed fail-safe world, and attitudes, as a consequence, are different.

Ten years ago, McDonough left his job as chief financial officer of First Chicago and took the presidency of the Federal Reserve Bank of New York. Although the New York Times described him as a "respected bank regulator," the primary concern of the Federal Reserve and its top officials is monetary policy and the big economic picture, not the nitty-gritty of regulation. This is particularly true at the New York Federal Reserve, which is the nerve center of the system's open-market operations that control the nation's money supply through the buying and selling of securities in the market every day.

McDonough's big moment in the sun and in the national headlines came in September of 1998 when he engineered (with the active support of Federal Reserve Chairman Alan Greenspan) a controversial $3.5 billion bailout of the Long Term Capital Management (LTCM) and its wealthy shareholders, which included one of Wall Street's most celebrated traders, John Meriwether, formerly of Salomon Brothers; two Nobel-prize–winning economists; and David Mullins, former vice chairman of the Federal Reserve Board.

Under McDonough's direction, the New York Federal Reserve sponsored an extraordinary meeting of Wall Street firms and commercial banks, including Bankers Trust and Chase, both state member banks under direct supervision of the Federal Reserve, to put together $3.5 billion to prop up Long Term Capital Management.

Representative James Leach, then chairman of the House Financial Services Committee who seldom finds any fault with the Federal Reserve, was incensed by the secret negotiations that led to the bailout and warned that the "application of the 'too big to fail' doctrine for the first time beyond a depository institution raises troubling public policy questions."

"From a social perspective, it is not clear that Long Term Capital, or any other hedge fund, serves a sufficient purpose to warrant government-directed protection," Leach told the House of Representatives in his usual understated rhetoric. "The LTCM saga is fraught with ironies related to moral authority as well as moral hazard. The Fed's intervention comes at a time when our government has been preaching to foreign governments, particularly Asian ones, that the way to modernize is to let weak institutions fail and to rely on market mechanisms, rather than insider bailouts."

McDonough and the Federal Reserve, of course, defended the intervention as fear of "systemic risk" if the hedge fund had been allowed to go under—a familiar rationale for most government bailouts of companies "too big to fail." Somehow, this doesn't seem to fit the "tough cop" label that the *Wall Street Journal* headline credited to the new chairman of the Oversight Board.

Let's hope that McDonough has put the soft "too big to fail" philosophy behind him and can lead the Public Company Accounting Oversight Board in an aggressive campaign to reform the accounting industry and restore some credibility and confidence in the nation's economic system. It is critically important that he actually becomes the "tough cop." At an annual salary of $560,000 (nearly four times the salary of Federal Reserve Board Chairman Alan Greenspan), that's the least the public should expect of the chairman of the Accounting Oversight Board.

April 24, 2003

Corporate America—Trading with the "Enemy"

For years, the Treasury Department's Office of Foreign Assets Control (OFAC) has run a very active enforcement program against major American corporations accused of trading with statutory enemies of the United States.

For years, OFAC would call corporate lawyers into their offices, demand that the companies pay to the Treasury Department thousands of dollars to settle allegations of doing business with countries like Iran, Iraq, Libya, or Cuba.

In exchange, OFAC did little to publicize the cases. One thing big corporations don't want is adverse publicity—especially when it comes to doing business with statutory enemies of the United States. A white-collar criminal defense lawyer told *Corporate Crime Reporter* (a newsletter based in Washington, D.C.): "It is not a badge that any financial institution or others who are tagged by OFAC wear proudly. These are very serious statutes. No bank or other financial institution likes to have any publicity or press on an enforcement action. So the defense bar is generally very pleased when our clients don't get press in this area."

Last year, OFAC's perverse protection racket came undone when *Corporate Crime Reporter* (www.corporatecrimereporter.com) and Public Citizen filed a Freedom of Information Act lawsuit and demanded that Treasury release information concerning the enforcement cases. The litigation resulted in the release of a slew of enforcement memos detailing big-name American companies like Goodyear Tire & Rubber, IKEA, CNA Insurance, Tyson Foods, and Boeing settling these cases. (The memos are posted at www.treas.gov/foia/reading-room/docs/ofac-index.html) As a result of the litigation, OFAC also agreed to begin to release information about the cases as they were released, on a weekly basis. On February 4 and February 11, 2003, OFAC released information on fifty-nine such cases, including ChevronTexaco in Iraq, the New York Yankees, Wal-Mart, ESPN, and Caterpillar trading with Cuba, and ExxonMobil and Wells Fargo trading with Sudan.

But the lists were buried in the bowels of Treasury's web site. And there was only one antiseptic line for each case—no information on dates, skimpy information on allegations of wrongdoing—and no enforcement memos.

While there is an ongoing public policy debate about who exactly is an "enemy of the United States" and whether the sanctions that support the law actually work in achieving their desired ends, there is little debate that when the government enforces the law against major American corporations, the results should be given widespread publicity. Adverse publicity is one of the greatest deterrents against corporate crime and wrongdoing.

When the Justice Department brings criminal prosecutions against major American corporations, press releases are distributed widely.

And yet, for years, OFAC would enforce the laws against major American corporations for trading with statutory enemies of the United States and not make the results public.

OFAC should follow the example set by its sister agency, the Commerce Department's Bureau of Industry and Security (BIS). BIS was formerly known as the Bureau of Export Administration.

BIS is in charge of administering export controls on goods and technology exported from the United States, controlled because they could be used in either commercial or military applications.

The former enforcement chief for BIS explained her agency's decision to publicize their settlements this way: "We posted our enforcement actions on our web site because there is a strong policy of letting the public know what you as enforcers are doing. We felt it was certainly in the public interest to release this information. And we also felt that it provided strong deterrence for the wrongdoers. And it provided guidelines for companies trying to comply, to understand what they could do to keep out of trouble."

To deter future corporate wrongdoing, OFAC must stop protecting major American companies from adverse publicity. After all, sunlight is the best disinfectant.

April 17, 2003

Shed No Tears for CEOs

A few of the bigger and more outlandish compensation packages for corporate executives may have declined last year in the wake of the Enron-style scandals and a falling stock market, but no one need shed any tears for the CEOs. They are continuing to do avariciously well at the pay window—in most cases much better than the investors in their companies.

Take the case of Michael D. Eisner, chief of Walt Disney. His total compensation in 2002 was up 498 percent to $6 million while shareholder returns plummeted by 18 percent. And Leo F. Mullin of Delta Air Lines raked in $13.8 million last year, a 104 percent increase, but the shareholders saw their investments sink by 58 percent. So much for the theory of corporate pay based on performance.

Nonetheless, the pay envelopes of Eisner and Mullin look thin alongside the bulging compensation packages of many of the corporate highflyers.

Miles D. White, CEO of Abbott Laboratories, for example, took home a compensation package totaling $25,545,490 in 2002—including base salary, bonus, restricted stock, long-term incentives, and options. That was an increase of 147 percent over his total direct compensation of a year ago. Stockholders saw their returns fall 27 percent over the same period. Tracking the bloated pay packages is tricky. At first glance the $1 million salary of James Dimon, the chief executive of Bank One looks modest when compared with the multimillion dollar compensation of many executives. But a closer examination reveals a $3 million bonus, nearly $2 million in long-term incentives and almost $6 million in stock options.

Sanford Weill, the chairman of Citicorp, a company that was a major participant in the Enron scandals, collected total compensation of $8.9 million last year, but Robert Rubin, chairman of the bank's executive committee and former secretary of treasury in the Clinton administration, more than doubled his chief's compensation with a bulging pay envelope containing $18.4 million for himself.

Departing chief executives often walked out with amazingly lush "good-bye" gifts. Honeywell International's CEO, Lawrence Bossidy, received a $4 million bonus as he left the firm even though the shares of the company dropped 27 percent last year. The Clorox Company gave its departing chief, Craig Sullivan, three years tax-free use of the company's plane plus other benefits.

A survey by the *New York Times* suggests that the focus of many of the company perks is being shifted under the glare of the accounting and other corporate scandals. The survey identified lucrative beefed-up pensions and life insurance policies, some worth tens of millions of dollars, as replacements for more direct compensation. Also on the favored benefit list were increased allowances for travel on private jets—rationalized by fears about terrorism on commercial planes. (The rest of the American public presumably will just have to continue to live with those fears while corporate executives are kept safe and sound in their private jets.)

For many of the U.S. Armed Forces, including members recently called up from civilian life in National Guard and Reserve units and sent to Iraq in recent weeks, the private jets and bloated compensation packages must seem strange, indeed.

With declared unemployment close to 6 percent, underemployment rising, and job losses rapidly expanding, the AFL-CIO has launched a campaign to promote shareholder votes on executive compensation, including stock options, at the annual meetings of 150 corporations.

"We think that CEO pay still continues to be totally out of line with company performance," Richard Trumka, secretary-treasurer of the AFL-CIO recently told the *New York Times*.

In the aftermath of the Enron and other corporate scandals, the move toward more stockholder democracy shows some encouraging signs. Last year, 33 percent of the 289 governance proposals voted on by shareholders won more than 50 percent of the votes cast, according to the Investor Research Center in Washington, D.C. A year earlier just 24 percent of the proposals that came to a vote won. The Center reports another increase in the number of corporate governance resolutions filed this year with compensation issues leading the list.

The Sheet Metal Workers National Pension Fund, which owns 44,800 shares of the San Francisco-based Charles Schwab and Company, has proposed that the company's board of directors set a policy of expensing the cost of all future stock options on its annual income statement.

The Academy of Our Lady of Lourdes in Rochester, Minnesota owns 1,509 shares of J. P. Morgan Chase. It wants the bank's board to prepare a report comparing the pay levels of the company's top executives with the lowest-paid workers in the U.S. as of January 1, 1982, 1992, and 2002.

Last year, 50.7 percent of the shareholders of Bank of America voted for a nonbinding resolution asking that the board seek their approval on any severance agreements that would more than double an executive's annual base pay.

These modest revolts against corporate excesses and the push for greater investor democracy are encouraging at the grass roots. But the message isn't reaching most members of Congress or the Iraq-absorbed Bush administration, which pays only lip service to reforms in the wake of Enron et al and continues to shamelessly push for greater tax breaks and generous welfare schemes for corporations and their top executives, in addition to allowing Bermuda-type tax havens for corporate tax escapees.

April 11, 2003

Corporate Freeloaders

The deepening federal and state budget deficits are causing cuts that affect the most defenseless and least powerful of Americans. That, of course, is the direct consequence of plutocracy—rule by the wealthy. Their ownership and control of the nation's private assets is growing while the poor and middle class are losing. The latest figures show wealth inequality is growing in America and is the worst in the western world.

If you've been reading the newspapers, you can see that the budget cuts are reducing health, education, housing, and many critical services for children. Safety programs are losing out. However, prisons are doing well, along with the welfare programs for the corporations.

Our politicians, with few exceptions, are not demanding that the cuts start *first* with the corporate welfare programs and corporate tax escapes costing the country hundreds of billions of dollars yearly.

California is one—albeit big—example. Facing a deficit of over $25 billion this year, the state and its cities are being squeezed. Oakland and Alameda County are paying Al Davis' Oakland Raiders NFL football franchise $25 million a year to service bonds issued to renovate the stadium and lure the Raiders from Los Angeles.

Oakland pays $12.5 million of this sum. By contrast, the annual budget of the city's library system is about the same dollar amount and is facing sharp cuts. The Raiders only play ten games a year there (including exhibitions), which hardly produce many jobs. To make matters worse, Al Davis is also suing Oakland and the county for $1.1 billion claiming they promised to guarantee a full stadium for every game. Imperiously, Davis orders television blackouts when the game is not sold out seventy-two hours before kickoff—an insensitive way to treat the taxpayers.

Corporate draining of the defenseless can be very direct. Pressuring or buying local officials to give tax abatements and other giveaways, these companies don't even care when the losers are public school children. In a brand new report entitled "Protecting Public Education from Tax Giveaways to Corporations" prepared by the nonprofit group Good Jobs First (goodjobsfirst.org), data from the fifty states showed that letting companies off the property tax hook costs the schools who rely on that revenue a great deal of money. One hundred million dollars in Ohio alone!

The same game of tax escape is played with ruthless precision in all the states. Companies dangle office buildings, hotels, retail chain stores or factories before state development agencies and ask for bids. The bids are a race to the bottom for exempting or abating these companies from paying their fair share to support the communities' services as do workers, homeowners, small businesses, and others.

These companies are shameless freeloaders, not free enterprisers. They say they want good schools for their labor force and a good community for their employees, but they participate in depleting school budgets through their avaricious demands for more corporate welfare.

In conjunction with the National Education Association, Greg LeRoy, director of Good Jobs First and author of the report, made three recommendations. First, improve disclosure of subsidies and enforce "clawback" provisions that require returning the subsidies given to developers "who have failed to meet their promises on jobs, wages, or capital investment."

Second, give school boards a formal say, with veto power, over subsidy decision-making.

Third, state governments should "prohibit the abatement or diversion of the school portion of property taxes." Today, only two states shield school funding from these subsidies.

Only two states enable school boards of elected members adequate participation in decisions about tax abatements and the diversion of tax increment financing.

Call or write Greg LeRoy (1311 L Street, NW, Washington, DC 20005) to find out where the corporate freeloaders are in your area so you can let them know that you know what they have gotten away with. This knowledge has many uses, including charity drives when these companies are asked to give to local charitable causes.

January 24, 2003

Seymour Melman: Overspending on the Military

I wonder how Seymour Melman feels these days. For over half a century, this Columbia University industrial engineering professor (now emeritus) has been researching, writing, and speaking about the massive overspending on the military portion of the federal budget and how this waste is deindustrializing America, costing millions of jobs and starving the investment in public works—repairing the crucial physical capital of America.

Recently, he prepared a memorandum called "The Pentagon Connection" where he recounted the massive redundancy and costliness of various weapons systems—such as the next wave of fighter planes, missiles, submarines, and aircraft carriers—and the budget impact on the domestic needs of our country. Remember, the U.S. no longer has a major opponent that used to justify huge military budgets. Both Russia and China are converting quickly to the state capitalistic-oligarchic model and the Soviet Union is no more.

First, Professor Melman cites the Report Card for America's Infrastructure that was issued by the American Society of Civil Engineers (asce.org/reportcard). One and one-third trillion dollars are estimated for the repair of twelve categories of public works, including schools, drinking water systems, sewage systems, airports, public transit, bridges, and roads.

The engineering society found what any person would find by observing great needs coming from great disrepair and decay. Adding $618 billion for repair of U.S. housing and railroads brings the capital improvement needs to a $2.0 trillion market, he notes.

Mr. Melman, whose knowledge of U.S. industry is legendary, adds: "Every manufacturing industry whose products are required for repairing and modernizing America's infrastructure is left out by the federal government's military plans." And expenditures.

The military economy drains the civilian economy and this trend has been accelerating into what Melman calls a "huge change" in the American economy. He writes: "This deindustrialization has happened so quickly that America's capacity to produce anything is seriously undermined. For example, last year the New York City government announced its plans to buy a new fleet of subway cars. Though this contract is worth $3 to 4 billion, not one U.S. firm responded. Of 100 products offered in this fall's L.L. Bean catalogue, 92 are imported and only 8 are made in the U.S.A."

"Closing U.S. factories has not only left millions without work, but has also diminished the U.S. production capability required for repairing our broken infrastructure," Melman says.

Melman doesn't mention it in his memo, but previous studies have demonstrated that a million dollars in civilian investment creates more jobs than a million dollars in military weapons systems.

The states and cities are reporting deeper deficits. This year, the states will be over $60 billion in the red. Taxes and tolls are going up. Necessities are being cut—outlays, Melman points out, for schools, libraries, fire and police departments, sanitation departments, child welfare, health care, and services for elderly people. But there are hundreds of billions for Soviet-era weapons driven by the weapons corporations and their campaign cash for key members of Congress who decide the distortions of your tax dollars.

Recently, Bob Herbert, a columnist for the *New York Times*, interviewed the well-known financier, Felix Rohatyn, who was involved in the response to the city's fiscal crisis in the 1970s. The current fiscal crisis of the states and cities is, to Mr. Rohatyn, very serious.

Mr. Rohatyn told Mr. Herbert that he believes that a $75 billion-a-year program of federal assistance to state and local governments combined with a $75-billion-a-year tax cut for working people would provide a substantial boost to the economy, and over time would result in the creation of several million jobs.

But, in spite of polls (as well as opinions expressed by military experts, like retired General Anthony Zinni) showing that a large majority of the American people do not believe that President Bush has made the case that Iraq threatens the U.S., nor do they want him to commit our troops unilaterally, the White House chief is willing to spend at least $150 billion and incur casualties pursuing this obsession, while ignoring life-saving needs in our country.

For a copy of the entire Melman memorandum, send a self-addressed, large stamped envelope to Professor Seymour Melman, Department of Industrial Engineering, Columbia University, 500 West 120th Street, New York, NY 10027.

Melman's article is also available on the web at: www.aftercapitalism.com/archive.html

January 17, 2003

Pay It Back and Go To Jail

Can the congressional Democrats draw a bright line between themselves and the Republicans over what needs to be done about corporate crime in the eight weeks before the November elections?

At first thought, the answer should be easy. The Republicans and their "whatever corporations want" subservient stance during the '90s reached levels somewhere between unconditional surrender and unconditional sellout. The former pesticide exterminator, House Republican Whip Tom DeLay (R-TX), once declared that he could not think of one regulation to keep on the law books. Deregulate everything in sight was their fevered mantra—including taking the federal cops off the corporate crime beat.

Getting rid of corporate law and order, pushing to lock up the corporate cops and throwing away the keys became the Republicans' inventory to raise huge piles of cash from the corporate malefactors. The Democrats, while as a whole not as obeisant, did not throw the gauntlet down then. Also some Democrats, like Senators Lieberman and Dodd, locked arms with the Republicans to take away important rights to sue held by shareholders until 1995.

Now during the past year's surge in corporate crime—Enron, WorldCom, et al—and its massive media attention, more Democrats than Republicans finally seem interested in reforms. So what do the Republicans tell the voters back home? That they're going to be tough on corporate crooks and demand that they should go to jail.

Bingo! The Republicans are even with the Democrats in the rhetoric game. When the Sarbanes reform legislation came to the Senate floor this summer, the Republicans, at first, bridled at its modest regulatory measures over accounting firms and corporate governance matters. Then cleverer heads prevailed. The Republican leaders in the Senate and House told their flock to jump on the Sarbanes bandwagon and make common identity with the Democrats.

Bingo! Blur! The Republicans become even with the Democrats in the legislation scorecard, including President Bush who signed it into law with the proper rhetoric.

At present, the Democrats know full well the stands that they can take and should take, which the Republicans will refuse to imitate.

Senator Byron Dorgan (D-ND) has one of them—a tough crackdown on U.S. corporations who renounce their U.S. state charter, reincorporate in Bermuda or other tax havens to escape gobs of taxes to Uncle Sam yet retain all the benefits as if they were still U.S. corporations. Dorgan says he will have hearings on this subject. One of the lead proposals will be to stop these companies from receiving government contracts and subsidies.

Another realm that the Republicans would never enter is to provide by law more powers and rights to shareholders to control the corporation that they own. Here the majority of Republicans are anticapitalist because they are in the hands of the corporate bosses who too often mismanage their companies, enrich themselves immensely, and contribute heavily to political campaigns.

Shareholders in large public companies must be given the authority to approve or disapprove executive compensation packages. It has been executive pay that provided the bosses with the incentives to cook the books and inflate company profits so as to make their stock options and other bonuses more lucrative.

Facilities to make it easier for consumers, taxpayers, and shareholders to band together voluntarily into powerful self-help associations are anathema to Republicans. If the Democrats drop their coolness or indifference to this proposal (see www.Citizenworks.org for information about this proposed Corporate Reform Act), they could broaden their appeal significantly to millions of defrauded or anxious Americans.

A more immediate bright line opportunity comes very soon when the House and Senate vote on the Justice Department appropriations bill. At least fifty million dollars should be added to expand the corporate crime prosecution section in the Department. There is no way that the Justice Department can go after corporate crooks with its meager staff and, certainly, no way it can respond to the recommendations for prosecution by the beefed up Securities and Exchange Commission.

More federal cops on the corporate beat and the establishment of a corporate crime database are necessary to make law and order happen and to help save millions of Americans their investments, savings, pensions, and jobs. Will the Democrats distinguish themselves from the Republicans and take the lead here in the next couple of weeks by amending this appropriations legislation on the floor of Congress? Isn't this the best way to respond to the most immediate demand of the voters—whether conservative or liberal—which is to make the corporate bosses "pay it back and go to jail."

Rolling back the failed deregulation of the financial industry that opened the floodgates to reckless, avaricious crimes and frauds in the '90s is also an area Republicans won't touch. Derivatives should be brought under regulation as should electricity (a necessity). It was deregulation that allowed the Enronitis disease, which gouged Californians and others and eventually brought down Enron and cost thousands of workers their jobs.

These and other positions that could be turned into bright lines between the two major parties are available on www.Citizenworks.org. Of course, one party has supported these sensible proposals all along. Color it Green.

September 12, 2002

Citigroup, Heal Thyself

Last week Citigroup, the nation's largest financial services holding company, trotted out one of its top executives, Robert Rubin, to spread some soothing words about how to clean up the corporate scandals and repair the sagging stock market.

Rubin's (and Citigroup's) message appeared as a lengthy op-ed in the *Washington Post* under the headline "To Regain Confidence." As former secretary of Treasury in the Clinton administration, Rubin commands a following, particularly in the financial press so important to Citigroup's vast empire.

The need for Citigroup to use Rubin to pose as an ally of reform became obvious two days later when the Senate Permanent Subcommittee on Investigations released hundreds of pages of documents that the Subcommittee Chairman Carl Levin said proves that Citigroup and J. P. Morgan Chase "knowingly assisted Enron Corporation in disguising debt by structuring sham financing vehicles."

The scheme not only facilitated Enron's deception, which cost investors and employees hundreds of millions of dollars, but earned more than $200 million in fees for Citigroup and J. P. Morgan Chase.

Citigroup's Rubin didn't provide an inkling of his bank's complicity in the Enron scandal when he penned his piece for the *Washington Post*. But he may well have had Citigroup's secret involvement in mind when he argued that "regulatory and legislative changes and enforcement should be balanced and appropriate."

With the revelations pouring out of the Senate hearing, it is understandable that Citigroup and its executives would be entering a plea for "balanced and appropriate" enforcement—a light tap on the wrist, perhaps.

At least one senator at the hearing, Peter Fitzgerald of Illinois, raised questions about how many of the current scandals could be blamed on Congress's decision in 1999 to allow banks, insurance companies, and securities firms to merge and form giant financial conglomerates such as Citigroup.

That question must have troubled both Citigroup and Rubin who played such major roles in the enactment of the legislation—Rubin as secretary of the Treasury and Citigroup as the biggest beneficiary of the action. Rubin left the Treasury in July of 1999 and Citigroup announced he had been hired by the corporation on October 26—four days after the final compromise was reached on the legislation.

In answering Senator Fitzgerald's question about the wisdom of the 1999 legislation that merged banks and securities firms, Lynn Turner, the former chief accountant of the Securities and Exchange Commission, said "securities firms and banking firms can't be working together, entering into transactions together and using the security arm to try to get banking business."

That echoed what many of us warned the Congress about repeatedly when the legislation was being hammered through by Rubin and Citigroup and the biggest players in the financial industry. The lobbying, greased with record campaign contributions from financial services corporations, drowned out all warnings about the dangers now so apparent in Enron and other corporate debacles.

For consumer and community organizations around the nation, the new revelations about Citigroup should come as no surprise. Community groups have been trying for years to get legislative and regulatory action that would halt predatory lending and other deceptive practices by Citigroup's affiliates.

Citigroup became the nation's largest predatory lender when it acquired Associates First Capital in September 2000 and merged it with another of its subsidiaries, CitiFinancial Credit. Last year, the Federal Trade Commission (FTC) filed a lawsuit against Associates First Capital, Citigroup, and CitiFinancial Credit Company seeking an injunction against unfair and deceptive lending practices.

Here is what Jodie Bernstein, director of FTC's Bureau of Consumer Protection, had to say about the practices of the Citigroup affiliates:

"They hid essential information from consumers, misrepresented loan terms, flipped loans and packed optional fees to raise the costs of the loans. What had made the alleged practices more egregious is that they primarily victimized consumers who were the most vulnerable—hardworking homeowners who had to borrow to meet emergency needs and often had no other access to capital."

Last year, Citigroup paid $20 million to North Carolina customers of Associates and $300,000 to the state to settle allegations that consumers had been tricked into buying expensive and unneeded credit life insurance as part of their mortgage loans. The *New York Times* reported last fall that Citigroup had settled two hundred lawsuits pertaining to practices of Associates with at least twice that number still pending in the courts.

But, these facts, like the funny money games now revealed in the Senate hearings, were strangely missing in Robert Rubin's lengthy rendition in the *Washington Post* about actions that were needed for the nation to regain confidence.

To paraphrase an old adage: Citigroup, heal thyself.

For information about what you can do to help create a Financial Consumers' Association, visit www.essential.org.

July 24, 2002

The Secret World of Banking

All the headlines about corporate disclosures and the need for transparency are sending shivers through the banking industry and its regulators who have always lived in a protected and largely secret world.

Hundreds of millions of dollars are expended on examinations of depository institutions, but most of the key findings are treated as inside information between the bankers and the regulators who see a mutual advantage in keeping the depositors and investors—and even members of Congress—in the dark about the gritty details of their performance. Only when an institution actually fails and taxpayer-backed deposit insurance funds are lost, do the hard facts of mismanagement and regulatory miscues become public knowledge.

The lack of timely disclosures about bank conditions arose a few weeks ago when a recess appointee to the Securities and Exchange Commission, Cynthia Glassman, suggested that the so-called "Camel ratings" of banks be made available to the public. Camel ratings compiled by the regulators are evaluations based on examiners' and supervisors' assessment of six factors: capital, asset quality, management, earnings, liquidity, and sensitivity to risk.

Performance is based on numerical ratings of 1 to 5—with five designated as the worst.

Ms. Glassman's suggestion produced an immediate uproar among regulators and the bank lobbyists. Comptroller of the Currency John Hawke, who spent most of his career as a big-time bank lawyer and lobbyist, immediately sent his spokesman out to denounce the idea of public disclosure, contending that the Camel ratings were an "internal tool of the regulators."

Other opponents suggested that disclosure of the ratings might cause a "run" on a bank by scared depositors. This brings back memories of the savings and loan collapse in the 1980s when the chairman of the Federal Home Loan Bank, Danny Wall, continued to paint rosy pictures and withhold bad news from the public while behind the scenes the savings institutions rotted and edged toward failure. At one point, Wall barged into the offices of the General Accounting Office in an attempt to block the release of a critical report citing mounting losses and increasing drains on the deposit insurance runs. And the friends of the savings and loans in key positions on Capitol Hill were all too happy to gloss over the worsening conditions until it was too late.

The costs to the taxpayers and the savings and loan industry increased greatly under this blanket of secrecy. The public release of the Camel ratings would make it impossible for regulators and banks to hide conditions and let problems mushroom into disasters ala the savings and loan collapse. And as the SEC's Ms. Glassman asks "why shouldn't investors [as well as depositors] have this information?"

Richard Carnell, a professor of law at Fordham University and former assistant secretary of the Treasury, wholeheartedly endorses the idea of public disclosure of the Camel ratings, arguing that the disclosure would "facilitate constructive criticism of how bank regulators measure risk." Carnell was one of the key staffers on the Senate Banking Committee who urged action on the savings and loan crisis in the 1980s and crafted many of the reforms after the collapse.

Rather than facing the market discipline, which full disclosure would help instill, the banks and other depository institutions prefer to utilize a costly deposit insurance system as a tranquilizer for the public. As the speculation by the savings and loans revealed in the 1980s, the taxpayer-backed insurance creates a moral hazard that encourages excessive risk taking.

Throughout this Congress, much of the banking industry has been on Capitol Hill in an intensive lobbying campaign to have taxpayer-backed deposit insurance increased from its present limit of $100,000 per depositor to as much as $150,000 plus indexing for future inflation. The present $100,000 limit was pulled out of thin air in 1980 by a handful of House-Senate conferees seeking a means of helping the ailing savings and loans attract deposits in competition with big money center banks. Actually, under loopholes, a family of four could keep as much as two million dollars in insured accounts in a single institution.

The secrecy maintained by federal regulators combined with the tranquilizer of the massive deposit insurance program effectively takes the public out of the debate about banking policy. As a result, it is difficult to build public opinion about legislative and regulatory actions that impact the safety and soundness—not to mention the efficiency—of banking corporations, and ultimately the health of the deposit insurance funds.

That was certainly the case in 1999 when the combined lobbying forces of banks, securities firms, and insurance companies pushed through a near total rewrite of the nation's financial laws, which authorized the formation of huge nationwide financial conglomerates—with little or no protections for consumers or the taxpayers who stand behind the deposit insurance funds.

So, the idea advanced by a lone member of the Securities and Exchange Commission for disclosure of the regulators' ratings of banks is a welcome development in this desolate desert of secrecy that surrounds the banking industry. But don't expect the banks or their regulators to agree voluntarily to come out in the sunshine. It is too convenient to leave bank regulation as an insider game. The same is true for the Congress—particularly the House and Senate Banking Committees—which prefers to legislate favors for the industry without being bothered with messy facts in the hands of their voters back home.

But the Enrons, the WorldComs and the Global Crossings, among others, are placing a new premium on open disclosure. Perhaps, the sunshine may ultimately reach the musty dark corners of the secret world of banks and bank regulation.

July 09, 2002

Money That Corrupts

Philip J. Purcell, chairman of Morgan Stanley, a Wall Street firm under investigation by New York Attorney General Eliot Spitzer for deceiving investors, visited Congress recently to peddle an amendment that Spitzer called "incredible." It would stop all state attorneys generals and state securities regulators from enforcing their securities laws against any company subject to the jurisdiction of the federal Securities and Exchange Commission (SEC).

Is this breathtaking audacity, arrogance, or what other words can be used to describe pushing to take the state cops off the securities industry's beat? Trillions of dollars are looted, defrauded, or lost through stockbroker and investment banking deceptions, conflicts of interest, and outright lying, while enriching the bosses through self-dealing. And the Wall Street lobbyists want to escape even more from any law and order that means business to protect innocent investors.

If you wonder how any senator or representative, knowing about what *Business Week* magazine called the current "corporate crime wave," can even tentatively entertain supporting Mr. Purcell's preemption of state authority, consider what was going on during the evening of June 19th at Washington, D.C.'s Convention Center. There, a large, wealthy crowd of 6,400 Republicans and lobbyists paid $2,500 each to dine and be entertained with President George W. Bush. They raised over $30 million for the party. Soon the Democrats will have their big bash with many of the same influence peddlers buying the same tables.

Masticating herb tenderloin, washed down with merlot/cabernet, and topped off with miniature raspberry paves, many Republican members of Congress chortled with the monetized minds of many corporate and industry representatives. Included among them was Morgan Stanley, J. P. Morgan Chase, Citigroup, Ernst & Young, the Bond Market Association, Fidelity Investments, and, of course, the powerful Securities Industry Association.

Corrupt money controlling politicians is the antithesis of deciding issues on the merits in a democracy. But corrupt money is the narcotic of most politicians, while public funding of public elections is their fumigator.

The most craven of politicians, like Senator Mitch McConnell (R-KY), say that the American people really don't care about campaign finance reform because the polls show this abstractly phrased topic way down on their list of concerns. The same polls show people worrying about social security, prescription drug prices, living wages, the environment, and health insurance. Well, dirty money in politics endangers all these concerns and many more. It steals the government from its people, demoralizes citizens who feel more powerless, and discourages good candidates from running for elective office.

So when the *New York Times* reports that proposals to go after these corporate crimes and prevent future depletions of pensions and investor equities are stalled in Congress by the crooks lobby, chalk up a lot of their success to the checks they write for the legislators' campaigns.

About 80 percent of the hundreds of millions of dollars poured into congressional campaigns comes from business interests.

Imagine the decay of our Congress. While the mainstream press is headlining daily the large and deep patterns of corporate crime, fraud, and abuse, the Congress has done nothing yet except fiddle, faddle, or often move bills in the House that weaken existing legal protections, not strengthen them.

What of President George W. Bush? He has contented himself with a ten-point list of prudent business practices and responsibilities that he sent up to Congress earlier this year. He has not provided even modestly regular attention and muscle by the White House, even with his own Republicans.

If you want to see the rising of workers and other citizens mobilizing to make Congress pay attention and join with them, check with www.CitizenWorks.org.

June 20, 2002

"A Fine Deal" for Merrill Lynch

New York Attorney General Eliot L. Spitzer called his settlement with Merrill Lynch for defrauding and misleading investors "a triumph for the investing public." Pulitzer prize–winning business reporter for the *New York Times* Gretchen Morgenson called the agreement "clearly" "a fine deal" for Merrill Lynch.

Who is right? Gretchen Morgenson.

First, give Spitzer his due. Tired of waiting for the Securities and Exchange Commission to act, he brought the first case of any state attorneys general against Merrill, citing a 1921 New York state law, the Martin Act, which regulates securities trading. The New York Attorney General obtained incriminating internal evidence from Merrill showing its stockbrokers would recommend that investors buy stock that those same brokers thought were "dogs," but lucrative for the firm's investment banking business, which in turn helped increase those brokers' bonuses. Early on Spitzer talked tough. He told Merrill that he would file criminal charges against the giant company if it did not provide restitution to the defrauded investors, admit wrongdoing, and restructure its business so that the stockbrokers have no relations with the investment banking side of the company.

More and more damaging information was flowing into Spitzer's office and the estimates of investor losses surged well over a billion dollars and counting. The media were reporting the deceptions, the greed, and the fraud almost daily. Spitzer caught Merrill Lynch red-handed. Then he caved.

The agreement provides no restitution to investors who were harmed. Spitzer not only let Merrill avoid his earlier stipulation—an admission of wrongdoing—he also agreed to the following description of his settlement: it "represents neither evidence nor admission of wrongdoing or liability." Instead Merrill merely apologized for failing to address conflicts of interest in the past. This language, of course, will undercut efforts by investors to take Merrill to court and win adequate restitution under the civil justice system.

Spitzer required Merrill Lynch to pay a $100 million penalty. This is less than one-third of what Merrill paid for office supplies and postage in 2001, according to the *New York Times*. Moreover, this money will be distributed to other states, whose attorneys general followed Spitzer's lead, and probably dissuade any efforts to go it alone. None of the money will go to the investors.

The core of Spitzer's agreement is the restructuring of Merrill's way of doing business, in effect separating the influence of investment banking fees from its stock recommendations. Merrill agreed to a list of reforms that will be supervised by an independent monitor to be approved by the New York attorney general's office. The business press, seeking comment by Wall Street types, found very few who thought that this agreement had any teeth or that it would change the corporate culture from the outside. In other words, it is up to Merrill to change from the inside. Perhaps the many forthcoming civil suits by investors and the shareholders' lawsuit, due to depleted stock value, will help.

For Merrill and other similar companies, the only deal that would work requires real separation of investment banking from their analyst divisions that provide investment advice to the public. Only if analysts are entirely independent of investment bankers can investors be confident they are receiving objective advice. This requires that Congress repeal all legislation from the last decade that has undermined New Deal safeguards from the 1930s for investors, and go on to broaden investor protections from predations that did not exist during the New Deal.

A few weeks ago, the cover page of *Business Week* asked: "How Corrupt is Wall Street?" The article inside answered the question by demonstrating that Wall Street is seriously corrupt.

No law enforcement agencies or legislatures will be able to stand up to the giant financial industry unless there is 1) public funding of election campaigns, and 2) mandatory paper inserts in communications between the companies and investors inviting the latter to form what has been long overdue—a national association of individual investors with full-time staff to represent them and be accountable to them.

There are millions of individual investors and until they organize, the companies will find ever new ways to take them to the cleaners. (For more information on a proposed financial consumer organization, see www.essential.org)

May 23, 2002

GM: Backwards Into the Future

Once again, General Motors shows how it can go backwards into the future. Its average new motor vehicle fuel inefficiency has been getting worse in recent years. Now it wants to unbundle many of its vehicles by dropping standard equipment side air bags and antilock braking systems (ABS) and charging its customers more for these life-saving devices as options.

So the new GM is like the old GM, which charged customers in the sixties and seventies extra for seat belts and air bags until federal law required or induced their standard installation.

Unless car buyers change GM's mind by showing their displeasure and moving away from GM to another manufacturer that builds these safety systems as standard equipment, GM's directive will have the following consequences:

1) Car buyers who go for the options will have to pay two to three times as much. Once a feature ceases to be standard equipment, it costs more to manufacture in more limited quantities. Also, car makers routinely overcharge consumers on options to begin with.

2) More lives will be lost, because these features will not be in all cars. To those rigid ideologues from the right who would leave almost all matters to choice, I would ask if they would include seat belts, doors, and padded dash panels under their ideology. The whole principle behind mandatory safety standards is to put a safety net under all vehicles sold, just like a good fire code does for building construction.

3) General Motors is exposing itself to losing more product liability lawsuits. Actively removing a safety feature from standard equipment strengthens the argument by innocent, injured motorists that GM knew better and acted recklessly by deleting a clearly feasible "crashworthy" safety feature.

According to USA Today, GM expects to save about $100 million a year on this move from standard to optional for ABS and side air bags. Last year GM grossed over $177 billion, by comparison. How many lives and injuries is that ill-advised decision going to cost motorists and eventually, in dollars, General Motors?

USA Today, in its report, seemed to lay this decision at the feet of GM's Product Chief, Robert Lutz, instead of the usual bean counters. I hope this is not the case.

Lutz is a freethinking former Chrysler executive recently brought in by GM bosses to shake up the staid or stagnant corporate culture and put exciting engineering functions and designs on the road. I held a joint press conference with Mr. Lutz about a decade ago to celebrate Chrysler's winning our celebrity buyer race by being the first to place air bags as standard equipment in automobile models affordable to middle-class buyers. Celebrities such as Phil Donahue, Paul Newman, Dear Abby, Steve Allen, and Bill Murray had pledged to buy such a vehicle and did.

It remains to be seen what the National Highway Safety Agency (NHTSA) will say about what Clarence Ditlow, the director of the Center for Auto Safety (Autosafety.org), called a "retreat from safety." It remains to be seen also whether GM will start a race to the bottom by other auto manufacturers who see greed and callousness in their "strategic planning" process.

Consumers can vote with their feet and send a signal to these companies not to follow GM into the pits. In the meantime, any citizen interested in safer roadways can convey his or her displeasure by writing to GM at GM headquarters, Detroit, Michigan or by logging into the company's web site—www.GM.com.

April 11, 2002

Large Corporations Lack Allegiance to U.S.

After years of indifference to reports of corporate crime and abuse in the mainstream media, a significant shift toward alarm, indignation, and revulsion is occurring in Congress by some senior members of both parties.

This does not mean that strong legislation and strong law enforcement are inevitably on the way; the Bushites in the executive branch remain indentured to their Big Business patrons. It does mean that more legislators are moving to aggregate the endless cases of corporate crime and fraud into a broader awareness that these represent patterns and trends, not just accurate anecdotes. In other words, it is not just Enron or Arthur Andersen.

Aggregation means that lawmakers take the conditions to the next stage, which invites, although it may not require, action and remedy. For years, politicians like Ronald Reagan would cite cases of welfare fraud by the poor, some not true. Then these politicians began to aggregate and pattern these abuses into a broader policy-producing plan. That's when the cause of "welfare reform" became irresistible.

Similarly, for years there were individual reports of street crimes in the cities. Then there came a time when these were aggregated into the battle accusation against politicians being "soft on crime." Tougher crackdowns were demanded. Thus were born a successful political hammer by Republicans that led to reinstatement of the death penalty, three strikes and you're out, zero tolerance, and a corporate prison building boom.

Now, could it be the corporations' turn? In March, the bastion of American capitalism, *Fortune* magazine, moved up to the aggregation stage. In its March 18th issue, *Fortune* devoted its cover story to the theme: "It's time to stop coddling white-collar crooks. Send them to jail." Inside, the pages rang with rage: "White-Collar Criminals: They Lie, They Cheat, They Steal and They've Been Getting Away With It For Too Long." Around these headlines were pages of details, data, and recounting of big-shot crooks who were rarely prosecuted and, if so, rarely jailed.

About the same time, *Business 2.0*'s April cover story listed dozens of documented cases of what the *Washington Post* called "an acid portrait of colossal avarice and stupidity in America's corporate suites." Big corporations are out of control, in large part, not only from the law, consumers, workers, communities, but from their own owners—the shareholders who long ago have been stripped of any power to control the company they own and the top management who decides its own massive pay through a rubber-stamp board of directors.

Beyond aggregation is looming a powerful critique of giant U.S. business corporations—they are unpatriotic, especially in their demonstrations of greed post 9/11 when they swarmed all over Capitol Hill demanding special privileges and handouts.

On March 22, the *New York Times* began its story on corporate tax shelters in Bermuda this way: "Senior Senators from both parties used blunt language today to denounce companies that use Bermuda as a mail drop to reduce their American income taxes by tens of millions of dollars, calling them 'greedy' and 'unpatriotic' tax evaders whose actions could not be tolerated 'in a time of war.'"

Both Senator Max Baucus (MT-D), chairman of the powerful Finance Committee, and the committee's ranking Republican, Senator Charles E. Grassley (IA-R), named names of companies, held up their products to ridicule, and promised to introduce legislation to end this flight from responsibility, while, in Grassley's words, "making profits off the taxes of middle-class Americans who are paying their taxes honestly."

Some of the named corporations, Stanley Works and Ingersoll-Rand, simply responded by saying that what they are doing is legal and necessary "to compete on a level playing field with international peers." Of course, corporate lobbyists drafted and lobbied this law through Congress. And please note the use of the "globalization pretext," which you will hear over and over again by U.S. corporations, keeping America down by saying they have to be globally competitive under "pull down" trade agreements that they helped write and enact.

Several years ago, I wrote the CEOs of the one hundred largest U.S. corporations, noting that they were created by government charters in the U.S. and rose to wealth and size with American workers, taxpayer subsidies and giveaways, and at times the support of the U.S. armed forces abroad.

In return, I requested that they signal their appreciation and loyalty, as corporations, by having the CEO rise at the annual shareholders' meeting and pledge allegiance of the corporation (not its directors or officers) "to the United States and the Republic for which it stands. . . with liberty and justice for all."

Only one company, Federated Department Stores, thought it was a good idea; the other sixty companies that responded rejected the idea outright, including, of course, General Motors and even Costco.

The charge that more large U.S. corporations have no allegiance to this country or community, other than to control them, use them, and milk them, will increasingly resonate throughout the land with workers, taxpayers, and, now more and more, elected officials.

So too will ring throughout the land the cry of comprehensive corporate reform.

March 28, 2002

Corporate Profiteering after 9-11

U.S. corporations aren't even subtle about it. Waving a flag and carrying a big shovel, corporate interests are scooping up government benefits and taxpayer money in an unprecedented fashion while the public is preoccupied with the September 11 attacks and the war in Afghanistan.

Shamelessly, the Bush administration and Congress have taken advantage of the patriotic outpouring to fulfill the wish lists of their most generous corporate campaign donors. Not only is the treasury being raided, but regulations protecting everything from personal privacy to environmental safeguards are under attack by well-heeled lobbyists who want to stampede Congress to act while the media and citizens are distracted.

Only a handful in the Congress—members like Senator Russell Feingold of Wisconsin and Representatives Peter DeFazio of Oregon and Barbara Lee of California—have shown the courage to question the giveaways and the quick wipeout of civil liberties and other citizen protections. In most cases, such as the $15 billion airline bailout and corporate tax breaks, legislation has been pushed to the forefront with little or no hearings and only fleeting consideration on the floor of the Senate and the House of Representatives.

One of the boldest grabs for cash has been by corporations seeking to eliminate the Alternative Minimum Tax (AMT), which was enacted during the Reagan administration to prevent profitable corporations from escaping all tax liability through various loopholes. Not only do the corporations want relief from the current year's AMT taxes, but they are seeking a retroactive refund of all AMT taxes paid since 1986.

This giveaway, as passed by the House of Representatives, would make corporations eligible for $25 billion in tax refunds. Just fourteen corporations would receive $6.3 billion of the refund. IBM gets $1.4 billion; General Motors, $833 million; General Electric, $671 million; DaimlerChrysler, $600 million; ChevronTexaco, $572 million. The fourteen biggest beneficiaries of the minimum tax repeal gave $14,769,785 in "soft money" to the national committees of the Democratic and Republican parties in recent years.

Soon to join the bailout parade is the nation's insurance industry, which is lobbying the Congress to have the federal government pick up the tab for future losses like those stemming from the attack on the World Trade Center. Proposals are on the table for taxpayers to either pick up losses above certain levels or to provide loans or loan guarantees for reinsurance.

The insurance companies want federal bailouts, but they continue to insist on regulation only by underfunded, poorly staffed state insurance departments, most of which are dominated by the industry. Any bailout or loan program involving the insurance companies must include provisions ensuring that insurance companies cannot refuse to write policies and make investments in low, moderate, and minority neighborhoods. Allegations about insurance company "redlining" or discrimination against citizens in these areas have been prevalent for many years. It would be a terrible injustice for citizens to be forced to pay taxes to help bail out insurance companies that discriminate against them. Congress needs to address this issue before it even considers public assistance for the industry.

People-concerns have been missing in all the bailouts. When the airline companies walked off with $15 billion plus in bailout money, the thousands of laid-off employees—airline attendants, maintenance crews, baggage handlers, and ticket counter employees—received not a dime. Attempts to include health benefits and other help for these employees were shouted down on the floor of the House of Representatives.

Last month, more than 400,000 employees lost their jobs nationwide and the national unemployment rate rose to 5.4 percent, the highest level since 1996. The Bureau of Labor Statistics said roughly one-fourth of the lost jobs were the direct result of the terrorist attacks of September 11. Bailouts, benefits, or other aid for these victims of the attacks? No, that's reserved just for the corporations under the policies of the Bush administration and the present Congress.

Yet it is the workers in the low-wage jobs—like those in restaurants, hotels, retailing, and transportation—who are bearing the brunt of the layoffs in the aftermath of the attacks on the World Trade Center, according to a report from the New York State Department of Labor. Almost 25,000 people told the department that they lost their jobs because of the trade center disaster. An analysis by the department of the first 22,000 of the claims found that 16 percent worked at bars, 14 percent worked at hotels, 5 percent worked in air transportation and 21 percent in a category termed "business services." Only 4 percent worked at Wall Street brokerage firms.

While more workers lose jobs, the administration is pushing for authority to expand the North American Free Trade Agreement (NAFTA) under new "fast-track" authority. The Department of Commerce concedes that at least 360,000 jobs have been lost under NAFTA, and private research groups estimate the total may be twice that number. Now, with unemployment rising to alarming levels, the administration decides to cave to pro-NAFTA corporate demands that will only make the labor picture worse. No bailout for laid-off workers, just a hard crack across the knees.

As Bill Moyers, the author and national journalist, commented: "They [the corporations] are counting on your patriotism to distract you from their plunder. They're counting on you to stand at attention with your hand over your heart, pledging allegiance to the flag, while they pick your pocket."

The present crisis cries out for shared sacrifice—not the opportunism so blatantly displayed by the nation's corporate interests. President Bush and the Congress must summon the courage to resist self-serving demands—the kind of courage and shared sacrifice that guided the brave rescue workers on September 11.

For more information: www.citizenworks.org

November 7, 2001

Runaway Compensation Packages

Sanford Weill, CEO of Citigroup, the giant multinational financial conglomerate, took home the fattest compensation package among the nation's corporate executives last year. $224.4 million. Weill may be the "poster child" for executive compensation excesses, but boards of directors of other major corporations have not been timid about dipping into their company's treasuries to shower lucrative salaries, stock options, and bonuses on their chief executives.

While the economy softened and many shareholders took their lumps in the market, the average CEO of a major corporation received $20 million in 2000, including 50 percent more in stock options and 22 percent more in salary and bonuses, according to the *New York Times*. In contrast, hourly workers averaged a 3 percent raise last year and salaried employees a 4 percent increase.

As a result of soaring executive pay, the gap between compensation for workers and executives is widening rapidly. In 1980, pay for corporate executives was 42 times that of blue-collar workers. By 1999, executives' compensation on average was 475 times that of workers and growing.

Beyond the annual news stories that follow the required corporate filings with the Securities and Exchange Commission (SEC), executive compensation gets little attention in the media. But the AFL-CIO has made a dramatic move through its updated web site to change that and wake up not only its members but the public to what is going on with these runaway compensation schemes and how they affect people who are saving for college, retirement, and other needs.

Not only does this well-designed Executive PayWatch web site provide links through which the compensation packages of major companies can be tracked, but it also contains a practical digital tool kit loaded with ideas about how citizens can effectively challenge the excessive compensation at various points such as in boardrooms, regulatory agencies, the Internal Revenue Service, Congress, and the community.

The PayWatch web site has proven to be a huge success. It has become the biggest draw on the AFL-CIO web site with 11 million viewers ("hits" in Internet language) last year, a testimonial to the growing concern Americans have about the inside games that executives and boards of directors (often dominated by cronies of the executives) play to hike executive compensation.

The web site provides fifty different "e-tools" for limiting runaway executive compensation plans. Here are some areas where PayWatch believes citizens can be effective:

• Pension funds, mutual funds, and 401(k) plans. Public and private pension funds own nearly one-third and mutual funds almost 12 percent of corporate stocks. As managers of workers' money, the entities, as shareholders, can have tremendous input on how corporations are governed. The directors and trustees of these funds can be contacted to initiate and support shareholder proposals to limit executive pay. The web site provides data on the funds that invest in companies with excessive compensation packages.

• Rally coworkers and the community. Organize allies in the workplace and community in campaigns against excessive executive compensation, including distributing fliers (automatic flier generator on the web site), contacting the company's board of directors, calling in to radio talk shows, contacting other media, initiating petitions, and urging public officials to support the campaign.

• Contact the IRS to tighten rules that limit corporate deductions for executive compensation. A 1993 law limits such deductions to $1 million unless the compensation is "performance based" and decided by an independent committee of outside directors. IRS defines both requirements loosely under current rules.

• Contact the SEC to require fuller disclosure of executive compensation packages.

The PayWatch web site has also injected some fun into the campaign. Visitors to the site can play a board game called "Greed" where they can win by grabbing a golden parachute, stacking the board of directors, cutting deals for extravagant perks, and covering up poor performance. Players lose points when shareholders revolt and file resolutions or lawsuits. PayWatch also allows visitors to the site to compare their pay to their own CEO's pay. The visitor can find out how many years it would take them to earn what their CEO earns.

Now that the rule that stock markets go down as well as up has been restored, and with the economic euphoria of the last few years wearing off, it is an opportune moment for sanity to be returned to corporate boardrooms on executive compensation. The AFL-CIO Executive PayWatch web site is a first-class tool to mobilize public opinion against corporate excesses. Every citizen who has a computer available should visit the site (www.paywatch.org).

April 18, 2001

NYSE and Greedy Grasso

Richard A. Grasso, chairman and chief executive officer of the New York Stock Exchange, and his merry band of traders must believe that Robin Hood had it all wrong. Grasso and company want to take from the working families, small businesspeople, and the other taxpayers of New York and give to the wealthy investors on Wall Street that make up the New York Stock Exchange (NYSE).

The 3,000 plus companies listed on the NYSE have a total market capitalization of more than $15 trillion. The NYSE limits its membership to 1,366 individuals or firms and the price for membership in this exclusive group fluctuates based on demand. Today's asking price for membership in this capitalist club is only $1,700,000. Despite the corporate and individual largess of the NYSE members, they want a $1.1 billion subsidy from New York State's big and little taxpayers.

One might ask why free-market boosters like New York State Governor George Pataki and New York City Mayor Rudolph Giuliani feel compelled to give the NYSE a gargantuan amount of corporate welfare. Well, the NYSE indicated it might move to New Jersey—that's right, New Jersey! The mayor and governor surrendered to this "laughable bluff," in the words of one veteran stock trader, and offered a pile of taxpayer cash, a big parcel of land, and other goodies like tax breaks and cheap energy.

Don't worry. The mayor and the governor did a swell job representing the taxpayer. They offered to purchase and demolish an entire city block at an estimated cost to taxpayers of $450 million, provide $480 million in outright grants to build a new 600,000 square-foot trading complex, and provide $160 million in tax breaks and low-cost electricity.

So New York gets to house the new NYSE for $1.1 billion. According to Good Jobs New York, a joint project of Good Jobs First and the Fiscal Policy Institute that tracks the use of corporate subsidies in New York City, this is by far the largest and most dubious corporate subsidy in New York State history.

The day after this proposed giveaway was announced back in 1998, former State Senator Franz Leichter said, "The mayor is playing Santa Claus with the city's treasury. The fact is, the city is paying an inordinate amount on the dubious proposition that the stock exchange would have moved to Jersey City. And all this has been done without any public debate." The entire process of moving tax dollars to the Wall Street Welfare Kings has given new meaning to the word "chutzpah."

Eighteen months after the deal was publicly announced, following a series of backroom negotiations, Governor Pataki employed a procedural sleight of hand to rush the bill through both the Senate and the Assembly on the second to last day of the legislative session.

The governor's "Message of Necessity" required Senators and Assembly members to vote on the legislation immediately, and waived the New York State constitution's requirement that no bill be passed or become a law unless it is printed and on the desks of the members, in its final form, at least three legislative days prior to its final passage. But the governor's message of "necessity" simply said the bill was necessary to authorize the state's development corporations to provide support to expand the NYSE—no emergencies, no explanation of why the legislation was being introduced so late, no grand theories, just bald circumvention of the democratic process.

The bill passed the Senate on June 22, 2000, the same day it was introduced, and on the very next day the Assembly followed suit. The legislators in each house approved this legislation without a word of debate or a single voice of dissent. Many were probably unaware of the cost. Amazingly, the bill was not signed by the governor until December 8, 2000. So much for the urgent need to move the bill through the legislature on an expedited schedule.

Some have questioned why the corporate sector doesn't bear the costs of this project, particularly given all the capitalist free-market boosterism on Wall Street. Alice Meaker, who directs Good Jobs New York—a project that promotes responsible use of New York State's economic development subsidies—said, "The securities industry in New York City, which is dominated by NYSE firms, paid out bonuses of nearly $12 billion in 1999. With a fraction of those bonuses, these firms could easily finance the new facility themselves." Ms. Meaker also notes that the $1.1 billion being offered to the NYSE "means much less for investments in public education, transportation, affordable housing, and job training."

New York taxpayers unite! It is time to send a message to the greedy NYSE titans and to cowardly public officials who lack the gumption to protect your interests. Conservative and liberal groups can band together and say no to this wasteful taxpayer giveaway to the Wall Street moguls.

For more information on how you can join this fight, visit the Good Jobs New York web page. The URL is: www.goodjobsny.org. You can also write to the Corporate Accountability Research Group, P.O. Box 19312, Washington, D.C. 20036.

January 24, 2001

Revolving Door Corporate Executives

Revolving doors, through which corporate executives glide effortlessly between private sector employment and government jobs and back again, seem to be a fixture of every national administration. Neither the Democratic nor Republican administrations are immune from the practice that blurs the distinctions between the interests of corporate America and the broader concerns of the public at large.

Former Secretary of Treasury Robert Rubin, a star player on the roster of the outgoing Clinton administration, is a perfect example of how thoroughly and profitably the personnel and interests of large international financial institutions and the federal government are meshed. Mr. Rubin moved into government as Treasury secretary in 1995, leaving the cochairmanship of Goldman Sachs, one of the nation's leading investment firms. In the summer of 1999, he went through the revolving door again, leaving government to return to the upper echelons of finance, this time as part of the three-person leadership team at Citicorp, the giant banking, insurance, and securities conglomerate.

A number of ethics laws have been enacted to lessen the possibility for conflicts of interest when former government employees return to the corporate sector. Most employees are barred from contacting their former agency on behalf of others for one year after they leave government. In the case of senior employees, like Mr. Rubin, a Presidential Executive Order extends the prohibition to five years.

Questions about just how vigorously these ethics laws are enforced came up recently concerning the role of Mr. Rubin in the passage of the far-reaching Financial Modernization Act of 1999. The *New York Times* quoted Mr. Rubin, who drafted and promoted the bill while Treasury secretary, as saying that he had a role in the final compromise that led to the passage of the bill after he left office and while he was in negotiations for his job with Citigroup, the major beneficiary of the legislation. In fact, Mr. Rubin's job was announced four days after the compromise was accomplished.

Mr. Rubin was obviously regarded as a major catch by Citicorp. In fact, during just the two months of his employment in 1999, Mr. Rubin received $21.4 million in salary and stock options—a livable wage even by Wall Street standards.

When the bill was reaching final passage, Mr. Rubin was also serving as chairman of the Local Initiatives Support Corporation (LISC), a leading community development group with a direct interest in the legislation. Lobbying on behalf of LISC or Citicorp would have been a breach of ethics.

In addition to the reports in the *Times*, the *Wall Street Journal* said Mr. Rubin acknowledged that he had "some conversations" with respect to matters relating to the Community Reinvestment Act (CRA). The article quoted Mr. Rubin as "confirming" that he spoke with his successor, Treasury Secretary Lawrence Summers.

After these stories appeared, several consumer and community organizations and I wrote Stephen Potts, director of the Office of Government Ethics, asking for an investigation of Mr. Rubin's post-employment conduct as it related to the financial legislation. In short, were the news stories about Mr. Rubin's role accurate? That letter set off a series of near-comical non-replies that eventually stretched from the Ethics Office to the inspector general of the Treasury Department to the Public Integrity Section of the Justice Department and back. None of the agencies wanted to provide us with straight answers or provide any factual basis for failing to pursue the case. It was classic "pass the buck" and "please don't ask me" answers out of the bureaucrats' survival manual. No one wanted to be caught answering specific ethics questions about a former Cabinet officer of a sitting administration.

Mr. Potts, chief of the government-wide Ethics Office even went so far as to plead that his was "not an investigatory agency" and, therefore, could not take up the case. This despite the fact of the office's own published regulations that state: "the director may initiate proceedings under this section for the purpose of making a finding as to whether there has been...a violation." After five single-spaced pages devoted primarily to renditions of various ethics statutes, Mr. Potts told us he thought it would be best for us to ask the Treasury inspector general or the Justice Department about ethics, not the Office of Government Ethics.

All this might be dismissed as simply one more case of timid bureaucrats who see no career-advancing potential in challenging high officials in government, including high former officials. But there is much more at stake. With corporate interests and big campaign donors dominating so much of government decision-making, it is important that ethics laws be vigorously enforced if public confidence is to be maintained in our democracy.

Dropping the issue without full public disclosure of the investigation and exposition of the findings casts serious doubt on the efficacy of government ethics laws and could have a negative impact on compliance by government employees of lesser rank than Mr. Rubin.

The Republican Party, which is assuming the presidency this month, has had much to say about ethics during the terms of the Clinton administration. It will be interesting to see whether the incoming administration will take steps to strengthen the ethics machinery in a manner that will keep the lobbyists and the corporate influence peddlers at least at arm's length from the decision-makers in the Cabinet and in the agencies.

President Bush should take immediate steps to put strong public-interest inspectors general in office in all departments and to beef up the Justice Department's public integrity section. It is time to prove that Republican rhetoric about ethics wasn't just another political ploy to be dropped when the inaugural bunting comes down.

January 17, 2001

Pension Takeaway

At a time when CEOs are paying themselves exorbitant salaries, stock options, and benefit packages, corporations are slashing the pension benefits of workers who have helped build their companies.

The most heinous of the pension takeaway schemes include switching to cash balance plans (which deprive workers of expected benefit increases from their final years of company employment), changing pension formulas with obscure "modifications" that are really cuts, and "wearaway," which can force employees to work many additional years to increase pension benefits beyond previously established levels.

These schemes reduce corporate contributions to pension plans or enable them to increase pension plan surpluses. Although employers by law cannot take pension surpluses directly for corporate purposes, they are allowed by dint of an accounting rule to show the earnings of the surplus on their corporate balance sheets.

A recent IBM 30 percent gain in operating income was due to such a pension surplus, according to the *New York Times*. Many IBM workers have been deprived of expected pension fund benefits and the number would have been much larger had protests not protected the pension rights of 35,000 other IBM employees, who faced losses of up to 50 percent of what they would otherwise have earned.

IBM, Bell Atlantic/Verizon, ATT, SBC, Boeing, Monsanto, RJ Reynolds, and Citibank, are among the companies that have opted for the switch to cash balance plans.

In the fall of 2000, Congress is set to make the problem worse with the Comprehensive Retirement Security and Pension Reform Act. Passed overwhelmingly in the House of Representatives, this "Tax Giveaway and Pension Takeaway" (H.R. 1102) bill would expand employer's ability to undertake pension fund rip-offs. A version in the Senate is even worse.

The Clinton administration has criticized the pension takeaways, but refused to lead the charge against the rip-off schemes. It remains unclear whether President Clinton will veto or block the Tax Giveaway and Pension Takeaway bill.

This corporate attack on workers' pensions must be stopped. Cash balance conversions should be prohibited unless older workers' benefits are truly and adequately protected. Companies should be prohibited from cutting back promised benefits following mergers, acquisitions, and sales of the division of a company. Surplus pension monies should be used to provide full cost-of-living adjustments. And investment accountability must be enhanced by giving pension plan participants the right to information on plan investments and a greater role in investment management.

Those workers not now covered by a pension plan must also be guaranteed a secure retirement. New pension plans to cover these workers should be simple, fair, and portable, with employers contributing the same percentage of pay for all employees, and lifetime monthly payments to retirees that are indexed for inflation and insured.

Of top priority right now is to strip the cash balance provisions from the Tax Giveaway and Pension Takeaway bill. Senator Tom Harkin (D-Iowa) is expected to propose an amendment that pension rights groups say would better protect workers' interests.

It is hard to overstate the cruelty of the corporate schemes to undermine loyal workers' pension benefits. Workers who have relied in good faith on company pension promises are left helpless in the face of cutbacks that deprive them of expected payments to support them in retirement and old age.

It is now fashionable to speak of the nation's "prosperity." What prosperity there is is the result of the blood, sweat, and tears of millions of working Americans, much more than the efforts of most corporate executives. The executives are paying themselves handsomely. They shouldn't diminish the nest egg workers who have made them rich expect.

The Washington, D.C.-based Pension Rights Center, the nation's only consumer organization working solely to protect the pension rights of workers, retirees, and their families, is among the organizations leading the campaign to stop adoption of the Tax Giveaway and Pension Takeaway bill. Contact them at: Suite 602, 1140 19th Street, NW, Washington, DC 20036, phone: 202-296-3776, e-mail: pnsnrights@aol.com.

September 21, 2000

Corporate Crime

On May 7, 2000, the Federal Bureau of Investigation released data on serious crime in the United States. The FBI notes that both murder and robbery registered 8 percent drops since 1988. Missing from the FBI news release were any data on crime in the suites.

That information vacuum is notable because corporate crime and violence are often the result of calculated, rational executive decision-makers—people who clearly could be deterred by stronger penalties and enforcement measures.

Corporate decision-making determines many of the key questions that affect our lives. These decisions are made not through the democratic process but in the private suites of major business corporations here and abroad. Decisions shaped by corporate power include: how our natural resources will be used; the kind and price of products and services; where toxic pollution will be released into the air, water, and soil; whether jobs will be created, taken away, or moved to other countries; whether conditions in workplaces will be safe; compensation levels for top executives as well as entry-level workers; whether women and minorities will receive truly equal opportunities to succeed in the corporate structure; which political parties, groups, and candidates will have enough money to saturate the airwaves prior to elections and key legislative votes; what technologies will be developed that fundamentally affect the natural world and the shape of our urban skylines; and the way crops are grown on our soil.

Many of these decisions are constrained by market forces and addressed by state and federal statutes and regulations. But market factors don't work where, as is often the case, various dimensions of competition are minimized and consumer access to information is weak. Moreover, due to corporate lobbying and the competition among states for corporate business, the laws governing corporate conduct set low standards, giving corporate executives plenty of leeway within the weak existing legal strictures.

The influence on corporate decision-making by shareholders—let alone by employees, consumers, affected small businesses, surrounding communities, and other stakeholders—is pathetically weak because our system of regulating corporate governance is a failure. Rules for corporate control have been left to individual states, and the result is well known: a "race to the bottom," in which states compete to offer the package of rules and incentives most attractive to the corporate managers who choose the state of incorporation.

Weak legal provisions and an imbalance of power between corporate management and shareholders are one thing, but what is worse is that even the relatively low standards set by the law—limits on corporate misconduct like fraud, toxic dumping, indifference to hazardous work conditions, and marketing of dangerous products—are often flouted. As bad as street crime is, the evidence is stronger than ever that business wrongdoing inflicts far more preventable violence and economic damage on society than all street crimes combined.

We don't know the precise magnitude of corporate crime due to the curious absence of Justice Department data on such lawlessness, but there is reason to believe it is enormous. The FBI reports that in 1999, burglary and robbery cost our nation approximately $3.8 billion. Meanwhile, according to W. Steve Albrecht, professor of accountancy at Brigham Young University, white-collar fraud—doctor and lawyer over-billing, defense procurement scams, and the like—costs us perhaps $200 billion per year.

Street criminals do not have a monopoly on violent crime, either. About 24,000 people in this country are murdered each year, says the FBI. But far more Americans—100,000, according to the National Institute of Occupational Safety and Health—die annually from work-related diseases like black lung and asbestosis. Sixty-five thousand die preventable deaths due to air pollution. More than 400,000 Americans die annually from tobacco-related disease—a product, to a considerable extent, of longtime tobacco industry marketing practices aimed at hooking adolescents into a lifetime of tobacco addiction.

Corporate environmental crimes are also widespread. Exxon, International Paper, United Technologies, Weyerhaeuser, Pillsbury, Ashland Oil, Texaco, Nabisco, and Ralston-Purina have all been convicted in recent years.

Against the backdrop of these factors—immense power and influence by the major corporations and weak controls by shareholders, labor, and other concerned constituencies; a disastrous race to the bottom in state corporate chartering; and an epidemic of corporate misconduct—citizens need to consider a Corporate Decency Act, a new approach to ensuring that our largest corporations act as good citizens in our society.

Where traditional federal regulation has focused on the external relationships of the corporation—don't pollute, don't fix prices, don't air deceptive advertisements—the Corporate Decency Act would seek to reform the internal governance structure of our largest corporations so that, in a manner consistent with our free-market economy, companies will exercise their power and discretion in more democratic and accountable ways.

It's time for corporate crime to be treated like street crime—as a dangerous affront to an organized, law-respecting society. Citizens interested in getting tough on crime in the suites can find a model Corporate Decency Act on the following web page: www.nader.org/modellaws/decency.html.

May 7, 2000

Microsoft Remedies

As the titanic antitrust case against Microsoft moves into its end-game, the question of the hour is what remedies will be effective in taming this wealthy and ruthless monopoly.

The goal of any set of remedies should be to ensure that there will, in fact, be innovation, competition, and reasonable prices in some of the most important sectors of our economy—software, computers, and telecommunications.

Consider the following remedies:

• Free PC manufacturers from Microsoft's grip. Microsoft has used its monopoly power to bully original equipment manufacturers (OEMs) into installing only Windows on computers. A court-ordered remedy of nondiscriminatory OEM licensing of Windows would go a long way toward solving this problem. Pricing and licensing should be "transparent," openly published, and evenhandedly applied.

• Don't let Microsoft use its other software monopolies to limit competition. Just as Microsoft used its Windows monopoly to threaten the competition, so it is using its Office franchise to scare off competitors and dominate new Internet markets. Its preferred strategy is the notorious "embrace, extend, and extinguish" gambit: embrace the new Internet authoring tools as part of the dominant Office software suite; extend control of the new market by introducing proprietary standards that are incompatible with competitors' standards; and extinguish competing software through manipulative licensing and bundling deals with OEMs.

The court should require Microsoft to separate Microsoft Office from Windows, and the new owner of Office should be required to port the entire platform to multiple non-Windows operating systems.

• Ensure that "Internet navigation" options remain open. Microsoft has insisted to OEMs that it retain control of the "first screen," or default choices for Internet navigation menus. It has done so in order to retain control over the time and attention of computer users, whose reliance on the default "first screen" can be used to channel them to certain e-commerce sites.

Here's the danger: If any single firm exercises too much control over Internet navigation, competition in e-commerce markets will suffer. Microsoft should be prohibited from imposing such terms.

• Protect interoperability of hardware, software, and network protocols. The usefulness of software programs depends upon their ability to work (and coexist) with other software programs, with hardware systems, and with the protocols of telecommunications networks.

It should come as no surprise that Microsoft frequently and deliberately introduces barriers to compatibility and interoperability, preventing competitors from working with Microsoft's monopolizing Windows or Office products. One remedy is to force Microsoft to support open standards for software and to provide extensive technical information in a timely manner to any requesting company in usable formats and protocols.

• Adopt structural remedies, because the record shows Microsoft cannot be trusted. The past six years of antitrust problems with Microsoft have demonstrated that the company cannot be trusted. Its conduct during the trial itself offers the best evidence of this point. The company subverted the intent if not the language of a 1995 consent order by integrating its browser into the Windows operating system.

Effective remedies should, as much as possible, avoid "conduct remedies" that require continuing court oversight. A better alternative is "structural remedies"—such as a breakup—that permanently alter Microsoft's organizational structure and the incentives by which it operates.

Ideally, a breakup of the company would go further than the Justice Department proposal to divide the operating system line of business from the application and other lines of business. The court could insist that Microsoft separate the Internet Explorer browser from Microsoft Office. That way, the browser market could become competitive again and the owner of Microsoft Office would find a way to function with more than one browser. This would be an important result in a world where the browser is key in setting web publishing standards and links to e-commerce sites, and where Microsoft is driving for dominance in Internet authoring tools.

The court should also consider forcing Microsoft to spin off, as a separate company, all of its online services and minority interests in networking companies. There is no legitimate tie between the software businesses and online/network services—only anticompetitive mischief.

The antitrust remedies that ultimately bring the marauding Microsoft to heel will have far-reaching consequences on future software design and choices, on consumer prices, on the competitiveness of e-commerce, on the very structure of the Internet and hence our culture.

The factual case against Microsoft has been made devastatingly clear. If Microsoft's long record of deception and untrustworthiness is to be ended, the public remedies must be as bold, sweeping, and effective as the company's private power.

May 3, 2000

No Cheerleader for Corporations

Nothing is more scarce than thorough, tough, or objective analysis of today's corporations. What little there is comes mostly from academics and public interest groups.

The majority of the mainstream media skims the surface and usually serves as little more than a cheerleader for the corporations. Rarely does anyone from inside the corporate world venture forward with anything but self-serving clichés about the values, glories, and ethics of corporate organizations.

But there is at least one exception. His name is Dee Hock. He doesn't play around with sugar-coated phrases in describing the shortcomings of the corporate structure or the immense power wielded by corporations throughout the world.

Dee Hock is no ordinary critic, and certainly no political radical. He comes to the arena with real credentials from inside the corporate world. He is founder and CEO Emeritus of VISA International, a credit card corporation owned by 22,000 member banks with 750 million customers who engage in $1.25 trillion transactions annually.

Here's the way Dee Hock sees the corporations of the twenty-first century: "The monetized commercial form of corporation has steadily become an instrument of those with surplus money (capital) and those with surplus power (management) to reward themselves at the expense of the community, the biosphere, and the many without surplus wealth or power, commonly called 'consumers' and 'human resources.'"

These "human resources," Dee Hock says, "are mined, smelted, shaped into products, worn out, and discarded with little more consideration on the part of monetary stockholders and management than they might give a load of ore or a pile of lumber."

Conservative "think tanks" and corporate public relations operatives turn out endless tomes about the heavy hand of government regulation over the corporations. Congress is lobbied for "regulatory relief" and much of the national media parrots the corporate line about the "burden" of regulation.

Dee Hock turns this argument on its head.

The "monetized shareholder" form of corporation, he says, "has demanded and received release from the revocation of its charter for inept or antisocial acts."

"The roles of giant, transnational corporations and government have slowly reversed," Hock argues. "Government is now more an instrument of such corporations than the corporations are instruments of government."

Dee Hock's critique of the organizational structures of corporations is contained in his recently published book *Birth of the Chaordic Age* (Berrett-Koehler Publishers, Inc., San Francisco, California). The book draws heavily on his experiences at VISA, a "chaordic" (simultaneously chaotic and orderly) structure involving "intense cooperation and fierce competition."

Looking not only at corporations, but at all forms of organizational structures, Hock says we're in an "accelerating, global epidemic of institutional failure" with organizations increasingly unable to achieve the purpose for which they were created, yet "continuing to expand as they devour scarce resources, demean the human spirit and destroy the environment."

Hock argues that our current forms of organization are almost universally based on compelled behavior, "on tyranny." The organization of the future, according to Hock, will be the embodiment of "community based on shared purpose calling to the higher aspiration of people."

Dee Hock debunks a ton of conventional thinking and lays out a challenging and exciting view of the future structure of corporations and society. It makes for exciting reading whether or not you buy into all of his theory.

January 19, 2000

A Groundbreaking Lawsuit against DaimlerChrysler

Increasingly, the citizens of Toledo, Ohio, are making connections between their daily lives and corporate welfare payouts, thanks to the recent provocations of DaimlerChrysler, which is sitting on $20 billion in cash, and its buddy, Toledo Mayor Carty Finkbeiner, who is sitting on a financially crumbling city government.

The residents are seeing the emergence of an enormous double standard where a giant, powerful corporation is given a ten-year tax-free holiday, free land, free water, and free site preparation for an expanded Jeep factory, while families, small businesses, and children suffer the burdens and pay the tax freight for the bosses from Stuttgart and Detroit. What's more, the people of Toledo are required by the one-sided November 1998 deal with the city to assume all environmental liabilities.

In return DaimlerChrysler agreed to maintain a declining number of jobs while making a whopping profit. If the company does not hold to its promise of retaining those existing 4,900 jobs, the city can do nothing and take back nothing from its huge $280 million giveaway.

The automaker knows something about building cars, but it knows far more about how to construct a one-way street.

The area that DaimlerChrysler coveted did have a problem, however. People lived in a corner—about eighty houses and several small businesses. There was in the rest of the 200-plus-acre tract plenty of space for the new plant and the truck staging areas. But the occupied corner nicely rounded out the geometry of the tract, and on one Chrysler map was designated for landscaping or shrubbery.

This did not sit well with longtime homeowners like Mary Ebright and the Robie family. For many years, this closely knit neighborhood never dreamed that the city could ever condemn their property and then turn around and give it to a big private business.

Well, they were mistaken. The mayor told them that their houses and small businesses would have to go, and that they better agree on a price before condemnation proceedings commenced. Most of the homeowners agreed to modest payments and some saw their homes bulldozed after they moved out. Others held on for months and ended up getting a better price from the city. Note that Toledo taxpayers had to pay for these properties, not the bulging treasury of DaimlerChrysler.

A few months ago, I called an executive at the auto company and asked why his firm would not agree to do what every homeowner and small business (that also generate jobs) have to do in Toledo—pay property taxes for the schools, police, fire, etc., and pay for their own improvements or expansions. His reply exuded the usual slogans about having to be competitive, meaning other big and powerful companies do this to their communities.

What this assertion boils down to is that a big and powerful corporation can bring a town to its knees and receive huge subsidies just by threatening to locate or move elsewhere.

Big Business freeloading is upsetting some Republicans in Congress, especially Representative John Kasich (R-OH), chairman of the House Budget Committee, who held hearings last June critical of many forms of corporate welfare.

But it is more specifically upsetting to the members of the Toldeo-based Phoenix Earth Food Co-op. They issued a statement of what the consequences to their town will be because the mayor decided to turn DaimlerChrysler into a tax escapee and immunize it from many other ordinary costs of doing business.

They said their public schools, badly in need of repairs, are running a $3 million deficit and the city government gives tax holidays to "mega bucks corporations. Residents pay more taxes, corporations go free."

The members' statement decried the rising rates for water usage, while DaimlerChrysler gets free water. They noted that their city, even with state and federal subsidies for the deal, may not be able to meet its fiscal obligations under the arrangement with the big automaker. As taxpayers they wondered about the cost of all environmental liabilities "now and in the future" and what incentive is that for the auto company to protect the environment?

Summing up their dismay, they declared: "Our tax dollars are used to downsize, worker-residents lose income (jobs) and the City loses even more tax revenue. Every one loses, except DaimlerChrysler."

Indeed, the declining number of jobs is already evident at the existing Jeep plant and the number of promised retained jobs has been cut as well.

On December 8, 1999, the people fought back. Represented by local attorney Terry Lodge and Law Professor Peter Enrich, taxpayers, residents, and small businesses filed a lawsuit against DaimlerChrysler, the city of Toledo, and the state of Ohio challenging the constitutionality of tax subsidies to companies that are conditioned on location of facilities in Ohio.

By conferring preferential tax treatment on in-state business, the suit maintains Ohio law "discriminates in favor of in-state business activity and against out-of-state activity, in violation of the restrictions imposed on discriminatory state taxation by the commerce clause of Article 1, section 8 of the U.S. Constitution."

This is a groundbreaking case based on a celebrated *Harvard Law Review* article (Dec. 1996) by Northeastern University law professor Peter Enrich. When politicians, laws, and corporate lobbyists run roughshod over basic rights of innocent people, the last resort for justice is our Constitution.

December 21, 1999

Curbing Microsoft's Monopolistic Practices

As the government's antitrust case against Microsoft winds down, the question is no longer whether Microsoft violated antitrust laws but rather what can be done to curb its most harmful monopolistic practices.

The case being tried by the U.S. Department of Justice and nineteen state attorneys general has been a textbook tutorial on how anticompetitive conduct harms consumers through higher prices, forced upgrades, degraded performance of competitors' products, and restricted consumer choice. However, there is no clear remedy for the hydra-headed problem, and public debate on the issue is nearly nonexistent.

The corrective measures currently under consideration go far beyond those imposed on Microsoft in 1995, when, after years of investigating anticompetitive practices, the Department of Justice first legally pressed Microsoft to change its ways. Some have a familiar ring, such as breaking the software giant into different lines of business, like the earlier AT&T or Standard Oil cases. Other remedies are more novel. Among other things, the government might require Microsoft to:

• Auction off several licenses for Microsoft's intellectual property, creating instant competitors for its main software products.

• Provide rival programmers with the technical information they need to make products work properly with Microsoft Windows or Microsoft Office.

• Stop using discriminatory pricing to discipline computer manufacturers who offer software from competitors.

• Support or not interfere with open or third-party protocols that run on top of Windows or Microsoft Office.

• Unbundle various components of Windows or Microsoft Office.

Some of these sanctions could be implemented on a "stand alone" basis, while others would work together.

Microsoft itself has not really joined the debate, its leaders perhaps thinking the lack of consensus will benefit the company by giving an impression that no one knows what to do to solve the problems.

But one thing is clear: Any settlement or court-ordered remedy will have enormous impact on consumers, the future of the Internet, and the computer and software industries. Any corrective measure should fit well with an industry that is rapidly changing, so that the technological stagnation that now prevails in areas dominated by Microsoft is replaced with innovation. This case should end with a strong measure of protection for the public against monopolistic practices, and the remedies should be forward looking, aimed at preventing future harm as well as addressing past transgressions. The outcome will be instrumental in defining the rules for competition in the next century.

Such groups as Essential Information and the Consumer Project on Technology are trying to promote broader debate on possible Microsoft sanctions and have scheduled a workshop on April 30 in Washington, D.C. The conference information is available at www.appraising-microsoft.org.

April 17, 1999

Bill Marriott Demands Corporate Welfare

Suppose, for a moment, you are a small businessperson. You employ six workers. You write a letter to your state's economic development agency. You insist that the state refrain from taxing you and offer you job training credits and an assortment of other bonuses. In return, you offer to hire two more people in addition to those currently in your employ. And you promise not to move your business to a neighboring state.

In all likelihood, the state agency would tell you to get lost.

Now change the scene and the scale. The Marriott corporation, which generated nearly $26 billion in revenue, last year recently announced that its corporate headquarters in Maryland would relocate to the state that offered it, in the words of CEO Bill Marriott, some "compelling financial reasons" to do so. Subsequently Virginia made an attractive subsidy offer and fostered what would soon become a bidding war between itself and Maryland.

Bill Marriott is a conservative, fervent free-enterprise advocate. He glorifies free enterprise in speeches made around the country. But he demands welfare for his hotel chain. And like the proverbial eight-hundred-pound gorilla, Bill gets what he wants.

State legislatures, pressured by threats like Marriott's, often give away subsidies at the expense of middle-class taxpayers, without demanding a reciprocal investment from the corporation benefiting from their actions.

As William Skinner, president of the Maryland Taxpayers Association, wryly said: "We didn't elect 188 legislators and all these county people to be venture capitalists." He urged companies that receive public money to issue stock to state residents. "They have my address. Where are my shares?" he asked.

When big businesses receive subsidies like these, they gain a substantial competitive advantage over smaller businesses. Worse still, property tax exemptions, or equivalent credits, diminish the tax base that funds schools, police, fire fighting, and a host of other public services. In the case of Marriott, the corporation benefits from the very services that it does not help pay for.

Corporations like Marriott justify their refusal to meet their community obligations by insisting that the economic impact of their investments in the community invigorates it. But isn't that true of other smaller businesses as well? What these big businesses are really saying is that sheer size and power demands privilege.

What are the possible remedies for this mega-billion-dollar corporate welfare epidemic?

State governments should agree among themselves not to engage in such races to the bottom. And the national government should work to abolish such subsidies entirely.

Until that time, the public should initiate a constitutional challenge to tax inducements designed to lure companies across state lines. In an article in the December 1996 *Harvard Law Review*, Professor Peter Enrich of Northeastern University Law School argues that such actions violate the interstate commerce clause. It's a sound argument, and one that activists need to pursue.

In the meantime, House Budget Committee Chair John Kasich (R-Ohio) will hold hearings in Congress on corporate welfare in May—the first of their kind. Send him your expressions of support. He's going to need them.

Honorable John R. Kasich
IIII Longworth House Office Building
Washington, D.C. 20515

April 9, 1999

Merger Mania

What do monopolistic practices and antitrust laws have to do with traffic congestion and commuter woes?

More than you might imagine.

In the late '30s and '40s, General Motors, with the help of a few oil and tire companies, purchased electrified mass transit systems in twenty-eight cities. It soon disabled these systems and began to lobby for new highways in the hopes of increasing its sales of vehicles, gasoline, and tires.

Ultimately, the U.S. Justice Department prosecuted these companies for criminal violations of the antitrust law that many called the "economic crime of the century." But the damage had already been done.

Fifty years after that incident our country is in the grip of monopoly mania. The new American Antitrust Institute (AAI) (202-362-8704) reports that there were 4,728 reportable U.S. merger transactions in 1998 totaling in value over $1.2 trillion. There were 1,529 mergers in 1991.

AAI argues that budgets for the federal antitrust agencies have not accounted for such a large increase in mergers. "Between 1977 and 1997 the total budgets of the FTC and the Antitrust Division decreased by 7 percent in constant dollars, while the GNP grew by 112 percent. Mergers have increased by 550 percent since 1992," says AAI President Bert Foer.

The concentration of economic power in a few giant corporate structures has been the stimulus for many populist and progressive revolts in our nation's history. Republicans authored the first federal antitrust law, the Sherman Act, in 1890. Teddy Roosevelt thundered against the "giant trusts." Franklin D. Roosevelt assailed the "malefactors of great wealth."

The trustbusters of yesteryear would be shocked at what has occurred in the past twenty years. ITT chairman Rand Araskog once said that merger mania "has more to do with the self-fulfilling prophecies of some egomaniacal financiers and overwhelming ambition of some investment houses than with business efficiencies. Too many deals are being done because of the ability to do them—not because they have sound economic logic or business validity."

Mr. Araskog should know. He spent years spinning off subsidiaries of ITT that were cobbled together unwisely. Today mergers proliferate by using inflated stock values to acquire other companies. As Federal Reserve Chairman Alan Greenspan told a House Committee recently, many of these large mergers don't work out. Workers lose their jobs, communities suffer, and consumers pay more and receive less service. In due time, some of these giant companies become too large to be allowed to fail, and the government is expected to bail them out.

Merger mania invites corporate welfare, a growing system of corporate socialism in which the taxpayers are forced to bail out mismanaged corporate giants.

Expanding by purchasing your competition does not create a quality economy. Instead it compromises service, products, and prices. Worse still, it undermines the public's ability to demand reform and corporate accountability.

Merger mania has become almost ubiquitous. It's occurring in the drug, telecommunications, airline, defense, auto, energy, electrical, cable, banking, and HMO industries. Will we allow it to continue? Or will we use it as a springboard for populist and progressive revolts?

March 26, 1999

Corporate Power and Measure

Arcata, California, a small town not far from the redwoods and wild rivers of northern California, made news in 1996 when an elected majority of its city council was members of the Green Party. Three years later, the town is about to find itself in the news again. Arcata is pioneering Measure F (the Arcata Advisory Measure on Democracy and Corporations), a piece of legislation that hopes to rescind corporate rule in California. Measure F calls on the Arcata city council to:

• Cosponsor (in cooperation with the drafters of this initiative) two town hall meetings in the five months following passage of this ballot measure on the topic "Can we have democracy when large corporations wield so much power and wealth under law?"

• Immediately act to establish, through the creation of an official committee, policies and programs that ensure democratic control over corporations conducting business within the city, in whatever ways are necessary to ensure the health and well-being of our community and its environment.

• Immediately forward copies of this ballot measure to all of our elected representatives at the county, state, and federal levels, and to members of the press.

Before cynics laugh at such local presumption, we must remember that major political reform movements in our country's history have often begun in rural areas. While it is the first such initiative in the nation, discussion of Measure F occurred across the country in local gatherings inspired by Richard Grossman and his associates (Program on Corporations, Law and Democracy).

Grossman and other proponents of Measure F—Paul Cienfuegos, Gary House, and Linda Mirelez—are asking Americans to examine nineteenth-century American history and the evolution of corporate privilege and immunity in this modern era.

The citizens of Arcata want to create an enlightened debate about the public's ability to reassert itself. They want to remind us that in the nineteenth century, states often revoked the charter of companies that broke the law. They want us to know that since all corporations are created by the state, it is within the public's power to modify and even revoke corporate charters.

In a pamphlet titled *Why Do Corporations Have More Rights Than You?*, Democracy Unlimited of Arcata argues that "this country's founders never intended for corporations to dominate our society and overwhelm our democracy."

There are more than fifty giant corporations currently doing business in Arcata, among them the Bank of America, Exxon, General Electric, Louisiana-Pacific, Maxxam, McDonald's, Media News Group, PepsiCo, Safeway, Pacific

Gas and Electric Co., and RiteAid. Measure F will ensure that these companies and their officials engage in a robust civic dialogue.

For more information, contact Democracy Unlimited at P.O. Box 27, Arcata, CA 95518 or visit its web site, www.monitor.net/democracyunlimited.

March 19, 1999

II

MEDIA AND COMMERCIALISM

Calvin Coolidge famously declared that "the business of America is business." Surely, there are grander purposes of our collective life than a simple measuring of the gross national product.

The commercial imperative permeates every aspect of our lives. Our food, entertainment, our electoral and political institutions—all of this and much more is controlled by corporations which care most about their bottom line.

The mercantile juggernaut has moved into area after area once wholly or largely off limits to commerce, including our schools and colleges, amateur sports, the arts, our holidays and rituals, religious institutions, and environment. Our major "public space" is the corporate shopping mall, which bars civic activity like petitioning. The columns in this section trace the extent and insidious effects of rampant commercialism and its subjugation of civic values.

If we take our Constitution and founding ideals seriously, the business of America is democracy. A well-functioning democracy requires diverse and vibrant media to ensure a "vigorous, robust, uninhibited democracy." Our country's founders understood that democracy cannot thrive without an open exchange of ideas that includes the ability to receive full information about the workings of government and viewpoints that challenge the official line.

The media is dominated by a handful of interlocking corporations with common political and economic interests, pursued daily by their paid vocalists. The Federal Communications Commission, funded by our taxpayer dollars and supposedly responsive to the public interest of the people's public airwaves, has taken action to make the situation worse, including repeal of the Fairness Doctrine and the Right of Reply.

Anyone doubting this should talk to Phil Donahue, whose program at MSNBC (which hired him, at least in part, as counterweight to conservative domination of the airwaves) lasted six months. From the beginning, the powers-that-be objected to Donahue's efforts to broaden public discourse. Before long, after harassing his program with dictates, they fired him, allegedly over less-than-soaring ratings.

In the columns that follow, you will encounter the stories of Donahue and *other voices muffled by the corporate media moguls. We own the public airwaves, but the media control what we see. A free and open society needs free and open media about what is going on in this country and the world—media that promote more than the narrow revenues of commercial interests.*

Signs of Societal Decay

Modern societies specialize in a dazzling number of indicators that mark the ups and downs of various activities, especially economic, health, and audience ratings. But when it comes to signs of societal decay that cannot easily be reduced to numbers, there is a void. So let's look at four "decays" that are trending downward.

Gluttony, no longer one of the seven deadly sins is rapidly becoming a competitive sport. In fact, gorging has become a contest with the gorgers riding circuit around the country performing in what its euphemists call "competitive eating." "Crazy Devin" Lipsitz, winner of the 2000 United Carnegie International Pickle Eating Contest in New York City, describes his skill as "a sport" played by "athletes."

There is even an International Federation of Competitive Eating that presides over dozens of events a year where contestants inhale hot dogs (the champion swallowed fifty hot dogs in twelve minutes), matzoh balls, chicken wings, and who knows what's next—mayonnaise?

The voyeuristic audience for such gluttony battles is growing fast. It may be only a matter of time before the first cable television show is launched. By the way, according to the rules, if an "athlete" vomits, he/she is disqualified. So much for the Peter the Great maneuver.

Next on the decay derby is Tyco under CEO L. Dennis Kozlowski, presently the defendant in a criminal trial. He held a $2 million fortieth birthday party for his wife in faraway Sardinia that featured a shrunken model of Michelangelo's David with vodka streaming from his penis into crystal glasses.

Videotapes also showed an exploding birthday cake with a replica of a woman's breast. Government prosecutors charge that Tyco paid for much of this party as a deductible business entertainment expense.

Parents cannot deduct their children's college tuition as an educational expense. Yet corporations can and do deduct liquor, lurid entertainment, and expensive, luxurious gifts as "ordinary and necessary" business expenses. They thereby reduce the revenues going to the U.S. Treasury, which could have been used to provide grants and loans to America's deserving students. Call this the decay of inverted priorities.

A third decay comes from the electoral arena. There was a time in our history when a resurgent citizenry gave itself the right to vote. So the oligarchs devised a "wealth election" and dollars began voting in ever greater numbers. But buying elections was not enough for the power brokers in the two major parties. Lately they are determined to pick their voters by increasingly precise computer-driven legislative redistricting.

In the past, redistricting came once every ten years after the decennial census. Now Republicans and Democrats can not resist the lure of more frequent redistricting because, depending on who controls the state government, the reward of making them one-party districts is obvious. In Texas, the state Republicans have broken cynical new ground in passing legislation that carves new zigzag congressional districts in order to pick the voters that would almost certainly replace up to five congressional House Democrats with Republicans. These elections are over before they start.

The courts have been too lenient in permitting such blatant electoral map-making that is turning most of the House of Representative Districts into areas of one-party domination. Both parties now believe that over 90 percent of House Districts in the country are not competitive, meaning that the other major party doesn't try to contest the incumbent's seat. This is worsening decay for voter choice and political competition in a weakening democracy.

The fourth "decay" is occurring in the midst of the nation's largest corporate crime wave (remember Enron, WorldCom, Health South, etc., etc.) that has drained or looted trillions of dollars from millions of workers, their pension funds, and small investors. Well, it seems that the corporate crooks so vastly outnumber the federal cops on the corporate crime beat that "accommodations" have become necessary.

Faced with a tiny enforcement budget and the "soft on corporate crime" attitude of the Bush administration, the Justice Department has developed ways to avoid traditional, straight-out indictment, prosecution, and conviction approaches of the past.

Presently, the Department initiates a criminal prosecution of a company and then settles for probation plus a modest fine. Or, the Department criminally prosecutes companies but then enters into a "deferred prosecution" agreement stipulating that the case will be dropped if the company shows good behavior over a year or two. Another lax approach is to file criminal charges but then not prosecute the company and instead enter into a "memorandum of understanding."

Large corporations with their giant corporate law firms skilled in battles of attrition and delay can routinely bring the small number of state and federal prosecutors to such levels of concessions, if they do not escape prosecution filings entirely in the first place.

Congressional and state legislators know this, as they raise money from these companies for their campaign treasuries. So these lawmakers return the favor to their business benefactors by starving the budgets of these federal and state anticorporate crime task forces. And you the consumers, workers, and investors of America continue to pay the Big price.

October 24, 2003

The Big SnApple

Mayor Michael R. Bloomberg held a news conference on September 9th that was described by the *New York Post* this way: "Looking more like a pitchman than a politician, the mayor bought an orange-mango juice drink from a Snapple machine, opened it and took a sip."

In so doing, the mayor's common sense snapped, as he committed New York City unilaterally to naming Snapple as the official water, juice, and iced tea provider for the nation's largest metropolis. The elaborate five-year agreement—not publicly available—transferred $166 million from Snapple to the city in return for exclusive selling rights of these and other products in the public schools and public buildings. Snapple's logo is to go on ferries and garbage cans.

About $40 million of this sum would go to the schools and the rest to the city's general budget. Snapple won the selection contest over seven other beverage sellers which the mayor refused to name.

The city's chief marketing officer (that's his title) said that the Snapple agreement was both "relevant" and "tasteful." The mayor flagged the future of selling New York City without asking its citizens: "This agreement is the first in a limited number of high-quality partnerships that we think will greatly enhance our efforts to promote and market New York City," he enthused.

Old-timers years ago would have wondered what the mayor means by marketing New York City. Cities were viewed more benignly when they were more livable, more employable at good wages, more replete with public institutions like good libraries, good public transit, good schools, good hospitals and clinics, and good recreational facilities in the neighborhoods. New York City is crumbling on these measurements.

Its officials, including the mayor, cannot even protect its poor children from the chronic, brain-and-body-damaging, lead-based paint poisoning in aging tenements. But he can provide them with Snapple drinks of dubious nutritional quality and water in the vending machines. Water??? Regular testing reveals that New York City delivers about the finest water of any city in the country, according to Consumers Union. The schools' water coolers dispense it.

Obviously in this age of overweening corporate commercialism and the placement of their executives in public office, marketing New York City means partnerships that promote products. What's next? Mayor Bloomberg isn't saying. Let's guess. Will New York City have its official cars, sports equipment, jeans, sneakers, computers, colas, hot dogs, pens, and cereal? And what intriguing new areas for corporate logos will be made available? In his fervent quest for budget dollars (never mind the massive tax abatements the city has given to corporations), Mayor Bloomberg might want to make city hall and his own backside available. Imagine what price a huge banner for GM or Apple Computer in front of city hall will fetch year after year?

Unlike his uncanny ability to think through the demand for financial information that marked the rise of his Bloomberg communications empire, the mayor has not thought through the slippery slope that the city is now on.

Giving a company a monopoly over certain products sold to the city means preventing better products from superior competitors coming along to demonstrate what free enterprise means. What will happen if your designated monopolist—say Snapple—or its parent conglomerate Cadbury-Schweppes (a British company) gets into trouble with the law—a criminal conviction, an Enron-type scandal, a covered-up product defect? Does the secret agreement with Snapple have an "out" clause? Who pays to remove the stigmatized company logos and signs all over the Big Apple?

What happens when the city government is wrestling with a policy that affects vending machine products? Will Snapple appear to have special influence in the mayor's administration? Will the mayor avoid doing the right thing for consumers because of some provision in the Snapple agreement that immunizes the company from some later public policy?

Already, the Snapple deal is making otherwise adult politicians look foolish. Mayor Bloomberg, according to the *New York Times*, announced the agreement "on the athletic field at John F. Kennedy High School in the Bronx, with a bright-orange Snapple vending machine and the high school's football team standing behind him." The mayor said: "Given the global popularity of Snapple products, this will present the city with countless new opportunities to make positive impressions on people around the world." So reassuring!

What happens when people and students take issue, as they surely will, with Snapple's president's blanket statement that "New York City loves Snapple," and start rebelling against this fiat by city hall, start wearing t-shirts in school saying awful things about Snapple, boycotting the products, examining the contents of the drinks, and showing that commercialism and public government do not mix. Who will Mayor Bloomberg's props be then?

For more information, log on to www.commercialalert.org.

September 14, 2003

Commercial and Civic Values at the Neighborhood Level

Public space, universal community services, and their historic traditions which bind our nation together are under assault. A presidential commission recommends that the U.S. Postal Service obtain commercial appraisals of their post offices and land with the view of selling the property off to help pay its expenses. The smaller postal services can find a place in a commercial mall to handle its "customers," advised this Bush-appointed commission, dominated by corporate executives.

The Government Printing Office (GPO), established by President Abraham Lincoln—who named it "The People's Printer"—to educate the public by providing all kinds of government documents, reports, and hearings at a very cheap price, just announced it is closing its twenty-three retail stores in major cities all over the country.

Reason? A GPO spokesman, Andrew M. Sherman, said that its online operation is draining the retail end of its operations. Sales have dropped 50 percent. The GPO said it would save the princely sum of $1.5 million annually with all the closures.

Aggressive real estate developers are eyeing public libraries and their urban branches with the aim of enveloping them under multiuse projects that include stores, cinemas, and condos. In return, these tax-sheltered developers will offer to pay for a portion or all of a new library structure.

Is there anything wrong with these trends? Plenty, and they revolve around the difference between commercial and civic values right down to the neighborhood level.

For over two centuries, freestanding post office buildings have anchored communities of all sizes. In small towns and rural areas, it is a vital force, a place to access all kinds of government information and notices, a gathering spot to chat briefly and meet your friends and neighbors, a place to send and receive mail and parcels. This is something both tangibly and intangibly different than going to an enclave in a sprawling corporate mall. People in small-town rural America see the post office as a symbol of Uncle Sam, of what the *New York Times* called "the national community." It is hard to imagine people rallying to save the postal enclave in a mall, as they do to save their little post office.

Budget-reduced public libraries are under increasing pressure to rebuild their libraries under multiuse projects. City Hall sees multiuse as relieving its library budget. And the federal government can continue to spend more every forty-eight hours in Iraq than its entire support of libraries in America over one year.

Again, the loss of freestanding library structures and their landscaping means families and individuals entering and leaving libraries must navigate between people with shopping bags and carts negotiating adjacent stores, parking, and all the noise. Commercial minds do not appreciate the sanctuaries of such public institutions. They do understand dependency, however, as well as the proverbial foot in the door toward privatization (better called corporatization).

The Edison company, which aspires to corporatize a goodly part of the $400 billion annual public school budget, has suggested that schools could be on floors of office buildings. What is so sacrosanct about a freestanding schoolhouse, anyway, it argues.

Then there are the GPO stores. Maybe if the GPO had a better sense of promoting the dazzling variety of fascinating and important government publications, it could have avoided these stores' closures all together. To be sure, there needs to be some enabling changes in the GPO's statutory base; but was there any excuse for the GPO shredding 1500 of the historic Watergate prosecutor's reports years ago instead of letting people know how to get this increasingly valuable historic document? Rather than discounting, or giving away its surplus reports, the GPO often shreds and gets a few pennies per pound for scrap paper.

The GPO store in Denver was twenty-nine years old. The manager, Kathleen Moss, said many of her patrons "are appalled that we're shutting down. A lot of people would still rather come in and see the books on the shelf."

This is otherwise known as browsing with others, something some human beings might prefer to a computer screen.

One patron of the store, who was looking for books on General George

Armstrong Custer, said: "they think everybody would rather have a computer in their lap than a book." All this to save $1.5 million, instead of actually expanding its market.

It is permissible to think that Abraham Lincoln would have disapproved.

August 8, 2003

Gardening

Question: What is the most popular hobby in America today? Answer: Gardening. Gardeners outnumber participants in amateur athletics.

Gardening gives off beauty and aroma. Gardening provides edibles worth over $15 billion annually in vegetables and fruits. Gardening provides exercise for those who cannot or will not exercise in other ways. Gardening is a communion with nature and with Earth's soil in an increasingly urbanized and pavementized society.

Gardening has ecclesiastical roots. From the Book of Genesis: "And the Lord God planted a garden eastward in Eden and there he put the man he had formed." Gardening has historical roots in our country going back to the earliest colonials from England, France, and Spain. Public gardens were integral to William Penn's plan for Philadelphia in 1682 and the layouts of Boston, Savannah, St. Petersburg, and Williamsburg.

In 1811 Thomas Jefferson wrote that "no occupation is so delightful to me as the culture of the earth, and no culture comparable to that of the garden.... But though an old man, I am but a young gardener."

There are active traditions in our country that bind society together, give meaning to life, and enjoyment to neighbors. They receive very little attention by the mass media because, perhaps, they are working or, more likely, because they do NOT represent violence, sex, addiction, or celebrities in trouble.

For garden lovers, there are many garden magazines, newsletters, catalogues, equipment, applications, and, of course, the estimable Garden Club of America. Its members include garden clubs in the city, town, and country embodying tranquil, genteel exertion of the human spirit and its aesthetic and utilitarian impulses. Is there a hobby so adaptable to space, so congenial to the demands of its practitioners, so predictably rewarding of one's diligence and expectations?

Whether private backyard gardens, public gardens, greenhouse gardens, or exotic gardens, we need to get our youngsters away from their addiction to television and video and computer screens hour after hour and introduce them to gardening and their own diverse senses. We need to stimulate communities all over our land to start arboretums, not just as oases of beauty and tranquility, but as living teachers of plant life and conservation.

It is fortunate that we have the public gardens that were in place before omnivorous parking lots took over.

During our contemporary struggles to define ecology as a way of life, not just a subject of study, the Garden Clubs could aspire to a larger role. In some places this has been happening, especially in the striving to de-chemicalize both gardens and lawns and introduce some old knowledge and new techniques to prevent the need for such reckless toxic applications. But much more can be done. And who has greater local credibility than Garden Clubs?

Commercialized, processed fruits and vegetables trucked for hundreds of thousands of miles before being slotted in supermarkets awaiting your purchase have made us forget what fresh tomatoes, pears, squash, carrots, beans, oranges, and kale taste like. Our very taste buds have been conditioned for the food industry's manipulation. Youngsters today actually turn away from natural soups or salads; their tongues belong to McDonald's and the sugar and fat pumps of the "fast food" industry.

There are bright signs appearing. According to landscape architect Catherine Mahan, "preservation of the environment is now considered by many to be the single most important factor in garden design." Such gardens are known as "xeriscape gardens," which can be, in her words, "abundant and lush or simple and spare. In either case the plant materials are selected for their capacity to adapt naturally to the specific site, their low water requirements, and their ability to thrive without chemical fertilizers and pesticides. The use of mulches and compost are encouraged, and turf areas are reduced or eliminated," she adds.

Now if we can design the highly automated, much touted productivity of our modern economy so that it does not squeeze every ounce of daylight time from harried commuting families, people would have more time with their children to experience the joys and nurturing embrace of gardening and more visits to our public gardens. Such gems as Dumbarton Oaks in Washington, D.C. and the glorious Cypress Gardens by Charleston, South Carolina, await you.

For the curiously interested, potential gardener, log onto www.gcamerica.org or write for information to The Garden Club of America, 14 East 60th Street, New York, NY 10022.

July 25, 2003

Giving Our Airwaves to the Media Moguls

There is little doubt that the Federal Communications Commission, by a split 3 to 2 vote, will open more doors for the giant media moguls to acquire more radio, television, and newspaper properties in cities, towns, and rural areas of this country. By the same decision, they will close more doors on ideas, speakers, writers, artists, and small businesses either because doing so makes them more profits or the moguls disagree with these various viewpoints.

FCC Chairman Michael Powell refused to hold more than one public hearing on this rule-making proceeding outside of Washington, D.C. So two other FCC commissioners, Michael Copps and Jonathan Adelstein, held over one dozen unofficial public hearings in numerous cities, including a recent one in Washington, none of which were attended by Chairman Powell.

The hearings were packed. People care. Whether they are the National Organization for Women or the National Rifle Association, or media magnates Barry Diller or Ted Turner, or Common Cause or William Safire, none want five or six chief executives to decide what they hear, read, or see.

Viacom's CEO Sumner Redstone once said on television that what keeps him and his often obstreperous, number-two man at Viacom, Mel Karmazin, together is their common interest in boosting the company's stock price. Not the company's programming, news staff diversity, localism, and innovative content for a more informed and enlightened audience. They sneer at such yardsticks, especially Karmazin—the ultimate monetary mind.

But the CEO of Clear Channel (owner of over 1,200 radio stations), Lowry Mays, is just as monetized. He once said: "We're not in the business of providing news and information. We're not in the business of providing well-researched music. We're simply in the business of selling our customers products."

Such commercialism would not be so appalling except that these media moguls are doing all this on our property—the public airwaves—and paying us no rent for exclusive use of our property. Yet they are deciding who says what and who doesn't say what twenty-four hours a day. The public airwaves are the property of the American people. The FCC is our hapless, industry-indentured (paid junkets are a way of life for FCC officials) real estate agent that gives away the spectrum.

There is an historic safeguard written into the Communications Act of 1934 that requires the FCC to regulate radio and television stations according to the public convenience, interest, or necessity. Chairman Powell will finish out his term without putting any modern content to this mandate for exercising the public trust in his deliberations as the chief manager of the public airwaves.

Interestingly, the broadcast and newspaper industry split on these concentration rules. Usually their trade association lobbies speak with one voice as they swarm over Congress and the FCC. Family-owned newspapers took a different position than that taken by Gannett or other newspaper chains, while locally owned independent television and radio stations did not like these monopoly enhancements. They believe, as Ted Turner wrote recently, that when you lose small businesses, you lose big ideas.

But the National Federation of Independent Business, which brags about its power to defend and promote small business, took no position. Apparently, its leaders are spending too much time huddling with big business to listen to the cries of small businesses whose cost of advertising on radio goes up in direct relation to the concentration of ownership of radio stations, such as in New York City.

This is no obscure regulatory rule-making. Hundreds of thousands of comments have arrived at FCC headquarters; there have been demonstrations and protests by groups who usually disagree on public policy issues. What they have in common is that they want a voice. They want to hear other voices beyond the canned entertainment and political party lines that they are receiving.

Were it not for the national absorption with the war in Iraq, the mushrooming opposition to Chairman Powell and the media moguls might have been decisive. As it was, the challenge moved toward critical mass too late for the June 2, 2003, decision, which Chairman Powell refused to postpone.

There remains the base of a large movement for recovering some diversity, localism, and competition from the mass media. It is bad enough that about 90 percent of what is carried on television and radio is advertising and entertainment. Our country needs serious talk, more good reporters, and citizen access to the great but unseen and unheard talent in our land—from artists to candidates for office.

Above all, the people need to stop having to beg. We own the public airwaves and, after charging the radio and television stations rent, there will be ample funds for a return to the people of their public airwaves for some time every day in the form of their own audience network. See www.csrl.org/modellaws/audiencenetwork.html.

May 31, 2003

MSNBC Sabotages Donahue

Monopolist Microsoft and oligopolist General Electric, the coowners of MSNBC, took their highest-rated show off the air and sent Phil Donahue away on February 25, 2003. After choosing Donahue to host his own daily show

8 P.M. only six months ago, the corporate managers micromanaged, mismanaged, and refused to let Phil Donahue be Phil Donahue.

About the only freedom Donahue had was the freedom to say what he thinks. Beyond that he was often told what kinds of subjects to showcase and what kinds of guests to have. And he was often chided for being too tough on some guests—shades of Fox's Bill O'Reilly, his competition for that hour, and the spitting, screeching, viper-like Sean Hannity.

In the past few months, the corporate "suits" even told Donahue that he had to have more conservative or right-wing guests than liberals on the same hour show.

Still, Donahue persevered. His ratings were slowly increasing, despite the regular lacerations that the top brass inflicted on a show that was supposed to be the liberal counterpart of the right-wing, bellicose Fox fare stitched together by Rupert Murdoch's media empire.

MSNBC, which was receiving ratings of about 440,000 viewers for Donahue, was aiming for 1,000,000 people. Were they interested in one million predominately liberal viewers attracted to the legendary talk show host who, starting in the sixties, broke apart on morning television the biases or taboos against women, minorities, gays and lesbians, downtrodden workers, consumer and environmental rights? Doubtful. For if they were, some of their promotional budgets would have gone for reaching liberal audiences of the kind who read *Utne* magazine, *Mother Jones*, or who watch various PBS outlets and other serious programming.

What emerged was quite different from that described by Steve Friedman, former producer of NBC's *Today* and the CBS *Early Show*, who told a reporter: "I think MSNBC felt the way to beat Fox was to do a liberal version of what Fox was doing, and Phil was a good person to do that. I don't know if they were really committed to that."

They were not. Instead, the top brass allowed other factors to shatter the identity and consistency of the show—which, by the way, would have always provided for contrary views to those held by Phil.

First, always hovering in their minds are the corporate advertisers, who do not exactly like a Dr. Sid Wolfe exposing the harmful effects of brand-name drugs. Right-wing radio and television talk show hosts dominate the electronic media because, unlike the rare liberal host, they attack government regulation, while the rare liberal may go after corporate crimes and abuse. Guess what? Corporations advertise and governments do not.

But there was more to the NBC officials' calculations. A commissioned report for NBC's internal purposes in December describes Donahue this way: "a tired, left-wing liberal out of touch with the current marketplace."

Continuing, the study said that Donahue is "a difficult public face for NBC in a time of war...he seems to delight in presenting guests who are antiwar, anti-Bush and skeptical of the administration's motives." Unmentioned was that there were more pro-war guests on the Donahue show than those espousing an anti-war viewpoint.

In a pointed but polite manner, Donahue issued a statement that indicated what was going on behind the scenes:

"We were hoping to break through the noisy drums of war on cable and become a responsible platform for dissenters as well as Administration supporters. The *New York Times* op-ed page features a variety of views regarding the Bush war on Iraq, including regular columnists who have been critical of the Administration's foreign policy team. MSNBC's voice should be no less diverse. The hiring of Mike Savage, Dick Armey and Joe Scarborough suggest a strategy to outfox Fox."

Starting last fall, leaks from top NBC sources bad-mouthed their own Donahue show, leading to regular trade press rumors about the demise of the show. This is no way to maintain morale, much less run a business supposedly endowed with at least some recognition of the public's right to diverse information and opinion.

Top NBC executives, given their enormous pay, should start paying attention to simple improvements. For example, in about half the country, MSNBC is not even listed in the daily and Sunday television cable guides, including Washington, D.C. If your programs are not even listed alongside CNN and Fox programs, there will be fewer viewers.

I notified a top NBC executive late last fall about this remarkable omission. His response: "I'm astonished to hear that," and he pledged to rectify the situation. Nothing has changed to date.

Donahue, in his gracious manner, paid tribute to the "worker bees" at MSNBC's Secaucus, New Jersey headquarters. These are the same workers whose state income tax payments are in effect refunded to profit-glutted Microsoft and General Electric under a corporate welfare scheme that the two companies demanded from then Governor Christie Todd Whitman. Now that would have been a great Donahue show!

February 28, 2003

Corporate Appropriation of Public Resources

Hundreds of billions of dollars of the nation's wealth—the people's resources—are being openly confiscated by corporate interests.

Government, the presumed protector of the public's property, has become, instead, the enabler of the plunder and theft. The media, the nation's self-professed watchdog, is apathetic, at best, in sounding the alarm about the people's loss of control over resources they have paid for or inherited from previous generations. These are the resources that citizens legally hold in common—their common wealth.

As a result, corporations have found it easy to lay claim to a wide range of public resources—from publicly funded medical advances to national forests, public spaces in cities, the Internet, software innovations, the airwaves, the public domain of creative works, the DNA of animals, plants, and humans. The appetite of Big Business for the appropriation of public resources is limitless. Even public education has not escaped the ambition of corporate control and takeover.

Surprisingly, corporate appropriation—privatization—of public resources has proceeded quietly with only sporadic public outcries against the most blatant thefts. One public interest activist and author, David Bollier, is making a valiant effort to change that. As Bollier argues, the abuses go unnoticed because the thefts are generally seen "only in glimpses, not in panorama, when it is visible at all."

Bollier's new book *Silent Theft—The Private Plunder of Our Common Wealth* (Routledge, New York and London) is a loud wake-up call for citizens interested in halting the steady exploitation and erosion of the nation's resources and values for short-term gains by the few. And the book does, indeed, provide the reader a wide, vivid, and scary panoramic view of what is happening to the public's resources, "the commons" as Bollier calls them.

"We have become a nation of eager consumers—and disengaged citizens—and so are ill-equipped to perceive how our common resources are being abused," Bollier says. He moves quickly to specifics—breakthrough cancer drugs that our tax dollars helped develop, and the rights to which pharmaceutical companies acquired for a song and for which they now charge exorbitant prices; the archaic 1872 law that gives mining companies the lucrative right to mine valuable mineral resources on our public lands for $5 an acre, a right that the mining industry preserves through what Bollier describes as "well-deployed campaign contributions."

Bollier is especially critical of the federal government's role in giving away its most promising drug research and development to the drug companies for a fraction of its actual value, with the companies then charging whatever prices they can make the desperately ill bear.

"It is a sweet deal for drugmakers but an outrage for millions of American taxpayers and consumers," Bollier says. "It is a scandalous fact that the fruits of risky and expensive scientific work typically do not accrue to the spon-sors/investors—the American people—until drug companies have extracted huge markups of their own. The American people pay twice, first as taxpayers reaping a lower (or nonexistent) return on their investments, and second as consumers paying higher drug prices charged by pharmaceutical companies."

Bollier reminds the reader that Americans own collectively one-third of the surface area of the country and billions of acres of the outer continental shelf. The resources are extensive and valuable: huge supplies of oil, coal, natural gas, uranium, copper, gold, silver, timber grasslands, water, and geothermal energy. The nation's public land also consists of vast tracts of wilderness forests, unspoiled coastline, sweeping prairies, the Rocky Mountains, and dozens of beautiful rivers and lakes.

"As the steward of these public resources, the government's job is to man-age these lands responsibly for the long-term," Bollier argues. "The sad truth is that the government stewardship of this natural wealth represents one of the great scandals of the 20th Century. While the details vary from one resource to another, the general history is one of antiquated laws, poor enforcement, slipshod administration, environmental indifference and capitulation to indus-try's most aggressive demands."

The increasing exploitation of the commons, Bollier argues, needlessly siphons hundreds of billions of dollars away from the public purse each year that could be used for countless varieties of social investment, environmen-tal protection, and other public initiatives. The public's assets and revenue streams are privatized with only fractional benefits accruing to the public in return, he says.

Bollier also contends that the enclosure of the "commons" by market forces (usually the bigger companies) tends to foster market concentration, reduces competition, and raises consumer prices. He says it also threatens the envi-ronment by favoring short-term exploitation over long-term stewardship—"the flagrant abuses of public lands by timber, mining and agribusiness companies are prime examples."

Despite his vigorous criticism of the exploitation and neglect of the public's resources—"the commons"—Bollier remains optimistic that people can be galvanized to reverse the current trend.

"Americans have a long tradition of creating innovative vehicles for ensur-ing fair return to the American people on resources they collectively own," he writes. "It is time to revive this tradition of innovation in the stewardship of public resources and give it imaginative new incarnations in the twenty-first century."

For anyone interested in joining the effort to reverse the corporate exploitation of our public resources, David Bollier's *Silent Theft* is a first-class starting point.

For more information on *Silent Theft*: www.silenttheft.com/

June 26, 2002

A Corporate State

What *Business Week* magazine calls "the corporate crime wave" shows every sign of worsening, as more major corporations scramble to admit massive deception of investors, looting of pension funds, self-enrichment of top executives, restatement of earnings, and giant farewell compensation packages to departing bosses who wrecked their companies to further their own mega-greed.

So much of these corporate cesspools are oozing into the public's view that it is difficult to piece them into an understandable reform movement for workers, consumers, and investors to support. The sanitation trucks can't begin to keep up with the spilling garbage of betrayed trust, pillage and plunder of trillions of dollars.

"Is Wall Street Corrupt?" headlined *Business Week*. Inside the reporters showed the answer to be yes, yes, yes! The founder of the giant Vanguard Mutual Fund, John C. Bogle, declared: "Our capitalistic system is in peril," and just started a shareholder-rights group with Warren E. Buffett. What communism could not do, the big business bosses are doing to the market system and the financial industry.

We are witnessing the corporate destruction of capitalism in favor of a corporate state. The law can't save it because the laws are controlled by politicians, many of whom are controlled in turn by these same business interests and campaign cash. For every honest politician like Congressman Henry Waxman or Senator Paul Sarbanes, there are scores of congressional and White House politicians huddling with business lobbyists to stifle prosecutions, reforms, and investigations.

The lead culprit is the retiring and shameless Senator Phil Gramm (Rep. Texas), whose wife just resigned from the Enron board and its audit committee. On May 16, he met with thirty corporate lobbyists to plan the surrender of Washington, D.C.'s national government against the crookery of Wall Street.

In American history, reforms usually followed scandals. Now over the past twenty years, scandals follow scandals because there are no reforms.

Sometimes the congressional reaction is to weaken the existing laws and safeguards against corporate crime, fraud, and abuse—even after imposing massive taxpayer bailouts of the culpable industries. Remember the S&L scandals that are costing taxpayers half a trillion dollars in principal and interest between 1990 and 2020.

Conflicts of interest are at epidemic levels in Wall Street and trust is being destroyed—the key confidence that investors must have in information and advice directed their way. Although it has received little notice, a devastating new report has been issued by the only major non-conflicted ratings firm left in the country (Weiss Ratings, Inc. from Palm Beach Gardens, Florida). It concludes:

> A deeper understanding of the crisis can be achieved through an analysis of "buy," "sell," and "hold" ratings issued to companies that went bankrupt in 2002: A total of 50 investment banking and bro-kerage firms issued ratings to 19 companies that filed for chapter 11 in the first four months of 2002.... 94% of the 50 firms continued to indicate that investors should buy or hold shares in failing companies right up to the day these companies filed for bankruptcy. Among the 19 bankrupt companies, 12 continued to receive strictly "buy" or "hold" rating on the date of bankruptcy filing.

Weiss Ratings receives no financial compensation from the companies it rates, unlike S&P, Moodys, and Duff & Phelps. Here are its unbiased ratings. "Among the 20 largest brokerage firms, 13 may be financially vulnerable if their finances deteriorate further, while seven have the financial wherewithal to withstand a severely adverse business environment."

Weiss Ratings gives low grades to JP Morgan Chase & Co, Lehman Brothers, Merrill Lynch, UBS Warburg LLC, Barclays Capital, and Credit Suisse First Boston Corporation. These firms have millions of customers who rely on their highly self-advertised, objective expertise. (For more details see www.weiss-ratings.com)

Before the November elections, there needs to be an aroused public to take control of their government and direct their public servants to enact systemic action for reform, not phony legislation that allows crooked business as usual. For suggestions on what these reforms can be, log on to www.citizenworks.org.

June 13, 2002

Corporations, Not Real People

In its celebrated cover story eighteen months ago, *Business Week* magazine asked, "Too much corporate power?" and answered yes in several detailed pages. It then delivered an editorial that urged corporations to "get out of politics." Last month, the giant British Petroleum Company (BP), having acquired the American oil companies Amoco and Atlantic Richfield, announced that it would do just that!

Starting April 1, 2002, BP's chief executive, Lord John Browne, said that the company would halt all political contributions from corporate funds "anywhere in the world." In his remarkable speech, which was almost unnoticed in the United States, Lord Browne based his decision on the belief that corporations "must be particularly careful about the political process, not because it is unimportant—quite the reverse—but because the legitimacy of that process is crucial both for society and for us as a company working in that society."

BP gave $1.1 million to the two major parties during the 2000 elections in the United States where it receives about half its income. Even though BP executives and employees are still able to contribute to political candidates, the decision to take this oil firm out of the political campaign rat race is quite significant, nonetheless. It allows a framework for providing additional reasons why BP did the right thing and stimulates a long-ignored distinction between artificial entities, which are corporations, and real people.

Corporations do not vote. Only real people vote and only real people should be able to participate in elections and campaigns.

Our Supreme Court, however, has decreed in the 1880s that corporations are "persons" for constitutional purposes and subsequent court decisions protect these "artificial" persons' right to contribute to referenda battles or to candidates indirectly. A ninety-year-old federal law prohibits corporations and, later, unions from contributing directly to candidates for federal office. At the state level, some states allow companies to contribute directly to candidates.

The idea that real people and giant corporations have equal rights under our Constitution makes a mockery out of the principle of "equal justice under the law." Not being humans, corporations can be in one thousand places at once, anywhere in the world; they can create their own holding companies (parents) for evasive maneuvers; they can lob off responsibilities on far-flung subsidiaries, diffuse or hide behavior that stymies law enforcement and tax collectors, pay their executives while going into temporary bankruptcy to get rid of most of their creditors' claims, shareholders' equity, and the claims of injured people or those under union contracts for their workers.

Corporations can hold patent ownership on the genetic inheritance of the world, including human genes. Under existing law they could genetically engineer and own humanoids some day, so long as those humanoids were sufficiently subpar in intelligence to avoid the laws against slavery. Corporations can dissolve (i.e., disappear), as did the coal mining companies that hollowed out the ground under many homes in Pennsylvania and West Virginia that subsequently sank, and have their assets reemerge in other corporate entities.

Once a public discussion begins on how corporations are treated differently and preferentially under our laws, as compared with real human beings, the examples of these double standards would proliferate into every nook and cranny of our society and demonstrate how they affect, cheat, deprive, harm, and control peoples' lives.

In that same *Business Week* issue, the magazine polled the American people. Seventy-two percent of those polled said that corporations have too much control over their lives. If freedom is participation in power, as the ancient Roman orator Cicero defined it so well over two thousand years ago, it is time for the American people to engage each other in conversations concerning what to do about such control—for themselves, their freedom, and their democracy.

March 20, 2002

Olympics: McDonald's and First Fry

Television advertisements during the recent Olympics were high-priced, but one by McDonald's reached a new low. It pictured a baby next to a parent with the message: "There will be a first step, a first word and, of course, a first french fry." The lethal impact—start clogging the tiny arteries at the earliest possible age. The baby appeared to be one year old!

Then there is the rapid increase in obesity—one in four children, nearly one in two adults. Just retired U.S. Surgeon General David Satcher stated that obesity is now approaching tobacco as a leading cause of preventable fatalities in the United States.

Much of McDonald's $3 billion a year television ad budget is directed toward children and its objective is to separate the children from their parents so as to get the children, as many parents know, to nag the parents into going to McDonald's. This fast fat company does not force children to eat its junk food; it is far more effective to seduce them with toys, Ronald McDonald fun, and tasty feelings, into clamoring for this bad and deadly diet that will plague them later in life.

A recent release from the Center for Science in the Public Interest (cspinet.org) says: "A typical [McDonald's] Value Meal (Big Mac, medium fries, medium Coke) delivers about 1,200 calories and three-quarters of a day's quota of saturated fat. That is exactly the type of diet that the federal government's 'Dietary Guidelines for Americans' and 'The Surgeon General's Report on Nutrition and Health' have recommended against." A professor of public health at Yale University, Kelly Brownell, told the Center's popular *Nutrition Action* newsletter that diet-related diseases are taking tens of thousands of American lives yearly. "I have asked myself," she said, "whether Joe Camel is different than Ronald McDonald. One could claim that they both encourage children to adopt habits that could be bad for their health."

McDonald's has weightier things on its mind than children's health, as it expands toward its goal of having a McDonald's less than ten minutes away from every American. It has been looking at its charts and the consumption of french fries after artery-bursting annual growth has begun to decline. Not much, perhaps 1 percent in the year ending this June 30th, according to the U.S. Department of Agriculture, but enough to alarm the burger bosses. One can imagine the bells ringing—quick! go down the age scale, start 'em on the grease before they are toddlers. Maintain that profit curve!

The *New York Times* attributes this decline in part to "health-conscious Americans' fear of fat," quoting Chandra Brooks, an office worker, saying "I don't even eat McDonald's anymore. I'm trying to get away from fatty food."

Gee Whizzerkers!! Information and education can work! But how can the truth about fatty diets and disease get to millions of youngsters and larger numbers of adults?

Well, there is the Center for Science in the Public Interest with their factual, readable posters, pamphlets, and newsletters reaching nearly a million people. But isn't there something wrong when the people own the public airwaves, the television stations control what goes on them around the clock as tenants who pay the FCC no rent for their lucrative license, and McDonald's gets its harmful products publicized without any rebuttal by nutritionists and other public health scientists. There isn't even a Phil Donahue Show anymore where the fat content in hot dogs and burgers can be openly discussed. Eric Schlosser, author of the best-selling paperback *Fast Food Nation*, has been on an extensive book tour and has received some good media getting his message out. He points to the reality that humans develop their tastes at an early age and have a difficult time changing course for certain foods heavy in salt, fat, and sugar. Knowing this biology and knowing how to turn the tongue against the brain at an early age, McDonald's and its fast food compadres zero in with relentless repetition, sensuality, and psychology.

Anyone with ideas about how to counteract this growing recklessness of the fast food industry ought to communicate them to the Center pronto. If you think that parents can effectively persuade their children by simply telling them to "just say *No*," try reading Pavlov's experiments about conditioned responses.

By all means, just say *No*, and grab your carrots, apples, and chick peas; but when in most cases that doesn't work, we have to look for other approaches.

March 6, 2002

Corporate Sin

For years I have wondered why religious sermons in places of worship focus so exclusively on excoriating individual sin while avoiding corporate sin in the business world. Well, those days of avoidance are being replaced with increasing attention to the gigantic, multidirectional Enron crimes and abuses against so many innocent people.

"The behavior of Enron executives is a direct violation of biblical ethics," writes the Rev. Jim Wallis, an antipoverty leader and editor of *Sojourner* magazine. "Read your Bibles. The strongest media critics of Enron call it putting self-interest above the public interest; the Bible would just call it a sin," he asserts.

Wallis, whose books relate religious principles to justice for humanity in the most eloquent language, brings the Bible's message on mammon and God to today's business crimes: "It's the second most prominent theme in the Hebrew Bible," and in the New Testament "one of every 16 verses" addresses "riches and God's concern for the poor." Decrying the imbalanced concentration of sermons on personal frailties, Wallis says: "I think people want to hear that faith has to do with money as well as sex."

Speaking to a *Washington Post* reporter, the Rev. John P. Burns, pastor of a Baptist church in Maryland said: "The people in the pews are appalled by it [Enron].... There is a general feeling among most people that they don't know what to do about this, other than to shake their heads and moan." Burns delivered a sermon recently on hubris and Enron. "Hubris," he declared, "makes the rich buy 10 homes—that is what Kenneth Lay of Enron had—while others sleep on grates. Right now it may only be the pensioners and the low-level employees who suffer.... But...hubris always brings the retribution of God."

The Rev. William J. Byron, pastor of the Holy Trinity Catholic Church in Washington, D.C., raises this ethical principle of corporate executives "having such disproportionate income relative to others in the same organization." He told the *Post*: "The principle I would use is that it's always wrong to take an unfair gain at the expense of someone."

Over at the Presbyterian Church in northwest Washington, D.C., the Rev. Roger Gench told the paper that the Enron case "speaks to me about what's gone awry with global capitalism. It's an example of a corporation that is so totally focused on making markets work and gaining wealth for a few people that it lost sight of how. . .to create wealth for the community in which it exists."

That community for Enron, a major tax escapee, was its pension holders, its investors, its gouged consumers, and eventually its thousands of employees who lost their jobs.

The Rev. John Mack, of the nearby First Congregational Church, summed it up: "The salient thing about the Enron case is the selfishness and greed of executives."

In the centuries before the creation of corporations, most marketplace wrongdoing emanated directly from individuals. The moneylenders driven from the Temples were individual businessmen. Now the complex corporatized economy, with its capacity to obscure or diffuse responsibility, has shielded the institutions as well as their executives from the judgments of sensitive clergy—until Enron and its executives spilled their greed and the media attached the necessary anthropomorphic attributes for widespread public revulsion.

When public sermons start treating corporate crime with biblical judgments, can Congress be far behind with secular reforms and remedies?

February 26, 2002

Online Education Pitfalls

The integrity of institutions of higher education has long been under assault by the growing collaboration between corporations and academia, particularly in the areas of scientific and technological research.

More than two decades ago, David F. Noble, a historian who now teaches at York University in Toronto, warned in an article in the *Nation* that corporations, in their search for legitimization, were buying into basic laboratory science, toxicology, epidemiology and other areas of public health, and policy-oriented disciplines such as economics and political and management science.

"The upshot has been the industrial connection with academia groomed for the role of legitimator for industry," he wrote.

Noble has proven to be prescient, as more of what he dubs as "leased scholars" provide reams of data, scientific publications, the cost-benefit analyses, and the policy recommendations that legitimize corporate policies.

Now, Noble has turned a piercing spotlight on another issue that threatens the integrity of academia—the automation of higher education—or as he calls it in the title of his new book, *Digital Diploma Mills*.

The title refers to the practice of developing and distributing digitized course material online without the participation of professors who draft the material—a technological version of the old correspondence school approach. Noble calls this "distance" learning or "commodification" of education, which he defines as the "deliberate transformation of the educational process into commodity form for the purpose of commercial transaction."

Debunking the claims of the online supporters about greater access and improved educational approaches, Noble says the digitized course material is not about education, but about profits of the vendors of the network hardware, software, and "content"—corporations like Apple, IBM, Bell, the cable companies, and Microsoft and publishing companies like Disney, Simon and Schuster, Prentice-Hall, and others who Noble argues view education as a market for their wares. He notes that the investment firm Lehman Brothers estimates that the market for educational commodities to be potentially worth several hundred billion dollars.

In Canada, the effort to develop the "Virtual U" customized educational software platform has been pushed by an industrial consortium that includes Kodak, IBM, Microsoft, McGraw-Hill, Prentice-Hall, Rogers Cablesystems, Unitel, Novasys, Nortel, Bell Canada, and MPR Teltech, a subsidiary of GTE.

The Canadian promoters predict a $50 billion market for their products, and Noble says the proposal emphasizes the adoption of "an intellectual property policy that will encourage researchers and industry to commercialize their innovations and anticipates the development of commercially marketable hardware and software products and services including courseware and other learning products."

Noble says that major promoters of the online education schemes are university administrators who see it as a means of giving their institutions a "fashionably forward-looking image" and a way to reduce labor and plant maintenance costs—fewer teachers and classrooms—while undermining the autonomy and independence of faculty.

Once faculty and courses go online, Noble contends that administrators will gain much greater direct control over faculty performance and course content than ever before and the potential for administrative scrutiny, supervision, regimentation, discipline, and even censorship will increase dramatically. In addition, the university administrators will be in a position to hire less skilled and hence cheaper workers to deliver the technologically prepackaged material.

Noble predicts that in the new regime of education as a commodity, educators will face harsh realities: speedups, routinization of work, greater work discipline and managerial supervision, reduced autonomy, job insecurity, employer appropriation of fruits of their labor and above all insistent managerial pressures to reduce labor costs in order to turn a profit."

But it is students who will be shortchanged the most if education becomes simply an online product. As Noble points out, "education is a process that requires interpersonal (not merely interactive) relationship between people—student and teacher (and student and student) that aims at individual and collective self-knowledge."

Noble notes that students' course work can be monitored and archived by company officials. This raises questions about what rights students have to privacy and the proprietary control of their work in this cyber world of education. Noble asks: What third parties (besides students and faculty) will have access to the student's communications?

While he paints a dismal picture of online education for profit, Noble does see growing and successful resistance to the trend by students and faculty at places like UCLA, the California State University system and his own institution, York University in Toronto. But with hundreds of billions of dollars on the line, don't expect the corporations to give up on the idea of turning education into a profit center. If you want to learn more about the corporate campaign to grab control of our colleges and universities, read David Noble's book, *Digital Diploma Mills, The Automation of Higher Education* (Monthly Review Press, New York, NY).

February 13, 2002

Privatizing Public Services

Corporations and their political friends have long promoted the idea that private enterprises could operate basic government services more efficiently and at less cost than government itself. Everything from schools to mass transit systems has been targeted by "government for profit" campaigns.

Today, many state and local governments rue the day that they fell for these slick claims about the glories of "privatizing" public services. Nowhere is this more true than in the efforts to privatize prisons—schemes that not only raise major questions about the validity of grandiose cost-saving claims, but about public safety and the quality of prison management.

A 1996 report by the General Accounting Office (GAO), which reviewed a series of academic and government studies, concluded that there was no clear evidence of cost savings when private companies took over prison management. Now a new study by Good Jobs First, a national research center that tracks state and local development practices, suggests that the "prisons for profit" projects have often been cesspools of corporate welfare at the expense of the taxpayers.

Good Jobs First studied sixty privately built and operated prisons in states and found that 73 percent of the prisons had received subsidies ranging from tax-advantaged financing to property tax reductions and tax credits. A total of $628 million in tax-free bonds and other government-issued securities was used to finance 37 percent of the prisons, and 38 percent received property tax

abatements or other tax reductions. Twenty-three percent received infrastructure subsidies such as water, sewer and other utility hookups, roads, and other
publicly paid improvements.

Judith Greene, writing in the *American Prospect*, says the private companies' search for profits through cost-cutting has resulted in significantly higher
employee turnover, with dramatic ill effects on quality and safety of the privately run prisons. She cites a survey conducted by George Washington
University that found 49 percent more inmate-on-staff assaults and 65 percent more inmate-on-inmate assaults in medium and minimum security private facilities than in similar prisons run by government. The turnover rate for
correctional officers was 41 percent for private prisons compared with 15 percent in government-operated institutions, according to data reported in *The
Corrections Yearbook*.

Greene's article cites a series of abuses and security lapses over the last year
at private prisons operated by Corrections Corporation of America (CCA), the
country's largest private prison company. Among these incidents:

• Last August, two prisoners escaped from a CCA prison in Bartlett, Texas.
State investigators found the doors had been left unlocked; no one was watching the closed-circuit television surveillance monitors. When the prisoners cut
their way through the prison's fence, a security alarm sounded, but staff in the
prison's control center turned it off and did nothing.

• In December, jurors in Columbia, South Carolina, found that guards at a
CCA juvenile prison had abused a youth confined there and that their use of
force was so malicious it was "repugnant to the conscience of mankind." The
jury awarded $3 million in punitive damages.

• In April, prison guards at CCA's Cibola County Correctional Center in
New Mexico tear-gassed nearly seven hundred prisoners who had staged a day-
long nonviolent protest of conditions at the facility.

• Good Jobs First reports a series of similar incidents in its survey of private
prisons. The organization describes a 1998 incident that involved the fatal stab-
bing of an inmate and a six-person escape from a CCA facility in Youngstown,
Ohio. In 1999, the company agreed to pay $1.6 million to settle a class action
lawsuit brought on behalf of prisoners who claimed they were abused, denied
medical care, and not properly segregated from more dangerous inmates.

• According to the survey, in April 2000 authorities in Louisiana, acting
under pressure from the federal government, took control of the Jena Juvenile
Justice Center away from Wakenhut Corrections, another major private prison
operator. The action came in the wake of revelations of widespread brutality at
the facility, some of it carried out by guards or encouraged by them. Conditions
were so severe at the Wakenhut facility that some youths mutilated themselves

so they would be transferred to the medical unit where they could more easily avoid beatings and rapes.

Many officials have lobbied to have private prisons built in their communities in the belief that the facilities would help bring jobs and development. But, Mafruza Khan, coauthor of Good Jobs First's study, says that there is an amazing lack of information available from local development officials about the impact of private prisons on local economies.

"Many officials did not know all of the taxpayer investments that had been made in local facilities," Mafruza said. "And despite granting hundreds of millions of dollars in subsidies, not one public official could cite a cost-benefit analysis or impact study on their facility."

The concept of privately operated prisons got a big boost with the pro-corporate, antigovernment philosophy of the Reagan administration in the 1980s. While the demand for private prisons is declining in many states, the big operators like CCA and Wakenhut are now looking to the federal government to pick up the slack in their business. The federal inmate population has grown as a result of harsh drug sentences and a crackdown on illegal activities, including many minor offenses by noncitizens, according to the Good Jobs First report.

Privatization of prisons was a questionable idea from the beginning. In practice, it has often proven to be a costly mistake and a drain on taxpayers to finance a growing list of subsidies to feed the profits of private corporations. Governing bodies from the local to the federal level should abandon this experiment in privatization.

October 31, 2001

Privatization of Government

Local, state, and federal governments, faced with complex problems in the delivery of services, increasingly are falling for schemes to let private corporations take over public duties. Behind the privatization of government functions is an ongoing propaganda campaign centered around the theme that corporations can manage and deliver services more efficiently at less cost than democratically controlled governments.

In many areas corporations have been allowed to take over prisons, schools, and community hospitals among other services on a for-profit basis. Many of the rosy scenarios predicted for this "corporations know best" management are fading in the real world of public services—at a heavy cost to citizens.

As part of the privatization craze, the federal government lets investor-owned commercial banks collect various payments for the Internal Revenue Service and the Treasury Department's Financial Management Service.

IRS contracts with four banks that maintain so-called lockboxes for tax returns and collections in ten locations. The banks are Mellon in Pittsburgh, Bank of America in Charlotte, N. C., Bank One in Chicago, and U. S. Bancorp in Minneapolis. The federal government pays the lockbox banks about $10 million annually for handling income tax returns. The amount varies from year to year based on a formula tied to the Consumer Price Index.

The corporate lockbox scheme was largely unknown by the American public until last month when thousands of taxpayers in New England and New York State started getting notices from IRS charging them with failing to file returns and pay income taxes due for 2000. IRS started levying heavy penalties and interest when the returns failed to show up with payments. Taxpayers insisted they had mailed returns and payments in a timely fashion, some weeks ahead of the April 16 deadline.

Finally the mystery began to unravel when security personnel at Mellon Bank found a box of discarded returns with checks attached. Initially, reports from the bank suggested only 1,800 returns had been "misplaced." Further investigation revealed that at least 40,000 tax returns and payments totaling $810 million may have been lost, hidden or destroyed by Mellon's downtown processing center operating under contract with IRS.

The Pittsburgh *Post-Gazette* said workers at the bank felt they were "under siege" and expected to process 80,000 checks and vouchers daily to meet an April 29 deadline. If the bank failed to meet the deadline, the bank would be hit with a penalty and supervisory personnel would not receive bonuses.

In an e-mail sent to employees last month, Mellon Chairman Martin McGuinn was quoted as saying that an "internal probe found that returns were hidden and in some cases destroyed."

The *Washington Post* said sources told it that the contract apparently penalized Mellon for unprocessed returns and checks rather than rewarding it for those it did process. "The system was flawed," the *Post* quoted a source as saying. "It gave them incentive to stick the payments in a drawer. It was almost cost-effective for them to do that."

In a letter to the Senate Finance Committee, IRS Commissioner Charles Rossotti said "whatever (tax) forms the guilty parties could remove for the staging with ease were taken, hidden and some destroyed." The Pittsburgh case occurred after the General Accounting Office (GAO) had issued reports in previous years identifying weaknesses in the Financial Management Service's monitoring of federal funds in lockbox banks.

But even if additional safeguards are installed and closely monitored, should taxpayers' tax returns be handed over to commercial banks for processing? What happens to the intimate financial and other personal details that all tax returns contain? Clearly this information cannot be successfully protected when tax returns are so carelessly treated as by the Mellon Bank in Pittsburgh.

Are the executives and employees of Mellon Bank concerned first and foremost about the timely, efficient operation of the federal tax system and the privacy of individual taxpayers? Or, is it profit that has first call on the performance and obligations of the operators of the corporation?

The same question can be asked of the corporations that are in the forefront of efforts to turn our schools, prisons, and community health facilities into adjuncts of the profit-making world where accountability to the public is secondary, at best.

September 10, 2001

Companies Can Have a Conscience

Most corporations measure their worth by their bottom-line profits. For some companies, like Working Assets Long Distance and Ben and Jerry's Ice Cream, profits, however, don't begin to measure their value to the public and communities.

Working Assets, for example, donates 1 percent of its long-distance phone revenue to progressive nonprofit organizations working for peace, human rights, equality, education, and the environment.

As the company tells its customers, every long-distance call helps to build affordable housing, clean up toxic waste dumps, protect a woman's right to choose, provide emergency relief to people devastated by AIDS in Africa, and expose corporate polluters around the world.

Among the organizations supported by Working Assets are Children Now, Doctors Without Borders, Fairness and Accuracy in Reporting, Handgun Control, Inc., Human Rights Watch, and the National Gay and Lesbian Task Force.

In addition, each month Working Assets (800-634-4150) sends out an alert on two urgent issues, and gives its customers an opportunity to make free calls to express their opinions to members of Congress and other government and business leaders. As an alternative to a telephone call, the company offers to write and send a low-cost "citizens' letter" on behalf of its customers.

Ben and Jerry's Foundation was established in 1985 through a donation of the ice cream company's stock. In addition, the company makes donations of approximately 7.5 percent of its pretax profits, part of it going into the foundation and other portions into employee-led community action teams, which make small grants to community groups in Vermont, the company's home state.

Ben and Jerry's Foundation offers grants to nonprofit grassroots organizations across the nation that facilitate progressive social change by addressing the underlying conditions of societal and environmental problems. The decisions on which organizations' requests are funded are made by a team of Ben and Jerry's employees.

Working Assets and Ben and Jerry's obviously are not the only companies that back up a social consciousness with money and other resources. The England-based Body Shop, for example, is similarly active. But, where do you find these community-minded companies among the mass of "business as usual" corporations that not only lack a social conscience, but are contributors to the exploitation of workers and consumers and polluters of our air and water?

One answer is provided by Co-op America, a nonprofit organization, that collects and publishes data to help its members buy socially responsible products, invest in healthy community development, and boycott corporate criminals who pollute the environment and exploit workers around the world.

Co-op America publishes the *National Green Pages,* a comprehensive guide to products that are ecologically sound and produced in a socially responsible manner. The Green Pages also contain information about investing in companies that respect the environment, protect their workers, and produce healthy products. Co-op America provides its members with assistance in divesting from companies that produce pesticides, tobacco, toxic waste, and other carcinogens.

As Alisa Gravitz, executive director of Co-op America, says: "We can blame irresponsible companies, unresponsive politicians or the 'system' for our problems. Or we can join together to do something about it. Nobody else is going to do it for us."

Consumers, equipped with the information provided by Co-op America (www.coopamerica.org) and other citizen organizations, do have the power to change the way corporations do business. There will be more companies like Working Assets and Ben and Jerry's with a social conscience if enough consumers demand them.

Consumers can speak loudly in the marketplace and at the ballot box. They have the power to make corporations and politicians deliver.

July 26, 2001

Low-Power Community Radio Stations

There is no greater place for mischief in Washington than budget and appropriations bills that slide through in the closing hours of a Congress.

These mammoth bills, often containing 300, 400, or more pages touching on a multitude of issues, are fertile ground for provisions sought by special interests—provisions that wouldn't survive the sunshine of open hearings, debates, and votes in committees or on the floor. Senior members with lots of political clout are especially adept at slipping amendments into these last-hour bills to award corporate interests and generous campaign contributors.

This year, provisions in an appropriations bill are being used to clobber an admirable plan by Federal Communications Commission Chairman William Kennard to issue licenses for low-power FM stations that could be used by schools, churches, and community organizations. Imagine a community group using low-power radio to share news about local issues and culture and to help rebuild the civic fabric of their neighborhoods. These nonprofit stations won't even compete with commercial radio stations for advertising dollars.

Why would there be opposition in Congress to efforts to enhance democracy by giving these groups a voice and adding diversity to an increasingly consolidated broadcast spectrum? As the FCC chairman said, this is "not about ideology, it's about money." It is also about blatant corporate power that seeks to use elected representatives and the influence of campaign money to stifle competition and provide special protection for an industry.

The lobbying effort against the low-power stations was led by the National Association of Broadcasters (NAB). As cover for a raw display of political power, NAB tried to argue that the 10- to 100-watt community stations would "interfere" with the signal of the full power commercial stations. Sadly, National Public Radio (NPR), which knows better and which, itself, was created to increase broadcast diversity, joined the commercial broadcasters in opposition to the community stations.

The argument about "interference" from the low-power stations was refuted by the FCC. The agency's engineering tests showed that interference, if it existed at all, was minimal. As Chairman Kennard noted, the broadcasting industry in the past has petitioned to allow full power stations to sit close to each other, some with 100,000 watt power. So, why would a 10-watt community station be the big concern that the broadcasters trumpeted to the Congress?

Once again, this episode illustrates just how the lobbying wars on Capitol Hill are stacked against citizen groups. Lined up in support of the community stations were the National Association of Evangelicals, the Leadership Conference on Civil Rights, the National Education Association, the National

Council of Churches and community groups. The interest in the establishment of the low-power stations is evident in the 1,200 applications that have been filed by nonprofit organizations in twenty states.

Yet, none of this counted when the broadcasters reached their congressional friends. In a report on the success of the broadcasters, the *New York Times* took special note of the fact that Senate Majority Leader Trent Lott, a leading supporter of the efforts to block the low-power stations, had been a friend of Edward O. Fritts, president and chief executive of NAB, since their college days at the University of Mississippi. Also included in the measure are provisions pushed by Senator Ted Stevens and Representative Billy Tauzin that release National Public Radio from obligations to offer free airtime to political candidates.

It is not accidental that issues like these end up in money bills at the end of the Congress. These bills always affect a broad set of issues and "must" items at the end of the session. The final passage is always on a House-Senate conference report that must be voted up or down without amendments. A direct vote on a separate provision such as the low-power stations isn't possible under the rules of the Congress. For similar reasons, such last-hour omnibus legislative packages are often veto-proof.

The wipeout of FCC's authority to license low-power community stations is an outrage that should be corrected in the next Congress. This bill is on the way to President Clinton. It would be wonderful if he would veto this bill. If he doesn't, President-elect George W. Bush, who has told the nation that he is a "compassionate conservative," could signal his concern about community needs by embracing the idea that communities, religious groups, schools, and citizen groups should have a voice through these low-power FM stations. This would be an excellent place for the new president to provide evidence of his desire to reach out to the people.

December 19, 2000

The Danger of Standardized Tests

For all the talk in Washington about the need to decentralize power and give authority to the states, in one of the core areas of state and local responsibility—education—there is a growing and dangerous sentiment among top officials in both the Democratic and Republican parties in favor of a new federal mandate: mandatory standardized testing of students and teachers.

It is obvious that our educational system is in need of significant improvement, but standardized tests won't help. In fact, they are sure to: exacerbate the worst educational tendencies toward rote memorization, bore students and turn them off to reading and intellectual engagement, and worsen racial disparities in the educational system.

Standardized tests fail to measure creativity, thoughtfulness, perceptiveness, judgment, diligence, critical thinking, communication skills, problem solving, or imagination—to name just a few attributes of genuine intelligence. What they do reward is thinking and memorization skills that have little importance in the world of work, higher education, family, or citizenship.

Exacerbating the problem, the tests exhibit persistent racial and gender bias, disadvantaging people of color and girls and women in competitive spheres from primary to graduate school.

Tests that measure narrow and unimportant learning skills—perhaps even penalizing those who think outside conventional boundaries—and also suffer from racial and gender bias should have no place in our educational system.

Despite reams of documentation—including the groundbreaking report "The Reign of ETS," published two decades ago—on how they are ineffective, biased, and counterproductive, standardized tests are finding ever-increasing usage. Beginning at very young ages, children throughout their educational careers are increasingly forced to pass standardized tests as a prerequisite to advancement. Access to advanced classes and later to colleges and graduate schools are overly dependent on standardized test performance.

The result is a corrupted educational system, in which teachers teach for tests, pushing memorization and multiple-choice skill-building, rather than foster children's critical thinking abilities. Those students who do poorly on tests—disproportionately children of color and children from low-income families—are vectored into special education, remedial or lower-level classes in which they are too frequently presented with boring and unchallenging material, ensuring that their academic performance will lag.

Teacher tests, which have little if any correlation with actual teaching ability but are also gaining in popularity, block tens of thousands of teachers of color from teaching in primary and secondary schools. African American teachers who do pass the tests score lower than whites on average, but beginning African American teachers earn higher performance ratings than their white counterparts, according to *The Effects of Competency Testing on the Supply of Minority Teachers*, by Dr. G. Pritchy Smith, professor at the University of North Florida.

The expansive utilization of standardized tests in more and more educational and other spheres is due, to a considerable extent, to the effective marketing of their fake objectivity by the Educational Testing Service and other testing companies. It also reflects a tragically misguided push by the Clinton/Gore administration to increase the use of testing as a facile marker for educational "reform."

As a first step, there should be a national ban on the use of "high stakes" standardized tests, where standardized tests are used as the sole measure to determine grade advancement, graduation, tracking, or other decisions. Federal incentives should encourage the progressive and rapid diminishment of reliance on tests. We can instead assess students primarily through integrated methods based in the classroom, including informal interviews, projects, classroom tests, and journals.

We certainly need national initiatives to promote educational reform—to engage students in critical thinking, to transmit citizenship skills that involve the application of classroom learning to the real-world challenges of building a more just and democratic society, to devote sufficient resources to ensure that schools are well maintained, to lower student-teacher ratios and more. But we don't need failed and discredited misnamed reforms that get in the way of authentic teaching. It is time to end the obsession in Washington and elsewhere with standardized tests.

To get more information on standardized tests, contact the National Center for Fair and Open Testing (Fair Test) at 342 Broadway, Cambridge, MA 02139, 617-864-4810, www.fairtest.org.

November 1, 2000

The Airwaves Belong to the People

The airwaves belong to the people. Yet the U.S. government gives them away to television and radio broadcasters for free, and demands virtually nothing in return.

We have forfeited many of the means of mass communication to concentrated corporate interests, consigning ourselves to homogenized low-grade entertainment and lower-grade copycat "newstainment" that barely aspires to inform let alone energize our eroding democracy. The major television networks are owned by giant conglomerates—General Electric, Disney, Viacom, Fox, Time Warner. Radio is even worse, with Infinity and Clear Channel dominating the airwaves.

Yet technology keeps offering us new opportunities to learn from the past, and ensure that new media deepen our democracy and serve public, noncommercial interests.

The Federal Communications Commission (FCC) has recently authorized noncommercial low-power FM radio broadcasts. Low-power FM (LPFM) has the potential to strengthen community organization and enrich public life, by permitting genuinely local broadcasting to serve the needs of local audiences.

Not surprisingly, the powerful National Association of Broadcasters (NAB) is trying to block LPFM. The NAB hopes to leverage its enormous political influence by including a provision to block the FCC's authorization of LPFM into a "rushed-through-Congress-at the-end-of-the-legislative-year" funding bill.

The NAB wants to make sure that grassroots challenges to its dominance of the airwaves do not emerge.

Right now most major market radio stations do not even produce their own news—if they air regular news at all. Instead, they rely on outside services that may be thousands of miles from the people they're supposed to serve. Some communities aren't represented in media at all: One news director doesn't bother to cover poor neighborhoods because they "might as well be in another dimension." Another dimension, he means, from the wealthier audience the station's sponsors and owners care about.

Low-power FM offers the opportunity to offset commercial radio's inadequacies, decentralize broadcasting, and empower neighborhoods and communities. Labor union locals will be able to broadcast to their members; communities will have a radio forum to debate and discuss local issues; ethnic groups will be able to air programming to meet their particular needs, including non-English broadcasting; senior citizen centers will be able to reach seniors who cannot make it to the centers' physical facilities; and local government meetings can be broadcast to the community. Under the FCC's plan, one thousand or more 100-watt stations serving areas with a 3.5 mile radius, plus additional 10-watt stations serving a 1 to 2 mile radius, could be licensed.

The NAB contends that low-power stations will interfere with the quality of existing stations' sound. But the FCC, which is not known for hostility to the industry it regulates with kid gloves, has concluded that its licensing arrangement for LPFM will not cause unacceptable levels of interference to existing radio stations.

There is every reason to rely on the FCC's assessment rather than the NAB's. But it comes as no surprise that political decisions in Washington are often made on factors other than the merits, and there is now a serious risk that Congress will override the FCC's plan. In the Senate, Senator Rod Grams (R-MN) has introduced S. 3020, which would drastically scale back the FCC's plan and is similar to a bill passed by the House of Representatives in April. Senator Judd Gregg (R-NH) has introduced a bill, S.2068, which would eliminate LPFM entirely. The greatest legislative threat, however, probably is posed by the possibility that anti-LPFM language will be inserted into a funding bill. That is the kind of backroom deal-making in which NAB-style fat-cat lobbyists specialize.

Whether a tiny fragment of the public's airwaves will be returned to the public for LPFM depends now on whether the public is ready to assert its interests. Call your senators, and tell them not to interfere with LPFM. A working democracy requires some public control of the means of communication.

For more information on LPFM and for breaking legislative news, contact the Media Access Project at (202) 232-4300, or check their web page at www.mediaaccess.org.

October 11, 2000

Stop Marketing to Kids

Step back for a moment and contemplate what corporate hucksters are doing to American childhood. Bypassing parents, these companies brazenly market directly to children, starting at age two. These marketeers (with the advice of the child psychologists on their payroll) wrap these youngsters in a commercial cocoon for an average of thirty hours a week.

Companies use three steps to avoid or neutralize parental authority over the children's spending. First, they urge the child to nag the parents. Second, the sellers take conscious advantage of the absence of parents who are commuting and working long hours away from home. Third, the marketers know that if they can undermine the authority, dignity, and judgment of parents in the eyes of their children, the little ones will purchase or demand items, regardless of their parents' opinions.

Most people, until the disclosures about how tobacco and alcohol companies court kids, had little knowledge about just how premeditated and calculated the efforts are. Children under twelve are increasingly being raised by these companies. Those kids spend far more time with corporate television, video games, toys, arcades, and now Internet games than they do with their parents and other adults. All this is fine with the companies—these boys and girls spent more than $25 billion last year, and what they got in return is violent, addictive, and tawdry sensuality.

These electronic child molesters have little sense of restraint or boundaries. Their odious fare is becoming more coarse, more violent, and more interactive to seduce these youngsters into an addiction of direct video game involvement in the mayhem. The euphemism is "interactive."

It has gotten so bad that Lt. Colonel Dave Grossman and Gloria DeGaetano have authored a new book, *Stop Teaching Our Kids to Kill—A Call to Action against TV, Movie and Video Game Violence.*

It took a while and some terrible school tragedies before President Bill

Clinton told the entertainment industry that "thirty years of studies" about this "daily dose of violence" demonstrate that it does "desensitize our children to violence, and its consequences."

Instead of our popular culture embracing children in a wholesome array of values, activities, and learning experiences with family, neighbors, and teachers, concerned adults have to focus on warding off this depraved corporate commercial saturation of the lives of millions of American youths. A saturation that is goading, exploiting, addicting, and harming children in order to sell, sell, sell.

Privately, more than a few business executives are holding their noses at what is being transmitted to these little customers. I've spoken to some of them. Their excuse: if we don't do this, someone worse will do it. In reality, they just don't have the courage to speak out as citizens.

But a new coalition of parents and friends—the Center for a New American Dream—is moving to organize public opinion and offer stiffer resistance. In a poll of parents commissioned by the center, 70 percent of parents, with children ages two to seventeen, say that marketing to kids is bad for their kids' values and world view, makes them too materialistic, and puts pressure on kids to buy things that are bad for them.

More telling, more than half of all parents polled admitted to buying things for their child that they disapproved of just because the youngster wanted the products to fit in with their friends.

The center is offering a free pamphlet called *Tips for Parenting in a Commercial Culture* to anyone who writes to Suite 900, 6930 Carroll Avenue, Takoma Park, Maryland 20912. Their web site is www.newdream.org. The struggle continues.

October 19, 1999

Privatization: Dangerous and Inefficient

The drumbeat to corporatize (a.k.a. privatize) essential facilities continues to beat from the business-funded think tanks in Washington, D.C. Recently, the government's uranium enrichment installations, which deal with national security matters, were corporatized and are now run by a company listed on the stock exchange.

Corporatization is supposed to be more efficient, more innovative, and reliable. Well, events this month in Japan and England contradict that.

A corporate uranium processing plant in Tokaimura, Japan, owned by Sumitomo Metal Mining, produced Japan's worst nuclear accident. Official investigators attribute the serious release of deadly radiation to a secret company policy that was illegal but reduced company costs. The workers who mixed this uranium cocktail were so ill-trained that one of them admitted he didn't understand the meaning of a "critical reaction."

The sloppiness was everywhere. The delivery of critical equipment—including a neutron measurer—to the power plant and the surrounding neighborhood was delayed for hours. The order to evacuate was also delayed, as was an order for more than 300,000 people to remain indoors.

According to the *Washington Post,* company officials admitted to investigators that "workers have been using the same illegal shortcut that caused the accident for the past seven or eight years. Company officials also said they had not made any preparations for this type of accident in which an excess of uranium poured into a mixing container triggered a nuclear chain reaction.

So far, three workers are in critical condition; many others have been seriously exposed to radiation, and each day brings more bad news. The accident has been raised to a Level 5 rating, which indicates higher levels of contamination outside the plant and in the surrounding community. The *Wall Street Journal* reported that, beyond bad management, the "enormous pressure to cut costs and compete with overseas rivals" was a major factor.

On the other side of the world, two crowded commuter trains collided in London resulting in more than one hundred deaths. Each train was run by a different company. The locomotives and passenger cars were rented from three other companies, while the track and signal equipment were the property of another corporation. Maintenance and repair work were contracted out to other companies.

Five years ago, British Rail, the nation's railroad system, was government owned. It has since been "privatized" by the conservative government. Now more than one hundred corporations own pieces of the national railroad network.

The national railroad regulator, Tom Winsor, sums up the result: "Punctuality and reliability are down, fares are up, complaints are way up, and government subsidies have doubled since privatization. Even the simple things don't get done: Why can't they clean the toilets?" And these companies get taxpayer subsidies to boot!

Whenever there are breakdowns or mishaps, the companies blame each other. What is noteworthy to remember is that Margaret Thatcher's other numerous privatizations have not worked out very well for consumers—lessons lost on the ideologues in the United States.

About sixty years ago, the noted author and journalist Walter Lippmann chided the market fundamentalists of his day by reminding them that there is a need for both private enterprise and public enterprise in our country. Wisdom is finding the right balance between what is best suited to one or the other.

Unfortunately that "balance" presently is out of balance in the rush to privatize prisons, water companies, fire departments, mental health facilities, background checks for public employees, municipal garbage collection, and spy satellites.

October 11, 1999

Kids and Advertising

In 1980, the U.S. Congress passed a law to protect adults who prey on children.

You read that correctly. Public Law 96-252 prohibits the Federal Trade Commission (FTC) from enacting rules that would protect the nation's children from commercial advertising that exploits their vulnerable and trusting natures.

This law is corporate power incarnate. It should be the role of Congress to protect children, not those who would prey upon them. Congress ought to repeal it.

Back then, the FTC was trying to respond to an increase in aggressive marketing aimed at children. Now, two decades later, that increase has become a deluge. Kids are literally assaulted from morning to night. Advertisers target them at home, school, and virtually all points in between.

According to Professor James U. McNeal, an expert on marketing to children, "Virtually every consumer-goods industry, from airlines to zinnia-seed sellers, targets kids."

Because of this, it has become nearly impossible for parents to control advertisers' access to their kids.

Some advertisers exploit children's weaknesses in order to get them to want products. For example, Nancy Shalek, president of the Shalek Agency, told the *Los Angeles Times* that "Advertising at its best is making people feel that without their product, you're a loser. Kids are very sensitive to that.... You open up emotional vulnerabilities and it's very easy to do with kids because they're the most emotionally vulnerable."

Some advertisers admit that they want to control children's minds. For example, Julie Halpin, CEO of Gepetto Group, which specializes in marketing to kids, explains that "Kids marketing in general is becoming more sophisticated" in competing for what she calls "share of mind."

Mike Searles, former president of Kids-R-Us, a major children's clothing store, said that "[I]f you own this child at an early age, you can own this child for years to come. Companies are saying, 'Hey, I want to own the kid younger and younger.'"

Marketers believe they are succeeding. Professor McNeal says that "Advertising targeted at elementary school children, on programs just for them, works very effectively in the sense of implanting brand names in their minds and creating desires for the products."

That's great for advertisers but bad for parents. The problem is that children appear to be developing health problems because they do precisely what the ads are urging.

For example:

Alcohol. Alcohol is a major cause of death among teenagers. It contributes significantly to motor vehicle crashes, injuries, suicide, date rape, and problems with school and family. It makes no sense to encourage children to drink beer or hard liquor. Nevertheless, the Federal Trade Commission recently found that the alcohol industry often advertises to audiences that include large numbers of children, including placing their products in PG and PG-13 films with significant appeal to teens and children, such as films featuring animals or coming-of-age stories. The industry also advertises on eight of the fifteen television shows most popular with teens.

Tobacco. The deadly effects of tobacco advertising on American children are well documented by the FTC and the *Journal of the American Medical Association.* RJR Nabisco's Joe Camel helped seduce hundreds of thousands of children into a lifetime of smoking. Each day another 3,000 children start to smoke. About one-third of them will have their lives cut short by smoking-related illnesses. Almost two-thirds of twelfth graders who smoke choose Marlboro. That is no accident. The Marlboro Man plays to the desires of young people for independence.

Violent entertainment. Following the school shootings in Jonesboro, Pearl, Springfield, Paducah, and Littleton, some media experts, psychologists, and elected officials have suggested that violent entertainment, including violent video games, movies, and television, may be contributing to the occurrence of such events. For example, Lieutenant Colonel Dave Grossman, coauthor of the new book *Stop Teaching Our Kids to Kill,* argues that first-person-shooter video games such as Duke Nukem, Time Crisis, and Quake "teach children the motor skills to kill, like military training devices do. And then they turn around and teach them to like it like the military would never do."

Junk food and fast food. Children are subjected to a barrage of ads for Whoppers, Happy Meals, Coke, Pepsi, Snickers bars, M&Ms, and other junk foods and fast foods. They are urged by these ads to buy these products directly themselves or, if they are too young, to nag their parents. These ads may contribute to skyrocketing levels of childhood obesity. About 25 to 30 percent of American children are now clinically obese. Severe obesity among young children has almost doubled since the 1960s. Similarly, childhood diabetes is also on the rise.

As a minimum response, Congress should now take the initiative to restore the full authority of the FTC to rule on marketing to children to cure these fundamentally unfair and deceptive practices.

Furthermore, Congress should now tell the FTC to make such rules, and give the FTC enough money to enable them to move quickly to protect children from this part of the advertising industry and its commercial molestations.

September 17, 1999

The Maternity Ward Marketplace

Throughout the country, mothers giving birth in hospitals are likely to receive a gift bag full of brand-name goodies and promotions. T-shirts, baby detergents, nursing pads, guides to infant growth, ice packs, and most prominently infant formula are some of the freebies for the new moms.

About a month ago, a mother gave birth to a baby daughter at George Washington University Hospital in Washington, D.C. She promptly received two bags of corporate products and marketing materials from the hospital staff. Our researcher, Tarek Ghani, proceeded to inventory the contents.

He found forty-nine commercial product or service endorsements. There were seven requests for more personal information to use in mailing lists and numerous product samples from multinational corporations, some of which have exhibited dubious reputations.

There were disposable "Huggies" diapers, unscented baby wipes, diaper rash ointment, three credit card offers, an offer for a "posture improving" bra and underwear for mothers worried about their appearance, and a slew of ads for baby books, films, toys, jobs, portraits, chocolate bars, life insurance, and bottles of children's Tylenol—to name a few.

In the mass of material, there were several surveys disguised as sweepstakes offers. Just answer a few questions, Mom, and you'll receive free samples, coupons, more special offers, an opportunity to win a $1,000 educational savings bond. And even free gifts, information, and coupons for the grandparents.

With the permission and implied okay of hospital authorities, the marketers are invading the maternity ward big time. Gone are the days when the wards were sanctuaries from commerce. These days, the business of birth starts as early as cutting the umbilical cord.

Tarek Ghani was not content with his inventory. He wrote a letter to the CEO of the hospital, Phillip S. Schaengold, asking him "exactly what GW Hospital gains from exposing new mothers to a manipulative culture of consumerism?"

He also inquired as to whether the hospital receives any compensation in any form from the two distributors of the bags, Giftpax and First Moments.

Finally, he asked: "Does the hospital consider its distribution of privately produced corporate products an implied endorsement of those products, and if not, how can you possibly justify the time hospital employees spend handing out those materials?"

There is more to this complaint than a charge of consumer irritation. Reaching the mother at the time of her child's birth has been a longtime marketing strategy of the infant formula industry.

In the bag presented to one Connecticut mother, the infant formula product and a baby advice booklet were from the same company. The booklet acknowledged that breast milk was best, but should the mother be unable or unwilling to breast-feed, why then the infant formula was ready.

Since new mothers are not often told about the pain that usually occurs during the first two weeks of breast feeding, a new mother becomes vulnerable to the interruptive availability of the commercial alternative. This approach has worked for years to turn away large numbers of women from breast feeding and is considered such a successful sales technique that marketing courses refer to it in the classroom.

Mr. Ghani's letter has a happy ending. With decisive promptness, CEO Phillip Schaengold replied with these words:

> In response to your letter, we examined the bags of materials that have been habitually distributed to patients at our childbirth center. Our staff receives these promotional bags free of charge from infant formula companies and with the best of intentions has distributed them to new mothers as gifts. After our review of the bags' contents we found your complaints to be valid. We too believe that the commercial products included in each bag to be inappropriate for distribution to our patients. The George Washington University Hospital does not endorse any of these products and will take immediate action.
>
> Over the next month, we will be working to create a GW Hospital diaper bag of our own which will include items such as: baby bibs and generic safety instruction cards. The purpose of this new bag is

twofold. It removes the need for the bags you found offensive and provides a gift for new moms who deliver their babies at our hospital.

Thank you for bringing this matter to our attention.

Good! Now what about the hundreds of other hospitals in the country? Why not ask them to do the same in your community?

August 23, 1999

Power (FM) to the People

Ever wonder why radio generally has become so canned, flat, and insipid, bereft of local news, and stuffed with commercials, mercantile values, and the same old, tired junk? Not to mention the downright offensiveness of Howard Stern and the other shock-jocks?

First, for years, more than 90 percent of all radio time has been composed of entertainment (music) and advertisements. Second, in the last three years, diversity in radio station ownership has been collapsing.

The Telecommunications Act of 1996 raised the number of radio stations that any single corporation may own in a particular market. This loosed a flood of radio company mergers. So, not only is station ownership concentrated in fewer corporate hands, but formulaic programming puts the few reporters left, and local coverage, in the backseat as well.

Two conglomerates own more than four hundred radio stations each, all over the country. One woman complained about the sameness of Cleveland radio following two huge radio company mergers: "It's as though McDonald's bought every restaurant in town, and all you could get was a Big Mac."

The purpose of these corporate radio mega-conglomerates is to maximize profits by reducing costs of reporters and editors—not to enrich public discourse or cover the news in their areas. Market forces have not led to a vigorous radio culture, or thoughtful programming, or programming that gives voice to the community. In their quest for larger audiences, more advertising, and greater profits, commercial broadcasters cater to the basest standards, with ever more blatant effusions of crassness, sex talk, and nihilism.

Commercial rewards drive the creation, production, and marketing of ever more Howard Sterns, Greaseman, and the rest of the shock-jocks. This inevitably leads to a coarsening of our culture, which has particularly harmful effects on children. Even "public" radio is becoming commercialized. National Public Radio now carries ever longer "underwriting messages," which are a form of advertisement.

Meanwhile, the public is mostly silent on the airwaves that we legally own.

Radio is supposed to serve the ends and purposes of the First Amendment. That means protecting public discourse, which is essential to our form of democratic self-government.

But the current regulatory regime for radio serves to thwart the First Amendment rights and the interests of most Americans. We speak little, if at all, on our own airwaves, while the wealthy may speak through radio by controlling who uses their stations and for what purposes.

What good is freedom of speech if nobody can afford it? Is speech truly free if only the wealthy can buy it?

Here's the good news: At last, the Federal Communications Commission (FCC) may come to the rescue.

Right now the FCC is considering whether to set up noncommercial, low-power FM (LPFM) radio stations of up to 100 watts, with a range of a few miles. That's a big deal. Imagine the new voices that could flourish on these microstations—service and advocacy groups, universities, community and civic organizations, ethnic groups, arts organizations, seniors groups, and others.

They could really liven up the radio dial. They could give us some choices.

But it is not enough merely to authorize LPFM service. The FCC should allocate more spectrums for low-power radio broadcasting and introduce it when radio switches from analog to digital signals.

These small stations could enrich the public's understanding of civic issues and social problems. They could be a modest but important step toward more cohesive communities, a renewed public discourse, and a richer and more realistic culture. It is not often that a federal agency can achieve so much with so little effort.

Americans are drowning in a sea of commercialism. Americans are immersed in advertisements, junk mail, junk faxes, television and radio ads, telemarketing, and billboards. There are ads in schools, beach sand, airport lounges, doctors' offices, hospitals, convenience stores, floors of supermarkets, toilet stalls, on the Internet, and countless other places. Advertisers even tried, unsuccessfully, to put ads in space and on postage stamps. Tom Vanderbilt, author of *The Sneaker Book*, writes of advertisers' efforts to "hang a jingle in front of America's every waking moment."

Three cheers for the Microradio Empowerment Coalition, a coalition of microradio stations, community and civic groups, organizations, and individuals that is working to make noncommercial LPFM radio a reality.

There is a profound need in America today for public spaces where people can talk to one another. We don't need more advertising talking at us. Can't we have just a few spaces—niches really—that are free from advertising? Sanctuaries, in effect. Is that too much to ask?

The FCC ought to use its authority to establish noncommercial LPFM stations to build a stronger democracy in America and to serve a vision grander than the profit-driven trivialization that largely characterizes the broadcasting and advertising. The FCC was not intended to merely protect the speech rights of broadcasters, advertisers, and the wealthy. It ought to uphold and protect the public's First Amendment interests in radio, to rededicate radio to the service of democracy in America. Noncommercial LPFM radio is one modest step toward that goal.

July 9, 1999

Channel One

Would you want your children to see propaganda that glorifies reckless driving or that reinforces the poor body image of teenage girls? That's exactly the kind of thing schoolkids are watching on Channel One, a so-called educational broadcast piped into classrooms across the country. Whether your main concern is quality of education, the role of corporations in our culture, or the commercial values children are exposed to, there is great reason to be concerned about Channel One. In essence, Channel One is run by a marketing company that uses the schools to deliver advertising to youngsters. Each school day, work comes to a halt in classrooms across the nation as teachers turn on a television show made up of two minutes of commercials and ten minutes of "news."

Currently, the MTV-like news show reaches about eight million middle, junior high, and high school students in 12,000 schools. Each year, students spend the equivalent of about one class week watching Channel One—including the equivalent of one full school day just watching ads. Advertisers love Channel One because, as its former president, Joel Babbit, puts it, "we are forcing kids to watch two minutes of commercials" in school. But many people take issue with using schools to deliver a captive audience of children to commercial advertisers. Many parents are worried about commercial culture and the way it pervades the lives of kids and reinforces values that are utterly contrary to the ones parents try to instill. So Channel One has hired high-priced Washington lobbyists and launched a P.R. campaign to convince parents that it's simply "an old-fashioned newscast that often reflects traditional values no longer seen on network news."

Nice try. The "news" is just filler. What Channel One really conveys is materialism: that buying is good and will solve your problems, and that consumption and self-gratification are the goals and ends of life.

Many of Channel One's ads also promote low-grade sensuality to children as young as eleven. Chew Winterfresh gum and kiss the Winterfresh babe. Shave with Schick razors and the Schick babe will hug you. There are ads for Blockbuster Video that portray kids playing video games nonstop for five days until they pass out from exhaustion. A Mountain Dew ad glorifies reckless driving. A Twix candy bar ad shows kids avoiding the consequences of doing badly at school by sending their report cards to the Eskimos so their parents won't read them. There are ads for Snickers that encourage kids to eat junk food. And then there are the ads for products, such as Gatorade, that show skinny models that make teenage girls feel badly about the way they look and encourage an unhealthy body image and an obsession with being thin.

Of course, Channel One says the ads are harmless. Never mind that Channel One's corporate parent is Kohlberg Kravis Roberts & Co., which used to own R.J. Reynolds Tobacco. That's the company that invented the Joe Camel ad campaign to hook hundreds of thousands of kids on cigarettes. A poll found that kids recognize Joe Camel as readily as Mickey Mouse. Are these the kind of people you want making images for your kids to see?

The Channel One broadcast also wastes both money and classroom time. Although Channel One loans the televisions to the schools, one recent study by Max Sawicky and Alex Molnar, "The Hidden Costs of Channel One," concluded that Channel One's cost to taxpayers in lost class time is $1.8 billion a year. And a 1997 study by William Hoynes found that the content of Channel One's "news" programming was shallow, filled with soft "news," mindless banter, music, useless "pop quizzes," and other fluff.

The U.S. Senate is currently scheduling hearings to investigate the effects of Channel One on children, schools, and taxpayers, and a broad coalition has been created to fight the broadcasts. The group, which includes the American Family Association, Center for a New American Dream, Commercial Alert, Family Research Council, and Eagle Forum, has asked the CEOs of companies that advertise on Channel One to pull their ads. For real education reform that protects children, costs nothing, and increases productive class time, tell your school board to kick Channel One out of class.

May 7, 1999

Opinion Oligopoly Dittoheads

Bob Woodward (of Watergate reportorial fame) once called Richard Cohen the *Washington Post*'s best regular columnist. But on January 31, Cohen wrote a regular column in the (Sunday) *Post Magazine* that is noteworthy for other reasons. Cohen fired himself from his Sunday column.

Cohen's explanation for abandoning his Sunday column (he still writes a column for the newspaper's op-ed page) marks him as unique among his colleagues. "I felt some time ago that I was out of ideas," he wrote. "Write this or that, people would say. I already wrote it, I would reply. I did it 10 or 15 years ago. I didn't want to repeat myself."

If only the Opinion Oligopoly of columnists and television pundits in Washington, D.C., would follow Cohen's lead. Week after week, month after month, year after year, decade after decade, they cling to their ever more redundant opinions.

Can readers learn much more from George Will, Charles Krauthammer, Anthony Lewis, the McLaughlin crowd, the Gordon Peterson circle, Cokie Roberts, Sam Donaldson, William Kristol, or George Stephanopoulos?

Why is the Opinion Oligopoly so stagnant? First, its members arrive at their positions based on their superiors' need to categorize them as conservative or liberal. They are pigeonholed by the publications that employ them. Then they're forced to feed their own stereotypes. Even if they bounce their ideas off the news of the day, their columns often become tiring. Richard Cohen told me that his editors around the country demanded that his syndicated column address the big headline stories of the day. This inhibited him from investigating new subjects that the news pages were largely ignoring.

A similar situation confronted Gordon Peterson, a first-rate television-reporting talent, who has been reduced to working as a "rip and read" anchor on a local television news program. What's most frightening about Peterson's situation is that the "rip and read" is issued not by the Associated Press or another wire service, but by station management, whose formulaic routines turn the advertising-saturated evening news into a contrived, depressing event.

The abundance of narrow opinions in American newspapers shocks many foreign journalists. Questions about corporate crime are rarer than hen's teeth. Opinions contrary to the corporate state and its autocratic governance of trade agreements are almost never heard. The Opinion Oligopoly sits heavily to the right of a very narrow divide while the tepid liberals shudder and adjust defensively. The conventional prattle of these journalists crowds out a rich diversity of opinion and experience in a city like Washington, D.C.

The Opinion Oligopoly needs to take a sabbatical, preferably a long one, and allow the public other frames of reference, so we can uncover important new opinions, voices, and stories that have too long remained unknown.

March 4, 1999

Privatizing Social Security

Social Security places government in one of its noblest roles: as an institution that offers a bedrock financial guarantee to all members of society that they need not fear the financial consequences of growing old or disabled. That's quite the opposite of the U.S. government's all too familiar role as a provider of corporate welfare, a patsy to narrow business interests that hijack government programs and agencies and convert taxpayer assets into private profits, with inadequate reciprocal benefits to the public.

So it saddened me to learn that our social security system is under attack. Relying on a trumped-up "crisis" in the social security program, a band of so-called privatizers want to convert our social security commonwealth into individual, private accounts.

The privatizers mislead the public. They distort returns we are likely to experience from a privatized system. They fail to mention the enormous administrative fees that stockbrokers and insurance agents might conceivably skim from private accounts, and they remain silent about the likelihood of millions of people losing their retirement income in the stock market. They ignore SEC Chairman Arthur Levitt's warning that stock fraud hucksters will inevitably take advantage of people who are encouraged to put their social security money in the stock market.

Worst of all, privatization will destroy one of social security's great assets—systemic tranquility. We know that in old age or disability, we can count on social security for financial support. If the system is privatized, this tranquility will be replaced by anxiety, as we worry about whether we will be winners or losers in the system's roller-coaster ride on Wall Street.

In his State of the Union address, President Clinton refused to accede to the privatizers' wishes for now. His proposal to allocate a portion of the federal budget surplus to a social security trust fund is a step forward in guaranteeing younger generations benefits similar to those that exist currently.

Unfortunately, the president also reintroduced a notion that seemed to have disappeared from the social security debate in recent months: direct government investment of portions of the social security trust fund in the stock market.

Under the president's proposal, at the end of fifteen years, the federal government will have invested about $700 billion in stocks. That means the government would basically own 4 to 5 percent of the entire stock market. This sort of initiative would further balloon an already dangerously inflated stock market and bring the country perilously closer to a corporate state, where corporations and government converge to serve big business interests.

What would happen if the market ever faced collapse? Would the president and Congress sit idly by as $700 billion in government investments shrank to $400 billion? That's hard to imagine. They'd almost certainly intervene. And any such intervention would primarily benefit private investors who will escape troubled waters without paying any rescue fees. That's free, de facto investor insurance, and it will raise risk-taking to new speculative highs.

Increased government interest in the stock market might also force Congress to legislate with even more of an eye to serving Wall Street than is currently the case. This sort of bias would inevitably result in a host of policies that would negatively affect the public and the environment: weak safety and health standards, suppression of the minimum wage, meaningless restrictions on greenhouse gas emissions, etc.

Proponents of the president's plan say it is not qualitatively different from federal, state, and local pension fund investment in the market. But those funds are diffused among hundreds of such investors. And they aren't invested by institutions which are able to bail out corporations and set national economic policy.

If Congress and the president do erroneously proceed with a plan to invest these funds in the stock market, the government must at the very least exercise the generic rights afforded to stock owners: the right to vote shares and influence company policy commensurate with its ownership stake. The government is not like other investors—it has certain policies and principles that it seeks to promote as a matter of law. It would be intolerable for it, as an investor, to ignore such corporate practices as consumer fraud, worker safety, and other corporate crimes that contradict broad public interest concerns.

For more information, contact the National Council of Senior Citizens at 1-301-578-8800 or www.ncscinc.org, or the Preamble Center at www.preamble.org.

January 27, 1999

III

ENVIRONMENT
AND HEALTH

If ever there was a simple fix in terms of public policy, it's the fuel efficiency of automobiles. Gas-guzzling vehicles pollute our air and contribute to a dependence on imported oil that distorts our foreign policy. And as much as some Americans may like their overpriced SUVs, polls show overwhelming public support for an increase in fuel-efficiency standards for all types of vehicles.

On top of that, in 1992 we elected a Democratic administration (with a vice president who had written a book trumpeting his passionate concern for the environment) that pledged to raise the fuel-efficiency ("CAFE") standard substantially. Yet nothing happened, and the standard remains just the same in 2004 as it was in 1985! Meanwhile, American energy policy remains in the grip of the oil, gas, coal, and nuclear industries, as practical renewable energy sources are neglected. The situation seems unlikely to improve with a president and vice president who are marinated in oil and see drilling in the Arctic National Wildlife Refuge (ANWR) as a solution to our energy problems.

Environmentalism is as much a matter of public health and ethics as it is about aesthetics or nature-loving. Today companies, and to a lesser degree governments, routinely pollute the water we drink and air we breathe, causing the spread of deadly diseases and the extinction of animal species. The columns in this section provide one example after another of a reckless plundering of the Earth's resources to the detriment of our health and well-being.

Other columns in this section deal with different threats to public health stemming from a failed health care system. The elderly and others often find drugs prohibitively expensive, and nearly forty-five million Americans have no health insurance. The Institute of Medicare estimates the loss of 18,000 American lives a year because there was no health insurance to cover their medical care. These and other health care problems are neither accidental nor inevitable. They result from deliberate economic and political actions by insurers, pharmaceutical companies, and HMOs that care a great deal about their profits and power and too little about our health.

A recurring theme in the columns in this section is the incompetence or indifference of the agencies charged with promoting sound public policy. In the face of environmental devastation, what remedial actions are taken by the Environmental Protection Agency, the Department of Transportation, and the Department of Energy? You may not like what you see. While the elderly suffer at the hands of price-gouging pharmaceutical companies, and the policies of agribusiness destroy fish and wildlife and contaminate our food supply, how do the Department of Agriculture and Food and Drug Administration respond? Like other regulatory bodies, they all too often respond to the whims and wishes of the very corporations they supposedly oversee.

In sum, those entrusted with protecting our health and environment are almost as much a part of the problem as the solution. As you read accounts of their negligence and their anticipation of later joining the companies under their scrutiny, remember that the power of these agencies is entirely delegated by We The People. Shouldn't we expect and demand better performance?

Pharmaceutical Prices

If Sam's Club can negotiate for lower pharmaceutical prices, why can't Uncle Sam? Because the approval by the Congress of a new pharmaceutical benefit for Medicare was saddled with a legal provision that prohibits the U.S. government from using its considerable consumer market power to negotiate for lower prices on medicines.

Our country is already spending more than 2 percent of GDP on pharmaceutical purchases, and these outlays skyrocketed long before the Medicare bill was passed. Because the U.S. government is obligated to provide some coverage for pharmaceutical drugs under the new bill, one would think it would seek to at least have the flexibility to restrain corporate patent owners from charging excessive prices for their medicines. In the absence of even the possibility to negotiate lower prices, there will be no price restraints and therefore less money for medicine.

Every European country and most industrialized countries have authority in domestic legislation to negotiate lower prices for medicines under government reimbursement programs, and/or the authority to order the issuance of compulsory licenses in cases of abuses by patent owners. (A compulsory license enables price-lowering generic drug competition for on-patent products.) Canadian economist Aidan Hollis notes that a legal requirement upon a government to provide coverage for drug purchases should logically be accompanied by powers to question or curb excessive prices—or patent owners can and will make unreasonable and costly demands on taxpayers.

While the U.S. government has long been a patsy for the powerful drug manufacturers industry, it does have powers outside of the Medicare program to negotiate for lower drug prices, for example, at the Department of Defense and at the Veterans Administration. And don't forget the case in 2001 when Secretary Thompson was able to cut the price of Cipro (an antibiotic used to treat people exposed to anthrax) in half, after threatening to purchase generic versions if Bayer did not offer the government an adequate discount.

The Medicare drug benefit will now take a different route. The federal government, acting on behalf of taxpayers and consumers, will be a passive consumer—accepting the prices offered by the drug industry. As Hollis predicts, the Medicare program will be exploited by drugmakers.

This is particularly galling because U.S. taxpayers already provide massive direct and indirect public subsidies, tax credits, and free donations of government research for the development of new drugs.

The defense of the "don't negotiate prices" provision in the Medicare bill is the familiar argument that any measure to protect taxpayers or consumers will undermine the development of new drugs. This argument is used time and time again to justify an ever expanding list of corporate welfare schemes and pricing abuses. Rather than simply accepting the notion that it is necessary to give unlimited pricing power to the patent holders and drug manufacturers (who spend more on marketing than on authentic research), Congress needs to explore more fiscally responsible alternatives.

Prudent negotiations of pharmaceutical prices will free up significant resources to provide greater coverage of seniors and will save taxpayers from being price gouged. The "don't negotiate prices" provision on the Medicare bill is the wrong approach. What we need is a new commitment to negotiate better terms for the money we spend (publicly and privately) on R&D. For more information visit: www.cptech.org.

November 28, 2003

The Energy Boondoggle

The only remarkable thing about the 2003 energy policy bill greasing its way through Congress has been the energy of the avaricious lobbyists for the oil, gas, coal, and nuclear corporations. But then there were tens of billions of dollars in it for them in tax escapes, loan guarantees, and outright subsidies along with weaker law enforcement for polluters of your air, water, and your public lands.

The legislation (H.R. 6) is 1700 pages of giveaways and contempt for the American people—their health, safety, and pocketbooks. It was debated all of one hour by the House of Representatives under the rule of dictator Representative Tom DeLay (R-TX), who raises more campaign cash from lobbyists the more he takes America down.

On November 21, 2003, the Senate had a showdown vote to cut off debate after two days on this bad bill. The bad guys lost—barely.

They're going to try again in a few days. However, in a way, the concentrated corporate powers over our government nearly achieved a new high dirty-water mark toward flooding Congress completely. They nearly defeated an opposition composed of both leading liberal and conservative groups. And they ignored editorials from dozens of leading newspapers, including a ferocious one by the *Wall Street Journal* acidly titled "Archer-Daschle-Midland."

The *Journal* meant to convey that most of the ethanol subsidies go not to farmers but to giant agribusiness companies, in cahoots with the leader of the Democrats in the Senate—Tom Daschle (D-SD). On the right in opposition were the Cato Institute, Heritage Foundation, National Taxpayers Union, and Citizens Against Government Waste, irritated over subsidies, giveaways, and other corporate welfare boondoggles, such as financing a shopping mall that included a Hooters restaurant in Louisiana.

On the liberal side were the auto and electrical workers unions (so much for Bush's jobs argument), U.S. Public Interest Research Group, American Lung Association, ACORN, Clean Water Action Project, Consumer Federation of America, Sierra Club, Union of Concerned Scientists, and Physicians for Social Responsibility. Among the reasons for their opposition were provisions letting manufacturers of the toxic chemical MTBE avoid liability for contaminating thousands of underground sites in the United States and leaving the taxpayers with an estimated $29 billion cleanup bill.

Weighing in to oppose the bill were the National League of Cities, the U.S. Conference of Mayors, the American Public Works Associations, the National Association of Counties, and the Association of Metropolitan Water Agencies.

And still the corporate Goliaths almost won!

Listen to the way the *Denver Post*—a conservative paper—described the legislation: "It eases environmental restrictions to promote drilling and mining on public lands, provides tax help to already profitable producers of oil, gas, coal and nuclear power, requires no progress on tightening emissions from vehicles or smokestacks, and adds insult to injury by subsidizing the purchase of monster gas-guzzlers, such as the Humvee."

The *Washington Post* wrote: "The House passed an enormous energy bill. . .that would remove tariffs from imported Chinese ceiling fans [for Home Depot], pay a half a billion dollars to chop down trees for fuel, ship bomb-grade uranium abroad. . . ." Regarding the uranium exports, top nuclear experts denounced that section because it would make it easier for terrorists to make a nuclear bomb. Where is George W. Bush to demand that this item be put on his cue cards?

One Senator from a mid-western state told me that the White House called him up and asked, "How many plants do you want in your state?" The White House becomes a peddler for corporate socialism.

The closeness of the vote was due to the expansion of ethanol production with a taxpayer subsidy. Usually stand-up Democratic Senators like Byron Dorgan (D-ND) and Kent Conrad (D-ND) caved in return for the ethanol provision and a gasification plant loan guarantee. Until that was offered, Dorgan was the most eloquent denouncer of the legislation. "If you put ear rings on a hog, it's still a hog," he said, before he got his necklace.

In coming weeks, the stench of this pork-legislation will emit from the newspapers and television programs digging into its many pages. The nearly seventy-year safeguard against public utility holding company speculation and the instability that kept electric companies stable would be repealed in this age of Enronitis and other drooling speculators in waiting.

Some day, stark paybacks for campaign cash by lawmakers will be considered illegal bribery. One provision in the bill gives a $100 million windfall for a large entertainment and retail complex near Syracuse. The boss of the development company is Robert Congel, who has raised more than $100,000 for Bush and recently hosted a major fundraiser outside Syracuse for Vice President Dick Cheney.

In the 1920s, Will Rogers, the satiric commentator, said that "Congress is the best money can buy." If he only knew how big the bargains have become.

For more information, see web site www.opensecrets.org.

November 22, 2003

The Energy Disaster

The word "chaos" cannot do justice to the omnibus energy legislation properly mired in something called the House-Senate conference. Inside tyranny by the Republicans and the outside full-nelson grip on Congress by the oil, gas, and coal corporations are driving the Democrats to think about filibuster. And deservedly, the bill merits defeat.

In fact, nobody but a few insiders even knows all that is in the bill. Where are the pages containing the changes, rejections, additions, and golden handshake insertions, ask the Democrats and the press. The Republicans have excluded the Democrats from many deliberations on this monster legislation, marinated in oil and driven by cash register politics.

Let's back up a bit to see what is at stake for the American people. Our economy wastes more energy than any other country—vehicles, lighting, heating, air conditioning, etc.—which is another way of saying, consumer waste means greater sales for the energy companies—your electric, gas, and oil company. So there is a conflict of interest here and the energy industry holds the trump cards of power, influence, and money in Washington, D.C.

On the other hand, there are all kinds of efficient technologies that are practical, working in some locales, or waiting on the shelf to be applied to production engineering. Back in the mid-seventies, energy efficiency engineers—hardheaded, practical types—were saying that the nation wastes over half its energy—for starters!

Today, the average fuel efficiency of your new vehicle is the lowest in over twenty years! GM is going backwards into the future, humming the noxious tune of the giant Hummer, with the Bushes giving owners a gigantic, first-year deduction if they are in some sorts of business.

Furthermore, with the CEO of BP (British Petroleum), Lord John Browne, referring to his big company as "Beyond Petroleum," selling solar energy ($300 million in sales last year), and warning about global warming, isn't it time to dredge up old solar energy technologies and new refinements as a core of future energy policy?

Now look at the omnibus energy bill's offerings. There are major but vague tax breaks for domestic oil exploration and development, as if this long pampered and subsidized industry needs more taxpayer "incentives" to make more mega-profits. The bill contains no significant increase in average fuel economy standards—a bill of rights for producing more gas-guzzlers that eat into your budget and pollute the air.

A huge new taxpayer-guaranteed Alaska natural gas pipeline, owned by big companies who want you to assure they get a price immune from market forces, is also in the mix. This one is too much for natural gas companies in our Southwest who recoil against future competitors' unfair corporate welfare.

The Republicans have supported provisions that open the Arctic refuge to drilling, but have met stiff opposition. More likely is yet another taxpayer subsidy for new atomic energy plants and more immunity for nuclear power in case of a catastrophic meltdown accident. There is more immunity for the makers of methyl tertiary butyl ether (MTBE), a gasoline additive that has polluted water supplies around the nation as it is being phased out.

A Senate-passed provision that would have made electric companies increase their use of wind, solar, and other renewable fuels (the way the publicly owned SMUD electric district is doing in Sacramento, California) was dropped.

The bill still contains some modest assistance to the poor to pay heating bills (certainly the oil companies like this assured payment), a very small program to assist consumers who conserve energy by weatherizing their residences, and a little research on climate change.

Significantly, the legislation does not regulate greenhouse-gas emissions from power companies and vehicles, which are connected to global warming, early melting of glaciers, and turbulent storms.

If you ask the people what they want, the answer is more clean, efficient, and, where practical, renewable energy. For many years, solar energy in all forms has scored very high on public opinion polls. But for a majority of Congress and its grasping hydrocarbon and nuclear lobbyists, it's more fossil fuels, uranium, your tax dollars, and environmental damage from the ground to the stratosphere.

Better to shelve the whole congealed greedy mess and start listening to the people next year. In the meantime, you all conserve wherever you can, and, if you are able, walk some more.

For more information, visit www.USPIRG.org, www.citizen.org, and www.ucsusa.org—it is not too late to let your members of Congress know your opinion on the energy legislation.

November 14, 2003

The Blue Frontier

It was a dinner gathering to remember. In a historic Washington, D.C. building, there was an assembly with such a variety of talents dedicated to saving our awfully overburdened oceans that Blue Frontier director David Helvarg remarked, "there's rarely been so much marine talent gathered in one place, since Jacques Cousteau dined alone."

The dinner was the official launching of our Blue Frontier campaign to connect and help organize over two thousand coastal and maritime communities and civic associations into a powerful force to roll back the devastations that spell misuse and overuse of oceans, beaches, estuaries, and bays.

Assembled were ocean-savers such as John Passacantando of Greenpeace, Andy Sharpless of Oceana, Roger Berkowitz, the far-seeing owner of the Legal Seafood restaurants, and Representatives George Miller, Sam Farr, and Wayne Gilchrist who are genuinely committed to effective legislation.

The oceanic crises were obvious. The decline in ocean fisheries has driven some species close to extinction. Giant trawlers scrape the bottom of the seas over a region equal to the size of the United States, wreaking eco havoc. Giant fish-catching nets and their accompanying technology shrink the giant oceans and their underwater denizens.

Environmentalist Barry Commoner's insightful phrase, "the technosphere against the ecosphere," comes to mind.

There is more. Nutrient runoff from factory farms and urban storm drains create massive algal blooms and dead zones (as in the Gulf of Mexico), spreading disease. Floods of chemicals are pouring into the seas, and the growing economies of China and India are seriously affecting their coastlines. India for years has been dumping radioactive waste into its seas in containers that do not last for more than a few decades.

David Helvarg, author of the brilliantly engrossing *Blue Frontier: Saving America's Living Seas,* told the dinner guests that "the chance to protect and restore our waters and wildlife are undermined by coastal sprawl impacting the nurseries and cleansers of our seas—our watersheds, estuaries, salt marshes, sea-grass meadows, barrier islands, and coral reefs...all these cascading disasters are being enhanced by fossil-fuel-driven climate change that's resulting in beach erosion, sea level rise, intensified storms, and coral bleaching from warming oceans."

Two major reports this year—one coming out this month from a presidential commission and the other published in June by the Pew Oceans Commission—contain many sensible recommendations for action. We may be the last generation (the next forty years) to save our oceans from an irreversible decline in performing their critical functions for the planet, animal life, and humans.

There are, to be sure, many vested interests, from the U.S. Navy to fishery companies to recreational users to beach property owners. But there are also many practical solutions, as described on the Blue Frontier web site (www.bluefront.org), if the "growing constituency of watermen and women who have solutions can build a seaweed rebellion of citizen activists," in Helvarg's words. Indeed such citizen rebellions have saved the Californian coasts from more oil drilling and have established marine sanctuaries, which are equivalent to wilderness areas for preservation of species.

As if to punctuate the urgency, dinner participants passed around a description of a notorious rider stealthily attached by Senator Ted Stevens (R-AK) in the final days of this congressional session, without any public hearings, to the appropriations bill for the Department of Commerce. This rider, if not stopped by a countermove led by Senators John McCain (R-AZ) and Olympia Snowe (R-ME), would allow the destruction of thousands of square miles of deep-sea coral habitat and open stellar sea lion refuges to exploitation by a small cartel of industrial fishing companies.

Interested citizens can contact "Sink the Stevens Rider" at www.oceana.org. For more information, go to the web site www.bluefront.org.

November 7, 2003

Government Purchasing Leverage

The federal government is by far the largest consumer in the land, spending hundreds of billions of dollars yearly. It buys many of the products regular consumers purchase, including motor vehicles, fuel, drugs, paper, clothing, food, computers, software, appliances, furnishings, and medical devices. It also buys less usual products, such as construction equipment, buildings, highways, and military hardware.

Connecting all these purchases with established national missions, rooted in law, to clean up the environment, promote consumer health and safety, advance job safety, and save taxpayer dollars can itself become a remarkable national mission. If the agencies and departments that do this buying could receive support and direction from Congress and the president, Americans would start seeing their dollars go further and their well-being improve.

This is not altogether a new story, but it is a largely forgotten one. How many people know that it was the U.S. Army that decades ago started legitimizing much cheaper generic drugs by using them in its hospitals? Until then, the big drug companies peddled the myth that much more expensive brand-name drugs were purer and safer.

Equally little known is that the opposition of the auto companies to air bags was significantly broken by the General Services Administration putting out a bid in the mid '80s for 5,500 air bag-equipped cars for government employees. GM and Chrysler refused to bid; Ford did and the rest is history. Back in Civil War days, standardized clothing sizes were introduced when Lincoln's Union forces had to purchase uniforms for its troops.

Here is the wonderful prospect. Government purchasing specifications, pushing forward the frontiers of innovation or available technologies that favor health, safety, and environmental protection, can quickly create large markets. This in turn offers producers or vendors early economies of scale, lower unit costs, and lower risks. This then makes it possible for companies to invest in innovations before a consumer market exists. The results are products that become available to a wider public, just like generic drugs and air bags.

Nearly thirty years ago, Professor Barry Commoner, the great environmental scientist, proposed to the Pentagon that it buy solar photovoltaics at a scale that would drop unit costs and create a growing solar industry. His proposal was not accepted. But in the nineties, on a smaller scale, the Navy was placing a projected 20,000 photovoltaics in remote installations for economic reasons. There is no need to refuel and it is good for the environment. The Pentagon did its best not to publicize this good deed.

Of course, longtime vendors to governmental agencies often oppose innovations that challenge the "not invented here" syndrome. And the more the federal government leases or outsources its activities to corporations, the less realizable is this potential of government buying for important innovations.

There is another reason why government purchasing is now so important to advance statutorily based national missions of health, safety, environment, efficiency, and care for posterity. Federal regulation is disappearing.

Why, you say, are there all those outcries by companies, trade associations, and think tanks about over-regulation. A skeptic would say, How else do these groups keep raising so much money from their members or benefactors? The skeptic is right. Most federal regulations on the books are years, if not decades, obsolete and long since surpassed by industrial practice. They are not upgraded. Other categories of regulations are: 1) those demanded by the industries themselves, such as agricultural marketing orders, 2)newer regulations watered down to levels acceptable to companies that brag about their meeting or exceeding federal regulations (like meat inspection standards), and 3) those that are completely written into law by corporate attorneys (like gas pipeline standards and railroad safety rules).

In the financial or commercial areas, the anemic nature of the rules is legendary. What's left are regulations that are often violated but rarely prosecuted (like water pollution violations).

So federal regulation as a force for pushing industries faster to become safer or better in various ways (as the first wave of federal motor vehicle safety standards did) is largely a myth. This leaves the massive consumer purchases of the federal government to meet these lawful purposes, as is now being done in modest ways for the buying of post-consumer content copying paper.

Even under the rubric of consumer sovereignty and the principle "the customer is always right," do not underestimate the corporate opposition. They know how consequential smart buying can be. Just ask Microsoft, whose monopoly power has pushed out competitors that can provide the federal government with software that is more affordable, usable, secure, and innovative.

So, Uncle Sam as smart consumer and shopper needs to become a widely discussed agenda among citizen and taxpayer groups and their political representatives in Congress and at the state legislatures. For more information, log onto www.gpp.org and become active.

September 5, 2003

Zoonotic Diseases

Unintentionally, the animal kingdom is striking back at Homo sapiens, who are not yet developing a "wise" response. Recently the *Washington Post* listed some of them in an article headlined "Why So Many New Infections are Coming from Animals."

AIDS, SARS, West Nile virus, hantavirus, influenza, Lyme disease, Creutzfeldt-Jakob (mad cow disease), and monkeypox are some of the diseases that animals transmit to humans.

All this is nothing new. You'll recall that the Black Death, which took millions of lives during the fourteenth century in Asia and Europe, came from infected rats. Smallpox, another slayer of tens of millions over the centuries, is believed to have been passed to humans from camels. And the massive toll of about fifty million lives in 1918–1919 originated in Chinese ducks and migrated to Chinese pigs before becoming a global human pandemic.

There was a period in the mid-twentieth century when a lull occurred, juxtaposed with the advent of modern antibiotics, which led to a period of complacency. Graduate students at the Harvard School of Public Health were advised not to go into the field of infectious diseases because antibiotics were rapidly eradicating them. Unfortunately, the good professors had not adequately recognized the mutational capability of bacteria and viruses.

The HIV virus struck in the United States in the early '80s followed by a number of new contagious entrants. Experts tend to concur that animals are more rapidly transmitting parasites, viruses, and bacteria than in previous decades. The reasons are more travel around the world, more trafficking in exotic pets, more disruption of habitats, climate changes spreading these hosts over newer geographic areas, and industrial agriculture feeding animal remains to animals, to mention a few.

To say that infectious disease specialists (and there are not enough of them) are worried is to engage in understatement. The *Post* quotes Dr. Robert G. Webster, a leading virologist at St. Jude Children's Research Hospital in Memphis: "There are probably hundreds, if not thousands—maybe even millions—of viruses out there. We don't even know they're there until we disturb them. SARS is probably just a gentle breeze of what one of these big ones is going to do someday."

Gentle breeze? Dr. Webster was referring to a fatality count that is still under one thousand worldwide from SARS. But look at the economic toll. It has cost China at least $30 billion in lost production (worker absences), lost export sales, and lost tourism. It has dampened the economies of East Asia and Toronto, Canada.

Just last week, Kodak said that the SARS epidemic in Asia has damaged its sales in China. Even the *New York Times* said that its second-quarter earnings would come in below Wall Street's expectations, citing the SARS virus and its impact on hotel and travel advertising among the leading explanations.

Modern-day economies increasingly are composed of "discretionary expenditures" that can be stopped because of anxiety, fear, or panic. People have to buy food, clothing, and shelter, for example; they don't have to be tourists or shop for modest luxuries or cater to their whims in the marketplace. This layer of instability adds another consequence to the actual sickness, anguish, and expense of these zoonotic diseases.

Get used to the phrase "zoonotic diseases"—sicknesses transmitted from animals like influenza, HIV, SARS, and monkeypox. George W. Bush also better get used to speaking out about zoonotic weapons of mass destruction. He has said and done very little about preparing the nation for these rapidly striking assaults by microscopic, lethal organisms.

President Bush needs to sit by himself and engage in some serious introspection about his insane expenditures and tax-cutting-for-the-wealthy priorities. The entire annual budget that nations have given to the World Health Organization amounts to what one, strategically outdated, B-2 bomber costs the Pentagon at a discounted price—just over 1 billion dollars.

The Centers for Disease Control—our country's frontline to alert, arouse, and respond to existing and fast looming zoonotic diseases—need more resources and more training of operational scientists and epidemiologists. The National Institutes of Health have been receiving more money for its previously languishing infectious disease research programs, but thousands of new infectious disease specialists across the entire continuum of challenges need to be trained.

Several billions of dollars a month are being spent to keep over 150,000 American troops in Iraq, where no use of Iraqi "weapons of mass destruction" or credible threats to the United States have either occurred or been found.

Come home, Mr. Bush, and get up to speed on the certain destroyers of American lives that can erupt into huge losses of life and a devastated economy. It's your responsibility and you will be held to it.

June 21, 2003

The Quest for the Fuel Efficient Car

Once again the congressional toadies for the auto industry have beaten back efforts by legislators such as Democrat Senator John Kerry and Republican John McCain to gradually increase fuel efficiency standards from the abysmally wasteful levels now inflicted on your pocketbook. Instead of choosing the path of reduced pollution, consumer savings, efficiency of engines, and less reliance on imported oil, these indentured lawmakers turned their back on automotive engineers who know how to do the job but are not allowed by their bosses.

The Sierra Club has decided to stop spinning its wheels on Capitol Hill and go directly to the people. In surveys of likely voters in Missouri and South Dakota, 79 percent of the people wanted the auto industry to be required to increase fuel efficiency and that included light truck owners. The voters do not buy the auto company propaganda that more fuel efficient vehicles mean less safety. Sixty percent of these voters say they would pay more for a higher mileage vehicle in return for its much larger dollar savings.

Longtime car owners know that fuel efficiency overall is no better than what vehicles did in 1980! They are wary of the sudden spikes in gasoline prices. They also know that companies spend lots of money on engine hyper-performance rather than on engine hyper-efficiency. Despite massive advertising by the auto companies to the contrary, they do not believe them.

Bolstered by public opinion, the Sierra Club announced a three-year campaign to pressure automakers to improve fuel economy. Executive Director Carl Pope said, "The technology exists today to allow the automakers to continue offering their most popular models, but with significantly improved fuel economy. These new safe, fuel-saving SUVs and pickups could be on the shelf very soon." (For specific examples see www.sierraclub.org.)

The Sierra Club is publicizing a "Freedom Option Package," which is a set of fuel-saving components that could be added to most standard models and that, taken together, could put the fleets of the Big Three on the road to 40 miles per gallon.

Dan Becker, the Club's Clean Energy director, says that "Detroit wants to sell option packages featuring seat warmers and cup holders" instead. He is mobilizing the Club's 700,000 members across the country to hold events at local auto dealers. Becker has enlisted a prominent Chevrolet dealer, Chuck Frank, in support of this initiative.

The Sierra Club, once enthralled by Bill Ford's environmental statements and assurances of major increases in Ford's SUVs, is now so disappointed with his company's joining the other auto giants to lobby against fuel efficiency laws that it has singled him and Ford Motor Company out for special pressure by motorists.

Soon to come (September 17) is the most jolting book against the auto company executives since *Unsafe at Any Speed* came out in 1965. I am referring to *New York Times* reporter Keith Bradsher's devastating expose of the SUVs that he calls the world's most dangerous vehicles and how they got that way. Titled *The High and Mighty*, this book explains how the auto industry's grip on

Congress got these SUVs (hiked-up, overpriced light truck) exempted from safety, fuel efficiency, and pollution requirements that were imposed on automobiles. That was accomplished when these vehicles were a small percentage of overall sales. Now they are a large part of sales; they kill their occupants in rollovers three times the rate of cars, are uniquely dangerous to other motorists, and will become more serious when drunks and teenagers (typically the worst drivers on the road) start buying the older used SUVs, Bradsher says.

With an impressive attention to detail and special documentation, Bradsher reports on the enormous advertising money spent ($10 billion since 1990) to deceive their customers and persuade Americans to switch from cars to the very profitable SUVs, while, he declares, "Gas-guzzling SUVs emit one-third more global-warming gases per mile than cars, and up to 5.5 times as much smog-causing nitrogen oxides per mile."

If the media grasps the importance of this book, September will be a hot month for the high and mighty in Detroit's executive suites. And long overdue.

August 8, 2002

GM Keeps Fuel Efficiency in the Dark Ages

General Motors should be renamed General Wasteful Motors for its decades of destructive resistance to improved fuel efficiency for your motor vehicles.

Never mind that you deserve, after all these years of industry stagnation (the last upgrade in fuel efficiency was 1985), more miles for your gasoline dollars. Never mind that our country is more reliant on imported oil (over 50 percent) than ever before. Never mind that as taxpayers you are being charged billions of dollars yearly for our armed forces to safeguard the flow of oil from the Persian Gulf. And never mind that you are breathing more polluted air from vehicle emissions, which are also contributing to global warming.

Giant GM, run by myopic executives, just won't let its engineers and scientists diminish the gas-guzzling nature of its infernal, internal combustion engines.

The last legislated standard on fuel economy was in 1975, which declared a phase-in by 1985 of average automobile economy to 27.5 mpg and light trucks to about 20 mpg. Today, average fuel economy overall has been dropping and now comes in at about 24 mpg—the lowest since 1980! It is reliably reported that General Motors is putting very heavy pressure on its suppliers to lobby Congress against long overdue stirrings by some Democrats and Republicans—most notably Representative Henry Waxman (D-CA), Senator John Kerry (D-MA), and Senator John McCain (R-AZ)—for higher, mandated fuel efficiencies.

GM is most upset with Senator John Kerry's proposal to boost fuel economy by 50 percent over the next twelve years. Imagine, after assuring decades
of delay both before 1975 and after 1985, garnished by futile futuristic promises of new engines and new fuel advances from its exhibit at the 1939 World's
Fair in New York to its contemporary propaganda, GM thinks going to 37 mpg
by 2014 is not possible. Some automobiles in the 1930s achieved that level. The
U.S. Department of Transportation in the mid '70s said that over 40 mpg average fleet levels could be yours by the year 2000. A few years later, a detailed
article in *Scientific American* showed how the average could be in the 80 mpg
zone by then. And, of course, Toyota and Honda are already selling thousands
of hybrids that average over 50 mpg already.

Talk fuel efficiency and you're sure to evoke from GM its sudden touching
concern with auto safety, as if you cannot have both. Clarence Ditlow of the
Center for Auto Safety (202-328-7700) and other engineers have pointed out
ad nauseam the corporate fallacy of having either a gasoline efficient less safe
car or a safer car that is less efficient.

The stubborn, dug-in-heels of General Motors and its allies have become
an ever greater national security, public health, and environmental problem.
One would think that GM would decide to be a little patriotic and think of our
nation's interest for a change.

The attitude of "*Nyet*" is too much even for the leading industry trade journal, *Automotive News*, whose journalistic integrity under the ownership of the
Crain family evoked the following editorial comment:

> It was a throwback to a darker era. On a Senate witness stand two
> weeks ago, Greg Dana of the Alliance of Automobile Manufacturers
> went mute when asked whether a 1-mpg increase in corporate average
> fuel economy standards during the next decade would be feasible.
>
> His questioner, Sen. John Kerry, responded "Don't you think that
> renders you sort of silly?"
>
> Indeed, it made the alliance look silly. Let's get real. It's time for
> automakers to deal forthrightly with fuel economy issues. . . . To
> deny—or refuse to admit—that there is technology that can reduce
> fuel consumption significantly is ludicrous. The industry's credibility
> is at stake.

Then *Automotive News* really turned the screw, noting that the 1.5 billion tax
dollars that Clinton poured into an engine research partnership with GM, Ford,
and Chrysler, as an alternative to raising fuel efficiency standards, was used by
the Big Three as a "cover to improve horsepower, not fuel economy."

It is also time for you, the motorist, to become more demanding of engines and fuel that are more efficient and cleaner. Detroit knows how to do it and has for many years, but once again profits come before patriotism, or even common sense.

February 20, 2002

Why is Industrial Hemp Still Illegal?

Why is the Drug Enforcement Administration (DEA) mounting an attack on pastas, cereals, and salad dressings, among other products? Instead of spending taxpayer money on more pressing and worthy issues, on October 9, 2001, the DEA issued rulings that effectively ban hemp foods. Industrial hemp is the nondrug cousin of marijuana.

Food is currently the largest U.S. market for industrial hemp. Estimated retail sales for hemp food and body care products in the United States exceeded $25 million in 2000, up from less than $1 million in the early 1990s. Hemp foods and body care products have penetrated the mainstream market and rapid growth was expected prior to the DEA's actions. Industrial hemp seed and oil are increasingly used in corn chips, nutrition bars, humus, nondairy milks, breads, and cereals.

Currently, the DEA treats industrial hemp as a Schedule I controlled substance—the most highly restricted category (more tightly controlled than opium or cocaine). Industrial hemp which contains only trace amounts of THC, the psychoactive component in marijuana, should not be regulated as an illicit drug, since it has no intoxicating effect when consumed. While the DEA effectively bans growing industrial hemp (largely on the fallacious grounds that agents cannot distinguish the crop from marijuana), until October 9, it permitted use of the product, which can be only imported, in food. Now, the agency is seemingly rolling back the common sense exemption. Last month, DEA issued new rules which prohibit human consumption of any hemp products containing any amount of THC.

The DEA's overzealousness in apparently banning products that are clearly not abused as illicit drugs is greatly misguided. The trace amount of THC in hemp foods and cosmetics (typically less than 1.5 and 5 parts per million, respectively) is far too low to produce a high and are about as likely to be abused as a poppy seed bagel, which contains trace amounts of opiates.

Virtually all hemp foods in the U.S. market do not contain detectable THC levels, according to the official testing method used on foods in Canada. A recent study published in the *Journal of Analytical Toxicology* shows that this minute amount is generally not enough for an individual to fail a highly sensitive drug test—purportedly one of the DEA's main concerns—even after eating an unrealistic amount of hemp foods daily.

Poppy seeds are more likely to cause the problems the DEA fears. Poppy seeds' trace opiates have sometimes led individuals, who have merely ingested poppy seed bagels or muffins, to fail a drug test. To this problem, the U.S. government responded sensibly, raising drug-test thresholds for opiates in the 1990s to accommodate the poppy seed industry.

The DEA states that it has "attempted to strike a fair balance between protecting the health and safety of all Americans and accommodating legitimate industry." In fact, the apparent ban on hemp foods is a strike both against the burgeoning industrial hemp industry and the health of Americans. It is an attack on the entire industry of industrial hemp, because while the greatest future market for industrial hemp products is predicted to be automobile parts—industrial hemp is an excellent and cost efficient replacement for fiberglass parts—the crop's current largest market is considered to be foods. It is important to maintain the industry now, so that when the United States repeals its irrational restrictions on industrial hemp, it can quickly expand use of this environmentally benign product. (Among its other environmental benefits, industrial hemp can be a particularly sustainable crop that minimizes toxics in our environment, because it can easily be grown with few or no chemicals and its natural brightness avoids chlorine bleaching in papermaking.)

Hemp foods offer real health benefits. Industrial hemp seeds are one of the best sources of omega-3 fatty acids in the vegetable kingdom, according to Dr. Andrew Weil, the Harvard-educated physician and noted expert on medicinal herbs. Omega-3 fatty acids are essential in the protection against many cancers, including breast cancer, and in the promotion of cardiovascular health. Other health specialists confirm the nutritional value of hemp foods.

Recognizing the various benefits of industrial hemp, in recent years numerous countries such as Canada, the United Kingdom, and Germany have amended their industrial hemp laws to legalize the cultivation of the crop and the production of a variety of end-products, such as fuel, paper, building materials, rope, foods, cosmetics, and automobile parts. Other countries, such as France, China, Romania, and Hungary, having never outlawed the crop, continue to cultivate, manufacture, and export industrial hemp.

As the rest of the world moves forward to capture the market potential of this useful and beneficial crop, the DEA has taken the United States a step backward.

Beware, your poppy seed bagel could be next.

Concerned citizens should urge their members of Congress to contact DEA and oppose its latest industrial hemp rule-making. Citizens can also write to the Deputy Assistant Administrator, Office of Diversion Control, Drug Enforcement Administration, Washington, DC 20537, Attention: DEA Federal Register Representative/CCD by December 10, 2001. For other action items, visit the www.votehemp.com site's Action Alert section. For additional information on the hemp food ban and industrial hemp in general, visit the www.naihc.org, www.thehia.org, and www.rca-info.org web sites.

November 27, 2001

Nuclear Plants Post 9-11

Nuclear power plants came on the scene in the post–World War II era with lots of official enthusiasm and a shortage of concern about safety. But much of that early excitement about the future of nuclear power faded after the accidents at Three Mile Island in Pennsylvania in 1979 and Chernobyl in 1986 and the high economic costs of this technology with its deadly wastes.

Now the attacks on the World Trade Center and the Pentagon are generating new fears that the nation's existing 103 nuclear power reactors may become our biggest nightmare in the event of new terrorist attacks. For over thirty years, watchdog organizations, which follow the nuclear power industry, have warned that a successful attack on a nuclear power plant—particularly one near a large city—could unleash an immense quantity of radioactivity that could cause hundreds of thousands of cancers and contaminate wide areas for generations. The former Atomic Energy Commission estimated that a "class-nine" nuclear power meltdown could contaminate an area "the size of Pennsylvania."

What would happen if a large jet airliner—such as those that slammed into the World Trade Center—crashed into a nuclear reactor? Here is the way Dr. Edwin Lyman, scientific director of the Nuclear Control Institute in Washington describes such an event:

> Well, the engines are one of the most rigid parts of the jet and would penetrate the containment, leading to a fuel spill within the building and likely a severe jet fuel fire or explosion, like we saw at the World Trade Center. Nuclear power plants are not well-equipped to deal with severe fires, · so if the containment has already been breached, the radioactivity released from the (nuclear) fuel as it is melting will have no barrier to the environment, and therefore a Chernobyl-type massive release of radioactivity is something that cannot be excluded.

The concern that nuclear reactors are potential targets for terrorist attacks was given credence by reports published in the *Sunday Times* of London, venturing that the jet airliner that crashed in western Pennsylvania on September 11 may have been headed for the Three Mile Island nuclear plant near Harrisburg, Pennsylvania. The newspaper quoted anonymous U.S. security sources as saying that the nuclear facility had been the subject of surveillance by some of the hijackers and their associates in the months before the terrorist attacks. So far, though, that is speculation.

The Nuclear Control Institute, along with another major monitor of the nuclear industry, Committee to Bridge the Gap, charge that the Nuclear Regulatory Commission (NRC) and other government agencies have failed to move decisively to impose "security measures that are needed to prevent a successful attack and avert catastrophic radiological consequences."

The organizations want immediate utilization of National Guard troops to deter attacks, deployment of advanced antiaircraft weapons to deter suicidal attacks from the air, and thorough "re-vetting" of all plant employees and contractors to protect against sabotage by insiders. These groups also want the NRC to "significantly upgrade its security regulations to protect against the larger numbers and greater sophistication of attackers posed by the new terrorist threat."

Representative Ed Markey of Boston, who has long expressed concern about the lack of vigor by NRC, says that neither the regulatory agency nor the nuclear power industry appear to have "fully awakened to the fact that we are living in a whole new world after September 11."

"The terrorist attacks require us to reexamine all of our security procedures and regulations pertaining to nuclear power plants," said Markey, who is a senior member of the House Commerce Committee that has legislative jurisdiction over NRC. "There is no greater single threat to our way of life than a successful attack on a nuclear power plant. It would be catastrophic."

Paul Leventhal, longtime president of the nonprofit Nuclear Control Institute, says NRC's responses to Representative Markey and the watchdog organizations suggest a "long bureaucratic review process" before new safeguards are placed into effect—something that Leventhal says is "simply unacceptable."

The concerns of Representative Markey and the watchdog organizations need to be given highest priority by the Bush administration as well as the National Regulatory Commission and the Congress. The consequences of an effective attack on a nuclear reactor are far too great to let the NRC drag its feet on imposing new security requirements for all 103 nuclear power facilities.

If these facilities can't be made secure, the federal government, as Paul

Leventhal suggests, has no choice but to shut down the plants. The risk is too great to do otherwise.

For more information: www.nci.org.

October 24, 2001

Senior Citizens Face High Drug Costs

Senior citizens have long been targets of cruel scams perpetrated by credit merchants, fast-talking telemarketers, fraudulent charities, and other sleazy operators who scheme to separate retirees from their meager pensions and savings.

But these devious "backdoor" merchants may not be seniors' worst nightmare. That title might be better attached to the "respectable" white-collar executives who run the nation's major pharmaceutical companies that continue to gouge senior citizens with inflated prices for prescription drugs.

Families USA, which closely monitors drug costs, found that the prices for the fifty drugs most often prescribed for seniors rose on average more than twice the rate of inflation last year. These increases are on top of price hikes that have consistently been above the rate of inflation throughout the 1990s.

While rising prices for prescriptions affect the entire population, seniors are the hardest hit. Although seniors represent only 13 percent of the total population, they account for 34 percent of all prescriptions dispensed and 42 percent of all prescription drug spending.

More than one-third of the most prescribed drugs for seniors rose in price at least three times between January 2000 and January 2001. The price of Synthroid (a synthetic thyroid agent) rose 8.5 times inflation; Alphagan, used to treat glaucoma, rose 8.4 times the rate of inflation last year; Glucophage, prescribed for the treatment of diabetes, went up 4.8 times inflation; and Demadex, a diuretic, 4.6 times.

The rising prices are increasingly making needed drugs unaffordable for senior citizens. This means that the health of millions of senior citizens, particularly those who exist on fixed incomes, is being placed at risk. Social security and pensions stretch only so far and, often, it is expensive prescription drugs—and health—that must be put aside to meet other basic necessities.

Some seniors who live near our northern border are resorting to bus trips to nearby Canadian cities where prescriptions can be filled for half the price charged in the United States. In addition to having a health care plan that covers all citizens, Canada doesn't allow drug companies to take crude advantage of their citizens. Not only does Canada have a health plan that can negotiate lower prices through bulk purchases, but it has a national price review board that ensures that drug companies can't get away with price gouging as they do in this country.

The pharmaceutical industry is adept at promoting the idea that the rising drug prices in the United States are the result of the companies' expenditures for research. The hard numbers don't support this transparent public relations ploy.

"The drug industry likes to claim that high prices are needed to pay for research and development, but these price increases have much more to do with corporate profits than the research costs for these drugs that occurred many years ago," the executive director of Families USA Ron Pollock says.

In fact, the pharmaceutical industry is the most profitable in the nation. Profit margins in the industry in 2000 were four times the average of Fortune 500 companies. What's more, compensation packages for their executives are lavish.

Merck and Company, Inc. allocated 15 percent of its revenue to marketing, advertising, and administration and only 6 percent to research and development. Pfizer allocated 39 percent of its revenue to marketing, advertising, and administration, 15 percent to R&D. Bristol-Myers Squibb and Company spent 30 percent of its revenues on marketing, advertising, and administration, 11 percent on R&D. In all, eight of the nine companies that market the top-selling drugs to seniors spent more than twice as much on marketing, advertising, and administration than on R&D.

The chairman of Pfizer, William C. Steere, Jr., led the pack of highest paid drug company executives with annual compensation (exclusive of unexercised stock options) last year of $40,191,845 followed by John R. Stafford, chairman and CEO of American Home Products Corporation, $27,008,927; Edward M. Scolnick, executive vice president of Merck and Company, $26,454,600; and Richard Jay Kogan, chairman and CEO of Schering-Plough Corporation, $21,444,020.

C. A. Heimbold, Jr., chairman of Bristol-Myers Squibb Company is champion holder of unexercised stock options in the industry with options valued at $227,869,513. Raymond Gilmartin, chairman, president, and CEO of Merck had unexercised stock options of $181,252,976 and William C. Steere, Jr., chairman of Pfizer, $130,944,439 in options. Consider further that George Bush and most Republicans want to cut the already low capital gains taxes on such bosses.

The pharmaceutical industry's claims about its research and development expenditures are diminished by the fact that the federal government has given the industry generous packages of tax credits, massive taxpayer-funded R&D support by the National Institutes of Health and other federal agencies, and subsidized loans from the U.S. Import-Export Bank and R&D monopoly patent extensions.

The idea of providing prescription drugs in some manner as a Medicare benefit is a live political issue both in the Congress and the White House. Clearly, there is a need to curb the pharmaceutical industry's appetite for high prices, high profits, and massive executive compensation if there is to be a workable, affordable solution.

July 17, 2001

Patients' Rights Legislation

The 180 million Americans with health insurance got a victory last month when the U.S. Senate adopted a long-sought set of rights for patients.

The legislation establishes federal standards for private health insurance, including that provided through Health Maintenance Organizations (HMOs), and allows patients to sue in federal and state courts to enforce their rights. In California, a similar state law providing the right to sue has proven a major deterrent to reckless denial of treatment by HMOs.

As one of the bill's key sponsors, Senator Edward Kennedy, commented: "This is a giant step forward in giving power to the powerless."

But left out of the celebration about patients' rights are 45 million citizens who have no health insurance. They remain the powerless in a scary world where even a relatively minor illness or injury can mean economic disaster and where preventative medicine, like a physical checkup or blood test, is an unaffordable luxury.

Even if patients' rights survive in the House of Representatives and avoid a presidential veto, health care in the United States remains a disgrace. We spend more on health care per capita than any other nation in the world, often double that of nations in western Europe who cover all their people. Yet, the World Health Organization ranks the United States as 37th in overall quality of health care.

Access to health care is distributed unequally among the rich and the poor. The disparities are even greater among the minority populations. Among whites, 11 percent lack health care insurance. This is too high, but 21 percent of African Americans, 21 percent of Asian Americans, and 33 percent of the Hispanics lack health insurance. More than 29 percent of young people between the ages of eighteen and twenty-four are without any form of health insurance.

Many of the 200 million citizens counted among the insured are actually "underinsured" with limited policies that often cover only catastrophic injuries or provide exclusions for a long list of health problems. There are serious gaps in many health policies that leave the insured with little or no coverage for prescription drugs and medical supplies and vision and hearing care. And many policies require large out-of-pocket "co-payments" from the insured, which make care unaffordable for low- and moderate-income families.

We can do better as a wealthy nation. Every other industrialized nation provides comprehensive care for its citizens and at a lower cost than our system, which leaves so many people out. Other nations spend between 6 and 10 percent of their gross domestic product (GDP) on health care while the United States spends 14 percent of its GDP on health care, much of it going to insurance company overhead, unnecessary (and often padded or fraudulent) billing and administrative costs, huge profits, and bloated executive salaries at large HMOs and other health care companies.

We need to face up to the need for a national health insurance program—a single-payer system ("full Medicare for all")—that would provide better and more affordable care for all citizens. Studies have shown that savings from a single-payer system would be more than enough to allow the nation to provide high-quality comprehensive health benefits for all Americans.

Under a model plan developed by the Physicians for a National Health Program (PNHP), the program would be federally financed and administered by a single public insurer at the state or regional level. Premiums, co-payments, and deductibles would be eliminated. Instead, employers would pay a 7 percent payroll tax and employees would pay 2 percent, essentially converting existing premium payments to a health care payroll tax. It would remove the bureaucratic middleman of the insurance-managed care industry from the health care equation. The General Accounting Office projects an administrative saving of 10 percent through the elimination of private insurance bills and administrative waste.

Under the PNHP proposal, everyone would be included in a single comprehensive public plan covering all medically necessary services and everyone would have access to personalized care with a local primary care physician and free choice of doctors and hospitals at all times.

The 59 to 36 vote in the Senate for a patients' bill of rights is strong evidence that the grassroots are beginning to make their voices heard on health care. The House of Representatives—where the Republican leadership plans to weaken, if not defeat, the Senate-passed version—is the next big test. President Bush has recklessly threatened to veto the legislation if the Senate bill is enacted. If the president does use his veto pen to wipe out rights of patients, it will be a monumental political mistake and one that will leave little doubt that the powerful lobbying forces of the health insurance industry have seized the White House.

Congress should use the momentum of the Senate vote for patients' rights to build support for a universal single-payer health insurance system. Citizens' groups across the nation also need to take courage from the Senate action, and renew campaigns to establish a health system that truly provides affordable care for all the people. We should not continue to lag behind the rest of the industrial world on such a vital issue. It has been fifty-one years since President Harry Truman proposed universal health insurance to Congress. It is time to act.

July 3, 2001

Closing Refineries and the Energy Crisis

If there is truly an energy crisis, why have so many of the nation's refineries been shut down in recent years?

Since 1985, a total of ninety-eight refineries have been taken off line. Fifty of these, with a crude capacity of 1,360,614 B/SD (barrels per stream day) were closed in the last decade.

The closures are just one more mystery in a muddled energy picture. Meanwhile, President Bush's clumsy efforts to take care of his oil industry buddies while fashioning what he hopes will pass for a national energy policy looks like an early disaster for the new administration.

The Bush-Cheney so-called solution to the nation's energy problems is weighted heavily on the side of more production with conservation and greater efficiencies tossed in as little more than afterthoughts.

But the heated debate over production versus conservation and efficiency obscures a lot of other steps that could be taken to give consumers a better break on energy.

The president should have the Department of Energy use its influence with the oil companies to get closed refineries back in production. In many, if not most, cases these refineries can be back in production without lengthy delay. For one thing, these refinery sites have been previously certified, which includes compliance with environmental standards. Reactivating these idle facilities should be a priority.

The administration also needs to take action to prevent refiners from spiking prices by withholding supplies of gasoline. As reported in the *Wall Street Journal*, Marathon-Ashland Petroleum LLC intentionally withheld supplies of gasoline for the Chicago and Milwaukee markets last summer to keep prices high. This is what happens when refinery capacity is deliberately tight when it does not need to be.

Based on findings by the Federal Trade Commission, the *Journal* said that, despite an excess supply, the company limited the gasoline it sold to keep prices high at the pump. FTC said the company, thus, found itself with "considerable market power in the short term."

The Portland *Oregonian* reported earlier this year that BP Amoco "systematically jacked up West Coast oil prices by exporting Alaskan crude to Asia for less than it could have sold it to U. S. refiners."

"There is no doubt whatsoever that they were in the business of shorting the West Coast market," a University of Texas economist hired by the FTC said in an interview published in the *Oregonian*. The newspaper obtained an e-mail exchange in which BP trading managers discussed the benefits of "shorting the West Coast market" to "leverage up" prices there. Motorists pay many dollars because of this corporate manipulation.

High on the must list of the administration should be a crash effort to investigate the degree to which unnecessary refinery closures, the withholding of oil and gasoline supplies, and collusion among the refiners may have contributed to this year's skyrocketing prices. Congress, too, has a very important role in getting to the facts behind the price increases and presumed shortages. Senator Carl Levin of Michigan is in a good position to investigate since he has recently assumed the chairmanship of the Senate Permanent Subcommittee on Investigations.

Certainly, these fact-finding missions should be carried out before the administration tries to get through a defiant Congress its ill-conceived plan to drill for oil in the Arctic National Wildlife Refuge in Alaska.

And on the question of Alaskan oil, the administration needs to take immediate steps to once again place a flat prohibition on the export of Alaskan oil, something that would take the pressure off plans to proceed with additional environmentally risky oil development.

In 1995, the Congress, with the enthusiastic support of the Clinton administration and the oil industry, passed legislation that wiped out the prohibition on exports of Alaskan oil to Japan and other Asian countries. The ban had originally been imposed in 1973 to guard against oil shortages on the West Coast, but with an excess of oil on hand in 1995, British Petroleum, ARCO, and Chevron lobbied to sell the surplus in Asia. And President Clinton and the Congress acquiesced.

When the merger of BP-Amoco with ARCO was pending before the Federal Trade Commission, the companies agreed voluntarily to stop the exports of Alaskan oil to the Asian nations. The agreement apparently has been kept. But it is a voluntary agreement that the companies could drop at any time. It has no force of law. Energy policies should not rest on such a thin reed, solely on the good faith of profit-hungry corporations. As long as his administration claims there is an energy shortage, President Bush should ask the Congress to reenact the export controls on an emergency basis.

Not only is it important to consumers and the nation's economy that a rational, fair, and environmentally sound energy policy be adopted, but it is also critical to the credibility of an administration whose top officials have deep roots and deep pockets in the oil industry.

June 14, 2001

Irradiation Craze

Is the cure worse than the disease? An old cliché perhaps, but it seems a particularly apt question in the current debate over food irradiation. Irradiation may appear to many as a miracle means of swiftly removing bacteria from food supplies, but underneath the hype lie major questions about the economic, health, and social costs of the process.

Before these questions were answered, the Food and Drug Administration under the Clinton administration loosened irradiation-labeling rules, lowered scientific standards the food industry has to meet, and abbreviated its review of requests by companies for irradiation approvals. Concerns about the wholesomeness of the irradiated food expressed by consumer and environmental groups were bluntly dismissed by the FDA. Not a single request for a hearing on the implementation of a food irradiation rule has ever been granted.

The irradiation craze has reduced the focus on cleaning up food processing plants. Instead of improving the filthy conditions endemic to factory-style slaughterhouses, food industry executives and government officials are embracing an under-studied technology to prevent food-borne bacteria from sickening people.

Irradiation does nothing to remove the sources of many harmful bacteria— the feces, urine, pus, and vomit often left on beef, chicken, and lamb as a result of dirty slaughterhouse conditions.

Dozens of research studies conducted over the past half century have shown that food exposed to radiation can cause serious health problems in laboratory animals, resulting in shorter life spans, chromosomal abnormalities, low birth weight, immune and reproductive problems, organ damage, and tumors.

We do know that irradiation destroys essential vitamins and nutrients in food, including substantial percentages of vitamin A in eggs and beta carotene in orange juice. Irradiation kills not just "bad" microorganisms, but also the "good" ones, such as yeasts and molds that keep botulism at bay. Irradiation might also spawn mutant forms of E. coli, salmonella, staphylococcus, and other bacteria.

If the irradiated food is not dangerous enough, the facilities where food is exposed to radiation provide even more cause for alarm.

Between 1974 and 1989 alone, forty-five accidents and violations were recorded at U.S. irradiation plants, including those used to sterilize medical supplies.

In one mishap, water laced with radioactive cobalt-60 was flushed down the public sewer system in Dover, New Jersey in 1982.

With all these dangers, why has the U.S. government legalized irradiation with so little study? And why did the FDA rely on only seven of the more than four hundred scientific studies to determine that irradiated food is safe for human consumption?

One answer might be found in the political muscle of the $460-billion food processing industry led by the National Food Processors Association and numerous allied groups. It is not an industry whose wishes are often ignored by official Washington.

But citizens can provide a countervailing force. They need to start demanding that their elected representatives raise questions with the U.S. Department of Agriculture and the FDA about this irradiation craze.

They need to insist on full studies of the dangers as well as the benefits. And long overdue are demands for a cleanup of food processing plants. Irradiation isn't the answer. Stricter standards vigorously enforced can make food safer and healthier without turning to unproven and dangerous technology lacking basic safeguards.

May 9, 2001

Dick Cheney and Energy Conservation

Vice President Dick Cheney is a dinosaur living in the age of mammals. Imagine a public official uttering the following:

"Conservation may be a sign of personal virtue, but it is not a sufficient basis for a sound, comprehensive energy policy.

"We...safeguard the environment by making greater use of the cleanest methods of power generation we know...that is nuclear power.

"The notion that somehow developing the resources in ANWR [Arctic National Wildlife Reserve] requires a vast despoiling of the environment is probably false."

It is time for the American people to insist Mr. Cheney stop talking nonsense and to tell Mr. Cheney and his fellow "oilman" President Bush that they have to wean themselves from the economically and environmentally costly energy policies that keep taxpayers, consumers, and environmentalists hooked on oil, coal, and nuclear power.

Federal policy over the past century has largely failed to promote an energy system based on safe, secure, economically affordable, and environmentally benign energy sources. The tax code, budget appropriations, and regulatory processes overwhelmingly have been used to subsidize dependence on fossil fuels and nuclear power. The result: increased sickness and premature deaths; depleted family budgets; acid rain destruction of lakes, forests, and crops; oil spill contamination; polluted rivers and loss of aquatic species; and the long-term peril of climate change and radioactive waste dumps, not to mention a dependency on external energy supplies.

There is an alternative. Three decades of detailed assessments, on-the-ground results, and research and development innovations in the energy-consuming devices used in our buildings, vehicles, and industries undeniably show that energy efficiency and renewable energy technologies are superior energy options for society. They offer a present and future path that is economically attractive, safe, and secure from large-scale or long-term risks or threats to public health, future generations, and the environment.

But embarking on that path requires overcoming the power of the oil, nuclear, and other conventional fuel industries to which both the Republicans and Democrats are indentured. Under the thumb of the dirty-fuel industries, Congress and the executive branch have refused to adopt even the most modest, commonsense measures. For example, when the President's Committee of Advisors on Science and Technology concluded in a 1997 report that doubling the Department of Energy's efficiency R&D funding would produce a 40 to 1 return on the investment for the nation, Congress responded by proposing deep cuts in the efficiency and renewables R&D budgets.

The Clinton/Gore administration nod to increased energy efficiency relied largely on corporate welfare. Rather than push for an increase in auto fuel efficiency standards, the administration established the Partnership for a New Generation of Vehicles (PNGV). PNGV is a $1.5 billion subsidy program for the Big Three auto companies that has done nothing to improve auto fuel efficiency but has served as a convenient smokescreen behind which the industry has been able to fend off new regulatory requirements for more efficient cars.

"Energy Innovations: A Prosperous Path to a Clean Environment," a joint study prepared by half a dozen of the nation's prominent energy and environmental research and advocacy groups, shows that a handful of simple and straightforward measures could produce a significant reduction in sulfur dioxide (SO_2) emissions (prime cause of acid rain) by 2010, compared to 1990 levels, and nitrogen oxide (NOx) emissions (a key precursor of ground-level ozone, smog), as well as deep cuts in emissions of other damaging pollutants, including fine particles, toxic metals like mercury and hydrocarbons, and carbon dioxide (CO_2) emissions.

President Bush could establish the United States as the model for other countries by adopting a sustainable energy policy that includes:

Ending fossil fuel and nuclear corporate welfare supports, including numerous special tax preferences.

Launching a robust federal research and development program in sustainable, renewable energy sources, so that the energy-independence promises of wind, solar, and other forms of renewable energy are finally realized.

Increasing auto fuel efficiency standards (at least to 45 miles per gallon for cars and 35 miles per gallon for light trucks) to be phased in over five years during a transition period to zero-emissions cars.

Adopting stronger efficiency standards for appliances and mandatory energy-performance building codes.

Ensuring electricity policies that promote efficient use of electricity through a range of measures, including "net metering" requirements that companies pay market prices for electricity generated by consumers and passed back to the utility, and elimination of clean air exemptions for "grand-fathered" fossil fuel facilities.

Establishing a well-funded employee transition assistance fund and job-retraining program for displaced coal miners, easily affordable with the savings from greater energy efficiency.

Our country has more problems than it deserves and more solutions than it uses. It is time for the United States to stop letting ExxonMobil, Peabody Coal, and Westinghouse shape our energy policy and for our misguided elected officials to adopt an energy strategy based on clean, renewable energy and conservation. Future generations will thank us for curbing our fossil fuel appetite.

May 2, 2001

Tritium Production, Nuclear Proliferation

Since World War II, citizens around the world have been deeply concerned about the proliferation of nuclear power. There has been increasing concern about nuclear technology falling into careless hands lacking regard for public safety or, worse, coming under the control of rogue nations bent on developing weapons of mass destruction.

The nuclear accidents at Chernobyl in the Ukraine and at Three Mile Island in Pennsylvania were stark reminders of the dangers, and the need for the tightest safety and nonproliferation safeguards possible.

But is our government actually serving as a watchdog over nuclear power facilities in the United States or is it retreating from safety and nonproliferation standards that have been the heart of national nuclear policy for fifty years?

With the nation focused on the holidays, on December 22, 1998, President Clinton's Secretary of Energy, Bill Richardson, quietly announced plans to produce tritium—a key element in the manufacture of hydrogen bombs—at the Tennessee Valley Authority nuclear plants, which, heretofore, had produced only electric power for consumer and commercial use. The administration's action violated policies that had firmly separated the commercial nuclear reactors from weapons production at the TVA under every administration after the end of World War II.

The license amendment, which would allow TVA to move into the production of material for military weapons, still must be reviewed and approved by the Nuclear Regulatory Commission (NRC). Rejection of the license has been urged by the Union of Concerned Scientists and other nuclear experts like Dr. Kenneth Bergeron who worked for twenty-five years at the Sandia National Laboratories performing or managing research on nuclear reactor safety and tritium production.

The clear separation of commercial from military uses of nuclear power is key to nonproliferation efforts in the United States and throughout the world. President Dwight Eisenhower's Atoms for Peace program in the 1950s firmly established the dual-track strategy of isolating peaceful uses of nuclear power from military weapons.

As Dr. Bergeron points out, this system "expanded into a vast nonproliferation regime that in one way or another touched each and every aspect of nuclear technology throughout the world."

For the United States to abandon this strategy, as the Clinton administration proposed, would be a dangerous precedent that would seriously interfere with nonproliferation efforts worldwide.

But, there are other big negatives in dragging TVA into the military weapons business. Front and center is the question of safety—something that appears was not on the administration's radar screen when it decided to produce tritium at TVA plants.

Dr. Bergeron says that the government could not have made a "worse selection" than the plants chosen to produce the hydrogen bomb ingredients. All three of the designated plants—two at Sequoyah and one at Watts Bar, Tennessee— are "ice condensers" that use giant wire baskets of ice chips to absorb heat and steam in case of a nuclear reactor accident. The buildings housing the ice baskets, according to Dr. Bergeron, are small and weak and would be "exceptionally vulnerable" to severe accident conditions. The buildings, Dr. Bergeron says, would "almost certainly rupture immediately after the nuclear core melted through its pressure vessel."

Dr. Bergeron says his study of the ice condensers found that the system "has a high likelihood of failing in the event of a serious accident, leaving the public completely unprotected against the kind of massive release of radioactivity that occurred at Chernobyl."

In addition, whistle-blowers have come forward to raise other questions about safety at the TVA plants. One of these is Curtis Overall, who was the plant expert on the ice condenser system at Watts Bar with the responsibility for keeping the system running properly.

Overall found that more than two hundred screws that held the ice condenser baskets in place were either missing or broken. When Overall recommended a visual inspection to make sure there were enough screws holding the ice baskets in place, he was removed from his position and ultimately fired by TVA.

Another employee, Ann Harris, who filed a half dozen whistle-blower complaints involving safety issues says she is convinced that TVA's plan to produce tritium at the Watts Bar and Sequoyah plants "poses serious and real danger to millions of people."

Recently, Dr. Bergeron and David Lochman of the Union of Concerned Scientists, along with the whistle–blowers, appeared at the National Press Club to sound the alarm about the dangers of converting TVA into a weapons producing enterprise. Sadly, but to no one's surprise, the national media largely ignored the press conference. Like so many health and safety issues, it apparently takes a Chernobyl or its equivalent to move the Washington press corps.

April 25, 2001

Mad Cow Disease

Is Mad Cow Disease just a European phenomenon or is it something that should trigger a significant upgrading of U.S. public health efforts? It is true that so far the U.S. has escaped the epidemic and its human counterpart, variant Cruetzfeldt-Jacob Disease (CJD). But is this the result of vigilance by our public health forces, or is it just good luck that the disease has not slipped through our defenses?

Testifying before the Senate Commerce Committee in early April, Dr. Peter Lurie, deputy director of Public Citizen's Health Research Group, made it clear we have no reason to be complacent or to think that Bovine Spongiform Encephalopathy (better known as Mad Cow Disease) is strictly a European problem.

As Dr. Lurie said, the disease has often found "a way to pierce small chinks in the public health armor." And there are plenty of chinks or perhaps full-scale gaps in the health defenses of the United States.

Pointing out that U.S. customs inspectors already face extremely heavy workloads from the dramatic increase in global trade, Dr. Lurie said there were serious concerns that these inspectors can adequately police the borders for shipments of animal products that might carry the Mad Cow Disease. Even with the best of customs inspections, the transshipments between countries can make it extremely difficult to determine the origin of meat and bone meal.

Deregulation of the dietary supplements industry in 1994 ripped another hole in our public health defenses, an action that now seems particularly foolhardy in the face of the Mad Cow Disease. Before the deregulation measure, Dietary Supplement, Health and Education Act (DSHEA) was enacted, the industry had the burden of demonstrating the safety of its products. But the act reversed the burden, requiring that the Food and Drug Administration (FDA) show that the product was unsafe before it can take action. Seven years later the FDA still has not adopted final regulations under DSHEA, but it has issued an "Import Alert" for dietary materials coming from countries with known Mad Cow Disease; compliance is voluntary.

How serious is this bit of deregulation? Here's what Dr. Lurie told the senators:

> For BSE (Mad Cow Disease), this means that an unscrupulous manufacturer could literally take a British cow brain, crush it, dry it out, formulate it into a dietary supplement and export it to the U.S.

Since 1997, the FDA has banned the feeding of mammalian parts to ruminants (cows, goats, and sheep), the main route by which the Mad Cow epidemic occurred in Britain. FDA prohibited the commingling of feed intended for ruminants and nonruminants (such as pigs, fish, and chickens), but Dr. Lurie found that some renderers and feed mills did not have adequate measures to prevent the commingling, and many others had yet to be inspected for compliance.

Dr. Lurie calls for the end of an FDA exemption that allows the feeding of so-called plate waste (leftover food that has been prepared for or served to humans) to cows and other ruminants. He notes that the European Union, Canada, and Mexico have banned such practices.

Dr. Lurie also wants changes in the way meat is processed to avoid infectious materials from the brain and spinal cord spreading to other parts of the animal. European countries require that the brain and spinal cord be removed before processing other parts of the animal, but Dr. Lurie said slaughtering processes in the United States vary widely and are not effectively regulated.

In blunt language, Dr. Lurie made it clear to the Commerce Committee that U S. surveillance efforts to detect the Mad Cow Disease and its human counterpart have been inadequate. He noted that only 11,954 brains of the forty million cows slaughtered in the United States had been examined in the ten-year period ending in 2000. In comparison, France is now testing 20,000 brains per week.

Dr. Lurie wants preventative measures activated, including the restriction of blood donations from those with extensive histories of residence in countries with a high incidence of Mad Cow Disease or its human equivalent. He calls for similar restrictions for cornea donors and wants regulations promulgated to prevent sourcing of materials for the production of vaccines from Mad Cow Disease-affected countries. He also urges the federal government to establish a network of regional pathology centers to do brain examinations for human CJD.

In 1997, Sheldon Rampton and John Stauber published a warning that Lurie's testimony now echoes. Their book, *Mad Cow USA: Could the Nightmare Happen Here?* (Common Courage Press), described how corporate agribusiness was putting American consumers at risk of contracting CJD. They've now made the contents of the book available online at no charge at www.prwatch.org/books/madcow.html.

We need quick tough action if we are to prevent Europe's experience from repeating itself in the United States. We need to make certain that inspections are increased at the border and that the U.S. Department of Agriculture and the Food and Drug Administration have the authority to issue mandatory regulations to ensure the safety of our food supply. This may mean that the Bush administration's aversion to regulation will have to give way to the health of citizens. However, the president, I believe, can find safe food and the prevention of disease to be consistent with his campaign pledge to be both compassionate and conservative.

April 11, 2001

Factory Farm Mergers

A concentrated food industry and concentrated factory farms have combined to throw rural America into one of the worst crises it has ever faced.

Federal and state regulators have failed to curtail the merger frenzy among livestock firms or the surge in factory farms that are polluting water supplies and poisoning ecosystems.

Now comes hope that the judicial system may offer some relief, at least from the worst excesses of the factory farm system. But while a new legal initiative launched by a coalition of environmentalists, family farm groups, and trial lawyers may begin to reverse the abuses of the factory farmers, by itself it will not be sufficient to save the American family farm—the primary source of knowledge and experience in this country on how to farm sustainably.

As a result of the past decade's merger mania, the top four cattle processors, IBP, Monfort (owned by ConAgra), Excel (owned by Cargill), and Farmland National, collectively control about 80 percent of the market—double the rate of two decades ago. The top five hog processing companies, Smithfield, IBP, Excel, Monfort, and Farmland, jointly control approximately 63 percent of the market. And Smithfield proposes to increase its market share still further, by merging with IBP. Regional concentration levels—often more important to farmers, especially small farmers for whom it is often impractical to ship livestock long distances—are even higher.

Accompanying the horizontal integration has been a vertical integration that has choked the open market for cattle and hogs. The big meatpackers now own and operate massive factory farms, or contract in advance with factory farmers for a specified supply. Small farmers find that the open market has shrunk so that there is barely any demand for their products.

And what goes on at the giant factory farms?

"A typical hog factory farm has several metal barns, each containing several hundred to several thousand animals tightly confined cheek by jowl," the Natural Resources Defense Council reported in a 1998 study, "Unlike traditional family farms, where pigs live in spacious barns in which straw bedding absorbs manure, or where they root about outside and leave their manure to decay in a pasture or open lot, these animals live in cramped conditions and may never see sunlight. They spend their lives standing on slated metal floors, beneath which their feces and urine are flushed. The manure is piped into open-air manure lagoons."

All too often, these enormous pools of manure leak into the rivers or contaminate underground aquifers, endangering public health and killing off fish and wildlife. Outbreaks of pfiesteria have been linked to manure contamination of water supplies.

A 1999 survey of ten states by the Clean Water Network and the Isaak Walton League found more than one hundred spillages in the previous year, with more than 4.5 million gallons of manure spilled or leaked into water sources. A single lagoon burst at a Murphy Family Farms factory farm in North Carolina pouring 1.5 million gallons into local rivers.

The odor from factory farms is also a major nuisance and public health menace, making life unpleasant for the unlucky neighbors of the monstrous farms.

Factory farms have sprung up around the country, with virtually no effective national or state regulation.

Earlier this month, a coalition of environmental and family farm groups, including the Water Keeper Alliance, the Sierra Club, and the National Farmers' Union, announced they were taking matters into their own hands. Partnering with leading trial lawyers, they pledge to use civil litigation to try to enforce the nation's environmental laws.

The Water Keeper Alliance says it has already initiated six lawsuits against factory farm operations for violations of the Clean Water Act and other federal environmental laws.

Success in this legal campaign should curtail the poisoning of water sources across the country. By forcing farm operations to respect the law and internalize some of their costs, it may deter the spread of factory farms and should create a more level playing field for family farmers.

But as important as this effort may be, it is not a cure-all. The industry concentration in the meatpacking sector is incompatible with a vibrant family farm sector, as are many federal farm policies. On the livestock side, groups like the Organization for Competitive Markets are encouraging the federal government to use its existing authority, under the Packers and Stockyards Act, to promote open and competitive markets, a moratorium on new agribusiness mergers, as well as other measures to counteract policy and market power biases toward the big meatpackers.

Time is running out to save the American family farm, and the rich family farm tradition of political populism and stewardship of the land. But with the Bush administration set to continue the corporate agribusiness bias of the Clinton tenure, the future does not appear bright—absent a rekindling of the spirit of the agrarian populist movement that forced major changes in America's politics and economy in the late nineteenth century.

For more information on how you can assist with the effort to save the family farm and stop factory farm abuses, contact the Organization for Competitive Markets at P.O. Box 6486, Lincoln, NE 68506, www.competitivemarkets.com, and the Water Keeper Alliance at 8 North Broadway, E Building, White Plains, NY 10603, www.keeper.org.

December 26, 2000

Environmentalist David Brower Remembered

David R. Brower was the greatest environmentalist and conservationist of the twentieth century. He was also an indefatigable champion of every worthwhile effort to protect the environment over the last seven decades. David Brower, who was eighty-eight years old, died from complications related to cancer on November 5th at his home in Berkeley, California.

David Brower once said, "We're not blindly opposed to progress, we're opposed to blind progress." He was masterful at bringing the appropriate framework to any environmental controversy, showing that the short-term economic gains are insignificant when measured against the long-term economic and broader societal benefits of proper environmental stewardship.

The monuments to his work dot the landscape of the nation's environmental movement. He founded the Earth Island Institute, the League of Conservation Voters, the John Muir Institute for Environmental Studies, the Global Conservation, Preservation, and Restoration (CPR) Service, and the U.S.-based Friends of the Earth. He also initiated the founding of Friends of the Earth organizations worldwide. Many of the leaders of the environmental movement outside the United States were personally recruited by David Brower and they were often financially supported by him. David Brower also helped establish the worker/environmental organization The Alliance for Sustainable Jobs and the Environment. And as executive director of the Sierra Club (1952–1969), he increased the organization's membership from 2,000 to 77,000 and transformed the organization from a mild-mannered conservation organization into a powerful environmental advocacy organization.

His ability to clear away the underbrush of polite discourse and focus on core problems was well illustrated by his views on the corrosive impact of special interest money on our political process. He said, "We don't have Democracy in this country. What we have is legal bribery, where politicians must raise so much money to get elected that by the time they do, they're bought and paid for by the companies and wealthy individuals who financed their campaigns."

His courage and dedication must be given credit in keeping dams out of Dinosaur National Monument, the Yukon, and the Grand Canyon and in establishing the National Wilderness Preservation System. The list of his accomplishments fills chapters in the history of the world's environmental movements. Future generations will be the major beneficiaries of his willingness to take up the tough battles for the preservation of the earth.

He was nominated three times for the Nobel Peace Prize and received numerous awards throughout his life, including the 1998 Blue Planet Award. He was, however, more proud of his mountain climbing accomplishments than his many awards and honorary degrees. In 1939 David Brower successfully scaled Shiprock, a 1,500-foot spire in northern New Mexico. In addition he had over seventy "first-ascents" of mountains and peaks worldwide.

David Brower brought as much passion to his climbing of the Sierra's peaks as he did to fighting reckless development. One of his greatest accomplishments was directing the fight to pass the Wilderness Act of 1964. This law was designed to protect millions of acres of public lands and to help keep these lands in pristine condition. David Brower was devoted to protecting our planet's natural habitats and he was in the forefront in helping to develop national parks and seashores in King Canyon, the North Cascades, the Redwoods, Great Basin, Alaska, Cape Cod, Fire Island, and Point Reyes. He led the way in protecting primeval forest in Olympic National Park and wilderness on San Gorgonio. David Brower was also one of the first environmental leaders to oppose nuclear power—something he believes led to his being fired by the Sierra Club in 1969 after working as the group's executive director for seventeen years.

He successfully developed the "exhibit format" books, which showcased nature photography and brought a sense of appreciation of wilderness areas to those who may never have visited the wild. These books helped raise environmental awareness among millions of readers and helped inspire many people to join in fights to preserve wild areas.

David Brower had little interest in quick compromise. He advised, "We are to hold fast to what we believe is right, fight for it, and find allies and adduce all possible arguments for our cause. If we cannot find enough vigor in us or them to win, then let someone else produce the compromise. We thereupon work hard to coax it our way. We become a nucleus around which the strongest force can build and function." This philosophy should be the foundation upon which today and tomorrow's environmental leaders build.

The environmental movement has lost a world champion and society has lost a man who placed enduring principle ahead of expedient deal-making.

He is survived by his wife Anne Brower; his four children Kenneth Brower, Robert Brower, Barbara Brower, and John Brower; his brother Joe Brower; and his three grandchildren Anne Katherine Olsen, Rosemary Olsen, and David C. Brower.

December 6, 2000

Genetic Engineering and the Taco Bell Crisis

The Taco Bell crisis and the mixing of genetically altered corn not approved for human consumption into the nation's corn supply reveals how poorly government regulators have been doing their job.

It was biotech opponents, not the FDA, who discovered that Taco Bell-brand taco shells—made by Kraft and sold in grocery stores—was contaminated with

Cry9C corn, marketed by the French biotechnology company Aventis under the name StarLink.

StarLink corn is spliced with a protein that kills insect pests. The U.S. Environmental Protection Agency approved StarLink in 1998 for use in animal feed or nonfood industrial purposes only. It withheld approval for introduction into the food supply on the grounds that it did not have satisfactory data to show it would not trigger allergic reactions.

This partial approval was bound to lead to contamination of the food supply. But the EPA and the FDA failed to monitor the situation properly. It took Genetically Engineered Food Alert, a coalition of health, consumer, and environmental groups, to collect samples, test the food, and discover the problem. Genetically Engineered Food Alert has since discovered genetic contamination of Safeway and Western Family taco shells.

The Taco Bell crisis is indicative of a much larger problem haunting biotech foods: Genetic engineering has far outrun the science that must be its first governing discipline. Many unknowns attend the insertion of genes across species, from ecological risks to food allergies. These uncertainties beg for investigation, before biotech corporations or their indentured researchers introduce unintended hazards into the natural environment.

In the industry, corporate greed has eclipsed the sound science that should be manifest in contemplations of *Changing the Nature of Nature*, as Martin Teitel and Kimberly Wilson titled a recent book that should serve as a primer on the biotech issue for all citizens and government regulators. Compounding the problem, government regulators have abandoned their duty to protect the public in exchange for a mission of industry boosterism.

The result has been a rush to introduce genetically altered seeds into the natural environment without adequate testing; a frenzy to patent genes, seeds, and life-forms and to extend monopolistic control over the very stuff of life; and an effort to foist genetically altered food on an unknowing public that would reject biotech foods if notified and given alternatives.

The federal regulatory budget for environmental and human health safety assessment has been tiny in comparison to research and other monies budgeted to aid industry aims. Recently, the administration supported only the voluntary labeling of genetically modified foods. Under the new plan, the FDA will require companies to disclose the planned release of genetically modified products into the food supply merely 120 days before their introduction. No testing will be required. This decision represents a staggering failure to recognize the precautionary principle and protect human heath and the environment.

It is time to reestablish priorities. Protection of human health and the environment must take precedence over corporate efforts to rush the latest product to market and please investors. We must:

• Halt the release of genetically altered plants into the environment until comprehensive, independent studies are performed as to environmental and food safety risks under a regulatory framework.

• Exempt life-forms from the purview of patent laws in order to allow broader research and safety testing opportunities by academia and government.

• Place liability for harm on the owners or licensees of biotechnology patent rights in the event of damages caused by environmental release.

• Label all food containing any genetically altered ingredients.

Of course, the biotech industry has a different agenda. Growing public outrage—as well as that of corn-purchasing and -selling companies—forced Aventis to stop, for now, sales of StarLink corn and to buy up this year's harvest of StarLink corn. But Aventis conceded only reluctantly to public concern, because it insists that StarLink is safe for human consumption. In late October, it requested the U.S. Environmental Protection Agency give time-limited approval for the presence of the corn in human food.

This is an industry with no sense of humility or caution. The biotech industry is intent on turning the entire consuming public into guinea pigs. For those not interested in participating in such an involuntary experiment, the time to act is now.

For more information, contact the Council for Responsible Genetics, 5 Upland Road, Suite 3, Cambridge, MA 02140, www.gene-watch.org, or Genetically Engineered Food Alert, 1200 18th Street, NW, 5th floor, Washington, DC 20036, www.gefoodalert.org.

November 8, 2000

Exxon Hasn't Paid Valdez Spill Victims

Justice delayed is justice denied. After the 1989 Exxon Valdez oil disaster, Exxon was found guilty by an Alaska jury and ordered to pay about $5 billion in punitive damages—this was about one year's profit for the oil giant. Eleven years later, Exxon has not paid a dime of the punitive damage award. Even the Rand Institute for Civil Justice, funded in part by insurance companies; recently noted the importance of such penalties: "Punitive damages are designed to punish a defendant for grossly inappropriate action and, in so doing, to deter further such actions by signaling that their consequences can be severe."

In a March 25, 1999, letter to Exxon CEO Lee R. Raymond, the National Association of Attorneys General said, "Each year Exxon delays payment of its obligation it earns an estimated $400 million from the difference between the statutory interest rate on judgments of 6 percent and the company's internal rate of return of about 14 percent."

For the forty thousand human victims of the oil spill and for environmentalists everywhere, this civil fine was modest for a corporate wrong that resulted in a massive spill of 11 million gallons of oil over Alaska's waters and more than 1,300 miles of shoreline.

The spill was extremely hard on the Alaskan natives on Prince William Sound and the long Alaska coast. Their subsistence and cultural lives, which had existed for millennia, were severely disrupted. The lives of commercial fishermen and their historical communities were rocked.

Eleven years later one can kick over rocks on the shore of Prince William Sound and find Exxon crude oil. Much of the cleanup was superficial.

When the Supreme Court decision was announced, many observers of corporate misdeeds were surprised that the fine was still unpaid. On the tenth anniversary of the spill, Exxon mounted a campaign with some supportive scientists to convince the world that all damage had been contained, and the Sound had returned to its pristine state. Mendacity often abounds when big oil companies talk about their oil spills. More than 200,000 birds and 2,000 sea otters died after the spill. Many scientists, including Dr. Ricki Ott, believe the damage to bird species, fish, and sea mammals is permanent. Some bird and salmon species essential to the region and its inhabitants are said to be "recovering," while others, like the common loon, cormorant, harbor seal, and harlequin duck, are faring less well.

Moreover, the chairman of the federal-state oil spill commission, Walt Parker, decried the failure of oil companies or the state and federal government to implement recommendations of the spill commission designed to prevent new disasters.

Despite the recent denial of an appeal by Exxon to the U.S. Supreme Court, Exxon company spokesman Tom Cirigliano said, "This is just one of several issues that needs to be resolved by the courts. It leaves our case very strong."

Exxon engaged in a legal war of attrition while thousands of Alaskans and others suffered. Exxon media flaks and other corporate "spin masters" often call litigation "frivolous" when they are defendants. What is truly frivolous is Exxon's legal foot-dragging in this case.

Federal and state government officials could have encouraged Exxon to pay the punitive fine when the oil giant wanted to merge with Mobil. No such pressure emerged from Alaska state officials, the Alaska congressional delegation, or the Clinton administration. Adding insult to injury, Alaska's Governor Tony Knowles worked hard to pass a tort "deform" bill that made sure that big punitive damage awards for future spills would have to meet even higher standards of proof than the ones applied by the federal court in the Exxon case. As the head of the oil support firm, appointed by Governor Knowles' citizen's task force, remarked to the head of an oil-and -gas lobbying group, "We don't want any more Exxon Valdez Jury Awards."

The tobacco, pharmaceutical, auto, oil, chemical, and health care industries, and their insurers, have fought to limit peoples' rights to sue and to further limit their own liability for the damages they cause innocent victims.

The civil justice system provides our society with its moral and ethical fiber. When the rights of injured consumers are vindicated in court, our society benefits in countless ways: by compensating injured victims and shattered families for unspeakable losses (and saving taxpayers from having to assist them); by preventing future injuries by removing dangerous products and practices from the marketplace and spurring safety innovation; by educating the public to unnecessary and unacceptable risks associated with some products and services through disclosure of facts discovered during trial; and by providing authoritative judicial forums for the ethical growth of law where the responsibility of perpetrators of trauma and disease can be established.

Exxon's negligence is almost matched by its shameless use of dilatory legal tactics.

October 4, 2000

Department of Energy Caters to the Needs of Fossil Fuel Industries

The late, great journalist I.F. Stone used to say that the evidence of government scandals lay in publicly available documents as much as in concealed material. Read what the government actually says, Izzy claimed, and you will find scandals aplenty.

That insight holds true today.

Consider the recent testimony of the acting director of policy at the U.S. Department of Energy, Melanie Kenderdine, before the House Judiciary Committee. In describing the Clinton administration's energy record in the context of soaring gasoline prices, Kenderdine offered an astounding list of subsidies, research giveaways, tax credits, loan supports, privatizations, and deregulatory initiatives to benefit oil producers. As described by Kenderdine, corporate welfare has been the intentional centerpiece of the administration's energy policy, notwithstanding some relatively minor efficiency programs.

"The President has proposed tax incentives for 100 percent expensing of geological and geophysical costs, and allowing the expensing of delay rental payments" [which would lower the cost of drilling on federal lands], Kenderdine testified.

"The administration has also supported and promoted virtually all significant energy legislation enacted by the Congress over the last seven years," she testified.

Then she launched into the stunning litany of benefits conferred on the oil industry in recent years. The handout legislation to the industry includes, as Kenderdine listed it, "Deepwater Royalty Relief; lifting the ban on the export of Alaska North Slope Oil; Royalty Simplification; privatization of the Elk Hills Naval Petroleum Reserve; the transfer and lease of Naval Oil Shale Reserves One and Three for production; and creation of a guaranteed loan program for small domestic oil and gas producers."

And how has the oil industry responded to the bountiful taxpayer handouts and subsidies? By asking the taxpayers to pay staggering prices for gasoline. Plunder at the pump is the way the rapacious, hyper-profitable oil companies "thank" consumers and taxpayers.

To pick just one item from that list, privatization of Elk Hills in California constituted the fulfillment of a long-standing dream of the oil industry. Bribes and a secret oil lease for Elk Hills, along with a lease to another federal property, the Teapot Dome field, led to the infamous Teapot Dome scandal that forced the resignation of two cabinet officials in the 1920s.

After the Clinton administration's auction of the land, the Tucson-based Southwest Center for Biological Diversity, the Sierra Club, and a Native American tribe governing council filed suit to block Occidental, the high bidder for Elk Hills, from acquiring it. They said Occidental's plans would potentially violate the Endangered Species Act by destroying valuable habitats, and might also disrupt Native American funeral grounds.

But there is more to the administration's generosity than just making it cheaper to drill for oil and making more federal lands available for drilling.

On the motor vehicle side, the administration has allocated more than a billion dollars to the Partnership for a New Generation of Vehicles (PNGV), a government-industry research venture that has done little more than provide a smokescreen behind which the industry can hide as it opposes more stringent fuel efficiency standards. Those standards remain unchanged since 1985, and overall vehicle fuel efficiency is at almost the same level as at the beginning of the Clinton administration.

Fortunately, Congress has been less interested in supporting several corporate welfare measures than the Clinton administration. Earlier this year, the House of Representatives narrowly approved an amendment introduced by Representatives John Sununu (R-NH), and Rob Andrews (D-NJ) to cut $126 million from PNGV. The House also approved cuts in dirty-fuel research programs that go nowhere.

The real solutions to energy issues—including the ever more ominous and pressing challenge of global warming—lie in energy efficiency and especially in renewables like solar and wind energy.

But you have to read deep into Kenderdine's testimony to find mention of solar and wind energy—a reflection of the shamefully and scandalously low priority attached to these technologies during the past two decades by a succession of administrations that have prioritized the needs and greed of the oil and fossil fuel industries, while failing to take measures to develop the technologies that could help us achieve a sustainable and prosperous future.

July 19, 2000

HMOs: Making a Killing

Imagine a well-written book on an important topic that you can read online for free. *Making A Killing: HMOs and the Threat to Your Health* by Jamie Court and Francis Smith (Common Courage Press, Monroe, ME)—www.makingakilling.org/—paints a troubling picture of what has become of our health care system.

Jamie Court and Francis Smith have written a searing, well-documented indictment of "corporate medicine" as practiced by HMOs. American medicine, the authors contend, has been taken over by the avarice of the corporate marketplace. "The doctor-patient relationship and its concomitant social values of trust and confidentiality have been eroded by the search for profits," the authors write. HMO doctors are frequently overruled on critical medical decisions by utilization reviewers in distant corporate headquarters. These reviewers are often little more than what the authors describe as "clerks with no medical license."

Not only does the search for profits endanger patients (and the book documents some truly horrifying examples), it also results in "colossal waste" of health care resources. The United States spends more per capita on health care and covers fewer people than any other western nation in the world. Where does the money go? Twenty to 30 percent goes to corporate overhead and profits, according to the authors.

Profits-before-patients is easily translated into corporate-dominated medicine. Greed and focus on stocks, stock options, and quarterly earnings rapidly degrade health care services. The professionalism of physicians and nurses is undermined by the juggernaut of commercialism uber alles.

The critical relations of care and compassion between server and patient are replaced by categorical protocols imposed by corporate bureaucrats commanded by monetized minds at the top of the corporate hierarchy.

The exercise of judgment, discretion, and mercy at the server/patient level is relentlessly eroded by the forces of mammon—the giant HMOs, their masterminding corporate law firms, and their political allies who safeguard their immunities and privileges in the face of growing public and professional outrage.

This was not the way it was supposed to turn out in the minds of the pioneers of prepaid medicine. Commencing with Dr. Michael Shadid's mobilization of poor farmers around Elk City, Oklahoma, in the 1920s to form the first cooperatively owned hospital in America, and then the Puget Sound and Kaiser Permanente health care plans, the ideal was quality health care with attention to preventive services within an affordable system of prepayment.

In the 1970s, the federal government began encouraging the formation of Health Maintenance Organizations (HMOs) whose nonprofit status and prevention orientation were believed to be well suited to curbing the excesses of the fee-for-service system, with its incentives to sell too much to patients. As costs annually far exceeded the general inflation rate and health care absorbed ever greater percentages of the GNP, the alternative of "managed care" emerged as a way to control costs. A dominant format also emerged—the giant, for-profit HMOs and their entrepreneurial billionaire bosses securing large clusters of customers and seeking more and more mergers.

A series of perverse economic incentives were insinuated from top to bottom so as to seriously compromise the independent clinical judgments of physicians and other health professionals, and often turned the pocketbook allegiance of the health care servers against the interests of their patients, as with gag rules, bonuses for not referring, and the like.

The giant HMO and its deepening swamp of commercialism over service, of profiteering over professionalism, of denial or rationing of care where such care is critically needed, of depersonalization of intensely personal kinds of relationships, are all occurring and spreading without sufficient disclosure, accountability, and structural responsibility to the detriment of life and health.

Workable alternatives are available. The underfunded Canadian universal health care system is still probably the best in the world, despite attempts by companies and corporate ideologues in North America to undermine and weaken it. For around 10 percent of its GNP, Canada provides health care for everyone from cradle to nursing home. Its administrative expenses are about eleven cents out of each dollar compared with double that in the United States, which this year may spend 14 percent of its GDP on health care, even as it leaves tens of millions of men, women, and children without coverage.

In *Making A Killing,* Jamie Court and Francis Smith make this story and its lethal consequences painfully clear. They searched and researched evidence, from inside the industry, the public records, the court judgments, and the documentation of personal tragedies flowing from HMO priorities, and they found patterns, not just episodes or examples. It is the system that swoops the savings from rationing and curtailment of needed care upward along the managerial ladders where the rewards grow larger and larger until they mock the very adjective "obscene." Venerable institutions and traditions in need of improvement are instead shut down and destroyed before the onrushing corporate Moloch.

This book moves from a description of corporations making medical decisions, the ensuing harm, the predictable frauds, the shunting aside of community servers, to institutional reforms and suggestions for self-help by patients and their families. The authors know well that while information is the currency of democracy, it will take a stronger democracy to achieve the desired changes.

As the only western nation without universal health care for its citizens, the United States is long overdue, and this highly motivating book should help band together a critical mass of citizens who are aroused and determined to forge a health care system as if patients and health care matter.

June 21, 2000

Partnership for a New Generation of Vehicles

It is time for the Clinton administration and Congress to end one of the most unnecessary corporate giveaways in recent times. The name is soothing—The Partnership for a New Generation of Vehicles (PNGV)—but the program is aggravating.

PNGV is a collaboration between the Clinton-Gore administration and the Big Three automakers—General Motors, Ford, and Daimler Chrysler. In return for federal funding and access to the research efforts of seven federal agencies and twenty federal laboratories, industry participants have pledged to create production prototype vehicles of a "Supercar" that would be, according to the Department of Commerce, "an environmentally friendly car with up to triple the fuel efficiency of today's midsize cars—without sacrificing affordability, performance, or safety."

The House of Representatives Committee on the Budget has publicly denounced the program as corporate welfare, asserting that the auto industry does not need the money, the same research is already being conducted by the

Big Three, any technologies that do emerge as a result of PNGV will mainly benefit foreign manufacturers and foreign consumers, and a "Supercar" is unlikely to ever be mass-produced. Members of Congress such as John Kasich (R-OH), John E. Sununu (R-NH), and Robert E. Andrews (D-NJ) are taking a pro-taxpayer stand by opposing this boondoggle.

The PNGV initiative has served as a smokescreen behind which the automakers have hidden for nearly a decade to protect themselves from more stringent CAFE (Corporate Average Fuel Efficiency) standards.

It is hard to imagine an industry less in need of government support for research than the auto industry, given that they raked in nearly $20 billion in profits in 1999. Through PNGV, the government is supporting research that the industry would or should do on its own in response to market competition, and should be mandated to undertake to meet tougher environmental standards. Instead, automakers insist that CAFE standards should not be raised since they are voluntarily participating in the PNGV initiative and are pursuing its long-term goal of developing a "Supercar" capable of achieving up to three times the fuel efficiency of today's vehicles. In the meantime, the automakers choose not to deploy existing technologies that could dramatically enhance auto fuel efficiency and reduce greenhouse gas emissions.

It is unconscionable that to date the cost of PNGV is larger than the yearly combined budgets of the National Highway Traffic Safety Administration and the Consumer Product Safety Commission. More than a billion dollars in taxpayer money has been thrown at the highly capitalized auto industry through PNGV. Furthermore, there is virtually nothing to show for this expenditure—except a lost decade in the quest for heightened fuel efficiency. The PNGV program does not even require the deployment in mass production of the technologies it seeks to develop. In March 2000, GAO concluded that "although PNGV has made progress toward building production prototypes that meet many of the PNGV objectives, at this point it does not appear likely that such a car will be manufactured and sold to consumers." Congress and the public should demand a much fuller accounting of what the auto industry has produced than that which was provided by the GAO in its March 2000 report on the PNGV.

The structure of PNGV creates special anticompetitive problems as the program provides the auto industry with an effective exemption for antitrust laws, with predictable and harmful consequences. Oligopolistic collaboration is prone to all kinds of pitfalls, from bureaucratic sloth to corrupt suppression of research—as the auto industry's own history makes clear. In the 1960s, the Justice Department filed suit against the automakers for product fixing—for refusing to introduce air quality enhancing technologies. Among other claims, the Justice Department alleged that the U.S. automakers and their trade association had conspired "to eliminate all competition among themselves in the research, development, manufacture and installation of motor vehicle air pollution control equipment." The 1969 consent decree prohibited the auto manufacturers from further conspiring to impede the development and marketing of improved air pollution control technology. The settlement agreement specifically barred the auto manufacturers from exchanging information on emissions control technology or from submitting joint statements to government regulatory agencies. Now PNGV is putting the government's imprimatur on this kind of collusive behavior even though competition in research and development is more likely to yield innovation than bureaucratized collaborative arrangements.

Why should the government waive antitrust laws and pay the highly profitable auto industry to collude on research that it could and should undertake on its own? What is the rationale for failing to extract guarantees that newly developed technologies will be deployed? Where are the procedural mechanisms to allow citizens to challenge this government-authorized and -funded corporate welfare collusion? What are the paybacks to taxpayers for this program? Seven years and $1.25 billion have gone into the program, and there is nothing to show for such taxpayer largesse. PNGV is corporate welfare at its worst.

June 13, 2000

Anti-Environment "Riders"

On May 19, 2000, the House passed a bill providing fiscal year 2001 funding of $55 billion for the transportation department. The vote wasn't even close—395 votes for and 13 against. Attached to this bill was a "rider" that prevents the Department of Transportation (DOT) from raising fuel economy standards for passenger vehicles and light trucks. A rider is a clause appended to a larger legislative bill. Appropriations bills that have significant support and are usually off limits for presidential vetoes are prime targets for anti-environment riders.

Since 1996, Congress, operating at the behest of the auto industry, has used riders to prevent DOT from developing new and improved Corporate Average Fuel Economy (CAFÉ) vehicle fuel efficiency standards, as chronicled in Jack Doyle's book, *Taken for a Ride*. The automakers lobbied to block improvements in fuel efficiency standards before and after 1975, when Congress enacted the Energy Policy and Conservation Act.

If the auto industry had spent as much time working on more efficient engines as it spent on lobbying against greater efficiency, cars would be driving many more miles per gallon than they are today. Perhaps the $11,528,816 in political contributions the auto industry gave in 1998 helped keep Congress in check.

The last major improvement in fuel efficiency standards came in 1985, which was the year Congress mandated that passenger cars meet a 27.5 mpg standard. Even the existing weak CAFÉ standards have helped reduce oil consumption and the output of global warming gases. The Union of Concerned Scientists notes that passenger vehicles and light trucks account for 20 percent of the carbon dioxide spewed into our air each year. Just imagine! Each gallon of gasoline produced and burned produces 25 pounds of carbon dioxide.

These standards are, however, no longer acceptable. In 1975, when Congress adopted fuel efficiency standards, there were about 133 million vehicles on the road. Today there are more than 203 million vehicles on the road. According to Center for Auto Safety Director Clarence Ditlow, passenger total fuel economy hit a high of 26.2 mpg in 1987, dropped to 24.4 mpg in 1997, and in 1998 moved up slightly to 24.6 mpg. In fact, the *Wall Street Journal* reports that the average fuel economy of all new cars is at its lowest point since 1980.

Environmental groups have been pushing Congress to raise the CAFÉ standard to 45 mpg for cars and 35 mpg for light trucks. This is a small but important step that our government needs to take if the United States wants any shred of moral authority when it talks to other countries about air quality.

Passenger cars and light trucks account for 40 percent of the oil used in the United States. Adequate mile-per-gallon standards for motor vehicles could reduce smog and alleviate some of the pollution exacerbating global warming, reduce consumption of foreign oil, and cut the trade deficit. Better standards could also save consumers money at the pump and lessen the toll air pollution takes on our health (according to several national studies, air pollution is responsible for 64,000 deaths each year). Moreover, improved vehicle fuel efficiency standards coupled with a strong commitment to renewable energy would eliminate our need to explore for oil in environmentally sensitive areas around the globe (less oil exploration and development also means fewer offshore oil spills and fewer leaky underground storage tanks to pollute our nation's groundwater).

The Center for Auto Safety has estimated that increasing CAFÉ standards for cars and light trucks by 60 percent (45 mpg for cars and 35 mpg for light trucks) by 2005 will result in a savings of three million barrels of oil each day, reduce hydrocarbon emissions by 500,000 tons, and cut 140 million tons in greenhouse gas emissions each year, and, on average, save new car purchasers $3,000 in fuel costs over the life of the car. Public Citizen estimates that since 1975 the CAFÉ standards have saved consumers more than $30 billion annually.

Existing technology can make cars 50 percent more efficient than they are today. Honda and Toyota have developed hybrid electric cars that get more than 60 mpg. The U.S. automakers could deploy existing technology tomorrow to increase fuel efficiency to much higher standards than are now required, if they chose or if they are mandated to do so.

Sierra Club's Dan Becker said, "Making vehicles go farther on a gallon of gas is the biggest single step we can take toward curbing oil consumption and global warming."

Unfortunately, the will of our elected officials to curb air pollution and the indifference of corporate polluters to the silent cumulative violence they inflict on our people through air pollution persists. Instead of supporting tougher standards on the automakers, the Clinton administration has been content to put forward the corporate welfare-heavy Partnership for a New Generation of Vehicles (PNGV). The PNGV program involves oligopolistic collaboration between the Big Three auto companies and a wide range of U.S. government agencies. They are researching a "clean car"—but the automakers have no obligation to deploy any technologies developed under the PNGV. For the auto companies, PNGV has been a perfect smokescreen behind which they can carry out their efforts to thwart mandated increases in CAFÉ standards. After eight years and $1 billion taxpayer dollars, the Big Three auto companies have little to show the public except that their already overflowing coffers have been bolstered by an unnecessary infusion of government funds. Given the ease with which this money came and went, taxpayers can be sure that the auto companies will be asking Uncle Sam to be Uncle Sugar and give them additional handouts.

We need to move well beyond the modest improvements in CAFÉ standards to truly provide people with the air quality they deserve. President Clinton can cease his passivity and tell Congress that he will veto any riders that make it impossible to increase vehicle fuel efficiency standards. The second step would be to close the loophole that allows sport utility vehicles to avoid the same CAFÉ standards that cars must meet.

May 24, 2000

Renewable Energy Now

Remember when the "energy crisis" was the big political issue? Remember the long gas lines and the sudden surge in gasoline prices— once in the mid '70s and once in the late '70s? Remember the politicians demanding that our country strive for energy independence, so that we would no longer need to be reliant on oil imports?

Well, what happened? Today, the politicians in Washington don't even have the energy question on their screen. Yet the United States now imports more than 50 percent of what the country uses. The Republicans in Congress are even moving to stop the Clinton administration from continuing its modest efforts to advance energy efficiency and use of renewable sources.

Despite the ubiquitousness of gas-guzzling SUVs on the highway, the Senate voted 55–40 on September 15 to continue freezing motor vehicle fuel efficiency standards at 1985 levels. With the exception of a few stalwart senators and representatives, Congress is mired in the dark ages when it comes to rejecting rational, efficient, and environmentally benign energy policies.

So, after some progress from 1975 to 1985 in conservation, which saved the country about $150 billion a year, the Big Stall dominates.

None of this discourages Ken Bossong, who is probably the most persistent solar energy networker in the country. Working out of a small office in a Washington, D.C. suburb, his Sun Day Campaign puts out a monthly update on the activities of his sustainable energy coalition. I find it a solar mine of encouraging information about developments and reports around the country that receive very little news attention.

Some information from "Sun Day Campaign":

Item: The giant accounting firm KPMG issues a report titled "Solar Energy: From Perennial Promise to Competitive Alternative," which calculates that one large-scale solar photovoltaic factory producing five million solar panels a year could reduce the cost of solar power by 75 percent or more. This drop in cost would make solar photovoltaics cost-competitive for domestic consumers who receive electricity from polluting sources.

How much would such a large-scale P.V. factory cost? Around $660 million, KPMG says. Or less than one-tenth of what is spent a year on dog and cat food in the United States.

Item: Albert Gore has not made a single speech on the need to make a renewable energy policy preeminent in this country if we are to be energy independent, efficient, and nonpolluting. Yet in a little-noted speech, White House Chief of Staff John Podesta told the National Press Club on September 1 that "ultraclean fuel cells and cars that get 80 miles per gallon are well within our reach."

Item: The U.S. wind industry set a record this last fiscal year by installing $1 billion worth of new generating equipment. Viewed by many energy experts as the new electricity-generating technology most frequently used, wind power now provides more than 1,000 megawatts of electricity a year, about the size of one large nuclear plant.

State laws in Iowa and Minnesota requiring modest amounts of renewable energy capacity have stimulated the wind electricity industry and the preparation of "wind velocity maps" all around the nation. Some day North Dakota's chief commercial export may be wind power. An interactive map showing new projects nationwide is available at the Wind Project Database site.

Item: The number of U.S. consumers and small businesses using nonutility natural gas and electricity suppliers has doubled to three million since January 1 and will increase by another third by the end of the year.

It is clear that there is interest in renewable energy throughout the country, despite the coal, oil, gas, and uranium lobbies egging on their Republican and some Democratic cronies to stop or slow the use of solar renewables.

Bossong is a public citizen laboring quietly in this crucial area, pushing for the use of more renewable energy sources. Neither the mass media nor the congressional majority is interested in energy subjects—that is until the next energy crisis. When that happens, they'll want to start calling civic leaders like Bossong.

In case you don't want to wait until then, you can write to him at 315 Circle Avenue, Takoma Park, MD 20912, call (301) 270-2258, or fax (301) 891-2866.

October 4, 1999

Smelly Business: Car Makers and Air Pollution

Back in 1969, the Nixon administration settled a civil antitrust suit against the Big Three automakers that charged them with conspiring since 1953 to "eliminate all competition among themselves in the research, development, manufacture, and installation of motor vehicle air pollution control equipment." (The Johnson administration originally brought the civil suit in 1968, after having decided against criminal charges.)

The settlement's consent decree included a promise by the Big Three—GM, Ford Motor Co., and Chrysler—and their trade association not to engage in the collusive behavior or take the joint-policy positions described in the lawsuit.

The companies got away without making any admissions of guilt, paying any fines, or having to put any extra effort into their pollution-control research and development.

All this happened at a time when people in southern California were choking on recurrent smog, largely caused by the photochemical mixtures of motor vehicle emissions. Physicians advised some ten thousand people a year to move out of the Los Angeles basin because of the serious danger to their health.

In 1981, under President Reagan, federal antitrust authorities did not pursue renewal of the consent decree, thus freeing the automakers to present a unified position on what can and cannot be done to control vehicular emissions. No one in government paid much attention to whether the auto companies were reverting to their old bad habits.

Then in August 1993 the naive Clinton administration entered into an agreement with the Big Three that committed $1 billion in taxpayer money to help the very profitable auto companies make their motor vehicles more fuel efficient—the so-called Clean Car Initiative. This joint venture with the government allowed the auto companies more leeway to do nothing. It gave them a buffer against long-overdue regulatory updates on fuel efficiency standards and any further antitrust action. And it gave them the argument that because they're in a partnership with Uncle Sam, there is no need for regulation and antitrust prosecution.

Predictably, the last six years have produced virtually no changes in this taxpayer-subsidized boondoggle, and by now the automakers surely believe the heat is off. So weak are the federal pollution standards that full-size pickup trucks and sport-utility vehicles are permitted to emit two and a half times the smog gases as cars. Next year, when tighter standards become law, they will be allowed to emit five times as much as cars.

Now Ford Motor has announced that, starting this fall, its full-size pickups will meet the current pollution rules for cars. It expects these same truck models to meet the stronger laws for cars next year. This news was reported in the *New York Times* on May 18, 1999, by *Times* reporter Keith Bradsher. But then Bradsher wrote a very disturbing paragraph that the Antitrust Division in the Justice Department should follow up on. He wrote:

> Some auto executives say that until the last couple years, there was a gentleman's agreement, at least among the Detroit automakers, not to compete on environmental issues. Ford has broken that informal understanding since early last year by repeatedly and very publicly going beyond what Federal regulations require, to the annoyance of executives at rival companies.

If this is what has indeed been going on, then the lawyers who pushed for a criminal case back in 1968 and lost the argument to those who filed a civil case will have been vindicated. Corporate executives treat criminal cases with far more gravity than civil lawsuits, which tend to end with not much more than a slap on the wrist.

Once again, the violation of "product fixing" comes to the forefront with its mockery of the competitive enterprise system. Maybe those annoyed auto executives need to get a call from the Justice Department.

May 31, 1999

IV

CIVIL RIGHTS, CIVIL LIBERTIES, AND CIVIL JUSTICE

"Civil rights" has a powerful resonance and privileged place in our country. But we shouldn't use the term too narrowly to refer only to the fights for equality for historically disadvantaged groups like African Americans, Latinos, and women (not to mention gays, the disabled, and others who have suffered pervasive legal and social discrimination).

The victories achieved by and on behalf of these groups deserve celebration. Nonetheless, these groups' quest for equality is far from over. African Americans and Arab Americans still endure racial profiling and other indignities at the hands of the justice system. Women remain second-class citizens in various places, ranging from professional suites to the amateur sports field. Some of the columns in this section deal with these and other instances of unequal treatment of groups not fully empowered within the political process.

But "civil rights," and the concomitant "civil liberties," mean much more. They entail the terms of association between a citizenry and its government, as well as the relationship among different parts of the citizenry.

The columns in this section address a wide range of civil rights and civil liberties issues. Several involve the systematic assault on our privacy from assorted sources, including telemarketers wantonly invading our homes; corporations gathering computer files on our personal lives; and an attorney general exploiting unprecedented powers to monitor and imprison people without traditional legal protections.

Some columns in this section deal with "civil justice" as well—the process by which people seek vindication of their rights in court. While our legal system often fails to provide justice for ordinary citizens who suffer at the hands of the powerful, the problem has been turned upside down; many indentured politicians in Congress and state legislatures complain that ordinary citizens receive too much justice at the expense of corporations. This response is backwardly tragic: they are enacting so-called tort reform (we call it tort deform) designed to limit the rights of victims to receive adequate compensation for devastating, wrongful injuries.

Other columns in this section address miscellaneous abuses of our rights and liberties. Several concern the predatory lending practices of financial institutions, and other economic crimes against the poor, one of the most underrated civil rights abuses today.

Still others deal with a pre-condition for a just society: open and equal political participation. Deprived of statehood, the residents of the District of Columbia are not afforded the voting rights provided to other U.S. citizens. The millions of Americans who decline to vote deprive themselves of their democratic birthright, and diminish our democracy. And a political system that rewards wealth with influence mocks the very notion of democracy and predictably produces the injustice of concentrated unaccountable power.

It is no accident that the section of the book dealing most directly with civil rights and civil liberties should range far and wide, for the threats to our civil rights and liberties are multiple and far-reaching. Eternal vigilance by We The People remains the only reliable safeguard.

MTBE Bailout

The past three years have demonstrated a disturbing trend: when tragedy befalls our country, we can count on the Republican leadership to capitalize on another opportunity to push its extremist agenda and reward its big business allies.

In the aftermath of the crippling northeastern blackout in August, Congress has been working feverishly to pass an energy bill full of supposedly beneficial energy solutions for American citizens. But behind closed doors, corporations, lobbyists, and leadership in both houses have been wrangling over just how far they can push the envelope of this bill to benefit their oily, deregulation-happy friends.

They have packed the bill with giveaways for the various big energy corporations. There are subsidies for atomic power, for Big Oil, and the repeal of a crucial historic law that has provided the regulatory framework for electricity companies.

One particularly egregious provision in the bill would shield producers of MTBE (methyl tertiary butyl ether) from any legal claims that the chemical is "defective in design or manufacture." MTBE is a little-known toxic component of gasoline sold in many parts of the country.

MTBE is added to gasoline as part of the Clean Air Act's efforts to require the use of "oxygenates" to make gasoline burn more cleanly and efficiently. But MTBE is only one kind of oxygenate and despite manufacturers' claims to the contrary, MTBE has never been specifically mandated as a fuel additive. Released into the environment from tens of thousands of leaking storage tanks and spills, it is one of the most ubiquitous pollutants in the nation.

There is only one reason that some legislators and their oil and chemical taskmasters have pushed so hard for this immunity bailout provision: MTBE is a defective product. Documents produced at a recent trial in California proved that gasoline manufacturers have long known the cold hard truth about MTBE: because of its extreme water solubility, this toxic chemical spreads in the environment farther and faster than other components of gasoline, and it is extremely costly to clean up.

Now companies that make and use MBTE are seeking absolution from cleaning up the mess they made. Lawsuits from coast to coast seek to hold them accountable. These companies should not be shielded from foreseeable negative effects of the products they create or employ.

Citizens concerned about the safety of their drinking water are outraged that Congress is seeking to shift tens of billions of dollars in toxic cleanup costs from the biggest oil companies in the nation to taxpayers and drinking water ratepayers. The MBTE provision is tantamount to a nationwide, $30 billion tax hike. If successful, this craven effort would be one of the bigger corporate bailouts in American history and a staggering rollback of the "polluter pays" laws that have cleaned up contamination hazards in every state in the nation. It would open a Pandora's box for manufacturers to seek liability immunity for a vast array of products with serious environmental or public health risks.

For over twenty years, U.S. decision-makers and courts have agreed that industries must bear the cost of cleaning up the environmental problems that they create. This is an appropriate remedy for damage caused by companies that pollute, and it deters future pollution hazards.

There is a lot of talk these days about "taking responsibility," which corporatists masquerading as conservatives use to refer only to regular people. Here the hypocrisy of the responsibility rhetoric is laid bare: The chemical and oil companies that make and use MTBE are specifically looking to escape their responsibility. But the usual conservative responsibility chorus is silent.

More than a few members of Congress have taken a turn singing from the responsibility hymnal. It's time for these members of Congress to fulfill their responsibilities—by refusing to relieve corporations of theirs.

Fortunately, there are some in Congress willing to take a stand. Having seen firsthand the value of the "polluter pays" framework in helping to clean the feculent toxic mess made by General Electric in the Hudson River, Senator Chuck Schumer has promised to filibuster if the MTBE provision remains in the bill. And last week, forty-two senators signed a "Dear colleague" letter initiated by Senator Barbara Boxer asking that the energy bill conferees remove the MTBE escape from liability protection.

And a coalition of national health, environmental, science, and consumer organizations have banded together to oppose the MTBE provision. Organizations of cities and water suppliers—including The National League of Cities, U.S. Conference of Mayors, Association of Metropolitan Water Agencies, American Water Works Association, National Association of Water Companies, Association of California Water Agencies, and National Rural Water Association—have also opposed the provision.

But in order to fend off this corporate bailout, our congressional leaders need to hear from you. Call the Capitol switchboard at (202) 224-3121, and ask to speak to your representative and senator about this dump-and-run liability protection provision in the energy bill.

October 17, 2003

Telephone Sales: Don't Call...

This week the American people were given a highly publicized free lesson in how they can become powerful against dominant corporate interests. It was the swirling dynamics around the Do Not Call registry established by the Federal Trade Commission which drew over fifty million people in a matter of weeks who don't like to be bothered by telemarketers while they're eating dinner.

The events started on September 23 when a federal district court judge, Lee R. West, ruled that the Federal Trade Commission did not have the legal authority to set up such a system. Members of Congress went, as they say, ballistic both as Republicans and Democrats. Back in February, 98 percent of the Congress voted to fund such a registry that they thought was already authorized in previous legislation. The reaction to Judge West's decision was bipartisan. The message was that this decision will not stand.

In little more than twenty-four hours, Congress overwhelmingly passed what Representative Billy Tauzin called the "This Time We Really Mean It Act." The vote was 412 to 8 in the House and 95 to 0 in the Senate. President Bush said he would sign it immediately.

It is fascinating to watch legislators turn away from their usual corporate grips when they hear the growing thunder of the people. Bill Tauzin, a certified cozy corporate carnivore in most instances, trumpeted "Fifty million Americans can't be wrong." He should have added "who spoke out," for he has been ignoring the subdued wishes of tens of millions of Americans on many other subjects that have come before his subcommittee and his own vote.

The powerful telemarketing industry whose campaign contributions and allies in Congress have made it a force to be reckoned with was also overwhelmed by the vote. It is in a bind. On the one hand, it doesn't want to appear too aggressive in taking away the right of the people to register "do not call;" on the other hand, it wants to overturn the FTC rule in court. Hours after the Oklahoma decision was countered by Congress, a federal district court in Denver ruled that the Do Not Call Registry violated the telemarketing companies' (who are not real persons, we should remember) constitutional right of free speech.

Judge Edward Nottingham ruled that the FTC burdened the commercial speech of the telemarketing companies by not applying the Do Not Call rule to nonprofit solicitations, such as those of the Red Cross, colleges, or public television. That burden, he said, was significant enough to violate the First Amendment speech right of these corporations.

There are two problems with the judge's reasoning. First, the FTC has no jurisdiction over many nonprofit group activities, so it could not adjust to his ruling even if it tried. More important, the courts have distinguished, although less than before, between the constitutional protection of commercial speech and what the attorneys call political speech—regular conversations. In a word, commercial advertisements or marketing talk are given less protection from regulation, especially when consumers don't want their privacy invaded.

The Supreme Court has already allowed consumers to block so-called junk mail. People can put a "no solicitation" sign in front of their house. Constitutional law specialists think the Direct Marketing Association—one of the plaintiffs—will not likely overturn the FTC rule on appeal.

Meanwhile, Congress is trying to figure out what to do when a court raises a constitutional issue—usually reserved for the courts—in time for the October 1 deadline when the Do Not Call Registry is to go into effect.

Feeling the public's heat, the Direct Marketing Association on September 26 advised its members to respect the national "do not call" list despite the two court rulings in its favor. Someone's getting smart. Corporate free speech does not extend to unwilling buyers who have registered their desire to keep the calls from coming to their homes.

All in all, the lesson is that should many Americans devote a tiny amount of time to convey their desires or displeasures, the thunder from that large community is heard in Washington. Civic morale in America should grow and give people a better feeling that when they act, they make the difference.

September 26, 2003

Privacy Rights

Congress has been slow to enact airtight protections for individuals' privacy. When there is a trade-off between the demands of corporations versus citizens' rights to privacy, our national legislators almost always come down on the side of financial institutions and their affiliates. Congress putted around the edges of the privacy issues when it passed the Financial Modernization Act in 1999. But the privacy provisions have done little to halt the wholesale access to financial records and other personal data of consumers.

A shocking report just released by the Federal Trade Commission (FTC) should disabuse everyone—and hopefully Capitol Hill—of the notion that the right to privacy is some nice esoteric concern with little real economic impact.

The FTC found that 3.3 million U.S. consumers had been victimized last year in identity thefts made possible by the easy access to personal information. The thefts were used to open fraudulent bank, credit card, or utility accounts and to commit other crimes.

The cost: $3.8 billion to consumers on top of losses of more than $32.9 billion to businesses, many of them small merchants.

In addition to these "identity thefts," the FTC found that 6.6 million became victims of a closely related crime, "account thefts," which involve the use of stolen ATM cards or financial records to steal from a victim's existing accounts.

These "account thefts" created $14 billion in business losses plus $1.1 billion in losses to consumers. The "account thefts" are outstripping the "identity thefts." FTC found a 71 percent increase in this type of theft last year.

In most cases, the thefts were used in purchases by the thieves. But about 15 percent of the thefts were used in other schemes including the utilization of stolen information to obtain government records. FTC cited cases where the thieves used the identifying information when stopped by law enforcement officers or caught in the commission of a crime.

Privacy is now before the Congress again. This time in legislation extending the override of state laws that in any way control how credit information is gathered, disseminated, and used by credit reporting agencies. These agencies maintain an estimated 600 million files on American consumers—a gold mine of data for the credit industry and a dangerous mine field for citizens wanting to protect their privacy. The preemption expires at the end of the year unless Congress acts.

The preemption of state laws involving the Fair Credit Reporting Act (FCRA) has passed the House of Representatives. It is now under consideration in the Senate Banking Committee. The financial industry had appeared likely to get what it wanted from the Senate without broader issues of privacy becoming a front-burner item.

In the interim, California, led by a spunky privacy rights advocate, State Senator Jackie Speier, has succeeded in passing a stronger state privacy law that allows consumers to block sharing of their information with affiliates. That's changed the equation. Now the privacy proponents want the California law to become a national standard and they are pushing the issue with the Senate Committee.

Complicating the issue is the fact that financial institutions in California agreed to the Speier bill this summer to head off stronger privacy provisions that were about to go on the California referendum ballot. That has made it tougher for financial lobbyists in the Senate and has given consumer organizations at the national level new leverage to bring privacy—not just extension of FCRA—to the forefront. They want the affiliate-sharing provisions in the FCRA bill brought up to California standards. California's two senators, Diane Feinstein and Barbara Boxer, have written the committee urging that the FCRA provisions be comparable to the tighter standards of the California law. Without that assurance, Feinstein and Boxer are expected to oppose the FCRA preemption extension.

Both Senate Banking Chairman Richard Shelby and the committee's ranking Democrat Paul Sarbanes have long been advocates of greater financial privacy. Will Shelby and Sarbanes support the California initiative and put it in the FCRA legislation? The financial industry has spent a ton of advertising and campaign money on extending the Fair Credit Reporting Act. The stakes are large.

As the FTC report on identity and account theft highlights, laws that are lax on privacy issues cost consumers and businesspeople—small and large—billions of dollars. Looking the other way on privacy is not cost-free. Write your senators and tell them to support the California privacy provisions as part of the FCRA legislation.

For more information:

Privacy Rights Clearinghouse: www.privacyrights.org U.S. Pirg: www.pirg.org/orgconsumer/credit/index.htm

September 19, 2003

The Triumvirate and Our Civil Liberties

George W. Bush, Dick Cheney, and John Ashcroft are testing the American people as to whether violations of the U.S. Constitution by the executive branch of government are to be viewed as mere technicalities or a growing threat to the fabric of liberty, privacy, due process, and fair trials in our country.

Of course, these men are verbally reassuring while they conduct their "war on terrorism." President Bush says, "we will not allow this enemy to win the war by restricting our freedoms." Last September, Attorney General Ashcroft said, "We're not sacrificing civil liberties. We're securing civil liberties."

Then, Orwellian-like, they swing into action. Arrests without charges. Imprisonment indefinitely without lawyers. Secret indefinite jailings for people who are just considered "material witnesses," not accused of any crimes.

If Bush-Cheney-Ashcroft want to shove the U.S. courts aside, then just call someone—even an American citizen—an "enemy combatant" and throw him into the brig without charges and without a lawyer. That way, neither the prisoner nor the courts will have a chance to question the all-powerful White House prosecutors. One can almost hear James Madison, who warned over two centuries ago, that "The accumulation of all powers, legislative, executive, and judicial, in the same hands, whether of one, a few, or many, may justly be pronounced the very definition of tyranny." Lucky for the Bush triumvirate that Madison and Jefferson are not around today!

Then there is the dragnet approach to law enforcement where all Americans are suspect until proven otherwise. The federal snoopers can search your house and business without notifying you simply by asking a secret court for a warrant—a court that to anyone's knowledge has never said no. The Triumvirate can go to libraries and bookstores to find out what you have been reading and prohibit the librarian or storeowner from telling you or anyone about their demands.

The Triumvirate can listen in on conversations between lawyers and their clients in federal prisons. They can access your computer records, e-mails, medical files, and financial information on what is essentially an enforcement whim.

Bye-bye to what the Constitution meant by that great phrase of restraint called "probable cause." Without "probable cause," the Triumvirate agents can covertly attend and monitor public meetings, including places of worship. This was even too much for House Judiciary Committee Chairman Republican James Sensenbrenner who objected vainly to such amorphous surveillance guidelines.

Brandishing the word "terror" in every direction, the Triumvirate is becoming a law unto itself—chilling the Congress, intimidating the Democrats (What, you're soft on terror?), seriously distracting us from domestic necessities, draining the federal budget into a great swamp of deficits to pay for a garrison state and its foreign adventures and, most important for Bush, scaring the public into nice poll ratings for the White House.

Conservative Republicans have opposed ever overreaching seizures by the

Triumvirate—such as setting up a TIPS program that would have enlisted millions of postal workers, delivery people, truckers, and service workers who have access to homes and offices to report on any "suspicious" talk or activities. Toward a nation of snoopers. Congressional conservatives and liberals joined together to stop both this craziness and the Rumsfeldian fantasy called a "Total Information Awareness Program" rooted in a gigantic computer dragnet of detailed information about all Americans so that a new computer software brain might find some actionable patterns.

Dragnets, once out of the neighborhood, are a notoriously inefficient and angering enforcement instrument. It makes for sloth while giving the impression of dutifulness.

Never one to miss destroying what he says he is protecting—our freedoms and fairness (due process)—John Ashcroft is ready to send Congress a draft proposal that is being called "Patriot II." It was named after the first so-called Patriot Act, which passed in a congressional panic on a day in October 2001 when no representative or senator had a chance to read the 342-page bill, except perhaps the only "no" vote in the Senate, Russ Feingold (D-WI), and a few House members flipping pages furiously.

Patriot II would turn the Triumvirate into a virtual junta. Among its provisions is one that could strip an American citizen of his or her citizenship if the government believes the person was providing "material support" to a group designated as engaged in "terrorist activities." Who defines these terms? Why the Ashcroft prosecutors. And you won't be surprised to learn that the provisions and guidelines allow almost total discretion for the Triumvirate to mean whatever it wants them to mean. With such license, the government can secretly search your premises in all suspected "criminal cases," not just ones deemed terroristic.

Who is speaking up? Besides the civil liberties groups, sometimes the American Bar Association, and a few stalwart law professors, there is what author Nat Hentoff calls the "gathering resistance" of towns. That's right! Over one hundred towns and growing are passing ordinances or resolutions saying enough is enough. They will not cooperate with officials—federal or otherwise—who are violators of the Bill of Rights and civil liberties. Many of these communities, which are being joined by spontaneous citizen gatherings, are urging repeal of the offensive parts of the Patriot Act.

Hentoff's new and spine-tingling book of what the Triumvirate has been doing—that is just the non-secret tip of the secret iceberg—is called *The War on the Bill of Rights* (Seven Stories Press, see www.sevenstories.com). Publication date is September 15 when Hentoff, a veteran civil-liberties defender, journeys around the country showing that Bush was right on one election promise—being a uniter, not a divider. Bush has united both liberals and conservatives in rising opposition to his government of men, not of laws and constitution.

August 29, 2003

Selling Victims' Rights

President George W. Bush takes off on our Air Force One to California, spends nine hours in that state, and comes back with $5 million in campaign money. He is on his way to raising a historic record $200 million in private, mostly business money. This is the price for selling the U.S. government to these fat cats and top dogs. Quite a bargain for the rich and the super-rich, but not quite what Thomas Jefferson or James Madison had in mind.

An illustration of what this plutocratic bargain does to tens of thousands of innocent victims of medical malpractice by negligent or incompetent physicians and hospitals is working its way through Congress. Keep in mind that a study by the Harvard School of Public Health estimated about 80,000 lives lost a year just in hospitals, not including emergency rooms, due to harmful medical practices.

Congressional legislation backed by the powerful insurance industry and many physician associations places a cap of $250,000 for a lifetime of pain and suffering, among other obstacles to these wounded Americans or their next of kin having their day in court.

No matter how serious the injuries or how outrageous the neglect or blunder (such as brain damage or removing the wrong organ), Bush and his congressional axis want to tie the hands of judges and juries with this one-shoe-fits-all cap. Only the judges and juries see, hear, and evaluate the evidence in these cases, not absentee Washington politicians pushing bills greased by cash.

The drumbeats for restricting the legal rights of victims have been loud and false. Lurid anecdotes of physicians being driven out of their practice by high insurance premiums were spread through massive advertising campaigns. The propaganda pointed to California where a similar cap has been in effect since 1976 as proof that caps restrain insurance premiums. In reality, what has restrained medical malpractice insurance premiums in California has been stronger regulation of rates due to a people-passed Proposition 103 in 1988.

Now, new data are available that put the lie to these cap supporters. Weiss Ratings, an independent insurance-rating agency in Florida, found that in the past ten years, those states with caps on noneconomic damage awards saw median doctors' malpractice insurance premiums rise faster than states with-out caps. Weiss thinks that regulation of premium increases made the difference.

About the same time, in written testimony before the California Department of Insurance, actuary James Robertson with SCPIE, the state's second largest medical malpractice insurance company, said that California's cap "did not substantially reduce the relative risk of medical malpractice insurance in California."

The Foundation for Taxpayer and Consumer Rights responded to this tes-timony, saying through its advocate, Douglas Heller, that "SCPIE admits that malpractice caps and other legal restrictions do not hold down doctors' rates." But this company says the opposite in other states to achieve legislated restric-tions on victims' rights. Heller added: "When SCPIE is pushing for caps in other states, they argue that California is less risky. But when they want to raise physicians' premiums in California, they say that California is still very risky. They cannot have it both ways," he concluded.

Whenever the insurance industry is faced with low interest rates and declin-ing stock investments, it starts the drumbeat against access to justice by harmed patients. Instead of demanding discipline or suspension of the licenses of the minority of recurring bad doctors (5 percent of the doctors are involved in about 50 percent of the malpractice payouts), instead of urging medical associations to police their own ranks, these insurers turn their doctor policyholders toward the state and federal legislatures to go after victims' rights and remedies in court.

Some of these victims, at great pain and expense to themselves, have been testifying about this assault on our civil justice system. But Bush and his con-gressional cohorts are not listening to the facts, morality, and justice of their pleas.

In their recent book titled *Bush's Brain*, authors Wayne Slater and Jim Moore recounted an interview with Karl Rove, Bush's top White House polit-ical adviser. Rove told them that he "sort of talked him (Bush) into that one," meaning so-called tort reform. Then the real motive came out. In Slater and Moore's words: "Rove wanted that issue elevated because he knew that its most ardent advocates in Texas could provide millions of dollars in campaign con-tributions needed to unseat [former Texas Governor Ann] Richards."

Back in 1989, Michael Hatch, then Commerce Commissioner of Minnesota, documented that two medical malpractice insurance companies had increased doctors' premiums 300 percent, even though neither the num-ber of claims against them nor the amount paid out by these companies had increased (see centerjd.org). This racket is not new.

Insurance regulation needs to be stronger. Enforcing the medical licensing laws against unworthy doctors needs to be expanded. In the meantime Bush and his political friends continue to raise big money while the "little people" suffer the results.

June 27, 2003

Level the Playing Field for Women's Sports

Title IX of the Education Amendments of 1972, one of the most important and successful civil rights laws in U.S. history, may soon be undermined by the Bush administration's Commission on Opportunity in Athletics.

Title IX bars sex discrimination in any educational program or activity that receives federal funding, including athletics. The law gave women access to classes, facilities, and opportunities that had historically been male-only.

While Title IX is not at risk of being repealed, it is widely believed that the Bush administration established the Commission on Opportunity in Athletics as a vehicle to push a predetermined agenda to weaken Title IX. The commission is to submit a written report to the U.S. Secretary of Education Rod Paige by February 28, 2003.

Prior to Title IX, if a woman wanted to pursue a professional degree in college, she could be passed over for a law school or medical school program simply because she was a woman. Since then, the thirty-year-old law has proven itself integral to women's rights. From the classrooms and playing fields to the executive suites, Title IX has been a vital tool in advancing equal opportunities for women and girls.

It is the college playing field where Title IX is now being threatened. Some athletic directors and commentators mistakenly blame the law for the elimination of some minor men's sports. To give women the same athletic opportunities as men, say Title IX critics, schools are forced to remove men's opportunities because of a lack of money to support added teams. They claim that Title IX's equality standard (commonly referred to as "proportionality"), which requires colleges to demonstrate roughly the same ratio for male and female athletes as for students enrolled at the school, results in discrimination against male athletes.

Contrary to the rationale of those who would like to weaken Title IX's equality standard, men's sports participation and funding have continued to grow.

The real expenses starving minor men's sports of funding are the disproportionate share of university athletic dollars spent on one or two teams—football and men's basketball—and not spent to add new teams for women or to support other men's sports. Title IX should not be the scapegoat for irresponsible, nonprofit institutions of higher education that operate their football and men's basketball programs like professional franchises.

Attention should turn to college presidents and athletic directors who fuel the growing arms' races in football and men's basketball with million-dollar coaches and excessive expenditures. The fact that these sports may bring in revenue (although some actually lose money) does not justify their bloated budgets, which take funds away from other men's sports as well as women's sports. Rather than sharing a little of what the football and men's basketball programs spend, the remaining men's and women's sports are forced to fight for the scraps, pitting the deprived against the deprived.

Despite the gains women have made under Title IX, resources for women's sports have never caught up to resources for men's sports at most colleges and universities. Women's athletic programs continue to lag behind men's programs by every measurable criterion, including participation opportunities, athletic scholarships, operating budgets, and recruiting expenditures.

While 55 percent of our college populations are female, female athletes still receive only 42 percent of all college athletic participation opportunities, 36 percent of sports operating expenditures, 32 percent of athlete recruitment spending, and 42 percent of athletic scholarship money amounting to $133 million less than male athletes receive in scholarships each year.

Why are women still second-class citizens in athletics despite a law guaranteeing that we treat our daughters as well as our sons? Because Title IX has never been adequately enforced. In fact, the federal agency responsible for enforcing the law, the U.S. Department of Education's Office for Civil Rights (OCR), has never initiated a single proceeding to remove federal funds at any school or college that fails to comply. Instead, OCR has served as a negotiator of settlements that are usually less than what Title IX requires.

In order to obtain the legal rights for gender equity in athletics guaranteed them under Title IX, women across the country have successfully filed civil rights complaints and lawsuits against institutions. But until women have the same opportunities as men to enjoy the psychological, physiological, and sociological benefits that sports participation can provide, we must all insist on the preservation and strengthened enforcement of Title IX.

If you'd like to help, visit the League of Fans web site at www.leagueof-fans.org, where you will find contact information for the key government offices and public officials involved in the Title IX fight.

January 29, 2003

The Malpractice Crisis

Have you been watching television news or television news magazine shows lately about the sharp increase in medical malpractice insurance premiums and agitated physicians walking off their jobs in some states? If you have, didn't they leave you with the impression that lawsuits against bad doctors were the cause? And these poor old insurance companies being forced to raise those premiums 30 percent, 40 percent, 70 percent all of a sudden!

Propaganda and slanting the news are going hand-in-hand these days, choreographed by the hidden persuaders hired by the American Medical Association together with the behind-the-scenes lobbyists of the gouging insurance companies.

Why in the world would some physicians be willing tools of the insurance companies who are gouging them regardless of whether they are competent, caring doctors or the negligent, incompetent few who account for most of the claims by injured patients? Part of the answer is that the insurance companies are scaring many doctors with specters of litigation volume that simply do not exist.

Malpractice cases filed and actual payments in constant dollars have been level for many years; about nine of ten malpractice incidents do not result in any lawsuits being filed, according to various studies. Yet the human toll is deadly. A Harvard study estimated that gross malpractice, just in hospitals, takes 80,000 American lives a year plus causing hundreds of thousands of serious injuries.

Good physicians should delve deeper into the way medical malpractice insurers do their accounting, their reserving, and their actual practices. If physicians would total the entire amount of premiums they paid last year and divide it evenly by all the physicians practicing in the United States, the average premium is less than $10,000 per doctor per year. Very manageable.

So why are some doctors paying $50,000 or $100,000 a year to their malpractice insurers? Because the companies have learned in the past thirty years to overclassify their risk pools, thereby reducing their number to specific specialties like obstetrics or orthopedic surgery in order to charge much more. In addition, by not surcharging the few bad physicians in these specialties (known as experience loss rating), the good specialists pay as much as incompetent ones with a large number of payouts to their wounded patients.

There is another political benefit for this kind of overclassification. When obstetricians are gouged, they scream loudly, threaten not to deliver babies or actually go on strike. This makes perfect visuals for television: crying babies and physicians in their garb blaming trial lawyers, who after all still have to persuade juries and judges (the latter being mostly former business lawyers). Meanwhile, the insurance companies are laughing all the way to the bank.

There are no visuals for the slowly dying and other human casualties who receive neither justice nor compassion nor compensation. Nor do people like Donald J. Zuk get any television time. Mr. Zuk, chief executive of SCPIE Holdings Inc., a leading malpractice insurer in the West, told the *Wall Street Journal* (June 24, 2002) in a very revealing analysis, "I don't like to hear insurance company executives say it's the tort injury-law system; it's self-inflicted."

Neither organized medicine nor the insurance companies are really going after bad doctoring. The AMA's web site does not report any data about incompetent or crooked physicians who give medicine a bad name. And loss prevention is something the insurance companies leave to professors of insurance to talk about.

Instead both lobbies are funding and pressing legislators to enact laws that politicize the courts, tie the hands of judges and juries (the only ones who see, hear, and evaluate the evidence before them) and make it harder for innocent men, women, and children to bring tragic cases to court and obtain an adequate award.

A favorite way to achieve this callous goal is to put a $250,000 lifetime cap on pain and suffering. Apart from the fact that some insurance executives make that much in one week, every week, from your premium insurance dollars, consider how such a cap wrecks the innocent in California.

Two-year-old Steve Olson, now twelve, became blind and brain-damaged because the hospital refused to give him a CAT scan that would have detected a growing brain mass. His mother left her job to take care of her son. A jury awarded Steven $7.1 million in noneconomic compensation for his life of darkness, pain, and around-the-clock supervision. But the judge was forced by a California law, that these lobbies now want Congress to enact nationwide, to reduce the amount to $250,000.

Don't think for a moment that restricting your court rights will reduce malpractice premiums for physicians. Not only have past restrictions not done so, but insurance industry and company spokespersons have openly said they will not do so and in some cases have raised premiums right after a state enacted restrictions.

There is an obligation for the many good doctors to speak out. Just a few weeks ago, nine of the doctors from Wheeling Hospital in West Virginia had cost their insurers at least $6.3 million in malpractice claims. Among the damage they caused, wrote the *Charleston Gazette,* was operating on the wrong knee, causing the need for a liver transplant by leaving a surgical clip on an artery, and causing a massive and fatal infection by inadvertently slicing into a patient's stomach.

The whole malpractice insurance premium business amounts to about what this country spends on dog food and is one-half of 1 percent of health care costs in this country. Isn't it about time to focus on malpractice prevention first and foremost, instead of pounding on the rights of hundreds of thousands of Americans who leave their doctors far worse than when they greeted them?

If you want to find out more about "questionable doctors" in your area and how little the state medical licensing boards are doing to protect you, log on to www.citizen.org/hrg/

For more information on the malpractice crisis, go to www.centerjd.org. And get ready to contact your members of Congress before it is too late.

January 3, 2003

Trent Lott—Words and Deeds on Race

Republicans were in a mad scramble earlier this month in a desperate effort to disassociate themselves from Senate Majority Leader Trent Lott's reiterated endorsement of the racist campaign of Strom Thurmond as a candidate for president in 1948.

The public suggestion by their Senate leader that the "country would be better off" if Thurmond's segregation campaign had carried the day fifty-four years ago struck political fear in the heart of Republicans who envisioned Lott's words spurring greater turnouts of African American votes for Democratic candidates and a loss of "moderate" voters on the fringes of their party.

With a roaring fire stoked by the news media talk show hosts and poorly disguised nudges from the White House, Lott was dumped. The Republicans are hoping the move will discourage any more serious inquiries into how the actions of President Bush and the Republican-controlled Congress are crushing the aspirations and the rights of African American citizens and other minorities.

While Republican senators raced to microphones and cameras to express their concern about the needs of minorities, the furor over Lott's remarks may well serve to uncover some of the less publicized secrets about Republican policies, which have continued to create and maintain economic and health divisions between the wealthy and African Americans and other minorities.

The monthly unemployment figures coming out of the Bureau of Labor Statistics are a constant reminder of the gaps. Consistently, the percentage of African Americans without jobs is more than double that of unemployed white citizens. Last month, the labor survey showed that 11 percent of African Americans were unemployed compared to 5.2 percent of white workers.

Before Congress adjourned earlier this month, the Republican leaders and President Bush were in the forefront of a successful effort to block the extension of unemployment benefits that expire after Christmas—a move that hits low-wage African American citizens with little savings particularly hard. The Lott furor led Bush to change his mind in mid-December. The lagging federal minimum wage stands at $5.15 an hour, which doesn't approach anything close to a living wage. Here again, Republican lawmakers—and certainly their leaders—have consistently turned their backs on attempts to provide minimum wage justice for low-wage workers, a high percentage of whom are African Americans and Hispanics.

Probably nothing defines the Republican Party—with or without Trent Lott as its Senate leader—more accurately than the mammoth 2001 tax cut, centerpiece of President Bush's economic policy. The $1.3 trillion tax cut went vastly and disproportionately to the wealthy—40 percent to the richest 1 percent of Americans and only 2 percent to the 20 percent on the lowest economic rungs, which includes a high percentage of African Americans and Hispanics.

Much more devastating over the long run is the fact that the size of the Bush tax cut jeopardizes vital economic and social programs, like health care, jobs, affordable housing, and education—programs so vital to minorities and other low-income citizens. These deprivations come on top of existing discriminatory practices that do not arouse John Ashcroft's Justice Department.

Of those who are HIV or AIDS positive, 43 percent are African American and 20 percent are Hispanic. The infant mortality rate for African American babies in 1995 was 15.1 for every 1,000 live births—nearly two and a half times the death rate for white infants.

Poverty rates for African American families run nearly four times those of white families. More than 28 percent of African American males will enter state or federal prison during their lifetime compared with 4.4 percent of white males, at least in part reflecting discriminatory treatment.

Yet, we have a Republican administration that believes tax cuts for the wealthy and many breaks for the big corporations are the national priority. That may not sound as harsh as Trent Lott's echoing the battle cry for segregation or commending a racist platform for a presidential candidacy. But in the end an economic and social policy that is designed largely for the well-to-do is discriminatory and destructive to the hopes of low- and moderate-income citizens, a high percentage of whom are minorities.

It is nice that so many Republican senators appeared on television and issued statements to assure the nation that they did not share the Senate Republican leader's belief that Strom Thurmond's 1948 racist Dixiecrat campaign was one of the highlights of our electoral history.

But, the repudiated words won't change the deeds—economic and social policies—that do discriminate and do hold back low- and moderate-income and minority citizens. Republican senators, who issued all those glowing words about their concern for African American citizens, need to realize that they will be judged not by their rhetoric, but by their deeds.

If there is to be no change in policy—no attempt to reach out to the poor and minorities with real programs like prevention of child lead poisoning, redlining or predatory lending, and other economic crimes in the ghettos—they might as well have kept Trent Lott in the saddle. He knows their drill well.

December 26, 2002

Predatory Lending

Sub-prime lenders have been marching up to state legislators around the nation with a stern warning—"enact protections for borrowers and you will trigger a quick and certain reduction of credit for thousands of low-, moderate-, and middle-income borrowers."

But the hard facts coming out of the states with the courage to stop predatory and other unfair lending practices are putting the lie to the lenders' scare campaign.

Last summer, Morgan Stanley, a major financial services firm, surveyed three hundred branch managers and loan officers from five of the largest sub-prime home equity originators and independent mortgage brokers. The conclusion from these frontline sub-prime operators was that predatory lending protections had not significantly dampened loan growth.

That was the finding for Georgia, New York, and North Carolina, which provide the toughest protections, as well as for Connecticut, California, Florida, and Pennsylvania, which have enacted more limited protections against predatory lending practices.

In fact, Morgan Stanley's survey concluded that the more consumer-friendly lending practices required in these states had lowered loan costs and appeared to be boosting volume, not drying up credit.

Morgan Stanley's survey is supported by a study of the North Carolina antipredatory statute conducted by the Center for Responsible Lending.

The Center said no major sub-prime lenders (lenders with more than 1 percent of the market) left North Carolina after enactment of the consumer protections. More important, the organization estimated that the curbs on predatory lending had saved North Carolina consumers at least $100 million in 2000.

Sub-prime borrowers with blemished credit histories are regarded as high risk and, as a result, predatory lenders take advantage of their vulnerability and weak bargaining position, charging them inflated interest rates and loan points, attaching costly "add-ons" like credit insurance, luring them into repeated fee-ridden refinancings and unaffordable repayment plans. Some of the predatory interest rates range up to 8 percent above the average sub-prime rates. The end result is often bankruptcies and foreclosures.

Consumer protections adopted by North Carolina and a handful of other state legislatures have been bright spots in this dismal world of predatory lending. Congress, in contrast, has been paralyzed by massive campaign funds from the entire range of financial interests, including predatory lenders. There have been some brave statements for the record, but nothing even remotely akin to remedial action in the federal legislature.

While Congress looks the other way, the Federal Trade Commission, at least, has weighed in on behalf of consumers. Its most noteworthy effort was a lawsuit against giant Citigroup, charging widespread abusive lending practices and violations of the Truth in Lending Act, the Fair Credit Reporting Act, and the Equal Credit Opportunity Act.

Jodie Bernstein, director of FTC's Bureau of Consumer Protection, said Citigroup's newly acquired affiliate, Associates First Capital, engaged in a wide variety of deceptive practices.

"They hid essential information from consumers, misrepresented loan terms, flipped loans, and packed in optional fees to raise the costs of the loans," Bernstein charged.

In September, Citigroup threw in the towel and entered into a $215 million settlement with FTC. The fund will be distributed among the victims of Citigroup's deceptive lending practices.

Despite FTC's effort against Citigroup predatory lending practices and the adoption of some protections in some states, consumers across the nation continue to be victimized by predatory and near predatory lending practices. The fast-buck, deceptive operators range from the established international giants like Citigroup to the back-alley loan sharks, which are equally adept at separating the poor and the near poor from their hard-earned money.

Knowing Congress is a safe haven against any meaningful federal sanctions on predatory lending, the financial industry—ranging from finance companies to multibillion dollar banks—will be chipping away at what state protections have been enacted and making sure that the idea of consumer protection doesn't spread to other states.

In Georgia, lenders like Chase Manhattan Mortgage Corporation, Ameriquest, Option On, and New Century Financial Corporation are launching new attacks on that state's Fair Lending Law, threatening to leave the state if the law isn't repealed. Hopefully, the findings of recent surveys like those conducted at Morgan Stanley will give state legislators the courage to stand fast on consumer protections for borrowers.

In addition to the state laws, consumers need the protection of a strong federal statute against all aspects of predatory lending in all fifty states. But the nation is faced with one of the most corporate-oriented anticonsumer Congresses in our history. The predatory lenders and other practitioners of deceptive and unfair credit practices fully expect that the Congress will continue to look the other way when consumer credit protections are mentioned.

Two and a half years ago, I asked Federal Reserve Chairman Alan Greenspan about the lack of action and he agreed that "enough was enough" on the excesses of predatory lending. Unfortunately, the Federal Reserve has taken only small steps to curb the practices. Not only the Federal Reserve, but the Comptroller of the Currency, the Federal Deposit Insurance Corporation, and the Office of Thrift Supervision need to place a priority on ending this outrageous gouging of innocent low- and moderate- and middle-income families.

November 22, 2002

Insuring Medical Malpractice

About eighty thousand Americans die every year (and many more are harmed) in hospitals from medical incompetence, neglect, or worse, according to the Harvard School of Public Health report. To make matters worse, the Republicans in the Congress are pushing to pass legislation to drastically restrict the compensation for pain and suffering that state and federal courts can award to the unfortunate plaintiffs.

Prodded and funded by the insurance and medical lobbies, these politicians, who always bray for states' rights, are callously handcuffing the judges and juries who are the only ones who actually see and hear the evidence on any individual case before them.

By absentee fiat, the House of Representatives recently passed a bill that says to parents of brain-damaged infants, people who are seriously misdiagnosed, and patients who are incapacitated for life, that they can only obtain $250,000 for their pain and suffering over a lifetime from the perpetrators of their harm. That is what some big-shot insurance CEOs make in one week!

The insurance companies are going through another one of their brutish economic cycles. Whenever interest rates and the stock market decline, sharply, reducing their return on investments, they move to sharply increase premiums over the doctors and hospitals. To justify their price increases they attack the civil justice or tort law system as out of control with huge verdicts doing them in. We have seen this cycle in the mid-seventies and mid-eighties; now it is happening again.

Amid the din of OBGYNs leaving their practices due to high premiums, and the insurance industry's huge propaganda machine with the rest of the wrongdoers' lobby, some critical facts are being obscured.

The medical malpractice crisis is, as *Business Week* magazine once pointed out, medical malpractice. But it is also the insurance companies' strategy of overclassification of different physician specialties, thereby reducing the number of insured people, for neurosurgeons, for example, which results in skyrocketing premiums for a few doctors. Instead of spreading the risk and using experience loss rating (surcharging the malpracticing repeaters), the companies like to squeeze OBGYNs and other specialties, in some cities with premiums that can exceed $100,000 a year. These physicians, instead of looking at why the insurance companies are gouging them, roar at the state and federal legislatures to curb the rights of patients to have their full day in court.

What the physicians should tell the insurance companies who are gouging them is this: "Insurance companies are paying victims of medical negligence, on average, approximately $30,000. Average payouts have stayed virtually flat for the last decade. According to the National Center for State Courts, there has been no change in the volume of medical malpractice cases in the last five years. Eight times as many patients are injured by medical malpractice as have ever filed a claim; sixteen times as many suffer injuries as receive any compensation. And get this: the average medical malpractice insurance premium per doctor in the United States during the year 2000 was under $8,000—less than half what an experienced medical receptionist made that year.

Granted there are some large verdicts and punitive damages, which are widely publicized and are almost always settled for far less before appeal or are cut back or reversed on appeal.

Read this especially. The sum total payment to victims of medical malpractice in verdicts and settlements, as a percentage of national health care expenditures, is at an all-time low, about one-half of 1 percent.

The medical profession and state licensing boards need to come down harder on the 5 percent of all physicians who account for the bulk of the malpractice. Prevention of malpractice in hospitals, nursing homes, HMOs, and drug companies could be one of the largest life-saving and injury reduction missions in the United States that has a chance of expeditious success. The physicians at Harvard estimated the cost of such malpractice to families and the economy annually to be at least $60 billion.

There is much more to learn regarding medical malpractice. For more information, log onto www.Centerjd.org, which is the web site for the nonprofit Center for Justice and Democracy.

October 17, 2002

"Bankruptcy Reform"

Margaret Dickens in University City, Missouri was having a tough time with mounting bills. She was a perfect target for a finance company that offered to refinance her 7.5 percent home mortgage with a $65,000 loan at 12.5 percent interest plus up-front fees of $11,600 including points and a single-premium credit life insurance policy.

But Mrs. Dickens isn't alone as a victim of predatory lending that often pushes borrowers into foreclosures and bankruptcies. Take the case of a sixty-eight-year-old former cleaning woman in Atlanta, Georgia who was coaxed into refinancing her home six times. In the end she had to default when the loan costs took more than 60 percent of her pension. A couple in Chicago was lured into an expensive loan consolidation to pay for the husband's triple by-pass heart surgery—a loan that carried up-front fees and charges representing 7 percent of the loan amount, all secured by a new $98,500 mortgage on their home at 12 percent interest. Millions of other consumers are being led into unmanageable debt by credit card companies that are using the mail and telecommunication solicitors to bombard consumers with unsolicited credit card offers promising easy instant credit.

Recent class action lawsuits and regulatory agency complaints against credit card companies have revealed a growing list of unscrupulous practices designed to rip off consumers, including charging late fees even when payments are received on time; advertising deceptive "teaser" interest rates that quickly skyrocket into unaffordable double-digit interest rates; worthless add-ons of high-cost credit life insurance; false promises to eliminate annual fees; charges for processing applications; and frequent increases in credit limits without regard to the ability of the credit card holder to repay.

So, what is Congress doing to protect consumers against these growing credit scams? The answer: nothing. In fact, Congress is on the verge of becoming a willing accomplice by making it easier for the credit merchants to collect from borrowers caught in impossible debt situations.

The legislation is going under the banner of "Bankruptcy Reform"—a classic euphemism in a Congress addicted to misnomers. In reality, the legislation guts the Bankruptcy Code and, in effect, turns the bankruptcy courts into collection agencies for the biggest financial corporations, credit card companies, car dealers, entertainment companies, and gambling casinos.

Eliminated by the legislation would be the concept that bankruptcy is designed to provide a second chance—a fresh start for citizens trapped in unmanageable debt, very often the result of illness, loss of jobs, and unscrupulous and predatory lending practices.

Key to the demands of the banks and credit card companies is a provision that imposes a tough and inflexible means test that will bar all but the most destitute from filing under Chapter 7 of the Bankruptcy Code, which now allows bankruptcy judges to grant consumers relief from impossible debt burdens.

"They've decided it's time to lock the door on the bankruptcy courthouse," says Elizabeth Warren, a Harvard law professor and bankruptcy specialist. "The point of this bill is to squeeze people out of bankruptcy altogether, turning debtors into annuities—they'll make payments to the credit card companies forever."

What this means is that thousands of wage earners, entrapped in these congressionally sanctioned "debtors' prisons without parole," will not be able to rebuild their lives as productive citizens with the ability to provide properly for their families. The long-term impact on many low-, moderate-, and middle-income families is likely to be devastating, not only in terms of human misery, but in consequences for the economy and future welfare costs.

Sadly, members of Congress aren't paying attention to independent experts like Harvard's Elizabeth Warren. Instead, they are listening to their generous benefactors—banks and other financial corporations that have poured millions of dollars into lobbying and campaign donations in the effort to eliminate protections for consumers facing bankruptcy. The National Consumer Bankruptcy Coalition, which includes Visa, MasterCard, the American Bankers Association, and the American Financial Services Association, contributed more than five million dollars to federal parties and candidates during the 1999–2000 election cycle, according to the Center for Responsive Politics.

MBNA America Bank, a giant credit card operator, contributed $3.1 million to political campaigns last year and was the overall top contributor to George Bush's presidential campaign.

The Center for Responsive Politics says that banks, credit unions, and finance companies contributed $30 million during the last election. Gambling interests, including some of Las Vegas's biggest casinos that are also pushing for the bankruptcy legislation, contributed $9.4 million. The Recording Industry Association of America, which has asked Congress to crack down on recording artists who file for bankruptcy and get out of record deals, contributed $451,488 in the last election cycle.

Congress apparently has swallowed a lot of the business propaganda about abuse of the current bankruptcy system. U.S. Chamber of Commerce President Tom Donohue, for example, lauded the Senate passage of the lenders' bankruptcy bill with these words: "The Senate took a critical step today to prevent wealthy debtors from passing the tab for mountains of debt on to businesses and consumers."

But the facts support neither the Chamber's statement nor congressional passage of the legislation. A national study conducted by bankruptcy judges in 1999 found that the median income of debtors seeking bankruptcy protection was $21,500—"wealthy" by no one's standards. The bankruptcy legislation is still in a House-Senate conference, but its proponents are pushing for a quick end to the conference and a vote on final passage in the next few weeks. The vote on final passage will speak loudly about where individual members stand on consumer justice versus the demands for special favors by the biggest financial corporations and a collection of their allies, like car dealers and gambling casinos. There is still time to let your senators and representatives know that you oppose wiping out key consumer bankruptcy protections. The telephone number for the House of Representatives is 202-225-3121; the Senate is 202-224-3121.

May 14, 2002

Payday Loans

Payday loans, refinancing schemes, and other forms of predatory lending have left many low- and moderate-income neighborhoods as financial wastelands. Sleazy lenders and the fast-buck merchants seem able to carry out their rip-offs with little or no effective opposition from authorities.

It may be infrequent, but every now and then there are thin slivers of light that give these neighborhoods renewed hope that someone is paying attention to the scams and is willing to help punish the bad actors who prey on the poor and the unsuspecting consumers.

One of these bright spots was furnished recently by Mel Martinez, the Secretary of Housing and Urban Development. Moving to enforce the long-unenforced Real Estate Settlement Procedures Act (RESPA), the HUD secretary obtained more than $2,250,000 in payments for violations involving illegal kickbacks and referrals in connection with home loans. The settlements include agreements with First American Corporation, Transamerica, Conseco Finance Corporation, ARVIDA/JMB Partners, and Central Pacific Mortgage Corporation.

The money from the settlements will be used to provide consumer housing counseling and education, refunds to home buyers, and payments to the government. Since the first of the year, HUD has brought thirty-eight other smaller cases and obtained monetary settlements from lenders found in violation of the antikickback provisions of RESPA.

Secretary Martinez's efforts to improve enforcement of RESPA have roots in his former job as a County Commissioner in Florida. He proudly describes his battles in Florida to stop lending and real estate abuses. So, there is reason to hope that the secretary will be encouraged to move forward from his recent successes to launch a full-scale nationwide campaign by HUD against lending and related housing scams. The secretary, I believe, would agree that HUD's effort to date is only a beginning.

There is also some light visible at the end of the tunnel on "payday lending" in at least two states, Indiana and North Carolina. A decision by the Indiana Supreme Court eliminated the ability of payday lenders to charge fees that translate into an annual percentage rate of about 420 percent.

In North Carolina, consumers were successful in getting the legislature to reject efforts by the lending industry to reenact a free-wheeling payday lending law that had expired under a "sunset" clause. The language eliminated by the sunset clause would have allowed fees that would have been tantamount to a 420 percent interest rate on an annual basis.

In North Carolina and Indiana, the legislative and court victories curbed abuses by small payday lenders. But the big interstate operators found a loophole. The larger payday operators may "partner" with out-of-state banks to circumvent state law under the "doctrine of exportation." This allows a bank chartered in a deregulated state to ignore the usury law in the borrower's home state, wiping out that state's ability to protect its citizens.

(Under "payday lending," the lender cashes a consumer's check and holds it against his next paycheck, often charging interest rates of 400 to 500 percent or more. And many lenders continue to allow the debt to be rolled over past the next pay day as interest charges mount.)

As encouraging as the actions are at HUD and in Indiana and North Carolina, predatory lending remains a huge—and cruel—problem nationwide. It is sapping the resources of already poor families and placing at risk the efforts to rebuild inner-city neighborhoods and depressed rural areas.

Congress spent six years rewriting the laws that govern the nation's financial corporations. When the bill was finally enacted in 1999, the sponsors called it "modernization," but it was little more than a Clinton-signed lucrative giveaway to the biggest banks, securities firms, and insurance companies. Efforts to provide protections for consumers against predatory lending were tossed aside as unnecessary in this new financial world. Consumers didn't even get the crumbs. As a result, the scam artists have been emboldened to extend their rip-offs across more of the population.

For more information on predatory lending, contact: National Consumer Law Center, 77 Summer Street, Boston, MA 02110

December 12, 2001

Ashcroft: Anti-Civil Liberties

Good law enforcement officials know that their success depends heavily on retaining the confidence of their communities. Blunderbuss police methods, which ignore citizen rights and single out racial, ethnic, and religious minorities for unfair and discriminatory treatment, risk losing public support so critical to law enforcement and public safety in a democratic system. They undermine the basic rule-of-law values that underlie our freedoms and democracy.

It is a lesson that the nation's chief law enforcement officer—Attorney General John Ashcroft—seems to have missed. In the wake of the September 11 attacks, the American public left little doubt that it wanted improved security measures. Instead of seizing on the sentiment to develop a responsible program to upgrade security, the attorney general is playing recklessly on the public's fear in an effort to gain support for draconian measures that skirt the Constitution and shred civil liberties.

Not only does the attorney general's program do damage to the very citizen rights that the nation has gone to war to protect in the past, but it deceives the public into believing that national security and adherence to our Constitution are incompatible. That is a false and dangerous philosophy that actually weakens our country, damaging the fabric of our democracy for years to come. It is regrettable that a high public official—who has sworn to uphold and defend the Constitution—would lead such an assault.

For many Ashcroft watchers, the attorney general's machinations are no great surprise. His record as a senator provided little hope for an evenhanded approach to civil liberties. The close 58 to 42 Senate vote for his confirmation as attorney general reflects the unease that many felt about giving him the reins at the Justice Department.

Ashcroft justice has included:

• The secret detention of more than 1,200 people with the Justice Department providing only vague and shifting explanations for the action. As the *New York Times* editorialized, the administration seems to have "no credible reason" to believe the detainees are dangerous beyond a vague concern that among them might be a "future law-breaker."

• Questioning by the FBI, under Ashcroft's authority, of more than 5,000 people, mostly men 18 to 30 of Middle Eastern background, in a random open-ended fishing expedition. The U.S. Attorney's office in Detroit is sending out letters in the area, which has a large Arab immigrant community, asking recipients to come in to be interviewed. The letter says, "Your name was brought to our attention because among other things you came to Michigan on a visa from a country where there are groups that support, advocate or finance international terrorism." Some local law enforcement officials have resisted efforts by the FBI to enlist them in the dragnet. The police chief of Portland, Oregon, for example, refused to participate in the random questioning on the ground that Oregon law prohibits the interrogation of immigrants legally in this country and not suspected of having committed a crime.

• Establishment of special military tribunals, which would replace civilian courts, to try any noncitizen that the president suspects is involved in international terrorism of any type or to be harboring or abetting terrorists. Unlike regular military courts, the special tribunals would be allowed to operate in secret, to withhold evidence from defendants, and to deny their choice of lawyers. The defendants in a special tribunal could be sentenced to death by a two-thirds vote of the military judges. In contrast, military courts may sentence a defendant to death only on a unanimous vote of the judges.

• Authorizing eavesdropping of lawyers' conversations with clients who are suspected terrorists—a clear violation of the attorney-client privilege and a major impediment to the preparation of a proper defense to the charges.

• Consideration of a plan to relax longtime restrictions on the FBI's spying on religious and political organizations in the United States.

• Abandonment of the long-standing principle that the Constitution and its Bill of Rights applies to all persons in the United States, including noncitizens. Our Bill of Rights and other constitutional guarantees are not mere conveniences to be discarded in time of crisis. They are carefully considered, fundamental rights that provide a measure of security for each citizen from abuses of government power. They represent the values we hold dear. And they are perfectly compatible with effective law enforcement and protection of national security.

We should not appear to be so weak as to destroy our own values in the fight against anti-American terrorism. People around the world support us because of freedoms and civil liberties that we promote and cherish. We do not help our cause in the court of world opinion if we walk away so easily from our real strengths as a free people. This is especially relevant to the credibility of our government's criticism of secret trials and human rights violations in foreign countries.

The attorney general is out of control. Rather than reassuring citizens,

Attorney General Ashcroft is scaring people who see him as a reckless official all too eager to abandon civil liberties and Constitutional protections. John Ashcroft is the wrong man, at the wrong time, in the wrong place. If he does not change his course and support due process and long-established legal practices, Ashcroft should step aside and allow the president to select a law enforcement official who believes in upholding the rule of law under the Constitution of our country.

December 6, 2001

Homeland Housing

President Bush is putting a big stake in the newly formed office of Homeland Security under the leadership of former Pennsylvania Governor Tom Ridge. The rationale behind the formation of the office is a belief that the coordination of the disparate agencies with responsibility for security will provide the nation with a more effective and focused net of protections in the wake of the September 11 attacks.

If the president sees coordination as a means of focusing attention and action on security problems, he should take a hard look at some domestic programs—particularly those that have an impact on inner-city neighborhoods and low- and moderate-income families. Millions of citizens continue to fall through holes in underfunded safety nets administered by a multitude of departments and agencies scattered across the federal landscape. Each agency manages to manufacture glowing reports of their accomplishments, but no single official or department has the authority or standing to pull together scattered efforts and mobilize funding and public opinion behind efforts to rebuild our inner-city neighborhoods.

As a result, efforts to develop inner cities continue to lag far behind. The Clinton administration was long on rhetoric, but short on developing a coherent urban policy that would have focused long-term congressional and broad public concern about the needs of low- and moderate-income and minority neighborhoods.

Housing is a good example of the federal government's uncoordinated approach to the problems of the poor. The nation is five to six million units short of needed units of affordable housing and millions of existing units are dilapidated and in need of major repair. In the organizational manual, the Department of Housing and Urban Development is listed as the lead agency on housing, but in reality what housing gets built and where is largely under the control of two heavily subsidized government-sponsored corporations—

Fannie Mae and Freddie Mac—whose political power has made them virtually untouchable. The coordination between HUD and these corporations is tenuous. The sad condition of many of our inner-city neighborhoods suggests just how well this coordination is working.

Nearly 20 percent of the nation's children live in poverty, most of them in inner-city neighborhoods and depressed rural areas. By adding the children in the "near poverty" category (below 200 percent of the poverty line), the figure rises to 43 percent, according to the National Center for Children in Poverty. The current rate of child poverty is higher than in 1979 and is two to six times higher than in most other major Western nations. For African Americans, the child poverty rate is 33 percent and for Latinos, 30 percent.

High rates of infant mortality remain a sad part of inner cities. African American mortality rates are nearly 15 for every 1,000 live births, nearly twice the average for the rest of the population.

The Department of Labor and the Health and Human Services Department have statutory responsibilities for programs that bear on the health, welfare, and job opportunities of inner-city residents. How could these programs and authorities be integrated in a coordinated assault on the ills that plague many low- and moderate-income neighborhoods?

While the nation is focusing on homeland security, is anyone really concentrating on what the growing economic downturn will mean to working families, the already poor, and the near poor? No one wants to reduce security to a "hit or miss" approach. But unless there is an immediate effort to repair and coordinate the safety nets, it is going to be just that kind of chancy life for the millions who lose jobs.

A time bomb is ticking on President Clinton's 1996 welfare bill, which set a five-year lifetime limit on continued welfare payments to needy families. Food stamps and unemployment compensation cover only part of the growing number of needy as jobs are lost.

The Bush administration and Congress have demonstrated that they can move fast in an emergency. It is an open secret that some of the speed has been generated by an overanxious desire to take care of corporate interests and wealthy taxpayers while the public is preoccupied with war in Afghanistan and the aftermath of the September 11 attacks.

Now let's see if they can get their act together to launch and coordinate government resources in a new effort to rectify an old problem—the neglect of inner-city neighborhoods and low- and moderate-income and minority citizens who populate many of these communities.

The president has made an appeal for pulling together all the government apparatus in a coordinated effort to strengthen security. True security rests with the people. The president should recognize that by assuring no one is left behind, including those who have long suffered the neglect of many inner-city neighborhoods, the nation will be stronger and more secure for it.

But as the recent lead headline in the Torrington (CT) *Register-Citizen* emblazoned—"It's Very Scary—No Food for the Poor." The nature of our national leadership's priorities remains seriously imbalanced.

November 20, 2001

Congress Hides Votes

Members of Congress are continuing to play hide-and-seek with their legislative records. Only two congressmen, Republican Representatives Christopher Shays of Connecticut and Frank Wolf of Virginia, have placed their voting records on the Internet in a searchable format easily accessible to citizens. Not a single U.S. senator has been willing to use the Internet in a manner that would give voters an open, accurate, and quick way to track their votes.

Thanks to the taxpayers, computers equipped with Internet access are available in the offices of every one of the 535 members of the U.S. Senate and the House of Representatives. Posting voting records on their web sites in a searchable citizen-friendly format would be a simple task.

So, why the reluctance to implement something that would make it easy for voters to understand how their elected representatives were performing their official duties? After all, members of Congress are famous for ringing "Fourth of July" pronouncements in favor of open government.

Flowery speeches about the public's right-to-know notwithstanding, most members of Congress are guided by the age-old political rule: "What the voters don't know can't hurt you on election day." If voters could pull up easy-to-read details on their computer screens about every vote a senator or a representative makes during a term, there might well be some very surprised voters and a lot of red-faced members of Congress in need of quick explanations.

This summer two members of my staff—Noel Dingboom and Mark Wittink—worked with congressional interns in a survey of Senate and House offices to determine attitudes about the posting of voting records in a searchable format on the Internet. The answers were disappointing with most members falling back on claims that votes were available on other Internet sites, including those managed by various private organizations. Some of the explanations for the failure of members to post their own records seemed to translate into something akin to "the constituents are too dumb to understand" an unvarnished straightforward rendition of a congressional voting record.

Reliance on private groups is tricky, at best. Most compile voting records in a manner to support their own policy positions. Others are very selective about the issues and votes they list. And members of Congress have a long history of attempting to discredit as biased any group that publishes a voting record that makes their record look bad. The welter of competing voting records by private organizations often serve only to further mislead the public, and make it easier for politicians to spin a false picture of their performance.

It is true, as many offices cited, that the Library of Congress, through a service dubbed "Thomas," carries votes in conjunction with its Internet tracking of activity on the floor of the House and Senate. The service is useful, but the process of extracting and compiling votes of individual members from "Thomas" is too cumbersome and time consuming to be practical for most citizens. The same is true for the Congressional Record printed by the Government Printing Office. Unfortunately, sometimes Congress is able to rig the parliamentary procedures so that some items can slip through without a vote. One of these was a $4,900 raise for all members which was allowed to go into effect earlier this month without a vote.

Representative Wolf, one of the two pro-voting record members of the House of Representatives, believes that the posting of how he votes on very issue is one of his responsibilities as a congressman. "I have always treated my office as a great public trust," Wolf says. "That includes letting the people I represent know how I have voted on all matters coming before Congress."

The need for Congress to make voting records available in the widest and most accessible manner is heightened by the media's failure to report individual votes on all but the most heavily publicized issues. Newspapers carry hundreds of column inches of stock market quotes, baseball box scores, horse racing statistics, and long lists of guests at White House dinners and major social events. But they deem it too difficult to compile and print the voting records of members of Congress who decide the fate of legislation that has a significant effect on wide segments of the population.

It is little wonder that frequently fewer than 40 percent of the eligible voters turn out in biennial elections to select their senators and representatives. And millions of those who do arrive at the polls have only the most surface information about what their sitting senator or representative has been doing in Washington. Incumbents like to keep it that way. That's one of the big reasons members of Congress aren't rushing to the computer to set up searchable voting record compilations on their web sites. Most of them think that their self-serving newsletters provide all the information that the voters need to know about how they are performing in Washington.

Information is the oxygen of democracy. It is also the basic ingredient that builds and maintains confidence and accountability in government. At a minimum, citizens have a right to know in detail the positions that their representatives take on legislation. Congress should adopt a rule that would require all members to list their voting record on the Internet in an easily accessed, searchable format by member name, bill subject, and bill title. This would be a giant step forward in efforts to ensure an informed electorate—and a more accountable Congress. Citizens should contact their senators and representatives and ask why this isn't being done. They can be reached through the Capitol switchboard—202-224-3121 for senators; 202-225-3121 for representatives.

November 14, 2001

Protecting Consumer Privacy

The Fourth Amendment to the U.S. Constitution spells out the right of citizens to be "secure in their persons, houses, papers and effects against unreasonable searches" by their government.

When that amendment was ratified in 1791, no one imagined that it would be corporations, not governments, that would use their vast power to invade the privacy of citizens and, in effect, carry out unreasonable searches of the most intimate personal data.

But that is exactly what is happening, particularly among newly formed giant financial conglomerates that have access to a mass of data collected about millions of individuals by their far-flung insurance, bank, credit card, and securities affiliates. Today, these giant corporations can assemble information to build a head-to-toe profile of most citizens and their buying and personal habits, including what prescription and nonprescription health products they use, as well as their investments, income, employment histories, and entertainment preferences.

For this, consumers can thank the Clinton administration and a bipartisan group of senators and representatives who lacked the courage to really defend citizens' right to privacy when the so-called Financial Modernization legislation moved through the Congress in 1999. This law is the vehicle that allows banks, securities firms, and insurance companies to merge as parts of financial conglomerates.

People like Democratic Representative Ed Markey of Massachusetts and Republican Senator Richard Shelby of Alabama fought hard to give citizens the right to control where and when their personal information was sold or used in any manner not authorized in writing in advance by you, the consumer-owner of the information. In short, under the Markey-Shelby approach consumers would have to "opt-in" in writing specifically authorizing the use of the information. Without this written affirmative permission from the consumer, the corporations could not sell, share, or use the data for any purpose beyond that specifically agreed to by the consumer.

The industry, however, believed (correctly) that few consumers would give permission to have their information shared with unknown persons and corporations. They lobbied, successfully, for an opt-out system, which would require consumers to send in a form indicating that they were opposed. The burden was on the consumer to "opt out." If they forgot the form or failed to send it in or could not understand the legal jargon, the company would be free to distribute the personal information anywhere or to anyone it chose.

The industry lobbyists threatened to walk away from the legislation if the Shelby-Markey opt-in was adopted. The Clinton administration and a bipartisan majority in the Congress surrendered to the threats and left privacy protections to the financial industry's demand for a weak, ineffectual, opt-out approach.

The industry has sent out more than a billion of the opt-out notices as required by law. Most of them have been stuffed in the envelopes with a variety of miscellaneous promotional brochures accompanying monthly billing statements. Financial consultants who are following the issue estimate that only about 5 percent of the opt-out notices are being returned—the remainder tossed in the trash unnoticed and unread.

Further rendering the opt-out approach nearly useless is the fact that many of the notices are written clumsily with little attempt to explain the consumers' rights in clear understandable language. Some appear to have been copied verbatim from technical federal regulations without translation into language that would help consumers take proper action to protect their privacy.

"People don't read them, and they don't understand them," Karen Petrou, a leading financial consultant, told a banking conference in Washington recently. That was exactly what the financial lobbyists were betting on when they pushed the opt-out language on a willing Congress.

Despite the shortcomings of the opt-out approach, consumer organizations and the media should do everything possible to publicize the existence of the opt-out possibilities and to encourage consumers to protect their privacy by sending in the opt-out forms immediately. But the only truly effective means of controlling the wholesale invasion of privacy is for Congress to flatly prohibit the distribution of personal information unless the consumer has specifically authorized it in writing in advance.

Your personal information belongs to you. You do not authorize its wholesale distribution just because you have provided information to a bank for a specific limited purpose such as a home mortgage. The bank should not have the right to sell or share that information for any other purpose unless you authorize it in writing and know specifically what information is being released and to whom.

Your personal information is your personal property. You should demand that the financial institutions you deal with so treat it. And you should demand to know how your senator or representative voted when the Financial Modernization Act was adopted in November, 1999 with a weak, industry-supported, opt-out provision attached.

For further information on privacy, contact: U.S. PIRG, 218 D Street, SE, Washington, D.C. 20003; www.pirg.org/consumer/optout.htm

June 21, 2001

Lending Rip-offs

Earlier this year, a magnificent joint investigative effort by the *New York Times* and the American Broadcasting Company's "20-20" program threw a rare spotlight on the shady practices that predatory lenders use to rip off citizens in low- and moderate-income and minority neighborhoods.

The series got enough national attention to prompt congressional Democrats and Republicans into producing piles of news releases lamenting the practices. Nine months later with the news releases long forgotten, Congress is preparing to adjourn without any meaningful action to curb the excesses.

The Federal Reserve conducted limited hearings and the Treasury Department and the Department of Housing and Urban Development issued a joint report on predatory lending. But, new regulations that might actually put teeth in the efforts to curb the rip-offs haven't appeared. Instead, there has been a lot of talk about collecting data and the "need for more evidence."

"We should be able to agree that more information is an important prerequisite to sensible policies in this area," Federal Reserve Governor Edward Gramlich said recently. Translated, the Federal Reserve is letting us know that tough action against the predators, if it's ever to happen, is a long way off.

This "go slow" approach is a far cry from the gung-ho attitude of Federal Reserve Board Chairman Alan Greenspan when he was lobbying for immediate passage of massive deregulation of the financial services industry last year. Then speed was the word of the day, and calls for more information on the impact of deregulation on financial stability and safety or on consumer and taxpayer protections were dismissed.

At the Federal Reserve and in Congress, it is one thing for the nation's biggest banks, insurance companies, and securities firms to want action on their desires. It's quite another when low- and moderate-income citizens want action to protect them against financial predators. Then the important question, as Governor Gramlich tells us, is the collection of more information, not quick remedial action.

While the Federal Reserve's leisurely collection of data inches forward, citizens continue to be ripped off by predatory lenders employing extortionate interest rates, outlandishly high fees, refinancing and home equity scams, balloon payments, and a welter of other deceptive practices. High-priced credit is pushed on unsuspecting borrowers who don't have the income to meet the mounting payments. At the end of all too many of these cases are foreclosures, bankruptcy, and further deterioration of neighborhoods.

Even without the scourge of this new generation of predatory lenders, the poor face a multitude of barriers when they attempt to obtain credit and other financial services at a fair and reasonable cost.

An estimated 22 million Americans do not have bank accounts. This means that these citizens must turn to check-cashing firms, liquor stores, loan sharks, and other costly means to carry out their financial transactions.

This has spawned a new rip-off enterprise—payday loans. Faced with the need for emergency cash, consumers borrow against their next paycheck, at annual percentage rates ranging up to 500 percent or more. Lacking cash, many low-income families obtain appliances, television sets, and other products from "rent to own" stores where charges usually amount to two and three times the value of the item. On a $200 television set, a consumer may pay $500 to $600 over the life of a rent-to-own contract.

Banks establish few branches in low-income neighborhoods. Even more difficult for poor citizens is the fact that banks, for the most part, don't make small loans, the kind of credit that low-income citizens need to avoid the high-priced loans peddled by "payday" operators and loan sharks. Credit unions, particularly community development credit unions, are an answer, but too little is being done to promote them. This should be a priority for the credit union movement, the next administration, and the Congress.

For too long, the agendas of the regulatory agencies, the Congress, and the executive branch have been oriented to the care and feeding of the biggest financial corporations. Washington needs to be shamed into devoting just a fraction of its time, money, and muscle to shape a financial system that serves everyone, including the poor on a fair basis.

December 13, 2000

Advancing Voter Participation

More than half of all voting-age Americans do not vote. If we are to prevent the further withering of our democracy and the entrenchment of plutocracy, we must take steps to spur dramatically enhanced voter participation.

Here are some steps we should take to revitalize our democracy:

• End legalized bribery and support publicly financed campaigns.

• Year after year, big business invests in politicians and political parties by giving them millions of dollars, and then, those businesses get corporate welfare and tax breaks worth billions of dollars. This must end.

The biggest single obstacle to honest, just government action—government of, by, and for the people—is the corruption of our election campaigns by special interest money. No one should have to sell out to big business in order to run a competitive campaign.

Political campaigns should be publicly financed, just like public libraries, parks, and schools.

• Take back the airwaves and provide free time for ballot-qualified candidates: The airwaves belong to the people, not the media corporations. We let them use the airwaves for radio and television broadcasting free of charge year after year, and then they collect hundreds of millions of dollars from political candidates paying for ads.

There should be some free time on radio and television for all ballot-qualified candidates during election seasons.

• Include everyone in elections by adopting same-day voter registration.

• Just when most people get excited about politics, in the few weeks before the election, it is too late to register to vote in most states. Millions of people who want to vote are turned away from the polls, simply because they didn't register a month ahead of time. We need election-day voter registration in all fifty states, not just the six states that use it now. Jesse Ventura, governor of Minnesota, says he wouldn't have won without same-day registration.

• Give voters the information they want by opening the presidential debates: The presidential debates are controlled by the corporate-funded, Democrat- and Republican-controlled Commission on Presidential Debates, which has set arbitrary, unfair rules to exclude third-party candidates and the issues they represent from the televised debates.

We must open the debates to legitimate third-party candidates who are on the ballot in enough states to actually win the election, who meet a minimal threshold of demonstrated support, or those whom a majority of Americans want to see in the debates. Polls show that 64 percent of Americans wanted to see a four-way presidential debate this year.

• Open up the two-party system by adopting proportional representation.

The two major parties, thanks to their addiction to special interest money, are converging into one corporate party with two heads. This leaves voters who are longing for alternatives without any significant choice on the ballot.

It is time to stop saying that we are going to surrender to a winner-take-all political system. We need a discussion about proportional representation, which gives electoral seats to those winning substantial vote counts that are short of a plurality. With proportional representation, more votes count, there is greater voter turnout, and the priorities of more citizens will be represented in government.

• Gauge public opinion at the polls by initiating a national nonbinding advisory referendum.

• We should put forth nonbinding referenda on salient national issues of the day to be voted on during election day.

• Make every vote count by allowing instant runoff voting.

• To win a presidential election, a candidate does not need a majority of votes, just a plurality. President Clinton, for instance, earned less than 50 percent of the vote. We should use the Australian system of instant runoff to ensure that the election winner earns a majority of votes. Voters get to rank the candidates: 1, 2, 3; if no candidate gets a majority of the votes in the first count, the second choices are then counted until one candidate gets a majority. This liberates voters to choose their favorite candidate and ignore the cries of "wasted votes" and "spoilers."

• When there is no one worth your vote, you should have a binding none-of-the-above option.

• In so many elections, there is only one major-party name on the ballot, or a choice between two candidates with few significant differences and little new to offer voters.

Voters should be able to reject the candidates put forth by choosing none-of-the-above, and force a new election with new candidates. This binding measure would give voters an escape hatch out of an unsatisfactory election and give the disaffected a chance to shake things up. Facilitating greater citizen participation can only strengthen our democracy.

November 15, 2000

Statehood for DC!

More than 500,000 people live in the District of Columbia. As the capital of this nation, the District is the symbol of the freedoms for which this nation stands. The light of democracy shines from the District, but does not illuminate this city. The core is hollow. The values of equality and political participation that the city promises are denied right here, in our nation's Capital.

Most Americans do not know, and many would find it hard to believe, that under our current system D.C. residents are second-class citizens. The District is denied local control—Congress must approve the District's budget, and can override any action of the city government. At the same time, District residents do not have even one voting representative in the Congress that controls them. D.C. is effectively a colony, with all local decisions directly subject to change by a Congress largely out of touch with local realities.

Most people who live outside of the District do not know that D.C. citizens pay about $2 billion a year in federal income taxes—more than several states—yet cannot elect people to decide how their money is spent. D.C. residents have served and died in our armed services over the last half century in disproportionately high numbers, but have no representation in the Congress that decides whether or not to go to war. The U.S. is the only democracy in the world that deprives the residents of its capital city the basic rights granted to other citizens.

Even more damaging than the lack of congressional representation is the colonial-style control that Congress exerts over the District. Adding one, or three, D.C. representatives to the 535 members of Congress would, by itself, do little to solve this problem.

Unaccountable power is by its nature abusive. The places where unaccountable power is exercised are, and must be, dysfunctional. Unaccountable power is uninformed. Members of Congress don't know this city. They don't know what's right for its people. They approve the budget and all the legislation, but they do not themselves have to live with their decisions. They foist pet projects on citizens who are perfectly capable of deciding these issues locally. They prevent the District from taxing income where it is earned. They regularly overturn the judgment of local elected officials—on public health, tax, budget, school issues—all with impunity.

Unaccountable power is destructive. It chokes the ability and destroys the responsibility of people to govern themselves. There is no place in the world where second-class citizens live side by side with first-class citizens and fare as well. It just doesn't happen. What happens to a community where the people cannot exercise authority, where there is no democracy? People stop participating. They don't run for local offices. The civic culture of the community withers away.

President Clinton has often objected to Congress's arbitrary use of its colonial power over the District. Last September, he wrote a veto message chiding

Congress for attempting to block District decisions that he correctly argued were local matters in the areas of: advocating statehood, access to special education, abortion, and drug policy, among other issues. But he has not publicly followed his argument to its logical conclusion and called for full local control and self-determination.

The results of congressional interference and the inefficiency of colonial-style management are as distressing as they are predictable. Poverty has increased during a time of economic expansion, with the percentage of residents in poverty going from 16.6 percent in 1988 to an appalling 22.1 percent in 1998. Even more astonishing was the growth in income inequality. The richest 20 percent of D.C. residents earned 16.4 times as much as the poorest 20 percent in the late '80s, and 27.1 times as much in the late '90s.

The voters of the District of Columbia should be allowed to hold a referendum to choose their future status.

Local control is what will make it possible for the District to start fixing its problems. With legislative and appropriations delays, regular governing confusion, and congressional interference eliminated, the District would be more able to deal with its pressing problems. The solution for the problems of democracy is more democracy!

October 18, 2000

Coca-Cola and Race

In a recent annual report, Coca-Cola assured its shareholders that there was plenty of room for growth. The company only sold one billion of the world's 48 billion beverage servings, the annual report noted. "A billion a day is just the beginning," the company proclaimed, "because people still say, 'for all the tea in China.'"

You might think that a company with these kinds of aspirations would be particularly sensitive to ensure that it was respectful of all ethnic groups, that it would go out of its way to avoid providing any basis for charges of racial discrimination.

Apparently, you would be wrong.

A lawsuit filed last year by Coke employees charges the company with a pattern and practice of racial discrimination against African American employees.

Last week, thirty current and former African American Coke employees took a "justice ride" on a bus from Atlanta, where the company is headquartered, to Wilmington, Delaware, where the company was holding its annual shareholder meeting.

The Justice Riders traveled to Wilmington to publicize their case and demand that Coke move to a quick and fair settlement of the dispute.

In their lawsuit, the Coke employees marshaled an impressive array of statistical and anecdotal evidence to buttress their claim of discrimination. They allege:

- African Americans' median salary at Coke's headquarters is about one-third less than those of whites at the headquarters. In 1998, the African American mean was $45,215 while the Caucasian mean was $72,045.
- A "glass ceiling" blocks African Americans from rising to top positions in the company. Although African Americans make up more than 15 percent of the employees at the headquarters, they are vastly underrepresented at top pay-grade levels—and not one member of the senior management team is African American.
- Coke's evaluation system "permits excessively subjective managerial discretion" leading to racial discrimination in evaluations. Since salary and raises are based on this performance evaluation system, this leads to race-based discrimination in pay scales.
- "Since at least 1995, Coca-Cola's senior management and officers, up to and including CEO M. Douglas Invester [since replaced], have known of company-wide discrimination against African Americans."
- In one poignant allegation, the Coke employees charge that "in or about 1996 or 1997, one of the few African American assistant vice presidents attended a meeting in Atlanta with some representatives of bottling companies. He was the only African American at the meeting, but high-level Caucasian marketing executives from Coca-Cola were present. The head of marketing of the bottling company for the state of Alabama introduced himself as the 'Grand Cyclops' of Alabama. Despite the obvious Ku Klux Klan reference, no Company employee responded to this outrageous comment at the Company meeting."

Coke denies the particular allegations in the lawsuit, but says it is "working hard" to resolve the suit quickly.

Company Chair Douglas Daft told shareholders, "This is the most diverse company in the world, and we will be the company that leads the world into a diverse business structure in the twenty-first century."

There is no mystery as to why Coke is eager to settle the suit. Not only does the suit present the company with a substantial outstanding potential liability, but a high proportion of Coke's U.S. sales are to African Americans (as well as Latinos). The employees estimate that about a quarter of Coke Classic and Sprite sales in the United States are to African Americans. Publicity about the case would endanger Coke's sales to these customers.

Indeed, in Wilmington, one of the Coke employee Justice Riders, Larry Jones, called for a Coke boycott.

"In 114 years, you've only had one black senior vice president," he said. "In 114 years, you only found one of us qualified? How long do we wait? We are never going to be anything but black employees. Let's stop buying Coca-Cola."

Unless Coke resolves the lawsuit fairly and quickly, it is likely to find the Justice Riders' boycott call gaining momentum around the country.

April 25, 2000

Congress Weakens Privacy Rights

Privacy is high on the list of rights Americans cherish. Now, the right to our privacy—like many of those rights we take for granted—is at risk.

Federal agencies, led by the Federal Reserve Board, have proposed a "Know Your Customer" regulation that would require banks to monitor their customers' accounts, presumably for the purpose of spotting "unusual" transactions.

Our sources of income would be identified; our transactions would be tracked from month to month to establish a "normal" pattern. Profiles of our financial activity would be assembled. If our financial behavior were to suddenly deviate from this bank-determined profile, we could become the subject of a report to law enforcement officials.

This wholesale invasion of privacy is ostensibly designed to help law enforcement agencies better track criminal activity, specifically the "money laundering" of drug traffickers. Successful prosecution of drug merchants and money launderers are goals supported by an overwhelming majority of the American people.

But vigorous and successful law enforcement in a free country should not depend on wholesale draconian scrutiny of the financial life of tens of millions of American families and businesses.

The public is already up in arms over this legislation. Bankers are concerned that their reputations might be tarnished if they were forced to become "government spies" as part of the Know Your Customer program. As one Indiana banker put it, "America is supposed to be the land of the free....Know Your Customer is a classic example of what this country revolted against."

And the worst is yet to come. An even bigger invasion of privacy is being cooked up in Congress as part of a big financial deregulation bill that is being packaged as "financial modernization."

The bill—H.R. 10—would allow banks, securities firms, insurance companies, and certain industrial corporations to form giant conglomerates. These financial behemoths would act as umbrella corporations for dozens of affiliates involved in everything from stock market transactions to health insurance.

Financial leaders lobbying for this legislation insist that these affiliates be allowed to exchange customer information freely among themselves in "cross-marketing" schemes. Such cross-marketing is the gold that the financial industry hopes to mine under the provisions of H.R. 10.

These newly created financial conglomerates will have unprecedented access to consumers' most sensitive financial information: account balances, CD maturity dates, sources of deposits, medical histories, and detailed data on personal assets. And they'll be able to share this information among themselves, use it as a sales tool, and in many cases, sell it to third parties.

"Financial modernization" has become a code phrase for "violation of privacy."

Efforts by privacy groups and consumer organizations to sound the alarm about this invasion of privacy have been ignored in the House and Senate Banking Committees, which seem determined to enact H.R. 10 regardless of the cost.

The American Association of Retired Persons (AARP) is concerned about what loss of privacy will mean in the lives of the nation's senior citizens. In a letter to the Senate Banking Committee, AARP warned:

"It is clear that elderly Americans are among the most vulnerable to the complex and fundamental changes already occurring in this period of financial transformation—and they will be put at further risk by the financial mergers permitted by this proposed legislation if the issue of information privacy is not addressed."

Unfortunately, federal regulators, members of Congress, and the financial industry are given little attention by the media as they craft these new regulations and laws. If Americans truly cherish their rights, they need to start paying attention to what goes on in the backrooms of Congress and the regulatory agencies, particularly regarding financial issues.

If you are concerned about your financial privacy, contact the Board of Governors of the Federal Reserve, 20th and C Streets N.W., Washington, D.C. 20551. (202) 452-3201; and members of Congress, U.S. Capitol, Washington, D.C. (202) 224-3121 (Senate) or (202) 225-3121 (House of Representatives).

February 3, 1999

V

GOVERNMENT— IMAGINATION AND STAGNATION

The founding period of our country produced a cluster of visionary states-men. The group included George Washington, Benjamin Franklin, John Adams, Thomas Jefferson, James Madison and Patrick Henry. It is inter-esting to compare this collection of talent to our current "leaders."

We are sorely in need of leaders with vision and the courage to take action in service of that vision. More often than not, we get the opposite: politi-cians who respond to the latest polls or sell out to their biggest campaign contributors. The columns in this section describe numerous profiles of cow-ardice and folly.

Much of it involves substantive policies, including corporate welfare and assorted government boondoggles. You may be surprised to learn how your taxpayer dollars are spent. Government has been privatizing military and prison functions—despite the problems with both. Congress has also dras-tically cut taxes for the wealthy while America's infrastructure (roads, bridges, public transit, schools, water systems, parks, libraries, and court-houses) crumbles.

An equally important concern is government process. The Supreme Court adopts stingy rules about who has "standing" to bring a lawsuit, thereby immunizing illegal governmental actions from court challenge. The Federal Reserve Board, whose decisions impact enormously on the econ-omy, acts in secrecy, and our representatives fail to protest.

Our state governments are often no better. Each state, wishing to attract people and business, should be motivated to adopt progressive policies. In real-ity, we often witness a race to the bottom where states outbid each other to kowtow to greedy corporate interests. To take just one example, states have rushed to deregulate lending institutions and the insurance industry—with costly results.

As you read all this, you may get indignant. This is our government, and the officials who commit various acts of commission and omission, as my father once said, work for us. We should be angry at them, but also upset with ourselves for letting them get away with it.

The Race to the Bottom

For years now, a commercial consulting firm has been releasing annual "business climate" rankings of the fifty states. The business press reports these rankings widely. Chambers of commerce and other lobbies raise the pressure on their respective states toward the lowest common denominator of the most corporate-indentured state jurisdictions.

This pressure usually means getting states to lower corporate taxes; increase corporate subsidies; go slower on law enforcement of existing consumer, environmental, and investor protection laws; repeal or weaken consumer and environmental laws; limit worker's compensation benefits; and enact anti–trade-union laws—to name a few indulgences.

The "hammer" is to point to the fifty state rankings and explicitly confront elected and appointed state officials with the specter or reality of losing industry and commerce to more permissive states.

This past year, a "tort deform" organization in Washington, D.C. issued its ranking of which states are more or less protective of corporate and professional "tortfeasors" (meaning perpetrators of wrongful injuries) when these businesses are sued in court by their victims.

Of course, this group uses the phrase "tort reform" to rank the states. But everyone who uses these state rankings knows that the top rankings go to states whose statutes and courts make it more restrictive for injured plaintiffs to have their full day in court against the defendant-perpetrators. These state rankings also receive wide publicity.

It should be axiomatic that those who control the yardsticks by which an activity or sector is measured will most likely control the focus or parameters of debate.

So, it is way overdue for some "people" yardsticks to be annually produced within the fifty-state format. Let's start with a "workers' climate" ranking of the states. Rank states based on better minimum wages, workers compensation, unemployment compensation benefits, safe workplaces, strong labor union laws, privacy laws, whistle-blower protections, health insurance, fair labor standards, and enforcement budgets against company abuses of workers and their pensions.

In an increasingly mobile workforce economy, blue-collar and white-collar workers could have a more informed choice about where to work. Also the publicity over these rankings would certainly shame, if not dissuade, state lawmakers and executive-branch officials from being so anti-worker. Moreover, a livelier public debate would result, instead of just being restricted to "business climate" agendas.

A second ranking of the states should be consumer protection. Which of the states do a better or worse job in dealing with protection of children, in going after or preventing abuses of home buyers by the bank-mortgage-real estate industry? Which states are more active in standing up for insurance buyers, bank customers, food buyers, telephone, electric, and gas customers, tenants, ghetto dwellers subject to immensely gouging payday loans, predatory lending and rent-to-own rackets? Maryland's consumer protections are generally better than those in nearby Virginia, for example.

A third ranking of the fifty states could relate to environmental protection. While federal laws here are often preemptive of states, there is still a brace of weaker or stronger environmental laws at the state level. I remember southern states being so lenient that they allowed pesticide-spraying trucks to go through residential areas with children running behind enveloped by the moving chemical clouds. This is not so likely in the northeastern and mid-western areas of the country.

There could be comparisons over drinking water safeguards, the level of permitted acidic runoffs, air pollution, nonsmoking areas, waste disposal, recycling, forest management, beach monitoring, availability of parks in good condition, encouraging solar and energy conservation, and preserving river purity and flow, for example.

There is available data to do this. For instance, the EPA reports that Texas polluters regularly release the most toxic materials into the environment. Louisiana and Ohio are often in the top tier also. For starters, see a report by Southern Exposure at www.southernstudies.org.

Comparative rankings that provide impetus or incentive for states to compete for the best, instead of "business climate" rankings that result in states rac-ing toward the bottom, are tasks that can be performed by existing institutions. For example, Consumers Union or the University of Wisconsin Law School con-sumer law section could undertake the consumer protection ratings. The larger environmental groups have the ability to evaluate the states in their area of expertise. "Workers' climate" would seem right up the alley of the AFL-CIO or labor studies institutes at universities, if the Department of Labor declined to be true to its name.

One ranking task would be simple. Earlier I mentioned the group repre-senting the tortfeasors' lobby ranking the states' treatment of wrongfully injured people in their courts. Assuming complete accuracy in their research, one only has to turn their list of the fifty states upside down.

August 19, 2003

Citizen-centric E-Government

Contracting out what the federal government does and what government needs is a large part of our economy. The former includes letting corpora-tions perform more military and intelligence functions; while the latter has included buying supplies like fuel, paper, food, medicines, and vehicles. Taken together, they amount to spending trillions of dollars over the past decade—your tax dollars.

The Bush administration seeks to go further by proposing to contract out the work of nearly 450,000 civil servants in various agencies and departments. Sometimes even the businesses on the receiving end of this "privatization" are a bit shocked.

A few years ago, a weapons company official asked incredulously about the Department of Defense's acquisition reform program giving the munitions industry the power to develop its own testing methods in order to determine whether Pentagon-purchased weapons are in compliance with specifications.

All these procurements and "outsourcings" involve written contracts some-times hundreds of pages long. It is not easy, to put it mildly, for citizens to get copies of these contracts.

Two of our staffers, during the month of May 1999, tried to obtain copies of eighty-one agreements with companies that the *Washington Post* reported had received federal government contracts. They called both the businesses and the government agencies that signed the contracts. In no cases were they able to obtain copies of contracts from the companies. None of the federal agen-cies voluntarily provided copies, prompting our associates to file a request under the Freedom of Information Act, which could take many months to process.

In January 2000 we sent a letter to President Clinton asking his administration to place government contracts above a certain minimum dollar amount on the web.

These agreements would include, for example, leases for mineral rights from public lands, research grants, government-industry cooperative agreements, joint ventures for the development of energy efficient cars, consulting contracts, agreements to dispose of nuclear wastes, concession contracts for national parks, licenses to government-owned patents, licenses to use the public spectrum for broadcasting and telecommunications services, agreements with firms that do security clearances for federal agencies, bank bailouts, loan guarantee agreements, and many more.

To our surprise, Bill Clinton personally wrote back saying it was an intriguing proposal and that he was sending it over to the Office of Management and Budget (OMB) for review. We never heard from OMB.

With the advent of George W. Bush, we contacted the new head of OMB, Mitch Daniels. We presented the reasons for putting these documents online:

1) it will enhance competitive bidding and give taxpayers both savings and higher quality performances;

2) it will let the media focus more incisively on this vast area of government disbursements to inform the wider public;

3) it will encourage constructive comments and alarms from the citizenry; and

4) it will stimulate legal and economic research by scholars interested in broader policy and structural topics related to government procurement, transfers, subsidies, and giveaways. For instance, how to use federal buying dollars to advance other national goals such as energy efficiency, recycling, safety, health, and innovation.

Many of these agreements are closed-door operations between government officials and the often close-knit vendor community. Government lawyers negotiating these contracts do not often drive strong bargains for taxpayers, especially if they are pressured from the politicians above them or they intend to work in these industries after they leave public service.

OMB's Mr. Daniels and his associates thought putting these contracts, grants, leases, subsidies, and so forth on the government's web sites was a good idea. Any sensitive information could be redacted. Many federal agencies already have internal systems for managing contracts in electronic formats.

OMB asked the General Services Administration (GSA) to place a notice and request for comments in the Federal Register (June 6, 2003) on a proposed pilot project "to begin making Federal contracts available to the general public on the worldwide web...to further the Administration's global vision of a citizen-centric E-Government."

This could be the beginning of the biggest window-opening on what government and corporations do in Washington in modern U.S. history. Unless, the vendor lobby squashes GSA and OMB. So in small or large ways, Uncle Sam needs to hear from you, the people. You can send written comments to General Services Administration, 1800 F Street, NW, Room 4035, Washington, D.C., 20405 or electronically file by e-mailing your comments to Notice.2003-NO1@gsa.gov.

July 16, 2003

Let Technology Work for People

Do new technologies trump power and decentralize it as some technophiles believe? Not if repressive power gets there first.

Here are three examples from the federal government where either corporate or political power has blocked technology from helping you assess your elected representatives and receive a more efficient government.

1) Log onto the web site of your congressional representatives. Over 95 percent of members of the House and Senate still do not place their voting record there in a clear, timely, and promptly retrievable fashion.

For an example of one legislator who does, see www.house.gov/wolf/VotingRecord.htm.

Now is there anything more important to be regularly placed on elected officials' web sites than their voting record? A PEW survey shows people want such information above all other. Fingertip access by voters back home, by the press, by students and scholars would change the dynamic of accountability between politicians and the people. But the politicians have other ideas. They want to communicate to their constituents through their slick newsletters, radio and television monologues, and other formats where they can shine, sloganize, and obfuscate.

For two years, some citizen groups, including ours, have been demanding that all members do what Congressmen Frank Wolf and Christopher Shays have done for years. I have written to the Democratic and Republican leadership in the House and Senate twice urging that their members publish their voting records. So adverse are the two parties to performing this simple service for the folks back home who pay their salary, benefits, and perks, that these leaders have not even bothered to respond.

The Technology is available. The Powers that be say No. So you try with your lawmakers. (Don't let them mislead you by links to the cumbersome Thomas database.)

2) Federal departments and agencies sign hundreds of billions of dollars in contracts with corporations each year. Technology permits them to put these contracts on their web sites in full view of potentially better competitors, scholars, media, and any citizen who wants to question them in whole or in part. Powerful corporations, in sync with bureaucrats who prefer to work in the shadows, says no.

So all kinds of deals with oil, gas, coal, hard rock mineral companies, drug and health care companies, weapons manufacturers, computer and assorted supplier firms, consulting outfits, and landlords—to name a few—would be exposed to the sunshine. Justice Louis Brandeis once called this kind of sunshine, "the best disinfectant."

Quite likely, there would be less waste, fraud, and corruption, and more quality competition. Fairer provisions for the taxpayers would start replacing these one-sided agreements and handouts that favor vendors and corporate welfare kings.

Now it looks like Technology has a backer. The Office of Management and Budget (OMB), under the leadership of Mitch Daniels, wants these contracts online above a certain minimum dollar amount and with due regard to redacting sentences involving national security. OMB will see to it that a proposed system to achieve an open government will be placed very soon in the Federal Register for public comment. At last, Power For vs. Power Against. Let's see who wins.

3) The U.S. government is a huge consumer of software. But Microsoft has huge monopoly power in the market for operating systems and also for applications like word processors, spreadsheets, and presentation graphics. The Justice Department let Microsoft off when it had the monopolist in a full nelson! Still, the U.S. government, as a Big Consumer, can use its vast purchasing power to break this Microsoft monopoly and save hundreds of millions of dollars yearly by dramatically changing software markets.

The source of Microsoft's power is its control over standards and, in particular, Microsoft's ability to constantly change the formats in which data is stored. People pay top dollar for upgrades to Microsoft Word and PowerPoint simply to be guaranteed that they can read, exchange, and edit files with others.

Yet there are competitive software programs that do a fine job of creating and editing documents and presentations. However, users are afraid these non-Microsoft products will not be able to properly read and modify documents created by Microsoft's dominant software.

The U.S. government can "solve" this problem by requiring, through a customer specification, that all software programs it purchases use as a default a nonproprietary data format that is approved by all competitors.

There is no reason for a monopoly on word processing or presentation graphics programs. People use dozens if not hundreds of different programs to create web pages, and this works for a simple reason. The World Wide Web is based upon open standards. If our government-as-consumer leads the way, it can stimulate competition and innovations for these important software applications. If the government does not lead the way, we may soon find there are no competitors left.

The Technology is there. Will the democratic Power be there to put it to work? Let's hear from you at info@essential.org.

May 21, 2003

Making Government Sponsored Enterprises Accountable

Fannie Mae and Freddie Mac, which dominate the nation's housing finance market, get most of the attention when the subject of Government Sponsored Enterprises (GSEs) comes up in Washington.

But, Fannie and Freddie are not alone in this growing world of government sponsored enterprises, which operate in a twilight zone somewhere between government and free enterprise. Financing for housing, students, financial institutions, and agricultural operations are among the functions that are being carried out through the government sponsored structure.

While the subsidies flowing from their links to the federal government vary, all the GSEs enjoy the implicit guarantee that the federal government would not allow the enterprises to default on their obligations. This means that the GSEs are able to reduce their debt costs substantially below that of similar corporations operating without government sponsorship. In fact, most of the GSE borrowing is at rates only a small fraction above that enjoyed by the federal government itself.

"The perception of government backing permits the GSEs to operate with much higher leverage than other companies: investors in GSE obligations look to the government's guarantee rather than to the financial strength of the GSE as the basis for repayment," says Washington attorney Tom Stanton in his new book, *Government-Sponsored Enterprises: Mercantilist Companies in the Modern World.*

Stanton, who has spent a lifetime studying the GSEs, describes the government as a "silent equity partner" of GSE shareholders by providing financial backing equivalent to tens of billions of dollars of equity—for which the government requires no financial return.

The big question for all the GSEs is whether a legitimate public purpose is being met through the use of this government benefit or whether the implicit subsidy is simply enriching the private shareholders and the executives of the GSEs.

The newest of the GSEs is the Federal Agriculture Mortgage Corporation, which has been dubbed Farmer Mac. Farmer Mac was created under the Reagan administration in 1988 as a vehicle to provide credit for farms and rural housing. In the mid 1990s, I raised questions about just how well this mission was being carried out.

In 1997, the General Accounting Office (GAO) confirmed that more than half of Farmer Mac's on-balance sheet asset holdings were in investments other than agricultural mortgages. So, Farmer Mac's advantages as a government sponsored enterprise were being employed to make investments outside the agricultural sector in order to generate profits for the corporation and its shareholders.

That year, Farmer Mac directors began awarding themselves stock options. The fifteen board members have average stock holdings valued at $816,249, according to a compilation by the *New York Times*. Nine of the directors made millions more selling shares, the report said. Last year, Henry Edelman, Farmer Mac's chief executive, received salary and stock options of $1.8 million. Edelman, according to news reports, controls $27.6 million of Farmer Mac stock.

More recently the *Times* has reported that Farmer Mac has generated income in the form of fees for guaranteeing loans already sitting on the books of banks. This seems far afield from Farmer Mac's mission to generate new credit sources for rural America.

In addition, the *Times* reports dissension between the board of directors and the management of Farmer Mac. One of the recently resigned directors charged that Farmer Mac was "taking outsized risks." Farmer Mac was defensive in its response to the news article, charging that the story had been prompted by "short sellers" of GSE's stock.

The new flap over Farmer Mac once again points to the weak oversight by Congress and the administration over the entire range of GSEs. All of the GSEs pose potential risks for the taxpayers. The market presumes correctly that the federal government will never allow any of the GSEs to fail. That means the taxpayers are the last line of defense. In the case of Fannie Mae and Freddie Mac, there is no question about the taxpayer liability. Each of these housing GSEs has a $2.25 billion automatic draw from the U.S. Treasury in the event they fall on hard times.

While Farmer Mac is subject to registration under the Securities and

Exchange Act, the giants—Fannie and Freddie—are exempt. In the wake of the Enron debacle, Representatives Ed Markey and Chris Shays have introduced legislation that would end the exemption and require Fannie and Freddie to register their securities. So far, it has generated little support from congressional leaders of either party.

The apathy of Congress and the executive branch is appalling in the wake of the size and the rapid growth of the GSEs. Here's the list: Farm Credit System, $94 billion in assets; Federal Home Loan Bank System, $654 billion; Fannie Mae, $607 billion in assets plus $707 billion of mortgage-backed securities guaranteed; Freddie Mac, $386 billion assets plus $576 billion of mortgage-backed securities guaranteed; Sallie Mae (student loans), $48.8 billion assets; Farmer Mac, $3.2 billion assets plus $1.5 billion of mortgage-backed securities guaranteed.

The Bush administration and Congress need to put a high priority on a top-to-bottom examination of all the GSEs to determine: 1) how well their statutory mission is being carried out; and 2) the safety, soundness, and adequacy of protections for the taxpayers against bailouts.

May 30, 2002

FDIC: New Bank Failures

Thanks to one of the biggest corporate giveaways during the Clinton administration, most of the nation's commercial banks have been enjoying the benefits of free federal deposit insurance since 1995.

Now the decision to let banks drop premium payments when the bank insurance fund's reserves reach the statutory minimum of 1.25 percent of insured deposits is coming back to haunt the Federal Deposit Insurance Corporation and the banking industry.

New bank failures, a growing number of problem banks, and an unanticipated surge in deposits are about to drop the reserves below the required minimum of 1.25 percent—an event that overnight could trigger a requirement for the banks to start paying premiums of 23 cents per $100 of deposits to build the insurance fund back to the 1.25 percent level. The number of problem banks rose to ninety-five in the fourth quarter of last year, an increase of 28 percent—the largest in a decade.

This is a huge shock to an industry that has been paying zero premiums. Only the most risk-prone—about 8 percent of the banks—have been required to pay premiums of any kind to support the fund since 1995. This has meant a bonanza of between five and six billion dollars annually for the industry. For a $100 million bank, the elimination of the 23-cent premium means about $230,000 savings annually, according to the FDIC.

When the free insurance went into effect in 1995, the bank lobbyists tried to quiet the controversy with suggestions that the savings would be passed along to the consumers of banking services. Another empty promise. In fact, bank fees have increased each year while the industry enjoyed free government insurance. Today, banks rake in an estimated $20 billion annually in fees on everything from charges for telephone inquiries to the use of deposit slips.

Last year, FDIC drafted a "reform" plan to remove the restrictions on the FDIC's ability to charge risk-based premiums to all depository institutions regardless of the level of the fund. Donald Powell, the new chairman of the FDIC, urges that any reforms adopted by Congress allow flexibility for the FDIC to set insurance fund targets based on economic and banking conditions. This would remove the "boom to bust" cycles of the current policy, which allows wild swings from zero premiums to 23 cents per $100 of deposits.

Typically, Congress is employing that overused and often misused word "reform" to hide new risks for the taxpayers. Representative Spencer Bachus, chairman of the Financial Institutions Subcommittee of the House Financial Services Committee, has succeeded in advancing his proposal for a hike in the insurance limit from $100,000 per depositor to $130,000. Others are pushing for the level of the insurance coverage to be increased by tying it to the consumer price index.

Using the current $100,000 insurance limit as a benchmark is ludicrous. The figure (raising the limit from $40,000 to $100,000) was slipped quietly into a House-Senate conference report in 1980 without hearings and minus any meaningful analysis. Its only purpose was to meet the demands of the lobbyists for a savings and loan industry desperate to compete with the big money-center banks for the deposits needed to fuel speculative investments.

Former FDIC Chairman William Seidman charged that the 1980 increase in insurance coverage gave the savings and loans "a $100,000 credit card issued by Uncle Sam and made the government a full partner in a nationwide casino."

Congress needs to find ways to limit the liability of the insurance funds and the risks to taxpayers, not increase them. There is no justification for an increase in the insurance coverage, which many experts feel is already excessive and a negative influence on the safe and sound operation of depository institutions.

But if the proposals for increases in the coverage seem dangerous, the banking lobby has another even more self-serving and lucrative proposal it would like to attach to that all-purpose word "reform." This involves "rebates" (refunds) paid out of the deposit insurance fund when the reserves grow beyond current needs. No "reform" could be sweeter (or more lucrative) from the viewpoint of the banks.

The proposal provides an insight into the banking industry's attitude about the insurance funds. Bankers regard the deposit insurance funds' reserves as their money, not the government's. As Fordham University professor and former assistant secretary of the Treasury Richard Carnell says, "for bankers to call the bank insurance fund reserves our money is no more true than for persons insured by AIG, Chubb, or Travelers to call those companies' reserves our money."

The value of the insurance fund in building confidence in the banking industry is priceless. It is the glue that holds the banking system together. The premiums paid by the banks now or in the future pale beside the role that the federal government and the taxpayers play in providing confidence in the system. The industry couldn't afford the premiums that would actually compensate for this backing. Nor could the industry afford—or even find—the private insurance that could match the stability created by the federal government's deposit insurance system. So, for the industry to suggest that it is owed a "rebate"—a refund—is the ultimate reach for corporate welfare.

Behind the idea of refunds is also the banking industry's belief that there should be a "cap" on the size of the insurance funds. That is the same concept that led the present unworkable cap of 1.25 percent of insured deposits. There is sentiment at FDIC and in Congress to replace that with a new "range" of caps between which the insurance funds could fluctuate. The fund should be allowed to continue to grow with the FDIC retaining the flexibility to adjust premiums according to banking conditions and risk. The idea of free insurance should be off the table for all time.

"Reform" is always a tricky word in congressional rhetoric. Especially so in the arcane world of banking. Don't be surprised if this latest banking reform deteriorates into little more than another version of the savings and loan deposit insurance reforms of 1980, which helped fuel that industry's demise and lightened taxpayers' pockets by several hundred billions of dollars.

March 13, 2002

The Federal Reserve's Power

The Federal Reserve wields enormous power over the national economy. Its decisions have a major impact on every citizen. Jobs, shelter, and the quality of life are greatly affected by what the Federal Reserve decides on monetary policy.

Yet, the Federal Reserve is allowed to make its decisions in secret. The transcripts and minutes of the meetings are carefully "sanitized" before they are released. When the Federal Reserve voted to lend money to Mexico, for example, the Federal Reserve's records were carefully redacted to keep the details of the transactions secret.

In a recent article in *Barron's* magazine, Dr. Robert Auerbach, who investigated the Federal Reserve as staff economist for the Banking Committee of the House of Representatives, recounts numerous incidents in which minutes were destroyed or heavily edited when the Federal Reserve made critical decisions.

Auerbach, along with other economists and longtime observers of the Federal Reserve, will be gathering at the National Press Club in Washington next week (January 7) to discuss what goes on behind those tightly locked doors at the Federal Reserve.

In sponsoring this conference, it is my hope that we can place a spotlight on this dark corner of our democracy and begin a campaign for a more open process in establishing economic policies that affect the daily lives of working families and the well-being of the entire economy.

The kind of secrecy and closed-door government carried out by the Federal Reserve has no place in a democratic system. In addition to exemptions from open-government requirements, such as the "Sunshine Act," the Federal Reserve does not face the normal checks and balances of the congressional appropriations and budget process. It drafts its own budgets and spends whatever it desires without seeking permission from Congress. It is little wonder that the Federal Reserve feels free to operate as virtually a separate government.

One of the experts who will appear at our January 7 conference is William Greider, a longtime journalist who wrote the book *Secrets of the Temple*, a carefully researched tome that has become a must-read for students of the Federal Reserve.

Keynote speaker for the conference will be James Galbraith, Ph.D. at the LBJ School of Government, University of Texas, who has written and lectured extensively on the Federal Reserve and who is rapidly becoming the nation's most outspoken and best-informed critic of the Federal Reserve and current monetary policy.

In addition to setting interest rates in carrying out monetary policy, the Federal Reserve has wide-ranging regulatory power over the financial community for consumer protection. It is strange, indeed, that this power would be exercised by the current chairman of the Federal Reserve, Alan Greenspan, whose past would give little comfort to anyone who believes in regulatory protections.

Greenspan was an early follower of Ayn Rand, the leader of the Objectivists, an antigovernment collective. Greenspan collaborated with Ayn Rand in writing *Capitalism: The Unknown Ideal,* in which he denounced regulation, particularly consumer protections and antitrust laws, which he described as "cardinal ingredients of welfare statism."

Later, Greenspan became a lobbyist for the financial industry against regulation and represented some of the high flyers—like Charlie Keating of Lincoln Savings—who plundered the savings and loan industry.

So, we plan for our conference to take a deep look at how well this ex-foe of regulation is representing the public in his current position as chief government regulator of banks, big financial services corporations, and the economy.

The conference is titled "The Federal Reserve—Reality versus Myth." We hope that our panel of experts will be able to unravel some of the myths that have allowed the Federal Reserve to escape accountability for so long to the detriment of the vast number of working Americans and our democratic system of government.

January 3, 2002

Congress Easy on Insurance Industry

I nsurance companies, fresh from their lobbying victories in the last Congress, are back on Capitol Hill with their hands out again.

Under legislation circulated by the insurance industry's favorite senator, Chris Dodd of Connecticut, taxpayers, not the insurance companies, in the future would be required to pay major insurance claims arising out of attacks like those on the World Trade Center. In addition, there are reports that the industry may get special tax breaks as part of the post-attack legislative rush.

None of this is surprising. The insurance industry has always lived a charmed life on Capitol Hill. This is the same industry that was given a free ride two years ago when Congress passed legislation to allow banks, securities firms, and insurance companies to merge and form giant conglomerates, which ultimately will dominate the financial sector in this nation and in much of the rest of the world.

Congress let insurance corporations enjoy the fruits of these financial services conglomerates without placing any demands on the companies. As a result, the insurance companies are allowed to remain outside of federal safety and soundness regulation. They face only limited supervision by the fifty state insurance departments, most of which are sadly underfunded, poorly staffed, and dominated by the industry they "regulate." Even the handful of well-run state insurance departments is in no position to regulate giant corporations that operate across state lines and in dozens of countries around the world.

For many communities, particularly low- and moderate-income and minority neighborhoods, Congress's refusal to regulate insurance companies is a crushing blow. Lobbyists for the companies threatened to scuttle the financial services legislation in 1999 if Congress included provisions to help curb redlining of inner-city neighborhoods by insurance companies. Court cases and studies by academics, fair housing councils, community organizations, and others have established that many companies resist writing policies or provide only limited overpriced insurance products in such areas.

More than three decades ago, the President's National Advisory Panel on Insurance in Riot Affected Areas outlined the problem:

"Insurance is essential to revitalize our cities....Without insurance, banks and other financial institutions will not, and cannot, make loans...housing cannot be repaired...efforts to rebuild our nation's inner cities cannot move forward....Communities without insurance are communities without hope."

A convincing case for a bailout of the insurance companies has not been made. But, if Senator Dodd moves aid for insurance forward, progressive members of the House of Representatives and Senate need to demand that anti-redlining measures be applied to the industry.

The Home Mortgage Disclosure Act (HMDA), adopted in 1977, requires banks and other depository institutions to submit annual reports about where they make mortgage loans by census tract. This has proven to be an extremely valuable tool in tracking and rooting out discriminatory lending practices in low- and moderate-income and minority communities. A HMDA-type requirement should be adopted that would require insurance companies to report where they write policies and make investments.

The Community Reinvestment Act (CRA) was enacted in 1979 to require banks to help serve all areas of their communities including low- and moderate-income neighborhoods. CRA has helped move billions of dollars of credit into inner cities and depressed rural areas. At the same time, it has opened new markets that many banks have found profitable. A CRA-type requirement should be included to require insurance companies to help serve and invest in all areas of their communities.

If Congress goes forward with an aid package, provisions should also be adopted to ensure that no federal monies, guarantees, or other bailout benefits will flow to insurance companies that have been found in violation of fair-housing laws or other antidiscrimination laws. Certainly, citizens should not be required to contribute their tax money to assist corporations that discriminate against them.

Enactment of anti-redlining reforms for the insurance industry should not be considered an impossible task. In 1993, Massachusetts Representative Joe Kennedy succeeded in moving a HMDA-style insurance reporting requirement through the House against stiff opposition from the insurance companies. The political muscle of the industry, however, kept the measure from being considered in the Senate.

During the consideration of the financial services legislation in 1999, the battle for HMDA-CRA responsibilities for insurance companies was led by three members of the House of Representatives—Tom Barrett of Milwaukee, Barbara Lee of Oakland, and Luis Gutierrez of Chicago. The insurance lobby eventually defeated these initiatives, but the three succeeded in putting a lasting spotlight on the issue.

Barrett, Lee, and Gutierrez should walk over to the Senate and insist that Senator Dodd, the point man for the insurance bailout package, and Senator Paul Sarbanes, chairman of the Banking Committee, incorporate federal regulation, including anti-redlining provisions, in any aid plan that might be considered by the committee. Congress needs to examine carefully all of the proposed post-attack bailouts with full hearings and full consideration on the floor. Congress's deliberations should go beyond the obvious self-interest of the companies and include people's concerns and needs, not the least of which should be statutory assurances that federally assisted corporations will not be allowed to discriminate against citizens and redline neighborhoods.

October 11, 2001

September 11 Attack: Transportation Infrastructure

The September 11 attacks on the World Trade Center and the Pentagon are changing the way Americans think about a lot of things. One critically important area of this rethinking must involve our national transportation system—how we move people safely and efficiently across this vast nation.

In the aftermath of the hijacking of four airliners on a single morning, Americans are rediscovering our often forgotten and shamefully neglected passenger railroad system. Suddenly, trains are looking very attractive as alternatives to airplanes and automobile-clogged highways.

But for the past half-century, passenger rail service has waged a tough battle for survival. For years, railroad corporations had a "common-carrier" responsibility to provide passenger service. The corporations, however, were much more interested in the lucrative business of hauling freight. Railroads let passenger service deteriorate (some actively discouraging it) so that the Interstate Commerce Commission would grant them permission to abandon their common-carrier responsibility and allow them to discontinue what they had created as an unprofitable service.

Faced with the sad state of passenger service, Congress adopted the Rail Passenger Act in 1970, creating the National Railroad Passenger Corporation that became popularly known as Amtrak. The following year, most railroads still operating passenger service turned their equipment over to Amtrak and the new company took on the responsibility of operating inter-city passenger train service.

It was a daunting task. Amtrak inherited passenger cars and locomotives that averaged more than twenty years of age along with dilapidated train stations. Despite being consistently underfunded, Amtrak managed to rebuild passenger service from the ruins left by the railroad companies. Last year Amtrak carried a record number of passengers—22.5 million.

The northeast corridor accounts for more than half of Amtrak's 60,000 passengers on most days. Passengers on those routes rose 17 percent in the days immediately after the attack and remain 10 to 13 percent higher than pre-September 11 totals. Amtrak was quick to respond to the emergency, putting on extra trains, honoring airline tickets, and adding extra support staff.

While the northeast corridor provides profits for Amtrak, the corporation must also maintain less-utilized and longer routes throughout the nation, including those that are decidedly unprofitable. Congress insists that the service be provided, but it has been tightfisted about providing subsidies to help maintain the system.

As the *Los Angeles Times* editorialized: "For years Congress has tried to have it both ways. It has insisted on Amtrak maintaining a nationwide passenger-rail operation—with several unprofitable routes—but it doesn't want to pay for it."

Congress has set a deadline of December 2002 for Amtrak to become totally "self-sufficient" or be dismantled. This is an absurd requirement. Congress cannot insist on Amtrak carrying out a needed public service role in transportation and at the same time issue an edict that it show a profit. Western European countries operate superb rail systems that their governments have continued to subsidize as an integral part of their transportation system.

The demand for "self-sufficiency" for Amtrak seems even more ridiculous in the face of huge transportation subsidies the federal government has willingly ladled out for airlines and highways through the years. Since the 1971 chartering of Amtrak, highways and airlines have received $750 billion in federal support. Amtrak has received only $11 billion in the same period.

Last week, Congress added to the subsidies with a $15 billion bailout package for the airlines. In contrast, Amtrak has asked for only $3.5 billion to fix problems with ventilation and evacuation routes in underwater tunnels to New York City, as well as rehabilitating other tunnels and providing additional security measures in the wake of the attacks.

Clearly, the emergency funds don't deal with the long-range needs of rapid rail passenger service for the entire nation. Despite the double standard that Congress has so often applied to Amtrak, there are some encouraging signs that legislators in both parties see the growing need for more investment in rail travel.

Don Young, Republican from Alaska and chairman of the House Transportation Committee, has introduced legislation to provide states with authority to issue $31 billion in bonds and to borrow $35 billion in low-interest loans to fund high-speed rail projects. In the Senate, a majority of members has cosponsored a bill to allow Amtrak to issue $12 billion in bonds to finance such a modern, speedy, and efficient rail passenger system.

"We desperately need a third leg to our national transportation strategy," Senator Kay Bailey Hutchinson, a Texas Republican conservative, told the Senate. "I believe passenger rail can function in that role."

These voices of support from conservatives for more investment in rail transportation may come as a surprise to many, but September 11 has been a call for the nation to think anew on a lot of issues. One memorial to the victims of the disaster would be to build a better nation that serves the needs of its people.

October 3, 2001

New Rules Publication on Banking

States' rights used to be the rallying cry for corporations, segregationists, and an assortment of special interests determined to blunt federal initiatives, particularly in the arena of regulation. Many state legislatures were underfunded, poorly staffed, and in session only for a few weeks or months, some meeting only biennially.

As a result, corporate lobbyists had a free run and, in effect owned many of the legislative bodies. It was no wonder that the lobbyists became so adept at running up the flag of "states' rights" whenever Congress looked like it might enact federal legislation that would protect consumers or curb the excesses of the special interests.

But today the balance is shifting in some states where legislatures, now better funded and operating with professional staffs, are taking the lead in proposing and enacting a number of consumer protections. Suddenly, the corporate lobbyists who talked so eloquently about states' rights only a few years ago are beating the drums for federal legislative dominance, insisting that state consumer initiatives be preempted by weaker provisions enacted by Congress, in effect giving the corporations a center for "one-stop injustice."

A major lobbying battle, for example, is being waged in the Financial

Services Committee of the U.S. House of Representatives where the rent-to-own industry is seeking to have Congress pass a weak regulatory bill that would preempt state laws providing protections for consumers against usurious interest rates and unfair practices, many transactions carrying interest rates of 200 to 300 percent on an annual basis.

At least five states—Minnesota, Wisconsin, New Jersey, Vermont, and North Carolina—have strong state laws governing rent-to-own contracts and have been aggressive in attacking predatory practices by rent-to-own firms. But these laws would be preempted—wiped out—if the federal legislation is enacted. Fifty-two state and territorial attorneys general have signed a letter to Congress protesting the effort to wipe out state protections.

Senator Paul Sarbanes of Maryland, who has recently become chairman of the Senate Banking Committee, has an opportunity to put his professed support for consumers into action by leading the charge against the preemption. It will be an early test of his new chairmanship.

Not only does Congress increasingly insert preemption language in federal legislation, but federal regulatory agencies, especially the financial ones, use their powers to wipe out grassroots initiatives in the states and local communities.

In 1991, New Jersey enacted legislation that would require all banks operating in the state to provide basic, low-cost checking accounts for low-income citizens lacking banking services.

Before the law went into effect, the Office of the Comptroller of the Currency (OCC) ruled that the National Banking Act preempted the New Jersey statute and authorized national banks to ignore the law. The preemption of the New Jersey law has chilled efforts by other states to enact legislation to help their citizens obtain banking services.

Local ordinances, as well as state legislative measures, have been targeted for extinction by the OCC. In 1999, San Francisco and Santa Monica, following mandates of referenda passed by the voters, banned extra surcharges, fees consumers pay to use automatic teller machines (ATMs) operated by a bank other than their own.

Bank of America and Wells Fargo sued the cities in federal court in a move to invalidate the ordinances. The two banks own 86 percent of the ATMs in San Francisco and 72 percent of those in Santa Monica. OCC entered the case on behalf of the banks and filed friend-of-the-court briefs arguing that the National Banking Act preempted the voters' decisions.

The citizens of the two California cities lost in federal district court and the case is now pending in Ninth Circuit Court with no decision expected until next year. Banks also are seeking to overturn Iowa's ban on surcharges, again with the muscle of OCC behind them.

"The OCC's actions on preemption appear to be more those of an indentured servant of the industry than a regulator concerned with the will of Congress," says Ed Mierzwinski, consumer program director of the U.S. Public Interest Research Group in Washington.

Consumer leaders like Mierzwinski have long complained about the aggressiveness of Congress and federal regulators in preempting stronger local and state laws designed to protect consumers against excesses of banks and other corporations.

Now *New Rules*, a quarterly publication of the Institute for Local Self Reliance (www.newrules.org), has come on the scene to catalog and question the growing efforts to override—preempt—citizens' grassroots decisions.

David Morris, editor of *New Rules*, lays out his concerns this way: "Increasingly higher levels of governments are overruling those closer to the citizenry. State legislatures override city councils and county commissions. Federal agencies and Congress override state legislatures. International agencies like the World Trade Organization override congresses and parliaments."

New Rules is providing a significant service in exploring the shifting power among levels of government and the ability of corporations and other special interests to seek and find the weakest links through which to gain their goals.

September 18, 2001

FDIC

One of the Clinton administration's more outlandish giveaways to corporate interests was its decision six years ago to provide free deposit insurance to about 92 percent of the nation's commercial banks. The move represented a five-billion-dollar annual bonanza to the banking industry and billions of dollars of new risk for taxpayers.

Before she left office earlier this year, the chairman of the Federal Deposit Insurance Corporation, Donna Tanoue, had her agency conduct a top-to-bottom study of the deposit insurance system. The study produced a mixed-bag of recommendations, but more importantly, it provoked a healthy debate in Congress and in the industry about the future of deposit insurance. Most of the debate has centered around the reforms' potential effect on financial corporations, but taxpayers who funded the bailout of the savings and loan industry in the late 1980s and early 1990s know they have a huge stake in the outcome.

By far the most important recommendation, from the standpoint of both risk and fairness, is the study's insistence on imposing insurance premiums on all depository institutions, ending the free lunch enjoyed by most of the nation's banks since 1995.

Under the present system, FDIC stopped collecting the premiums when the insurance funds on hand represented 1.25 percent of the insured deposits, the absolute minimum reserve allowed by law. Under the system, if reserves drop below the minimum of 1.25 percent (for example, because of bank failures in an economic downturn), FDIC would be required by law to once again impose premiums to rebuild the fund.

Thus, the existing system could force banks to pay high premiums during periods of financial distress and none when they are enjoying fat profits, as they have in recent years. Payments like that have the potential to reduce credit and exacerbate "boom and bust" banking cycles at exactly the wrong time. Instead of keeping reserves at a minimum, FDIC proposes that all banks continue paying premiums and that the insurance fund be allowed to shrink or build gradually around broad targets or ranges. This proposal is in keeping with recommendations I made to the FDIC in 1995, objecting to the agency's proposal for free insurance for banks.

Much more questionable, however, is a FDIC recommendation that the current insurance coverage limit of $100,000 per account be increased through a formula tied to the Consumer Price Index. The insurance coverage was raised from $40,000 to the current $100,000 level in 1980 in a surprise move by a House-Senate conference without economic analysis, hearings, or even a recommendation from the FDIC. The figure was simply pulled out of the air during negotiations among various conferees. Behind the move was an intense lobbying effort by the savings and loan industry, which wanted the additional insurance to help it attract large deposits that were flowing to big money-center banks.

Not only do higher limits of insurance coverage make the resolution of failed institutions more costly to the insurance fund and potentially to taxpayers, but they create a "moral hazard" by which the public, Congress, regulators, and financial institutions are lulled into complacency.

While the current limit is technically $100,000 per account, deposits can be maneuvered in a manner that could conceivably allow a family of four to keep as much as two million dollars under insurance coverage.

The talk of change in the deposit insurance system has prompted some independent banks to lobby for an immediate increase in the limit. Some of their friends in Congress are urging an overnight doubling of the coverage to $200,000 per account, shades of the efforts by the savings and loans in 1980 that led to the present $100,000 coverage.

FDIC's study also raised the possibility of gradual rebates to banks when the insurance fund exceeds the outer range of targets established by the agency. Rebates, however, could endanger the growth of a "rainy day" fund that would protect the insurance fund and taxpayers against unforeseen and hidden problems in the financial system and in federal and state regulatory agencies.

When the fund amasses a significant reserve and a stronger, coordinated regulatory system is in place, Congress can worry about rebates. That shouldn't be up-front in a bill designed to develop a more sound, more rational deposit insurance system.

The new FDIC Chairman Donald Powell was sworn in August 30, and he should place deposit insurance reform at the top of his agenda. His predecessor opened the door with a study. The Bush administration should now move reform forward in a legislative form, and, at a minimum, make certain that financial institutions pay premiums on the insurance that generates public confidence and provides the glue that holds the system together and helps generate its considerable profits. Corporate welfare in the form of free deposit insurance for banks is a prime candidate for elimination. Taxpayers have been bilked enough by massive bailouts of financial institutions in the past.

September 5, 2001

California Insurance Deregulation Debacle

California often serves as the nation's laboratory for new public policy initiatives. Some of the initiatives have been disasters. This is particularly true in the area of regulation where California has bounced from pro-consumer initiatives to "free-market" solutions favored by the state's corporate powers.

In 1996, California's Republican Governor Pete Wilson led a successful bipartisan campaign to support the demands of the state's electric utilities for deregulation. That was one of California's disasters, and today, as a result of deregulation, the state faces record high-energy costs, rolling blackouts, poorer service, and taxpayer-financed bailouts.

Other initiatives have provided significant benefits, as with automobile insurance reforms. Here the state's voters seized the initiative in 1988 and passed Proposition 103, which has led to the strongest pro-consumer insurance regulations in the nation.

"California regulations are the state-of-the-art regulations in the nation, far and away the best," says J. Robert Hunter, director of insurance for the Consumer Federation of America and former commissioner of insurance for the state of Texas. Hunter's findings were based on a study of the results of regulation of automobile insurance in the fifty states.

The numbers lend support to Hunter's words. Under Proposition 103's rate rollback requirement, refunds totaling $1.3 billion were paid to consumers. During the decade after Proposition 103 was adopted by the people of California, automobile insurance rates in the state went down 4 percent while rates nationally rose by more than 25 percent.

The consumer savings under Proposition 103 did not come at the expense of the insurance companies. In fact, profits of the California insurers actually were higher than those enjoyed by their colleagues in other states.

From 1990 to 1999, California insurers, for example, amassed profits (return on net worth) of 15.40 percent on personal automobile liability compared to a return of 8.80 percent for insurers nationwide. On personal automobile physical damage, the rate of return on net worth was 18.70 percent for California companies; 17.20 percent nationwide.

In addition to the premium savings, Hunter points to other consumer benefits flowing from Proposition 103. These include fairness requirements, regulation of rating factors, such as large good-driver discounts, full disclosure, the availability of data by zip code to help determine if redlining is present, public scrutiny of filings, accountability through consumer participation in the process, and an end to the industry's exemption from state antitrust laws.

Under Proposition 103, regulations were adopted to disallow unnecessary costs, such as excessive expenses, fines, bad-faith lawsuit costs, bloated executive salaries and related outlays.

"Proposition 103 was a shot across the bow of the insurance industry," Hunter says. "Prior to 103 the industry saw itself as a 'pass through' operation."

The old system created what Hunter calls a "perverse incentive" in the ratemaking process by allowing the companies to pass through unjustified and excessive costs to the consumers. It also provided no incentive to aggressively combat fraud or to promote highway safety.

Proposition 103 required insurers to open their books to justify rate increases before they were imposed. For the first time, insurers were provided with financial incentives for efficient performance, rather than simply being able to pass on costs (justified or not) to consumers.

The study found that Proposition 103's "Good Driver Protections" provided strong incentives for driver safety. "Clean" drivers with good records receive a 20 percent discount and the right to buy insurance from the company of their choice through the program.

The success of California's Proposition 103 haunts the insurance industry nationwide. If rates can be slashed while insurers continue to enjoy healthy profits, why can't this be duplicated in other states? If full disclosure, prior approval, and consumer participation work in California, why won't they work in other states? If companies can compete while adhering to state antitrust laws, why can't they do so in other states?

These questions may soon be front and center at the federal level. In the wake of the so-called financial modernization bill of 1999, some elements of the insurance industry, for the first time, have begun talking about seeking federal charters. If this becomes a reality, Congress has an excellent model in California to provide the basic structure for a federal charter and federal regulatory agency. Congress should accept nothing less.

June 26, 2001

Rebuild Our Infrastructure

Economic policy is taking on a surreal appearance in Washington. President Bush has gambled everything on a massive tax cut based on the quicksand of long-term projections of yet-to-be-achieved budget surpluses. A bipartisan majority in the Congress has enthusiastically endorsed the president's philosophy of "tax cuts cure all" with the Democratic opposition chipping away only at the margins.

The final version of the tax cuts seems certain to be another bonanza for the wealthy. The richest 1 percent of taxpayers—citizens with annual incomes over $375,000—would receive one-third of the benefits of the cuts while the bottom 60 percent of the taxpayers would get only 15 percent of the benefits.

Leaving the fairness issue aside, the decision to place tax cuts at the top of the nation's economic agenda seems unreal even in the fantasy world of Washington. It is as if President Bush and congressional leaders see no unmet needs across the nation. In the real world there is a mounting backlog of delayed solutions to national problems ranging from health to affordable housing to a decaying infrastructure. The ability to deal with these and other unmet needs is placed at risk by a policy that puts tax cuts for the wealthy ahead of investments in the economic future of the nation.

The neglect of the nation's infrastructure—everything from water plants to transportation systems—is a national disgrace that threatens not only the economy, but the health and safety of the entire citizenry.

The American Society of Civil Engineers recently published a report card (www.asee.org/reportcard) that came up with a near failing grade of D+ across twelve critical areas of the nation's infrastructure. Ironically, the engineers estimated that $1.3 trillion was needed in the next five years just to repair current and looming infrastructure problems—a sum just about equal to the amount that President Bush plans to push out the door in the form of tax cuts.

"Without these resources, we gamble America's prosperity on an infrastructure whose pipes, schools, and airports are literally at the bursting point," says ASCE President Robert W. Bein, a civil engineer from Irvine, California.

Here are some of the areas that the engineers cited as candidates for immediate action:

Roads: One-third of the nation's roads are in poor or mediocre condition, costing American drivers an estimated $5.8 billion and contributing to 13,800 fatalities annually.

Bridges: As of 1998, 29 percent of the nation's bridges were structurally deficient or functionally obsolete.

Transit: Transit ridership has increased 15 percent since 1995—faster than airline or highway transportation. Capital spending needs to increase at least 41 percent just to maintain the system in its present condition.

Schools: Seventy-five percent of the school buildings are inadequate to meet the needs of school children.

Drinking water: The nation's 54,000 water systems face an annual shortfall of $11 billion needed to replace facilities nearing the end of useful life and to comply with federal water standards.

Wastewater: Some sewer systems are one hundred years old. There is more than a shortfall of $12 billion annually in investment needs of the systems.

Dams: There are more than 2,100 unsafe dams in the United States with sixty-one failures in the past two years.

Not only are these critical needs for health and safety, but public monies that would go into these improvements would provide local jobs and stimulate a slowing economy. As Louis Uchitelle writes in the *New York Times*, Democrats used to carry the flag for critical public investments to meet these needs, but the emphasis shifted under the Clinton-Gore administration to keeping government less involved and preserving surpluses.

Uchitelle also makes note of recent polls by Louis Harris and Associates, which indicate that citizens do favor more spending on services they want, such as education, health care, medical research, highways, police, and air traffic control.

But neither the Bush administration nor Congress has the courage to test the waters and do the right thing in investing in programs that build the nation and meet real needs of the people. It is easier to pass out candy in the form of tax cuts than to go to the people as a community of citizens with a real economic program for the future. The nation will pay dearly for a White House and a Congress that dodged the hard choices and left our country in poor repair.

May 22, 2001

Children's Defense Fund

The Children's Defense Fund (CDF) has long run on the motto "Leave No Child Behind." But that phrase was given much higher visibility as the slogan of the presidential campaign of George W. Bush, who as governor left more than a few children behind in Texas. CDF was not pleased with the appropriation of these words by candidate Bush. Its attorneys had more than a few words with Bush's campaign lawyers. But to no avail.

Now Marian Wright Edelman, founder and president of the CDF, is set to mount a massive coalition of organizations with millions of members to enact an "Act to Leave No Child Behind." This movement will wrap the "Leave No Child Behind" phrase squarely around George W. Bush's shoulders, and my guess is that he is not going to like it.

Most politicians want their lofty campaign slogans forgotten by the time they take their oath of office. Turning slogans into realities is going a bit too far. When the realities include prodding President Bush to protect children from the toxic chemicals of the companies that have funded his campaign, or to provide all children and their parents with health care coverage, or increase the supply of affordable housing units, Mr. Bush is likely to punt.

But Ms. Edelman and the large, resolute staff at CDF are nothing but determined. You take our slogan, then you better mean it. Starting on May 23 right through June 1, which is Stand for Children Day, a barrage of initial publicity, including events in fifty states, will be deployed to raise "public awareness of children's needs." In CDF's words, this includes a multimillion dollar "TV, radio, and print media campaign; town meetings, prayer vigils, and study circles; and house parties. Coalition building, nonviolence, and media-skills training to build a critical mass of effective spokespersons and advocates will be an ongoing and integral part of our movement building."

Children do not come in pieces, says CDF, so the "Act to Leave No Child Behind" (this time a registered trademark) is comprehensive. It includes health care, not just health insurance. It embraces needed federal standards that take into account small children's vulnerability to environmental hazards and toxins, to environmental racism, and such hazards in the schools. It pays fuller attention to helping hard-pressed working parents and the destitute to care for, nurture, and protect their children. Early childhood development and education receive high priority, along with insuring quality education in well-kept schools. A major poverty reduction program taking into account tax laws, raising the minimum wage, and broader usage of existing programs unknown to the poor is detailed.

Housing and nutritional deficiencies, child abuse, after-school programs, juvenile justice, and gun safety are confronted with the carefully thought-out programs that CDF has been well-known for throughout the years. This nearly thirty-year-old organization is a wellspring of field experience, hard data, and creative thinking that show how more justice can replace more charity. It is beginning to turn more attention to corporate exploitation of children and teenagers in the marketing excesses and outrages that are alarming both conservatives and liberals.

That latter point is one George W. Bush and his strategists should take note of in coming months. They won't be able to ideologically or politically bait the large CDF-led coalition. Marian Wright Edelman and associates are far too smart to let them do that. The wave of righteous but not dogmatic people she is banding together will come at the White House and Congress from all parts of the political spectrum. It is a wave that must overcome.

Interested readers can reach CDF at 25 E Street, N.W., Washington D.C., 20001. 800-CDF-1200, www.childrensdefense.org.

May 16, 2001

John Graham and OMB

When a new administration comes to Washington, the media devote a lot of resources to coverage of appointees to Cabinet-level positions. The American public quickly gets a pretty good idea about who these officials are, what they have done, and what they might do as key members of an incoming administration.

Unfortunately, this same media scrutiny is often missing in the coverage of so-called second-level appointees—the under and assistant secretaries of Cabinet offices, the heads of bureaus and agencies and key employees slipped quietly into other decision-making roles in the bureaucracy.

It is unlikely that many citizens following the formation of the Bush administration have heard the name of John Graham uttered. No headlines and no prominently displayed biographical sketches in major media have given the public any clue about this nominee.

Yet, Mr. Graham, if he is confirmed by the U.S. Senate, will hold enormous power as director of the Office of Information and Regulatory Affairs in the Office of Management and Budget (OMB). He will, in effect, be a regulatory czar with authority over the fate of regulations issued by all government agencies, including those involving public health, safety, and environmental protections.

At OMB, Mr. Graham would be the classic example of the old cliché about the "fox guarding the henhouse." As founding director of the Harvard Center for Risk Analysis, he has supported major corporations in efforts to halt or delay the issuance of protective regulations across a broad front.

His center is funded by more than one hundred large corporations and trade associations, including Dow, 3M, DuPont, Monsanto, Exxon, the Chlorine Chemistry Council, the American Automobile Manufacturers Association, the American Chemistry Council, and the American Petroleum Institute. The center's executive board is similarly dominated by corporate executives with a self-interest in undercutting health and safety regulations.

These investments in John Graham's center have paid big dividends for Corporate America's campaign against regulation. In the early 1990s, for example, Graham solicited contributions from Philip Morris and let the company's public relations staff review draft chapters of his book on secondhand smoke. Internal memorandums at Philip Morris later revealed that the company relied on Graham's strategy to discredit the Environmental Protection Agency's correct assessment of the cancer-causing effects of secondhand smoke.

As Public Citizen says in a report on the Harvard Center, Graham's methodology "appears to be informed more by the wishes of his corporate backers than by anything recognizable as 'science.'" The report—accompanied by ample supporting data—finds that Graham's research conclusions have been frequently marred by his inflation of industry costs and underestimation of public benefits.

The record is clear. John Graham, using Harvard's prestige, has been front and center as a critically important player in a long industry-supported campaign to discredit federal agencies and to block the regulatory process. And as Public Citizen says, the debates over the safety of pesticides, injury prevention, pollution, secondhand smoke, toxic chemicals, and contamination of our food and water have all been victims of the so-called research of Graham's Harvard Center.

The prestige of the Harvard name obviously gave Graham's arguments—and thus the positions of his corporate donors—great weight in the battle against health, safety, and environmental regulations. Should he be confirmed by the Senate, these same arguments will have the weight of the White House behind them when the decisions are made about the health and safety of the American people.

The Senate should reject this nomination and shut one of big business's backdoors to the Bush White House.

March 22, 2001

Greenspan Speaks

When Bill Clinton headed out of town last month, political pundits were anointing the former president as Washington's master politician. Perhaps not the most ethical, but the most skilled was a near unanimous verdict.

Did these pundits overlook Alan Greenspan, the Federal Reserve chairman, who has had everyone from right-wing conservatives to staunch liberals sitting reverently at his feet waiting for words of economic wisdom for the past eight years? If not the most skilled politician of our time, surely he has a solid claim on being the most flexible.

Last year, Greenspan dumped a lot of very chilly water on the idea of a big tax cut. What to do with the projected budget surplus? Pay down the debt was the pronouncement of the Federal Reserve chairman.

Now, Greenspan has undergone a miraculous and much ballyhooed conversion. Suddenly, big tax cuts, according to Greenspan circa 2001, are just the right medicine for the economy. Gone are the cautionary warnings of last year.

What brought about the change? True the economy has slowed slightly, but a bigger change, in the eyes of the Federal Reserve chairman, was the arrival of a new occupant of the White House who had placed a truly big tax cut— $1.6 trillion (largely for the wealthy)—at the top of his political-economic agenda.

Greenspan's conversion produced headlines in newspapers across the nation, and changed the odds in favor of the new president's agenda. Greenspan's embrace of Bush economics stung Democrats who had hopes of modifying the Bush plan or, at least, targeting some of the cuts lower in the tax brackets. Privately, Democratic leaders were infuriated that Greenspan had so openly and so quickly used his considerable clout to tilt the battle in favor of Bush.

If the Democrats are unhappy with the turn of events, they have only themselves and their recently departed President Clinton to blame. Despite Greenspan's long, high-profile work in Republican vineyards, President Clinton reappointed Greenspan twice to the chairmanship of the Federal Reserve, giving up opportunities to replace him with someone who would move the policies of the Fed on a more progressive, more consumer-oriented course.

Not only the White House, but the congressional Democrats wrapped their arms around Greenspan in loving embraces every time the Fed chairman appeared on Capitol Hill in the 1990s. When the nomination for Federal Reserve chairman was up during the first Clinton term in 1996, the Democrats on the Senate Banking Committee—led by a leading liberal, Paul Sarbanes— voted unanimously to endorse Greenspan. Ditto when the nomination was up again last year. Only a handful of Democratic senators like Tom Harkin, Byron Dorgan, Harry Reid, and Paul Wellstone have ventured forth to criticize the Greenspan policies when his nominations were on the floor of the Senate.

President Clinton and the congressional Democrats can't claim ignorance about Greenspan's conservative, pro-corporate, anti-consumer background. His views have been quite visible as an economic guru for the Republican Party, a leading disciple of Ayn Rand, and a lobbyist for financial corporations, including such notorious operations as Charlie Keating's Lincoln Savings that failed at a cost of $2.5 billion to the taxpayers in the 1980s. In between, he sat on boards of directors of many major corporations including Mobil Oil, Alcoa, and J. P. Morgan and Company. He served as an advisor to President Nixon and was chairman of the President's Council of Economic Advisers under President Ford. He was appointed to the Federal Reserve chairmanship by President Reagan and reappointed by President George Bush, father of George W. Bush.

In an article published in 1963 as part of Ayn Rand's book, *Capitalism: The Unknown Ideal*, Greenspan lashed out at government regulation, declaring that the protection of the consumer "against dishonest and unscrupulous business was the cardinal ingredient of welfare statism."

Faced with filling the federal chairmanship in 1996 and 2000, President Clinton apparently saw no major differences between his social and economic policies and those espoused through the years by Alan Greenspan in service to various Republican leaders and corporations. And if there were doubts among Democratic members of Congress, they, for the most part, kept them to themselves.

So, now the Democrats on Capitol Hill face the daunting task of convincing their colleagues and the American public that there are important differences in tax policy between the major parties—the words of President Clinton's Federal Reserve chairman notwithstanding.

The lack of congressional oversight, secrecy and a fawning unquestioning press have combined to encourage Greenspan to assume a role in economic policy-making that goes beyond the Federal Reserve's statutory assignment as monetary czar. The debate over fiscal policy involves broad political as well as economic and social issues that are outside the more narrow responsibilities that are assigned by the Federal Reserve Act.

Because of the inordinate political clout that the Federal Reserve has amassed, pronouncements by Greenspan threaten to short-circuit much needed congressional and public debate over economic policy involved in the tax cut proposals. Greenspan's testimony before the Senate Budget Committee in late January was an overt attempt by the Federal Reserve to intervene in congressional policy deliberations and undermine the legislative branch's authority to decide the fate of fiscal policy initiatives put forward by the president.

Clearly, there is an overriding need to restrain wide ranging policy excursions by a Federal Reserve Board that operates largely in secret, avoids the checks and balances of the appropriations process, and receives a pass from all but the most pro forma congressional oversight.

February 7, 2001

Deregulation—Beware

Next time some major industry starts talking about the glories of deregulation, consumers should hold tightly to their billfolds.

The rush to deregulate has intensified over the past twenty-five years as lobbyists for airlines, cable television, financial institutions, and telephone, natural gas, and electrical utilities have succeeded in convincing compliant local, state, and national legislative and regulatory bodies to let corporations escape consumer protections.

These well-financed campaigns for deregulation invariably center around grandiose claims about consumer benefits of "free-market" competition. Against an onslaught of high-powered corporate lobbying, warnings and questions from citizens' groups are either ignored or buried as afterthoughts in news stories and legislative hearings. All too often the rosy scenarios about "consumer benefits" have faded into horror stories of higher prices, poorer service, and taxpayer-financed corporate bailouts.

California, the nation's most populous state, has become the "poster child" for electric utility deregulation gone bad. A 1996 state deregulation plan that was supposed to make electricity cheaper has resulted in vastly higher energy costs for consumers and businesses. California residents and businesses paid nearly 11 billion dollars more for electricity last summer than the previous year. The state now faces the possibility of power shortages manipulated for price maximization. This possible manipulation was pointed out by the California Public Utility Commission last summer.

Even California's current Democratic governor, Gray Davis, who has tiptoed cautiously into the controversy, calls the state's deregulation "a colossal and dangerous failure." But now the big question is how the mess is to be cleaned up and, more important, who pays? Consumers or the big utilities that promoted the deregulation scheme in the mid 1990s?

Two investor-owned utilities—Southern California Edison and Pacific Gas and Electric—have turned their public relations and lobbying teams loose around the state with sob stories about their financial plight. Lurking behind all the corporate hand-wringing is the hope that the politicians can be cajoled into providing a bailout financed by the taxpayers. High on the corporate wish list is authority for a bond issue to be financed by consumers through higher electric rates—a scheme that would burden electric ratepayers for years to come.

The governor has called for the establishment of a California Power Authority and more state control over power generated in the state along with increased production and conservation measures. As yet, he has not endorsed the utilities' bond scheme, but the final chapter on the utility lobbying efforts will be written in a special session of the state legislature.

What should make California consumers (taxpayers) nervous is Governor Davis's inordinate concern about the possibility that the investor-owned utilities might be required to face up to their mistakes in a bankruptcy.

"I reject the irresponsible notion that we can afford to allow our major utilities to go bankrupt," Davis told the legislature in his annual "State of the State" message. "Our fate is tied to their fate."

That is the kind of dangerous philosophy that, too often, has fueled the costly idea in state and federal governments that the taxpayers are responsible for bailing out the mistakes of corporations. Contrary to the fears stoked by the utilities, the companies will not disappear in a bankruptcy. The corporate entities simply will be restructured with new management under supervision of a bankruptcy court. There may well be losses for the shareholders, but that risk is part of being an investor in our economic system.

At least one California consumer organization, The Foundation for Taxpayer and Consumer Rights, has come up with data that suggests the utilities have vast worldwide assets that could more than cushion their financial problems in California—without reaching into consumers' pockets for higher rates and a bailout.

As Harvey Rosenfield, president of FTCR, said: "Edison can bail itself out."

Figures compiled by Rosenfield show that Edison International's assets are valued at $37.9 billion. Rosenfield says that some of these assets—like Edison's Massachusetts' trading affiliate ($45 million), the logo on the Anaheim Angels' baseball stadium ($25 million), investments in Mission Windpower Italy, B.V. ($43 million), a 40 percent stake in Contact Energy, New Zealand ($676 million), and plants purchased from Commonwealth Edison of Illinois ($4.9 billion), among others—should be sold before the well-being of the company becomes the responsibility ("fate" in the words of Governor Davis) of California taxpayers. The consumer advocate also urged the company to cut the bloated salaries of its top executives ($7.5 million) and $371 million of shareholder dividends as further buffers against bankruptcy.

Consumers should not be coerced into a monstrous bailout as this electric drama unravels in California. It will be interesting to see who stands up for the consumers against the utilities in California. California has an opportunity to set an example for the nation—an example clearly establishing that consumers should not be required to pay for failed deregulation schemes, corporate mistakes, and greed. Citizens in other areas of the nation should realize that their states are not immune from the type of deregulation disasters that have befallen California.

January 9, 2001

The Future of Fannie Mae and Freddie Mac

Fannie Mae and Freddie Mac are the envy of the corporate world. When it comes to corporate welfare–subsidies and implicit government guarantees—they are in a league all by themselves. Increasingly, the two corporations dominate the mortgage finance market and largely dictate the terms and conditions on which home buyers may obtain shelter, while using their links to the federal government to enrich their private stockholders, officers, and directors.

Any substantive criticism of this cozy juxtaposition of government subsidies and private profits triggers the immediate deployment of lobbying swat teams from the two government-sponsored enterprises to quell any idea that change is needed. Fannie Mae, in particular, is quick to unleash its well-financed public relations and political muscle against anyone or any group that raises a serious negative question about its operation.

Embarrassed by its surrender during the 1980s to the savings and loan industry and fearful of a repeat in other financial sectors, Congress did adopt some limited reforms for the government-sponsored enterprises in 1992, establishing machinery to monitor Fannie and Freddie's contributions to affordable housing and a separate agency as regulator for safety and soundness. Despite some well-meaning administrators, these efforts remain incomplete and underfunded and receive only timid support from a Congress fearful of stepping too hard on the toes of its friends at Fannie and Freddie. Fannie and Freddie have learned to live with the 1992 reforms without drastically changing their approach or their profits.

Fannie and Freddie provide a classic story of what happens in a democracy when a commendable goal—such as the provision of housing—is corrupted by power and greed and, most of all, by lack of accountability. Both Fannie and Freddie were originally government instrumentalities designed to boost financing for housing. Ultimately, both were moved out of government and given "private" charters, which did not fully sever their umbilical chords to the federal government.

Despite their seeming invincibility, some storm clouds have been forming over the GSE's corporate horizon in recent months. It is far too early to know whether these clouds will produce storms that will uproot long-standing policies at Fannie and Freddie and produce better and more equitable protections for the taxpayers and the seekers of homes at affordable prices.

Here are some of the forces at work that may affect the future of Fannie Mae and Freddie Mac.

1) FM Watch, a recently formed industry group dominated by banks, insurance companies, and other financial institutions. They see Fannie and Freddie as competitors that use quasi-government powers to encroach on the private sector role in the mortgage market. The group is staffed and well financed and is having an effect on Capitol Hill and in the media. The big shortcoming in the credibility of this organization, especially for housing and community groups, is the fact that big players in FM Watch have a poor record of meeting affordable housing needs of low- and moderate-income families. In addition, many of FM Watch members contribute large sums to financial trade associations that actively oppose efforts under the Community Reinvestment Act (CRA).

2) The House Banking Committee where Representative Richard Baker, a rising Republican star on the committee, has introduced legislation that would curb Fannie and Freddie and has conducted well-publicized hearings that highlighted a host of GSE shortcomings. How far Baker will push his efforts is still a question, but at the moment he is the most painful burr in the side of Fannie and Freddie. An even bigger question may be the ability of Baker to gain support from the incoming administration of George W. Bush.

3) The Federal Reserve Board chairman has written, in answer to Baker's inquiries, two letters that raise questions about Fannie and Freddie's competition with private lenders and the degree to which government subsidies are passed on to home buyers. Greenspan, riding the crest of a popularity wave, adds new heft to Baker's efforts and increased media coverage of the issue. However, many wonder whether Greenspan wrote the letters as a political move to curry favor with a prominent Banking Committee Republican, rather than in a real effort to fan the flames for GSE reform.

A countervailing force is the fact that many senior Democrats in both the Senate and House sought assignment to the Banking Committee because of the Committee's housing and urban development jurisdiction. Many of these Democrats readily accept the often stated, but never proven, claim by Fannie Mae that any change in the GSE's status would raise the cost of housing. Some middle-level Democrats, like Representative Ken Bentsen of Texas, however, have raised questions about Fannie and Freddie and many of the junior members have stayed out of the fray. So, the ultimate party split on GSE reform is still a question mark.

The support among the Democrats for reform may hinge largely on how strong a case can be made that Fannie and Freddie are failing to meet afford-able housing needs, particularly in low-income and minority areas. A key quid pro quo for the GSE's continued existence as freewheeling users of the government's credit has been support for affordable housing. If oversight hearings establish that Fannie and Freddie are falling short in this area, the tide could rise for basic reforms in the public interest.

These reforms should ensure that:

1) any government subsidy is passed on to home buyers, not pocketed by Fannie and Freddie shareholders or used for public relations, excessive executive compensation, or political purposes;

2) housing goals are set high enough to end the continuing shortfall of affordable housing and that these goals are rigorously enforced;

3) patterns of purchases of home mortgages by Fannie and Freddie are nondiscriminatory;

4) capital standards and regulatory oversight are sufficient to protect tax-payers against bailouts;

5) Fannie and Freddie's charters are amended to clarify the role of the GSEs in housing and that oversight is sufficient to ensure that the companies do not stray from their assigned mission.

January 2, 2001

Financial "Modernization" Legislation

L ast year's deregulation monster—the so-called financial modernization leg-islation—was riddled with anti-public interest provisions, but nothing illus-trated congressional recklessness more than the way safety and soundness of the nation's financial system was ignored.

In its rush to deliver for the financial corporations, a bipartisan coalition in both the Senate and the House of Representatives turned its back on demands to strengthen the antiquated federal regulatory system.

Unfortunately, the legislation was taken up at the height of economic eupho-ria with a skyrocketing stock market, mounting corporate profits, and rising income at the upper levels of society. With their typically shortsighted view, Congress and the financial lobbyists crafted the legislation on the fairyland premise that these "good times" would last forever.

But the prosperity bubble may be receding for some of the nation's big banks. Bank of America, the nation's largest bank, for example, revealed earlier this month that its loan losses could more than double in the fourth quarter from the $435 million the bank reported in the third quarter. Analysts on Wall Street were even more blunt, predicting that the losses would translate into charge-offs of about one billion dollars for the quarter. First Union, the nation's sixth largest bank, said it expected to write off $125 million on a single large loan.

James Dimon, head of Bank One Corp, the nation's fourth largest bank, told executives in Chicago that "credit is deteriorating quarter by quarter and we expect it to continue."

To their credit, bank regulators have been warning for months about the erosion of lending standards, cautioning that an economic slowdown will make it much tougher for highly leveraged companies to make good on their loans. But regulatory hand-wringing isn't going to save the taxpayer-backed insurance fund or prevent taxpayer bailouts.

What is needed is a modern coordinated regulatory system that can deal with and properly monitor the mega-banks and financial conglomerates that are being created under last year's financial modernization legislation. As I recommended during the hearings on the legislation, we need a single regulatory body to replace the overlapping, conflicting, and disjointed system composed of six different federal regulators plus a Heinz 57 variety of state regulatory agencies.

Regulators, banking officials, financial analysts, key members of Congress, and the General Accounting Office have repeatedly pointed to the inefficiencies, conflicting interpretations of rules, and the lack of accountability created by the current system. Through the years, bills have been introduced to create a single coordinated agency that would have the sole responsibility of regulation, but the legislation has failed in the face of opposition from segments of the financial community wanting to keep their own agency and from agencies, themselves, wanting to hold on to their turf.

During the 1990s Charles Bowsher, head of the General Accounting Office (GAO), often pled with Congress to upgrade and coordinate the regulatory system.

Here's what he told the House Banking Committee in 1993: "The current regulatory structure has evolved over more than 60 years as a patchwork of regulators and regulations...we question the ability of the current regulatory structure to effectively function in today's complex banking and thrift environment."

This warning was issued six years before passage of the financial modernization legislation of 1999—a measure that creates huge financial conglomerates combining the biggest of the insurance companies, banks, and securities firms. If the GAO in 1993 found the financial system too complex to be monitored by the present regulatory system, then certainly the new, much larger, and infinitely more complex system created last year cries out for immediate action to craft a modern, more nimble, and more accountable regulatory system.

Congress also needs to return to the drawing board to ensure that there is an adequate deposit insurance system and to make certain the "too big to be allowed to fail" conglomerates don't become candidates for taxpayer bailouts.

The deposit insurance fund has only about $32 billion in reserves, a totally inadequate sum to cope with the sagging fortunes or the outright failure of banks that are part of conglomerates with nearly a trillion dollars in assets—and growing. The deposit insurance system needs to increase deposit insurance premiums paid by the banks to build a "rainy day" fund that will protect not only the soundness of the banking system, but the taxpayers who are inevitably left holding the bag when the big corporations fail.

November 30, 2000

The Insurance Lobby

The insurance lobby, one of the most powerful special interest forces in the United States, has launched an all-out campaign to emasculate the nation's already weak insurance regulatory framework. If the insurance lobby gets its way, it will be much easier for insurers to raise your rates, cut your coverage, and use deceptive sales methods.

The industry's campaign for deregulation follows the passage of the Gramm-Leach-Bliley Act (GLBA), which allows insurers, banks, and securities firms to merge into the money trusts of the past. The insurance lobby perversely calls this process "financial services modernization."

There is, however, nothing modern about the GLBA. The act is a piece of special interest legislation repealing New Deal reform legislation that kept financial sectors such as banking, insurance, and securities separate because the combined economic and political power of these industries threatened to undermine competitive enterprise and democratic government.

The passage of the GLBA has spurred consumer groups to redouble their efforts to strengthen the insurance regulatory system and reject insurance industry demands to weaken the already inadequate consumer safeguards in the insurance marketplace. Consumer advocates are also concerned about the misuse of political and economic power that is likely to come with further consolidation of financial services.

On September 10, the Consumer Federation of America's director of insurance, J. Robert Hunter, led a coalition of consumer advocates in calling for public interest-oriented insurance regulatory reform. The consumer coalition released a white paper that provides specific guidance to public officials with regard to reinventing insurance regulation to benefit consumers. The paper listed seventy pro-consumer principles by which the public can judge whether the changes being proposed meet consumer needs. These principles fall into eight broad categories: timely and meaningful disclosures for consumers, user-friendly design of policies, access to adequate coverage, nondiscriminatory marketplace, privacy protection, meaningful right of redress, competent regulatory structure, and consumer representation in all processes.

The AFL-CIO and Consumers Union, among others, endorsed the white paper and the American Association of Retired Persons (AARP) issued a similar list of principles by which to measure the proposed changes.

Mr. Hunter has succeeded in building a strong coalition, but he has a tough battle to fight. The insurance lobby has picked a battleground that is inaccessible to most consumer advocates and concerned citizens.

Rather than debating the merits of deregulation in Congress or the state capitals nationwide, the insurance lobby has taken its plans to two private forums: the National Association of Insurance Commissioners (NAIC) and the National Conference of Insurance Legislators (NCOIL). The NAIC, an association of state regulators, is heavily influenced by the insurance industry. The NCOIL membership consists of state legislators who often side with the insurance industry in state legislatures.

The NAIC and NCOIL are cozy clubs where insurance lobbyists and the public officials they control meet without being bothered by inefficiencies of democratic government. Both organizations like to hold their meetings in high-class hotels. State officials can afford to be there because their expenses are subsidized, or paid for outright, by insurance lobbyists' attendance fees. Hospitality suites abound for the regulators. And, there is no shortage of insurance industry lobbyists wanting to treat the regulators to fine dinners.

Insurance reform has never come easy. Usually, reform has only followed financial failure. The financial panic of 1907 resulted in the Armstrong and Merritt Committees in New York. The lingering effects of the Great Depression resulted in the Temporary National Economic Committee (TNEC) Investigation. A series of great antitrust cases initiated by Thurman Arnold following the TNEC Investigation nearly succeeded in forcing insurers to comply with the same consumer protections as other national businesses.

There have been successes in the fight for insurance reform, such as the 1988 landmark pro-consumer ballot initiative in California. Consumers voted to reject excessive auto, homeowner, and business insurance premiums and curb a variety of abuses by insurance companies in California.

Unfortunately, insurers are shielded from federal antitrust law and Federal Trade Commission oversight because state officials promised, in 1945, to replicate these consumer protections at the state level. Unrelenting pressure from insurance lobbyists has prevented the states from producing meaningful pro-consumer insurance regulation.

We should not wait for another Great Depression to bring insurance under the same regulatory framework as other sectors of interstate commerce. Fair and reasonably priced insurance is important for economic growth and security. Consumers beware! The insurance industry campaign for insurance deregulation is primarily designed to benefit the insurers, not consumers.

For more information about this issue, write to: Robert Hunter, Consumer Federation of America, Suite 604, 1424 16th Street, NW, Washington, D.C. 20036.

September 27, 2000

"Standing" to Hold Government Accountable

It is time to expand the rights of citizens to hold government officials accountable for misdeeds or unacceptable behavior.

Americans have a right to hold companies and government officials accountable when there are violations of the laws of this country—laws protecting the environment, prohibiting racial discrimination, or otherwise affecting the purposes of the people acting through their elected representatives in Congress.

Unfortunately, a series of wrongheaded Supreme Court decisions has twisted the law of "standing"—the court rules that determine whether a particular person or group has the right to bring a lawsuit—in a manner that has undermined the intent of Congress, the provisions of the Constitution, and the will of the people.

What has emerged from the Supreme Court is a complex and convoluted body of "standing" law that is too arcane for most citizens to want to even try to understand and too demanding to allow legitimate grievances to be heard in court. Using such esoteric terms of art as "injury in fact," "redressability," "logical nexus," and "zone of interest," the law of standing has become an obstacle to ensuring that the public will, as enacted by Congress, is carried out. Much court time is spent on preliminary skirmishes over this complex, confusing, and often contradictory "standing" law instead of proceeding to decide the actual merits of a lawsuit. Moreover, there are many instances in which no citizen would have standing to complain, even if the executive branch of the government or a private party openly and deliberately violated laws passed by Congress.

This is no way to promote official compliance with the law or citizen confidence in the operation of government.

In the environmental area, Congress has enacted a series of "citizen suit" provisions to improve enforcement. Recognizing that federal enforcement resources would never be a match for the sprawling activities and enormous resources of industry, Congress decided to fill the gap by allowing citizens who detected violations of law—either by regulated industries or by the regulatory agency itself—to bring suit to fix the problem. Nearly every major environmental statute contains a citizen suit provision. The Clean Water Act, the Clean Air Act, the Safe Drinking Water Act, the Community Right-to-Know Act, the Toxic Substances Control Act, and at least nine other environmental statutes have such a provision.

Professor Cass Sunstein, a respected constitutional law scholar, has proposed a legislative solution that should meet the Supreme Court's most demanding and formalistic approach to the constitutional requirements of standing. This proposal is the basis of the Citizens' Bounty Act.

The Citizens' Bounty Act simply provides that anyone who sues either the government or a private party under the "citizen suit" provision of a statute and prevails in the suit will receive a $250 cash bounty. (Few people will bring a suit for just $250 dollars—this provision is designed to overcome the obstacles to getting standing.) Such a provision would give any citizen suit plaintiff a direct financial interest in the outcome of the suit, thus providing a concrete basis for standing—the first step in allowing a citizen to have his or her day in court.

Such an approach is similar to that undertaken in *qui tam* provisions, such as the False Claims Act, under which a citizen who exposes wrongdoing against the government by a government contractor and prevails in court is entitled to a share of the recovery. People using the False Claims Act have gone after defense contractor boondoggles, Medicaid rip-offs, and other misuses of taxpayer dollars.

This simple fix will eliminate the need to waste valuable time arguing about standing and allow cases to proceed efficiently and on their actual merits. It will allow citizens who can prove that private parties or the government are violating federal law to make their case in court and enforce the will of the people, as reflected in the laws enacted by Congress.

August 23, 2000

Aviation Industry Failing to Upgrade Safety Programs

The tragic crash of a Concorde near Paris on a flight to New York City, killing all 109 on board and four on the ground, has shocked the world and brought public attention to an issue being quietly debated by aviation safety experts and officials: Should old aircraft face mandatory retirement?

Airline corporations and the federal government mandate that airline pilots must retire at age sixty, yet at the same time oppose any mandatory retirement for aircraft. Currently, aircraft have clearance to fly even if they far exceed their design life (the number of years or takeoffs and landings for which the manufacturer designed the aircraft). Some airlines take advantage of this by continuing to fly passengers as long as the planes can be repaired and pass government inspections. However, many safety experts and engineers—including some in the aircraft manufacturing industry and aviation safety organizations such as the Aviation Consumer Action Project (ACAP) (which I founded in 1971 to give consumers a voice and ear on major aviation issues)—are worried that airlines do not decommission airliners after their planned twenty-year life. This poses a growing danger to the traveling public. So far, the only action taken by the U.S. and other governments is to "study" the problem.

Meanwhile, the U.S. aircraft fleet of about 4,900 airplanes is rapidly aging, according to a 1998 report by the White House Commission on Aviation Safety and Security, chaired by Vice President Al Gore. The commission also concluded that airline crash fatalities would double by 2007 unless major improvements in air safety were implemented. Historically, old airliners were made obsolete by improved, newer aircraft and rarely remained in service past their design life. But, today, deregulated profit-hungry U.S. airlines have about 3,000 aircraft, or 60 percent of the total fleet, in service that have already exceeded their design life. Some in the industry advocate that aircraft designed for twenty years of service (or about 40,000 takeoffs and landings, called cycles) should be allowed to continue indefinitely in public passenger service—thirty, forty or even fifty years. This is taking the aviation industry into uncharted territory where passengers and flight crews unwittingly become the test subjects to see how long old airliners can fly before they literally come apart.

The supersonic Concorde fleet, which now consists of only twelve planes in service, was built between 1969 and 1979. Contrary to some media reports that the Concorde has had a "perfect" safety record, there have been a growing and disturbing number of safety incidents, at least six since 1998. They include the near disastrous loss of 40 percent of a Concorde's lower rudder during a flight to New York City on October 8, 1998; a wing problem on May 28, 1998, over the Atlantic that caused the aircraft to turn back to London; an engine failure resulting in an emergency landing and a fire alarm on another Concorde causing another emergency landing, both on January 30, 2000. And most recently, on July 24, 2000, one day before the Concorde crash near Paris, there was an announcement of the discovery of cracks in the wing supports of all seven British Air Concordes, resulting in the mandatory grounding of only one. This record is particularly distressing considering the very small number of Concordes in service and the very high level of maintenance they constantly receive.

Paul Hudson, ACAP's executive director, points out that the use of jetliners far beyond their design life is also retarding the adoption of modern safety systems that could make flying much safer. Such systems include fire and explosion suppression systems that have been used successfully in military aircraft for over a decade (three of the past five air disasters in North America were due to uncontrolled in-flight fires or explosions—Swissair 111, TWA 800, and ValuJet).

In 1999, the high cost of retrofitting existing airlines was cited by industry as the main reason for its opposition to installing fire and explosion suppression systems in fuel tanks after the TWA 800 disaster. The National Transportation Safety Board (NTSB) recommended, after finding that the TWA 800 disaster was due to an exploding center fuel tank, that the Federal Aviation Administration (FAA) should implement measures to eliminate or substantially reduce the risk of such explosions.

Last year an industry-government task force report on fuel tank safety found that existing aircraft, which often contain center fuel tanks with adjacent heat sources, were in a potentially explosive condition about 30 percent of their operating time and calculated that it could be expected that six hundred persons would die in such accidents over the next ten years. The FAA typically has agreed with the industry to "study" the problem, but has not required that any currently available explosion or fire suppression technology be installed on commercial airliners.

Many state and local fire codes for large buildings and even restaurant kitchens are now under stricter standards in the United States (which generally require automatic fire suppression systems) than those for airliners. Of course, most air travelers do not know that when traveling at 30,000 feet there are few, if any, fire suppression or detection systems.

The aviation industry and government claim that existing maintenance and inspection programs are adequate, but they fail to require replacement of basic systems, such as old wiring (insulation has been shown to wear out with age and use), hydraulic systems that power aircraft controls, or even most electronics.

Ultimately, consumers have real power to determine whether old aircraft will be taken out of service before they become older than their pilots, regardless of corporate greed or government inaction. Air passengers should ask the age of the aircraft when booking flights, avoid aircraft that have far exceeded their design life, and support a mandatory retirement regulation for aging aircraft. You can find out more about this growing menace to aviation safety and what you can do by contacting ACAP. Web site: www.acap1971.org; telephone: 800-588-ACAP; address: 529 14th Street NW, Suite 1265, Washington, D.C. 20045; e-mail address: acap71@erols.com.

August 1, 2000

Consumer Protection Agency Still Needed

More than ever, politics and policy decisions in our nation's capital are dominated by big money. Contributions from U.S. and multinational corporations heavily influence the outcome of elections. And lawyers and lobbyists representing wealthy business interests dominate proceedings in Congress, in the courts, and before federal agencies. It is time for Congress to do something to level the playing field—to provide citizens, in their roles as consumers, homeowners, and small business owners, with better representation in the halls of Washington.

It is time to create a modest-sized agency whose mission would be to protect the interest of citizens in the rough-and-tumble of Washington politics. It is time—in an age when both major parties speak eloquently of curbing the role of special interests and returning government to the people—to create a Consumer Protection Agency.

A Consumer Protection Agency would be a tremendously lucrative investment for our government to make. The agency would be an internal trim-tab—a tiny rudder within the government but also aimed at the government. It would more than finance its tiny price tag by creating enormous economic benefits for the public.

The purpose of a federal Consumer Protection Agency would be to improve the way government decisions are made—to make them more responsive to the needs of the people, to make them fairer, in order to improve the functioning of our market economy. Corporations have the wealth and power to make their views known in Congress, in the courts, and in agency proceedings. The ordinary citizen does not. Corporations can deduct their lobbying expenses on their income tax returns as necessary business expenses. Members of the public who get themselves to Washington to express their concerns on vital issues, even issues of direct economic concern to them, must do so at their own expense, with no tax break provided. These imbalances, time and time again, result in decisions that favor the multinational corporations over individual American consumers and taxpayers.

When the Food and Drug Administration decides whether to approve for sale or to remove from the market a drug or medical device, medical supply corporations weigh in heavily; consumer interests are overwhelmed. When the Securities and Exchange Commission considers regulations regarding the fraud on shareholders or insider trading, corporations, brokers, and investment banks provide detailed suggestions and arguments; small shareholders may never know the SEC proceedings have occurred. When the Department of Transportation decides whether to order a recall of a potentially dangerous automobile model, the manufacturer can launch a heavily funded offensive, while disaggregated consumers have little influence. When the Federal Aviation Administration considers new air travel and airport safety rules, the major carriers weigh in, but airline passengers have little representation. When banking agencies turn a deaf ear to a virtual crime wave by rogue savings-and-loan operators, millions of taxpayers and savers have no one to speak up for them, although they will eventually pay for a huge bailout designed with the help of power lobbyists. When federal departments and agencies give away vast public resources in one-sided sweetheart deals with corporate contractors, the public is rarely consulted or heard.

A small Consumer Protection Agency—staffed leanly but expertly by economists, accountants, scientists, engineers, and lawyers—would press the agencies and the courts to fully consider the consumer perspective in making the decisions that affect our daily lives.

The Consumer Protection Agency would not add a new layer of federal regulation. The agency would have no power to regulate business activity. Instead, it would investigate, develop facts, and present consumer interests to legislators, regulators, and courts. It would participate in agency proceedings and challenge federal agency nonenforcement of statutes passed by Congress.

The concept of a federally-created voice for consumers has been around at least since 1959, when Senator Estes Kefauver of Tennessee sponsored legislation to secure effective representation for the consumer, whom he called the "forgotten man in our Government structure." In the 1970s, both Houses of Congress approved legislation to create a Consumer Protection Agency—in some cases by a wide margin. But although President Jimmy Carter promised to sign the legislation, aggressive, well-financed corporate opposition ensured that it was never passed by both Houses in the same session and sent to the president.

The agency would help promote the safety, quality, and availability of consumer products and services; protect consumer choice and competitive markets; prevent unfair and deceptive trade practices; and advance the legal rights of consumers.

And the Consumer Protection Agency would more than pay for itself. The benefits to the public as consumers—in the form of better, safer products and services, more competitive markets, and lower prices—would far outweigh the modest costs. Who speaks for patients confronting high drug prices that drain billions of dollars from ailing people?

Also the potential for Consumer Protection Agency watchdog actions would make federal departments and agencies utilize taxpayer dollars more productively.

Recent history is full of examples of situations where a federal consumer protection agency could have saved taxpayers millions—and also saved precious lives. Imagine if a full-time consumer agency could have weighed in before bank regulators approved the operations and actions of the sharp operators who ran the savings-and-loan industry into the ground—forcing a massive $500 billion federal bailout.

Or if consumers could have been fairly represented when the Department of Transportation cancelled its announced plan to recall six million General Motors pickups with vulnerable fuel tanks that have cost hundreds of lives?

Or if a consumer agency could have participated in FDA proceedings before that agency granted approval to market fatally defective medical devices, where companies hid key safety information. In those cases and many more, the presence of a robust, independent Consumer Protection Agency could have made a major difference. And no doubt there are many more such cases on the horizon. The need for the agency is clear. Write your senators and representatives to find out where they stand on this proposal.

July 26, 2000

Corporate Lobbyists and Their Government Buddies

It never seems to end—this relentless merger of corporate lobbyists and their government buddies.

The latest display of cushiness was at the annual summer meeting of the National Governors' Association (NGA) at Pennsylvania State University. The NGA is a private association on the corporate hospitality take. And, man, do these corporations give to get inside the gated community.

Forget about everyday Americans and their citizen groups. They can't afford the tickets of admission to hobnob with the governors. But corporations, paying up to $150,000 each, get inside the gates. Seventy companies paid the top price.

Larry Makinson, executive director of the Center for Responsive Politics, based in Washington D.C., commented: "Talk about an investment. This is a golden opportunity for these companies to rub shoulders with the CEOs of virtually every state of the Union." Right, Larry, and he who has the gold gets the opportunity.

Unions, environmental and consumer groups need not apply. But corporations, such as Aetna and Wal-Mart, can send their executives to a special "corporate fellows" program that spends time with governors and their staff who are often the companies' regulators.

It doesn't matter to politicians how often these companies violated the laws. ExxonMobil, DuPont, the illegal monopolist Microsoft—all receive deferential treatment.

Outside of the governors' meeting, over one hundred protestors gathered for a rally-demonstration to challenge abuses of corporate power. Philip Morris, the giant nicotine dealer, got inside, but the police kept the peaceful demonstrators away from even the entrance of the conference center. Out of sight, out of media opportunity.

One of the discussion topics at the NGA meeting where President Clinton, Colin Powell, and Federal Reserve Chairman Alan Greenspan spoke was how state governments should react to the information-age economy. You can bet that putting all major state government contracts and grants on the state's web site was not on the agenda. Or urging the state legislatures to put their voting records in an understandable, retrievable manner on the states' web sites for citizens to easily discover.

At its conferences, the NGA passes resolutions, which are often very pro-corporate. The one that took the cake was a resolution in the mid '90s. It supported federal preemption of the state common tort law for purposes of restricting further the rights of wrongfully injured Americans to have their day in state court against the perpetrators of their harms.

Yep, the NGA is the best money can buy. And it comes without even any shame over appearances.

National Governors' Association, Hall of States, 444 North Capitol St., Washington, D.C. 20001-1512. (202) 624-5300.

July 12, 2000

Make the Fed Follow the Rules

The Federal Reserve has always acted as a separate government. Normal checks and balances that apply to other federal agencies are simply ignored by the Federal Reserve Board.

The board sets its own budget and operates off the billions of dollars collected in buying and selling government securities as part of its control of the money supply. The spending is not even subject to a formal congressional review. With the exception of an occasional perfunctory hearing, congressional oversight is largely a joke or nonexistent. Rather than probing the operations of the Federal Reserve, hearings invariably become contests to see which member of Congress can utter the most fulsome praise for the Fed and its current chairman, Alan Greenspan.

The Federal Reserve picks and chooses the laws it follows. It claims, for example, that it is not subject to the Civil Rights Act and the provisions of the act that outlaw job discrimination. In 1980, Congress passed the Monetary Control Act in an attempt to eliminate the subsidies that the Federal Reserve was handing out to commercial banks in the form of below-market pricing of check clearing and other services. The Fed processes and transports more than 17 billion checks annually, largely carried out through a contract fleet of fifty-three airplanes.

Instead of changing its pricing system to comply with the law, the Fed has engaged in some "creative bookkeeping" and some less than straightforward explanations to Congress in an attempt to obscure the subsidies.

A handful of members of Congress and their staffs have refused to fall for the Fed's flimsy explanations. They believe that the Federal Reserve is continuing to thumb its nose at the law and the clear intent of Congress that services be priced at market value and subsidies ended for the banks.

During the mid-1990s, former House Banking Chairman Henry Gonzalez and his chief economist and Fed-tracker extraordinaire, Dr. Robert Auerbach, conducted detailed investigations that revealed "waste and fraud" in the Fed's payment system. Among other things, the Gonzalez report documented what it called "corrupted bidding procedures," interference with competitors, and overcharging the U.S. Treasury for hauling its cleared checks—all of which helped mask the subsidies. The report cited, as well, cases of the Fed paying for "phantom aircraft" and double paying for aircraft that the Federal Aviation Administration had permanently grounded due to falsified maintenance reports.

Fed officials tried to play down the report and portrayed Gonzalez's findings as simply "differences of opinion about management decisions." Despite this attempt to dust off the report in public comments, the Fed behind the scenes did make some limited internal changes in its check transportation system. Now the Federal Reserve has come up with a new scheme to maintain the fiction that it is recovering the costs of the payment system, rather than subsidizing the services in violation of the 1980 Monetary Control Act. The Fed is now transferring part of the excess in its employees' pension funds to subsidize the services. Dr. Auerbach, who is now a professor at the University of Texas Lyndon B. Johnson School of Public Affairs, estimates that the Fed offset $87 million of the payment system's costs in 1998 by using the pension funds.

After learning of the pension fund gimmick, Senator Harry Reid of Nevada quietly attached as an amendment to last year's financial modernization legislation that prohibited the Fed's use of pension fund money to balance the books on the payment services.

But the amendment was short-lived. During the House-Senate conference, Fed Chairman Greenspan—who appeared to serve an ex-officio member of the conference—lobbied House Banking Chairman Jim Leach, a longtime apologist for the Federal Reserve, to get rid of the Reid amendment. Without any debate, recorded votes, or public announcement, the amendment suddenly disappeared from the bill's text, leaving the Fed free to continue to play with pension funds to hide payment services subsidies.

The treatment of the Reid amendment is the latest illustration of how subservient the Congress is to the Federal Reserve and how weak-kneed the banking committees are in resisting pressure from Alan Greenspan. Congress is letting the Monetary Control Act of 1980 become a nullity, by allowing the Federal Reserve to openly hand government money to the banks in contravention of the law. It is time for the voters to demand a Congress that doesn't cave to the every whim of the Federal Reserve. It is a disgrace when Congress cannot summon the courage to see that the laws it passes—like the Monetary Control Act of 1980—are carried out. No wonder that Chairman Greenspan openly thumbs his nose at congressional oversight and operates the Fed as a private preserve for the banks and Wall Street.

February 15, 2000

Consumers Seeking Airline Leg Room

Alert for the millions of airline passenger knees—American Airlines will give them three to five extra inches of space in about a year.

Hooray for small favors. One would think that buying an airline ticket for a seat on the plane would include knees along with toes and torsos. But since airline deregulation over twenty years ago, passengers who do not fork up the dollars for a first-class seat are treated more as cattle than as customers when it comes to space.

But the six-footers have been grumbling ever more loudly as their lower extremities move from being cramped to being crushed (especially when the person in front of them reclines that seat), to losing circulation and sometimes going numb.

One physician, traveling from the U.S. to London a few years ago, had such circulation problems from cramped quarters that he came close to losing his life. Fortunately he recovered.

For the airlines, cramped seats mean more seats per linear foot and therefore more people in the cattle car. Since all the airlines did the same, give or take, letting people continue their circulatory functions was not a competitive advantage for coach class.

If you want to separate your knees from the firm upholstery, you have to pay extra for first class, business class, or something United Airlines calls Economy Plus.

Last August United Airlines announced more leg room for a price, or if you have special frequent flier totals. Not good enough, for it defies the basic principle of equal opportunity knees and undermines the widespread desire by passengers for whole-body tickets.

The Federal Aviation Administration has no minimum leg-room standards. Pain, bruises, and blood clots are not viewed as part of the FAA's concerns.

But within the next sixty days the Aviation Consumer Action Project (ACAP) will file a petition with the FAA and the Department of Transportation to set minimum leg standards, unless the "industry follows American Airline's lead in increasing coach class leg room to tolerable levels."

ACAP is working on one more initiative—a Six Footers' Club to advance normal comforts for tall passengers. For more information, write to ACAP at P.O. Box 19029, Washington, D.C., 20036, or call 1-800-588-ACAP.

February 8, 2000

Oil Companies Defraud U.S. Government

"America's big oil companies have been ripping off federal and state governments for decades by underpaying royalties for oil drilled on public lands. The Interior Department tried to stop the practice with new rules, but Congress has succeeded in blocking their implementation."

So wrote the *Los Angeles Times* in an editorial this summer. Indeed, this larcenous behavior by the large oil companies has been a routine practice since the early years of this century.

Unlike simple burglaries, big oil thefts are complex and varied. There is the geological type, where the company siphons off oil underneath adjacent property so that it comes up on the property the company is legally entitled to produce from. Then there is the type where the company undercounts the barrels it produces. Indian tribes, among others, have been ripped off with the latter technique for years.

At times the companies would buy and sell from their subsidiaries, or to and from each other, to establish a sweetheart price lower than the actual market price, so they could underpay royalties to the federal and state governments, which are the trustees of the public lands.

The controversy in Congress for the past four years has been over the accounting practice of assigning a posted price to the oil that is well below market price. This, claim oil industry whistle-blowers and senators including Barbara Boxer (D-CA), violates the contractual agreements between the lessor governments and the lessee oil companies. The agreements with the U.S. government require that "the value of production for purposes of computing royalty on production from this lease shall never be less than the fair market value of the production."

Congress is too full of oil-industry senators and representatives taking tens of millions of dollars in campaign contributions to stand up for the taxpayers' assets in these public lands. So the last bastion of democratic government—the courts—has been witness to many lawsuits filed by numerous states and the federal government, as well as some initiated under the False Claims Act by private citizens.

This act allows citizens who have evidence of fraud practiced on the federal government by corporate contractors or lessees to sue to recover the sums defrauded. Often the Justice Department will join these suits. The state lawsuits alone have already recovered about $5 billion through settlements. A number of big companies are settling their share of a lawsuit that was brought by two whistle-blowers and the U.S. government in Texas. That suit aimed to recover a total of $5 billion for alleged violations reaching back for years.

Pressed by the state of California since 1981, the federal government finally agreed to publish a final revised rule on the royalty valuation of crude oil on federal lands to stop the underpayments. But led by the oil-marinated Senators Tim Hutchinson (R-AR), Pete Domenici (R-NM), John Breaux (D-LA), and Don Nickles (R-OK), Congress has blocked this crude oil valuation rule for two years. The same senators are pushing for another year-long delay, which Interior Secretary Bruce Babbitt estimates will cost the federal treasury, the states, and Indians nearly $6 million a month.

The federal and state lands, owned by the American people, have long been plundered by the oil, timber, mining, and grazing companies that manage to get these valuable natural resources for a fraction of their real market value. And, in the case of the 1872 Mining Act, gold and other hard-rock minerals entirely for free.

The struggle to get fair market value for these resources should be won through omnibus federal and state laws that prohibit these multibillion-dollar giveaways of the people's heritage to corporations. How? By applying the same yardstick that corporations do when they deal in the marketplace for their goods and services. It is called fair market value.

September 23, 1999

Putting Public Works First

New projections of a federal budget surplus have left Washington abuzz with proposals on how the government should allocate hundreds of billions of dollars.

Strikingly absent from the debate are recommendations to revitalize our commonwealth by investing in a public works program.

At no time in recent history has a program to construct, rebuild, or repair crumbling bridges, schools, drinking water facilities, sewer lines, docks, parks, mass transit systems, libraries, clinics, courthouses, and other public amenities and infrastructure been so urgent or achievable. Too many of our roads and bridges are decrepit; school roofs across the nation are leaking or falling in; the public water system does not deliver safe drinking water for millions; the reach of public transportation systems is dwindling; the great national park system is seriously decaying—and this is only the beginning of the list. It is past time to commence a major public works initiative to repair this great storehouse of shared wealth.

Federal, state, and local governments already spend substantial funds on various public works projects, most notably highway construction. And a modest debate is now percolating on federal support for school building construction. But current expenditures are hugely inadequate to meet many of our most pressing public works needs.

Consider the following:

• One in three schools across the United States is "in need of extensive repair or replacement," according to a 1995 General Accounting Office report. Fixing the schools, the GAO estimates, will cost $113 billion over three years.

• The Centers for Disease Control estimates 1 million people become sick every year from bad water, nine hundred of whom die as a result. The EPA estimates nearly $140 billion will be needed over the next twenty years for water system investments to install, upgrade, or replace failing drinking water infrastructure.

• Maintaining the public transit system at current levels, the Department of Transportation estimates, will cost $9.7 billion a year. Improving the infrastructure to a condition of "good" would require upping annual expenditures to $14.2 billion a year. But maintaining or slightly upgrading the public transit is not nearly enough. Bold new investments are needed to create a modern mass transit system conducive to livable cities, one that will bring community residents closer together, combat the momentum toward sprawl, guarantee lower-income groups the ability to travel efficiently in metropolitan areas, abate air pollution, and improve transportation safety.

• As a society we have failed to respect the foresight of Theodore Roosevelt, John Muir, and other conservationist founders of the national park system, neglecting to invest sufficient resources to maintain, let alone properly expand, the parks. A National Park Service-estimated funding gap of nearly $9 billion has left animal populations at risk, park amenities in substandard or unusable conditions, and many national historical artifacts in danger of being lost to posterity.

Investments in public works—those mentioned here, plus others, such as construction of public health clinics, libraries, sewers, and courthouses; bridge and road repair; and cleanup efforts of military and nuclear waste sites—make our communities stronger and more closely knit. While many of these community benefits do not accrue in citizens' personal bank accounts, they do register in direct and discernible improvements in every person's life. Investing in and protecting our great public assets makes us richer as a nation and a people.

Public investments also strengthen the economy through a better-educated and healthier workforce and through efficient transportation of goods and people.

Historically, investments in public works have been a key spur to private wealth creation. A national public works plan, Franklin Roosevelt said in his 1934 State of the Union speech, "will, in a generation or two, return many times the money spent on it....More important, it will conserve our natural resources, prevent waste and enable millions of our people to take better advantage of the opportunities which God has given our country."

This—an era of burgeoning private wealth and large projected public surplus—is the time to reinvigorate our public investments.

July 27, 1999

Corporate Welfare

The first-ever congressional hearings critical of corporate welfare—the hundreds of billions of dollars given annually in subsidies, bailouts, giveaways, tax escapes, etc.—were held June 30 by House Budget Committee Chairman John Kasich (R-OH). And most of the major media organizations did not show up. But C-SPAN did and relayed a remarkable array of witnesses and testimony to the American people who are paying these bills.

The Kasich hearing was public education by Congress at its best. No sound bites. Instead the testimony was detailed, the questions thoughtful, and the proposals for ending these boondoggles were numerous.

In a rare moment of agreement, both conservative and progressive groups lined up to criticize the looting of Uncle Sam and the very big business that such looting has become.

My testimony described several categories of corporate welfare. These included: the giveaways of hard-rock minerals, such as gold and molybdenum to domestic and foreign mining companies; the giveaway of the public airwaves, which belong to the people, to private radio and television stations (including the latest $70 billion gift of the digital spectrum); taxpayer subsidies for giant defense corporation mergers and commercial weapons exports to governments overseas; and making patients pay twice for drugs, once as taxpayers to develop the medicine and again as patients, after the federal government gives monopolistic control over the chemical's manufacture to a price-gouging drug company.

The impact of these handouts to corporations on taxpayers is sad. A woman with ovarian cancer contacted us with her desperate story of having to pay about $14,000 for six treatments of Taxol, sold by Bristol-Meyers Squibb. Thirty-one million dollars of taxpayers' money developed this drug, right through the human clinical trials.

Bristol-Meyers owns the rights to make Taxol. No other company can produce it. So there is no price competition to drive the price down. If patients with cancer have to go on Medicaid because they cannot afford this gouge, then the taxpayers again pay Bristol-Meyers for Taxol.

By the way, Bristol-Meyers is not obligated to pay Uncle Sam any royalties on what this year will be $1 billion in sales. Do you know any private business that develops and gives away its assets like that?

Then there is the Partnership for a New Generation of Vehicles (PNGV), which Clinton and Gore announced in August 1993 at a White House ceremony with Detroit bigwigs. Under this deal, taxpayers give $1 billion to General Motors, Ford, and Chrysler to entice them to build a more fuel efficient vehicle. These giant companies are reporting record profits year after year and should be competing on their own to develop more efficient engines.

It gets worse. PNGV effectively gives the auto companies immunity from the antitrust laws in this area, takes away the competitive pressures, and staves off overdue consumer protection regulation. After six years, what is the result? A few technical papers, no model cars, and no competition. Guess which automakers will market a car next year that will get over 60 miles per gallon? Toyota and Honda, which are not part of this do-nothing partnership.

My testimony contained many proposals, both procedural (disclosure of corporate beneficiaries on the Internet, sunset provisions, and competitive bidding for taxpayer assets) and substantive (an outright repeal of the corporate hand-outs, charging fair market value for inventions and natural resources, and reasonable pricing provisions on government-developed products such as Taxol).

It will be interesting to see if the presidential candidates, including Kasich, will strive to make corporate welfare a major issue. For in addition to its other symptoms, corporate welfare breeds corruption in politics and often presents unfair competition to taxpaying small businesses that have to coexist with the Chryslers, Intels, Marriotts, and others. These corporations, and others like them, have demanded and received huge property-tax holidays for their buildings.

To obtain copies of the Kasich hearing testimonies, go to www.house.gov/budget/hearings/hrglist.htm. You may wish to contact Representative Kasich's office with your opinion. His phone number is (202) 225-5355.

July 2, 1999

Truckin' Past Safety Regulations

It happens week after week in the nation's capitol and often goes unnoticed by the media. After suffering a family tragedy due to a preventable act of corporate negligence, a group of Americans find one another in their grief and travel to Washington, hold a press conference with a supportive safety group, and visit their members of Congress urging corrective action.

A few days ago, it was the relatives of adults and children who had lost their lives due to large truck crashes and the abysmal nonregulation of truck safety by the Federal Highway Administration's Office of Motor Carrier Safety (OMC). Their gathering in Washington, D.C., called Sorrow to Strength 1999, was sponsored by CRASH—Citizens for Reliable and Safe Highways (www.trucksafety.org).

Thirteen-year-old Ryan Hensley from Ohio spoke up: "My dad was one of over 5,000 people killed in a heavy truck crash in 1997 when a big-rig truck ran a stop sign and hit his car. Too many politicians take a lot of money from the trucking industry. What does the industry expect to get in return? Heavier trucks? Fewer safety inspections? More hours behind the wheel for tired truck drivers?"

A mass of documentation backs up Ryan's lament. In April the Department of Transportation's inspector general issued a report that tore into OMC for not enforcing safety regulations and not deterring repeated violations by some trucking companies with adequate fines and other sanctions.

Public Citizen issued a report in June titled "Truckloads of Money for

Congress," showing the trucking industry's millions of dollars in political contributions to members of Congress by name, and millions more for lobbying
expenses. It reported a flood of exemptions, waivers from existing federal safety
requirements, along with blocked legislation to improve truck safety.

With more than one hundred people killed each week in large truck crashes
and nearly three thousand injured each week, the venerable issues of inadequate
maintenance and equipment, excessive hours of driving, overweight vehicles,
and hazardous cargo violations remain largely ignored by the OMC. Its budget
is tiny, its inspectors few, and its willpower flaccid. It is subservient to the giant
trucking lobby in Washington.

Public Citizen's Joan Claybrook wants the safety functions transferred from
OMC, which she calls "a wholly owned subsidiary of the trucking industry," to
the National Highway Traffic Safety Agency, which she believes will pay more
vigorous attention to this carnage on the highways.

As if the present situation on the highways were not bad enough, from south
of the border there looms an even more horrifying prospect. The NAFTA trade
agreement will allow Mexican trucks, operating under even more neglected or
reckless conditions, to operate in the United States.

Under NAFTA, Texas, California, New Mexico, and Arizona were supposed
to be open to Mexican trucking companies by December 1995. The rest of the
country would be opened by January 2000.

This proved to be too much for Bill Clinton—the leading NAFTA booster—
because he was told about the miserable condition of many aging Mexican trucks
and did not want major crashes to occur before the 1996 elections. He stopped
Mexican trucks from coming into those states beyond the border staging areas,
even though this was a violation of NAFTA. The ban has continued since.

In Mexico, large trucks can weigh 175,000 pounds, compared to the 80,000-
pound ceiling in the United States. And Mexican truck drivers can operate
these giant trucks at age eighteen without proving they are skilled in driving the
particular rig and that they can handle the particular cargo. Also, insurance
coverage is deficient. In the United States, drivers must be twenty-one years old
and proficient with both rigs and cargos.

On June 25, 250 members of Congress, along with the Teamsters Union and
numerous safety groups, demanded that Clinton continue the ban on such
Mexican truck traffic.

The General Accounting Office and the Department of Transportation's
inspector general have issued detailed warnings about the inadequate inspection facilities to monitor Mexican trucks in the border states.

The DOT report found that during 1997, 3.5 million commercial trucks
entered the United States from Mexico through twenty-eight border crossings.

There were only sixty-eight full-time federal and state inspectors to inspect those vehicles. Only one-half of 1 percent were inspected and of those, 44 percent were placed out of service due to serious safety violations. Mexican trucks are routinely violating U.S. and state axle- and gross-weight limits. Then there are the added problems of smuggling illegal hazardous waste and contraband into the United States.

Corporate lobbies behind NAFTA want Mexican trucks in the United States (the drivers get less than $10 a day) in order to also allow U.S. trucks to travel through Mexico.

These business executives should consider what they will see in the rearview mirrors of their limousines in New York, Pennsylvania, California, Illinois, etc., if they too don't start demanding full safety inspection and solid operating standards, with insurance and legal authority, by the federal and state governments.

Otherwise there will be anxious motorists all across America who can turn into angry voters.

June 28, 1999

The Corporate Culture of Violence

Following last week's tragic homicides at Columbine High School and the mourning over the loss of life there, House Speaker Dennis Hastert and Senate majority leader Trent Lott announced they would convene a national conference on youth and culture.

That's good. Such a conference is sorely needed.

But it must not be an empty dialogue. Our country needs better. Throughout the last week, politicians and the media have searched for the causes behind the disaster in Littleton, Colorado, and have been quick to ascribe it, in part, to the violence in video games, music, the Internet, pop culture, Hollywood, movies, and television.

Such comments, although understandable, do not go far enough. They stop at the symptoms, fall short of the cause. They fail to grasp the central fact of our commercial corporate culture: it is produced by corporations that are getting rich by promoting products to teenagers, corporations governed by profiteering that impels them to respect no boundaries in their exploitation of teenagers' vulnerable minds.

Every day hundreds of companies work in pursuit of one goal: manipulating children and teenagers to purchase video games and music and watch movies and television endlessly and mindlessly.

In their quest for larger audiences and greater profits, the commercial media predictably races to the lowest and basest standards, with ever more blatant displays of violence, sex, crassness, and nihilism on television, cable, movies, radio, video games, and music. Our society, even ten or twenty years ago, would not have tolerated such youth-beamed depravity. These are the motivations that relentlessly drive the creation, production, and marketing of ever more Doom, Quake, *Basketball Diaries*, Marilyn Mansons, Mortal Kombat I and II and III and IV, Jerry Springers, Howard Sterns, South Parks, and the rest of it.

This poison has got to stop. Enough is enough.

There is a crying need in this country to redraw the lines, establish the boundaries, declare to the media industry in no uncertain terms: "Thus far and no farther." It is time to say that our children matter more than this brutalizing entertainment. There are few critiques that Congress or President Clinton could start that would have such a salutary effect upon our children and, therefore, on our nation's future.

After all, the people own the public airwaves and should be given the time to challenge such video muck. It is easy to point the finger at the Marilyn Mansons. But they are merely instruments. Speaker Hastert and Senate Majority Leader Lott ought to focus on the deeper problems. Behind every Marilyn Manson are corporations and corporate executives who cynically draw their large compensation packages from the fruits of such work.

The Hastert-Lott national conference on youth and culture will be a charade unless they discuss the corporations and the powerful, moneyed interests that produce this dominating corporate culture and vigorously insinuate it into the minds and pockets of American youth.

Will Speaker Hastert and Senator Lott have the courage to trace the problem to its source, to focus their national conference on youth and culture upon the commercial rewards that give rise to this destructive culture, and on how we might alter these dynamics? Can they enable corporations and civic institutions to produce a culture that nourishes and doesn't harm its teenagers? If so, they will provide an important service for this country, its parents and their children, who are surrounded by debasement and conscripted into violence by methodical, calculating corporate huckstering that our teenagers may not understand.

There is nothing Congress could do that is more important than making America's children safe again from the interests that would rob them of their childhood. Many teenagers and children are powerless to defend themselves against the clever media magnates, their advertising and marketing firms, and their hostility or total disregard for teenagers' health, happiness, and well being.

Families and children need help. The question is, will Speaker Hastert and Senator Lott help them?

April 30, 1999

A Free Ride for Insurance Companies

The insurance industry continues to live a charmed existence in state and federal legislative halls.

Even banks—no slouches at using corporate money and muscle to gain legislative favor—appear incompetent when compared with large insurance companies that regularly escape regulations designed to protect the public.

Adequate credit on reasonable terms is often the lifeblood of many communities. Equally important is insurance. You don't build homes, operate small businesses, or buy automobiles without insurance.

Thirty years ago, the President's National Advisory Panel on Insurance in Riot Affected Areas stated:

"Insurance is essential to revitalize our cities.... Without insurance, banks and other financial institutions will not—and cannot—make loans; ...housing cannot be repaired; ...efforts to rebuild our nation's inner cities cannot move forward.... Communities without insurance are communities without hope."

The Home Mortgage Disclosure Act (HMDA)—a law adopted nearly a quarter of a century ago to combat redlining of low- and moderate-income and minority neighborhoods—requires banks to make annual reports of where they make mortgage loans. The law has helped move credit into underserved rural and urban areas and to detect discriminatory lending patterns.

In 1993 the House of Representatives passed legislation to extend HMDA-type reporting to insurance companies, but the insurance lobby rolled out the big guns in the Senate and prohibited the legislation from being considered by the Senate Banking Committee. Later, in 1996, big insurance companies maneuvered behind the scenes to scuttle a proposal by the National Association of Insurance Commissioners to conduct an industry-wide study of redlining.

Financial deregulation legislation now pending in Congress (H.R. 10) provides a great opportunity to extend an HMDA-style anti-redlining requirement to insurance companies. But the House and Senate Banking Committees have ignored or dismissed the issue.

Amazingly, deregulation legislation is moving forward in both the House and Senate with provisions that will allow insurance companies to form and become members of federal financial holding companies—without being subject to safety and soundness regulations by any federal banking agencies.

According to the pending legislation, insurance companies would continue to be regulated—if that term can be used—by fifty separate state insurance departments, most of which are understaffed, underfunded, and far too often influenced by the industries they monitor and supervise. The Federal Reserve, which would serve as an umbrella regulator of holding companies, would be prohibited from examining or setting capital standards for insurance company subsidiaries. Even the interpretation of regulations would be left solely to the states. Only in extraordinary circumstances could the Federal Reserve intervene in the machinations of an insurance company to prevent the collapse of a holding company.

A few years ago a congressional report evaluating state insurance regulation found a number of weaknesses in this system, including lack of coordination and cooperation, infrequent examinations based on outdated information, insufficient capital requirements and licensing procedures, failure to require independent audits and the use of actuaries, and improper influence on regulators.

Even in the handful of states where insurance departments are reasonably funded and staffed, the emergence of thousands of companies that do business across state lines, as well as in overseas markets, would make it impossible for a single insurance department to monitor and assess risks. Adding to the difficulty of tracking the financial health of insurance companies is the growing complexity of their investments.

Why is this important to taxpayers? Because many of these insurance companies are big enough to compromise an entire financial holding company should they fall on bad times. If that should occur, taxpayer dollars may be used to bail them out.

H.R. 10 is becoming another sad example of the insurance industry's influence over state and federal legislators. As Congress seeks to deregulate the financial industry, insurance companies have taken a prominent position in trillion-dollar business that could dominate the financial world.

March 31, 1999

VI

GLOBAL AND
LABOR CONCERNS

Much of this section deals with one of the saddest developments of the last several decades—the gradual, relentless decline of organized labor. Major factors behind this development include the Taft-Hartley Act; many bureaucratic labor leaders insulated from their rank and file; a concerted campaign by corporate management; and a Republican Party that is so bad on labor issues that the Democrats can easily take labor for granted.

If you doubt that organized labor plays a key role in promoting positive working conditions, consider that its decline has coincided with the following: the spread of globalization that costs millions of American jobs as corporations find cheap labor overseas; the failure of the minimum wage to keep pace with the cost of living; the decline of traditional pension contributions; and the weakening of the Occupational Safety and Health Administration (OSHA) and consequent evisceration of regulations promoting workplace safety.

The globalization trend has hurt the American worker, and amounts to a lose-lose proposition, harming not only America but also the nations overseas where our corporations shift manufacturing. Workers in those countries are paid minimal wages and suffer horrific conditions in export boom and bust industries. The sweat shop and child labor are alive and well in the third world. Globalization also contributes to environmental degradation and deteriorating health around the world. Just ask the fast-food and tobacco industries, which are delighted to find vast new markets for their health-damaging products. (The "progressive" Clinton Administration made the problem worse, adhering to a policy that prevented dissemination of affordable medication.)

As the emphasis on globalization suggests, many of the columns in this section cross America's borders. Our government's shortsighted policies have devastating effects all around the globe. This point extends to the Bush Administration's reckless foreign policies, its unilateral rejection of disarmament, arms control and environmental treaties, and much more. But the problems go way beyond any one administration. Assorted international bodies, including the International Monetary Fund, World Bank, and United Nations, have adopted corporate-first policies that wreak havoc on the third world.

Despite the depressing trend, there are a few heroes in the pages that follow, men and women who refuse to accept defeat. They include the late Anthony Mazzocchi, the founder of the Labor Party and an indefatigable fighter for a new labor agenda that emphasizes worker power, health insurance, wages, and affordable college education.

We need so many more like him. We need a renaissance of organized labor.

The Job Export Machine

In the past four decades, many millions of manufacturing jobs in this country have been shipped overseas or to South America. This transfer was supposed to be part of the "win-win" process of free trade. But twenty-seven straight years of growing trade deficits with the rest of the world makes one wonder: Who's winning?

Conventional economists and their Republican and Democratic converts try to cushion this job export machine by saying that the large majority of jobs in this country are white collar not blue collar. The implication is that white-collar jobs are not as easy to export.

Well, welcome to the computerization age. U.S. companies are rushing headlong to export computer programming work to countries like India and Malaysia and now China where English-language proficiency and cheap labor cut costs by more than two-thirds. Payroll processing, airline passenger billings, insurance computer applications, and new software designs are only some of the labor that is done in foreign countries for U.S. companies.

Last week's *Computerworld* magazine calls "Offshore's Rise" relentless. By next year, the article reports, "Forty percent [of U.S. companies] will have completed some kind of pilot program or will be using nearshore or offshore services. IBM and Accenture, Ltd. were named as firms pushing the dominant trend in the Information Technology services industry, says the research firm IDC. IDC adds that 42 percent of the application management contracts now contain some offshore component."

It is difficult to find any estimates regarding the total number of American jobs displaced in this sector. But Gartner, Inc. uses the jargon "human resources outsourcing services" and puts a $46 billion price tag on them for this year.

Moreover, U.S. firms are opening subsidiaries in countries like India to compete with Indian firms for outsourcing business. Accenture CEO Joe W. Forehand is reported by *Computerworld* as comparing the trend to the previous exodus from the United States of many manufacturing operations. "The way we look at it, the industrialization of IT [information technology] is a reality and we have to embrace that," he said.

It has been in a bit of a slump, not to mention the rest of the computer industry. So, when outsourcing is combined with massive layoffs in this country and the continuing inflow of lower-wage computer technology workers under H-1B and L-1 work visas, it is not surprising to see the gloom besetting American technology workers.

Unlike H-1B visas, which are supposed to receive prevailing wages (but often do not), the L-1 does not oblige employers to pay workers prevailing wages and there is no cap on the number of these visas that can be awarded foreign workers.

With over 500,000 workers in this country on "temporary" H-1B visas, supposedly meeting a domestic dearth of skills, the L-1 visa workers are supposed to be just transfers between subsidiaries and parent companies. In fact, reports the *New York Times*, "They are now routinely used by companies based in India and elsewhere to bring their workers into the United States and then contract them out to American companies—in many instances to be replacement for American workers." The number of workers replaced is unknown, according to the *Times*.

All of this upsets the Organization of the Rights of American Workers, a nonprofit group based in Meriden, Connecticut. Its president, John Bauman, believes that a recovery in this industry will not bring back the American jobs due to both outsourcing and these special visa programs so strongly desired by Silicon Valley companies.

When these concerns are raised to international economists, one of their replies is: "Don't you know what an extraordinary job machine the U.S. economy is?" Well, it has lost 2.6 million jobs since February 2001. More important is that at least one-third of our economy's full-time workers—nearly 50 million—do not earn a living wage! The federal minimum wage, adjusted for inflation since 1968, would be around $8 an hour. Instead, it has remained at $5.15 an hour, exerting a downward pull on lower-income wages generally.

Someday the Pollyanna belief that the U.S. economy always replaces the jobs it loses overseas with new jobs here, as we keep racing ahead of other countries with modern technology and new or redundant services, may run into a contrary riptide that no set of spurious statistics can obscure.

July 9, 2003

Bush Dodges Iraq Meeting with Civic Leaders

Over the last six weeks, major civic groups with deep concerns about the impending war with Iraq have requested meetings with President Bush, who not once in the past year has met with a domestic antiwar delegation.

Astonishingly, not one of these groups, which collectively represent millions of Americans, has received an invitation to meet in response to their written requests.

After the completion of Bush's long overdue news conference on March 7, Senator Robert Byrd remarked: "He spoke like a man who has stopped listening." There are many engaged citizens who wonder whether President Bush ever started listening or has directly heard views of civic leaders who don't want a war, an invasion, or a lengthy occupation of Iraq.

Many commentators and reporters—having spoken with people inside the Bush administration—have noted the isolation, the solitude, and the exclusionary nature of the Bush White House on this subject. Others, such as *Washington Post* reporter Bob Woodward who interviewed President Bush, say the president views himself as a "black-and-white" type of person, a man who makes decisions "from the gut" or from instinct.

Combined with isolation from many informed contrary views, this attitude is made more disquieting by the president's continual invoking of God and God's will when it comes to Iraq. Viewed from abroad, this messianic militarism appears to millions of people as if President Bush is embarking on a religious war.

Now is the time for President Bush to spend a few hours listening to cogent presentations by these Americans of widely different backgrounds and insights, but mostly similar in their opposition to war-invasion-occupation.

Meeting with representatives of these groups, which oppose the president's proposed policies, would afford President Bush an opportunity for a two-way exchange. There have been too many monologues, which serve their purpose, of course, but a dialogue tends to probe and clarify the issues and test the strength of opposing views.

Leaders of veterans' groups and former military leaders are anxious to convey to the president details of the horrific toxic aftermath of the war-invasion to both Iraqis and U.S. troops. They know about the first Gulf War firsthand

and have been closely associated with the treatment of over 200,000 soldiers who were disabled and have been receiving disability payments. Even if the president takes this country to war, he would benefit from knowing how under-trained and inadequately equipped U.S. soldiers are to defend themselves against what the president has said is the likely prospect of chemical warfare by Iraq's brutal dictator.

From women's groups, including those back from numerous trips to Afghanistan, he would learn about the terrible effect on the civilian popula-tion long after hostilities ended, due in part to the lack of promised follow-through assistance by the United States to the Kabul government. They can also convey the likely consequences on Iraqi families whose elderly, mothers, and children will especially suffer from lack of food, spreading disease, fires, and score-settling.

From the perspective of working families, the president would hear why this is the first time that major labor unions, with the encouragement of the AFL-CIO, have ever opposed a war by the United States, in part because it is an unprovoked war.

From the business leaders, he would hear concerns about the further insta-bility and decline of our economy with its effects on standards of living, employ-ment, and neglected domestic budgets.

From representatives of the clergy, the president would hear why the broad religious community believes there is no moral justification for this war and the chaos it will bring.

From leading physicians having experience with poor health conditions and healthcare capacity in Iraq, the president will be informed of the scale of civil-ian mortality and morbidity, including contagious diseases that come from war and its aftermath.

The additional organizations requesting to meet with the president rep-resent a broad cross-section of the American people. They include: elected rep-resentatives of city councils representing tens of millions of Americans; environmental organizations knowledgeable about the environmental dev-astation to the region and the planet on a level even greater than 1991 that is likely from this proposed war; international intelligence specialists with past governmental experience who will tell the president what many dissenters can-not say about consequences and alternatives; specialists inside the Pentagon and the State Department; prominent academics, historians, and civic lead-ers; and groups representing millions of college students, our hope for the future.

They seek a dialogue with President Bush, not out of political partisanship, but because they have not been convinced that war with Iraq is necessary.

The texts of the letters from the civic groups to President Bush are available at: www.essentialaction.org. (See Spotlight on Iraq.)

March 13, 2003

Ignoring the Caution Signs in Iraq

As the drive to war in Iraq races toward a precarious endgame, the lead-footed Bush administration shows no signs of heeding the caution flags flying in from all sides.

Urgings to go slow are not just a phenomena of "Old Europe." At home, retired General Anthony Zinni, a consultant to Colin Powell, and many other retired generals, admirals, and officers have warned about the potential for "blowback." They argue convincingly that this pending war diverts and distracts from the war on terror and is likely to catalyze further acts of terror against the citizens and security of the United States. Retired General Wesley Clark told the Senate Armed Services Committee that a war would "supercharge recruiting for Al Qaeda."

With U.N. Security Council members France, Russia, and China still unconvinced of the need for immediate military action, international support for "preemptive strike" seems unlikely to materialize. Even governments that support a U.S.-led war in Iraq, such as Britain, Turkey, and Spain, do not have the support of their people. If the United States chooses to go it alone or with the help of only a few allies, the already present strains of international anti-Americanism will become even more virulent.

Meanwhile, the Bush administration has been less than forthcoming in providing the public estimates of the actual costs of a war, both in terms of troops and money. The American Academy of Arts and Sciences estimates that over ten years, war and the reconstruction of Iraq could cost as much as $2 trillion—almost the equivalent of the entire annual federal budget. In the *New York Review of Books*, Yale Professor William D. Nordhaus puts the low estimate at $120 billion and a high estimate at $1.6 trillion, given a combination of "different adverse effects."

Despite the costs and dangers to innocent civilians, one powerful administration constituency stands to benefit from a unilateral war in Iraq that results in a U.S.-led regime change. That constituency is the oil industry, whose slick influence and crude ambitions permeate the administration from top to bottom. Both the president and the vice president are former oil executives. National Security Adviser Condeleezza Rice is a former director of Chevron. President Bush took more than $1.8 million in campaign contributions from the oil and gas industries in the 2000 election. All told, forty-one members of the administration had ties to the oil industry.

U.S. oil companies, banned from Iraq for more than a decade, would like nothing more than to control the production of Iraqi oil. With reserves of 112.5 billion barrels, Iraq sits on top of 11 percent of the world's oil.

Vice President Dick Cheney and Senator Richard Lugar (R–IL) are two of the many politicians wondering who will control Iraq's petroleum.

Plans for control of the oil fields are already being laid. The *Wall Street Journal* reported on January 16 that officials from the White House, State Department, and Department of Defense have been meeting informally with executives from Halliburton, Slumberger, ExxonMobil, ChevronTexaco, and ConocoPhillips to plan the postwar oil bonanza. But no one wants to talk about it. Larry Goldstein, president of the Petroleum Industry Research Foundation told the *Journal*, "If we go to war, it's not about oil. But the day the war ends, it has everything to do with oil."

The American people have a right to know what role the oil industry is playing in Bush's increasingly frenetic drive to war. What is being discussed in these meetings regarding the oil industry's designs on this gigantic pool of petroleum?

The American people also have a right to know what was discussed in the numerous secret meetings Vice President Cheney's national energy task force held with oil and gas executives. Cheney has been adamantly secretive about these meetings, despite repeated attempts by Congress and public interest groups to learn what was discussed.

Cheney's energy policy casts as inevitable that we will have to import 17 million barrels of oil a day (two-thirds of our supply) by 2020 and subsequently recommends "that the President make energy security a priority of our trade and foreign policy." It does not recommend specific goals for conservation anytime in the near future.

Just as Cheney refused to meet with anybody but industry cronies in formulating the national energy policy, Bush is now refusing to entertain the counsel of anyone but war hawks. Repeated entreaties by national peace groups, including veterans, clergy, and business groups, for meetings with the president have fallen on ears deaf to anything but the constant beating of war drums.

While it would be naive to label this purely as a war for oil, the apparent connections are enough to raise some serious questions. And when coupled with the administration's frighteningly stubborn insistence on ignoring the caution signs pouring in from all sides, those questions become even more serious.

February 14, 2003

The West Texas Sheriff

George W. Bush has this thing about laws—domestic or international—that disagree with him. He likes to operate outside their embrace or withdraw from them or try to repeal them. It is not just personal—as when he costs taxpayers millions to pay for his political trips on Air Force One before elections—it also involves the health and safety of Americans and people abroad.

Bob Woodward relates in his new book, *Bush at War*, that the president admits to being a black-and-white person who makes decisions from his gut. A dubious enough personality type for a football coach, this trait raises serious concerns when imbedded in the commander-in-chief of the most powerful arsenal on earth.

Consider what this gut instinct has done to our constitutional framework and the tenuous architecture of international law. Earlier this year, Bush launched an all-out offensive on Congress to have it selectively surrender its exclusive constitutional authority to declare war against Iraq. Despite heroic efforts from legislators led by Senator Robert Byrd (D-WV), Congress supinely gave up its war-making power to the White House.

Jefferson, Madison, Adams, and company had distinct reasons for refusing to lodge this power in the presidency and instead wanted many legislators in open session to make this awesome decision. They did not want another King George emerging with this single-power launching war.

Throughout the year 2002, Bush made no secret of his desire to unilaterally overthrow the Iraqi dictatorial regime (called "regime change"). But the opinion polls were unflagging: the American people in sizable majorities did not want the United States to go it alone.

Okay, said Mr. Bush; he'll go to the UN and have the Security Council resume a rigorous inspection process in Iraq of weapons of mass destruction. The other nations then insisted that if Iraq materially breaches the UN resolution, the United States would go back to the Security Council for any further action. Yet Bush made it clear that if the UN did not act, the United States and its very few allies would do so unilaterally.

It should be noted that in responding to Iraq's invasion of Kuwait in 1990, Bush's more deliberative father, then President Bush, first asked the UN for a resolution, then asked Congress, after the November elections not before as did his son, for its approval the following January.

Treaties that deal with arms control or a real weapon of mass destruction called global warming are irritants to our White House-based West Texas sheriff. The Bush administration has rejected the Kyoto Protocol on climate change, declined to support the small arms treaty, the land mines treaty, and the verification protocol for the Biological Weapons Convention. Mr. Bush refuses to submit the Comprehensive Test Ban Treaty for ratification by the Senate, which rejected it under President Clinton. There are other similar avoidances.

Even in the area of health, Mr. Bush is indifferent. The International Covenant on Economic, Social and Cultural Rights, which 130 countries have signed, has not received Mr. Bush's willingness to send it to the Senate for ratification. What is objectionable about the Covenant is that it has a "right to health" within its terms, along with steps to attain this right to health incumbent on signatory nations. The United States is the only western democracy without universal health care.

Prior to 9/11, perhaps no other area of American law aroused more anger in Mr. Bush's mind than the American civil justice system, which enables wrongfully injured children and adults to sue, among other parties, the president's corporate friends when they sell dangerous or defective products.

As governor of Texas and as president, Bush has wanted to limit corporate compensation for unlimited injuries, take away the authority of the states and put it in Washington, D.C., and federally tie the hands of state judges and juries who are the only ones who hear and see the evidence in trials. Note, however, none of his so-called "tort reforms" would take away the right of corporations to sue people or other companies.

It is the daily behavior of this one-track president that is irritating even the usually compliant White House press corps. Day after day, his repetitively belligerent sound bites and his unrevealed "intelligence" declarations about Iraq have been wearing thin. A *Los Angeles Times* poll on December 17 found that 72 percent of respondents, including 60 percent of Republicans, "said the President has not provided enough evidence to justify starting a war with Iraq."

On October 11, the *Washington Post* reported that the former military commander for the Middle East, retired Marine General Anthony C, Zinni, is opposed "to a U.S.-led invasion of Iraq." Zinni believes Iraq is already contained and that the United States has other priorities in the Middle East. Adding that General Zinni is "widely respected in the U.S. Military," the *Post* concludes its report by saying that a retired three-star general said that Zinni's concerns "are widely shared by many in the leadership of the military but aren't universal."

There are few doubts, however, among the covey of "chicken hawks" surrounding Mr. Bush. These men, including Vice President Dick Cheney, supported the Vietnam War in the '60s but wanted other Americans to do the fighting.

There is not much time before Mr. Bush declares a war with scenarios far more costly, harmful, and devastating then the "cakewalk" scenario that is the premise of Mr. Bush's airborne electronic posse. It could be a war fraught with severe longer-term "blowback" impacts on the United States and one that could seriously affect the economy, as Yale Professor Nordhaus warned recently in the *New York Review of Books.*

It is testimony to the inherent sense of the American people that, even in the midst of the Bush propaganda barrage, when asked if they would support a U.S. unilateral invasion with large civilian casualties in Iraq and significant casualties among our military personnel, a large majority says no.

More Americans are wondering why Bush wants peaceful dialogue with a North Korea that has more advanced arms, yet seeks war with a contained, weakened and surrounded Iraq. But then, when decisions are made in the gut, such inconsistencies can abound.

December 20, 2002

Outsourcing Accountability

George W. Bush wants to transfer some 800,000 civilian jobs in the federal government to private business. That is about half of the civil service; such a move is urged in order to save the government money and do the work more efficiently.

Whatever you call it—contracting out, outsourcing, privatizing, or corporatizing these governmental functions—there is no escape from managing the corporate contractors in order to prevent spreading waste, fraud, and abuse. So, President Bush, walk over to your Department of Energy and see what has happened to 90 percent of its entire budget, which is contracted out regularly to firms with a total of 100,000 employees.

On Sunday, November 24, 2002, Joel Brinkley of the *New York Times* wrote a description of how government bureaucracies and their corporate contractors can combine to produce a long-standing disaster of nonperformance and colossal loss of taxpayer dollars.

Notice who is cited by Brinkley to make his story. The evidence comes from within the Department of Energy itself in official reports and commentary. Also, the evidence comes from outside the department by authorities whose legal mission is to investigate government waste.

Yet, year after year, nothing of any consequence changes the radioactive waste left by the nuclear weapons programs, which themselves involved heavy outside contractors. An internal report coupled with auditors' reports documented thirteen years of mismanagement that wasted "much of the $460 billion it has spent over that time," writes Brinkley. One example: a project to deal with 34 million gallons of stored liquids in South Carolina was supposed to take three years and cost $32 million starting in 1985. Fourteen years later, the department ended the project as unworkable due to mismanagement. But not before the taxpayers were taken for $500 million. (Imagine that sum spent on safe city playgrounds for our children in America's cities.)

Others have weighed in to denounce the mess. The General Accounting Office (GAO) regularly exposes what it has called the "high risk" nightmare of the contract management debacles. The White House's Office of Management and Budget, under both Democratic and Republican administrations, have repeated each other's tedious conclusions that there are two strata to the department—the top where new relays of appointees promise change and reform, and the netherlands where contractors and their government procurement staff cook their dysfunctional deals.

Just last September, a GAO audit said the situation was worsening with greater cost overruns and deadlines delayed. Brinkley reports a memorable, amazing statement by Jessie Roberson, the current assistant secretary of energy for environmental management, who said that critical investigations become so redundant that they actually encourage agencies to stay with the offending practices. "There has been a learned pattern of co-dependency between the department and the GAO and the inspector General [of the department]. When they identify problems, our job is to stand firm and explain the problems away. And with that posture, the problems don't get better over time." Ms. Roberson promises new initiatives and expects to hire two hundred more trained supervisors.

Other mainstream institutions have weighed in on Secretary Spencer Abraham's hapless Energy Department, apart from his own audits. The National Research Council (NRC) sharply observed in a report last year that the department awards contracts to clean up radioactive sites without looking back.

The NRC, responding to a congressional demand, minced no words, accusing the Energy Department of wasting half of the $17 billion it spends on contracts and of having "virtually abdicated its role of owner in project oversight."

Even the Office of Management and Budget, which has great powers to affect departmental practices, seems resigned to another round of pledges and promises from high officials that change is coming. One OMB official is quoted by the *Times* as saying "so far, we've had more discussions about what they are planning to do than anything they have actually done."

Brinkley could write a follow-up story about how year after year this institutionally corrupt tryst between vendors and vendees can be so resistant to budging, so impervious to Congress, OMB, the GAO, its own leadership, its own internal auditors, its own chief financial officers, and to media exposés.

The easy answer is that a "corporate state" situation produces the corporate control of government and leaves the politicians at the top with lip service outrage but with heads who find it rewarding to look the other way.

All the myths about how government can be made accountable are punctured by this outsourced Department of Energy. Except, that is, getting rid of outsourcing essential governmental functions, thus ending this passing of the buck to corporations with billions of dollars.

Listen up, Mr. President. The buck stops at your desk, as Harry Truman once said.

December 13, 2002

Anthony Mazzocchi: A Working-Class Hero

Rose Ann DeMoro, executive director of one of the nation's fastest growing unions—the 45,000-member California Nurses Association—called him "the greatest labor leader I have ever known." She was referring to Anthony Mazzocchi, a mentor and strategist to thousands of labor activists over the past fifty years. He lost his struggle with cancer on October 5, 2002 at age seventy-six.

For over thirty of those years I knew and worked with Tony on labor, health, and safety matters, environmental toxins, gas pipeline safety legislation, and various corporate abuses. These concerns were only a few of the many injustices where this unsung labor giant was leading the way.

Although he never attained any higher post than secretary-treasurer of the Oil, Chemical and Atomic Workers Union (OCAW), Mazzocchi's influence spread in all directions. At a time when union membership was declining and union leaders were largely moribund, he broke new ground in one area after another.

He pioneered the collaboration of scientists with organized labor on matters ranging from the asbestos epidemic to the radioactive fallout from atomic bomb tests. While in his mid-twenties, as president of his union local in a Long Island cosmetics plant, he negotiated equal pay for women workers in the factory, ending the two-tier wage system there in 1952.

Another bridge he built was between labor and environmentalists who were often at odds. His winning argument was that toxics in the workplace and toxics in the environment were both forms of deadly silent violence that had to be stopped. For his tireless efforts, he was chosen to chair New York City's first Earth Day rally in April 1970.

A wide-ranging reader, Mazzocchi quickly recognized the devastation of the corporate globalization juggernaut on industrial jobs, the lowering of worker and environmental standards, and the stripping of union bargaining power.

After traveling hundreds of thousands of miles meeting with groups of blue-

collar workers in our country—what labor leader does that year after year?—
Mazzocchi founded and organized the Labor Party at a huge convention in
Cleveland, Ohio six years ago. Delegates from hundreds of union locals and some
national unions forged a labor agenda with strong emphasis on national health
insurance, living wages, and a free college education for students.

Sound utopian? Not after you listened to Tony show how a change of priorities
and a jettisoning of corporate bureaucratic rake-offs in the health industry can
comfortably pay for these services. Tony would always ask doubters to remember how our country passed and implemented the GI Bill of Rights right after
World War II to its dazzling successes at a time when the national debt was a
much higher percentage of the gross national product than today.

The Labor Party to date has run no candidates; it keeps building support
and membership and presses its pro-labor agenda for the day when it can run
competitive candidates for various offices.

Mazzocchi had the courage of speaking the truth to his own union members.
He opposed atomic energy's hazards and wanted it replaced with labor-inten-
sive solar energy, even though his own union—the OCAW—had members
working at atomic power plants. His stance cost him the presidency of his
union in a close contest.

Watching workers getting beaten down with employers' threats to move
their jobs to third-world countries, Mazzocchi said "The very existence of the
World Trade Organization, with all its ramifications, is the reason we need a
Labor Party. I am consistently amazed that my brothers and sisters in the
American labor movement, after all that has been done to them, continue to
support the very politicians who have brought this about."

With the exception of a few major unions, such as the United Mine Workers,
the Labor Party has received little support from organized labor. One would think
that the conscience of the labor movement would have been treated with more
grace and recognition.

Tony Mazzocchi returned to his country after seeing combat in Europe during World War II with a vision of more than economic justice for working people. He wanted them to have time to educate themselves throughout their lives,
spend more time with their families and communities, and engage their own
culture of music, plays, and other arts.

Would Tony have had an even bigger impact on the America he loved so
much and worked so hard to make more lovable if the mass media covered his
achievements and proposals? Of course the answer has to be yes. Instead, they
squandered their sense of news and integrity with massive repetitive coverage
of the O. J. Simpson, Tonya Harding, and Monica Lewinsky–type stories.

Before he died, both ABC's *Nightline* and PBS's Bill Moyers were prepared to do a feature on his life and activities for millions of their viewers. But they waited too long. Pancreatic cancer got there before they did.

For more information about the Labor Party, see www.thelaborparty.org or call 202-234-5190.

October 24, 2002

IMF, Deregulation, and the Tobacco Industry

B lind adherence to ideology can get you in some sticky places. That's where the International Monetary Fund (IMF)—the Washington, D.C.-based agency that makes loans to developing countries facing balance-of-payment and fiscal difficulties—now finds itself.

The IMF believes in unregulated markets, and pushes for policies of deregulation, privatization, and marketization without regard to specific context. In nearly every country, in nearly every sector of the economy, the fund's message is always the same.

More often than not, however, markets do need to be regulated. Sometimes, privatization has harmful consequences. Some matters should not be left to the market (like people's right to education, healthcare, and clean water).

One example of the deleterious consequences of privatization is illustrated by the tobacco industry.

Although the tobacco industry has been firmly in private hands throughout U.S. history, in many countries, including in the developing world as well as in Eastern Europe and the former Soviet Union, state-owned enterprises have had responsibility for tobacco product manufacturing and distribution.

If these enterprises are privatized, they will likely be sold to Philip Morris, BAT, or other giant multinationals. These companies swoop in, gain dominant market share, crank up their slick marketing machines to replace the sleepy marketing operations of the somnolent state-owned enterprises, bulk up their political leverage to block implementation of antismoking policies, and introduce flavorings and product manipulations that make smoking more appealing.

Nonetheless, the IMF supports tobacco privatization around the world. In recent years, according to a new report, "Needless Harm," issued by the group Essential Action, the IMF has supported privatization of tobacco enterprises in Bulgaria, Korea, Mali, Moldova, Thailand, and Turkey.

All this comes despite an abundance of research from the World Bank, the IMF's sister institution, on the economic costs of smoking and the economics of tobacco—including research strongly suggesting that the privatization pushed by the IMF will lead to increased smoking rates.

The World Bank has recognized that tobacco use is an impediment to development. The health costs of tobacco are severe, and lost work time due to illness and death saps societies of labor power. Its econometric reviews have reiterated that excise taxes work to reduce smoking rates and advance public health. The Bank has also published important information on tobacco trade liberalization, finding that reduced tobacco tariffs and freer trade in tobacco products has dire consequences, raising smoking rates and increasing preventable death and disease.

Of crucial importance, the bank has examined the results of the opening of tobacco markets in East Asia. In the late 1980s and early 1990s, the United States threatened trade sanctions and forced open tobacco markets in Korea, Japan, Taiwan, and, to a lesser extent, Thailand.

Following the U.S.-forced opening of East Asian markets to foreign tobacco imports in the late 1980s and early 1990s, smoking rates in the region surged. World Bank studies estimate smoking rates rose by 10 percent as a result of the tariff reductions. A GAO study found smoking rates among teenage girls quintupled the year after the market opening in Korea.

Now the IMF seems intent on repeating the market-opening disaster in East Asia. Privatization will replicate and deepen the harms from market opening, as the multinationals are able to entrench themselves. Reduced tariffs enable the multinationals to compete on price, the World Bank points out. Privatization will enable Big Tobacco to avoid tariffs altogether. After market opening, the Bank finds intensified advertising by multinationals; post-opening gains enough market share to justify increased marketing expenditures. After privatization, with a giant gain in market share, the multinationals have even more incentive to step up their advertising and marketing campaigns. Privatization confers other benefits on Big Tobacco: the ability to take over local brands and enhance them with new flavorings, to operate a full product line and exert control over a full-fledged national distribution system, and to gain expanded political influence.

There is no reason to believe that the IMF wants to promote smoking or advance the interests of Philip Morris—although that is the impact of its policies.

The IMF seems to be completely oblivious to these matters, simply not giving attention to the public health ramifications of its policies.

With tobacco, however, the public health consequences could not be higher. The stakes are life and death. So far, the IMF has put itself on the wrong side of this equation, recklessly endangering millions of lives.

For more information, see www.essentialaction.org/tobacco.

September 26, 2002

GATS, the WTO, and Society

The ultimate downfall of the corporate globalizers may be that they know no limits.

Not satisfied with imposing pull-down agreements on the trade in goods, Big Business is looking to do the same thing for services through the General Agreement on Trade in Services (GATS). Services includes such economic sectors as finance (banking, insurance, pensions), healthcare, telecommunications, construction, travel and tourism, the professions, education and training, express delivery, and energy and environmental services. GATS is part of the World Trade Organization (WTO) and is now undergoing renegotiation to become more encompassing.

The Wall Street banks and the other service multinationals first want to ensure that countries do not discriminate against foreign service providers. The United States does not let foreign airlines service domestic routes, for example. Such restrictions to protect domestic firms are prevalent in developing countries and an impediment to the expansionary dreams of the rich country multinationals.

But the multinationals want much more than nondiscrimination. Their real goal is to use the language of nondiscrimination (they talk about "market access" and "national treatment" for foreign companies) in order to force deregulation and privatization.

A key priority for the service companies is to place a burden on all countries to show that their regulations are the "least trade restrictive" means to achieve a legitimate purpose.

What does this mean? In case after case, the European Union has suggested that the U.S. federalist system—with overlapping regulatory powers between the states and federal government—is an impediment to trade. The argument goes like this: American companies with a bigger presence in the United States can more easily manage to deal with separate regulatory agencies in each state. Foreign companies with a smaller presence cannot negotiate this terrain as easily. Thus, goes the EU argument, regulation should be done at the federal level.

Do we really want to sacrifice important state-level consumer and civil rights protections—for example, interest rate caps, limits on corporate discriminatory practices like redlining, restrictions on predatory lending—because they are inconvenient for European companies? Of course, the real point is not that they are inconvenient for Europeans, but for business. The U.S. companies hope to use GATS to eliminate U.S. regulations—just like the European corporations want to get rid of rules in the EU.

There are relatively weak GATS rules in place now, but ongoing negotiations between nations under corporate influence to tighten them and apply them to more and more services raise serious concerns.

What might a strengthened GATS mean for the United States? It's too early to say with certainty, but based on a careful analysis of existing proposals, Professor Patricia Arnold of the University of Wisconsin-Milwaukee has raised a set of disturbing questions:

Will GATS weaken efforts to regulate financial markets in the aftermath of the financial and accounting scandals? Already foreign companies are complaining about the reach of the modest Sarbanes-Oxley accounting reform bill, which would require foreign as well as U.S. CEOs to attest personally to the validity of their companies' financial statements, if they sell stock on the New York Stock Exchange.

If Wall Street gets its way and achieves a partial privatization of Social Security, will GATS make it impossible to ever bring the program back fully into the public sector? GATS requires countries to pay compensatory damage if they grant new public rights over the supply of a service, she notes, making privatization a one-way street.

Would GATS limit efforts to regulate the health insurance sector? The insurance industry argues that service agreements should prohibit restrictions on the types of insurance products allowed on the market. Might this mean a ban on legal requirements that health insurance policies must cover certain medical conditions?

Some will argue these are Chicken Little sky-is-falling concerns. But if the NAFTA-WTO experience shows anything, it is that corporate lawyers will grab onto any crevice in trade rules to hoist corporate interests above the public interest.

Consider the "Chapter 11" investment protections in NAFTA. In a case closely paralleling what might occur in other countries with a GATS agreement, UPS is suing the Canadian postal service for offering express delivery service. The postal service is subsidized for mail delivery, and that subsidy unfairly advantages Canada Post over UPS in the express delivery market, UPS claims.

If Canada Post wants to compete in the market, they should set up drop-off boxes separate from mailboxes, employ delivery and sorting staff separate from the people who handle the mail, and handle delivery packages at separate facilities from the mail, UPS argues. Since Canada Post had the temerity not to pursue this economic irrationality, UPS is asking for hundreds of millions of dollars in compensation.

This is actually happening, and other companies are filing lawsuits in each others' countries against safety regulations, court verdicts, and other expressions of domestic sovereignty.

Enough cases like this—and a more dominant GATS will make sure there are many more—may eventually produce a backlash that will bring down the whole WTO-NAFTA edifice. But the damage inflicted in the meantime is too severe. Better instead to prevent new agreements that diminish our living standards and roll back existing ones.

For more information on how to stop the GATS, contact Global Trade Watch at www.tradewatch.org.

September 20, 2002

The Labor Party

The Enron scandal, followed by revelations about World Com and other corporate shenanigans, has produced a lot of instant experts who for the first time are actually finding fault with the ethics of the nation's biggest enterprises.

For Tony Mazzocchi this must seem a strange turn of events. For decades, Mazzocchi has sounded the alarm about corporate power and its damaging effect on the well-being of low-, moderate-, and middle-income families. For the most part, the media—and certainly the Republican and Democratic parties—have taken a see-no-evil, hear-no-evil attitude about the performance of the corporate giants that dominate the economy. Six years ago in Cleveland, Ohio, Mazzocchi was the prime mover behind the formation of the Labor Party. Under Mazzocchi, the Labor Party has been a strong voice for progressive causes ranging from universal health care to worker safety and civil rights.

Mazzocchi's creation is a growing national organization made up of international unions, hundreds of local unions, AFL-CIO councils, and community organizations. Mazzocchi is blunt in his criticism about the deleterious effect of the unchecked power of corporations.

"We have witnessed an industrial and social meltdown advanced by and for corporate and moneyed interests," he said recently.

Mazzocchi isn't any kinder in his evaluation of the performance of the major political parties. In his view both the Democratic and Republican parties "have failed working people." He sees the parties as too timid in facing the nation's problems.

The Labor Party is specific about the failure of politicians to face national problems. Here are some of the Labor Party's often-stated criticisms:

• Our decades-old health care crisis continues. More than 44 million people lack access to health care and premiums for health care insurance continue to rise.

• The wave of corporate mergers and acquisitions across national boundaries has continued unchallenged, and as a result, the nation is facing a growing concentration of global corporate power.

• The price for the North American Free Trade Agreement (NAFTA): 400,000 jobs lost and 40 percent real wage drop for Mexican workers.

• Rights guaranteed to all citizens—freedom of speech, of assembly, and of association—are not fully available to American workers under the restrictive anti-labor Taft-Hartley Act. As a result, the nation has the smallest proportion of private sector workers covered by union contracts of any western democracy.

The Labor Party has not run candidates for public office. Instead, it has focused its efforts on generating debate on the issues that affect working people. And Mazzocchi hopes that the Labor Party's constant drumbeat will force the major parties to take up the causes of working families despite the parties' long and profitable links to corporate movers and shakers.

While that may seem an optimistic goal to many, certainly the Enron and Enron-like scandals have provided credibility to the efforts of Mazzocchi and others who have sought to rein in corporate excesses and free up resources to meet critical social and economic needs. While Mazzocchi has never spared the tough words, he and his Labor Party often exude a positive attitude about the future. A recent Labor Party publication described its vision of America in this manner:

"An America where everyone who wants to work has a job at a living wage, where laws protect our rights to organize and strike, where the wealthy and corporations pay their fair share of taxes, where quality health care is a right and where solidarity puts an end to bigotry."

In six short years, Mazzocchi has positioned the Labor Party and its allies to reach for these goals. And now—thanks to a greedy band of executives—a few more people understand what Mazzocchi is talking about when he warns about the dangers of a nation and a political system that allows corporations to usurp the power and rights of the people in a democracy.

For more information about the Labor Party, visit www.thelaborparty.org.

July 31, 2002

The Taft-Hartley Act and Union Organizing

This year marks the fifty-fifth anniversary of the passage of the Taft-Hartley Act, one of the great blows to American democracy.

The act, which was drafted by employers, fundamentally infringed on workers' human rights.

Legally, it impeded employees' right to join together in labor unions; it undermined the power of unions to represent workers' interests effectively; and it authorized an array of antiunion activities by employers.

Among its key provisions, Taft-Hartley:

• Authorized states to enact so-called right-to-work laws. These laws undermine the ability to build effective unions by creating a free-rider problem—workers can enjoy the benefits of union membership in a workplace without actually joining the union or paying union dues. Right-to-work laws increase employer leverage to resist unions by enabling them to benefit from free riders. Vastly decreased union membership follows, dramatically diminishing the unions' bargaining power.

• Outlawed the closed shop, which required that persons join the union before being eligible for employment with the unionized employer. (Still permitted are provisions that require any member of a bargaining unit to pay a portion of dues to that union.)

• Defined "employee" for purposes of the act as excluding supervisors and independent contractors. This diminished the pool of workers eligible to be unionized. The exclusion of supervisors from union organizing activity meant they would be used as management's "frontline" in antiorganizing efforts.

• Permitted employers to petition for a union certification election, thus undermining the ability of workers and unions to control the timing of an election during the sensitive organizing stage, forcing an election before the union is ready.

• Required that election hearings on matters of dispute be held before a union recognition election, thus delaying the election. Delay generally benefits management, giving the employer time to coerce workers.

• Established the "right" of management to campaign against a union organizing drive, thereby scuttling the principle of employer neutrality.

• Prohibited secondary boycotts—boycotts directed to encourage neutral employers to pressure the employer with which the union has a dispute. Secondary boycotts had been one of organized labor's most potent tools for organizing, negotiating, and dispute settlement.

The political damage of Taft-Hartley was just as severe. In addition to starting an era of red-baiting with the American labor movement that led to harmful internal divisions (a now-invalidated provision of Taft-Hartley required union leaders to sign anticommunist affidavits), the act sent a message to employers: It was okay to bust unions and deny workers their rights to collectively bargain.

In short, Taft-Hartley entrenched significant executive tyranny in the workplace with ramifications that are more severe today than ever. Union membership is at historic sixty-year lows, with only 10 percent of the private economy's workforce unionized. Employer violations of labor rights are routine, and illegal firings of union supporters in labor organizing drives are at epidemic levels.

It is past time for the repeal of Taft-Hartley. That would be one important step in restoring workers' right to organize into unions, achieving a living wage in the Wal-Marts, McDonald's, and other workplaces, and revitalizing American democracy.

July 18, 2002

The Fast Food Legacy

Dr. Roberto J. Gonzalez, an anthropologist who teaches at San Jose State University, recently completed a study entitled "Latino Overweight and Obesity: Marketing Disease to Minorities." He found that "Immigrants once came to the U.S. and watched their children grow taller and stronger. Today many come and watch their children grow fatter and weaker." One of his explanations is that immigrants' children adopt diets laden with fats and sugars and a more sedentary life.

Before he left office, U.S. Surgeon General David Satcher announced a national action plan for reducing the prevalence of being overweight and obese, noting the acceleration of this major indicator of health hazard.

"The prevalence of overweight and obesity has nearly doubled among children and adolescents since 1980," he declared. "It is also increasing in both genders and among all population groups of adults," he added. About 60 percent of adults are either overweight or obese, a trend toward the ballooning of America that the relentlessly advertising fast fat and sugar food industry can take some credit for. Children learn fast food logos before they reach twenty-four months or so.

McDonald's motto, "It's a child's world" (to get youngsters to nag their parents), denotes a world where being overweight and obese, in Dr. Satcher's longer-term diagnosis, "substantially raise the risk of illness from high blood pressure, high cholesterol, type 2 diabetes, heart disease and stroke, gallbladder disease, arthritis, sleep disturbances and problems breathing, and certain types of cancers. On average, higher body weights are associated with higher death rates.

After more than thirty-five years of advancing consumer interests toward food safety and nutrition, I sense a high level of public interest in matters of food and what corporate processors are doing to it, an interest as strong as ever before. A book on the subject, *Fast Food Nation*, has been a best-seller for months. There are calls for greater regulatory vigilance by the Food and Drug

Administration, the U.S. Department of Agriculture, and their state counterparts. There are mobilizations against filthy food-processing conditions, against irradiation as an incomplete and risky (to workers and consumers) cop-out from traditional sanitation practices, and against the unknown of unlabeled genetically modified crops. Organic fresh food consumption contrasts with the avalanche of supersized fat and fatty meals whose ads and cartoon characters seduce youngsters into a lethal diet immersion. These meals, Gonzales says, "begin to resemble addictive substances."

Corporate fast fatty foods are replacing traditional diets all over the world and giant fast food franchises are spreading their web of low-grade sensuality into one country after another. The results are remarkably similar, regardless of culture, because consumers' sensory points of contact are the same almost everywhere.

A new World Health Organization (WHO) study reports that there is an emerging global epidemic of obesity among children and junk foods are its roots. Dr. Gro Brundtland, director general of the WHO, stated that "the real drama is that they are becoming more prevalent in developing communities, where they create a double burden on top of the infectious diseases that always have afflicted poorer countries."

WHO experts want to continue emphasizing more education and more exercise, but also are eager to connect with the food companies and persuade them to switch to foods with less fat, sugar, or salt. One regular can of Coca-Cola contains over nine teaspoons of sugar, for example. (Check www.who.int for public comment on proposed WHO healthy-eating guidelines.)

Clearly, first and foremost, we need a continual and robust public discussion, debate between consumers, nutritionists, and the food industry, which does not like debate. It is fine to hear Secretary of Education Rod Paige exhort youngsters to turn "off the TV" and go "swimming instead" or eat "nutritious vegetables instead of fatty french fries" or "do whatever, just move your body." But this does not get heavy media coverage repeatedly.

In the '70s and early '80s, there were many daily television talk shows that invited discussion on fast food more than once and helped several million people change their diets. Now with Jerry Springer, Sally Jesse Raphael, Rikki Lake, and others, there is not enough room for such programs and guests. Thousands of junk food ads are not rebutted.

Consider the barriers against sane and healthy rebuttals. Talk shows are either not open to such subjects or have long been discontinued, such as the Phil Donahue, Mike Douglas, and Merv Griffin shows. The government is not aggressively moving toward a steady public information campaign that shows both the hazards of and the alternatives to fatty, sugary, salty foods. Many schools are too busy showing Channel One, in return for free television equipment, to millions of youngsters; the advertisements promoting junk food and junk drink make the seductions more likely.

Politicians in elections, saturated with food industry contributions, avoid the subject. And Congress, which used to lead with the likes of Senator George McGovern's famous public hearings on nutrition, is not even bringing up the labeling of genetically engineered foods, desired by 95 percent of the American people, due to the influence of the food industry lobbyists, which includes Monsanto, Philip Morris, and others.

So it is time for intensive conversations between people directly, over the picket fences and the web sites, in the schools and on the playing fields. Good exercise does not go well with bad food.

June 6, 2002

Taking on the Corporate Government in an Age of Surrender

A t civic rallies we are holding around the country, the talk is of the need for change, for the pursuit of greater justice as a precondition for the pursuit of greater happiness. Filling large arenas, such as the Rose Garden in Portland, Oregon or the Sundome in Tampa, Florida, these gatherings, together with tables by hundreds of local and state social justice groups, are conveying that more citizen time is needed, that if millions of Americans could devote a small amount of time, major changes long overdue would occur to add fairness, productivity, respect for the environment, and community cultural revival for more sustainable self-reliance, as in energy, food, and shelter.

There is nothing out of reach or utopian about these objectives. They are well within the resources, intelligence, and values of our society. I summarized them in my new book, *Crashing the Party: Taking on the Corporate Government in an Age of Surrender*, on page 319 where these first-stage goals for a better America and for stronger democratic tools are listed:

1) Enact legislation that mandates publicly financed public elections and broad reforms of the electoral process. Facilitate the ease of banding together as consumers, workers, and taxpayers. Strengthen citizen participation in our political economy.

2) Enact living-wage laws, strengthen worker health and safety laws, and repeal Taft-Hartley and other obstructions to collective bargaining and workers' rights.

3) Issue environmental protection standards to systematically reduce damaging environmental toxins and to promote sustainable technologies like solar energy and organic farming.

4) Provide full Medicare coverage for everyone and revamp our national programs for prevention of disease and trauma.

5) Launch a national mission to abolish poverty, as some other Western democracies have done, based on proposals made long ago by conservatives, liberals, and progressives.

6) Design and implement a national security policy to counter the silent mass violence of global diseases, environmental devastation, and extreme poverty. Reduce waste and corporate domination of defense budgets—a wasteful defense is a weak defense. Vigorously wage peace and advance nonviolence by education and by foreseeing and forestalling global perils.

7) Renegotiate NAFTA and GATT to be democratic and to be "pull-up," not "pull-down," trade agreements that subordinate labor, consumer, and environmental standards to commercial trade matters.

8) End criminal justice system discrimination. Reject the failed war on drugs, in favor of rehabilitation and community development. Replace for-profit corporate prisons with superior public institutions.

9) Defend and strengthen the civil justice system, apply criminal laws against corporate crime, and fully prosecute consumer fraud and abuse. Expand consumer, worker, and children's health, safety, and economic rights.

10) Strengthen investor-shareholder rights, remedies, and authority over managers, officers, and boards of directors so that those who own the companies also control them. End the massive corporate welfare schemes that distort and misallocate public budgets. Reintroduce the historic function of corporate chartering as an instrument of ensuring corporate accountability and the sovereignty of the people.

The sorry political record of the last several years, marked by one capitulation to corporate demands after another, reminds us of how pressing the work is to strengthen our American democracy.

For more information on how you can become involved in this civic effervescence, visit our web pages: www.democracyrising.org and www.citizenworks.org.

April 18, 2002

United Students Against Sweatshops

It is a long distance from college and university campus stores in the United States to the wretched overseas factories with indentured sweatshop labor that make products that find their way to student consumers. But the United Students Against Sweatshops (USAS) has built a network of students across our country to bridge that distance with organized consumer power and citizen pressure.

The companies whose brand names are on the items in the campus and other stores do not generally put their brand names on the grim factories in Central America, Mexico, southeast Asia, China, and in other authoritarian regimes whose serf-labor and health and safety conditions are jeopardizing workers daily.

Several dozen college and university administrations, both shaken by and admiring of the students' ethics-in-action, have joined a Workers Rights Consortium (WRC) through which visitations are conducted to these factories in various nations. Students return with far more than facts and eyewitness accounts; they make arrangements for some workers to visit the United States to give firsthand testimony.

Some of these manufacturing facilities use child labor to make products for international commerce—a situation that is legal under the World Trade Organization (WTO) rules. You cannot buy anything made by child labor in this country, because such labor is illegal in the U.S.A.; but ironically, our government cannot ban such imports without violating the WTO trade agreement and subjecting the United States to monetary fines or other trade penalties.

This is just one reason why a growing coalition of labor, church, human rights, environmental, consumer, and student groups oppose corporate globalization.

Over the past three years, USAS has been doing more than arousing the campuses, holding training conferences, and enlisting faculty to their cause. They are pressing U.S. companies to insist that their contracting companies in foreign countries upgrade their miserable working conditions and demonstrate proof of that result. For example, USAS reports a recent victory following its coordinated effort with organizing efforts of workers at the large Kukdong factory in Puebla, Mexico, which makes collegiate apparel for Nike and Reebok. The laborers now have their own independent trade union. In the United States, USAS is active as well. Presently, students are mobilizing behind factory workers at the New Era cap factory in Derby, New York—a facility that makes baseball caps for over four hundred universities and is the exclusive supplier for major league baseball. Workers have been on strike to oppose a 30 percent pay cut, an increase in workload, and unsafe working conditions.

For decades consumer leaders have dreamed of organized consumer power—whether by boycotts or promises of one through more intricate networks and corporate campaigns—to reshape company misbehavior along more decent pathways. These students are pioneering new territory in turning such dreams into reality.

There are many workers, sweating under terrible bosses, devoid of any rights or legal protections, unable to feed their families, and exposed to the arbitrary actions of tyrants and their business partners in these third-world countries. It is their plight and their needs that keep these students expanding their mission of justice.

USAS has its offices in Washington, D.C., where Rachel Edelman, Amber Gallup, and Bhumika Muchhala run a beehive of activity. Readers who want more information or who wish to support this committed organization with tax-deductible contributions should contact USAS at Suite 303, 888 16th St. NW, Washington, D.C. 20006 or through their web site: www.usasnet.org.

December 27, 2001

Pro Baseball: No Lockout, No Strike

This autumn, major league baseball has a unique opportunity to display to the American public and its sports fans that there is still reason to call baseball its national pastime.

The occasion has nothing to do with the extraordinary record-breaking team and individual accomplishments of this season. Nor does it involve celebrating the completion of the memorable careers of two distinguished future Hall of Famers. In fact, these achievements will be seriously tainted if major league baseball overlooks this significant event.

The owners and players of baseball now have the chance to show unity in negotiating and signing a new collective bargaining agreement immediately following the World Series. A quick settlement between franchise owners and the players' union would assure us all that baseball will be played come spring. No lockout, and no strike.

Major league baseball has failed to negotiate any of its eight previous agreements without some kind of work stoppage. And having yet to recover the overall popularity it had prior to the strike of 1994 and 1995, baseball would forever lose countless supporters if it failed them now. In a time of grief and uncertainty, a joyful release like professional baseball becomes important to public morale.

What major league baseball Commissioner Bud Selig and Players''s Association Director Donald Fehr have done is to keep the issue quiet and out of the press so as not to disturb the present season and play-offs. But with the expiration of the current collective bargaining agreement scheduled for the end of October, now is the time to move aggressively to resolution.

Baseball has experienced incredible financial prosperity since the work stoppage of 1994–1995, with owner revenue increasing by over 200 percent and player salaries climbing by 61 percent. But since the stoppage, greed and overreaching have become expected from major league baseball. Team owners flourished in large part by manipulating and threatening state and local governments into taxing the public so the owners didn't have to pay for their own new ballparks.

Baseball, like some other industries, has capitalized on the boom in concentrated wealth over the last several years and has changed its operations to cater to the new white-collar luxury market. This is easily exploitable with the business and entertainment tax deductions for luxury seats, allowing corporations and wealthy individuals to share 50 percent of the cost of their exclusive locations with federal taxpayers.

Team owners have discovered that they don't have to please the average fans anymore to enjoy tremendous profits. Instead of building their new ballparks with sports fans in mind, owners choose to build for their business partners and the corporate executives who gladly shell out big bucks for tax-deductible luxury boxes—a nice place to do business. Average fans across the country have learned that going to a baseball game has become either a once-a-year treat or a corporate perk.

However, despite the reckless behavior of the baseball industry that has caused the alienation of so many fans, baseball has an important chance to weave itself back into the fabric of this nation. The time has come for major league baseball to show some of the character that deserved so much respect from society during World War II. Baseball pulled us through by helping to ease the anguish of our country; some players were even regarded as heroes.

It would be offensive to everyone for baseball's powers-that-be to even consider a work stoppage this time around. If bickering between the owners and players were to drag on into the winter, with spring training right around the corner, the tolerance for such selfishness would be nil. Baseball would learn that it can no longer sustain itself while taking the fans for granted.

This is an unmistakable crossroads for major league baseball that will define its status in this country for years to come. But at this point, the thought of labor negotiation is being treated like stacks of overdue bills that no one wants to touch, as reflected by Commissioner Selig's threat to fine any franchise owner $1 million for speaking publicly on the topic. If Selig cannot now find the motivation to begin a dialogue to save baseball for millions of loyal fans, then shame on him and the other baseball executives.

Will major league baseball pull through this autumn giving us justification to call baseball our national pastime? Or will it turn its back on us again and further disgrace this once celebrated and heroic game?

October 17, 2001

A Voice for Labor

Increasingly, America's working families are questioning how well their interests and needs are being represented by the Democratic and Republican parties. And a lot of union members aren't meekly accepting the apathy of the major parties. They are demanding action and taking action on their own.

One of the most creative and effective vehicles for change and spurring efforts on important social and economic programs has been the formation of the Labor Party. The Labor Party was launched in Cleveland, Ohio in 1996 by more than 1,400 delegates from 250 international and local unions, AFL-CIO councils, and community organizations and is continuing to grow—despite the fact that it has received little notice in the "mainstream media."

Today, the Labor Party is a growing national organization made up of international unions and thousands of local unions representing more than two million workers plus supporting organizations and individual members.

This month, the Labor Party, under the seasoned leadership of longtime unionist Tony Mazzocchi, celebrates its fifth anniversary with a variety of meetings and organizing drives in cities across the nation. These meetings will address actions on topics from universal health care to workers' safety and civil rights.

Mazzocchi doesn't hide his disgust about the timidity and inaction of the major parties. His blunt assessment: "both the Democratic and Republican Parties have failed working people."

"We have witnessed an industrial and social meltdown advanced by economic and trade policies designed by and for corporate and moneyed interests," Mazzocchi wrote in an open letter to supporters of the Labor Party. Indeed, Mazzocchi and the Labor Party note many of the policy failures that were raised by the Green Party in the 2000 election.

Among the failures cited by the Labor Party:

• Our decades-old health care crisis continues. More than 44 million people lack access to health care, and premiums for health insurance continue to rise.

• Under legislation granting China Permanent Normal Trade Relations (passed by Congress and signed by President Clinton), ultimately about 900,000 jobs in the United States will be lost.

• The wave of corporate mergers and acquisitions across national boundaries has continued unchallenged, and, as a result, the nation is facing a growing concentration of global corporate power.

• The price for the North American Free Trade Agreement: 400,000 jobs lost and a 40 percent real wage drop for Mexican workers. Fast track legislation for a Free Trade Area of the Americas (FTAA) is scheduled to be brought up in the Congress with active support from the Bush administration.

• Rights guaranteed to all citizens—freedom of speech, of assembly, and association—are not fully available for American workers under restrictive labor laws like the Taft-Hartley Act. The nation has the smallest proportion of private sector workers covered by union contracts of any western democracy. Health and safety protections are declining as evidenced by the recent congressional override of regulations to protect workers from ergonomic injuries.

The Labor Party describes its vision as:

"An America where everyone who wants to work has a job at a living wage, where laws protect our rights to organize and strike, where the wealthy and corporations pay their fair share of taxes, where quality health care is a right and where solidarity puts an end to bigotry."

The Labor Party has not run candidates for public office. Instead, it has focused on generating debate on the issues that affect working people. Mazzocchi's efforts are challenging the major parties to summon up the courage to take tough stands for workers' rights, even if it means stepping hard on the toes of their corporate benefactors.

"I'm for a party that begins to create a tempo, that changes the nature of the political dialogue and, ultimately, will vie for electoral office, but that's way down the line," Mazzocchi said in an interview with the *Multinational Monitor*.

The growing trend toward independent candidates and progressive third parties is furthered by the energies of the Labor Party on this fifth anniversary of their establishment.

For more information on the Labor Party, write: Tony Mazzocchi, The Labor Party, P.O. Box 53177, Washington, D.C. 20009.

June 6, 2001

Democrats' Role in OSHA Repeal

Columnists and commentators who view themselves as Democratic Party supporters are in an uproar over George W. Bush signing the congressional repeal of the ergonomics rule. This OSHA regulation is designed to urge and press employers to reduce repetitive stress injuries, such as carpal tunnel syndrome.

There are over one and a half million such injuries in this category a year. Conditions producing these injuries range from chicken processing plants to office workers using computers eight hours a day. A few months ago the National Academy of Sciences issued a report concluding that the link between workplace activities and these types of painful and sometimes disabling injuries is real.

Along with other safety regulations, President Clinton issued this ergonomic rule after Bush's election and, in this instance, just three days before he was to leave office. This two-minutes-to-midnight activity avoided losing business contributors to the Democrats' political campaigns, but exposed these standards to false Republican accusations that they were hastily and sloppily issued.

A brief look at the history of the repetitive stress disorder rule will show that it took both parties to produce this result, not just the Republicans. The proposed ergonomics rule started under the first Bush administration. Industry immediately attacked it. The criticisms and responses went back and forth for years between the business groups and OSHA. A total of six weeks of public hearings—almost unprecedented for OSHA—was scattered over the Clinton years.

By 1995, Dr. Barbara Silverstein, working on the rule, believed it was ready to be issued in its final form. But the 1996 election was coming up. The rule was delayed. After the 1996 election it was delayed again and again until its pre-midnight issuance as Bill Clinton was leaving the White House.

Had Al Gore become president, there was no guarantee against even further delay. After all, under Clinton and Gore, OSHA did not issue one toxic control regulation in all eight years of their administration. But George W. Bush—the corporation disguised as a person—is in the White House and the expected occurred.

Here again, the Democrats were complicit. Bush and congressional Republicans speed-tracked the repeal of the rule through the Senate and the House under a law called the Congressional Review Act (CRA) of 1996.

This legislation passed unanimously by the Senate in 1996 and was signed into law by Bill Clinton. It gave Congress a fast-track procedure to overturn health and safety regulations within sixty days of their issuance. Under this law, there are no public hearings in Congress and no amendments permitted. Also, debate on the House and Senate floor is time restricted.

Just like the fast-track law that propelled NAFTA and GATT through Congress in the mid '90s, the CRA is profoundly undemocratic. Yet the Democrats handed Bush and the Republicans in Congress the very tools they used to give the omnipresent business lobbyists their victory. For good measure, six Democratic senators helped the Republicans do this by crossing over and voting to abolish the ergonomic rule.

Are Democrats having second thoughts about this CRA? Will they file legislation to repeal it? There is no indication at all that they are preparing to go this route even though the Republicans are ready to use this law again to go backwards into their future.

"If it came up again today, I'd vote for it again," Senator Christopher J. Dodd (D-CT) told the *Washington Post*. "I don't agree with the results, but I agree with the law," remarked Senate Democratic Whip Harry M. Reid from Nevada, who teamed up with his Republican counterpart, Senator Don Nickles (R-OK), to ram it through Congress in 1996.

The Democrats and their supporters need some introspection. While some Democrats, like Senator Paul Wellstone, vigorously fought the bankruptcy bill that favors credit card businesses over debtors whose budgets are destroyed by loss of employment or expenses from illnesses, it passed with the votes of eighty-three senators, including thirty-three Democrats.

Is there a party here or just a collection of senators who call themselves Democrats and follow the corporate money?

The same party dissipation among Democrats is at work over Bush's tax cut for the wealthy, his self-serving drive to end the estate tax, the effort to enact some campaign finance reform by McCain-Feingold, and more.

Bush rode to the White House on slogans, one of which was that he is "a uniter, not a divider." Arriving in Washington, he soon learned that it is much easier to divide the Democrats in order to rule them.

March 27, 2001

The Need for Unions

There can be no vibrant American democracy without a vibrant labor union movement. Unions enable working people to band together to enliven our modest political democracy, and they are by far the most important institution working to infuse at least a modicum of the nation's democratic values into the economic sphere. Whatever their limitations and imperfections, there should be no dispute that our nation is far stronger than it would be in the absence of a labor movement.

That makes the latest figures on unionization rates a matter of serious concern, not just for union leaders or even all union members but for all Americans. Despite an increased investment in union organizing in recent years, the number of unionized Americans declined last year, not just as a percentage of the workforce but in absolute numbers.

Over the last two decades, Corporate America has waged a sustained campaign to weaken unions in the United States.

Employing union-busting consultants and motivated by an anything-goes antiunion animus, employers regularly confront union organizing campaigns with threats to close plants, harassment, intimidation and firings of key union supporters, captive meetings, supervisory one-on-one meetings with fearful employees, threatening literature, use of surveillance technologies, and much more. Strike-breaking techniques, including the use of scab replacement workers and armed guards, are now so evolved that unions are fearful of using what at least once was their most powerful tactic, the strike.

The two-party duopoly, featuring one party that too often takes labor unions for granted and another that wants to take them out altogether, has aided and abetted Corporate America. Lawmakers and the executive branch have not interfered with a legal regime that tremendously disempowers workers and they have worked hard for passage of key policies further undermining worker power.

Much of U.S. labor law, on the books and even worse in practice, is a disgrace.

Although it is illegal for employers to fire striking workers, it is legal to "permanently replace" them—a distinction without difference to any worker or employer, but one the Supreme Court has embedded in the law and which Congress has not seen fit to remedy.

Although it is illegal for employers to fire workers for supporting a union, approximately one in ten union supporters in union organizing drives are in fact fired. The chilling effect from such practices is obvious and the insignificant penalties for illegal firings are little deterrent whatsoever to employers.

And then there is Taft-Hartley, the labor law deform that remains on the books fifty years after passage. Taft-Hartley's sweeping antiunion provisions deprive workers of many of their most important tactics, including calling boycotts of those who continue doing business with boycotted companies.

Corporate globalization, with rules included in the corporate-managed trade agreements that go by names like GATT/WTO and NAFTA, has tilted the labor-management playing field further in corporations' direction.

New technologies and ways of organizing business did not inevitably lead to an international system of laws and regulations that leave workers ever more defenseless; that result has come from the business manipulation of the emerging norms and rules.

The rules of the World Trade Organization are so skewed that they make it illegal for the United States to ban the import of goods made with brutalized child labor.

Most serious for U.S. workers, NAFTA and the WTO have ensured that U.S. employers can pull up stakes and move operations without restraint. The well-documented record of U.S. employers closing plants and moving to Mexico, China, and other low-wage havens casts a pall over most U.S. contract negotiations. American workers must always deal with the threat that, if they ask for too much, they will lose their jobs. Even worse, U.S. employees seeking to exercise their rights to unionize routinely find themselves facing threats that their employers will close their plant and move. Cornell researcher Kate Bronfenbrenner has found in her pathbreaking research that employers issue such threats in more than half of all union-organizing drives.

As yet another blow, U.S. unions are now forced to devote resources to addressing extraordinarily aggressive investigations and congressional saber-rattling. There can be no tolerance for corruption in the labor movement, of course. But one cannot help but question the motivation of tough-talking members of Congress who focus their rhetorical salvos and investigative authority at some of the most aggressive members of organized labor's leadership, while regularly ignoring massive defrauding of shareholders and consumers and a broad corporate crime epidemic—not to mention the massive corruption in their legislative/lobbying midst.

Organized labor—and all who understand the importance of labor unions to American democracy—needs members of Congress to stand up on behalf of working Americans and their representative unions.

February 21, 2001

Minimum Wage—Time for a Raise

Despite all the talk of prosperity, many communities between Silicon Valley and Silicon Alley are still waiting for an economic upturn.

In the United States the difference between those who are poor and those who are wealthy has moved from unseemly to obscene. Most of the economic gains of the past three decades have gone to the wealthiest segments of the population. From 1979–1998, the inflation-adjusted income of families in the poorest fifth of the population did not improve at all, while incomes for the whole population increased by 20 percent. Incomes at the very top have increased even faster. As *Business Week* magazine puts it, "people feel overworked and underpaid, especially in contrast with their CEOs, who now make nearly 500 times the average employee's wages." The net financial wealth of the top 1 percent of households now equals the combined wealth of the bottom 95 percent of American households.

This has not been an accidental outcome of patterns of economic growth, but instead the result of deliberate government policies that have had the effect of redistributing income upwards. Such policies include the erosion of workers' rights to organize unions and bargain collectively and the pursuit of free-trade agreements that put corporate interests above the interests of workers, putting U.S. manufacturing workers in direct competition with the lowest-paid workers anywhere in the world, including child laborers.

Income inequality is also the result of erosion in the minimum wage. The buying power of the minimum wage has fallen by more than 20 percent since a peak in 1979, even as productivity has increased by more than 35 percent. A recent study by the National Low Income Housing Coalition shows that nowhere in the United States is a modest one-bedroom apartment "affordable" for a single, minimum-wage worker, and in most places two minimum-wage workers together would have to pay more than they could afford to rent a two-bedroom apartment.

Increasing the minimum wage is good for the economy. Moving working families out of poverty will improve children's health and education, helping to build a strong future. And recent research shows that increasing the minimum wage does not lead to increased unemployment. In 1967, when the minimum wage peaked in real purchasing power, unemployment was at 3.8 percent, and remained low the next year. If the minimum wage had kept up with increases in productivity since 1967, it would now be around $11 per hour.

It is time to reconfirm our national commitment to ensuring that workers can afford a decent standard of living by substantially increasing the minimum wage. If the minimum wage had kept pace with inflation and productivity increases since 1979, it would now be in the range of $9 per hour; if it had kept pace since 1967, it would be much higher. Since government policy has been one of the main causes of growing inequality, it is appropriate to design a government policy to reduce inequality and ensure that all workers get a share of the gains from the growing economy.

First, we should tie the minimum wage to inflation, so that minimum-wage workers get automatic cost-of-living increases. It is outrageous that low-wage workers have to fight, often unsuccessfully, just to keep even against inflation, while members of Congress, who make fourteen times as much, give themselves automatic increases.

Second, we should provide a long-delayed increase in the purchasing power of the minimum wage to ensure that working families earn a living wage. One proposal for discussion would be to raise the minimum wage to $7.30 as soon as possible, and then gradually increase its real value until it reaches at least $9 in inflation-adjusted 1999 dollars within a few years. After this point, the inflation-adjusted value of the minimum wage should be periodically increased to ensure that all workers share in the gains from the economy's productivity growth.

A major goal of our national economic policy should be to ensure that everyone shares in the gains of growth. Providing a living wage to all workers would be an important step in this direction. And, raising the minimum wage would make a significant difference in the lives of tens of millions of workers.

November 22, 2000

Strengthen OSHA

The American mission of safe and healthy workplaces should be highly visible, heralded and backed by an adequately funded and enforced program. After all, far more Americans have lost their lives due to trauma and toxics in places of employment—especially the factories, farms, construction sites, and mines—than the number of Americans lost in all the nation's wars.

Nonetheless, for generations it has been a reluctant push and a strained pull to eke out the most minimal governmental safety initiatives in these arenas.

The failure to act is all the more tragic because it is clear that occupational health and safety regulation works. For all their limitations and crises of underfunding, the Occupational Safety and Health Act (OSH Act) and the agency it created, the Occupational Safety and Health Administration (OSHA), have dramatically reduced the death toll from workplace hazards in the United States. Since the passage of the Occupational Safety and Health Act in 1970, and despite the lax enforcement of OSHA rules, overall industry fatality rates from trauma have fallen by 75 percent. Construction fatality rates have been cut by almost 80 percent, mining rates by 75 percent, agricultural rates by nearly two-thirds, and manufacturing rates by 60 percent.

With the occasional leadership of people like Eula Bingham, OSHA, through its actions and its looming potential, has steered the country toward successes in reducing deaths on the job. But the injury and death toll remains shamefully high. In 1998, over 6.2 million workplace injuries and illnesses were recorded in the private sector. More than 6,000 workers die annually from workplace trauma; the National Institute of Occupational Safety and Health conservatively estimates that another 50,000 workers die every year from workplace-related disease.

Over the last twenty years, OSHA has suffered by equal turns from administrative and congressional neglect and hostility.

According to a 1999 Public Citizen report, the Clinton administration's record on protecting worker safety is the worst since passage of the OSH Act in terms of the number of annual inspections and the percentage of proposed serious, willful, or repeat (SWR) violations that were dismissed or downgraded. The administration's record is worse than the Bush administration's in terms of SWR violations and total penalties ultimately assessed. And it is no better than the Bush administration in terms of the ratio of unprogrammed to programmed inspections, the number of SWR violations per inspection, the percentage of proposed penalties ultimately assessed, and the average penalty per inspection.

The real-world effects of this neglect are tragic.

With the administration deprioritizing worker safety and health and unwilling to buck an extremely hostile Republican Congress, it has issued only a handful of new occupational safety and health standards. As a result, workers are exposed to deadly levels of chrome and other toxic hazards every day—leading to preventable death and disease.

Guaranteeing people's human right to a safe workplace must again become a top national priority. The current OSHA administrator, Charles Jeffress, says the OSHA budget should be increased twenty times, to $7 billion. He's right. That would put the OSHA budget on par with that of the Environmental Protection Agency.

We need to see a beefed-up inspection system, a heightened willingness to use criminal sanctions against employers who put their workers' lives at risk, and higher available penalties.

And we must make sure that workers have the legal right to defend themselves from workplace hazards. They need stronger whistle-blower protections so that employees are not fearful of losing their jobs or other retaliation if they report dangerous working conditions, and a Right to Act—an unambiguous statutory right to refuse dangerous work.

It is time for the nation to focus its attention on the gap between safety and health regulatory promise and actual corporate performance, and to resolve to turn around a situation that for too long has been in the backwaters of politics and press.

October 25, 2000

The UN—Cozy with Corporations

The last few years have witnessed the increased blurring of corporate and governmental roles in the international sphere—none more worrisome, perhaps, than the United Nations cozying up to big business.

With a surge in private-public partnerships among various UN agencies, UN Secretary General Kofi Annan is leading the international organization into ever more intrusive and entangling ties between the UN and multinational corporations.

One recent misstep is the UN's "Global Compact." With the disappointing support of some international human rights and environmental organizations, the UN has asked multinational corporations to sign on to the compact's unenforceable and overly vague code of conduct.

Companies are able to sign on to the compact and "bluewash" themselves, as critics at the Transnational Research and Action Center (TRAC) in San

Francisco have labeled the effort by image-impaired corporations to repair public perceptions by hooking up with the UN.

"The UN must not become complicit in the positive branding of corporations that violate UN principles," warned a coalition of sustainable development activists organized by TRAC in a July letter to Annan. "Given that there is no provision for monitoring a corporation's record in abiding by UN principles, the Guidelines' [the Guidelines on Cooperation between the United Nations and the Business Community, issued to clarify which companies are eligible for UN partnerships] modalities for partnerships are quite susceptible to abuse. For example, a company with widespread labor or environmental violations may be able to join with the UN in a relatively minor cooperative project and gain all the benefits of association with the UN without any responsibilities. The UN would have no way to determine whether the company, on balance, is contributing to UN goals or preventing their realization."

This kind of bluewashing is already taking place. Among the early supporters of the compact are Nike, Shell, and Rio Tinto. Nike has employed sweatshop workers in Asia and elsewhere to produce its overpriced athletic wear. Shell has been targeted by activists for its ties to the Nigerian government, which has a dismal human rights history. Rio Tinto, one of the world's largest mining companies, has been associated with environmental and human rights disasters around the world. These are three of the last companies you would expect to see on a list of responsible businesses.

As troublesome, Kofi Annan has framed the compact in the context of acceptance and promotion of corporate globalization—a kind of plea to business leaders to recognize their own self-interest in restraining some of their worst abuses.

In exchange for corporations signing on to the global compact, he said when first announcing the initiative, the UN would seek both to make it easy for companies to enter partnerships with UN agencies and to advocate for speeding up corporate globalization.

"You may find it useful to interact with us through our newly created website, www.un.org/partners, which offers one-stop shopping for corporations interested in the United Nations," he told business leaders gathered in January 1999 at the Davos World Economic Forum. "More important, perhaps, is what we can do in the political arena, to help make the case for and maintain an environment which favors trade and open markets."

The promise of the United Nations, if only sometimes realized, is to serve as an intergovernmental body to advance justice, human rights, and sustainable development worldwide. Not long ago, the UN's Center on Transnational Corporations collected critical data on multinationals and published incisive critiques of growing corporate power. That growing power eventually was sufficient to force the closure of the Center on Transnational Corporations, thanks to the demands of the United States.

Now, with the UN permitting itself to become perverted with corporate sponsorships, partnerships, and other entanglements, it risks veering down the road of commercialization and marginalization.

An effective United Nations must be free of corporate encumbrances. Its agencies should be the leading critics of the many ways that corporate globalization is functioning to undermine UN missions to advance ecological sustainability, human rights, and global economic justice, not apologists and collaborators with the dominant corporate order.

September 13, 2000

Return to the Jungle

Just about the last government function you would want to see privatized is meat inspection.

But under recent and proposed regulatory changes, that is the direction in which the U.S. meat inspection program has been moving.

The results, documented in "The Jungle 2000: Is America's Meat Fit to Eat?," a report issued by the Government Accountability Project and Public Citizen's Critical Mass Energy Project, have been horrifying.

One federal meat inspector summed up the situation like this: The new regulatory system "ties our hands and limits what we [federal inspectors] can do. If this is the best the government has to offer, I will instruct my family [and] friends to turn vegetarian."

The problem with meat inspection and food safety is rooted in agribusiness concentration and new technologies. The giant meatpacking firms—including IBP, ConAgra, and Cargill—now control an increasingly dominant market share (the top four beef firms controlled 79 percent of the market in 1998); these mega-firms have ushered in the use of new technologies that push carcasses down the assembly lines at increasing velocities. Similar changes have taken place in the poultry industry, dominated by Tyson, Gold Kist, Perdue, and Pilgrim's Pride, plus ConAgra and Continental Grain.

Faster line speed means less opportunity for workers to do their jobs in a thorough and sanitary way, and less opportunity for inspectors to evaluate meat for cleanliness.

On top of these problems, the Clinton administration in 1996 announced the adoption of the Hazard Analysis and Critical Control Point (HACCP) system. As originally designed, HACCP was supposed to supplement the traditional meat inspection process, in which inspectors could demand that a product be condemned or trimmed as soon as they saw a problem. HACCP was supposed to involve additional company inspections at self-identified critical points.

In fact, as "The Jungle 2000" shows, HACCP has become a substitute for the traditional food inspection system. Now the meatpackers themselves are in control of the inspection process in processing plants. Inspectors find themselves limited to observing at company-determined critical points—or, even worse, confined to reviewing company documents showing that the company has complied with sanitation requirements.

A survey sent by the Government Accountability Project to meat inspectors shows widespread concern among inspectors that the new system has undermined their ability to do their job and guarantee a safe food supply.

• Two-thirds of inspectors said that since HACCP began, there have been instances where they have not taken direct action against contamination—including feces, vomit, and metal shards—that they observed and would have taken action against under the old system.

• More than 85 percent of inspectors responding to the survey said that company employees secretly asked them for help with problems in the plant, because they feared supervisor reprisals for speaking out against dirty conditions.

• More than three out of four respondents said that they cannot enforce the law as well under HACCP as before.

• More than half of responding inspectors in plants that are required to test for E. coli report that they never see actual lab results of company testing and are only shown a plant summary.

As bad as things are now, they may get worse. The U.S. Department of Agriculture has proposed extending the system of privatized self-inspection to cover slaughterhouses (involving killing, skinning, cleaning, and chilling the carcass) as well as processing plants (where carcasses are further processed for consumption). A federal judge has ruled this illegal, but the meat industry is lobbying Congress for new legislation to authorize privatized inspections.

Instead of trying to address worsening sanitation problems, USDA and the meat industry are trying to paper over them. Their "solutions" involve efforts to sterilize dirty food—including food contaminated with fecal matter—through chemical treatments and irradiation. These treatments, which pose potential safety problems of their own, are sad substitutes for clean food.

Privatization of meat inspection has been an unadulterated failure. It is time to halt the trend toward more self-inspection, restore the authority and budgets of federal meat inspectors, and demand that the meat and poultry industries deliver sanitary products to consumers.

"The Jungle 2000: Is America's Meat Fit to Eat?" is available free of charge on the web at: www.citizen.org/cmep/what'snew.html or for the print version send a $15.00 U.S. check or money order to: Public Citizen, Publications Dept. Box, 1600 20th Street NW, Washington, D.C. 20009.

September 7, 2000

Business War on Labor

During the post–World War II era fifty-three years ago, a pro-business Congress passed the Taft-Hartley Act in an effort to slow, if not stop, the growth of the American labor movement. The fondest dreams of its corporate sponsors are being realized today.

John L. Lewis, the president of the United Mine Workers, was prophetic in his remarks in the following passage of the legislation: "This Act was passed to oppress labor, to make difficult its current enterprises for collective bargaining, to make more difficult the securing of new members for this labor movement, without which our movement will become so possessed of inertia that there is no security for its existence."

As Lewis predicted, union members have fallen to less than 10 percent of the workers in the private economy today—the lowest in sixty years and far below the percentage of organized workers in comparable western democracies.

As we approach Labor Day 2000, there is a critical need for the labor movement and progressives to once again pick up the battle against the restrictive antilabor provisions of Taft-Hartley. There is a need to adopt labor laws that end the tilt toward employers and provide a fair opportunity for workers to organize without intimidation. Today, nearly one out of every ten workers involved in union organizing drives is fired by employers who wage a campaign of fear, threats, and slick propaganda to keep workers from exercising a genuinely free choice.

Any reform of the labor laws should include a provision that would impose treble damages against employers who unfairly fire employees because of their efforts to organize unions. The current law is essentially a meaningless deterrent as it relates to such incidents. It calls only for reinstatement with back pay, minus other interim earnings of fired workers, if you can afford a lawyer to win your case.

The need for fair labor laws goes beyond the interests of the unions themselves. As union membership falls so do the wages of all workin~ ~ and nonunion alike. This is particularly true for low-wage work States, who historically have earned less than their counterpa

European economies. The typical low-wage worker in Europe earns 44 percent more than in the United States. One in five children exist at a poverty level in the United States, more than twice the rate of child poverty in western Europe. More than one-fourth of Hispanic and African American children in the United States live in poverty.

Much is made of the increase in income of married middle-class couples, but a significant part of this increase comes from growth in family work hours, which are up 182 hours to 3,600 hours—nearly 4.5 extra full-time weeks a year since 1989. And much of the "extra" earnings of two-worker families is offset by increases in costs for child care, transportation, and related items.

We spend more on health care than any other nation in the world, but a poorly regulated, corporate-dominated health care system eliminates choice, erodes care, and inflates administrative costs while boosting profits and executive compensation. Yet, more than 45 million Americans have no health insurance. Eighty percent of these uninsured are working families and their dependents. Universal health care, as well as enactment of fair labor laws, should be a priority on the labor agenda.

Labor Day 2000 should also mark a new resolve to end abuse of trade by corporations under the guise of "free trade." Free trade sloganeering has been a means to hide corporate efforts to evade labor and environmental standards and, with the support of dictatorial regimes, to exploit workers throughout the world.

Trade policies should be based on "pulling standards" up around the world, not on "pulling down" our standards. Labor, joined by environmentalists and human rights advocates, should make clear the differences between corporate-managed trade and what is truly "fair trade," which provides decent protections for workers and the environment.

Labor Day 2000 should be a moment for the nation to focus new emphasis and new action on the rights of the nation's workers—the real strength of our economy.

August 28, 2000

Third-World Smoking

For decades, the multinational tobacco companies have known that their future rests in the third world.

All of the growth in global tobacco consumption in coming years is expected in the developing countries, with the world's 1.1 billion smokers expected to rise to 1.64 billion by 2025. The World Health Organization estimates four million people die annually from smoking-related disease; by 2030, that number is expected to climb to 10 million, with 70 percent of the fatalities occurring in the third world.

As one of the most politically vulnerable and therefore most politically engaged industries, Big Tobacco has long kept an eye out for potential threats to its plans to spread death and disease.

Philip Morris, BAT, and the other tobacco giants have viewed the World Health Organization (WHO) as a particularly grave threat to their interests.

The industry's response, a new WHO report shows, has been to attack WHO's credibility, turn other UN agencies against the health organization, seek to undermine its funding base, undertake surveillance of WHO's operations, and even seek to infiltrate WHO.

Based on a review of internal industry documents made public as a result of U.S. litigation against the tobacco companies, the report documents industry efforts—in the companies' words—to "attack WHO," "undertake a long-term initiative to counteract WHO's aggressive global antismoking campaign and to introduce a public debate with respect to a redefinition of WHO's mandate," "allocate the resources to stop [WHO] in their tracks" and "work with journalists to question WHO priorities, budget, role in social engineering, etc."

Industry tactics throughout the 1980s and 1990s, according to the WHO report, included:

• Influencing the UN Food and Agriculture Organization to oppose WHO's tobacco control policies.

• Secretly funding "independent" experts to publish papers and comment on WHO research in an effort to manipulate the scientific debate on the health effects of tobacco.

• Using a U.S. lawyer with strong ties to the tobacco industry to divert WHO away from focusing on tobacco control. Appointed to the development committee of the Pan American Health Organization (PAHO, a health organization for the Americas that serves as a regional office for WHO), the lawyer tried to redirect PAHO away from focusing on tobacco issues. The lawyer, Paul Dietrich, denies his efforts at PAHO were funded by tobacco companies.

These dirty-trick stratagems, along with weak leadership at WHO, for years succeeded at diverting the World Health Organization from devoting proper attention to the smoking epidemic.

Now, finally, things have changed. Under the aggressive leadership of Director General Gro Harlem Brundtland, WHO is pushing a bold Tobacco-Free Initiative with a proposed international treaty on tobacco control as its centerpiece.

The WHO's proposed Framework Convention on Tobacco Control would properly frame tobacco control as a global problem requiring a global response—focusing especially on containing the predatory activities of the multinational tobacco companies. Through their introduction of slick advertising and marketing, promotion of smoother blends, and association of smoking with perceived American values of freedom, the multinational companies' lethal contribution is to increase smoking rates among women and young people.

The Framework Convention would obligate signatory countries to pursue a wide range of tobacco control objectives, including preventing tobacco addiction, promoting smoke-free environments, stopping exposure of youth to tobacco promotions, and other general measures to reduce the toll of tobacco-related disease and death. Protocols to the Convention would require countries to undertake specific commitments, such as banning all or certain categories of tobacco advertising or taking identifiable steps to end cigarette smuggling.

Such a treaty and the accompanying protocols will surely not put an end to the unconscionable activities of the tobacco merchants, but the treaty and protocols do have the potential to curtail Big Tobacco's activities and to steadily advance a health agenda in meaningful ways.

WHO hopes to have completed treaty negotiations as soon as next year. Rapid completion of the negotiations, however, will have to overcome objections from the industry—albeit an industry with declining credibility, as the WHO report and other searches of the companies' internal documents highlight case after case of deceitful and deceptive industry schemes.

Whether WHO can succeed in its efforts to achieve a strong and effective treaty and protocols that include specific commitments will also depend in significant part on the stance of the United States. So far, U.S. delegates have shown a disturbing proclivity to favor watering down the treaty and to exclude public health advocates from the treaty negotiation process (itself a sure means to weaken the final result).

There is no excuse for an even partially obstructive negotiating posture by the United States or any other country. The deadly consequences of the spread of smoking are now beyond debate; the ability to reduce smoking rates through comprehensive tobacco control policies has been demonstrated by the examples of Singapore, South Africa, California, Massachusetts, and other jurisdictions; and the vital need to constrain the activities of the multinational tobacco companies is indisputable.

August 17, 2000

Free Trade in Executive Talent from Third-World Countries

Imagine the following:

The *New York Times* announced today that it was replacing columnists Thomas Friedman and Paul Krugman with the two leading bilingual writers from the *Beijing Daily*. A *Times* spokesman explained that the move was necessary to meet global competition.

The two prize-winning Chinese newspaper columnists—Li Gangsun and Mao Yushi—pledged to work hard, write four columns a week, if desired, for $25 a column. Media analysts estimated that the *Times* would reduce its costs by over 95 percent.

An accompanying *Times* editorial urged other companies and think tanks to consider opening up their ranks to free trade in executive talent from third-world countries. "It is time to practice what we preach and join the globalization movement," said the editorial, "and achieve the long-hidden efficiencies from these markets."

The *Times* cited two examples of CEOs from Boeing and General Electric, who, at retirement, replaced themselves with highly regarded, experienced executives from Shanghai and Cuernavaca. The replacement executives are taking office with an unheard of pay package of $19,000 a year. These two gentlemen have long experience with Boeing factory outsourcing in China and GE factories and suppliers moving to Mexico. With today's on-line technology, they expect to remain where they are, with occasional visits to the States.

Tom Friedman's last column had a wistful tone—given his past paeans to corporate globalization—but it had a defiant note when he concluded by writing: "I regret that my editors failed to recognize both my long service to the *Times* and my double Pulitzer prizes. It seems that the intangibles of quality and place have no value anymore. Apparently, everything now is for sale!"

At a departure ceremony, his editors gave Friedman an award for the reporter who has traveled the most and predicted that he would have a fine prospect for employment with the fast-expanding global Chinese media.

Professor Krugman's good-bye column was totally different. He developed an amended theory of comparative advantage to rebut the very thought of replacing him. "Totally unique commodities like myself," wrote the noted economist, "can only adhere to a doctrine of superior advantage. My eminence cannot be compared to the exchange of early nineteenth-century Portuguese wine for British textiles."

Krugman declared that he will return to his full-time faculty post at MIT where he will research how the practice of monopolistic competition can be exempted from world trade agreements and the imminence of widespread distance learning.

Li Gangsun's first column recommended that the Chinese government bring a number of WTO complaints against the non-tariff trade barriers erected by the upper classes of U.S. corporations and universities. "Since everything is for sale," he wrote, "then all these positions should be considered 'commerce and trade' and opened to vigorous competition worldwide."

As for those "tenured economics professors at Harvard and Stanford, who are always testifying for total free trade between nations," he wrote, "they are the essence of impermissible barriers to trade. There are numerous Chinese academics who could do a better job, either in situ or by Internet instruction, at far lower salaries, thus lightening the tuition and debt load for American students."

Word was leaked out that the upcoming meeting of the Business Roundtable, which will be closed to the press, will have on its agenda a debate over the topic "Globalization: If It's Good for Our Workers, Why Not Our Top Executives?"

Meanwhile, over at the offices of the U.S. Chamber of Commerce near the White House, CEO Tom Donohue is huddled with his aides. The Chamber was planning a joint press conference with its counterpart, the Mexican Chamber of Commerce, to protest President Clinton's clear violation of NAFTA by banning Mexican truck driver's from access to all fifty states.

Already the Teamsters Union and consumer safety groups have been emphasizing the traffic safety hazards of such poorly maintained trucks. Moreover, Teamster drivers are angry over having to compete with $7-a-day Mexican drivers.

The aides have new information for Mr. Donohue that is furrowing his brow. It seems that the head of the Mexican Chamber, Jorge Zapata, after reading the *Times*, is preparing an offer to replace Mr. Donohue. Zapata, a hard-driving, Harvard Business School-trained economist, is willing to work for one-eighth of Mr. Donohue's executive compensation package and move to Washington before the year's end. This could lead to reductions in management salaries at the Chamber below Mr. Donohue's level, argues the memo, and result in an overall reduction in membership dues.

Mr. Donohue heaved a sigh and, deferring comment, suggested that they all go out for a three-martini lunch.

July 5, 2000

China and Trade

The China lobby is on the march—and posing serious problems to citizens in the United States and China alike.

Big Business is pulling out all the stops to encourage Congress to grant Permanent Normal Trade Relations (PNTR, formerly known as permanent most favored nation) status.

The many corporations that have endorsed PNTR are primarily interested not in making goods in the United States for export, but in investing in China, where they can sell services to the Chinese and make goods for Chinese and U.S. markets.

Of course, U.S. companies are already moving to China in large numbers. But the investor guarantees connected to a PNTR deal would speed the migration—and the migration of well-paying factory jobs.

It is true, as PNTR proponents argue, that much of this investment—especially by financial and service companies—will be to serve the Chinese market. But it is equally true that these investments will do almost nothing to create jobs in the United States. New Citigroup branches in Shanghai or Aetna's expanded ability to insure businesses in China will do very little to create jobs in New York or Connecticut.

Much of the investment will shift jobs from the United States to China, especially in the manufacture of goods like clothing, auto parts, and consumer electronics. PNTR will exacerbate the trend of U.S. factories shutting down, moving to China, and then exporting their goods back to the United States.

Why does this happen? The story is familiar. U.S. businesses, or their contractors, can pay dramatically lower wages and get away with far inferior working and environmental conditions in China than they can in the United States.

How big are the savings? Here are some wage figures recently published by the New York City-based National Labor Committee: workers making Kathie Lee handbags for Wal-Mart in China are earning 3 cents an hour; Nike contract workers putting in eleven to fifteen hours a day are earning 20 to 22 cents an hour; some women sewing Nike bags are making as little as 8 cents an hour; workers making Huffy bikes, Timberland shoes, Alpine car stereos, and RCA televisions are earning as little as 22 to 27 cents an hour—well below a living wage.

Before the PNTR vote, corporations should be asked to release their plans for new factories in China, so the public and Congress can consider the PNTR issue with full knowledge of the consequences of its passage.

If the Chinese were to benefit from PNTR, the issue might be more complicated. But it is not the case that further opening to the United States and the West will bring prosperity and good times to China.

The phase-out of price supports and protections for farmers will throw 10 million peasants off the land, according to Chinese government estimates. Competition from foreign businesses will likely lead to a wave of state company layoffs, downsizing, and bankruptcies, throwing millions more out of work and undermining the social protections that many Chinese companies now provide to their employees.

Passage of PNTR will also eliminate a crucial lever to advance democracy and human rights in China. Wei Jingsheng, one of China's leading democracy activists, explains that the annual congressional review of China's human rights record plays an absolutely crucial role in restraining the Beijing government from committing even more egregious human rights abuses.

Listening to Wei should put to rest the fallacious claims of PNTR proponents that removing pressure on the Chinese government will somehow improve its human rights practices.

Many of these basic facts are not in dispute.

If PNTR passes Congress, it will not be because of proponents' substantive arguments. It will be because the Chamber of Commerce, the National Association of Manufacturers, the Business Roundtable, the insurance industry, the automakers, and many others donated enough money, hired enough lobbyists, paid for enough advertising and—in combination with the Republican congressional leadership and the Clinton White House—twisted enough arms and cut enough deals.

If PNTR is defeated, as it should be, it will be because labor, consumer, environmental, human rights, and other citizen groups joined together and refused to let the China lobby steamroll Congress. The key vote in the House of Representatives may be as early as May 25. To see how you can help stop PNTR, see www.tradewatch.org.

May 17, 2000

IMF/World Bank Protest

Six months ago, who could have imagined a crowd of 20,000 or more gathered in Washington, D.C. to protest the policies of the International Monetary Fund (IMF) and World Bank? What were the odds that such a demonstration would accompany thousands more in the streets engaging in festive civil disobedience during the spring meetings of the IMF?

Things have changed dramatically in the movement against corporate globalization in the last six months. However unlikely such large-scale protests against international financial institutions that cultivate secrecy might have seemed last year, they now appear to have emerged as part of the political landscape.

The growing protest movement against the IMF, World Bank, and the World Trade Organization—and the even broader public disenchantment with these organizations—in part reflects a demand for minimal accountability from public institutions.

What are the standards of failure for the IMF? How much economic ruin, corruption, and embezzlement must it permit before it is stripped of authority to do more harm?

In the last three years alone, the IMF has:

• Contributed to and worsened financial crises in Asia and elsewhere;

• Watched as billions of dollars of its money was stolen in Russia;

• Failed to respond in meaningful ways to the growing global demand for debt cancellation for poor countries;

• Bailed out big banks while impoverishing the poor; and

• Continued to push its environmentally destructive export-led development model.

How about the World Bank? It too has compiled a record of failures. Unlike the IMF, the World Bank regularly undertakes internal review studies (a good thing), which lead to very critical reports (also a good thing), with little discernible effect on Bank policy (a bad thing).

For example:

• A 1992 report found that nearly 40 percent of Bank projects were judged unsatisfactory, using the Bank's own narrow measures.

• A 1999 review of Bank structural and sectoral adjustment lending (making up about two-thirds of the Bank's lending) found that "the majority of loans do not address poverty directly, the likely economic impact of proposed operations on the poor, or ways to mitigate negative effects of reform."

• A 1999 report on forests determined that despite a Bank goal of reducing tropical forest destruction, "Bank influence on containing rates of deforestation of tropical moist forests has been negligible in the 20 countries with the most threatened tropical moist forests."

• Bank lending in support of big dams and other projects often leads to mass, forced resettlement of thousands of people. The Bank tries to alleviate the worst effects, with minimal success. "The core objective of resettlement planning, namely the restoration or improvement of incomes and standards of living, is still not being achieved, except in a few projects," a 1994 Bank report found.

Having seen the IMF and the Bank contribute to increasing poverty, deepening economic inequality and environmental degradation—all while opening up developing countries to exploitation by multinational corporations—a broad coalition came together in Washington to demand an end to the institutions' destructive practices.

Among the many important features of the coalition is the increasing surge of student understanding and opposition to corporate globalization. Young people are on the cutting-edge of the movement, providing it with creativity, energy, vitality—and hopefully long-term staying power.

Also critical is the changing role of the labor movement. Where organized labor was a primary organizer of the rally in Seattle, labor unions played a much smaller role in the Washington, D.C. rally. But labor has a more direct stake in trade debates, and so the unions' involvement in the April 16 protests was in some ways more significant than in Seattle. It illustrates an important evolution in labor's approach to global economic issues, and a new willingness to pose fundamental challenges to corporate globalization.

What's next for the movement against corporate globalization? In the U.S. Congress, there is an important upcoming vote on whether the WTO's powers should be expanded by permitting authoritarian China to join the organization. Beyond that, there are numerous campaigns to be waged on sweatshops, global warming, biotechnology, and countless other issues.

It may be premature to say where the next large-scale demonstration will occur, but it is certain that corporate globalization is facing a brewing citizen reaction in developing and industrialized countries alike. The call is growing for new economic arrangements that emphasize accountability, democratic control, ecological sustainability, and the leveling of economic inequality.

April 18, 2000

Anti-Bribery Law Rarely Enforced

When twenty years ago Senator William Proxmire (D–WI) was championing the Foreign Corrupt Practices Act (FCPA) that prohibited U.S. companies from bribing their way to sales in foreign countries, many large U.S. corporations were outraged and opposed. Unfair, they cried; other western countries allow foreign bribes (in fact, such bribes were deductible in some countries) and that will take business away from U.S. shores.

Senator Proxmire would then challenge them to cite any examples where U.S. companies lost contracts overseas because a European or Japanese company bribed their way to a deal. Tellingly, U.S. companies could not supply the senator with any evidence.

Although the anti-bribery law was rarely enforced by the Justice Department, the act established a standard of business practices on merits instead of on greased money in the hand. U.S. businesses managed to survive, while the pressure rose on the European nations to pass legislation that would outlaw such foreign bribes as well.

Well, last year thirty-four countries agreed to an OECD Anti-Bribery Convention that makes the bribery of foreign officials a criminal offense. The United States exerted an upward pull by not joining the race to the bottom of its legal barrel.

These laws are still largely lip service. Their enforcement is not a high priority and naturally evidence is hard to obtain for prosecution. But lip service is a start and encourages action.

And, according to the business-oriented Transparency International (TI), which, on January 20, 2000, issued an unprecedented Bribe Payers Survey, action is indeed needed. Peter Eigen, TI's chairman, introduced the survey with these words:

"The scale of bribe-paying by international corporations in the developing countries of the world is massive. Actions by the majority of governments of the leading industrial countries to curb international corruption are modest. The results include growing poverty in poor countries, persistent undermining of the institutions of democracy, and mounting distortions in fair international commerce."

The survey itself was quite ingenious. It was based on 779 lengthy interviews with business leaders in fourteen mostly third-world countries, from Indonesia, India, Argentina, Brazil, Morocco, Nigeria, and South Africa. Many of those interviewed represented major foreign companies or national companies, along with executives at accounting and law firms and chambers of commerce.

Among the more interesting questions are those relating to perceptions of bribe-paying in these third-world countries by companies from the nineteen leading exporting companies, mostly in the industrialized West.

Those interviewed were asked to rank companies from these exporting countries on how likely they would bribe to win or retain business. The United States did not fare that well, ranking ninth, below Sweden, Australia, Canada, Austria, Switzerland, Netherlands, United Kingdom, Belgium, and tied with Germany.

The survey showed that the industries most likely to bribe or be extorted to bribe by senior public officials were, in declining order of corruption levels: 1) public works contracts and construction, 2) arms and defense industry, 3) power (including petroleum and energy), 4) industry (including mining), 5) health care, 6) telecommunications (equipment and services), 7) civilian aerospace, 8) banking and finance, and 9) agriculture.

To illustrate how much more work needs to be done by international companies, TI's interviews found that most of these executives either had not heard of or were only dimly aware of the OECD Anti-Bribery Convention. Their companies were likewise lagging behind in their compliance plans. For more information, log onto www.transparency.org.

February 2, 2000

Seattle and the WTO

The media called it "the battle of Seattle" last week.
Certainly it was clear once again that the media often wait for street demonstrations before conveying the message of the demonstrators—in this case composed of labor, church groups, environmental and consumer organizations, family farm delegations, human rights advocates, students against overseas sweat-shops, and others never before so united behind a common cause.

President Bill Clinton also read the political and civic strength behind the demonstrators and their intense workshops and press briefings during that exciting week.

After ignoring the articulate pleas of these groups back in 1994 when he was ramming the latest revision of the GATT trade agreement and its World Trade Organization (WTO) through Congress, Mr. Clinton started repeating their concerns. He came out for openness, instead of the secrecy of the WTO that he pushed through Congress. He came out for more consideration of labor and environmental rights by the WTO, after brushing them off five years ago.

Finally, after condemning some window-smashers, he praised overwhelmingly peaceful marchers and activists for compelling the world's nations to consider whether they are going in "the direction we all want to go."

Well, well, well, Mr. Clinton—a WTO reborner! What's that old saying about "when the people lead, the leaders will follow!" Even right-wing columnist Bill Safire, writing in the *New York Times,* said it "was Clinton's finest hour." Safire noted that trade should be about more than money. Other values counted. Other conservatives agreed and marched along with liberal groups in Seattle.

Seattle was a fork in the road, and as Yogi Berra once said: "When you reach a fork in the road, take it." Quo vadis? The global corporatists preach a model of economic growth that rests on the flows of trade and finance between nations dominated by the giant multinationals—drugs, tobacco, chemical, oil, nuclear, munitions, biotechnology, autos, textile, banking, insurance, and other services.

For third-world nations, export-dependent economies become too dependent on international finance and its speculative instability, on non-sustainable or seriously polluting technologies, and on cash crops instead of growing food for their own people.

The global corporate model is premised on the concentration of power over markets, governments, mass media, patent monopolies over critical drugs and seeds, the workplace, and corporate culture. All these and other power concentrates, homogenize the globe and undermine democratic processes and their benefits.

Far better for countries to focus on building domestic markets through land reform, micro-credit for small businesses, use of local materials for housing, and renewable energy solar-style. For developing countries, it is far better for bottom-up capital formation to encourage local economies that are more job intensive—generating purchasing power—than adopting highly capitalized and chemical plantation type agribusiness with destructive technologies. Just look at American economic history and recall the enormous multiplier effect of growing more food and fiber by small farms following the great Homestead Act of 1863.

Obviously, the domestic markets' priority requires more democracy while the global corporatist approach is quite congenial with dictatorial regimes.

The very successful financier and civil society supporter, George Soros, wrote that the major threat to democracy in the world today—post–Soviet Union—is what he called "the market fundamentalism" of the multinational corporations.

That "market fundamentalism" dominates the commercial mandates and autocratic procedures of the World Trade Organization. With about 134 countries that are members, the domestic environmental, consumer and workplace health and safety regulations have to prove they are "least trade restrictive."

What that omnipresent phrase means is that one country can challenge another country's safety laws or standards for allegedly obstructing imports. So far these cases, brought before the WTO's secret tribunals in Geneva, Switzerland, usually have been decided against health and safety under the tribunal judges' yardstick of "trade *uber alles.*"

When this practice is combined with the harmonization (downward so far) of health and safety standards worldwide, which is WTO's objective, what country can lead in safety as the United States did in auto crash protection years ago? Now our country's auto safety officials go for harmonization meetings under WTO—that are secret—instead of pioneering the lifesaving frontiers for its people.

On November 20, 1994, *New York Times* reporter David Sanger wrote "Over the past year the Administration tried desperately to keep anyone from noticing GATT." That arrogance by the Clintonites then presents the president with vast redemptive opportunities now. It is in the hands of the people to show him the way.

December 7, 1999

Anti-Sweatshop Movement

There used to be a time when big corporations were worried about rebellious and anti-corporate students on university and college campuses. Rallies, teach-ins, boycotts, and other forms of protest took on corporations for polluting, discriminating, exploiting consumers, backing military dictatorships, and other misbehaviors.

In 1970, Earth Day events involving nearly 2,000 colleges shook and exposed corporate polluters. It was a mass media event, because then the media took the issues seriously.

Big Business Day in 1980 concerned Irving Shapiro, CEO of chemical giant DuPont, so much so that he collaborated with his friend Lane Kirkland, head of the AFL-CIO, no less, to dampen organized labor's passion for this teach-in.

But in the past twenty years, with the exception of the movement advocating divestment in South Africa and some student public interest research groups, the campuses have been more than quiet. They have succumbed to the temptations of the computer economy and the investment bankers. Students by and large have viewed college as on-the-job training for what they hope will be lucrative employment after graduation. They have not wanted activism on their résumés.

Well, executives can start getting worried again. This fall, on more than two hundred campuses, the anti-sweatshop, anti-child-labor movement will likely be strong. In concert with labor and religious groups, students will focus on large retailers, such as Wal-Mart, that buy merchandise from third-world nations that grind their workers to the ground.

Textile workers in a Bangladesh factory that makes clothes for Wal-Mart are paid between 9 and 20 cents an hour—far less than the country's legal 33-cent minimum wage—seven days a week.

The National Labor Committee (NLC), based in New York City, is documenting these abuses. It investigates brand-name products and companies, such as Liz Claiborne, with their celebrity endorsers, and encourages students to trace the money from purchases in on-campus shops to miserable dungeon-like factories in Asia and South America. And from Duke University to Harvard

University to the University of Wisconsin, students have linked their knowledge to action. They have pressured retailers on campus and off to publicly disclose the factory names and addresses.

Finally, students are realizing the power of their purchasing dollars. They're telling these U.S. multinationals to start disclosing more information about the brutal conditions imposed on the young women and children slaving for their business partners in other countries.

Charles Kernaghan, director of the NLC, has calculated that Salvadoran women are paid 74 cents for each $198 Liz Claiborne jacket they sew. That means their wages are less than one-half of 1 percent of the retail price that American consumers pay for the jacket.

In the United States, the labor cost to sew a garment typically is 10 percent of the retail price. By moving production abroad, Kernaghan says, "the companies have almost wiped out the cost involved in sewing a garment."

The coming year will see a more intense focus on the booming practice of using child laborers under conditions unimaginable to most Americans—the same Americans who unwittingly buy the fancy items. International trade in products made by children, in many cases under indentured servitude, is legal under the World Trade Organization established through the GATT treaty, which President Clinton and the congressional Republicans turned into federal law in 1994.

Together with student groups at many colleges and the People of Faith Network, the NLC is planning demonstrations, world petition drives, the release of thousands of pages of internal company records, educational videos, and student reports on overseas conditions. The NLC will ask politicians to support linking trade to human rights.

High school students will be closely involved in these drives as well. All these activities will culminate December 9, Human Rights Day, with candle-light vigils and walks for conscience across America.

Linked to standards of justice for the oppressed children and young adults laboring for the massive profits of Wal-Mart, Nike, and other giant companies, consumer dollars can speak power and truth. The alternative is for unknowing shoppers to keep allowing these abuses that lead to obscene profits for corporations.

To obtain an action kit for the coming events, write to the National Labor Committee, 275 Seventh Avenue, New York, New York 10001. The NLC web site is www.nlcnet.org.

August 11, 1999

Gore: AIDS in Africa

For years, consumer activists have asked Al Gore to reverse the U.S. policy of punishing developing country governments that tried to make essential medicines more affordable for sick people. And Gore ignored the calls.

Matters suddenly changed on June 16 when a small group of AIDS activists began clamoring and demonstrating at events by Vice President and presidential candidate Al Gore.

The activists focused on Gore because he oversees a U.S.-South Africa binational commission. The United States has used the commission meetings and structure to exert enormous pressure on South Africa, urging the country to abandon efforts to promote generic drug competition in AIDS and other essential medicines that are priced out of reach of most consumers. (The United States has similarly imposed or threatened trade sanctions against other countries seeking to take steps to make essential medicines more affordable.)

With the protests prompting some of the major media to wake up and pay attention to this critical issue, Gore and the pharmaceutical industry have issued a series of defenses of the retrograde U.S. position on the pharmaceutical access issue. The underlying question is countries' rights to employ compulsory licensing and parallel import policies.

Compulsory licensing involves a government giving a manufacturer a license to produce an item for which another company holds a patent or exclusive rights, in exchange for the payment of a reasonable royalty to the patent holder. The effect is to introduce generic competition and drive prices down.

Parallel imports involve a government or other party shopping on the world market for the lowest-priced version of a product, rather than accepting the price at which it is sold in their country. In the pharmaceuticals market, prices tend to vary dramatically between countries.

Gore and the industry's first defense was that compulsory licensing and parallel imports are bad because they decrease drug companies' profitability and thereby hurt their research efforts. But Gore, at least, soon abandoned that argument—an especially weak claim given that Africa constitutes on the order of 1 or 2 percent of the global drug market, hardly enough to affect the industry's R&D expenditures. Now the industry is emphasizing that lower prices for drugs will not be sufficient to solve the global AIDS plague, which is now killing more than 2 million a year. This is surely true—poor countries desperately need to emphasize AIDS prevention and education. But for those infected—up to 25 percent of the population in some African countries—access to affordable drugs is vital. Without access, virtually all people with AIDS are sentenced to die.

The industry trade association, PhRMA, is also trotting out the line that making drugs affordable to poor people may create drug-resistant strains of the AIDS virus. The concern is that poor health care systems will prevent proper administration of the drug treatments, and mutant strains will develop that are not susceptible to pharmacological treatments.

But as Dr. Peter Lurie of Public Citizen points out, virtually everyone now who goes without drugs will die—drug-resistant strains, which are no more aggressive than nonresistant ones, can't make things worse for them. "If the problem is lack of infrastructure, the solution should be improving infrastructure, not denying poor people lifesaving medicines," says Lurie. "One would never withhold effective therapy for tuberculosis or malaria for fear of inducing drug resistance. Why should AIDS be any different?"

Moreover, some kinds of treatments, for particular AIDS-related infections or short-course treatment to prevent mother-to-child HIV transmission, are easier to administer and could save many lives and ease considerable preventable suffering.

In late June, with pressure building, Gore told the Congressional Black Caucus that he supported South Africa's right to use the controversial policies of compulsory licensing and parallel imports. But, he said, in employing these policies, South Africa must comply with the international trade rules established by the World Trade Organization (WTO).

That was a disturbing caveat, which leaves unclear the real meaning of Gore's statement. At times, the United States has argued that compulsory licensing and parallel imports are not permitted by the WTO. No serious and honest trade lawyer believes this to be the case, however. Is Gore still making this claim?

It is true that the WTO sets certain technical conditions for countries to employ compulsory licensing. But South Africa has repeatedly pledged that it will ensure that its compulsory licensing policies comply with WTO rules. Since South Africa has not yet issued a compulsory license, it is hard to know what more the government could do to satisfy Gore—if his proclaimed respect for South Africa's right to use compulsory licensing and parallel imports is genuine.

In the policy world, talk is cheap. One in seven South Africans is HIV positive. Twenty-two million Africans are estimated to be infected with HIV/AIDS; eight million more are infected in Asia and Latin America.

Yet the U.S. Trade Representative (USTR), Charlene Barshefsky, insists on placing South Africa on the "watch" list for countries supposedly interfering with U.S. trading rights, and is even conducting a special, out-of-cycle review of South Africa. Other countries have received similar treatment for pursuing policies similar to South Africa's.

If Vice President Gore wants the public to believe his claims of compassion for those with HIV/AIDS in the developing world and his asserted respect for countries' rights to undertake policies to make drugs more affordable and to save lives, then he must see that the abhorrent U.S. policy is changed.

July 23, 1999

Affordable HIV/AIDS Drugs for Africa

S outh Africa and the rest of Africa is experiencing an HIV/AIDS catastrophe, which the U.S. Surgeon General has likened to the plague that decimated Europe in the fourteenth century.

South Africa wants to take steps to lower the extraordinary prices of essential medicines to treat HIV/AIDS and other diseases. ("Drug cocktails" to treat HIV/AIDS can cost $12,000 a year per patient in Africa.)

Vice President Albert Gore thinks this is a bad idea. As chairman of the United States/South Africa Binational Commission, Vice President Gore has engaged in an astonishing array of bullying tactics to prevent South Africa from implementing policies, legal under international trade rules, that are designed to expand access to HIV/AIDS drugs.

According to a recent State Department report to Congress, Gore has led "an assiduous, concerted campaign" by "all relevant agencies of the U.S. government"—including the Department of State, the Department of Commerce, the U.S. Patent and Trademark Office, the Office of the United States Trade Representative, and the National Security Council—to coerce South Africa into abandoning measures to make pharmaceuticals more affordable.

Why does Gore oppose sensible South African policies? Because this is what the pharmaceutical industry, led by its trade group, the Pharmaceutical Researchers and Manufacturers Association (PhRMA), wants him to do. The industry does not care too much about drug prices in South Africa or Africa. Because of the African continent's poverty, sales are quite limited, and lower prices might actually increase industry revenues by spurring a much higher sales level. But the drug companies do fear that steps to lower prices in South Africa will generate pressure to lower prices in the United States and Europe.

Gore and the U.S. drug industry argue, incorrectly and insincerely, that South Africa's Medicine Act violates international trade law by permitting what is known as compulsory licensing and parallel imports.

Compulsory licensing enables countries to instruct a patent holder to license the right to use its patent to another party. This introduces competition in the market for the patented good, thereby bringing prices down. In the case of pharmaceuticals, compulsory licensing can lower the price of medicines to consumers by 75 percent or more.

Parallel imports involve imports of a product from one country and resale, without authorization of the original seller, in another. (The South African government, for example, might buy a drug sold by Bristol-Myers-Squibb at a lower price in France than the company charges in South Africa, and then sell it at the lower price in South Africa.) In the case of pharmaceuticals, where prices differ significantly by country, parallel imports can be a tool to enable developing countries to lower prices for consumers.

Under the rules of the World Trade Organization, compulsory licensing is permissible, so long as the government follows certain procedures to protect the interests of the patent owner, including the payment of reasonable royalties. Parallel imports are also legal under World Trade Organization rules.

Gore and the pharmaceutical industry know that the South Africans are playing by international trade rules. Indeed, when pressed by knowledgeable inquirers, U.S. officials are willing to acknowledge that—public claims to the contrary notwithstanding—South Africa's policies are permitted by World Trade Organization rules.

Gore and the industry also know that the United States itself regularly issues compulsory licenses for products ranging from pharmaceuticals to chemicals to computer chips, to nuclear safety to clean air technologies.

As for parallel imports, the United Kingdom and several European Union countries have extensive trade in parallel imports of pharmaceutical drugs, a practice affirmed by the European Court of Justice.

But, U.S. officials say, the United States feels justified in demanding more stringent patent protection from South Africa and other developing countries than is required by the World Trade Organization rules—even more than the United States itself or European countries provide.

The Gore position is worse than hypocritical. Africa is confronted with a public health crisis of historic proportions. Of course South Africa and other countries should take steps, such as compulsory licensing that is legal under international trade rules, to expand the affordability of essential medicines. This is an emergency; millions of lives are at stake.

Why should President Nelson Mandela and the South Africa government permit their population to be defenseless simply because Glaxo Welcome, Bristol-Myers Squibb, and other multinational drug companies want the power to set prices for HIV/AIDS drugs—even for receiving free U.S. taxpayer-funded and government-developed medicines—in Africa?

How should Al Gore be assessed if he cannot take time out from his frantic political fundraising to recognize the immorality of his government's policy toward the South African people on this issue?

April 23, 1999

VII
CONSUMERS AND
THE ECONOMY

To some people, especially those who worship at the altar of the free market, the collapse of communism in the 1980s and 1990s conclusively demonstrated the wonders of capitalism. That assumption is akin to the notion that the moral bankruptcy of the Republican Party implies proof of the greatness of the Democratic Party.

This is a false dichotomy. It is possible that capitalism and communism, at least as we know them, are each failures of a different kind. If we're talking about corporate capitalism American style, there are many reasons not to celebrate. In fact, America's political economy, when it has suppressed democratic processes, has failed us in many important areas chronicled in this section of the book, including (but by no means limited to):

Failure to provide a living wage to tens of millions of able-bodied workers and their families.

Failure to provide a decent safety net that ensures minimally acceptable housing and health care for all citizens.

Failure to produce lending institutions, an insurance industry, and a securities market that are even close to free of corruption.

Failure to prevent and prosecute widespread corporate crime.

Failure to protect consumers from assorted frauds and predators, as well as unsafe and unhealthy products and services.

Corporate capitalism has not succeeded even on its own theoretical terms—providing a free and open market without government bailouts and controlled by its owners. A properly functioning market must be open and competitive, as opposed to dominated by one or a few companies. According to economic theory, in cases of market failure, the government must step in and enforce antitrust laws to break up monopolies and oligopolies. Some radical free marketers, discussed in this section, consider even antitrust laws to be an improper intrusion into the sanctity of the marketplace. Numerous industries, including agribusiness, drugs, cable, telecommunications, and computers, are highly concentrated. The wave of mergers and acquisitions throughout the 1980s and '90s violated the letter and spirit of the antitrust laws, and clever ways of price-fixing, product fixing, and bid-rigging have become commonplace. In the face of all this, the Justice Department and various regulatory agencies do little or nothing.

America's brand of corporate capitalism has produced unprecedented wealth if we measure by gross national product. And there's no doubt that it has proven to be a superior economic system to that which dissolved in the Soviet Union and other communist countries. Is that the standard we wish to be judged by? Are communism and our current version of corporate capitalism the only viable alternatives? The columns below reject such a pessimistic view, and offer a vision of more just economic arrangements that help make capitalism more humane, more available, and more accountable to its investor-owners which include worker pension funds.

USDA vs. John Munsell and Safe Meat

Imagine a businessman, consumer advocate, and whistle-blower all in one person. He is John Munsell, owner of the family business Montana Quality Foods, Inc.

Mr. Munsell charged that the U.S. Department of Agriculture (USDA) tried to drive him out of business because he exposed the department's failure to act on evidence that the giant ConAgra beef packing company was shipping E. coli contaminated ground beef carrying the USDA's own seal of approval as wholesome.

The USDA's aggressive "do not look, do not tell" noninterference policy with ConAgra backfired when it was finally required to recall over 19 million pounds of ground beef and related trim during the summer of 2002. The reason: Laboratory tests confirmed E. coli 0157:H7—the same deadly germ that had taken lives and hospitalized many in previous contamination tragedies.

When John Munsell found that the hamburger he ground from ConAgra-provided meat contained the pathogen E. coli, he informed the USDA. Whereupon the department launched an inspection of his operation, but not the source of the contamination—ConAgra. They closed Munsell's plant for four months.

USDA's delay in going after ConAgra's Greeley plant resulted in the death of an Ohio woman and sickness for thirty-five other consumers before ConAgra recalled 19 million pounds of beef.

Back in 1967 when we were exposing dirty meat plants throughout the nation that led to the media and congressional furor that in turn led to the 1967

Wholesome Meat Inspection Act, I heard similar complaints about USDA. Meat inspectors who did their job often lost their job or were transferred. Dirty or cancerous meat was funneled into the poor inner cities where consumers had the least power. The 1967 act then gave USDA more authority to regulate this industry and for a time conditions were improved.

But never count out the lobbying power of the meatpacking industry and their allies in the councils of government. They do not want regulation; they want self-regulation under the guise of regulation so as to reassure people that the USDA seal means something.

So in the '90s they started beating the drums to get rid of continuous daily USDA inspection of meat plants' assembly lines. During the Clinton administration in 1996, USDA started a new Hazard Analysis Critical Control Point (HACCP) system that was described as a modernization movement. HACCP was touted as placing the responsibility on the companies for their products, supplemented by laboratory tests to detect invisible microbial contamination. It hasn't quite turned out this way.

According to the Government Accountability Project (GAP), which is championing Munsell's cause, the USDA has "left the public ignorant of and vulnerable to ongoing shipments of government-approved, tainted meat." USDA is "not enforcing the HACCP rules for industry's duty to maintain accurate, complete public health records to protect America's consumers," charges GAP. This deficiency reduces the ability to trace products when recalls are necessary, GAP asserts.

GAP is a highly credible organization (see www.whistleblower.org) that defends whistle-blowers in court. When it declares that USDA "engaged in persistent, ugly retaliation against anyone who attempted to expose the ongoing cover-up, whether the whistle-blower is government or corporate, employee or small business," "consumers better take notice. Congressional hearings and continued oversight is crucial. Congressman Henry Waxman (D–CA) conducted an investigation of the ConAgra recall. But the majority House and Senate Republicans seem to care far more about big business than consumers' rights to clean and safe meat.

Munsell, a Republican, is on the move—demanding action from Congress, writing detailed letters to the USDA, and agitating in every direction he can think of for safer meat products and effective regulation. Thousands of USDA meat inspectors are cheering him on. They are fed up with the large companies contacting the higher-ups in the USDA and in Congress to pressure inspectors to lay off or be transferred out. Tough enforcement and USDA have not mixed.

On December 16, 2003, one of our affiliated groups gave John Munsell of Miles City, Montana, the Joe A. Callaway Award for Civic Courage. He should have gotten an award from the National Federation of Independent Business if the NFIB knew anything about the courage of small business to take on big business and risk all in the name of conscience.

December 19, 2003

Shelving the GSE Reforms

Fannie Mae and Freddie Mac, the giant government-sponsored housing finance corporations, apparently haven't lost any of their political clout despite the front-page stories about their accounting scandals and mismanagement.

Members of Congress issued a blizzard of press releases of the standard "shock and dismay" variety last June when Freddie Mac's top executives were forced to resign in the wake of revelations that the company had misstated its income by $4.5 billion. Not to be outdone, Fannie Mae admitted in October that it had misstated its stockholder equity by $1.1 billion in a third-quarter report.

Congress, which has always treated Fannie and Freddie with the softest of kid gloves, was finally forced to look like it was taking its oversight responsibility of the Government Sponsored Enterprises (GSE) seriously. For six months, members of Congress drafted a variety of reform proposals and the Senate and House Banking Committees dutifully conducted well-publicized hearings.

But when Congress adjourned this month, the reform bills were still sitting in committee. This means that reforms will have to wait until next year. Congress always moves at a snail's pace at the beginning of a new session. As a result it is likely that spring flowers will be in bloom in Washington before the committees pick up the politically hot potato of GSE reform again.

The GSEs are not happy with proposals that would allow regulators to establish minimum capital standards, require prior approval of new products, or put the companies in receivership in the event of a failure or a general tightening of ongoing oversight and greater transparency.

Despite the revelations of accounting problems and other shortcomings, the GSEs remain a potent political force and that fact is not lost on either the Bush administration or Democrats and Republicans in Congress. So while reforms may be politically necessary, Congress isn't inclined to step too hard on the GSE toes.

Congress, particularly the members of the two Banking Committees, is well aware that the GSEs have been adept at selling the idea that Fannie and Freddie are the keepers of the "American Dream of Home Ownership." And the GSEs are very solicitous of members of Congress, never failing to include them in well-orchestrated press conferences called to announce housing finance projects in their home districts.

During the 2002 federal elections, Fannie Mae and Freddie Mac contributed $6.57 million to candidates, according to the Center for Responsive Politics. Astonishingly, Fannie hired fourteen lobbying firms and Freddie Mac paid the tab for twenty-six other lobbying firms. Lobbying expenses for the two GSEs totaled $9.7 million in the first six months of this year, according to data compiled by FECInfo.com, which monitors lobbying on Capitol Hill. The boards of directors and the staffs of Fannie and Freddie have always been populated by former officials and political activists from both the Republican and Democratic parties, who are given huge pay packages.

Part of the delay in moving the reform legislation has been the Bush administration's insistence that the Office of Federal Housing Enterprise Oversight (OFHEO) be dissolved and the regulatory functions assigned to an office within the Treasury Department.

The Treasury Department is a mammoth bureaucracy with 160,000 employees carrying out duties ranging from the secret service to the management of the fiscal affairs of the federal government to the collection of taxes, to mention just a few of the myriad assignments of the department. GSE regulation would be buried in this bureaucracy and no one would judge the performance of the secretary of the Treasury on how well the regulatory duties were carried out. Accountability for GSE regulation would suffer greatly.

Treasury secretaries are part of the inner circle of any president's administration, Democratic or Republican; they are often political confidants as well as Cabinet officers. Faced with cracking down on Fannie and Freddie for safety and soundness reasons versus letting the GSEs roar forward with a politically attractive finance scheme might prove to be a difficult dilemma for a Treasury secretary. In addition, placing responsibility in Treasury for regulation of GSEs (which are major players in the money markets) increases the perception that Fannie and Freddie are quasi-governmental entities.

Fannie and Freddie each already have a $2.25 billion draw on the Treasury Department should they fall on bad times. This link, which gives the GSEs great benefits in raising funds in the market, should not be enhanced by assigning the Treasury Department direct responsibility for the safety and soundness of the corporations.

Rather than reinventing the wheel, Congress should leave OFHEO, the present agency, in place with statutory assurances that it is an independent agency with the sole function of regulating Fannie and Freddie.

OFHEO, under the direction of Armando Falcon, has assembled a small, but capable staff. It has been handicapped, however, by lack of funds with both the Senate and House Appropriations Committees keeping a tight lid on the agency. The Office of Management and Budget has been less than courageous in pushing for more funding for fear of antagonizing key figures on the Appropriations Committees. The regulatory reforms need to include assurances that OFHEO will be given enough staffing and adequate money to carry out its job.

Fannie Mae is the nation's second largest corporation measured in terms of assets. Freddie Mac is the fifth largest. Not only do these two each have a draw of $2.25 billion from the Treasury, but they are obviously high on the list of corporations "too big to be allowed to fail." That means they are candidates for taxpayer bailouts. Congress should not have left town this year without enacting the GSE reforms. When it gets back next month the legislation needs to be sent to the president on an expedited basis. It will be a great test of how much courage the Congress and the president can muster in an election year.

December 12, 2003

Binding Arbitration Traps

" Americans are in love with their cars" is a badly overworked phrase, but it is a cliché that rings the cash registers at car dealers to the tune of $650 billion of new car sales annually.

That's why many consumers are so vulnerable when they roam the car lots.

Suddenly, they just have to get behind the wheel of that magnificent red convertible or that mammoth SUV. Caution diminishes and basic questions that might be asked, even for the purchase of a $100 microwave—much less a $30,000 automobile—are forgotten.

New car dealerships, already with all the advantages in their corner, are increasingly locking the door on consumers who might raise a dispute after the purchase of a car—even where outright fraud may have been involved.

This is being accomplished by requiring consumers to sign an agreement to forgo their constitutional rights to ask the courts to settle a dispute with the dealer. Instead of an impartial judge or a jury of randomly selected jurors, the consumers are required to place their fate in the hands of an arbitrator. This is called binding arbitration, keeping the consumer from seeking justice in the courtroom even after the arbitrator's decision.

In theory, the arbitrator is supposed to be neutral and agreed on by both parties, but many dealers designate the arbitration company in the sales contract when the automobile is purchased. And common sense suggests the arbitration company isn't likely to come up with decisions that might cut off future business from the dealer.

If the binding arbitration clause is in the contract, why doesn't the consumer simply refuse to sign the contract? One big reason is that many consumers don't realize the requirement for binding arbitration is in the contract, and dealers aren't likely to mention the issue until the buyer has signed the contract and the consumer is about to drive away with the shiny new car.

In the cases where the consumer does become aware of the binding arbitration clause, the dealer often tells the buyer that they can't sell him the vehicle unless the binding arbitration clause is signed.

At this point, all the advantages—certainly all the emotions—are on the side of the dealer. The buyer is salivating at the thought of driving away with that beautiful 220 horsepower monster and, too often, surrenders to the dealer's claim that the clause is a "must sign" agreement before the car leaves the lot. Car dealers, by definition, are negotiators and consumers should remember this when they lock horns over questionable claims about the mandatory nature of binding arbitration clauses.

Remar Sutton, the president of the Consumer Task Force for Automotive Issues (www.autoissues.org), lists some of the frauds that binding arbitration lets car dealers commit:

1) A dealership buys wrecked vehicles, repairs them, sells them to unsuspecting customers without disclosing the damage. The vehicle becomes a repair nightmare for the consumer and the dealer refuses to accept responsibility.

2) A dealership employee forges the consumer's credit statement and forces the consumer into an automobile loan that the consumer can't afford. When the forgery is discovered, the consumer is sued by the finance company. The consumer's credit is ruined.

3) A dealership trades in the consumer's old car, but never pays off the loan on the old car. The consumer is sued by the finance company and forced to pay thousands of dollars in damages.

4) A dealership buys lemon vehicles from the manufacturer, destroys the papers that show the vehicles' histories and sells the cars to consumers.

Under arbitration, the clear, well-established, consistent discovery rules followed by courts are lacking. This makes it difficult for consumers to obtain the information they need to establish their claims, in contrast to court procedures that provide for "discovery." Unless the arbitrators commit fraud, their decisions cannot be appealed and, in most cases, there are no reviews or other oversight mechanisms to ensure fair procedures. In short, binding arbitration is anything but consumer friendly.

While automobiles represent big investments for consumers (usually second only to purchases of homes), they are far from the only area where binding arbitration is imposed on consumers. Credit card companies, computer firms, electronic equipment sellers, insurance companies, home improvement contractors, and large employers, among others, frequently slip in the binding arbitration clauses that take away consumers' rights to address their grievances in courts of law. Consumers need to read these contracts closely to make certain they aren't giving away their rights to settle disputes in court. If companies insist on a binding arbitration agreement, just walk away from the transaction. You don't have to give away your rights as a citizen just for the privilege of purchasing an automobile or obtaining a credit card. It may take a little shopping, but there are choices in the marketplace where you can purchase a product and still keep your rights as a citizen. If more and more walk away, the vendors will start shaping up.

For more information, see the December 5 , 2003 "*Dateline* NBC's Hidden Camera Investigation" with Remar Sutton, president of the Consumer Task Force for Automotive Issues and read the January/February 2002 issue of the National Consumer Law Center publication *NCLC Reports* on binding arbitration clauses. www.consumerlaw.org/.

December 5, 2003

Consumer News

August is supposed to be a slow month in Washington, D.C. but two public reports released by two news conferences on August 12 seem to indicate it is the press that is slow.

Eight thousand doctors called for national health insurance and outlined their detailed single-payer plan in an article published by the *Journal of the American Medical Association*. The signers included two former U.S. Surgeons General, the former editor of the *New England Journal of Medicine*, hundreds of medical school professors and deans, and many practicing physicians throughout the country.

Dr. Marcia Angell of the Harvard Medical School said, "In the current economic climate, we can no longer afford to waste the vast resources we do on the administrative costs, executive salaries, and profiteering of the private insurance system." A factual predicate for her statement was given by Dr. Steffie Woolhandler, also of Harvard, who stated that "we are already spending enough to provide every American with superb medical care—$5,775 per person this year. That's 42 percent higher than in Switzerland, which has the world's second most expensive health care system, and 83 percent higher than in Canada."

In essence an expanded and improved version of traditional Medicare, the proposal, they assert, would save at least $200 billion annually on paperwork and administration. This sum alone would cover all the uninsured and upgrade coverage for those who are underinsured.

These thousands of physicians are "taking a stand on the side of patients and repudiating the powerful insurance and drug lobbies that block wholesome reform," said Dr. Quentin Young, former head of the Department of Medicine at Chicago's Cook County Hospital.

The physicians' plan would provide universal, comprehensive coverage without increasing overall health spending and give patients their free choice of doctor and hospital (which today's HMOs prohibit). Most hospitals and clinics would remain privately owned and operated.

What is unique about this proposal by the Physicians for a National Health Program is not only its lifesaving potential, its increase in efficiency, and its restraint on greed and poor quality care. It is also its detailed explanation on how it is to be paid for, how savings will result, and how a much more benign reallocation of where the money now goes to where it should go if patients' needs are first. See www.pnhp.org for more details or call 312-782-6006.

The other event was about the failure of cable deregulation and its skyrocketing cable bills (just another example of the miserable failures of so many deregulation schemes and their broken promises).

Remember the promises of the cable industry. In the '50s and '60s, a small cable industry promised no advertisements and vibrant local programming in return for a modest monthly fee. Then, it was composed of many small firms that were indeed locally rooted—community cable, it was called. Now three giant cable conglomerates control 56 percent of the entire national marketplace. Deregulation was a setup for a spate of mergers slouching toward wider monopolization.

Guess what happened after the last full-stage deregulation in 1996—voted by many liberal Democrats, such as Congressman Ed Markey (D–MA), along with the Gingrich crowd? Consumers were price-gouged more than 50 percent. This was after Congress and Clinton promised that deregulation would bring competition and lower prices, according to Ed Mierzwinski of the U.S. Public Interest Research Group—the prime sponsor of the new report (See www.uspirg.org for more details).

But according to Jay Halfon, who wrote the report, the reach of the cable company giants is boundless. They continue "to deny competitors access to critical programming, wireline competition is virtually non-existent, and the industry now dominates the broadband Internet market, giving it enormous and unregulated influence over America's digital future," he writes. Andrew Jay Schwartzman, longtime president of the Media Access Project, was direct: "The Internet as we know it is in jeopardy. If the cable television model is extended to the Internet, the open and interactive system which characterizes the dial up Internet will be lost."

What does the report propose? Return regulation to the states and local governments and away from the pathetic Federal Communications Commission. Require as a condition of franchise renewal that cable operators include billing inserts that invite consumers to join a local Cable Action Group that would operate a local Audience Channel, well-funded and equipped by the cable company—a modest quid pro quo for the franchise.

Introduce a la carte programming to expand consumer choices rather than being force-fed the programming bundles the cable operators demand. Empower state public utility commissions to regulate all cable rates and charges for video services until real competition emerges.

Jeff Chester, executive director of the Center for Digital Democracy, summed up the crisis: "Cable's threat to democracy and diversity on the Internet, our virtual town square, cannot be overstated."

Two fresh reports by prominent organizations and civic leaders about important matters on a slow news day and the major media looked the other way. It happens all the time in Washington, D.C.

August 15, 2003

Credit Card Crunch

What's the most self-destructive thing that consumers carry around in their pockets? It's those little pieces of plastic—credit cards—that are becoming the greatest menace to the financial health of low-, moderate-, and middle-income Americans.

There was a time when the "plastic money" was considered a convenience for consumers and a boon to the small merchants who couldn't afford to establish elaborate credit programs to compete with the national chains. Today, the credit card industry has become a hungry monster that is devouring the hopes and dreams of low-, moderate-, and middle-income families across the nation.

Credit card companies are rapidly moving to the front of the pack of predatory lenders. They are targeting sub-prime audiences, the working poor, college students, and people with blemished credit histories.

This segment of the unsecured credit market is a rich lode of fees—over-the-limit charges, late payment fees, and cash advance fees. Desperate for any kind of credit, lower-income borrowers are willing to pay outlandish fees to establish an account. Deceptive offers of easy credit combined with the desperation of credit-starved consumers too often end up in foreclosures, bankruptcies, and devastated families.

The "come on" is sometimes a promise of a relatively low interest rate on the outstanding balance each month. But, the "low rate" disappears quickly under the terms hidden in the fine print of the mandatory disclosures accompanying the credit card. A payment arriving a day late or a charge that exceeds the credit limit by a few dollars can trigger a 300 percent increase in the interest charges. A 9.9 percent interest rate trumpeted prominently in the credit card advertisements can become overnight a costly 28 percent on outstanding balances. When cardholders reach their borrowing limit, the companies frequently offer to increase the limit for an additional fee, all the while pushing the cardholder deeper in debt with increasing fees and interest charges.

Dr. Robert Manning, author of *Credit Card Nation*, who monitors the credit card industry closely, says that the companies market the sub-prime borrowers because they are more likely to keep high balances on their accounts month after month, often paying only the minimum finance charges. In contrast, the wealthier cardholders pay off the balances each month and, as a result, pay the least in interest charges and fees.

In the back rooms of credit card companies, Professor Manning says these more affluent quick-paying cardholders are referred to ironically as "dead beats." Manning notes that the largest increase in consumer credit card debt in recent years is among households with incomes of less than $10,000, according to the Survey of Consumer Finance conducted by the University of Michigan.

Some of the offers that fill mailboxes would make a common pickpocket thief blush. The First Premier Bank of Sioux Falls, South Dakota recently sent out a massive mailing, telling recipients that they had been preapproved for a 9.9 percent fixed rate gold Master Card. In the fine print of the disclosure form, the bank revealed that the credit would be limited initially to $250. From that sum, the bank would deduct an annual fee of $48, a "program" fee of $95, account setup fee of $29, and a monthly participation fee of $6. After the bank pockets these fees, the holder of the preapproved card would have $72 available for credit. Credit card solicitations continue to grow. From 1997 to 2001, the mailings rose 66.7 percent from 3.5 billion in 1997 to 5 billion in 2001. Credit card debt rose from $554 billion to $730 billion in the same period. Net revolving credit card debt climbed from $51 billion in 1980 to over $610 billion in 2002.

In addition to targeting the sub-prime market, credit card companies have been zeroing in on college students and, in some cases, even high school seniors. Dr. Manning says college students are a lucrative market for the card companies because the students lack knowledge of personal finance and are largely free of consumer debt. Dr. Manning's research finds that three out of five college students had maxed out their credit cards during their freshman year. Three-fourths of the students, according to Manning, were using their student loans to pay for their credit cards.

The credit card industry has become increasingly concentrated. In 1977 the top fifty banks controlled more than 80 percent of the credit card market. Today, only ten banks control more than 80 percent of the market. These banks and their credit card affiliates wield heavy influence in Congress, particularly in the House and Senate Committees with jurisdiction over the financial industry. And this is an industry that dumps generous bags of cash in the campaigns of key politicians in a position to block any attempt to provide consumers protections against gouging by the credit card operatives.

MBNA, the nation's second largest credit card company, was the number one contributor to President Bush's 2000 campaign and inaugural festivities. Not only the president but both Democratic and Republican members of Congress, particularly those on the Senate and House Banking and Judiciary Committees, have shared in the campaign largesse of the credit card industry. A coalition of banks, automobile finance companies, and credit card companies distributed $20 million in individual, PAC, and soft money to members of Congress in the 2002 election cycle.

The aggressive tactics of the industry and the reach into the lower-income market has created a few problems for the industry. Not the least of these is the fact that the deceptive practices and the gouging with high fees and unconscionable interest rates have destroyed many working families, forcing them into bankruptcy. The credit card operators are now fearful that protections in the bankruptcy courts may prevent them from collecting all their ill-gotten gains.

As a result, the banks and credit card companies are demanding that Congress change the bankruptcy laws, remove consumer protections, and make certain that they will be able to collect every dime from the people they have pushed into bankruptcy. In effect, consumers would be placed in a virtual debtors' prison and left with no chance to resume their lives as productive citizens. The bankruptcy courts would be converted into glorified debt collection agencies.

The House of Representatives, which has become an easy rubber stamp for the banks and other corporate interests, has already agreed to the wipeout of bankruptcy protections. It is still in the Judiciary Committee in the Senate, but the heavy pressure is on to send this pro-bank, anticonsumer legislation to the president this session.

Congress should be concentrating its fire on the banks and credit card companies that have lured so many hard-pressed low-income consumers into costly unmanageable credit card debt. Instead of going after the perpetrators of the credit abuses, Congress, led by the dictatorial Texas Representative Tom DeLay, wants to punish the victims. In this Congress, the only thing that talks is money—money that is given with greedy expectations of legislative booty.

July 3, 2003

Tax Cuts and the Homeless

Two views of the nation's capital were on display last week.

At 1600 Pennsylvania Avenue, the main event was the ceremony for President Bush's signing of still another massive tax cut designed primarily for the wealthy. On hand were the usual bevy of reporters and cameras to record the event. There were Republican leaders from the House and Senate full of self-praise for their legislative achievement that will balloon the deficit and drain funding from critical federal programs.

A dozen blocks away, some five hundred health workers from all over the country were gathered in a hotel ballroom to discuss ways to meet the desperate need for housing and health care for the nation's growing population of homeless Americans. None of the Republican leadership brass was in sight and no media showed up to carry forth the message of the desperate plight of people without shelter or health care or hope.

High on the agenda of the advocates for the homeless, whose organization is formally known as Health Care for the Homeless (HCH), is the closing of the enormous gap in the supply of affordable housing. The nation is five to six million units short of the demand for the barest affordable housing. This fact places heavy pressure on the effort to find decent shelter for low- and moderate-income families.

Fourteen million families spend more than half of their entire income on housing, much of it crowded and substandard, leaving little for other necessities such as food, clothing, and medical care. The Department of Housing and Urban Development has long urged that families try to keep their housing outlays to less than 30 percent of their income. Any payout for housing beyond that often leads to serious economic problems that push families into bankruptcy and homelessness—not to mention the fact that many forgo proper nutrition and medical care in an attempt to keep their homes.

Meanwhile at Bush's White House tax cut ceremony, it was obvious that the political oligarchies were not thinking about affordable housing or, for that matter, any other pressing economic need of the nation. Needs? What needs? It's party time for the wealthy as the Treasury is emptied for them.

This means that critically important social and economic programs will be put off for years while the nation struggles out of budget deficits created by the 2001 and 2003 tax cuts and the rising costs of the invasion and prolonged occupation of Iraq. This will have a serious negative impact on the national economy in coming years. Future administrations and future generations will have to struggle with the consequences long after George W. Bush has left office and is lounging under a mesquite tree in Crawford, Texas.

But the impact on homeless people and families is immediate. Not only will affordable housing programs be pushed to the background, but the other big need of the homeless—adequate universal health care—will slide further down the national agenda if the budget deficits balloon.

Sadly, people without homes are not on the decline. Homelessness is increasing and along with it a growing number of serious health problems, some contagious. It is difficult to pin down the exact number of homeless at a given moment, but a 2001 study entitled "Helping America's Homeless" estimated that 842,000 people were homeless in a given week and 3.5 million became homeless over the course of a year. A 1995 study reports that over a five-year period 2 to 3 percent of the U.S. population will experience at least one night of homelessness.

Many of the homeless are the working poor who earn only the minimum wage of $5.15 an hour—totally inadequate in today's housing market. The purchasing power of the minimum wage is less than one-third of the minimum wage of 1968. How can minimum wage families exist—putting proper food on the table and clothing their children—much less pay rent in today's market? A worker would have to earn $14.66 an hour to provide enough income to afford a two-bedroom home at the national weighted Fair Market Rent (FMR). With the unemployment rate at 6 percent and rising, the problem of homelessness is only going to worsen.

A survey by the U.S. Conference of Mayors found that requests for emergency shelter increased an average of 19 percent in major cities last year. In many cities—often having gleaming stadiums subsidized with tax dollars—the requests had to be rejected because the cities lacked sufficient beds.

Lack of a stable place to live is traumatic for adults, but for children the experience is particularly cruel. More than 1.35 million children are homeless at some point each year. They exist in shelters, cars, parks, or pushed into already badly overcrowded quarters. The homeless life disrupts their education, exposes them to communicable diseases, malnutrition, depression, and drug addictions.

It is difficult to imagine a worse environment for a child or young adult. What kind of nation do we have when we allow children to be dropped through the safety nets and left on the streets or in crowded shelters? Of course many of the safety nets have been shredded through welfare reform efforts, benefit retractions, and the declining value of the frozen minimum wage. The growing income gap between the poorest and wealthiest citizens has left an increasing number of families at risk of homelessness, including those with young children.

We can solve the problem of poverty and homelessness. But it will take more than the "Alice in Wonderland" economics of the Bush administration, which believes there is only one solution to all problems—cut taxes for the wealthy who, unlike working families, do not spend their Bush bonus.

We need to get off this plutocratic tax-cutting binge and start grappling with real solutions to real problems.

June 3, 2003

Wiping out State Protections for Consumers

Never try to cut a deal with the lobbyists for the credit and banking industry. Whatever the compromise, they always come back with their hands out for more favors and bigger loopholes to gut protections for consumers and leave them defenseless against both price and privacy exploitation.

They're proving it once again with a massive lobbying campaign to stampede Congress into shutting out state legislatures and attorneys general from any say on key elements of how credit information is gathered, disseminated, and used by credit reporting agencies that maintain an estimated 600 million files on American consumers—a gold mine of data for the credit industry and a dangerous minefield for citizens wanting to protect their privacy.

When Congress updated the Fair Credit Reporting Act in 1996, the financial lobbyists made impassioned pleas for a temporary preemption of related state laws until they had a chance to absorb and work with the federal changes. Senator Richard Bryan of Nevada, the lead sponsor of the legislation, reluctantly agreed but with the firm understanding that the preemption was to be temporary. Ultimately, Congress agreed on January 1, 2004, as the end of the preemption. After that date, states were to be free to adopt stronger protections for their citizens. Now the financial lobbyists have tossed all that legislative history out the window and have descended on Capitol Hill with demands that the preemption of state laws be made permanent in important areas of the credit reporting business, such as sharing information with corporate affiliates.

Operating under the euphemistic name of "Partnership to Protect Consumer Credit," the credit bureaus and credit pushers have launched an all-out public relations campaign—including full-page advertisements in major newspapers plus hundreds of radio spots—claiming that the preemption of state laws is needed to ensure accuracy, fairness, and confidentiality for consumers and to "protect the national consumer credit system."

The claim about ensuring "accuracy, fairness, and confidentiality" sounds like a bad joke up against the real facts of the credit reporting industry. The Federal Trade Commission (FTC) issued a report in 1993 saying that the most common type of consumer complaint received was about credit reports, with the majority related to accuracy. After the 1996 amendments, FTC revisited the issue in 2000 and found that complaints about credit reports were still among the most numerous, with the issue of accuracy leading the pack.

Consumers have a tremendous stake in the accuracy of credit reports. Most of the reports are prepared and maintained by three major firms, Equifax, Experian, and Trans Union. The reports contain identifying information, such as name, last known address, marital status, social security number, names of dependents, and employment information. The credit information includes account numbers, the payment history on loans and charge accounts, and public information, such as court judgments, liens, and bankruptcies.

Consider the personal uses of credit reports under the Fair Credit Reporting Act. They include your applications for credit, insurance, and rentals for personal, family, or household purposes. The price of credit and insurance are often determined from the data collected in credit reports. They are also used in employment evaluations (with the consent of the applicant) as well as in reviews of existing charge and bank accounts.

Federal, state, and municipal agencies can obtain basic identifying information from a consumer reporting agency. The USA Patriot Act, passed in the wake of the September 11, 2001 attacks, deepened access to the reports by law enforcement agencies.

Some parts of an individual's credit report—the so-called "headers" containing the name, address, and telephone and social security numbers—are not considered "credit information" by FTC. This has allowed consumer reporting agencies to sell this information with no legal protections for individuals. A 1997 report by the Public Interest Research Group (PIRG) described the unrestricted sale of these "credit headers" as one of the main causes of identity theft, which leaves 40,000 consumers each year "fighting to clear their names and correct their credit reports after thieves establish fraudulent credit accounts in their names."

Clearly, the credit reporting system remains badly flawed despite the amendments adopted in 1996. States should be allowed to protect their citizens' rights to fair access to credit and reasonable safeguards of their privacy.

Congress made it clear in 1996 that preemption of states' rights on regulation of credit reporting was to be temporary. Congress should keep that promise! That can be accomplished by simply letting the sunset date of January 1, 2004 remain on the books. In this case, Congress can help consumers by doing nothing. Even this Congress should be able to manage that task.

May 16, 2003

The Bankruptcy Shuffle

If you are facing financial difficulties and heading toward bankruptcy, it is all so much nicer to be a corporate executive than just an ordinary hardworking citizen. And if the financial lobbyists and their friends in Congress have their way this year, the disparity between the kid-glove treatment of corporate bankruptcy and tough bankruptcy for beleaguered consumers will grow by mammoth proportions.

Under legislation already passed by the House of Representatives earlier this month, hard-pressed consumers in bankruptcy will face a draconian means test that will leave them in a virtual debtors' prison for years.

Gone will be the concept of a second chance for consumers who fall into impossible debt situations because of illness, loss of job, or divorce.

While rushing to meet the demands of daily lobbying by credit card companies, banks, finance companies, and predatory lenders for a scorched earth policy against consumers in bankruptcy, Congress is leaving in place bankruptcy laws that provide corporations and their executives with a soft landing in the event of financial troubles.

Unlike the punitive penalties that Congress wants to impose on consumers, a corporation can use Chapter 11 of the Bankruptcy Code to "reorganize" its business and try to become profitable again. Management continues to run the business and is only required to seek approval from the bankruptcy courts for "significant" decisions of the corporation. Chapter 11 provides a process for rehabilitating the company's faltering business—in effect providing the "second chance" that Congress is now trying to strip from the bankruptcy process for consumers.

A recent article in the *Wall Street Journal* illustrated just how well corporate executives make out in a bankruptcy. Twelve executives of Pacific Gas and Electric Corporation of California, including its chairman and chief executive officer, Robert Glynn, Jr., are expected to receive $34 million in bonuses this year despite the fact that the company is deep in bankruptcy proceedings and lost $2.2 billion in the fourth quarter of 2002.

Contrast this corporate executive bonanza in bankruptcy with the pending consumer bankruptcy legislation with its tough means test and provisions that endanger child support payments, increase the likelihood of evictions, foreclosures, and loss of automobiles needed for work, and leave bankruptcy judges with little discretion to provide relief even in the most extreme family hardship cases.

The pending consumer bankruptcy legislation is truly a war on women who represent the largest group in bankruptcy and on African American and Latino home owners who are 500 percent more likely than white home owners to find themselves in bankruptcy. Senior citizens are now the fastest-growing group in bankruptcy.

While the human misery certain to flow from the legislation will be a tragedy for many families, one of the worst effects may be the encouragement of reckless, abusive, and predatory practices by lenders.

With the bankruptcy courts serving as virtual bill collectors and with most of the consumer protections stripped from the process, lenders will find it worth engaging in unfair and unscrupulous practices. So what if the borrower is forced into bankruptcy? Under the pending law, the predators know that the bankruptcy courts will be required to turn the screws on the borrowers and collect for the lenders.

Consumer groups pled repeatedly for Congress to clean up the credit industry and stop the deceptive practices, excessive fees, and outright fraud before considering an overhaul of the bankruptcy laws. There is no question that the abusive tactics of lenders are the root cause of many of the consumer bankruptcies in recent years. Instead of cracking down on the lenders, Congress seems determined to reward them with a grossly unfair and punitive bankruptcy law.

While the proponents of the lenders' bankruptcy bill have filled the Congressional Record with stories of real or imagined abuses of bankruptcy by consumers, they have remained silent about the ease with which many corporations glide through bankruptcy and emerge as viable companies with bloated executive salaries intact. We don't see any consumers in bankruptcy waving multimillion dollar bonuses like the top executives at PG&E.

Consumers aren't seeking these corporate-style handouts. All they are asking for is a fair chance to straighten out their finances and to regain a toehold as productive citizens. Historically, the bankruptcy system was constructed on the idea of a second chance for hard-pressed families caught in impossible debt situations, almost always because of unforeseen difficulties stemming from health problems, loss of jobs, and divorce. If corporations get a second chance to reorganize, what is the rationale for depriving consumers and their families of a fresh start? In coming weeks, the U.S. Senate will have an opportunity to stop the rush to shred consumer bankruptcy protections. Millions of campaign dollars have poured into the Senate and the House from the credit merchants over the last three Congresses.

Preserving a fair bankruptcy system and saving protections sorely needed by consumers may seem difficult in the face of the power and the money of banks, credit card companies, finance companies, and predatory lenders.

But it can be done if enough citizens will let their senators know that they don't want the bankruptcy system converted into a glorified collection agency working for the avaricious merchants of consumer debt.

March 28, 2003

Preempting States' Rights

For decades Republicans and conservative Democrats were vehement in their defense of states' rights. Federal legislation on everything from civil rights to gun control to environmental and health safeguards—and a host of other consumer protections—has faced vigorous opposition centered around the argument that such issues were the province of the states, not the federal government.

Now we see the players rapidly changing game jerseys. Coalitions formed among Republicans and conservative Democrats are attacking states' rights and beating the drums for federal laws to preempt—wipe out—state laws, particularly those that might in any manner involve regulation of financial corporations and other business interests.

Weary of watching Congress consistently sell out to business interests, consumers have been going to their state legislatures and state attorneys general in an effort to enact and enforce state and local laws that will fill the gap and provide citizens basic protections in the marketplace.

This has angered the Washington lobbyists who see the grass roots movements threatening what they have bought in recent Congresses. Some state governments, once patsies for whatever the dominant economic interests wanted, have been showing some backbone and a willingness to provide consumers with basic safeguards involving such things as privacy, lending scams, arbitrary and excessive fees, access to financial services, health care, control of tobacco, stock fraud, and other deceptive practices.

As a result, preemption of state laws is becoming a cottage industry for corporate lobbyists in Washington. Members of Congress and their campaign contributors, who used to play homage to the sanctity of "states' rights," are now more likely to be talking about the need for "national uniform standards." Translation: the indentured U.S. Congress has become much more dependable than many state legislatures in bending to the desires of corporations and other special interests.

The regulatory agencies have picked up the same tune. The king of the preemption campaign at the regulatory level is Comptroller of the Currency (OCC) John (Jerry) Hawke, a longtime Washington bank lawyer-lobbyist who now regulates national banks. Hawke has his legal staff working overtime defending banks and arguing that the National Banking Act allows federally chartered institutions to thumb their noses at state and local consumer laws.

Hawke has gone so far as to issue a directive warning national banks to immediately notify him if any state law enforcement official tries to obtain information on their operations. The warning is aimed at blocking efforts by state attorney generals who have launched vigorous efforts to protect consumers from lending scams and deceptive practices.

Hawke's agency, of course, has a vested interest in using his office to help banks wipe out protections for consumers. By using the National Banking Act against consumers, Hawke has a giant carrot with which to encourage federally chartered banks to remain under his jurisdiction and continue to pay millions of dollars in fees to fund his office. Hawke and his predecessors have always been very sensitive to the ease with which banks can switch charters and slip out from under his regulatory power.

While OCC and its sister agency, the Office of Thrift Supervision, have attempted to preempt a variety of state laws on credit cards, ATM fees, and lifeline bank accounts, the present focus of the banks and regulatory agencies is on the increasing efforts of states to control predatory lending practices and their outrageous gouging. Under attack by the lending industry are strong antipredatory efforts by states like Georgia, North Carolina, and New York as well as more limited moves in Connecticut, California, Florida, and Pennsylvania. Legislatures and state attorney generals in other states are eyeing the chances for the adoption of safeguards to protect consumers—particularly low- and moderate-income citizens—from the lending predators. Facing these grassroots efforts, the predatory lending industry is coming to Congress in an effort to preempt the state and local laws. Point man for the effort is Representative Robert Ney of Ohio. In press releases and newsletters back to his constituents in Ohio, he claims that his bill is actually an effort to set "national standards" against the scam lending operations.

Not so, say most of the nation's leading consumer, community, and civil rights organizations. They see the Ney legislation, instead, as a Trojan horse designed to enact a limited and loophole-filled federal law that will end any chance for states and local governments to provide tough protections that will close the door tightly against predators.

In a letter to Congress, the consumer organizations warned: "Congressman Ney's bill will not address the predatory lending problems facing our communities while it undermines existing statutes and any future attempts by state and local legislators to protect consumers from predatory lenders."

On March 17, the National Association of Attorneys General (www.naag.org) will meet in Washington; federal usurpation of state authority will be very much on their minds.

Congress has done nothing to stop the unfair, destructive, and cruel exploitation of borrowers by predatory lenders. Now, it appears poised to wipe out whatever protections local and state governments can provide for their citizens. With special interests dominating this Congress, it is hard to identify any single attack on consumers as "the most outrageous," but the Ney bill can certainly claim a prominent place in the anticonsumer hall of shame.

March 7, 2003

The Cost and Confusion of Real Estate Settlements

For most families, the purchase of a home represents the single largest financial obligation of a lifetime. It's all part of the "American Dream," according to the pitchmen for builders, lenders, brokers, and other assorted players who make up the lucrative real estate industry. Too often, the "dream" becomes something closer to a nightmare when the home buyer—already facing the daunting prospect of long-term mortgage payments and moving costs—reaches the moment for signing the final papers only to learn that it's not just those huge principal and interest outlays, but an array of fees called "settlement costs" that must be paid before the front-door key is handed over.

Here's the way Mel Martinez, secretary of the Department of Housing and Urban Development, described the problem recently in testimony before the Financial Services Committee of the U.S. House of Representatives: "After agreeing to the price of a house, too many families sit down at the settlement table and discover unexpected fees that can add hundreds if not thousands of dollars to the cost of their loan. And at that point, they have no viable options. On the spot, the borrower is forced to make an impossible choice: either hand over the extra cash and sign or lose the house."

This is no nickel-and-dime problem. Americans spend an estimated $50 billion each year in real estate settlement costs. It is a dizzying list of charges added for such things as loan originations, appraisals, credit reports, various inspections, mortgage insurance applications, mortgage insurance premiums, hazard insurance premiums, flood insurance, title fees, title examination, title insurance, document preparation, attorney's fees, lender's title insurance, recording and transfer fees, surveys, courier fees for the delivery of documents...the list goes on and on.

The cost and confusion of real estate settlements has long plagued home buyers. In an effort to provide more timely disclosures and other reforms, Congress adopted the Real Estate Settlement Procedures Act (RESPA) in 1974. But there have been dramatic changes in the housing industry and in lending practices. The need to update the twenty-eight-year-old law has long been obvious.

Secretary Martinez has proposed new regulations that he contends can simplify the settlement process and save home buyers as much as $8 billion annually—an average of $700 per closing. The regulation, among other things, is designed to significantly improve the "good faith" estimate of settlement costs provided to home buyers prior to settlement and would allow lenders to offer guaranteed mortgage packages covering interest rates and lender-required settlement costs. Under the guaranteed package approach, settlement costs cannot vary from the time the offer is made. The interest rate guaranteed in the package can vary only on the basis of an observable index or yardstick. The package, which must remain open for thirty days, would be simplified to provide easy cost comparison with competing offers.

The public comment period on the rule ended in October and a final version of the regulation will be published early this spring.

It may take legislation to save another of Secretary Martinez's initiatives on RESPA. The 8th Circuit Court of Appeals ruled against HUD's attempt last month to use RESPA to ban markups (padding) of some closing cost fees—the so-called "junk fees." The court ruled that while HUD had authority to ban kickbacks and fee splitting under RESPA, the law did not give the department the right to ban surcharges—even unconscionable markups—that some firms were placing on closing costs. Ken Harney, who does a remarkably thorough job of tracking housing developments around the nation, predicts in his latest nationally syndicated column that Congress will be asked by HUD for explicit authority over such markups when it reviews Secretary Martinez's broader reform of RESPA later this year.

Unless Congress does act, Harney noted that lenders, title companies, mortgage brokers, and other settlement service providers will be left free to continue practices like charging $65 for a credit check that actually costs $9 or charge $350 for "full appraisal" which, in reality, was performed electronically and cost the lender only $50 or allowing a $55 courier fee for delivery services that only cost $15.

While HUD's proposed reforms for RESPA need some fine-tuning and clarification in some areas before the final version is published, it is becoming increasingly clear that Secretary Martinez is very serious about ending the gouging of home buyers at the settlement table. His public statements make it clear that not only does he feel this a "fairness" issue for consumers, but also a fundamental need if we are to increase home ownership, particularly for low- and moderate-income citizens.

"The mortgage finance process and the costs of closing are major impediments to home ownership," he says emphatically. And he ties that statement directly to the Bush administration's announced goal of creating 5.5 million new minority home owners by the end of the decade.

It will be interesting to see how a Republican-led House and Senate will respond to Republican Secretary Martinez's initiatives to end the long-standing and gigantic rip-offs of homebuyers.

February 5, 2003

A Banking Agenda for the Senate

Washington is in the midst of its biennial guessing game about what legislation will get the green light when the 108th Congress convenes next month. Many committee chairpersons, of course, are just waiting to get their marching orders from the White House and their friends among the army of lobbyists (aka campaign contributors).

But at least one new committee chairman, Senator Richard Shelby of Alabama, is making it very clear that he isn't waiting on instructions from anyone. The votes had hardly been counted from the November 5 election when Senator Shelby announced an agenda for his Banking Committee that sent an early wintry chill through the ranks of big lobbying firms on K Street in Washington.

Shelby is talking about "safety and soundness" of financial institutions, a phrase that had been all but dropped from the vocabulary of most of the members of the House and Senate Banking Committees in the rush to meet the demands of the financial industry for more power and less regulation. And he is making it clear that federal regulators charged with safety and soundness responsibilities meet those responsibilities. It sounds like the regulators better be prepared to make lots of trips to the Senate next year.

In interviews, the new chairman has announced plans for hearings on whether Congress went too far in the passage of the financial modernization legislation (Gramm-Leach-Bliley Act) in 1999 and, in the process, jeopardized the safety and soundness of the banking system and the taxpayer-backed deposit insurance funds. The key component of the legislation was authority for banks, securities firms, and insurance companies to merge and form giant financial conglomerates.

Now the corporate scandals involved in the collapse of corporations like Enron and WorldCom are raising new questions about the conflicts of interest created by the legislation. Are banks making risky loans to corporations to assure that their securities affiliates can peddle lucrative investment banking services to the same corporation? Are there other tying arrangements involving loan and investment products that could jeopardize safety and soundness of insured banks? Shelby is giving every indication that he intends to explore these questions fully.

His inquiry will add new heat to various investigations of lending and securities underwriting relationships already underway involving banks such as Citigroup, Suisse First Boston, and J. P. Morgan Chase.

Senator Shelby was assigned to the Senate Banking Committee in the late 1980s just as the savings and loan industry was collapsing, something that undoubtedly influences his concern over the safety and soundness of banks and the health of deposit insurance.

"It all goes right back to the insurance funds," he said in an interview with the *American Banker*. "I believe that we have to look at setting banking policy from the context of making sure the funds are sound, so we will not visit the taxpayers again, like we did in the thrift debacle."

Shelby opposes increasing the current $100,000 insurance limit on individual accounts and questions the "free ride" that banks are receiving through the 1995 suspension of premiums for deposit insurance for all but the most risk-prone banks.

"I never have insurance on any building I have unless I pay the premium.... I don't know what the premiums should be, but to just let a few people pay the bank insurance premium and give everybody insurance...that ought to be looked at," Shelby said when asked about deposit insurance by a reporter.

Shelby is right. There is no legitimate rationale for the banks to escape paying for their own insurance when the taxpayers are on the hook for hundreds of billions of dollars for a bailout when the fund is depleted. As the senator points out, that is exactly what happened in 1989 to the savings and loan insurance fund. Although largely overlooked at the time and seldom mentioned, the bank insurance fund also fell into the red in 1991, forcing Congress to adopt provisions for a $30 billion contingency fund for commercial banks that is still on the books.

But for all of his concern about safety and soundness and the viability of deposit insurance funds, very high on his agenda is privacy—the safeguarding of financial, medical, and other personal data of individuals.

During the consideration of the financial services legislation in 1999, he and Representative Ed Markey, Democrat from Massachusetts, fought hard to include a strong privacy provision that would have required consumers to agree in writing before any personal data could be released by a bank, credit card company, or other financial institution. The consumer would have to "opt in" specifically to any data being sold or otherwise distributed to any third party under the Shelby-Markey provisions.

After strong privacy language failed on the floor of the Senate, Shelby renewed the battle when the House and Senate versions of the bill were being reconciled in a joint conference.

Once again, the pro-bank forces from both the Senate and House, pushed hard by a horde of financial lobbyists, blocked Shelby's efforts and adopted a privacy provision that provides no real privacy for the personal information of financial consumers.

The weak privacy language was one of the big factors in Shelby casting one of only eight votes in the Senate against the adoption of the conference report for final passage of the financial services modernization bill. Opponents of financial privacy may find the going much tougher with Richard Shelby wearing the chairman's hat.

None of this is to suggest that consumers will not have reasons to disagree with the senator from Alabama on issues in coming months, for example, items like bank redlining and the Community Reinvestment Act. But Senator Shelby does come into the chairmanship with a solid understanding of the Senate Banking Committee's responsibility for insisting on the safety and soundness of insured financial institutions, tough oversight of regulatory agencies, and the protection of citizens' privacy. Those are some welcome and big steps forward.

November 27, 2002

Punishing the Poor to Bail out the Credit Pushers

When the current Congress convened last year there were lots of promises to curb predatory lenders that peddle credit on outrageous terms to poor, elderly, and unsophisticated borrowers.

Not only is Congress reneging on its promises, but it is rushing to reward the lenders whose scams have devastated low-, moderate-, and middle-income families and forced many into foreclosures and bankruptcies.

Congress's gift to the predatory lenders is a scam artist's dream under the guise of "bankruptcy reform." The sponsors hope that this "lenders' relief" bill can be shoved through Congress in the last days of the session—before the American public realizes its elected representatives are rewarding the banks, credit card companies, finance companies, and other financial corporations that have provided Congress nearly $30 million in campaign contributions to promote "bankruptcy reform" in recent years.

The financial industry, along with its allies like gambling casinos and car dealers, are attempting to convert the nation's consumer bankruptcy law, which has served consumers and business well for decades, into a punitive debt collection enterprise that will keep hard-pressed consumers in what amounts to "debtors' prisons" for years.

The lobbyists for the credit merchants have consistently resorted to the tactics of the "big lie" with claims that the long-standing consumer bankruptcy protections are being abused by "dead beats" attempting to escape their debts. The hard facts gathered from surveys of bankruptcy filings show that 90 percent of all bankruptcies are triggered by the loss of a job, high medical bills, and divorce.

Bankruptcy law has always been based on the principle that debtors facing impossible financial situations be given an opportunity for a new start—a second chance—to regain their role as productive citizens rather than being thrown on a human trash heap to satisfy the demands of the creditors.

Not only is this sensible and humane for the family trapped in unforeseen financial troubles, but it makes the utmost economic sense for local communities and the nation as a whole. Crushing families through a harsh bankruptcy law means more people on welfare rolls, off tax rolls, and dependent on already hard-pressed local charities.

Congressional supporters of the repeal of bankruptcy protections know quite well that many of the money problems faced by families today are the result of runaway credit card schemes of the past decade that have duped so many unsuspecting consumers. Credit card offers have filled mailboxes with come-ons of easy credit. Introductory offers of a low interest rate are quickly converted into double-digit charges plus a mounting list of fees. As the cardholder falls deeper into debt, the credit card companies continue to up the ante by offering bigger and bigger credit limits. Ultimately, the consumer is sucked into cascading debt multiplied by high interest rates and hidden, deceptive charges and fees.

And Congress—now so eager to enact a punitive consumer bankruptcy law—has consistently rejected efforts to reign in credit card abuses. Instead, they want to punish the poor to bail out the credit pushers.

Congress's timing adds an extra note of cruelty to the conversion of bankruptcy into a punitive anticonsumer device. Thousands of workers are losing their jobs, savings, and pensions as a result of fraudulent management at Enron, WorldCom, and other large corporations. Many of these workers are left with only a few hundred dollars in the bank, no jobs, and facing outlays for mortgages, education, transportation, and other necessities in an economy where unemployment is at 6 percent and rising.

Members of Congress have turned out reams of news releases and uttered thousands of words of lament about the workers caught in the whirlwind of massive corporate fraud. But now many of these same congressmen are ready and willing—and eager—to enact a bankruptcy law that will truly clobber these same workers. The next time you hear your senators and representatives express sympathy for the victims of corporate fraud, ask how they voted on the repeal of consumer bankruptcy protections.

And you might ask them how they justify shredding consumer bankruptcy protections while leaving corporations free to continue to avail themselves of an easy route through bankruptcy, shedding investor equity and reorganizing as viable companies. A soft, easy landing for corporate bankruptcy versus a harsh, punitive, rocky route for consumer bankruptcy—an atrocious double standard.

How serious is Congress about protecting citizens against corporate excesses and unfair, unscrupulous, and deceptive lending practices? The vote on wiping out consumer bankruptcy protections will come up in both the Senate and the House of Representatives in September. It will be a major test of Congress's ability to summon the courage to stand up to the massed lobbying forces of corporations. Forget the well-honed news releases and speeches for or against repealing protections for consumers on bankruptcy and watch for the actual vote of your senators and representatives. This will be the hard-telling evidence of who your elected representatives really represent in Washington.

Let your congressman and senator know how you feel about wiping out consumer bankruptcy protections. Senate, 202-224-3121; House of Representatives, 202-225-3121.

August 13, 2002

The Better World Travel Club

For decades, the American Automobile Association, better known as Triple A, has grown up with the American automobile. Millions of travelers have joined to ensure themselves of roadside service in emergencies and to gain access to trip tickets (maps), travelers' checks, insurance, and other travel offerings.

Beneath its benign image as a "travel club," AAA has become a big-time lobbyist that mimics the agenda of the nation's giant automobile manufacturers. Travelers who pay dues to AAA find themselves supporting lobbyists who fight the "Clean Air Act," public transportation, stronger safety standards, and even bike paths.

"What they [AAA members] don't know is that AAA is a lobbyist for more roads, more pollution, and more gas guzzling," says Daniel Becker, director of Sierra Club's Global Warming/Energy program.

Now, a couple of entrepreneurs from Portland, Oregon, Mitch Rofsky and Todd Silberman, are challenging Triple A's comfortable perch at the top of the travel club business. Rofksy and Silberman have formed "The Better World Travelers Club," which not only competes head-to-head on basic travel services, but actively supports programs for a clean environment.

Rofsky was a consumer activist in Washington who later became president of Working Assets Capital Management where he managed a widely acclaimed, socially responsible mutual fund and was the first chairman of Business for Social Responsibility. Silberman headed Lifeco, which became the nation's third largest travel company before its sale to American Express in 1993.

For starters, the Rofsky-Silberman team is donating 1 percent of its annual travel agency and club revenues to environmental cleanup efforts. They are also promoting big discounts on what they have dubbed "eco-travel services," including such things as green lodging and eco tours. The club also offers a 20 percent discount on electric and hybrid car rentals and discounts on bicycles and electric car purchases.

In its promotional material, The Better World Travelers Club reminds its customers that each time a passenger takes a domestic airline flight, more than a ton of harmful greenhouse gas emissions are released into the atmosphere. Rofsky and Silberman trumpet the fact that their club is the only U.S. travel agency to offer a "clean air" program—"Travel Cool"—certified by the Climate Neutral Network for its efforts to offset greenhouse gasses generated by air travel. A portion of each airline ticket purchased through The Better World Travel Club will be earmarked for programs to save energy and reduce CO_2 pollution. The club also offers "Travel Cool" automobile insurance that supports programs to help offset carbon produced by automobiles.

The pro-environmental stance of this new travel club is throwing down the gauntlet to other travel services, not only AAA, but to the multitude of other travel clubs promoted through new car warranties and credit card companies. It is a highly competitive field, but consumers and the environment can only gain if the competition turns into a battle for cleaner air.

The news about healthy new competition in the travel business is welcome in the overall business community, which has been clearly stung by the sleaze revealed by the investigations of Enron, Tyco, WorldCom and other corporations. Lawyers and public relations operatives are working overtime in efforts to restore badly tattered corporate images.

But, it is going to take tangible action—not just slick public relations campaigns—to convince the American public that real change and real reform are being undertaken. The newspaper headlines and the television news programs are giving the public the impression that con artists have invaded boardrooms and executive suites en masse.

The Rofsky-Silberman effort in blazing a new trail in the travel business should be a reminder to American business that profit-making enterprises can operate with a conscience and with an authentic concern about the environment and health. The Better World Travelers Club's business plan is based on the concept that profit and the public interest can be compatible goals in our enterprise system. For more information on The Better World Travel Club: www.betterworldclub.com.

July 03, 2002

The Meat Monopoly

Once in a while Congress takes on a powerful corporate lobby that has overreached and is squeezing the little guys. Remarkably enough, the Senate has already passed a farm bill that prohibits meatpacker ownership of livestock. Since four giant companies control 83 percent of the nation's cattle slaughter and about 63 percent of the hog slaughter in the country, this ban is directed at the vertical integration of this industry at the expense of small farmers, consumers, and the environment.

The bill now goes to the House of Representatives where it invites grassroots support from all citizens and carnivores who care about the domination of our economy by big business.

The Organization for Competitive Markets (OCM) (Competitivemarkets.com), a civic advocacy group composed of farmers and university academics, has documented the disturbing trend that rebuts the industry's claims of efficiency through ever growing Bigness. Farmers' prices are plunging while consumer prices for meat are rising at three times the rate of general food price inflation.

How is this so? First, rapid consolidation of meatpackers, through mergers and acquisitions, has meant fewer buyers for livestock at the farm gate. In fact, today, many small and midsized farmers in this country have one bidder for their production. Moreover, these large meatpackers are also moving into livestock production like those massive hog farms that lead to environmental havoc and pollute water. This vertical integration facilitates supply manipulation in order to engage in price declines for the produce the meatpackers purchase.

The packers then turn around and pocket the growing spread between farm gate prices and what is sold to wholesalers or chain supermarkets. The meatpackers have reported record profits in the last four years as the rate of family farm loss continues to increase. Consumer beef prices rose 9 to 11 percent from November 2000 to November 2001—three times the rate of general food price inflation. The consumers are not receiving the benefits—whether by lower prices or higher quality—of the asserted efficiencies of Bigness.

A majority of senators came to the conclusion that prohibiting packer ownership of livestock is a necessary first step toward regaining competition and reducing barriers to new competitors in the food chain system. Many decades ago, Congress prohibited railroads from owning coal mines for much the same reasons.

The Senate farm bill contained an overall "Competition Title," which also required country-of-origin labeling, a ban on agribusiness-imposed arbitration clauses in livestock contracts, and a limited prohibition on agribusiness-imposed confidentiality clauses in livestock contracts. Over two hundred organizations across the nation have signed a statement in support of these pro-competition provisions.

There is an unprecedented crisis in rural America that has nothing to do with locusts and droughts. It has everything to do with monopoly, duopoly, and oligopoly. As OCM's recent letter appealing for support writes: "Biotech seed companies like Monsanto and DuPont/Pioneer have more monopoly power than ever as they buy up competitors' patent seed and make agreements with one another. Retail chain supermarkets are increasing their market share, increasing profits, and forcing down the farm share of the consumer dollar. The two dominant milk processing firms in the country, Suiza Foods and Dean Foods, were allowed to merge by the U.S. Department of Justice last December."

The takeover of farm production through enormous hog farms or through "contract agriculture," which has produced the poultry peonage of chicken farmers to the giant processors like Tyson and Perdue, sketches the future end of a small farm economy and its regenerative rural culture.

We should never forget that the greatest political reform movements, the producer coop subeconomy, much of our music and festivals and other connecting traditions came from rural America.

"Lend a hand" is one of those traditions between farm neighbors. So lend a hand and call your representative (202-224-3121) to support the "Competition Title" in the farm bill.

April 25, 2002

Cable and Telephone Industry Abuses

Gene Kimmelman of Consumers Union has been following the telephone industry for many years before and after the notorious deregulatory Telecommunications Act of 1996. This act was supposed to increase quality competition between local, long distance, and cable operators, which would benefit consumers. Here is Kimmelman's shorthand evaluation of the result of the act on your pocketbook and precious time:

"Cable rates, since deregulation, are up almost three times faster than inflation, more than 30 percent, local phone rates are up, and the majority of consumers are actually paying the same or more for long distance, and no sign of meaningful competition in the local phone market."

He rendered these judgments on the December 16 edition of CBS's *60 Minutes.* Anchor Steve Kroft produced an excoriating report of a law, backed at the time by the industry, that boomeranged against consumers in favor of the selling companies, including the biggest telephone companies.

Connecticut Attorney General Richard Blumenthal has been investigating the abuses. "Scams and schemes," "competing by cheating" are the ways he described the rip-offs by AT&T, MCI, WorldCom, Spring, and Quest whom he has sued. One such scheme, experienced by large numbers of residential consumers, is switching their telephone service to another company without their permission. This is known as the illegal practice of slamming.

Blumenthal has also taken AT&T to court for continuing to send people bills after they indicated their termination of the company's service.

Deceptive television advertising is another widespread practice. Recall the 7 cents a minute come-on. Kroft gets to the nub: "But it's not 7 cents a minute anytime, anywhere, when you factor in the restrictions, the monthly fees, the charges and the surcharges that appear in fine print, which you would need a remote control, slow motion and high-definition television to read." "The fine print is illegible and meaningless," says Blumenthal.

Kroft spent "months trying to get interviews with AT&T, MCI, Sprint, and Quest." They refused to be interviewed and referred his request to their trade association as befits a cluster of corporate hucksters too often plying the same fraudulent trade.

The 1996 act was supposed to deconcentrate the telephone industry from that year when 94 percent of local phone service was controlled by the seven regional giants called the Baby Bells. Well now, after the post–1996 merger wave, just four of these Baby Bells control 93 percent of all local phone service.

You used to be able to get through quickly to a human being in the phone company. Now you're hanging on the phone with "press one, press two...," and once you get a voice, it is increasingly a robot who doesn't know discretion, judgment, or answers to unprogrammed questions. Then there are the deliberately inscrutable bills you receive. As Mr. Blumenthal himself says: "I don't understand my phone bill a lot of the time. I know a lot of people, very informed, very smart who don't either. And I think that's the result of a deliberate strategy on the part of the phone company."

Most people give up on understanding their phone bill. Why does Sprint charge its customers a 1 percent monthly surcharge to pay for its property taxes? Phone companies are required by law to pay 6.9 percent of their long-distance revenue to subsidize rural phone service and Internet service for schools, libraries, and hospitals. So, what do phone companies do? Turn the charge into a profit center by charging customers 10 to 12 percent.

The hapless Federal Communications Commission asks the carriers why the markup. According to the FCC's Dorothy Attwood, the so-called regulatory agency hasn't gotten satisfactory answers yet.

Whatever fines are exacted from these corporate crooks by state attorney generals, state commerce commissions, or the FCC, are just a cost of doing gouging business. The gouging goes on and on. Congress continues to do nothing about this problem. Television programs like *60 Minutes* do their job with clarity; law enforcement against these corporate crimes and fraud scratch the surface; and private civil lawsuit litigators, like John Bell of Augusta, Georgia, achieve sizable settlements after years of persistence.

But at the end of the day, little changes. The companies—big and small alike, with few exceptions—pocket illicitly far more zillions of dollars than they have to give back. These corporations are not just mostly above the law; they are beyond the law.

Nothing seems to stop these abuses until state and federal governments require these companies to insert printed invitations to their customers to band together into full-time consumer protection groups in state after state with full-time staffs.

As the old saying goes, it takes organized people to take on organized money!

December 20, 2001

Lemon Laws for Computers

Decades of consumer advocacy have built an impressive, if still inadequate, array of consumer guarantees in the common law and statutory allocations of rights to consumers. It is unclear however, if the integrity and effectiveness of these norms and structures of consumer protection will continue in the digital age.

Certainly, electronic commerce is posing many challenges to conventional consumer protection arrangements. If a consumer in Denver purchases a software product over the Internet and downloads it from a server based in Buffalo from a company based in Toronto, where did the transaction take place? Whose law applies? In what venue can a lawsuit be filed? Clicking on a button saying "I agree" that all disputes will be governed by the law in Toronto may not seem important to the average consumer at purchase time but can become very important when a dispute arises. Even more troubling are shrink-wrap licenses, designed to bind the consumer to sale terms, just by opening a software package.

Computers can make many aspects of life easier, enabling people to do things they otherwise couldn't do and perform a variety of tasks more quickly and effectively. But computers, and the accompanying software, only make our lives more difficult when they don't work. The purchase and use of computer goods are enormously stressful for many people, because defects are common, repairs often short-lived, and warranties limited.

There is, however, a ready solution to this problem. A suitable model is already on the books. Starting with Connecticut in 1982, states across the nation enacted "lemon laws" to protect purchasers of automobiles. Under these laws, if an automobile must be repaired multiple times for the same problem within a specified time period, the consumer has the right to a full refund of the purchase price or replacement of his or her "lemon."

Although lemon laws have proven successful, they have not been enacted with respect to most products. However, there is a compelling case for lemon laws in the area of computers and computer software. The situation facing software and computer consumers resembles the situation facing consumers of automobiles.

As with automobiles, defects are common and recurring. So, too, manufacturers are often uncooperative when confronted with lemons. As with automobiles before the advent of lemon laws, remedies for defective computer goods are generally inadequate. And manufacturers have crafted an array of contract provisions that shift the risk of computer and software failure to the user. The typical terms specify "(i) that the contract (usually drafted by the vendor) is the exclusive statement of the parties' agreement, (ii) that the vendor extends no warranties other than a narrow one stated in the contract, and (iii) that the user's remedies for breach are limited."

Although computers and software are typically less expensive than automobiles, they are far too expensive for consumers to ignore when hardware or software is defective. And the market has not worked to ameliorate the sale of lemons. The recent successful antitrust action against Microsoft belies any suggestion that competitive market conditions prevail in this industry.

In short, it is time for state legislators to start passing computer and software lemon laws that can help consumers deal with recalcitrant vendors.

Our associates at Essential Information and the Consumer Project on Technology have drafted a model computer and software lemon law that can be adopted by any state legislature.

The model law does the following:

• Requires a computer seller to correct any defect that substantially impairs the use or market value of a computer during the first two years after its purchase;

• Gives the consumer the choice between a replacement or refund if a manufacturer refuses to make repairs, or is unable to correct a substantial defect; and

• Mandates clear and conspicuous labeling listing the legal rights of the consumer to be displayed on each computer.

To obtain a copy of the model law write to Todd Main, Essential Information, P.O. Box 19405, Washington, D.C. 20036 or visit the web page: www.essential.org.

August 22, 2001

ATM Fees

Emboldened by a complacent Congress and regulators who serve as little more than industry cheerleaders, banks continue to pile more fees on consumers.

The latest evidence of the fee gouging comes from a nationwide survey conducted by the U.S. Public Interest Research Group, which found that surcharges imposed on automated teller machines (ATMs) have nearly tripled over the past five years for consumers who use an ATM not owned by their bank.

In reality, the ATM fee structure represents a blatant double-dipping scam at the expense of consumers who are only attempting to gain access to their own funds. When consumers use another bank's ATM—dubbed by the industry as a "foreign" ATM—they pay a fee to their own bank plus the surcharge imposed by the ATM's owner.

According to the data collected by U.S. PIRG, this two-handed grab by the banks is costing consumers an average nationwide of $2.86 per transaction in 2001. In 1996, before the surcharges were slapped on, the cost was $1.01 per transaction. Even the surcharge is not satisfying the appetite of many banks. Eighteen percent of banks are now adding an annual "rental fee" averaging $13.76 for use of the ATM card.

As noted in earlier PIRG surveys, big banks, despite years of record profits, continue to be the leading offenders in imposing higher fees. Twenty-four percent of the big banks, for example, have started imposing annual rental fees for use of an ATM card compared with only 12 percent of small banks. ATM fees charged by big banks averaged $3.07 against a national average for all banks of $2.86.

The average big bank surcharges in 2001 were $1.55, up from $1.42 in 1999. Small bank surcharges averaged $1.36, up from $1.30 in 1999. Credit unions, only half of which imposed any surcharge, were the lowest with surcharges averaging $1.24 in 2001, up from 98 cents two years ago. Ninety-seven percent of the big banks surveyed by PIRG impose surcharges. To their credit there are a handful of banks, like the Amalgamated Bank of New York and Washington, D.C. (founded seventy-five years ago by the Amalgamated Clothing and Textile Workers Union), that continue to refuse to become involved in the surcharging schemes.

The bank fees skyrocketed while the Banking Committees of the House of Representatives and the U.S. Senate devoted most of their agenda over the past three Congresses to legislation to provide banks, securities firms, and insurance companies with vast new powers and lucrative profit centers.

Efforts by a few progressive members of Congress, like Representatives Maxine Waters of California and Bernie Sanders of Vermont, to halt the fee gouging were tossed aside by committees that were clearly more interested in fulfilling the wish list of bank lobbyists than in protecting consumers. With this blatant pro-bank attitude prevailing in Congress, it is little wonder that the banks pile new fees on consumers at will.

But there is evidence of a grassroots movement that may change Washington attitudes. San Francisco and Santa Monica, California, for example, have banned ATM surcharges, but their efforts have been blocked pending an appeal. Iowa continues to enforce its ban against surcharging and cities like New York and Chicago are considering bans.

Unbelievably, these citizen initiatives at the local level are facing major obstacles thrown up by federal regulators who feel their first responsibility is the care and feeding of the banks. In battles to preserve their surcharges, banks have been aided and abetted by friend-of-the-court briefs and agency opinion letters prepared by a federal regulator, the Office of the Comptroller of the Currency (OCC), which long has been aggressive in preempting state consumer protection laws. OCC has also proposed amendments to some of its regulations to give greater strength to the banks attacks on the San Francisco and Santa Monica ordinances.

In addition to local ordinances, several networks and alliances of small banks and credit unions are marketing their own "no surcharge" and "selective surcharge" policies. The New England SUM Program, an alliance of several hundred community banks with over 1,700 ATMs, now has members in New York, Ohio, and Puerto Rico. Similar alliances include the Pennsylvania Freedom Alliance, the Louisiana area Community Cash Network and numerous credit union networks. Members of these alliances do not surcharge each others' customers.

Despite these commendable efforts, the great majority of citizens are going to continue to be faced with rising bank fees. Members of Congress, particularly those on the House and Senate Banking Committees, need to get some strong messages of outrage from consumers who are being fleeced daily by rising ATM charges and other fees. And Congress needs to rein in unwarranted efforts of federal regulators, like OCC, to preempt local consumer protection laws. After all, OCC is supposed to be a federal agency that protects consumers, not just banks.

Until heat can be put under Congress and the regulators, consumers need to avoid surcharges where possible by using ATMs only at their own bank or using machines with a "no surcharge" logo. As PIRG recommends, bank at a credit union, not at a bank, if possible. Or consider a community bank to avoid the higher fees imposed by big banks.

High bank fees are not inevitable. They have become easy profits, unearned profits, for the banks. They will continue to rise unless enough citizens sound off and let Congress and state legislatures know enough is enough, the money and lobbying power of the banks notwithstanding.

April 4, 2001

The Poor Still Pay More

Some thirty years ago David Caplovitz wrote about a situation that the poor have known for years. He called his book *The Poor Pay More*. At the time, his documented evidence created quite a stir and many articles were written in the press about these intensive consumer abuses against people least able to endure them or fight back. Some protective legislation was passed and some good court decisions were written.

Now in the year 2000 comes the National Consumer Law Center (NCLC) out of Boston to report that business crime, fraud, and abuse are thriving on the backs of poor Americans. The laws are not enforced very much and can not keep up with the creative scams that pour forth, not just from retail sharks, but, in impact, far more from larger companies and their law firms.

Here is a sample of NCLC's findings.

1) Auto fraud: "an astonishing percentage of car sales involve fraud, deception, or unfair conduct. Consumers are sold both new and used cars that are "lemons" or are defrauded by car dealers who do not give a full disclosure of

the car's wreck or salvage history, its prior use as a rental vehicle, history of mechanical problems, or other defects."

2) Auto title pawn: "These transactions are a recent phenomena in which the car-owner pawns title to the car in exchange for a sum of cash. The effective interest rate of an auto title pawn can be astronomical (sometimes over 900 percent APR). If the consumer falls behind on the monthly payments, the car will be at risk of repossession no matter how much has already been repaid on the loan."

3) Home equity fraud: "Home improvement scams and deceptive lending practices are among the most frequent problems experienced by low-income home owners. In many communities they lack access to traditional banking services and rely disproportionately on finance companies and other less regulated lenders. Often in desperate need of home repairs (e.g., roof replacement, structural reinforcements), unsophisticated home owners fall prey to unscrupulous home improvement contractors who premise easy access to credit. Many of these loans have inflated interest rates, outrageous closing costs, and unaffordable repayment terms."

4) Payday lending: "This exploitive form of short-term lending can devastate the finances of cash-strapped consumers. The consumer provides the lender a post-dated check and receives an amount less than the face value of the check. The check is then held for one to four weeks (usually until the customer's payday) at which time the customer redeems the check by paying the face amount or allowing the check to be cashed. Payday lenders charge exorbitant fees for the loans, and the effective interest rates can top 1,000 percent."

5) Rent-To-Own (RTO): "RTO businesses are essentially appliance and furniture retailers that arrange exorbitant lease agreements for those customers who cannot buy goods with cash. Consumers who buy from rent-to-own businesses often pay two to three times the cash price for their purchases. The RTO industry aims its marketing efforts primarily at low-income consumers by advertising in ethnic media, public transportation, and housing projects."

6) Arbitration of Consumer claims: "Creditors and merchants are increasingly inserting clauses into the fine print of their contracts that prohibit consumers from filing lawsuits and force all disputes to mandatory arbitration hearings. Arbitration clauses are carefully drafted to stack the deck against the consumer: they allow companies to select the arbitrators, arrange for the arbitration in places convenient for the companies but not the consumers, forbid class actions, limit discovery, and prohibit recoveries, such as punitive damages and attorney's fees."

The center has also embarked on an initiative to help distressed older Americans who lose billions of dollars a year to home improvement fraud, scams involving medical aids, useless supplemental insurance, and high-pressure door-to-door sales and telemarketing schemes.

What opened the door to unconscionable interest rate gouges that form the core of many of these rip-offs was the repeal of the usury laws in state after state during the 1970s. This allowed what was once illegal and severely punishable to become legal. The companies called this law reform.

Weaker enforcement of existing laws and sharp reductions in public funding for civil legal aid programs (the latter accomplished by the Republicans who control Congress) permit fertile soil for business frauds.

Even this is not enough for corporate predators. By these fine-print binding arbitration clauses, consumers give up their constitutional right to go to court. The standard form contracts, uniformly used by alleged competitors, have reversed what contracts are supposed to be—namely, a meeting of the minds. Instead the seller minds and the consumer signs—on the dotted line.

For more information about NCLC, log on to consumerlaw.org or write to 18 Tremont Street, Boston, MA 02108.

February 22, 2000

Overbilling by Utilities

Unlike the sleazy headlines in some tabloid newspapers, the *Detroit News* often has sensational headlines on page one that reflect important, substantive stories. This certainly was the case on January 4, 2000, with the lead story blazing the headline "Report: Edison over bills $248M."

The "Report" refers to a study done by Moody's Investors Service for a Detroit-area business group, which includes the major auto companies, and is called "Associate of Businesses Advocating Tariff Equity." These companies don't like being overcharged for electricity anymore than residential customers, and they complained to the Michigan Public Service Commission. Moody's analysis took the commission to task for allowing Detroit Edison to collect too much for the "stranded costs" of its Fermi II nuclear plant in anticipation of the coming of electricity competition. Broken down, Moody's put the annual average overcharge at $43 a year for residential customers, $456 a year for commercial customers, and $82,600 for industrial users.

The business group is demanding a rollback in electric rates for Edison's two million customers who already are paying among the highest prices in the Midwest.

Michigan has not yet joined the nearly two dozen states that have passed so-called full electricity deregulation laws opening up the markets to supposed competition. I say "supposed" because in California, there has been very little competition to the erstwhile electric utility monopolies due to the huge "stranded cost" subsidies and other advantages exacted from the state legislature in return for giving up their monopolies.

Enron, a large energy company, was planning to compete with Pacific Gas & Electric and California Edison, but dropped out because of this unlevel playing field. Nearly two years into California's electricity deregulation and only 1.7 percent of households have switched to what competition there exists.

The looming question arising out of the Moody's report is: Are other electricity companies overcharging in other states under the non-watchful coziness of their state regulators? If so, then billions of dollars are being taken from customers under the accounting formula applied to the "stranded costs" doctrine—i.e., making consumers pay again for the uneconomic investments in nuclear and other inefficient plants as a condition for open competition.

A clue to the likelihood that Detroit Edison may not be the only utility overcharging on this basis was contained in the Moody's study, which noted that similar conditions in other states may be allowing the electric utilities "to charge ratepayers for costs they don't need help covering," according to the *Detroit News.*

When the twenty-three states passed their electricity deregulation laws in the past three years, there was very little reporting on these topics and very little knowledge among the legislators whose votes were whisked through their chambers by electric industry lobbyists. The large industrial electricity users supported deregulation because they could more easily bargain for big volume discounts.

Now, it seems, one utility's gouging behavior is too much for one group of businesses in Michigan. Will other business associations in other states also commission studies similar to Moody's in order to find if and how electricity customers are being overcharged in their states?

Why not ask your state Chamber of Commerce?

January 4, 2000

Electronic Signature Problems

An elderly woman is visited at home by a window salesman who talks her into buying ten windows for $10,000. She signs a number of pieces of paper, including the sales contract, the financing agreement, and a form on which she consents to receive the contract and all notices relating to the sale over the Internet at an e-mail address established for her by the window salesman. She does not

own a computer and has no knowledge of how to use one. The window salesman does not provide the woman with any paper copies of these documents.

A savvy young man walks into a car dealership. After driving a number of
cars, an agreement is reached regarding the purchase and financing of a particular model. The young man sits down to sign the papers. Among the contract and disclosures, he finds a consent form under which he would agree to
receive his copies of the papers he is currently signing, and all other notices and
disclosures relating to the transaction (such as the warranty information and
recall notices), at an e-mail address. He objects to this. The salesman points out
that if he does not agree to receive everything electronically, the price for the
car will be increased by $1,000.

A professor at a major university shops the Web for the best price for a personal computer. He finds just what he wants and enters into a contract to purchase the computer and make twelve monthly payments of $150 each, for a
total price of $1,800. He agrees to receive the contract and all other notices
and disclosures electronically. His copy of the contract is sent to him in Word
Perfect 6.0 format. After considerable difficulty, he is able to open and print
the contract, but in the process he has to save it as a Microsoft Word file. The
computer arrives at his home, and it is not the one he ordered and not the one
referred to in his contract. He contacts the computer dealer and is told that he
received what their version of the contract indicates. He contacts an attorney
for assistance, but is told that he does not have a copy of the contract that he
can use to prove its terms in court, so he is stuck. The terms in the contract he
was sent do not match the terms on the web page.

All of these scenarios are currently illegal, but would be made legal under H.R.
1714, the Third Millennium Digital Commerce Act, that passed in the House of
Representatives two weeks ago. Under the guise of facilitating electronic commerce,
the House passed a bill that would eviscerate numerous state and federal consumer
protection laws. Unfortunately the financial services industry used this bill as a
way to avoid providing required and important information to consumers. If this
bill becomes law, states would be prohibited from passing laws to protect their
own citizens. Despite the strong warnings from the Democratic leadership that
this bill hurts consumers and is not the way to assist e-commerce, as well as the
threat of a veto from the president, the bill passed overwhelmingly.

A much more judicious bill on the same subject also passed the Senate last
week. The Senate version, S761, only allows the practice of consenting parties
to enter into contracts using electronic records and electronic signatures. States
are permitted to protect their consumers as they deem fit.

The Federal Trade Commission and numerous consumer groups have
raised objections to the overreaching provisions of the House proposal. The

consumer groups have proposed the following basic standards for a federal law governing electronic commerce:

1) Electronic disclosures should only be permitted when the transaction is initiated and consummated electronically and not in person.

2) When signatures are required, the electronic signature technologies used must be reasonable, tied to the consumer's actual intent to sign the document, and only be attached to documents that are unalterable after the signature is attached.

3) The consumer should be given the specific and optional opportunity to consent or to refuse to accept disclosures electronically without surcharges for rejecting the electronic notices.

4) If the consumer is wrong about the capacity of the computer to print and/or retain the electronic record of the disclosures, the consumer must be able to request paper copies to be provided at reasonable and bona fide cost, and in a reasonable and timely manner.

5) The disclosures must actually be delivered to the consumer's e-mail address with a manual reply return requested, or they must be retained on the seller's web site for the duration of the transaction.

6) When disclosures are provided to consumers through a seller's or creditor's web site, they must be retained for the duration of the contract.

7) The electronic record must be accessible and retainable by the consumer and must be provided in a format that prevents alteration after it is sent, so that it can be used to prove the terms of the record in a court of law.

8) There should be a separate consent for each type of disclosure made after consummation. The consumer's failure to respond to the consent request should trigger paper disclosures before the failure to respond to an electronic disclosure triggers default.

November 29, 1999

Microsoft Settlement Should Be Kept Public

The historic Microsoft monopoly trial took an odd twist on November 19 when Federal Judge Thomas Penfield Jackson secured the agreement of the Justice Department and Microsoft to accept mediation by 7th Circuit Chief Judge Richard Posner.

For most jurists, being a chief judge of a busy federal circuit court of appeals would be a full-time job. But Judge Posner, often called a brilliant workaholic who grinds out a book a year on different subjects, thinks he can stimulate a settlement between the two warring factions.

The stock market believes in Judge Posner's conservative reputation and his numerous writings scathingly critical of most past antitrust doctrines enough to jump Microsoft's stock nearly five points in after-hour trading Friday (adding another $5 billion to Bill Gates's fortune).

Are the boys on Wall Street being precipitous? After all, Posner's colleagues and several law professors consider him unpredictable and his own man. They point out that as a mediator, he cannot force a settlement nor can he divulge any of the discussions to Judge Jackson or anyone else.

But then Judge Posner is not like any other prominent judge. He seems never to have had an opinion that he did not want to publish. His thirtieth book was a sharp denunciation of President Clinton's lying in the Monica Lewinsky scandal and a general defense of Special Prosecutor Kenneth Starr's handling of the case. No one would accuse him of having the conciliatory temperament that a mediator should possess.

One of his law students tells the story of Judge Posner, a part-time professor at the University of Chicago Law School, coming in the first day of class and writing the word "Justice" on the blackboard. He then turned and said to his class that he did not want to hear that word in his course.

As one of the founders of the "law and economics" school of monetized thought, what Judge/Professor Posner meant was that quantitative economic reasoning could explain legal issues by a cost-benefit analysis. For example, in one of his books he argued for parents' rights to sell their children for adoption to the highest bidder.

Throughout his career, Judge Posner, businessman Posner, and law professor Posner have challenged many a conventional attitude, and antitrust law has been no exception. He has written that "The evils of natural monopoly are exaggerated, the effectiveness of regulation in controlling them is highly questionable, and regulation costs a great deal."

It takes a deliberate price-fixing scheme between competitors or a tight cartel to get his antitrust dander up. Years before he became a judge, Posner started a consulting firm, called Lexecon, that advised corporations how to defeat antitrust law enforcement and undermine regulatory actions.

Given his voluminous antagonism to government regulation, it is not likely that Judge Posner will nudge his sparring parties toward "conduct" changes by Microsoft that need regulatory oversight. But then, would he encourage "structural" changes, such as Microsoft's breakup into two or more companies that separate its operating systems business from its applications business?

Certainly Judge Jackson's findings of fact would support a breakup remedy. But it is difficult to envision Judge Posner recommending such a move. He would probably prefer some self-executing remedies upon Microsoft that would presumably unleash competitors against the giant software company's anti-competitive monopolies.

In his book on antitrust law (1976) Posner doubted whether any company could have enough persistent market power over time to actually impose predatory pricing.

Since Judge Posner, as mediator, has no decisional power and cannot publicize his views, what is Judge Jackson's exercise here all about? There is about a ninety-day window for the mediation to conclude before Judge Jackson issues his long-awaited findings of law.

It appears that Judge Posner's function is to move the government and Microsoft to a settlement by the force of his intellect and his probabilistic assessment of both parties' chances on appeal. All in private, subject to his influence.

How much better it would be to continue the open judicial process, now that the trial phase is over, to an open judicial conclusion under the public's watchful eye. A full record and precedent would contribute to the development of antitrust law in these new fields of monopolistic technology networks.

November 22, 1999

Greenspan Doesn't Represent America

Alan Greenspan, chairman of the Federal Reserve—an agency serving purposes that officials in other western countries would call "central banking functions"—must keep saying to himself these days that "It doesn't get any better than this." Here he is, head of the most powerful federal regulatory agency in the government and all conservatives can do in Congress is to praise him effusively every time he goes there to testify. Here he is, the boss of the powerful Fed, which is funded by private banks, not by congressional appropriations, and whose regional divisions are actually run by private bankers; yet none of the liberals in Congress object to this troubling business influence.

And here he is, widely known as a fierce watchdog against inflationary trends, yet he is remarkably selective in what kind of inflation he is against.

For example, he now recognizes stock values along with housing values as mainstays of our economy. The prices of stocks have risen vastly more than the prices of housing over the past six years. Yet apart from some vague mumblings, he seems to be viewing prices of stocks as outside the realm of an inflationary trend.

Other numbers are also going up but they are clearly outside the conventional definitions. Corporate welfare disbursements and preferences are proliferating in every direction at all three levels of government, totaling hundreds of billions of dollars a year. The percentage of the working poor that is under the poverty level is at a record high. The number of Americans without any health insurance continues to go up—nearing 50 million children, women, and men.

More families are making less in inflation-adjusted income than families did in 1970. The figures on corporate and economic crimes continue to rise sharply. Just read the *Wall Street Journal* and other business publications that report on stockholder, consumer, tax, and government contract frauds.

Could it be that Mr. Greenspan is a willing prisoner of his own skewed economic indicators—the kind that led one economist this month to say "this economy is close to perfection"? Nor is he above inflating one indicator—interest rates—in order to deflate other parts of the economy, a maneuver that doesn't affect large corporations as it does consumers and small businesses. The Fed chairman does show consistent concern about one inflationary indicator—any rise in ordinary wages—and he is regularly relieved to see that they have been "stable," even though labor's productivity has been up sharply recently. It is clear that he loses little sleep over workers not sharing in the massive profits that their companies are reaping.

If only just once Mr. Greenspan would testify before a congressional committee as if he represented the American worker, consumer, and small taxpayer, instead of the Wall Street establishment, he might open his testimony this way:

"Mr. Chairman and distinguished members of the Joint Economic Committee, I come before you to declare that the state of our economy is not very good. I realize that this conclusion is at odds with my previous testimonies in recent years, but an entire new set of indicators has come to my attention.

"Please consider that nearly 25 percent of our children are growing up in poverty—the highest percentage by far in the western world. The bottom 80 percent of the workforce is making less in inflation-adjusted dollars than was made twenty-five years ago. The same is the case with inflation-adjusted income of the median family.

"What's more, these Americans have additional consumer expenditures they must reluctantly make because more members of the average family have to work outside the home, often commuting longer distances and having to maintain more cars and pay for more household functions.

"Consumer debts are at record highs, vastly greater in relative as well as absolute terms than in 1970 and this has led to record personal bankruptcies. The low-income housing stock is in a shabby and inadequate state. And many of the public structures, such as schools, clinics, and mass transits, are old and in terrible repair, all of which depress the standard of living of the nation's majority.

"In addition, while I am not worried about a few years of foreign trade deficits, about twenty-five years of uninterrupted trade deficits are indeed worrisome.

"Mr. Chairman, the sharp increase in wealth inequality—now at a seventy-year high and greater than any other western nation—certainly suggests that the growth of the economy during the past decades has not been advancing the long-term security of many families. This widening gap, enhanced by tax-payer subsidies, results in the top 5 percent of the wealthiest people receiving the bulk of the economic gains since 1973, including those from stock ownership and appreciation.

"I do not begrudge the wealth of Bill Gates, but it does tell us something to learn that his net worth is equal to the combined net worth of the bottom 120 million Americans. After years of hard work, these people are essentially broke, living at best from paycheck to paycheck. In my next testimony, I hope to elaborate these "people" economic indicators and suggest some directions for economic policy-making. Thank you."

November 15, 1999

Health Care Fraud

When it comes to the tens of billions of dollars of annual health care fraud that all of you eventually pay for, the sophistication of the private criminal enterprisers is ahead of the government's law enforcers.

The usual figure for the amount of billing fraud and abuse that the government estimates is 10 percent of what is spent, which amounts to over $100 billion this year alone. Some specialists believe this is the minimal figure and that it could be much higher if the government devoted modest resources to finding out.

The Clinton administration proudly reports that it has cut 45 percent of the Medicare overpayments and that this has helped curb the inflation in health care costs. But Malcolm Sparrow, who is on the faculty of Harvard University's Kennedy School of Government and an expert on fraud control, says that the control systems do not go deeply enough to reach the criminal practices.

The more automated and efficient the claims processing systems are, the easier it is for the criminals to achieve their objectives. He says: "Most of the control systems essentially assume that the information content of incoming claims is true—they don't question it. They merely ask questions like: Does the diagnosis match the procedure code? Is the price about right for this procedure in this region of the country? Is this procedure covered by the insurance policy that is operative?"

Sparrow, who has experience in police fraud detection and a doctorate in applied mathematics, avers that these questions are important medical utilization inquiries. However, they do not test the truth of the claim itself. "None of them check to see whether the patient knew anything about the diagnosis or whether the patient was even sick," he says, adding "that's the basic flaw in the up-front detection systems."

As he explained in his groundbreaking book *License to Steal: Why Fraud Plagues America's Health Care System* (Westview, Boulder, Colorado), the rule for criminal perpetrators in the health care industry is to "bill correctly." If the outlaws bill correctly, "matching the diagnosis to the procedure code, making sure they are within the confines of policy coverage, making sure the treatment is medically orthodox, then the crooks are mostly home free."

Sparrow believes that fraud control is a much harder problem than anyone understood or imagined. Academia has paid remarkably little attention to this subject, he notes. The science here is weak, especially since "fraud control is a game played against intelligent opposition" that is always trying to outwit the law enforcers who have very few cops on this beat to begin with. And computers are not the answer, he insists, explaining that he believes in "a long-term role for humans in a fraud control operation...any fraud control strategy that relies heavily on automated prevention is going to be a sitting duck for fraud perpetrators."

Well, then, is managed care the answer to fraud? Sparrow replies that "under capitated systems, fraud changes its form. Instead of billing for services not provided or billing for unnecessary services, fraud takes the form of diversion of capitation payments—where a lump sum is paid per patient per month—away from frontline medical provision . . . the net result is that patients who need treatment are not going to receive it. . . .When that happens, patients die as a result of fraud."

In the meantime, there is a growing business in firms that specialize in advising payers how to detect and recover overcharges on hospital and other medical bills. About 90 percent of hospital bills have mistakes, with overcharges comprising two out of three of the errors, according to business surveys. Unlike in Canada where everybody has health insurance and no one sees a bill under this system of single payer, in our country, complex, inscrutable, duplicative, phony, sometimes un-itemized bills devour huge amounts of time for consumers and other payers and processors.

This morass is why administrative expenses as a percentage of the health care dollar are over twice as high in the United States as they are in Canada.

Whether the abuse is the "non-self-revealing" health care fraud or the invisible billing overcharges, the legal, economics, and accounting-auditing professions need a wake-up call to seriously pay attention. Most law schools still do not even have a course or seminar on corporate crime.

To contact Malcolm Sparrow, write him at the Kennedy School of Government, Harvard University, Cambridge, Massachusetts 02138.

November 9, 1999

"Financial Modernization" is a Consumer Rip-Off

The financial services industry spent millions on public relations, opinion polls, and advertising to promote legislation in the current Congress that would allow the merger of banks, securities firms, and insurance companies under common ownership in financial conglomerates. All of this in addition to the more than $30 million in campaign contributions that can be traced to the various industry Political Action Committees plus soft money donations to the Republican and Democratic parties.

The slogans used in the campaign were varied, but no word was used more often than "modernization." It appeared frequently in congressional testimony and in the lobbying handouts that landed on the desks of members of Congress and the news media.

But it's hard to find "modernization" in a piece of legislation that hands vast new powers to financial institutions without strengthening (or modernizing) the regulatory machinery needed to protect the public interest and, incidentally, the deposit insurance funds that are backed by the taxpayers.

That's hardly modernization. We've tried that before in the savings and loan debacle. The cost of that bit of deregulation (or modernization, in the words of the financial services flacks) was about $500 billion including interest and a lot of disruption in financial services in communities.

It is equally difficult to spot the "modernization" in legislation that rolls back the Community Reinvestment Act (CRA), which has brought badly needed credit to underserved areas and housing, small business, and other development without using a dime of taxpayer funds. Where's the "modernization" in adopting legislation that ends up creating more urban problems and ultimately forcing communities to turn to tax sources to fund development efforts that could have been financed by CRA lending if the so-called modernization legislation wasn't enacted?

Where's the "modernization" in a bill that promotes the interests of the telemarketers? We've been hearing those salesmen on the telephones for quite a few years, and there aren't many citizens who look at these intrusions as anything close to the definition of "modernization." Yet the proponents of "modernization" legislation worked to keep the privacy invaders in business and up to date on your personal life. The affiliates of the conglomerates created under the legislation will now be free to share with other corporate affiliates every intimate detail of your life—buying habits, investing patterns, health records, entertainment choices, employment data, just about any detail of an individual's existence.

If that's modernization, there may be a whole lot of people who want less of it.

Rip-offs of consumers' rights and property seem like a practice that has been around for an awfully long time. But the proponents of the deregulation bill apparently see this as all part of "financial modernization."

That is apparently why the members of Congress were so eager to include a provision called "redomestication." That sounds something more akin to taming a wild animal than to a financial issue. But what it means is that mutual insurance companies, which are owned by their policyholders, will be allowed to sign a piece of paper declaring that their headquarters are now in another state. And, of course, that other state will just happen to have some lax laws that will allow the management of the mutual insurance company to convert to a stock company and in the process take the equity that the policyholders had in the company.

To a great many people this might sound a lot like old-fashioned highway robbery. But the proponents of the legislation tell us that it is just part of that wonderful idea of "financial modernization." The mutual policyholders may want their rights and their equity a little more than they do the "modernization" that the Congress is forcing on them.

"Modernization" is also intended to encompass something that the advertising writers have labeled "one-stop shopping centers." The idea is that the customer, once inside the premises of the bank (and perhaps just seeking to cash a check), can be lured, and maybe coerced, into buying some annuities, a little more life insurance, and perhaps convinced to take a flyer on some "sure thing" stock in an international conglomerate. Before Congress decided that this was part of "modernization," there were a number of consumers and not a small group of economists who believed that consumers got the best deal and the best price when they shopped around for products among a variety of financial services providers.

But the congressional sponsors of the financial services legislation have their own definitions. To Congress one-stop shopping centers are "modernization." Never mind if that means fewer choices and higher prices.

Financial modernization, crafted by the corporate lobbyists and sold by their public relations flacks, is the new world that Congress and the Clinton administration is delivering to the American people. Can consumers survive this heavy dose of "modernization"?

November 2, 1999

Publicly Owned Local Utilities Work

Solar energy advocate Dan Berman has sent me news of a development for electricity consumers in Davis that millions of households may find interesting during these times of energy deregulation.

A group of citizens is moving toward a referendum in Davis to establish the town's own municipal utility district. If the voters pass this proposal next year, the town will own its own electric company, will be able to bargain with suppliers for lower prices for its citizens, and will be able to enter into agreements with other communities that have their own utility districts, such as one covering much of the greater Sacramento area.

With states passing laws restructuring the electric utility industry in ways that bail out the utilities' costlier projects—such as decommissioning nuclear power plants—in return for their accepting competition, towns and cities across the country are thinking about purchasing their own energy systems. For years, about 1,000 electric co-ops serving some 30 million people in forty-six states have already aggregated consumer bargaining power.

The NorCal Electric Authority that serves Del Norte, Siskiyou, and portions of Modoc and Shasta Counties will begin providing more than electricity to its 41,000 ratepayers next year. This co-op is considering offering Internet, satellite, television, solar equipment, and other energy services in its territory. Just what is driving the citizens of Davis? Besides lower prices, they want "to control their own destiny." Right now the big California utility, Pacific Gas and Electric, charges Davis residents $56 for 500 kilowatt hours of electricity. The same amount costs $39 in Sacramento, a public power city.

The people of Davis want to be able to choose the type of power they buy. The Sacramento Municipal Utility District (SMUD) covers all of Sacramento County and a tiny portion of nearby Placer County, and is governed by an independently elected seven-person board. SMUD let the voters decide to shut down its Rancho Seco nuclear power plant and to explore the feasibility of solar energy.

Other complaints the citizens of Davis have against PG&E involved ongoing reliability problems year after year and the absurdly low fees that the giant utility has paid the city for erecting utility poles and stringing wires on city streets.

A Davis ordinance passed in 1959 gives PG&E the "indeterminate" franchise to, for example, only pay Davis about $269,000 for selling $26.9 million worth of electricity sales in 1997. This is a little-noticed giveaway by municipalities to the electric company monopolies that has been going on for decades all over the country. Talk about cheap rent! In short, the city government has been willing to require PG&E to pay one penny for every dollar of sales by this corporate distribution monopoly.

Under the California constitution, cities can buy out the local private utility and the Davis citizens' proposal intends to do just that. If passed, the city will take out bonds to pay for the buyout.

With twenty states already passing laws that deregulate electric utilities, presumably hoping that significant competition would be able to challenge these behemoths, how can individual, unorganized consumers be protected? The answers have to be either a local public power district or, in lieu of that, a vigorous city effort to represent citizens' interests during an aggressive bidding process among utilities.

If you live in a city or town and want to consider what those in and around Sacramento did years ago, or what Davis and other municipalities are thinking of doing, contact the Coalition for Local Power at 645 C Street, Davis, CA 95616 or call (530) 753-5959. If you wish to learn about the differences between electric rates under public power as compared with corporate electricity, look at the web site of the NorCal Electric Authority, www.norcalelectric.com.

Finally, a nationwide coalition of consumer and environmental groups has formed, Ratepayers for Affordable Green Electricity (or RAGE for short), and will be pleased to send you much good information. Write to them at RAGE, 215 Pennsylvania Ave. SE, Washington, D.C. 20003.

Now is the time to organize and forestall a serious decline in consumer protection, especially for low-income and rural consumers.

October 17, 1999

Internet Retailing

The virtual-reality marketplace of the Internet is booming with sales. Transactions between businesses are in the tens of billions a year. And retail revenues are also in the billions already. Economic forecasters are predicting that the first annual trillion dollars of sales will be reached in two or three years. If more and more people and businesses start buying off the Web instead of going to stores and offices, what will happen to the value of commercial real estate?

This question came to me most recently near Oakland when I saw a truck (labeled something like Van.Com) drive up to a house. Two energetic young men jumped out, went to the rear of the truck, and carried two crates of groceries to the front door. I found out that if you order more than $50 worth, they'll deliver to your residence. No need to get into your car, drive to the supermarket, and fight the crowds, lines, and parking. This new Internet company is undercutting prices at Safeway in some cases.

Turn to the other side of the country—42nd Street in New York City. According to the *New York Times*, the Hotalings News Agency, whose store sold newspapers and magazines from around the world since 1926, is closing shop. The main culprit, according to the family, is the Internet. Newspapers across the country have put their news and worse, their help-wanted and real-estate ads on the World Wide Web. Foreign papers and magazines are also available online.

Susan A. Carey, who owns the business with her brother, told the *Times*: "We never had any competition; now the Internet is our competition." There are already 3,744 newspapers with Web sites, including 1,500 overseas papers.

Hotalings did not close down easy. The store survived the Depression, wars, blackouts, and the longtime decay of the Times Square area. The owners of Hotalings cut expenses, shortened hours (closing at 6 P.M. instead of 9 P.M.), upgraded its premises, and expanded its selections. But the Internet won.

Marvin Cohn, an employee, saw the "beginning of the end" when people looking for jobs in Silicon Valley stopped coming in to buy the *San Jose Mercury News* right after the paper started its site.

The switching of customers to the web sites seems so unstoppable that real marketplace companies are opening web sites of their own. This is good news for warehouses and express delivery companies. But it has to be bad news for malls and Main Street, USA.

Still, few commentators are pointing to this zero-sum situation between real stores and Internet stores. The country is being fed a euphoria bred of these bustling economic times. For example, Internet companies lose money and see their stock skyrocket. Why? Because investors believe that down the line, the Internet is the place to be for commercial supremacy.

Will there be fewer real stores and offices when people and businesses make banking, insurance, real estate, food, clothing, furniture, toys, medicine, and other transactions from the computer? Will there be less traffic and pollution and time away from the children when people shop on the Web? Will the physical interactions between businesses and individuals decline similarly and reduce the value of their premises and the number of their employees?

I remember when television was supposed to empty the movie houses of

America. It did not. But the motor vehicle did empty the sidewalks and the stores next to residential areas. Cars got people to distant shopping centers or cities.

Shifts in physical space are not the same as shifts from physical space to Internet space. The difference may be seen in two-year-old comments by executives at American Airlines and the Bank of America, who called Microsoft their main future competition.

August 1, 1999

Real Estate Industry Cashes in with Stealth Strategy

The last hours of a state legislative session is a paradise for avaricious corporate interest groups. This is the time when they can sneak through, without public debate or even public notice, some of the most craven laws against consumer or small-taxpayer interests ever enacted.

Among the lobbies that ply this just-before-midnight stealth strategy is the real estate industry. With its alliances of banks, lawyers, title companies, and appraisers, the industry has managed to gouge home buyers and sellers for billions of dollars each year, according to the Consumer Federation of America.

The realtor lobby struck again recently in Hartford, Connecticut, June 9—the last day of the legislative session. Lobbyists convinced legislators to ram H.B. 6981 through the state senate. The proposed law would further erode any allegiance that real estate agents must pledge to either the buyer or the seller of a home.

Most home buyers do not know that their real estate agent legally represents the interests of sellers, unless he or she is a buyer broker who only represents buyers. H.B. 6981 would effectively permit licensed real estate agents to enter into relationships with buyers and sellers during the same transaction—a conflict of interest.

The opposition of numerous consumer groups and others supporting the rights of property buyers defeated the real estate industry's effort to push a similar bill through the Massachusetts legislature.

Having lost the battle in Massachusetts, the real estate industry leadership ensured that the Connecticut bill was kept very quiet. The industry did not mention it during its one-day mass lobbying effort in the capital, nor did trade publications mention it. After they finally learned about it, opponents labeled it the "Stealth Bill."

These disreputable tactics are par for the course for the real estate industry, which has one of the most powerful trade associations in the country—the National Association of Realtors. NAR's legislative cronies have systematically weakened real estate consumer protections throughout the country to minimize the industry's liability to the consumer.

In Connecticut, NAR weakened consumer protections by authoring and ensuring the passage of H.B. 6981, a bill that allows "designated agency." The bill would limit consumers' access to fair representation in real estate transactions while ensuring that mega-brokers maintain their profits. "Designated agency" enables one real estate firm to simultaneously "represent" both sides of a real estate transaction—ensuring the largest possible commission for the firm. It's analogous to one law firm "representing" both the defendant and the plaintiff. Under "designated agency," both the buyer and the seller may be "represented" by a different licensed person, within the same firm, although that "representation" will be significantly reduced.

Neither licensee would be adequately overseen by his or her supervisor (the broker and often the owner of the firm), as occurs in the majority of transactions where different firms are used. Licensees are required to be supervised by the broker, who must pass more stringent requirements to practice.

"Designated agency" is particularly dangerous for consumers because licensees largely learn their profession through on-the-job training provided by the broker, rather than through classroom education. Although real estate licensees are dealing with houses, which are the largest financial investment for most American consumers, the classroom education requirements are much lower for a real estate licensee than for a hairdresser (30 hours versus 1,500 hours).

Proponents shepherded H.B. 6981 by hiding it in another real estate bill, H.B. 6954. The latter exempts real estate licensees from obligations to disclose to prospective home buyers any information they have concerning ex-convicts living in the neighborhood. This exemption may be a prelude to future industry efforts around the country to reduce real estate agents' common law duty to disclose all material facts—matters such as leaky roofs, termites, or environmental liabilities.

H.B. 6954 and its "designated agency" amendment is the real estate industry's latest successful attempt to reduce its allegiance to the consumer and the diligence it must practice in protecting the consumer's interests. Since pro-corporate Connecticut Governor John G. Rowland will sign this bill, it will be yet another shield for the real estate industry against responsibility and legal liability.

Maybe there should be a citizen task force that figures out how to stop the heavy-handed, last-minute misbehavior of legislators that has become an odious tradition in most states.

June 21, 1999

No-Fault Car Insurance—No Bargain

The Senate Commerce Committee recently held a hearing to consider a new bill that is designed to replace state auto insurance laws with a no-fault system backed by a coalition of insurance companies led by State Farm.

The bill, S.B. 837, can be simply explained this way: Consumers would give up their right to compensation for pain and suffering in the event of an accident and agree to other drastic reductions in benefits. Based on that cut back benefit schedule, the federal government predicts (but does not guarantee) savings for motorists of $35 billion a year. It would be up to the insurance companies to pass the savings along to consumers.

Imagine: The insurance companies are lobbying Congress for a law that will save you money. Of course, there is a catch.

Ten states already have mandatory no-fault insurance laws, and another dozen have hybrid no-fault systems under which civil lawsuits and compensation are not restricted. No-fault states are consistently among the most expensive for auto insurance premiums in the nation.

Statewide referendums in California (twice), Arizona, and Florida have defeated no-fault proposals that were heavily funded by the insurance industry. No state has adopted no-fault since 1976. Because no-fault insurance pays both the victim and at-fault driver, it is not surprising that states with no-fault insurance often have higher rates for coverage.

Giving up pain and suffering compensation is no small matter. No-fault systems treat human injuries much like a damaged fender, allowing only a pittance to be recovered for medical and wage-loss expenses.

J. Robert Hunter is an advocate of the type of no-fault insurance Michigan offers—it includes unlimited medical benefits. As an actuary for former federal and Texas insurance commissioners, Hunter's advice is influential. Two years ago he testified before a congressional committee about a proposal similar to S.B. 837: "Savings outside of benefits are little under Choice.... In order to achieve an overall 30 percent reduction in personal auto costs...benefits paid victims must be reduced by over 50 percent to achieve the bill's price goals."

To Hunter, the legislation being proposed now is altogether the wrong kind of no-fault program because the vast majority of purported savings come not from increased efficiency but from sharp cuts in benefits to accident victims.

Hunter also believes that no-fault and fault systems cannot coexist for long in any state, because collisions between different vehicles—one with a fault insurance policy and the other with a no-fault policy—would lead insurers to surcharge policyholders until they are driven into the no-fault policy arena.

That stacks the deck in favor of the insurance industry. It also abandons the basic notion of driver responsibility, and it requires careful drivers to subsidize their negligent counterparts.

In 1988 voters in California passed a referendum to reform automobile insurance laws. The referendum imposed a rate rollback and a temporary freeze on rate increases. It also required regulatory approval of future rate increases, opened up the insurance companies' books, eliminated the antitrust exemption for the insurance industry, and made a driver's record a key factor in the price Californians pay for auto insurance, among other reforms.

The result was that auto premiums actually fell one-tenth of 1 percent in California between 1989 and 1995 while premiums throughout the rest of the country rose 32.2 percent. California went from having one of the fastest rising auto insurance rates to one of the slowest in the past decade. Between 1989 and 1995 California motorists saved about $14 billion.

California has always been an expensive place for auto insurance, but since 1989 a measure of price sanity has prevailed and insurance companies have reduced their bureaucratic waste to stabilize what was once an endless downward spiral.

For more information write to Harvey Rosenfield, 1750 Ocean Park Blvd., Santa Monica, CA 90405. Rosenfield has led the consumer drive to reform California's auto insurance system.

June 13, 1999

Enforce Antitrust Laws Now

Albert A. Foer is scratching his head these days. As president of the American Antitrust Institute, he is puzzled why Congress keeps the budgets so low for the federal cops on the anti-monopolistic, price-fixing, corporate beat. Not only do the Justice Department's Antitrust Division and the Federal Trade Commission (FTC) have the duty to stop and punish business practices that rig markets to cheat consumers, but their tiny combined budget of just over $200 million a year cannot keep up with an $8 trillion economy, plus more foreign companies violating American antitrust laws.

Yet even with their anemic resources, look at the deserved fines they bring to the U.S. Treasury. For example, Foer reports that in the first eight months of this fiscal year, the Antitrust Division has collected $913 million in criminal fines. That is nine times the division's annual budget.

The United States is in the middle of a fast-rising merger wave. The number of mergers that had to be reported under federal law to Uncle Sam rose from 1,529 in 1991 to 4,728 in 1998. And mergers of companies are getting larger all the time, not to mention the very neglected area of thousands of joint ventures between competitors such as General Motors and Toyota.

Enforcement resources are way behind the growth in GNP, which rose by 112 percent between 1977 and 1997. During the same period, the antitrust budgets actually decreased by 7 percent in constant dollars. You read about these mergers every day—AT&T merges with the cable company TCI, giant drug companies merge, now the big oil companies are joining together, along with massive consolidations in one industry after another (automobiles, airlines, railroads, food processors, banks, health maintenance organizations).

As Bert Foer stated recently, "Health care is not sufficiently competitive. Airlines monopolize hub terminals, international cartels cost consumers dearly, price-fixing and bid-rigging are a continual abuse of the system. New technologies are creating persistent monopolies [like Microsoft]. Agricultural and meatpacking industries are unduly concentrated."

What does enforcing the anti-monopolistic practices have to do with your standard of living, you may ask? Well, a single antitrust case can save millions of dollars for consumers, as when the FTC blocked the Staples-Office Depot merger and, according to economists, saved consumers $200 million a year. How? Because with both those companies competing head-on, they give you better prices.

Just last month the Justice Department broke up a massive nine-year international price-fixing conspiracy covering vitamin supplements that affected more than $5 billion of commerce in these products just in the United States. The lead corporate price-fixer, pharmaceutical conglomerate Roche Holding A.G., pleaded guilty and paid a $500 million fine to the U.S. government.

Then there were the domestic auto companies in the '50s and '60s, led by General Motors, that were charged by the Justice Department with "product-fixing." The antitrust enforcers filed a lawsuit declaring that those companies conspired to "eliminate all competition among themselves in the research, development, manufacture, and installation of motor vehicle air pollution control equipment."

Millions of Americans were breathing more toxic air because competition for cleaner cars was suppressed. The companies signed a consent decree in 1969 to avoid a trial.

So antitrust law affects health as well as the pocketbooks of Americans. In just one year, 1964, the Los Angeles County Board of Supervisors reported that physicians had advised 10,000 persons to move away from their county due to the intensity of motor vehicle pollution.

If you think all this antitrust jargon is beyond comprehension but you want to understand the importance of this century-long history, you can obtain a very clear booklet, issued free by the Federal Trade Commission, titled *Promoting Competition, Protecting Consumers: A Plain English Guide to Antitrust Laws,* by writing the FTC, Washington, D.C. It is also available on the Web, at www.ftc.gov/bc/compguide/index.htm.

Bert Foer would also like you to contact your member of Congress about expanding the antitrust enforcement budgets, which pay off big in dollars saved for consumers and in more competitive quality. The collected fines from the corporate culprits, who have made a tragic mockery of the free enterprise system, more than pay for the law enforcement expenses.

Specific information from Foer's nonprofit, Antitrust Institute, can be obtained by writing to 2919 Ellicott St. NW, Washington, D.C. 20008, or by accessing www.antitrustinstitute.org.

May 27, 1999

How to Beat High Insurance Rates

Twenty years ago, consumer advocate J. Robert Hunter studied insurance rate filings in the District of Columbia and found that, other things being equal, the same consumer could pay as little as $350 or as much as $900 a year for the same coverage from different companies.

Comparative shopping for auto insurance is a good way to save significant money every year. But how do you go about getting reliable information to comparison shop? For years we have been urging state insurance departments to provide such information to the public. There is no question that the data exists, but state insurance departments have yet to put it into an understandable format that can be easily accessed and distributed. While some departments have made efforts in this regard, it clearly is not a high priority. With the availability of the Internet, it is even more inexcusable not to have this information at the touch of the consumer's fingers.

Now comes the Progressive Insurance Company out of Cleveland, Ohio— the sixth or seventh largest auto insurer in the nation—with a new study that shows drivers could be saving an average of $481 every six months on auto insurance "if they took the time to compare rates." The study adds that "the same driver could receive a quote of $1,256 for a six-month auto insurance policy from one company, and a quote of $775 for the identical policy from another company."

If you live in Kentucky or Texas, the average six-month variance is over $700. In New York and Vermont, the average six-month variances were narrower than other states—averaging $192 and $210 respectively. Progressive

Insurance Company also commissioned a study that found that, based on interviews with 1,800 drivers, a majority of drivers were not aware of how wide the price variances are in their community.

Progressive started publicizing a comparison of its rates with those of the top three competitors in each market a few years ago. Sometimes, Progressive did not come out too well in these rankings, but its CEO, wavemaker Peter Lewis, just expanded the areas of the country reached by the comparisons (accompanied, of course, by Progressive's toll-free telephone number).

What Lewis sensed earlier than most of his peers is that new technology is making comparative data services inevitable, so why not gain the first credibility for his company? Although Progressive is on the right track by offering comparisons on its web site www.progressive.com., the information could be greatly expanded. Send Progressive an e-mail asking that the company expand its list of companies from the top three to the top ten auto insurers. (Smaller companies may have a better deal and should not be left out.)

Indeed Internet technology will soon make price, service, and quality comparisons available for many other products (autos, home appliances, clothing, housing, furniture, food, health care) and services (banking, home repair, transport, communications, medical, dental, rentals, hotels, etc.).

These comparison shopping futures won't come without problems; they will come with the usual assortment of deception, fraud, error, as well as inaccuracy. They won't come into being online quickly either, until consumers begin to demand such information from government, business, and nonprofits that could collect such information as part of their overall missions.

Most folks realize that shopping around usually will produce a better deal than going for the first "do I have a deal for you" smiling insurance agent. It takes informed, aggressive consumers to make competition more effective. The best are brought forward and the worse are driven out by a tough, intelligent selection process by consumers. Saving your consumer dollars is equivalent to getting a raise at your workplace. Comparison shop and give yourself a raise.

May 22, 1999

Taxpayer Appreciation Day

I'm going to go out on a limb here and suggest that April 15 of each year be designated Taxpayer Appreciation Day, a day when corporations receiving taxpayer subsidies, bailouts, and other forms of corporate welfare can express their thanks to the citizens who provide them.

Although it may not be evident, quite a few industries—and the profits they generate—can be traced back to taxpayer-financed programs whose fruits have been given away to (mostly) larger businesses.

Taxpayer dollars have often funded discoveries made by NASA, the Department of Defense, the National Institutes of Health, and other federal agencies. In many instances the rights to those discoveries were later given away to companies that brag about them as though they were the fruits of their own investments. Taxpayer dollars have played a major role in the growth of the aviation and aerospace, biotechnology, pharmaceutical, and telecommunications industries—to name only a few.

Although corporate America insists it must file yearly income taxes just like everyone else, it is responsible for a sharply decreasing portion of federal tax dollars—despite record profits. Corporations have paid only between 7 to 10 cents of every federal tax dollar in recent years, because of the loopholes they have driven into our tax laws. The average citizen pays more than four to five times that in federal income tax revenues (with the single exception of payroll taxes).

Clearly corporations that believe they are self-reliant are often, in fact, dependent on taxpayer funds to maintain their financial viability. The least they could do is thank us. Which is why we need something like Taxpayer Appreciation Day. Consider the following:

• General Electric bought RCA (which owned NBC) in the mid '80s with funds it was able to save by using an outrageous tax loophole passed by Congress in 1981. That loophole allowed GE to pay no federal taxes on three years of profits, totaling more than $6 billion. It also gave them a $125 million refund! That gave GE the money to buy RCA. GE should arrange a media extravaganza on NBC to say "Thank you, taxpayers."

• Pharmaceutical companies constantly ballyhoo their discoveries in advertisements. What they don't tell us is that many of the important nonredundant therapeutic drugs—including most anticancer drugs—were developed, in whole or in part, with taxpayer money and then given to them by the NIH and the Defense Department.

• Bristol-Meyers Squibb, for example, controls the rights to Taxol, an anticancer drug developed all the way through human clinical trials at the National Institutes of Health with $31 million of taxpayer money.

• Pharmaceutical companies spend billions on advertisements each year. Perhaps they should consider a big "Thank You, Taxpayers" ad campaign every April 15, if only to remind them where their drug research and development subsidies come from.

• Mining companies often receive vast sweetheart deals from taxpayers. Under the 1872 Mining Act, hard-rock mining companies are allowed to purchase mining rights to public land for only $5 an acre, no matter how valuable the minerals on (or in) that land might be.

• A Canadian company recently mined $9 billion in gold on federal land in Nevada after using the Mining Act to purchase the mining rights to it for about $30,000. Mining companies owe the taxpayers their gratitude.

• Television broadcasters were given free license to use public airwaves (worth around $70 billion) by a supine Congress in 1997. They too should thank us.

• What about all those professional sports corporations that play and profit in taxpayer-funded stadiums and arenas? The owners and players should thank the fans/taxpayers who—in spite of their largess—still must pay through the nose for tickets.

• For years McDonalds received taxpayer subsidies to promote its products overseas as part of a foreign market access program. Now McDonalds is a ubiquitous brand name worldwide, but has it ever thanked the taxpayers who underwrote its efforts?

• Then there are the HMOs, hospitals, and defense contractors that have had their legal fees reimbursed by the taxpayers when our government prosecutes them for fraud or cost overruns. Those companies have great public relations firms that can help them show us their gratitude.

Corporate America has taken too much from us for too long. It's time it shows us a little bit of appreciation.

February 18, 1999

The Fed as Regulatory Czar

The Federal Reserve—already one of the most powerful and least accountable entities in the federal government—is about to become even more powerful.

It's all part of a scheme to rewrite the nation's financial laws and allow banks, securities firms, insurance companies, and, in some cases, industrial firms to merge under common ownership in giant conglomerates.

Under the plan now being considered in Congress, the Federal Reserve would become king of the hill among the federal financial regulatory agencies. It would, in effect, become the regulatory body, with the Federal Deposit Insurance Corporation, the Office of Thrift Supervision, and the Office of the Comptroller of the Currency taking a backseat on critical issues involving the safety and soundness of the financial system.

This legislation raises a big question about just how well the present members of the House and Senate Banking Committees truly understand how far the Fed operates outside the rules that govern the conduct of the rest of the government.

Ironically, the proponents of the new financial legislation, H.R. 10, are promoting their plans by insisting that we need to change Depression-era laws—as if the mere date of these laws and statutes were sufficient rationale for their wholesale eradication.

If H.R. 10's proponents are worried about these outdated laws, they might take a look at one that's older still—the Federal Reserve Act of 1913. It is doubtful that such a law, riddled with conflicts of interest and absence of accountability, would be taken seriously today as a proper framework for a federal regulatory agency in a democratic government.

Enacted in 1913, the Federal Reserve Act allows commercial banks to select two-thirds of the boards of directors for each of the twelve federal reserve banks. As a result, these boards are populated not only with bankers but also with representatives of securities firms and insurance companies, all of which will come under some degree of Federal Reserve jurisdiction if H.R. 10 becomes law.

Each of the twelve federal reserve banks—operating under the guidance of these bank-controlled boards—supervises and polices those holding companies and state banks that are members of the Federal Reserve. Tough regulatory decisions that protect the safety of financial institutions and taxpayer-supported deposit insurance funds do not always coincide with a central bank's concept of what promotes its economic policy at any given moment. It is difficult to imagine a clearer picture of conflicts of interest.

When the Long Term Capital Management hedge fund collapsed last fall, the problems with the Federal Reserve board became all too apparent. The Federal Reserve, led by Chairman Alan Greenspan and William McDonough, president of the New York Federal Reserve Bank, engineered a $3.5 billion corporate bailout of the hedge fund, claiming that the stock market was in danger of a meltdown. In the process, the Federal Reserve used its regulatory power to lean on three big commercial banks under its day-to-day supervision—Bankers Trust, J. P. Morgan, and Chase—to put up $300 million each for the bailout.

It doesn't take much analysis to realize what was really going on here. In an op-ed article in the *Washington Post,* Jim Leach, chair of the House Banking Committee, wrote: "it is difficult not to be struck by the fact that the shrewdest in the hedge fund industry could commit such investment errors; that the most sophisticated in banking would give a blank check to others in an industry which they are also considered to be experts; and that the U.S. regulatory system could be so uncoordinated and so easily caught off guard."

Such conflicts of interest between monetary policy and bank regulatory policy are why many nations separate the two functions. Some of these nations are Great Britain, Austria, Belgium, Canada, Denmark, Finland, Germany, Japan, Mexico, Norway, Sweden, and Switzerland.

The Federal Reserve certainly doesn't have an untarnished record as a banking regulator. The General Accounting Office raised a number of questions about the Federal Reserve's performance, noting a lack of minimum inspection standards that led to superficial approaches to inspections of bank holding companies.

Now Congress is planning to pile huge new duties and powers on the Federal Reserve. If the Fed's inspection standards have been lax under its present responsibilities, one can only imagine what will fall between the cracks if it's allowed to supervise the trillion-dollar conglomerates created under H.R. 10.

February 10, 1999

Financial Industry "Nickels and Dimes" Consumers

"Nickel and diming" the consumer is now a big, booming business in the financial arenas of corporate greed and fraud. Bank charges, currently numbering over two hundred varieties, bring in nearly $20 billion a year to the banks. First Union even charges its customers 50 cents for a deposit slip and $2 for each call to an employee beyond two a month.

The General Accounting Office, the auditing arm of Congress, estimated that 10 percent of health care expenditures are drained away through billing fraud and abuse. That is about $100 billion this year.

The credit card industry works overtime in the nickel-and-diming business. One company, Advanta, announced a charge of $25 when you quit them!!! Another company charges you if you pay your balance on time!!!

Now comes San Francisco-based Consumer Action (CA), a twenty-eight-year-old, nonprofit consumer education association, with a list of profit-maximizing impositions on credit card users. Late fees have risen nearly 75 percent since 1995. Although general interest rates have declined significantly in recent years, the average APR (annual percentage rate) on all cards in a survey of 117 cards from seventy-four banks was 15.25 percent—slightly higher than in recent years.

Since 1995, Bank of America has increased its late fees from $7 to $25 and Wells Fargo from $5 to $29—clearly reflecting profit-center mind-sets rather than increased bank costs.

The increases in penalty rates, beyond the late fees, ranged from 16.25 percent to 24.95 percent or an average of 4.5 percentage points higher than the regular rates of thirty-five bankcards surveyed.

Next on the spiral list are higher "over the limit" fees, charged each month that your balance exceeds your credit limit. In 1995 Consumer Action found only one bank charging as much as $20. By 1998, CA found eighteen cards that had over-the-limit credit fees of $20, thirty-one charged $25, and thirteen billed cardholders for $29.

On and on goes the squeeze. "Grace periods" get shorter, "leniency periods" are curtailed, "minimum payments" lowered. CA Executive Director Ken Eldowney added: "If you have a card with an introductory rate and you make a couple of late payments, your APR could jump fifteen percentage points. We see plenty of direct solicitations with 4.9 percent teaser rates, but if you're not careful, you can get zapped with a penalty rate of close to 25 percent."

Instead of answering their phones with real staffers, banks are sweating their creativity on overcharge strategies. One consumer, whose Chevy Chase card went from 11.9 percent to 19.9 percent, finally got an explanation of sorts. She was told it could have been triggered by several factors, including—get this—"too few bank promotional inquiries on the account."

According to CA, the bank did not appear to know that when credit reports are "prescreened" prior to a promotional offer, credit bureaus are not allowed to reveal prescreening inquiries to other creditors.

Corporate regulations are controlling more and more of peoples' own money. Increasingly, when they overcharge with this "nickel and diming," your account is either debited immediately or charged to your credit card and, if you object, your credit rating or rates or penalties may go against your desires.

The consumer finance system is rigged so one-sidedly that even reading the fine print doesn't matter. All the so-called competitors have the same fine print and your newest choice may soon change the terms and cause you to experience the observation, "They got you coming and going."

Members of Congress occasionally speak up against anticonsumer practices of credit card companies and urge corrective legislation. All these bills, so far, have been proposed by Democrats, but the chairperson of the relevant subcommittee in the House of Representatives, Representative Marge Roukema (R–NJ), has not yet taken them up.

All of this shows why improved consumer class action rights and better state antitrust laws, which allow private rights of action in court, are needed. Some portion of any government penalties exacted from the culprits should be devoted to facilitating the organization of nonprofit consumer advocacy groups specializing in fighting these abuses and pushing toward more balanced fine-print agreements between credit card issuers and users.

For more information from Consumer Action, either write to 717 Market Street, San Francisco, CA 94102 or e-mail: info@consumer-action.org.

January 5, 1999

VIII

OBSERVATIONS AND INSPIRATIONS

History books as well as chroniclers of current events focus attention on those at or near the seat of power. But a healthy society also depends on the daily public-spirited actions of citizens whose names we rarely learn.

Many of the columns in this section celebrate seemingly ordinary Americans with an extraordinary devotion to the public good. We will meet a courageous paraplegic who designs safer, less expensive wheelchairs and promotes their construction in third world locales; an astonishing ninety-year-old woman who works and walks relentlessly across the country for campaign finance reform; and other exemplary citizens and tireless volunteers.

Other columns also revolve around inspiring, public-spirited citizens with a somewhat higher profile, such as Gene Stilp, an activist lawyer with a genius for provocative props spotlighting abuses of power; Herb Kelleher, CEO of Southwest, who built a rare consumer-friendly airline; Craig McDonald, director of Texans for Public Justice, who perseveres in the fight for open, honest government in Texas, Dr. Nabil Moukheibir, who pioneered reliable software to diagnose kidney disease; and Jeff Gates, author of several creative books about ways to combat obscene economic inequality.

A very special column eulogizes Senator Paul Wellstone from Minnesota, whose moral courage and passionate concern for those most in need of assistance put most of his colleagues to shame.

Finally, uniquely gifted athletes and artists can and should inspire us. One column describes my chance encounter with Joe DiMaggio, the Hall-of-Fame baseball player who epitomized athletic grace and greatness, which made him a legend for all time.

My goal in this section is to spur each reader to tap the best in themselves, to draw inspiration from the special people who grace these pages, and in turn find, sustain, or deepen, their own commitments.

The eclectic observations about some less-than-inspiring developments in our society, including automated phone calls from telemarketers; a growing obsession with meaningless statistics; and luxury shopping, provide a contrast between the heroes featured in some columns and the mundane myopia confronted in others reflecting the juxtaposition of the grand with the gross.

Important Tidbits

This is a column of tidbits—to be sure, important tidbits. I think they are part of a mosaic of our times. But I'll let you decide your favorite theme that runs through them.

1) Congress refuses to raise the federal minimum wage to the level of purchasing power that existed in 1968. At $5.15, it is over 33 percent less now in the goods and services it can buy than what workers received thirty-five years ago. Yet Congress increases its own salaries just about every year—presently indexing them to inflation at over $75 per hour plus great benefits and perks.

2) After deceiving investors of tens of billions of dollars, ten Wall Street firms were slapped on the wrist by the SEC and the New York Attorney General. The "settlement" amounted to a total of $1.4 billion (much of it deductible), which is the equivalent of two drops in the bucket.

There were no signs of any prosecution of the big boys. No signs of investors getting much money back, although the bidding arbitration clauses make any real litigation unlikely. No interest in facilitating the banding together of millions of investors through compulsory notices in mailings from these firms to their customers that invite investors to join together and become a powerful group for a change. The best senators could do at a recent hearing on this fraud was to wonder whether "Wall Street gets it." Hope rather than tough sanctions is what springs eternal on Capitol Hill.

3) D.C. Mayor Anthony Williams issues two statements in four years on his grand vision for the D.C. library system, declares doing something about the

District's 37 percent functional illiteracy rate, and then cuts the tiny budget of the starved library system with its twenty-six branches even further. At the same time, he announces a $338 million tax package for a desired new major league baseball stadium.

4) The *Wall Street Journal* reports that some insurers and critics believe that the giant insurance company—AIG—is overstating the severity of the medical malpractice litigation crisis as a way of justifying large rate increases inflicted on physicians and hospitals. No kidding! This is what the insurance companies have been doing every time the stock market and interest rates go down on their investments.

Since the physicians never want to be sued and since organized medicine, like the American Medical Association and its state counterparts, refuses to crack down on the small percentage of bad doctors who account for the lion's share of the liability payouts, they become willing tools of their insurers.

Abandoning their patients in gross violation of medical ethics, all too many physicians march on the state houses demanding variations of immunity from the less than one in ten litigating victims of incompetence or negligence that is taking 80,000 American lives a year, according to the Harvard School of Public Health studies. "Patients Face Cancellations, Delays, Prescription Hassles," headlines the *Wall Street Journal.*

Lost in these mindless manipulations is insensitivity to the enormous loss of life and preventable injuries from medical and hospital mayhem.

As for those costly insurance policies for physicians, take all their premiums and divide the dollars by the number of practicing physicians, the average premium would be under $10,000 a year for each doctor—about one-third of what physicians pay for a seasoned receptionist. Instead, insurers break out physicians into over twenty classifications to reduce the insurable pool—as for OBGYNS—and skyrocket the premium.

5) President Bush wants to bring democracy to Iraq but stubbornly refuses to support congressional voting representation for the people of the District of Columbia whose sons and daughters are in Iraq. Residents of the District pay full federal income taxes but have no senators or representatives.

6) The biotechnology industry's grip on the Food and Drug Administration continues to deprive American consumers of their strong desire to have biotech food labeled as such in the supermarkets. The fish farms growing salmon oppose any disclosure and labeling of the dyes they are using to color the salmon pink from their real color, which is gray. Unlike ocean salmon whose pink color comes from their consumption of crustaceans, expanding farm-grown antibiotic-doused salmon have no such luck.

So what do you make from these snapshots of our economy and politics? What do they add up to? What is your mosaic of interpretation?

May 9, 2003

Addiction, Substance Abuse, and the Gender Gap

Despite some encouraging statistics about recent declines in substance abuse, the use of drugs, alcohol, and tobacco by teenagers and young adults remains one of the nation's most serious and destructive health problems.

A lot of time, money, and words have been expended on prevention programs. So why haven't we made more progress in reaching young people about the dangers of drug abuse and addiction?

The National Center on Addiction and Substance Abuse at Columbia University has come up with an intriguing answer to at least part of the puzzle. It's a gender gap. The prevention efforts have largely been designed with males in mind, ignoring the unique needs of females and, thereby, failing to influence millions of young girls and women, according to a three-year study and a 231-page report, "The Formative Years: Pathways to Substance Abuse Among Girls and Young Women, Ages 8–22," issued by the Center earlier this month.

"The findings from this study cry out for a fundamental overhaul of public health prevention programs," says Joe Califano, president of the Center and former secretary of the U.S. Health, Education and Welfare Department. "The women of America have paid a fearful price in premature death and destroyed lives for our failure to craft programs aimed at their unique needs."

The numbers bear out Califano's alarms. More than 4.4 million women are alcoholics or abuse alcohol. More than two million use illegal drugs. Thirty-one million women smoke. At the high school level, 45 percent of girls currently drink alcohol and 26.4 percent binge drink. One in five smoke marijuana. More than one-quarter of female high school students smoke cigarettes and nearly 4 percent are users of cocaine while another 4.2 percent use inhalants.

The study cites a long list of risks and consequences of smoking, drinking, and drug use that are unique to women. Among these:

• Girls typically experience puberty at an earlier age than boys. Girls who experience early puberty are at greater risk than boys of smoking, drinking, and using drugs.

• Girls are likelier than boys to have been physically or sexually abused. These girls are at increased risk for substance abuse.

• Substance use can sink into substance abuse more quickly for girls and young women than for boys and young men.

• Girls are likelier than boys to diet and to have eating disorders. These girls are at increased risk for substance abuse.

• Key transitions, such as frequent moves from one home or neighborhood to another, pose greater risks of substance abuse for girls than boys. Similarly, the transition from high school to college creates greater risks of substance use for young women.

• Girls using alcohol or drugs are more likely to be depressed or suicidal, increasing the risk for substance abuse.

• Girls and women are more likely than boys and men to experience adverse health consequences from smoking, drinking, or using drugs.

• Females have greater smoking-related lung damage than males and are more susceptible to alcohol-induced brain damage, cardiac problems, and liver disease.

Tobacco and alcohol manufacturers come in for heavy criticism for their practice of spending billions of dollars each year on advertising and promotions, sponsorships of events, and product placements in movies and television shows in an effort to promote use of their products by women.

"The tobacco industry has a long history of targeting its marketing efforts to young women, exploiting women's desire for independence and sophistication, and appealing to perennial female concerns about weight and appearance," the report says. "Alcohol industry advertising makes drinking, and by association women who drink, appear fun and sexy." What can be done to reduce the risks for women, particularly young women in their formative years? Not unexpectedly, the report cites parents as the "first line of prevention."

In a survey of 1,220 girls, nearly 62 percent who had conversations with their parents about substance use said the conversation made them less likely to smoke, drink, or use drugs. The report urged health care professionals to be alert to signs of substance abuse in routine screening of young female patients and to encourage those in need of help to seek treatment.

The report also says that prevention programs should target girls at times of highest risk and should be sensitive to the reasons they use drugs, how they get them, and the very overlooked conditions, such as depression, that increase their risk. The report calls for more government investment in research, prevention, and treatment that focuses on the special needs of girls and women.

Despite the deplorable findings of the study, the Center's president, Joe Califano, is optimistic that a properly crafted prevention program that recognizes the unique needs of women can bring about a major change in the outlook for a reduction of substance abuse. Califano projects that a reduction of only 25 percent in the number of women abusing and addicted to substances could mean saving 8 million women from smoking, one million from alcoholism and abuse, and one-half million from drug abuse and addiction.

Under Califano's leadership, the National Center on Addiction and Substance Abuse has produced an extremely valuable document that should alert the nation to the need for a major change in the way we approach women's health, particularly in the critical arena of substance abuse.

For more information on The National Center on Addiction and Substance Abuse: www.casacolumbia.org.

February 18, 2003

So Many Calls, So Few Answers

There was a time when specialists in time-and-motion would take great pride in shaving five minutes off a production line in a factory. Time was money and time saved was money saved.

Clearly, these time-saver experts would not have any idea of what to do about the billions of hours Americans have to waste every year just trying to get through to someone on the phone for a two-way conversation.

Let's call the people receiving calls the "callees" and the people making the calls the "callers." Depending on the call you can be either. There is little doubt that the "callees" have the advantage over the "callers." They have technology on their side. They can refuse to take the call and let you resort to voice mail or e-mail. Not quite the same.

About a dozen years ago, the *Wall Street Journal* reported on a survey that said it took an average of six business calls to get one returned. It has to be much worse now. Last month I asked my assistant to make a call to Matt Groening, the main creator of *The Simpsons* television show. No human being answered at their main telephone line—only voice mail. This went on for call after call, at all times of the day. Then I asked him to call anyone—other producers, clerical workers, anyone. No answer. Also no answer from anyone who was left a voice mail.

Now it could be said that no one wanted to call back. Not likely. I am a *Simpsons* fan, within limits, and gave out Simpson calendars last year.

The success of the callees' strategy is sometimes enhanced by not even giving out a phone number, like a business magazine I know. Then there are callers who pay a monthly fee to block the callees from seeing their phone number. Now callees are fighting back with an automatic message that informs such callers that their call cannot be taken as a result.

And so the game goes on to obstruct great telecommunications technology with technological blockers, diverters, or suspended messages. All this back and forth over and over again reminds me of the pre-rotary telephone days when one would pick up the phone and the operator would come on and ask, "What number, please?" One would give the number, the phone would ring and, unless the line was busy, the person would answer if the person was at home or at work.

Today, automation allows immensely more calls to be made with fewer workers, but can you get through?

Now, there are newspaper reporters who have voice mail on all day! There are businesses who keep you pressing layers of one, or two, or three, or four, until, either your finger slips and you have to try again, or you're often put on a diet of music or advertisers while you wait.

Certainly, their practice is not inevitable or courteous. Try calling Southwest Airlines or Federal Express and a real human being answers after just one, two, or three rings. If they can do it and make good profits, why can't other companies whose staffers are required to attend customer satisfaction training sessions? How about just answering the phone satisfactorily?

There is an information overload that most people feel is getting worse. Callers do need to be more considerate in the frequency of their calling. With cell phones, pedestrians seem to be saturated walkie-talkies. Before cell phones I rarely saw lines of people in front of pay phones.

The callees are hardening their position by ignoring phone calls altogether and using e-mail for peers and subordinates. One of my former coauthors, now an editor of a successful business magazine, ignores the telephone calls. So it is nearly impossible to have an extended conversation with him from time to time, other than via e-mail. Which, again, is not the same thing.

If you've had such an enduring experience with friends or colleagues like that, there is more than a loss of time involved. There is a loss of content and motivation that comes from person-to-person conversation.

Where is all this heading? Readers, please write me if you think you know (P.O. Box 19367, Washington, D.C. 20036). As for my continuing attempt to reach Matt Groening at "The Simpsons," I finally used the post office and sent him a letter—airmail.

January 10, 2003

Senator Paul Wellstone

The memorial service for Senator Wellstone, his wife Sheila and daughter Marcia at the Washington Hebrew Congregation in Washington, D.C. on

November 13, 2002, was a fitting and diverse tribute from their two sons, Mark and David, senatorial colleagues, staff, and friends.

With each heartfelt expression, the assemblage understood what Senator Tom Daschle meant when he said "so much was lost in that crash."

Paul and Sheila Wellstone were always there for the poor, the homeless, the sick, and the defenseless. They championed justice for millions of people and traveled to their places of distress to see their plight firsthand. Senator Wellstone always wanted to see situations for himself—in Bosnia, Thailand, Colombia, American prisons.

Yesterday the Associated Press called me to ask who I thought would take the place of Paul Wellstone in the U.S. Senate. I had no answer because now there is no one with his sense of consistent, determined energy on so many issues, so many networks, so many strategies.

Anyone who visited him in his Senate offices was greeted so warmly and authentically that it was like coming home. His phrase "Never separate the lives you live from the words you speak" is one for the book of quotations. It is also a self-description of Paul and Sheila.

In the Senate, Wellstone was identified by his support for raising the frozen minimum wage, for renewable energy, and for opposition to corporate lobbyists who demand corporate welfare, tax escapes (to Bermuda tax havens), and lax enforcement of the corporate crime laws. He took on the tobacco companies, the drug companies, and the health insurance giants.

But perhaps Paul and Sheila Wellstone's greatest passion was legislation that would give mental health patients health insurance parity with those suffering from physical illness. At the memorial service, Republican Senator Pete Domenici tossed aside his prepared remarks to speak about how he met Paul Wellstone at a meeting of mental health advocates. His affection for the Minnesota senator was apparent when he vowed that the parity bill he and Wellstone have coauthored would be enacted by the Congress next year and would be known as "the Paul Wellstone Memorial Mental Health Parity Law."

Senator Wellstone's desk in the Senate is now shrouded in black. His Senate colleagues unanimously passed legislation to apply $10 million to establish the Paul and Sheila Wellstone Center for Community Building in St. Paul, Minnesota. The Wellstones understood to their core the meaning of Jean Monnet's words: "Without people nothing is possible, but without institutions nothing is lasting." The essence of community is the banding together of people to do for themselves and posterity what they could not do alone—both in the civic society and in government.

The last bill Paul Wellstone introduced was S.3143, known as the consumer and shareholder protection association. It was legislation that would facilitate through inserts in mailings of large publicly traded corporations, including financial institutions, invitations to their customers to join together voluntarily in nonprofit associations that would defend their interests (for full text, see essential.org).

The corporate crime wave and the looting of the pensions and 401ks of millions of Americans losing trillions of dollars worried Wellstone. He wanted to help build institutions of investor and consumer influence to prevent recurrences in the future.

After the fatal airplane crash, commentators were awed by the outpouring of praise for Wellstone by friends and adversaries alike.

What was it about this politician that led his strongest opponents in the Congress to weep when they heard the news? Certainly, it was his friendly personality and his personal interest in their family tragedies. They all had a Paul Wellstone story dear to their heart. But it was mainly what Senator Daschle called the rarest of traits—"his moral courage." Something maybe they had wished on themselves long ago.

Garrison Keillor commemorated Wellstone in his nationally syndicated public radio program with these words: "Paul Wellstone identified passionately with people at the bottom, people in trouble, people in the rough. He was an old-fashioned Democrat who felt more at home with the rank and file than with the rich and famous."

At the short end of some 99 to 1 or 95 to 5 votes in the Senate, Wellstone's problem was that he did not have enough "old-fashioned Democrats" with him in the Senate. There may come a time when his statement that "politics is not about power; it is about people" will attract many more dedicated adherents throughout the land.

November 14, 2002

Whirlwind Wheelchairs

Corporate scandals, the threat of war in the Middle East, and a sagging stock market are squeezing the flow of funds from foundations and other charitable donors across the nation. As a result, many worthwhile nonprofit enterprises that depend on the generosity of these donors for survival are facing perilous times.

One of these organizations is Whirlwind Wheelchair International (WWI), a true jewel among the nonprofits that is giving new hope and mobility to millions of disabled persons in the third world.

Whirlwind is the brainchild of Ralf Hotchkiss, a MacArthur Genius Award winner. Working out of the WWI Center at San Francisco State University, Hotchkiss has traveled around the world setting up workshops and training workers to make low-cost durable wheelchairs out of locally available materials.

Hotchkiss, himself rendered a paraplegic in a motorcycle accident in high school, recognized that providing U.S. manufactured wheelchairs was impractical and unworkable for third-world countries. First, the wheelchairs were too expensive, most costing $1,000 to $2,000. Second, the standard wheelchairs were built for paved sidewalks and ramps, not the rough, rocky, and steep paths of third-world countries. Third, parts for the wheelchairs were unavailable or prohibitively expensive, making repairs virtually impossible.

In his travels, Hotchkiss is constantly designing and redesigning to meet special needs in the developing countries. He has come up with new specifications for wheelchairs that can provide mobility in mountainous regions. He has designed special wheelchairs for women and separate configurations for children. And most importantly, he searches out available local materials that are affordable and easily adapted to wheelchairs.

Currently, Hotchkiss is completing the design and testing of an off-road chair designed for ultra-rugged terrain. It meets all the standard indoor and outdoor criteria, but it can travel on slopes twice as steep as those deemed safe for a standard chair. A unique X-brace feature allows height and width flexibility so that the chair can "grow" as its owner grows from child to adult.

Hotchkiss explains the importance of using local components this way: "it's much better to start with wheelchairs built in the country made out of bicycle parts that are available locally, tubing that's available locally, canvass, and then whenever anything breaks, you don't have to send it to the factory for spare parts, you just go to the local blacksmith and while you wait they can make any part."

Workshops with citizens trained by Hotchkiss are operating in two dozen developing countries, including Zimbabwe, Sri Lanka, Uganda, Vietnam, Cambodia, Palestine, Guatemala, and Honduras. And Whirlwind Wheelchair is continuing to reach out and liberate the disabled in remote parts of the world.

The need for wheelchairs—affordable, durable, and easily repaired wheelchairs—is staggering, particularly in countries ravaged by polio and preventable amputations. Whirlwind Wheelchair International estimates that twenty million people in developing countries need wheelchairs, yet only 1 percent own or have access to such transport.

In many of the countries that lack adequate supplies of workable wheelchairs, the disabled must be dragged, carried, or left behind.

Whirlwind Wheelchair International at San Francisco State College has proven its worth. It has what is perhaps the world's most creative and imaginative designer and technical director of wheelchair technology in Ralf Hotchkiss. And WWI is fulfilling a clear and demonstrated need to provide mobility for the disabled—a necessity for a full and productive life for our fellow citizens around the world.

Yet this great success story may have a sad final chapter unless funding can be maintained. Not only is Whirlwind Wheelchair facing reductions in contributions from foundations and other donors as the stock market drops and economic uncertainties mount, but its home base of San Francisco State University has been hit by cuts in the California state funding of education. That means funding cuts for Whirlwind Wheelchair International as well.

Despite the concern about the stock market and other economic uncertainties, it is inconceivable that this rich nation would let such a wonderful and successful project as "liberation for the disabled" wither for a lack of funds.

If you want to make a charitable contribution or want more information on Whirlwind Wheelchair International, write them at 2600 Holloway Avenue, San Francisco, California 94132. The web address is http://whirlwind.sfsu.edu.

October 9, 2002

Consumers "Get No Respect"

Workers and consumers these days could echo Rodney Dangerfield's line about not getting any respect. Labor Day has come and gone with very little mention of its significance by major newspapers or television networks. It is not for lack of news. Nonunion labor has been slipping behind in their inflation-adjusted wages since 1973, while many union workers are finally confronting management with intentions to strike.

From the possible strike by dockworkers from San Diego to Seattle to the threatened strike by hotel workers in Chicago's convention business to the standoff between the machinist union and Boeing to the possible work stoppage by janitors in Boston's downtown office buildings, the issues of living wages, job security, give-backs and the ultimatums of mismanaged bankrupt companies could fill many a news hole for the Labor Day media.

No way, say newspapers, which have cut their labor beat all over the country; only a handful of full-time labor reporters are left. No way, says ABC's *Nightline* program that reran on Labor Day. When I called to seek an explanation, an ABC person shrugged and said that the staff just wanted to take the holiday off.

Of course, the AFL-CIO and its large member unions could have made some news themselves for Labor Day, such as mounting a determined drive to repeal the fifty-five-year-old Taft-Hartley Act, which is a chokehold on workers' right to organize. Having done nothing about this repressive law for almost half a century, such an announcement by the trade union movement would have truly been news!

Now consider the way the major airlines are "regulating" consumers in order to secure more dollars from them. These airline bosses are issuing orders in a rather peculiar manner if that is their goal.

See if you can follow this logic. US Airways, which has survived in recent years largely from their de facto monopoly routes (like charging $900 for a round trip from Washington, D.C. to Syracuse, New York), decides to bring its employees and its creditors to their knees by declaring bankruptcy this summer. In its airplane magazine (August issue), CEO David Siegel writes, "Our challenge is to run our business in a way that will make you want to fly with us again and again." So, in the past few days, US Airways imposed several unilateral "regulations" effective immediately with no invited feedback from its supposedly revered customers.

The airline announced, along with American Airlines (the major airlines like to do these things at the same time), that passengers with discount nonrefundable tickets will have their tickets confiscated if they do not take the designated flight on the ticket. These tickets cannot be used toward another US Airways' departure. They are rendered worthless. Never mind that people often have to change plans or miss planes due to emergencies, traffic tie-ups, or weather. Too bad. Just shut up and patronize US Airways more and "again and again."

For good measure, US Airways announced the same day that it will charge you $25 for each paper ticket you use (instead of online) and, if you're upset by that on a transatlantic flight, relax, there will be no more alcoholic beverages in economy class.

Northwest Airlines similarly raised its penalty for leisure fares using paper tickets to $25.

I won't burden you with a host of other Mickey Mouse rules imposed on the airlines' customers, other than to say that these and other companies using uniform, standard-form contracts have become private legislatures. Whether you are dealing with credit card companies, landlord leases, insurance policies, bank deposit cards, hospital waivers, you just sign on the dotted line. Going to a competitor merely shows you a similar fine-print contract, so there is normally no escape.

In the airline business, there is one notable escape, although it has limited routes due to the ways the major airlines control airport slots.

I'm referring to Southwest Airlines, which somehow is making more money selling cheaper tickets every year than the top three largest airlines combined.

Southwest doesn't have all these rules and regulations to afflict, discomfort, and irritate you. True, you can sometimes get a small discount if you buy your ticket online but there is no penalty for using a paper ticket. The staff is cheerful, helpful, knowledgeable, and actually seeking to make life easier for its passengers. That is why Southwest is gaining market share and, if it had the slots, would mop up the top-heavy, overcharging, bureaucratic, money-losing major airlines.

These must be difficult times for US Airways' director of Consumer Affairs, Deborah Thompson, and the airline's volunteer Consumer Advisory Board. Just wait until passengers with discount tickets worth hundreds of dollars find out that US Airways has confiscated them if they missed the flight through no fault of their own.

Maybe US Airways' motto should be—"Take that, passengers, and be sure to come back again and again."

Mr. Siegel and his boss, Mr. Steven Wolfe, need to recover a sense of shame for still paying themselves handsomely while their company is in bankruptcy. Their recent disrespect toward their customers is sure to generate more rage than revenue.

September 4, 2002

Needed: Leaders with Fortitude

Two leaders—one the Secretary of Defense and the other the president of the U.S. Chamber of Commerce—need to put their fortitude behind their recent acknowledgments of major problems in their domains.

Donald Rumsfeld, who was a class ahead of me at Princeton and vibrating with energy even then, has been reported in the press to have said "we are not spending our tax dollars wisely." He was referring to the military budget. Official studies, reports, and public hearings over the past thirty-five years have documented the huge waste in the Pentagon, driven by bureaucracy, interservice rivalries, and above all, the outside corporate military weapons industry that places its executives in high positions at the Defense Department as a matter of bipartisan routine.

In addition to mounds of studies that could reach part way to the moon, the mainstream media have reported ad infinitum on waste, fraud, and redundancy costing hundreds of billions of defense dollars. Almost no enduring changes or reforms have occurred as a result. It takes someone in charge, with high public acclaim, to get matters of structural frugality and efficiency under way. That man is Rumsfeld.

The problem is that President Bush has just demanded of Congress another

$48 billion in defense programs on top of the roughly $331 billion already allocated to the Pentagon. This budget never gets squeezed of its waste; it just gets piled on like the layers of Pompeii.

And the pile after 9/11 is immense. As Senator Robert Byrd (D–WV), a longtime, self-described hawk declared, this will come at the expense of important and serious domestic programs, including health and safety.

Rumsfeld is now a television media star, given both his almost daily press briefings and an adoring covey of reporters. If the experienced Rumsfeld, on his second tour as Secretary of Defense, cannot step up to this challenge of reform and respect for taxpayer dollars being wasted, stolen, or defrauded, no one in his position can. He'll have to take on the "military-industrial complex," in President Eisenhower's words, by demonstrating that a wasteful defense weakens our country.

Thomas J. Donohue heads the sprawling U.S. Chamber of Commerce. Last month, at a television studio, he said off camera that Enron executives "are thieves" and that he threw the company out of the Chamber. But where has he been, since taking the helm at the Chamber more than three years ago, on the corporate crime wave reported regularly by the *Wall Street Journal, New York Times, Washington Post, 60 Minutes, Barron's Financial Weekly,* and other major publications? Nary a peep from the Chamber condemning very bad business practices that, unprosecuted or unregulated, drive out honest business practices. Its energies are directed toward reducing or jettisoning the federal cops on the corporate crime, fraud, and abuse beats. The Chamber lobbied incessantly to erase law and order with a deregulatory brush.

As a supermarket of thievery, greed, and power, Enron's practices are, as conservative commentator George Will put it the other day, "a systemic crisis of capitalism in this country." Enron just had more tentacles and drooling jowls as its executives inflated earnings, sold out high, and left its workers, pensionholders, and investors with a bankrupt corporation.

Mr. Donohue needs to publicly denounce these practices and accounting shenanigans in a major statement and support corporate crime reform in Congress with adequate prosecutorial authority and budgets for a change.

The budgets on commercial crime enforcement are tiny in the various agencies covering major areas of consumer, worker, environmental, investor, and taxpayer protections. One year's budget on the failed war on drugs towers immensely above all the many years of corporate violations budgets put together.

So "law and order" says to the feisty Tom Donohue, boldly proclaim that you and the Chamber are supporting the efforts of the federal police (with their congressional backers) to pursue, prosecute, and convict the corporate criminals in our economy. Over the past ten years, all you would have needed is a robust clip file from the business press to make your case before your membership.

January 30, 2002

Solutions to Rising Health Care Costs

Premiums for health care insurance in the United States are expected to increase by 15 percent this year—a staggering sum, adding tens of billions more dollars to the trillion-dollar-plus price of year 2001. The industry is rife with waste, duplication, mistakes, billing fraud, and malpractice. Countless studies have documented these patterns from the General Accounting Office to the Harvard Medical School.

But there are many solutions—some in pilot projects, others blocked by the rigidities, greed, and lack of accountability in this sprawling business. A widespread problem in clinics, hospitals, and HMOs is wrong diagnosis and the costs associated with unnecessary testing and treatments that flow from it, often resulting in injuries, fatalities, and, less frequently, litigation.

A longtime practicing nephrologist, Dr. Nabil Moukheibir, spent three decades observing these problems in the area of kidney ailments. While practicing in Tennessee, he began to develop a unique, now patented, software system, which he demonstrates is "capable of scanning the medical file of a patient and responding within seconds by displaying a highly accurate diagnosis, a suggestion of appropriate tests, and the treatment of the condition." Its level of accuracy is based on a proprietary concept that does not rely on probabilistic approaches that impose a rigid "yes/no" system of questions on the patient.

In his field of kidney diseases, Dr. Moukheibir tested the accuracy of his system in front of leading specialists and computer medicine experts at Harvard Medical School, Johns Hopkins, and Baylor Medical School, among others, and they were very impressed with its speed, accuracy, and conceptual elegance. Dr. Warner Slack, a pioneer in computer medicine associated with Harvard Medical School, saw how it works and called it "an excellent program which should help physicians in caring for their patients."

The benefits are directed toward increasing the quality of care and reducing the cost of patient diagnosis and treatment. General practitioners are overwhelmed by the exponential growth of information. When patients come to them, these physicians need immediate assistance from a body of specialized knowledge that is up to date. So too do nurse practitioners, physician assistants, and other skilled personnel on the frontlines.

Early competence in diagnosis and treatment squeezes out tens of billions of dollars now expended on mistaken decisions and their harmful effects. It will improve productivity in the best patient sense and reduce the number of unnecessary referrals to specialists.

Since the overarching objective is to deliver higher quality of care to the patient at a lower cost, one would think that the large HMOs, the federal and state health agencies, and the insurance companies would be beating a path to Dr. Moukheibir's door. So too, one would expect the health sections of newspapers, magazines, and medical publications to be curious. He has spoken to some of these institutions and written or called others who have not returned his calls. All to no avail. Yet trivial or dubious studies regarding healthy lifestyles make the national print news and television regularly.

A company that has a distinctly inferior product received a $3 million grant from the federal government. A lone inventor doesn't get the time of day with a real breakthrough, tested product. The Department of Energy for many years has had a small invention evaluation unit to receive and evaluate good ideas of products fostering energy efficiency. The Department of Health and Human Services should have a similar unit for healthcare inventions. There are an abundance of them languishing.

If you wish to learn more about Dr. Moukheibir's software and its applications to other medical specialties, contact him at Connectance.com (e-mail: connectance@msn.com).

January 9, 2002

Texans for Public Justice

As a state dominated by the oil and gas industry and other large corporations, Texas has generated little excitement about government reforms. That's changing, and much of the credit goes to the bright light that a public interest group, Texans for Public Justice (TPJ), has focused on the state's judiciary, legislature, and the governor's office.

Organized just four years ago by Craig McDonald, TPJ's five-person staff has been releasing a veritable blizzard of reports on everything from corporate influence in Texas elections to how big money buys access to the Texas Supreme Court.

Last April, McDonald's organization released a report entitled "Pay to Play," revealing that lawyers and parties to court cases who contributed to the elections of state supreme court justices were four times more likely to have their cases accepted by the court. Cris Feldman, staff attorney for TPJ, says "even when

Justices don't face an opponent they still raise money hand over fist and most of that money comes from those with cases on the docket."

The report received major attention in the Texas and national media and generated public debate throughout the state. TPJ also testified on the issue before a committee of the American Bar Association, which has now issued its own report calling for tax-funded elections in states where the judiciary is elected.

A separate report produced by Texans for Public Justice took a major swipe at another practice of the Supreme Court, allowing its judicial clerks to take "hiring bonuses" from law firms before they start their one-year clerkship at the court. TPJ's report showed that four big law firms hired thirty-three of the seventy-six clerks and "accounted for 70 percent of the conflicts of interest at the court." These were Baker Botts, Vinson and Elkins, Fulbright and Jaworski, and Bracewell and Patterson.

With the TPJ report gaining lots of publicity and editorial support in the state, the Texas Ethics Commission is expected to adopt an advisory opinion against the law firm subsidies, dubbed "clerk perks" by the TPJ report.

Last fall, TPJ released a devastating report revealing that Texas was lagging behind most of the nation on a wide range of socioeconomic indicators that measure the quality of life.

"Texas has a resilient character and natural beauty that have survived massive abuses by its government and industry," the report said. "Still the quality of life in Texas compares poorly with the rest of the nation. Texas leads the nation in hazardous waste and air pollution, falls behind most every state in health care access, and treats its poor as if it was a third world country."

TPJ regularly exposes the tactics of the army of special interest lobbyists who descend on the state capitol and details how these lobbying groups harm consumers, the environment, and workers.

"Legislators are rubbing shoulders with 1,579 lobbyists, almost all of whom hustle for business interests," McDonald said in a 1999 report entitled "Austin's Oldest Profession: Texas Top Lobby Clients and Those Who Service Them." "While our legislative process is dominated by corporate interests, there is virtually no counterbalancing lobby to represent Bubba. Nowhere on the list of Texas' biggest lobby spenders will you find a single group dedicated to the interests of consumers, the environment or human services. No wonder these citizen interests repeatedly get steamrolled in Austin."

That same year, TPJ released a report on the Texas Chemical Council, a trade association of chemical companies operating in Texas. The report's conclusion: "Texas Council Members dump 187 million pounds of toxins in Texas (EPA data 1996) and up to $10 million into state politics." The report listed then Governor George W. Bush as the "Number One Recipient of Texas Toxic Cash."

"Pollution and political clout are closely linked in Texas," McDonald says. "The Texas Chemical Council is a prime example of how a special-interest group harnesses big money in order to dump on average Texas citizens. Cleaning up state politics is the first step towards cleaning up the air we breathe and the water we drink."

Texans for Public Justice (www.tpj.org) is doing a magnificent job with limited resources. It is up against some of the biggest corporate interests in the nation and some of the toughest lobbying organizations and law firms to ever occupy a state capital. The successes of TPJ should be a source of encouragement to other citizen organizations around the nation that are seeking social and economic justice against great odds. Interested in learning more about how TPJ operates as a public watchdog in Texas? Write: Texans for Public Justice, 609 West 18th Street, Suite E, Austin, Texas 78701.

August 28, 2001

The Refreshing Southwest Airlines

At a time of rising customer complaints, sagging airline profits, and cutbacks by major carriers, Southwest Airlines stands above the pack as brash and adventuresome as it was thirty years ago when Rollin King and Herb Kelleher launched the company as a three-airplane enterprise carrying passengers between Dallas, Houston, and San Antonio.

From that modest start, Southwest has grown dramatically. Today it has 353 jet airplanes serving fifty-eight airports in twenty-nine states. In 2000, it carried 63.7 million passengers and last month declared its 100th consecutive quarterly dividend on profits of $175.6 million in the second quarter. In terms of domestic customers, it is now the nation's fourth largest airline.

Southwest is truly a phenomenon, not only among airlines but among corporations generally. The ingredients of Southwest's success may be numerous, but they certainly include a ton of notions about good customer relations, a heavy dose of innovative management, and the ability to operate a big corporation with a sense of humor.

Here's the way Southwest, itself, describes Rollin King and Herb Kelleher's philosophy in launching the airline:

"They began with one simple notion: If you get your passengers to their destination on time at the lowest possible fares and make darn sure they have a good time doing it, people will fly your airline."

And people in the airline industry privately agree with the Southwest philosophy even if their own airlines don't practice it.

Recently, I had an employee of United Airlines tell me that the Southwest success in insisting on good customer relations "comes from the top." Traveling occasionally on Southwest, the employee said she recently arrived just minutes before departure as the gate was being closed for a Southwest flight. "They couldn't have been nicer about getting me on the flight," she remarked.

Southwest is continuing to expand aggressively. One of its means for expansion has been centered around finding sleepy out-of-the way regional airports. A recent example of this was its entry into the New York-New Jersey market by gaining access to MacArthur Airport at Islip, NY on Long Island. Southwest's share of the passengers has steadily increased over the last two years, and it now appears to be winning in head-to-head battles with Delta's subsidiaries that fly out of Islip.

Southwest is creative in finding ways to cut costs. For one thing, it flies Boeing 737s exclusively. This means that its inventory of parts can be better and more cheaply managed. Similarly, its ground crews work every day on 737s and learn the intricacies of these planes while crews for other airlines often face the daunting task of learning an array of systems on different aircraft, jet and non-jet, used by their companies. This means lower training and maintenance costs for Southwest—and undoubtedly fewer mistakes.

Southwest also holds fares down by twenty-minute airport turnarounds for its aircraft, ten minutes faster than the industry average.

Southwest doesn't try to compete with other airlines on the basis of "gourmet" meals. In fact, Southwest doesn't serve meals. On most flights it's a choice of peanuts or raisins. Last year, the airline served 90.9 million bags of peanuts and 7.3 million bags of raisins. On longer flights, this menu is varied with the serving of plastic-wrapped snacks.

Southwest's seating is purely democratic. Seats are not set aside for "first class" or "business class" or any other class. It is all one class with passengers queuing up according to when they arrived at the boarding counter. Passengers are free to take whatever seat is available when they board the plane.

Southwest has won a long list of awards. In May, the *Wall Street Journal* reported that Southwest ranked first among airlines for the highest customer service satisfaction, according to a national survey conducted by the American Customer Satisfaction Index. Southwest came out on top as the most admired airline in the world for 1997, 1998, 1999, and 2000 in a *Fortune* magazine survey.

Herb Kelleher, Southwest's chief, was listed by *Business Week* as one of the nation's top twenty-five executives and was named CEO of the Year by *Chief Executive* magazine.

Southwest's personnel are 82 percent union members. Employees own about 12 percent of the company's stock through a profit-sharing plan that the company initiated in 1974.

Southwest Airlines is proving that a corporation can treat its employees fairly, earn ample profits [total operating revenue of $5.6 billion and a net income of $625.2 million in 2000] and serve the public's need for low-cost service with good humor. The growing success of Southwest is also proving that the public can differentiate between the delivery of solid transportation and the unnecessary frills that are employed to paper over the often poor service delivered with a frown by some of the nation's more illustrious air carriers—many of which don't come close to matching Southwest's record of consistent earnings.

August 9, 2001

Walter Miller: A Community Leader

Walter D. Miller, 70, was pumping gas into his vehicle on July 17, when he collapsed and never revived. His hometown, Winsted, Connecticut, lost more than the owner of the forty-year-old Miller Air Conditioning and Heating business. The community lost a many-splendored public citizen—a pillar of local democracy and service.

There were times when Walter seemed to be everywhere. He was involved in many controversial issues that come up in little towns, talking up his views, writing letters to the editor, making special visits to get information and impart it. There was no rigid ideology to his thinking. Like a good umpire, he called them as he saw them, which meant he was not easy to predict. But then he never was part of the political cliques that often are found in hamlets where many people know each other.

During a heated struggle over whether to demolish and build a new elementary school or remodel the stately large Red School House, Walter came down on the side of refurbishing. He knew about flat roofs and elongated motel-type school buildings of recent vintage. And he didn't like either design.

Fiscal discipline in town government was one of his specialties. In 1987, he helped revive the Winchester Taxpayers Association and for a time served as president. Unlike many of the national taxpayers groups, which are antigovernment per se, he viewed a taxpayers' group as a practical way to assure the competent and prudent use of tax dollars for the public's benefit.

Such an attitude was represented by a former town manager, Wayne Dove. So when the selectman cut Dove loose in the late '80s, Miller printed bumper stickers, "Remember Dove," and spread them all over town, including his own van. He never got the talented and enlightened Wayne reinstated, but then he never gave up either. Dove became his standard for evaluating the performance of town managers. (Dove went on to make his fortune in international finance.)

In no way was Walter Miller the consummate outsider. He plunged into the political system and was elected to the board of selectmen and was elected chief of the fire department four times. A former fire chief, Frank Smith, was right on when he described his friend of forty years as "somebody who took the community's interest to heart. You don't see too many guys like him come around anymore."

There was nothing circuitous about the old firefighter. You always knew where he stood and the reasons for his positions. Outspoken people often irritate others and he had his share of detractors who often never really said where they stood. Inwardly they disagreed and outwardly they just didn't like his style.

A joyful person, a gardener of beautiful flowers, and a red-hot baker, Miller turned his hobbies into generosity. He would pop into a friend's office with a freshly baked loaf of bread.

Youngsters who learn about democracy in their schools are rarely taught about the few citizens who hold up our democracy for the rest of us in communities across the nation. They are usually unsung, get very little media in the larger cities, and are not long remembered by those who come after them and regularly benefit from their good civic deeds and vigilance.

Someday, authors will turn their attention to these practitioners of community civic responsibility and profile them in collections. Their legacy deserves a long spotlight into the future.

For now, Walter Miller would want any contributions to go to the volunteer-based Winsted Fire Department, Central Fire House, Elm Street, Winsted, CT 06098.

August 2, 2001

Our Nation is Obsessed with Statistics

In our nation there is an accelerating obsession with public opinion polls, standardized tests, employee evaluation systems, and a multitude of numerical measurements of every aspect of human existence.

Television and newspaper coverage of national elections has become little more than a blizzard of polling data. Education policy is influenced heavily by tests that purport to measure student performance and potential. Our preferences for everything from beauty products to food are endlessly surveyed as corporations compete to be the first to market what they hope will be the next profit blockbuster.

Do all these constant measurements, polls, and statistics add up to a true picture? Do they really produce reliable data on which to base national policies that affect every citizen? Do they measure the right factors or do they measure the wrong things and miss the values and complexities of human life?

One person who raises serious questions about our preoccupation with mathematical measurements of human behavior is David Boyle, editor of *New Economics* magazine and frequent writer on economics for *The Guardian, New Statesman,* and other newspapers and magazines. Boyle has put his theory forward in a highly readable (and often humorous) new book: *The Sum of Our Discontent–Why Numbers Make Us Irrational* published by Texere of New York and London.

"The trouble is, brandishing numbers doesn't work anymore," Boyle says. "They mean little and they have plunged us into a world packed full of figures where almost every aspect of our lives is measured—from our purchases to our insurance risk—and transformed into numerical half-truths."

Boyle argues that the process of "counting everything is changing human nature and making us mechanical." He pictures a dismal future:

"We will soon have a workforce recruited by categorizing aspects of personalities on a scale of 1 to 10. We will have our nannies graded for their caring abilities on the basis of some kind of check list. We will have children who can pass exams but have no judgment. We will measure all our institutions by numerical 'best practice' standards and wonder vaguely why nobody innovates anymore. And we will have doctors who translate our symptoms into numbers before feeding them into the computer. We will be turning ourselves so slowly into machines."

Corporations have already found the era of "numbers first" useful in their battles against regulations, including those involving public health, safety, and environmental protections. These regulations must pass a "cost-benefit" test at the Office of Management and Budget and, all too frequently, the costs are inflated and the benefits to society underestimated.

Here's the way Boyle views the effect of cost-benefit analyses:

The problem, as the cost-benefit people found, is that economists measure and celebrate the wrong things because money isn't a very good measuring rod. Somehow you have to use it as a guide, but if you take it too seriously, it can have a perverse effect on the world. It measures Wall Street pretty well, but it ignores some of those things that are most important—bringing up children, looking after seniors, creating a good and healthy environment—because they're not measurable with money. Then it forgets them altogether.

Boyle says that while the modern world tries to measure everything, the hard fact is that "only when laboratory conditions are precise can you ever get anything like precision." And he argues that "laboratory precision" is never possible on important issues involving people, such as education, economics, health, or voting.

Nonetheless, the number crunchers are not deterred. In Boyle's words, they continue to "measure, measure, measure, knowing that what they measure is alive and will not keep still, and suspecting also that—however much they count—they will not capture the essence of the question they are asking." Things have to keep static if you're gong to count them—and real life isn't still, he notes.

As Boyle points out, numbers dominate the lives of citizens:

There are personal calculations to be made each day, about investments, journey times, bank machines, and credit cards. There are professional figures at work in the form of targets, statistics, workforce percentages, and profit forecasts. As consumers we are counted and aggregated according to every purchase we make. [Something that privacy advocates well know.] Every time we are exposed to the media, there is a positive flood of statistics controlling and interpreting the world, developing each truth, simplifying each problem.

A book about "numbers" may seem an odd selection for a summer reading list. But don't let the title fool you. The book is as entertaining (and funny) as it is serious about the shortcomings and tyranny of numbers, public opinion polls, testing, marketing surveys, and cost-benefit analyses.

When everything is numbers, then numbers become everything.

July 11, 2001

Living Wage May Lower Street Crime

Crime rates—street crime rates, that is—have registered dramatic drops in the last decade.

Politicians clamor for credit. We've built more jails, some boast. We've made sentences longer, brag others. We've cracked down on minor offenses, say others.

Perhaps these punitive measures have contributed to the declining crime rates. And there is reason to believe that the increasingly popular community policing methods have strengthened law enforcement. Perhaps putting more police on the streets has cut into crime rates, as well. But with all of the focus on law enforcement measures (again, for street crime only; corporate crime law enforcement remains pitifully weak), politicians, the news media, and most purported experts have ignored a strikingly obvious contributor to lower street crime rates: declining unemployment.

Now come economists Jared Bernstein and Ellen Houston of the Washington, D.C.-based Economics Policy Institute with a short booklet,

"Crime and Work: What We Can Learn from the Low-Wage Labor Market," that aims to remind us of the commonsense notion that perhaps the best crime deterrent is ensuring the availability of jobs that pay a living wage.

Although over the past year the Federal Reserve has moved to raise interest rates, declining and then relatively low interest rates for much of the past decade permitted the unemployment rate to decline to well under 5 percent—far below the 6 percent level conventional economic wisdom had predicted would start an inflationary spiral. And in the last few years, persistently low unemployment rates have finally translated into (small) real wage increases for those at the bottom of the income ladder.

Bernstein and Houston show that these employment gains and wage improvements for those at the bottom end of the wage scale correlate very closely with declining street crime rates.

A series of charts comparing regional crime and unemployment for young men with a high school degree or less—the population committing the bulk of street crimes—reveals that year-to-year downturns in the street crime rate are typically simultaneous with declines in the unemployment rate.

The good news is that reducing and keeping unemployment low—a vital social goal and something well within the reach of policymakers, should they seek to achieve this objective—has the ancillary benefit of making a significant contribution to low street crime rates.

Jobs occupy potential criminals, take them off the street, and vector them away from law-breaking. And employment earnings enable families and individuals to make ends meet, lessening the financial crunch that can encourage street crime.

But the cautionary note from Bernstein and Houston is that the benefits of an expanding economy are delivered last to those at the bottom of the class hierarchy, and that unemployment remains far, far too high among specific demographic groups.

"Even with the wage growth of the mid-to-late 1990s, the wage levels for young black males generally remained at or below their 1989 peak in 1998," they note. Moreover, even with an official 4.2 percent nationwide unemployment rate in 1999, unemployment among 16- to 24-year-old black males was 26 percent.

The lesson they draw is that sustained periods of low unemployment are needed to deliver real benefits to low-wage workers. It is only in the latter half of the 1990s that young male African-American workers began to register notable wage increases, and significant declines in unemployment rates.

"To lift the economic prospects of all low-wage workers is not only a worthy economic and social goal," Bernstein and Houston conclude, "it is one that will pay off in the long run by offering potential [street] criminals a legitimate alternative."

There is no secret about how to improve low-wage workers' prospects. Key measures include: low interest rates; an increased minimum wage designed to ensure all workers earn a living wage, tied to the inflation rate; and increased unionization, so that workers can join together to defend their interests in the workplace and the policy sphere. For the corporate lobbyists who resist these measures, perhaps knowing that these policies can cut street crime rates will persuade them to drop their opposition.

To see the executive summary and introduction to the Economic Policy Institute report, go to www.epinet.org.

August 8, 2000

Jeff Gates: Democracy at Risk

"No sensible democracy would opt for an economic system in which the financial wealth of the top 1 percent of households exceeds the combined wealth of the bottom 95 percent."

That is the commonsense observation with which Jeff Gates begins his provocative new book, *Democracy at Risk: Rescuing Main Street from Wall Street* (Perseus Publishing, Cambridge, MA).

Noting that the nation's four hundred richest families increased their wealth on average by $940 million each from 1997 to 1999—an increase of $1.28 million every day—Gates then asks the provocative question: "Who voted for that?" He asks, "How many wage earners in a true democracy would endorse a system in which 1998 wages are 7 percent lower than in 1973—when Richard Nixon was in the White House."

These questions are rhetorical, but they are provocative because they highlight a critical insight: how wealth is distributed is a function of conscious policy choices. The business pages and financial magazines are flush with accounts of this or that entrepreneur or innovator, but as important and desirable as entrepreneurialism may be, major shifts in how wealth is allocated are due in large part not to the workings of the free market, but to the political market in Washington, D.C.

Tax policy over the last twenty years has shifted the tax burden off the shoulders of the wealthy, large corporations, and increasingly on to the middle class, spurring the massive wealth concentration of the last two decades.

Federal corporate welfare policies shift more than two hundred billion dollars annually from American taxpayers to Big Business.

Moreover, depreciation rules and other tax policies encourage rapid depletion of natural resources, with the costs of cleanup and environmental degradation foisted on to the public. National and international accounting rules ignore the real costs of ecological destruction, facilitating more intense pollution and resource extraction.

Once you accept Gates's point that society's rules significantly influence how and where wealth is generated and how it is distributed, the next step is to ask the question now off the political radar screen: What measures can be taken to deconcentrate economic power?

Gates offers a range of intriguing proposals, among them:

• Create a legal requirement for pension fund managers to invest not only with the purpose of achieving competitive returns, but also to enhance broad-based ownership of major assets. Why should pension funds be invested to turn Sam Walton's family into multibillionaires, he asks, rather than using their investment leverage to demand that Wal-Mart stock be broadly shared among workers and others?

• Encourage customer-owned utilities, with customer service payments buying not only electric, water or other utility services, but also a progressively larger share of equity in the utility.

• Use the power of government purchasing to reward companies that are broadly held—and, it should be added, meet other public interest standards.

• Create a commission, made up largely of the superrich, to propose ways to more evenly distribute the nation's wealth.

To encourage the public to think boldly and creatively about wealth questions, Gates recalls Huey Long's "Share Our Wealth" program. Long wanted to impose a "capital levy" on family fortunes in excess of $5 million ($62 million in 1999 dollars). The "surplus wealth" would be turned over to a corporation that would issue stock to the American people according to a congressionally devised plan. The relevance of this plan today? "Though the times are very different," Gates writes, "Huey remains correct on his key point: Ways must be found to Share Our Wealth."

We live now in an era in which massive disparities of wealth subordinate democracy to plutocracy. To break the grip of today's oligarchs and shift to policies to encourage broad-based prosperity will require a status quo-shaking political movement on both a national and international scale. There are many signs that such a movement is now nascent—the student campaigns against sweatshops, the protests in Seattle and Washington against corporate globalization, and in many local innovations to disperse ownership and establish local control over local wealth.

As Jeff Gates has written, we know that capitalism routinely expands without expanding the ranks of those called capitalists.

What remains is for a growing political momentum to generate more innovative thinking, local experimentation, and a maturing public movement that demands a renewed commitment to wider ownership of capital resources and a subordination of manic mercantilism to democratic values.

June 7, 2000

Luxury and Excess

Thorstein Veblen, the turn of the nineteenth-century social scientist who coined the term "conspicuous consumption," would blush if he were to witness today's consumption patterns.

Luxury and excess have been taken to new flights of fancy and have become the object of desire for an ever greater portion of the population. In her recent book, *Do Americans Shop Too Much?*, Harvard professor Juliet Schor points to a "new consumerism," the centerpiece of which is "upscaling of lifestyle norms" irrespective of ability to pay.

Much of the luxury buying is of course being done by newly minted millionaires, as the Reagan-Bush-Clinton regimes promote the ever greater concentration of wealth in the hands of the few at the top. But Schor's important point is that even those who haven't benefited from the boom at the top are engaged in a flurry of frivolous spending.

Driving the current luxury and other excessive consumption binge are the marketing mavens—the consumer product companies, the Madison Avenue advertising firms, the new marketing consultants, and the hyper-commercialism the marketers and their clients have entrenched in the cultural landscape.

The credit card industry, for example, sends out 2.5 billion solicitations each year; credit card advertisements urge consumers to, simply, spend. The result has been a sharp upsurge in credit card use in the last decade—and a simultaneous increase in consumer debt. Does anyone doubt that the credit card industry's aggressive marketing efforts have fueled the skyrocketing provision and use of credit cards?

Or consider pharmaceuticals, where the drug industry's investment indirect- to-consumer (DTC) advertising has risen from $25 million in 1988 to more than $225 million in 1994, $610 million in 1996, and more than $1 billion in 1998. The purpose of DTC advertising—which appears on television, in magazines, over the Internet, and in any other forum the industry can use—is to convince patients to badger their doctors to prescribe brand-name drugs—drugs they may not need, drugs that may be unsafe, or drugs for which there may be better or cheaper substitutes. No one, least of all the pharmaceutical industry, seriously questions that DTC advertising bumps sales.

To the marketing push, Schor adds other social factors as contributing to today's luxury fever. She argues that an increasingly skewed income distribution has stretched out the consumer comparison hierarchy. Those aspiring to emulate those one, two, or three notches above them on the income ladder must now reach higher, because the space between the rungs has expanded in the last two decades.

Meanwhile, television programming has delivered portrayals of the lifestyles of the wealthy into homes of every social group. Along with the breakdown in neighborhood cohesiveness and the entry of women in the workforce, she contends, the television factor has led consumers to shift their point of reference from their next-door neighbor (likely located in the same income group) to the increasingly remote upper-income groups.

The trend of ever more conspicuous consumption will not be reversed through a series of individual choices. It will require a shift to a culture of civic engagement, a seeking of value and purpose in a realm other than things. This shift will not just happen. It will require, among other things, a revitalized consumer movement built on institutional arrangements that encourage consumers to reorient their buying practices.

Independent consumer organization will give rise to new values, new modes of analysis, and new policy ideas—and generate the political momentum for new policies.

Some of the forms of consumer organization that require nurturing:

• Banding together for group buying: Wholesale group buying operations—where tens, hundreds, or thousands join together to negotiate bulk purchases and lower prices—exist in patches around the country, especially in home heating oil markets.

• Banding together for group information sharing and complaint handling: The Internet offers unprecedented opportunities to create clearinghouses of consumer-generated information on product quality, defects, billing frauds, etc., with equally promising opportunities for victimized consumers to negotiate as a group for redress.

• Banding together for group negotiating: Voluntary, mass-based consumer policy organization could remake the terrain of consumer-seller interaction. Utility consumers in Illinois, for example, are able to join a consumer group that has saved them billions of dollars in electric bills. In conjunction with state government mailings, consumers receive a notice asking them to join a membership organization, controlled by dues-paying members, that advocates on consumers' behalf before utility regulatory bodies. This model, based on a simple solicitation insert in mailings that would otherwise be sent (and therefore add no postage costs), needs to be replicated around the country, and for many other industries—cable, banks, insurance, auto companies, etc.

These and other forms of independent consumer organization would work not only to redress specific consumer demands, but to help create a consumer culture that places value on quality, good value, and ecological and social considerations in production processes. Banding together as consumers broadens horizons, creates countervailing political power to oligopolistic sellers, and contributes to a shift in the buyer paradigm from conspicuous to conscious and conscientious consumption.

May 31, 2000

Gene Stilp: A Prop for Any Protest

Imagine a public interest artist using the town square as a canvas. Now comes Gene Stilp, a forty-nine-year-old lawyer with a keen sense of advocacy, a nose for news, and the creativity and skills to symbolically present a complicated public policy initiative with a prop guaranteed to generate media coverage and capture hearts and minds at the same time. Gene is more at home in the workshop than the courtroom.

Stilp's gallery includes some unusual works:

• A thirty-foot ear of corn. This mutant vegetable greeted the participants at a Food and Drug Administration hearing on genetically modified foods in Washington, D.C. in late 1999. With about $400, Gene Stilp and his activist associates assembled the enormous ear of corn with fencing and 1,000 recycled milk cartons and twine. The prop was featured in the *New York Times*, *USA. Today*, and a myriad of electronic and print sources throughout the country.

• A twenty-four-foot SUV. Stilp supplied the U.S. Public Interest Research Group with a twenty-four-foot long, fourteen-foot high, ten-foot wide inflatable SUV to help the group dramatically call attention to the gas-guzzling SUVs that are crowding the nations' highways. The SUV prop is hard for the media to avoid and it helps jolt the public into thinking about the consequences of wasting energy on oversized vehicles.

• The PECO burnt-toast toaster. In 1998, the Pennsylvania state legislature debated electric deregulation. In order to call attention to a proposed bailout of the nuclear industry, Stilp refashioned a 1963 Airstream trailer into a twenty-foot long, twelve-foot high toaster. Two ten-foot long, four-foot high pieces of blackened toast were popping out of the toaster. With the flick of a remote switch, smoke poured out of the top of the toaster to replicate burning toast. Signs adorning the toaster proclaimed, "Don't Get Burned By PECO."

Gene Stilp has been an outspoken activist for over two decades: from hunger issues to safety concerns about nuclear power, he is always ready to help concerned citizens make their voices heard in the corridors of power.

Stilp's motivation to build props stems from his desire to help groups that can't afford to buy television time for commercials or full-page newspaper ads to advance the public interest agenda. Most Stilp creations start with a creative impulse followed by a quick trip to the local hardware store or junkyard. With baling wire and two-by-fours, he begins the job of making an issue move from the mimeograph machines of local and national activists to the daily newspapers and evening news shows. His props are as varied as the issues of the day.

To call attention to global warming Gene produced the first "global warming groundhog." Capitalizing on the national attention generated every February by Groundhog Day, Gene used February 2, 2000, to launch the first official Global Warming Forecasting Groundhog. With the U.S. capitol as a backdrop, "Globbie," a small but effective groundhog sculpture, predicted adverse climate changes for the coming year.

The corrupting influence of special interest money on politics is an important matter. Stilp's special approach to this issue prompted him to spend about $200 to build a full-scale replica of the Lincoln bed. (This was after President Clinton's campaign contributors were offered a chance to sleep in the real Lincoln bedroom in the White House.) As the U.S. Congress gathered in Hershey, Pennsylvania for a "civility retreat" in 1997, is was greeted by the Lincoln bed prop—with an attached meter that recorded donations for time spent in the bed. This prop focused attention on campaign finance reform and the congressional and presidential campaign finance abuse investigations, and resulted in national media coverage of the need for campaign finance reform from a citizen perspective. Stilp was interviewed by a host of national correspondents while he lounged in the "Lincoln bed."

In the coming year, Stilp hopes to transform his lifelong passion for building props for causes into an enduring institution called the National Prop Shop. This nonprofit enterprise will help public interest groups make use of creative props and incorporate props into their campaign efforts. Gene Stilp wants the activist community to use the National Prop Shop but ultimately he would like to see every community have the ability to assemble local talent to build the props they might need to dramatize local issues.

People interested in contributing ideas, materials, or funds for this unique public institution should contact Mr. Stilp at The Prop Shop, 1550 FVCR, Harrisburg, PA 17112.

March 12, 2000

Governor Davis and Civics 101

It is remarkable how someone like Gray Davis can be elected governor of California without knowing the basic elements of Civics 101.

Yes, Governor, our state and federal governments are divided into three branches—the legislative, executive, and judicial branches. They were designed both to balance one another's excesses and to perform functions unique to their design, according to state and federal constitutions.

Now comes Gray Davis's Civics 101. Last year, in a typical fit of public temper, he told the *San Francisco Chronicle*'s editorial board that the state legislature's job is "to implement my vision." Davis declared he was elected on a platform, and the legislators should take his marching orders because only he was elected on a statewide basis.

Davis was roundly criticized for this imperviousness by commentators and in editorials around the state.

No matter. A few days ago, at a meeting of state governors, Davis turned his attention to the judges. He said that the judges he appoints "should reflect my views. They are not there to be independent agents—they are there to reflect the sentiments that I expressed during the campaign."

And what if they arrive at an opposite position, he was asked? Davis quickly replied: "They shouldn't be a judge. They should resign."

The "sentiments" that Governor Davis mentioned were his position in favor of abortion rights and individual (not corporate) capital punishment and his opposition to same-sex civil partnerships.

Reporters, listening to Davis demand that all three branches of government come under the governor's domain, rushed to their phones for scholarly comments. University of Southern California, Erwin Chemerinsky, declared: "That's outrageous. A judge is not a Cabinet member who is there to carry out a governor's or a president's policies."

The Associated Press also called Berkeley law professor Stephen Barrett, who described Gray Davis's comments as "bizarre," adding that judges frequently must rule against majorities and on the facts of specific cases.

Senate President John Burton (D) told AP that the governor "doesn't support an independent legislature, so why should he support an independent judiciary. It's consistent with his view that the other two branches are irrelevant."

Davis is no novice. He was chief of staff for Governor Jerry Brown in the '70s where, according to his colleagues, he began laying the groundwork for his political career. Later he was elected to the state legislature and then won the lieutenant governorship under Republican Governor Pete Wilson.

As governor, he immediately started shaking the business money tree. In a frenzy of political fundraising right after he was elected, the money poured into his coffers at the rate of $1 million a month!

Recently, he stepped up his conference calls urging powerful corporate interest groups in the insurance, utility, and banking circles to contribute big dollars to oppose Proposition 25, which would set some limits on the "skies the limit" cash register politics that now prevails. It did not seem to bother the governor that some of these same corporate interests were funding a campaign against Propositions 30 and 31 to overturn auto insurance reforms he signed last year.

During his telephone calls, the governor warned the business lobbyists that if Proposition 25 passes, it will make it easier for consumer and other citizen groups to win ballot initiatives against them. Yuk! For this, Democrats waited sixteen years to elect one of their own as governor.

There was once a report on a poll of high school students that found more of them knew the names of the Three Stooges then of the three branches of government. It is an open question whether Governor Davis of California knows more about stooges than about the historic separation of powers within our state governments.

March 7, 2000

Granny D Wants to Clean Up Politics

"Granny D, you speak for me."

That was heard on the streets of Washington, D.C., as they followed ninety-year-old Doris Haddock on the last leg of her cross-country march to rally support for meaningful campaign finance reform.

Granny D began her cross-country trek at the Rose Bowl parade in Pasadena, California on January 1, 1999. She steadily made her way on a 3,200-mile journey—traversing California, Arizona, New Mexico, Texas, Arkansas, Tennessee, Kentucky, Ohio, West Virginia, Pennsylvania, Maryland, Virginia, and the District of Columbia—walking ten miles a day.

She called her march a "pilgrimage" for social justice, relying on strangers for food and shelter. Thousands of people have supported her, she says, a testament not only to their generosity, but to their passionate commitment to ending the corruption of our democracy by big money interests.

Along the way, Granny D has proved that one person can make a difference. Her walk has generated enormous media interest, and she has appeared on NBC "Nightly News," "Good Morning America," National Public Radio, and many other programs to issue a clarion call for campaign finance reform.

Finally, her fourteen-month pilgrimage concluded in Washington, D.C. She began her final day's trek in Arlington cemetery, beginning, she said, "among the graves of Arlington—so that those spirits, some of whom may be old friends, might join us today and that we might ask of them now: Did you, brave spirits, give your lives for a government where we might stand together as free and equal citizens, or did you give your lives so that laws might be sold to the highest bidder?"

She ended her march on the steps of the capitol, where she said she came to deliver a consistent message from across America, from young and old, and from people of every color: "Shame on you, Mitch McConnell, and those who raise untold millions of dollars in exchange for public policy. Shame on you, senators and congressmen, who have turned this headquarters of a great and self-governing people into a bawdy house." (Senator McConnell of Kentucky is infamous for his defense of large campaign contributions as a boon to democracy, and his call for removal of existing restraints on campaign donations.)

As she walked through downtown Washington, it was apparent that Granny D did in fact speak for the generations-spanning crowd that followed her on the last leg of her trek. Many had traveled from all over the nation to join her in the last steps of her march. Carrying "Go, Granny, Go" and "End Legalized Bribery" signs, they reverently looked on as she completed her inspirational journey for justice, and they listened carefully as she spoke truth to power.

But unlike so many of our elected politicians, Granny D does not pander to her audience. She paused in her remarks to remind her fellow citizens of the need to recognize our own complicity in the withering of our democracy and the need to re-engage in civic life.

"Along my walk, I have seen an America that is losing the time and the energy for self-governance," she said. "We must energize our communities to better see our problems, better plan their happy futures, and these plans must form the basis of our instructions to our elected representatives. This is the responsibility of every adult American."

"If we are hypnotized by television and overwrought by life on a corporate-consumer treadmill, let us snap out of it and regain our lives as a free, calm, fearless, outspoken people who have time for each other and our communities."

Her programmatic agenda is straightforward: Pass a ban on the use of soft money in federal election campaigns as a modest first step, and implement more comprehensive reform thereafter, including full public financing and free television time. Citizens must push for and win reforms at the local and state level, so that political momentum for comprehensive campaign reform becomes unstoppable nationwide.

The ultimate goal, she says, is to devise ways "for a great people to talk to one another again without the necessity of great wealth."

Few distill the civic challenges or embody civic commitment as does Granny D. She relies on social security payments for financial support and has no money to leave her twelve great-grandchildren. "So," she told the *Washington Post*, "I said, 'I can leave the legacy of a democracy. I want them to be brought up in a democracy.'"

March 1, 2000

George Sherwood, the Public Citizen

The local articles describing the life of George L. Sherwood, who passed away at age eighty-two on July 28, were accurate and kind but could not do justice to this remarkable resident of Winchester, Connecticut for his profound contributions to local democracy.

The civic fiber of local communities has always relied on a small number of active citizens who speak out, participate, and contribute in ways that are silently supported by larger numbers of their neighbors. If you had to make a checklist of civic contributions, the activities of this retired aeronautical engineer, this consummate public citizen, George Sherwood, would provide quite a comprehensive guide. After his service as a glider pilot in World War II, Mr. Sherwood worked for thirty years on airport planning and design for the state of Connecticut. That was his day job. His other hours were devoted to his wife and seven children and to his public responsibilities to make his town a better place to live.

The town of Winchester is nestled in the Litchfield Hills. Around 12,000 live there in a heavily forested area the size of Manhattan. Within a short walk from their homes, the residents can find schools, stores, libraries, the town hall, the movie theater, the fire and police departments, ball fields, rivers, lakes, parks, and trails. This is my hometown, and I knew Mr. Sherwood for many years.

He was funny and blunt and creative and brought people together. He coordinated neighbors to establish a land trust for conservation. With my brother in the '60s, he helped establish a community college. With his wife, he started the Winchester Center Kerosene Lamp Museum, the only place in the country that featured these lamps that were made between 1856 and 1880. Some of these fine products were donated to the Smithsonian by the Sherwoods.

Mr. Sherwood was the designated town historian. He gave us context and background about how our community came to be.

For conversation, he and his wife ran the little post office that served more communication purposes than just the collecting and sending of mail. He had a tradition for several years of inviting townspeople to a Friday "salon" in his pretty eighteenth-century captain's house, where all shared in good food, drink, conversation, and friendship. At his home he experimented with energy-efficient ways of heating.

When mismanagement collapsed the town's nearly one-hundred-year-old hospital, Mr. Sherwood volunteered his time and knowledge on the Code Blue Committee to oppose its closing and restart a health care center. He traveled to various parts of the world, bringing back an enriched perspective and an impressive collection of photos. He offered his home to foreign students, and year after year he learned from them and taught them how to be a part of a community. One, now an international economist at Case Western Reserve University, drove from Ohio to his memorial service and wept openly at the loss of the man he thought of as his second father.

This citizen of Winchester was about more than civic highlights. He embodied the principle that daily democracy requires daily citizenship. No shirker of his civic duties, Mr. Sherwood was always there at town meetings, at the town hall, on the zoning board of appeals, in the Winchester Grange, with the Winchester Volunteer Fire Department, wherever there was a little or big proposal or project to make life better, more fair, and more pleasant.

A man from the pre-television era, he believed in personal interaction. He loved to show youngsters what he thought they should know about their community, their past, their world.

There are not many young George Sherwoods coming around as public citizens in local communities and staying for fifty years or more. We live in increasingly rootless, mall-filled, withdrawn communities, whether large or small. We stare at electronic screens of virtual realities instead of making our own realities, in our own communities.

One of my recollections of Mr. Sherwood, not long ago, was his almost plaintive question: Where are the young people?

Refusing to be discouraged, George Sherwood and his civic life recall the words of the famed scholar Max Weber, who decades ago wrote that anyone working for change requires "the steadfastness of heart which can brave even the crumbling of all hopes."

August 8, 1999

Giuliani Plants Corporate Welfare

Although New York City owns some 10,000 empty lots throughout the city, in a triumph of impulse over judgment, Mayor Rudy Giuliani has announced the pending sale to commercial developers of twelve lots that support community gardens.

Apparently the mayor wants to add to the city's coffers by placing these small oases of productive greenery and mutual self-help on the property tax rolls. Giuliani is using what Justice Louis Brandeis long ago called "other peoples' money" to make the rich even richer at the expense of small taxpayers.

When the people who were tending these gardens in mostly lower-income neighborhoods protested, the mayor uttered another characteristic provocation: "This is a free-market economy. Welcome to the era after Communism."

What rescued Giuliani from a burgeoning public relations fiasco was his allowing private philanthropies to buy the community gardens for about $4 million. The entire episode, however, served to highlight the side of Giuliani that grovels before the demands of corporations for all kinds of privileged subsidies.

There may have been a few among the corporate welfarists in the skyscraper canyons of Gotham who squirmed when they read the details of the community gardens fiasco, but they need not worry that they are next on the mayor's list of welfare reform. After all, they are not $300-a-month welfare mothers. They're powerful billion-dollar corporations that feed at the public trough.

George Steinbrenner, owner of the New York Yankees, wanted Giuliani to build him a $1.5 billion stadium and move the Yankees to Manhattan from the Bronx. Giuliani agreed—that is, until public outrage and critical economic analysis turned the tide back toward renovating the present "House that Ruth Built."

Other corporate welfarists had no such trouble convincing a cowed city hall that a mere bluff of moving to Hoboken or Jersey City garners multimillions of dollars in goodies. These typically include sales tax exemptions, property tax abatements, and discounted electricity prices. Even Donald Trump, whose super high-priced condominium projects aren't selling anywhere, still manages to wrest such tax breaks from New York City.

The King Kong of corporate welfare also rattled the high temple of capitalism—the New York Stock Exchange. Again bluffing about considering a move across the Hudson River to Jersey, the Stock Exchange secured a $900 million subsidy package from Mayor Giuliani to build a new headquarters near its present location. The subsidies amount to about $200,000 per retained job!

Other financial exchanges—the American Exchange, the Mercantile Exchange, and the Coffee, Sugar, and Cocoa Exchange—demanded similar largesse. And more Giuliani sugar sweetened the pot for media corporations, including ABC, NBC, Ziff-Davis, McGraw-Hill, Reuters, Condé Nast, Time Warner (shortly), and Rupert Murdoch's News America. And even after CBS announced it would remain in the city until 2008, Giuliani still gave it $10 million in tax escapes and other subsidies.

Erosion of the city tax base means fewer municipal services and/or higher taxes on small businesses and individuals than would otherwise be the case. The corporate welfarists use the police, fire, schools, and other services but don't want to pay the taxes that make them possible. That sounds a lot like freeloading.

When big corporations escape taxes, it also gives them an unfair competitive advantage against small businesses. Some well-regarded legal scholars believe that local and state governments that use tax escapes as bait for locational decisions by businesses violate the commerce clause of the U.S. Constitution. Peter Enrich, professor of law at Northeastern University School of Law in Boston, wrote a legal analysis behind such a conclusion in the December 1996 issue of the *Harvard Law Review*. A test case in federal court is expected to be filed soon.

Other ways to stop this frenzied bidding for business is through compacts among the states. The federal government can also play a key role by legislating policies that either prohibit such tax incentives and other strip mining or neutralize state giveaways by surcharging companies that received such subsidies. The latter approach is in a bill introduced by Representative David Minge of Minnesota.

On June 30, the first congressional hearings on corporate welfare will commence under the aegis of Republican John Kasich, chair of the powerful House Budget Committee. He welcomes your opinions and suggestions. Stay tuned.

May 17, 1999

Joe DiMaggio

The Yankee Clipper, Joe DiMaggio, lost his struggle with cancer on March 8, 1999. The next day newspapers were full of memories by his friends and teammates. As a boyhood fan of DiMaggio back in the forties, I always looked forward to meeting him. That occurred in the spring of 1990 and I promptly wrote about it in my June 1, 1990 column, which is reprinted here for interested readers:

I finally met Joe DiMaggio, one of my boyhood sports heroes. He was sitting quietly in the Green Room waiting for his turn to go on to the stage at Radio City Music Hall in New York City during a gala benefit for retired actors and actresses of the theater called Night of the Stars.

Back in my hometown of Connecticut, baseball was serious stuff for boys in the 1940s. You were either a Red Sox fan or a Yankee fan, a Ted Williams fan or a Joe DiMaggio fan. The town was split down the middle by the two factions. Ever since Dodger catcher Mickey Owen dropped a third strike in the 1941 World Series and the Yankees rallied to win the game, I was a fervent fan of the Bronx Bombers.

At seventy-five years of age Joe DiMaggio appeared in good shape, lean and lithe. A quiet, reserved man with an unbending sense of privacy, he seemed quite willing to talk on that day. My first question was about his early teammate, the great Yankee first-baseman and iron man, Lou Gehrig. Joe spoke highly of Gehrig: "He wasn't all that agile a fielder," he said, "but when he got up to the plate—wow, the pitchers feared him, especially in the clutch."

The Yankee Clipper observed that whenever Gehrig had a bad day, such as going 0 for 4, he would sit in the locker room dragging on a cigarette and blaming himself if the team lost.

I asked DiMaggio if he plans to write a book. He replied that he often thinks about it but doesn't have the kind of detailed memory like Tommy Henrich (another clutch Yankee hitter) who is writing a book.

I urged him to put pen to paper so he could convey the spirit of the game before it became so hyper-commercial, where owners buy and sell players from one another instead of relying on farm teams, and players charge kids for autographs. I said the younger generation needs to know and he wondered whether the younger generation cared to know.

Joe did not seem to approve of Yankee owner George Steinbrenner's approach to winning by buying players at a frantic rate. Coming from teams when players stayed together for years, Joe felt that few owners have succeeded in buying winning teams, including, of course, Steinbrenner. "Winning teams need continuity and the familiarity of playing together," he said.

He sees Mickey Mantle from time to time. Recalling the famous Mantle fall at age twenty that started his string of knee injuries, Joe observed that Mantle, who fell in a hole in the Yankee outfield during an important game, was on his back crying from the pain and his missing the fly ball.

Joe holds one of the most unbreakable records in professional sports—the sensational fifty-six-game hitting streak. I offered a more unbreakable record by Joe Sewell, who played thirteen years for Cleveland and then the Yankees between 1920 and 1933. Sewell was almost impossible to strike out, as Joe related. And in thirteen years, Sewell used only one bat! He was such a line-drive, precision hitter that he never broke the bat he started out with in 1920.

Joe acknowledged that this was a pretty astonishing performance. Howard Cosell came over and started talking to DiMaggio and I knew that my chance interview was over.

March 9, 1999

Detroit's Snow Policy

The collapse of a community surfaced with a vengeance in Detroit, Michigan recently when the snow started falling on January 2, 1999. Twenty-one inches of snow fell over the next two weeks and city officials still had not plowed the residential streets.

That is not an oversight. It is a policy of many years standing. "Side streets" are not plowed. To illustrate the policy, regardless of weather extremes in a regularly wintry city, there are only fifty-nine plows for 2,400 miles of roadway—far, far less than other northern cities of comparable size.

This studied incapacity to perform a vital city service for its residents has led to predictable outcomes. Emergency vehicles cannot reach homes. People slip and fall in the snow hardened with ice. Many cannot get to work on time, if at all. Schools are closed. The elderly are endangered.

The postal authorities announced on January 14 that mail carriers will honk their horns, like the Good Humor man, to let residents know they are there so that people can hazard into the drifts to pick up their mail—their bills and notices.

At the same time, the city Department of Public Works says the storms have cost $2.5 million—$1 million more than the department had budgeted for snow removal all year. Note that this sum is for the nation's tenth largest city with a population of one million. This sum is also equal to what Chrysler's president, Robert Eaton, makes in less than ten days from his huge compensation package.

The mayor, Dennis Archer, behaves as if he is out of central casting for a movie about bumblers. He finally asks the city council for more money two weeks after the storm froze Detroit. He asks the state of Michigan for financial assistance. He asks the federal government to declare a state of emergency in order to obtain federal funds to plow the residential roadways.

Run this scenario of metropolitan incapacity and desperation past the good burghers of the Snow Capital, Buffalo, New York, which already has received nearly five feet of snow, and you'll be greeted with disbelief or worse. I've been in Buffalo during and after large snowfalls years ago, before the stunning technological developments of late-twentieth-century America, and the streets were cleared quickly. So were the sidewalks by people who owned homes and stores and believed that doing this was just doing what comes naturally in a civil society.

I grew up in a hilly Connecticut town of 10,000 people. After great snowfalls, the streets were cleared faster than they are now with far more modest equipment. But even now, my hometown gets the job done overnight or the following day for an area almost the size of Manhattan Island.

What's going on then in Detroit—the Motor City for the world's largest automobile industry? Abandoned by its corporate rulers and its political governors, that's what.

The corporate bosses do not live in Detroit. They live in nearby wealthy Grosse Pointe or Bloomfield Hills where their streets are smooth and clear. GM headquarters in Detroit is accessible to these executives because they are on main thoroughfares that are plowed.

GM is more experienced in getting rather than giving. What these bosses have demanded from city hall are subsidy packages and property tax abatements, including one amounting to $350 million for one factory. Reporting hyper-record profits for years, GM and Chrysler (Ford Motor Co. is in Dearborn) could have donated the money for more plows and/or contributed more trucks for a week or two. These companies are, after all, in the transportation business. But they lack civic pride and civic responsibility.

As for the city officials, so much discredit has been heaped upon them by the people that they cannot get enough volunteers out to clear the streets and some of the remaining schools that are still snowbound. What are we paying our taxes for, declared some Detroiters.

Here and there were demonstrations of community spirit. For a week, 150 homeless men, working with a group called Operation Get Down, have been "digging out the homes of pregnant women," the *Detroit Free Press* reported. Several small businesses lent their trucks, snowblowers, and shovels.

The Detroit city government has been pressured repeatedly to produce federal, state, and local corporate welfare packages for its big corporations. Now when the city is overwhelmed with snow, these big companies are content to watch the hapless Mayor Archer beg for federal disaster assistance—for snowfalls that cities for decades have been able to handle routinely by themselves.

Today, Detroit means community breakdown.

January 19, 1999

IX

POLITICAL GAMES AND SHAMES

The stealth pay raises Congress has passed for itself over the years are shameful. Starting in the 1980s, Congress has been plagued by a bitter partisanship that often produces gridlock. During this acrimonious period, however, Democrats and Republicans have consistently agreed on one subject: the need to reward themselves (despite their many manifest failures) and fatten their own wallets, notwithstanding the fact that their income exceeds that of more than 97 percent of their constituents. Imagine the leadership of the two parties agreeing not to support any challenger in their own party *who made an issue of the congressional pay raise.*

The conspiracy to hike their own salaries and benefits at the taxpayers' expense, and as secretly as possible, tells us a lot about our so-called representatives. But it hardly represents the only example of their shameful behavior and game-playing. The columns in this section highlight other actions that should make your civic blood heat up, including:

- *Congress abdicating its war-making responsibility while a messianic militarist President, spurred by former draft-dodgers, leads the nation into a preemptive war and quagmire, based on false pretenses (including nonexistent weapons and an alleged alliance between mortal enemies), that exacts staggering human and economic costs.*
- *Democrats, in the 2002 mid-term elections, going out of their way not to criticize or challenge the President (notwithstanding the damage his policies inflicted on workers and consumers), making a mockery of the notion of an opposition party—and going down to defeat.*
- *Members of Congress rushing to condemn corporate crime in the wake of the Enron and Tyco scandals, despite the fact that they had eviscerated the regulatory apparatus designed to prevent such lawlessness.*
- *The Bush tax cut, tilted heavily to the wealthiest Americans and justified by absurdly optimistic projections of economic growth, which predictably sparked major deficits that make us less able to address the nation's most pressing necessities and injustices.*

- *Yielding control of presidential debates to the Commission on Presidential Debates (CPD), a front for the major parties devoted to preventing the American people from seeing converging Tweedledum and Tweedledee forced to defend their ideas against outside challengers or thoughtful questioners.*
- *Congress and the President enacting modest campaign finance reform (McCain-Feingold), and then doing everything possible to circumvent it.*
- *The refusal of both parties to make easily available on the Internet the voting records of each member.*
- *The resistance of government agencies to placing final government contracts online.*

Note that neither party has a monopoly on shameless shenanigans.

"The Platform is the Party's Contract with the People"

"The Platform is the Party's Contract with the People." This noble sentiment has been used by both Republicans and Democrats in characterizing their state and national party platforms over the decades. It can become an embarrassing yardstick for any party that lives a double life.

Consider President Bush and his Texas State Republican Platform of 2002 that is still in effect. The authors and endorsers of this lengthy document were taking no chances. It says crisply that each "Republican candidate for a public or Party office shall be provided a current copy of the Party platform at the time of filing. The candidate shall be asked to read and initial each page of the platform and sign a statement affirming he/she has read the entire platform."

Signing on the dotted line is connected with the party giving the candidate financial and other support.

Then follows policy after policy of great specificity in direct opposition to what the Bush administration is doing and not doing. For example, the Texas Republican Party demands that Washington repeal NAFTA and GATT and get out of the World Trade Organization and the United Nations. It is adamant against any gathering, accumulation, and dissemination of personal data and information on law-abiding citizens by business and governments. It wants "all citizens" to be free from government surveillance of their electronic communications.

In a slam against Attorney General John Ashcroft, the Texas Party believes that "the current greatest threat to our individual liberties is overreaching government controls established under the guise of preventing terrorism."

Remember, this is the Texas State Republican Party. It is President Bush's party—the organization that launched his political career to the governorship and beyond. His friends and political allies run this party.

So it is remarkable to read that the platform demands the "elimination of presidential authority to issue executive orders, presidential decision directives. . . and a repeal of all previous executive orders and administrative mandates." This policy would handcuff both George W. Bush and John Ashcroft.

In opposition to President Bush, his state party insists that social security funds "should not be commingled or spent with general revenues or invested in private or public corporate stock." And it adds, social security benefits should "be non-taxable," until private pensions replace social security.

Talk about abolishing government! The Texas Republican Party wants to terminate the U.S. Department of Education (there goes Bush's Leave No Child Behind hoax), the Internal Revenue Service, along with the elimination of the personal income tax, inheritance tax, corporate income tax, payroll tax, and the minimum wage. That is not all. The party wants to close down the Department of Health and Human Services, Commerce, Labor, the Environmental Protection Agency, the Bureau of Alcohol, Tobacco and Firearms, and for good measure, the "position of Surgeon General."

The platform has one demand that is quite sensible—namely "The Party does not support governmental subsidies, tariffs, bailouts, or other forms of corporate welfare [including sports stadiums] that are used to protect and preserve businesses or industries that have failed to remain relevant, competitive, and efficient over time."

President Bush made his fortune by getting Texas taxpayers to pay for the Texas Rangers' new baseball stadium. His government now expands corporate welfare on the backs of individual taxpayers, while allowing huge tax escapes for large multinational corporations.

If you want to read more, log onto www.texasgop.org/library/RPTPlatform2002.pdf. But if you've read this far, you may be asking: How did this astonishing Texas GOP vs. Bush come about. It has to do with the double life of the Republican Party—the main party dominated by corporatists and the adjunct party relying on conservatives and libertarians to produce the margin of votes for victory in elections.

The corporatist Republicans give the platforms and the core ideological issues to the conservatives, pat them on the back at convention time, and then move into office with the welcome mat for Big Business lobbyists and their slush funds.

This duplicity is illustrated by the large contributions that the national Republican Party takes from the gambling industry in return for political support. In contrast, the Texas party platform states that "gambling has had a devastating impact on many Texas families" and opposes "any further legalization, government facilitation, or financial guarantees relating to any type of gambling."

In a letter to President Bush, I called on him to engage in truth-in-advertising and let the voters of this country know which provisions of his own state party's platform he endorses and which ones he opposes. For all their faults, the media do not like forked tongues and will sooner or later demand "clarification."

As for the Democratic Party, why didn't it make hay with this platform, as the Republicans surely would have if the shoe was on the other foot. Why? Because the Democratic Party *is* hay.

October 4, 2003

The Corporatist Democratic Leadership Council

Al From, the founder and soul of the soulless Democratic Leadership Council (DLC), assembled his flock in Philadelphia recently and warned his comrades about a takeover of the Democratic Party by "the far left." Launched in 1985, the "far right" DLC grew to have a controlling interest in the party through the efforts of then-Governor Bill Clinton, Senator John Breaux, Senator Al Gore, and Senator Joseph Lieberman.

If there were a superlative to the word "hubris," it would come close to describing Al From and his DLC cohorts. With unseemly regularity, they take credit for all Democratic victories as having been rooted in their philosophy of turn-your-back-on-organized-labor and open-your-pockets-to-corporations (who fund the DLC, incidentally). All Democratic defeats are explained as owing to losing candidates being too "left" or too "populist."

The DLC brags about one of their own—Bill Clinton—developing the message that brought the Democrats the White House in 1992, after the disastrous failure of the supposedly ultraliberal candidacies of Walter Mondale in 1984 and Michael Dukakis in 1988. Clinton insiders will tell you that Ross Perot (and his 19 million voters) was more responsible for beating President George H. W. Bush than the DLC strategy.

So what is the explanation when two of their very own, Gore and Lieberman, lost what should have been a landslide election in 2000? Soon after the election was stolen by the Bushites and the Supreme Court, From's group gathered to post-mortem the reasons why Gore lost (although he won) and concluded it was because he chanted populism ("I will represent the people, not the powerful"). A few months later, Lieberman agreed with From, saying he would not have campaigned with words that criticized industries like the oil, insurance, drug, and HMO barons. (To his credit, From has not blamed the Greens.)

But Gore won the election—both the popular and, as subsequent reviews documented, the electoral vote in Florida as well. (See Jeffrey Toobin's book *Too Close to Call*.) Instead of going after the still-operating perpetrators of this theft in Florida and pushing for national electoral reform that not only accurately counts all the votes but eliminates the disenfranchisement of citizens from the voting rolls, the DLC continues its ideological tautologies.

Observers are still waiting for the DLC to explain how, with Democratic candidates espousing its protective imitation of Republicanism, the party could lose more governorships, more state legislatures, and both the U.S. House and Senate. Overall, it has been downhill since the DLC drove the party into groveling haplessness beneath corporate lobbies and their corrupting campaign contributions.

As the *New Republic*, a fan of the DLC, reported, the party deliberately chose conservative Democratic challengers to win back the House in 1998 and 2000, only to have them go down in defeat. DLC-type Democratic Senate incumbents went down to defeat in 2002, plaintively expressing their support for George W. Bush's warmongering and pro-super-wealthy tax policies.

To the DLC mind, Democrats are catering to "special interests" when they stand up for trade unions, regulatory consumer-investor protections, a pre-emptive peace policy overseas, pruning the bloated military budget now devouring fully half of the federal government's entire discretionary expenditures, defending social security from Wall Street schemes, and pressing for universal health care coverage.

So right-wing is the DLC, mounted imperiously on its sagging party, that even opposing Bush's tax cuts for the wealthy that cause huge federal deficits and program cuts in necessities such as health, education, environmental protection, and the well-being of children, is considered ultraliberal and contrary to winning campaigns.

"Special interests" to the DLC means defending the rights of African Americans, Hispanics, and blue-collar workers, and securing a full day in court for wrongfully injured Americans. Being serious about consumer justice and environmental protection also raises DLC's eyebrows.

It is hard to discern how much is left of the Democratic Party's raison d'e-tre when these activities are excluded.

In 1995, Al From emerged from a closed-door meeting with Silicon Valley executives and announced his support for their restrictive legislation, which passed and made it harder for defrauded investors to hold the responsible outfits accountable. Al From was on another mission that day—raising money from these same computer industry moguls.

Small wonder that the DLC is not exactly hard on the ensuing corporate crime wave that has looted or drained trillions of dollars from millions of investors and pensions.

So far right is the corporatist DLC that it believes that the party can move toward Republican positions and still maintain its voting base among labor and minorities because they have nowhere else to go. Maybe that is one reason so many of these voters are staying home.

Liberal Republican senators in the '70s, such as Jacob Javits (New York) and Chuck Percy (Illinois), would now be considered on the left wing of the DLC-dominated Democratic Party.

Besides, what does the Democratic Party win if it loses its historic principles as the party of working people and the downtrodden? Nothing more than the right to take marching orders from its corporate paymasters.

August 1, 2003

The All-Knowing, Instinct-Driven President

With the chicken-hawk-driven war on Iraq in high gear, Bush and Cheney have learned that the best way to silence the Democratic Party, distract from their miserable domestic outrages, and provide the corporate and rich classes with favors is to envelop our nation in fear.

Using false or distorted statements, contrary to the findings of U.S. intelligence agencies, to exaggerate Iraqi threats, weapons, and terrorist (al-Qaeda) connections as reasons for the war, the invasion and prolonged occupation may produce greater risks of stateless terrorism in the United States. Last fall, the CIA informed Congress of just this higher probability resulting from an Iraqi invasion.

Watching reports describing our draft-dodging president as totally immersed in the scope and details of his Iraqi invasion, a number of puzzling questions arise:

1) Why is Bush pouring half of the entire U.S. military at huge cost into the Persian Gulf while rejecting the frantic requests by cities and states (such as New York City) for overdue monies for homeland security?

2) What will Bush say to Americans if no weaponized nuclear, chemical, or biological materials are found in Iraq or, if found, not used? The CIA told Bush that Saddam would be more likely to use these chemical and biological weapons if the United States invades. (*60 Minutes* World War II vet Andy Rooney

believes we ourselves would use these weapons if a powerful foreign invasion was overwhelming our country.)

3) With domestic necessities of the American people being ignored, why is Bush pushing Congress for yet another huge tax cut for the wealthy while Alan Greenspan is warning about larger budget deficits this year and afterwards?

4) Albeit surrounded by his little clique of ideologues, why has Bush refused requests for a meeting from thirteen major antiwar groups representing tens of millions of Americans? They include labor, business, clergy, human rights, war veterans, academics with national security experience, physicians, and elected city officials—all with important information for him. Some have battle experience in the Gulf and know about toxic exposures to our troops. Others have returned from Iraq with firsthand knowledge about conditions. Still others are steeped in the boomerang effect of ill-advised belligerence and distraction from more serious global conflicts and struggles against sabotage.

Tony Blair in London spoke for nearly an hour with a delegation from the National Council of Churches headed by former Congressman Bob Edgar. Yet the Council leaders have been rejected by their own president for the past year. There is the cause-and-effect of history that Bush needs to know about in the Middle East. Maybe he would not have used the word "crusade" or have invoked God's will and his divine guidance regarding overthrowing Saddam. Such references are viewed in Islamic societies as meaning a religious war.

But Bush does not seek any advice, information, or insights from these informed Americans. He ignored all their written requests.

5) Immersed in Iraq, Bush pays little attention to America. He is spending far more time on the Middle East, and destructively so, than on the manufacturing decline of the Middle West. And he wants to cut veterans' benefits. His unchallenged domination of the mass media leaves little space for others to raise these issues.

Have you heard about opportunity cost (or opportunities lost) of his messianic militarism lately? No attention to a long frozen minimum wage, worsening poverty, skyrocketing drug prices along with soaring consumer bills for oil and natural gas. Have you heard about advances needed for energy efficiency and solar power and less gas-guzzling motor vehicles? Bush has put America on hold!

6) What is a weapon of mass destruction anyhow? Ask Iraqi families whether or not Bush has sent weapons of mass destruction from the air, from the sea, and on land, to smash their country and destroy tens of thousands of lives in order to topple one man. Haven't the economic sanctions blocking medicines, surgical materials, and sanitation purifiers for clean drinking water

taken the lives of enough Iraqi children over a decade? Deliberately making civilians suffer for a military overthrow of a dictator happens to be a violation of international law.

7) Why did know-it-all Bush, who ironically brags about making decisions from his gut, stifle dissent from his war policy and its likely aftermath that still simmers at sub-cabinet levels inside the Pentagon, the CIA, and the State Department? Leading retired generals, admirals, diplomats, and national security officials tried to articulate the same criticism publicly over the past few months.

Except for the oil and munitions industries, the war is a downer on the economy. A few business executives have spoken up strongly. Most are not prone to speak publicly for fear of retaliation by the Bush administration, which, in this area, is believed to be vindictive against corporate dissenters.

From the big Geneva, Switzerland auto show last month, *Automotive News'* executive editor, Peter Brown of Detroit, talked to many European auto executives. He writes: "Personally, most of the executives oppose the war as unnecessary and likely to lead to greater terrorism and instability." This is pretty much the judgment of most of the U.S. foreign policy establishment whose prominent ex-government officials are also being ignored by the all-knowing, instinct-driven president.

April 3, 2003

A Judicially-Selected Dictator

As this is written, the campaign known as "shock and awe" has begun over Iraq and the five million civilian inhabitants of Baghdad. Bombs indeed shock, but why the word "awe"? This is Defense Secretary Donald Rumsfeld's way of turning the Iraq bombardment against what he knows is a defenseless country, run by a brutal dictator, into a metaphor for the rest of the world. He wants the whole world in "awe" of the mighty military superpower in preparation for the next move against another country in or outside the "axis of evil."

This is truly an extraordinary time in American history. A dozen men and one woman are making very risky consequential decisions sealed off from much muted dissent inside the Pentagon, the State Department, the CIA, and other agencies that have warned the president and his small band of ideological cohorts to think more deeply before they leap. They are launching our nation into winning a war that will generate later battles that may not be winnable— at least not without great economic and human costs to our country.

But let's back up a moment. Our founding fathers most emphatically placed the war-making power in the hands of Congress. They did not want some arrogant or brooding successor to King George III to plunge the country into war. They wanted a collegial body of many elected representatives to decide openly (Article I, section 8).

Last year, Congress, with leaders of both parties, surrendered its war-making power to George W. Bush. This itself is unlawful. But unfortunately, there is no judicial remedy for any citizen to challenge assigning the war-making power to the president. Senator Robert Byrd (D–WV) eloquently and repeatedly objected to this constitutional abdication. The large majority of Congress just shrugged. They knew that there was no punishment for this institutional crime.

Mr. Bush, on the other hand, was only too eager to strip the Congress of such authority, just as the attorney general, both by action and by demanding and receiving such crushers of civil liberties as the so-called U.S. Patriot Act, was eager to diminish the role of the judiciary. Having turned our federal system of separation of powers between three branches into a one-branch hegemony, Mr. Bush proceeded to flout the U.N. Charter, which the United States mostly drafted and signed on to in 1945.

His preemptive war—the first in U.S. history—against a nation that has neither attacked nor threatened our country cannot be construed as self-defense and therefore violates international law. Washington would certainly make exactly this point were another nation in the world to attack a country it finds noxious.

Then how do the arguments for going to war that Bush has made endlessly in the mass media for a year, without a steady rebuttal by the cowering Democratic Party, stand up? Bush's assertion that Iraq is reconstituting its nuclear weapons program is based on evidence that Congressman Henry Waxman called a "hoax." In a blistering letter to the president on March 17, Congressman Waxman all but called Bush's assertion that Iraq was seeking uranium from Niger a lie, citing both the CIA and the International Atomic Energy Agency as his authorities. Neither agency has evidence of a rebuilding nuclear weapons program.

President Bush has repeatedly tried to tie Iraq with Al-Qaeda. There is no evidence to support these allegations. The two are mortal enemies—one secular and the other fundamentalist. The CIA informed Congress that confronted with a U.S. overthrow attack, Saddam Hussein, the ally we formerly supplied, "probably would become much less constrained in adopting terrorist actions." Even then, analysts have published articles casting doubt on the efficacy of whatever mass destruction weapons he may have against a modern air and missile attack followed by spread-out armored vehicles racing toward a surrendering army.

The UN inspectors found nothing in their forays inside Iraq before Bush stopped their increasing penetration of that regime.

On March 18, the *Washington Post,* which avidly favors the war, felt obliged to publish a story by two of its leading reporters titled, "Bush Clings to Dubious Allegations About Iraq." The article questioned a "number of allegations" that the Bush administration is making against Iraq that "have been challenged—and in some cases disproved—by the United Nations, European governments and even U.S. intelligence reports."

Now that the short war has begun, it is hoped that there will be minimum casualties on both sides. But after the U.S. military prevails, the longer battles during occupation begin. They are fires, disease, hunger, plunder and looting by desperate people and roving gangs, and bloodletting between major religious and ethnic factions.

U.S. intelligence agencies say the Iraq war will likely increase global terrorism, including inside this country. Respected retired military generals and admirals, such as Marine General Anthony Zinni, believe it will destabilize the Middle East region, undermine the war on terrorism, and distract from the Israeli-Palestinian conflict. "King George" is not listening to them or to other prominent former leaders in the State Department, Pentagon, or the major intelligence agencies, including his father's own National Security Advisor, Brent Scowcroft.

This must be the only war in our history promoted by chicken hawks—former belligerent draft dodgers—and opposed by so many of those inside and outside of government who served in the armed forces.

Still the messianic militarist in the White House refuses to even listen—either to opposing viewpoints held by tens of millions of Americans or to viewpoints counseling other nonwar ways to achieve the objectives in Iraq. Indeed, he has refused to meet with any domestic antiwar delegation. Groups representing veterans, labor, business, elected city officials, women, clergy, physicians, and academics with intelligence experience have written requesting an audience (See www.essentialaction.org).

Michael Kinsley is a sober, bright columnist who said that "in terms of the power he now claims, George W. Bush is now the closest thing in a long time to dictator of the world." One might also use a Canadian phrase—an elected dictator. Correction—a judicially-selected dictator.

March 21, 2003

The Robo-Candidate

Walking down a busy street in downtown Washington recently, I began to hear interesting words coming from an excitable conversation between two gentlemen briskly walking behind me. "Do you have any idea what is emerging?," one said to the other. "We're perfecting the robo-candidate from Washington, D.C. and making it seem like it's local."

It turned out the latest robo-candidate they were talking about was Republican Senate candidate Suzanne Haik Terrell who, at this writing, is in a runoff race with a Louisiana Democrat, Senator Mary Landrieu. "We now can select the candidate from any state to beat the Democrats, frame the issues, convey the slogans, raise the money, buy the television ads, and even provide the robo-rebuttals for the debates. Hah, hah, hah, whoopee," said the fast-walking fellow who was the younger of the two.

The other fellow was no less exuberant. He added: "And we bring in Bush and Air Force One for the finale with total media coverage totally unchallenged. It's working again and again. The Dems are in a panic, falling all over themselves to agree with the president. Landrieu even has a television ad showing how many times she agrees with Bush." As they turned the corner, they couldn't stop laughing.

The duo was actually understating what the Republicans are doing to the Democrats who years ago forgot who they were. All kinds of national Republicans—Vice President Cheney, Urban Development Secretary Mel R. Martinez, Senate Minority leader Trent Lott and others—have gone into Louisiana to campaign for Terrell. Landrieu doesn't want any national Democrats to do the same. Only her fellow Democrat, conservative Senator John Breaux, is doing the honors from campaign event to campaign event.

Robo-politics, Republican style, is also quite visible. Terrell's campaign headquarters in the state capital, Baton Rouge, is tiny, reports the *Washington Post*. She made only one appearance the weekend before Saturday's election day, while relying on huge television buys to get her robo-message (smaller government, less taxes, bigger military and, surprise, she's against terrorism).

Meanwhile, back in Washington, D.C., the Republican National Committee offices are "Terrell Central." The RNC is running the show right down to the words used in the debates: "You're 100 percent wrong, Mary, and you are so negative." Where have we heard those words before November 7 around the country? Everywhere!

After losing more seats in the House and losing control of the Senate, the Democratic strategists seemed to have learned nothing. Enron is close to Louisiana; so is WorldCom. Yet, corporate crime, fraud, and abuse, looted pensions, laid-off workers and depleted 401ks are not made into major issues where the corporate-indentured Republicans are at their weakest. All kinds of corporate crime crackdowns and reforms of Big Business and health care-denying HMOs, could appeal to pollution-drenched Louisiana and its past populist traditions. So could the living wage issue.

Somehow, the Democrats believe they can beat the opposing Republican Party by never criticizing its leader—George W. Bush—America's burgeoning Big Brother whose snooping, liberty-violating, and anti-worker ways are getting a free ride on the backs of our crumbling democracy, while giant corporations are laughing all the way to the bank on the backs of the small taxpayers who are forced to subsidize them.

And there is Suzie Terrell sticking to her RNC-inspired lines: "He will know when Suzie Terrell doesn't agree. I'm going to stand firm and strong for Louisiana," she told a smiling George W. Bush at the rally on December 3. In Republican circles, this is called the "independence streak" line to counter charges that she and other such choreographed candidates by the RNC and the White House's Karl Rove are going to be rubber stamps for the president.

The RNC even knows when to let the robo-candidate switch back on cue. Will the Democrats ever free themselves of all that corporate money and wake up?

December 6, 2002

The Tweedledee and Tweedledum Midterm Elections

The midterm elections are over. After spending hundreds of millions of business dollars, the Republicans now control the Senate and hold on to the House of Representatives. It is amazing that the Democrats did not do worse. They had decided months ago on a strange strategy—they were going to defeat the Republicans by not criticizing their belligerent leader, George W. Bush.

In their ads, literature, and debates between congressional candidates, mention of Mr. Bush by them was to praise, not to challenge or expose the hypocrisy and the damage to American workers and consumers by this corporation president.

Listening to the debates from around the country on C-SPAN radio, I was astonished to hear Democratic candidates in tight races eager to show their support for Bush's 2001 tax cut for the wealthy, for the giveaway war resolution authority on Iraq, and for Bush's federal drive to take over the historic role of the states in personal injury law by restricting Americans' right to their full day in court.

And what did Senate Democrat candidates such as Jean Shaheen in New Hampshire and Senator Max Cleland of Georgia get for their support of

President Bush? Why he roared into their states on Air Force One and campaigned against them, as he did against other Democrats who voted with him on these and other Republican litmus paper tests.

The morning after election day, reporters asked Senate Majority Leader Tom Daschle why the Democrats lost. He replied, because the Democrats were "up against a very popular president." That's a self-fulfilling point. Asked the same question, Democratic Party Chairman Terry McAuliffe answered: "Because they [the Republicans] outspent us." But it was the Republican House speaker who gave the accurate response: "Because the Democrats did not have a message."

At a time of rising unemployment, a shaky economy, and growing Republican deficits, it would seem that the Democrats had opportunities. Yet while the Republicans were shamelessly touting ending the estate tax for the four thousand estates a year that are in the multimillion dollar category, the Democrats were not highlighting the desperate need for raising the federal minimum wage (now about one-third less in purchasing power than it was in 1968!) and extending unemployment compensation benefits.

Most Democrats, with the prominent exception of the late Senator Paul Wellstone, took a dive on making Republican softness on corporate crime a major issue, coupled with solid reform proposals to crack down on corporate scandals that stole billions from pension funds and 401ks and cost many jobs.

Namby-pamby was the Democratic routine on the increasing millions of Americans without health care coverage and on the staggering inefficiency, waste, and greed of many giant HMOs and the drug industry.

Although the Democrats had in their possession finely tuned economic stimulus plans, they tied their own hands by declining to go after a bloated military budget (now half of the U.S. government's entire nondiscretionary budget) and the tens of billions of dollars in yearly corporate welfare subsidies and handouts.

Instead, the Democrats' economic agenda was the raising of big bucks from business interests—a sure way to silence championing the peoples' necessities.

When the Democratic Party adopts a look-alike strategy vis-a-vis the Republican Party, some of their voters may prefer the real thing and vote Republican. After all, only a shift of less than three hundred thousand votes in key states would have given the Democrats control of both Houses of Congress.

Amidst the din of endlessly repeated political television ads, it wasn't made very clear that the Democrats were going after the Republicans on down-home consumer protection issues, such as insurance and food safety and affordable housing. Environmental positions regarding cleaner air and water were not prominent either.

Lessons for the future? Don't give your major political opponents a free ride between and before elections. Challenge the corporate takeover of elections, including the sudden surge of political television advertising paid directly by industries like the big price-gouging drug companies. And get down to the neighborhood level with visible stands for the people.

Otherwise the Democrats will become even better at electing very bad Republicans.

November 7, 2002

Open Letter to the Democratic Party

The Democrats should have an easy time winning control of the House of Representatives and the Senate in next week's election. Recession is deepening, unemployment is rising, and corporate corruption headlines are proliferating. Health care costs, drug prices, and the number of Americans without health care coverage are all increasing. Median household incomes are falling. Corporate crime has heavily depleted 401Ks and other pension losses.

These should all help the Democrats win against the corporate-indentured Republicans marinated in corporate cash, soft on corporate and environmental crimes, and demonstrably antilabor.

Why then is the overall contest for party control of Congress too close to call? Because Democrats are not clearly, relentlessly, and aggressively emphasizing these fundamental issues to distinguish themselves from the Republicans. Why? Are they unaware, neglectful, or torpid? No, their chronic ambiguity flows from being largely indentured to the same monied commercial interests as the Republicans.

So Governor Shaheen of New Hampshire, running for the U.S. Senate, refers to corporate crime as "corporate mismanagement" and other Democratic candidates are allowing the Republicans to blur key poll-tested issues like prescription drug benefits, tax cuts for the super-wealthy, and corporate crime enforcement.

Voters want to know whose side candidates are on in their daily struggles as workers, consumers, patients, small taxpayers, and savers, on the one hand, and, on the other hand, the giant corporations that pay for control of our government in order to get all the goodies that come out of the hides of working families. Fairness is the great issue in American politics, stupid!

Franklin Delano Roosevelt and the Democrats won election after election by conveying one singularly clear impression—that the Republican Party was beholden to the wealthy and the Democratic Party represented the working people. Karl Rove, in the Bush White House, understands this history. That is why he is engaged in the "blur and spur" strategy of fuzzing the hot-button issues to portray the Republicans as fighters for ordinary Americans, instead of the big businesses that own them. This is also why the Republicans are using the spur of the drumbeats of war to distract the country away from pressing domestic necessities, injustices, and hazards.

By a margin of nearly two to one the American people do not want a war against Iraq that involves an invasion, American casualties, and essentially having the United States go it alone. Not when rigorous UN inspectors can go to Iraq first.

Even more Americans would join these citizens if the mass media relayed the facts about how boxed in the militarily weakened dictator of Iraq is, surrounded by more powerful enemies (Iran, Turkey, Israel), two-thirds of his country out of his rigid control (no fly zones), deterred, contained, and under twenty-four-hour satellite surveillance.

More voters would be antiwar if there was greater media discussion about the likelihood of awful civilian casualties and sickness among the innocent children and adults of Iraq. Voters would also be antiwar if Americans were given the facts about the opposition to the touted conduct of this war from inside the Pentagon among retired military officers and other experts who believe the risks of undermining the effort against terrorism, of generating a boomerang of domestic terrorism around the world and an endemic civil war in Iraq (where the United States stays as expensive occupier) are not worth toppling the government of Iraq by a unilateral invasion.

When a group of Gulf War veterans had a news conference at the National Press Club in Washington on October 24 to point out some of these consequences (which included conditions leading to the sickness of 128,000 Gulf War veterans in 1991), the media did not show up. (For their statements, see www.veteransforcommonsense.org).

The "cakewalk" view of the planned war, widely espoused by the circle of chicken hawks surrounding George W. Bush, is obscuring serious public debate about another possible outcome—diverse human and economic consequences adverse to U.S. and global security during and after the war.

The Democrats can still raise their voices for the people in the next few days before November 5, if they understand that waffling rarely wins campaigns. The people want straight talk and real action.

October 30, 2002

Holding Political Candidates' Feet to the Fire
on Corporate Crime

When the revelations of crime and deception poured out of the executive suites of Enron, Tyco, WorldCom, and other corporations earlier this year, politicians—particularly sitting members of the Senate and the House of Representatives—unleashed a blizzard of news releases to denounce corporate crime.

Never mind that many of these same politicians had long been neck-deep in schemes to weaken (if not outright eliminate) regulation and remove the regulatory cops needed to uncover and stop the kind of corporate shenanigans that destroyed the Enrons and left thousands of workers without jobs and pensions—and investors holding worthless stock of bankrupt companies.

The politicians were betting that some well-honed news releases and a few speeches expressing outrage back home would be enough to take voters' minds off the scandals and the human misery left in the wake of the corporate excesses.

Unfortunately, it is probably a good bet. Too often in the past that has been the case—a quick outburst of anger and concern and then back to business as usual.

When hundreds of savings and loans failed in the 1980s followed by the greatest rash of bank collapses since the Depression, there was a national uproar and a string of congressional investigations. Some regulatory reforms did get through Congress, but less than a decade later the financial industry was back on Capitol Hill demanding deregulation once again. Despite the recent financial disasters, Congress agreed to the new deregulation in 1999 and many of the financial combinations created by that deregulation are intertwined in the current corporate scandals.

Are we about to repeat this same sad cycle in dealing with the current corporate fraud and crime wave that has cost millions of Americans trillions of dollars? Will this year's headlines, a few limited reforms and a tap on the wrist be the end result—with no real protections in place for the public, investors, workers, and the economy? We should not allow such a result. We need to prove that our political and economic system is better than that. We can make lasting, effective change as citizens. This time, we need to keep the issues on the front burner until we have true reforms, not fake facsimiles that do nothing but lull the public into a false sense of security.

As part of that effort, this year I am asking candidates for the U.S. Senate and the House of Representatives to sign a ten-point pledge that contains provisions that will put teeth in the crackdown on corporate crime. The pledge includes a promise that the candidate will support legislation that would give shareholders the right to democratically nominate and elect the board of directors and approve all major business decisions, such as mergers and acquisitions above $1 billion in value and the compensation packages of top executives. The pledge would also promise support for a ban on corporate criminals obtaining government contracts and banning government contracts for companies that relocate their headquarters offshore to avoid taxes.

Signers would also pledge to strengthen pension reforms and rein in excessive pay for corporate chief executives as well as establishing a federally chartered nonprofit Financial Consumers Association joined by millions of American investors that would represent consumers before legislative and regulatory bodies.

The pledge also contains a promise to repeal the notorious Private Securities Litigation Reform Act (1995) that shields the aiders and abetters of corporate crime, such as accounting and law firms, from civil liability. The pledge also calls on signers to support the regulation of derivatives trading.

Candidates would also pledge to support the establishment of a Congressional Commission on Corporate Power to explore various legal and economic proposals that would rein in unaccountable giant global corporations. The commission would seek ways to improve on the current state corporate chartering system and propose ways to correct the unfair legal status of corporations such as the doctrine of corporate personhood.

In addition to holding political candidates' feet to the fire on corporate crime, we need to continue to energize and enlist citizens in the effort to crackdown on corporate crime. An upcoming effort in mobilizing citizen support will be a rally on Wall Street on Friday, October 4.

The rally, sponsored by Democracy Rising (See www.democracyrising.org) is designed to focus attention to ongoing corporate crime and to propose remedies to help shareholders, taxpayers, workers, and consumers. The rally will be on the steps of City Hall directly facing the New York Stock Exchange. Reformers are going to take the issue right to the New York Stock Exchange.

Citizens across the nation have the power to change corporate behavior if they will stick with the issue over the coming weeks and into the next Congress. We will be pushing forward with "The Candidate's Pledge to Crackdown on Corporate Crime," but citizens should raise the issue of corporate crime directly with congressional candidates in their hometowns and demand that they produce more than news releases and speeches. This time we need to get real reform before the issues fade and the politicians find another convenient rug under which the crimes can be swept.

October 1, 2002

The Highway Robbery Lobby

Ever since the first public transit—a ferryboat near Boston in 1630—got underway, a broad variety of carriers has emerged—buses, trolleybuses, vanpools, jitneys, heavy and light rail, cable cars, monorails, tramways, and automated guideway transit. Rarely did these transports ever attract private investment—that was reserved for The Car on publicly funded and maintained highways.

In the year 2000, Americans took 9.4 billion trips on public transportation, an increase of 3.5 percent from 1999. But in 1946 Americans recorded 23.4 billion trips, which is still unsurpassed even though the population was only half of what it is today. What happened to account for the decline of public transit, which is safer, more efficient, less polluting, and reduces highway congestion while stimulating nearby economic development?

The major answer to this question is the long-standing opposition of The Highway Lobby—the auto, oil, tire, and cement industries. You don't hear much these days about "The Highway Lobby" as such. The reason is that it has done its destructive job, which is to make America an occasion for ribbons of crowded highways carrying millions of motor vehicles as the only "practical and direct" way to get around on the ground.

At times the lobby has had to resort to crime to achieve its assaults on public transit, while at other periods, it just used its money, muscle, and propaganda with state and Washington lawmakers. Twenty-eight crimes were committed by General Motors and its oil and tire company co-conspirators in the '30s and '40s leading to their convictions in federal district court in Chicago during the late '40s. The U.S. Justice Department's charge, upheld in court, was that these large companies, in order to eliminate their major rivals—the trolley industry—bought up these firms, tore up the tracks in and around twenty-eight major cities in the United States, including the biggest one in Los Angeles, and lobbied legislators to build more and more highways to sell more and more vehicles, gasoline, and tires. Earlier, GM tried to pressure banks to reduce credit to these trolley companies and when that did not succeed sufficiently, the conspiracy to buy out their competitors and shut them down was hatched.

This is more than corporate crime history. Everyday, today, tomorrow, and the next day, millions of Americans find themselves on clogged, bumper-to-bumper commutes because there is no convenient mass transit or no mass transit at all where they live and work.

Lots of people have little or no idea of all the flexible and super-modern modes of public transit that reach all the way toward something called "personal public transit," which would allow you and fellow passengers to call up a mono-rail car to take you to your destination in some future resurgence of public transit technology.

First, change must replace the dominant highway lobby imagery with sleek public transit imagery. For example, have you ever seen a television advertise-ment for a new car stuck in congested traffic? By contrast, have you ever seen an ad for public transit showing people zooming to work in a modern transit train, while they were snoozing, chatting, or reading the newspaper, and rac-ing ahead of a parallel highway clogged with trucks, vans, and cars moving in slow motion? Fifty years of this bias and it is not surprising how low the pub-lic's expectations have become.

Second, the bias has translated into the reality of residential, shopping, and other developments geared to the car and inimical to public transit in a vicious circle of reinforcement for the highway lobby's designs for America.

Still, there are the public transit optimists. Every other month I receive and read a magazine called *Transit California*, published by the California Transit Association.

The current issue is full of news regarding innovative advances and expan-sions in public transit from Santa Monica to Santa Clara Valley to Contra Costa County and various kinds of public transportation delivered to residents.

The Association will be having its thirty-seventh annual fall conference in Ontario, California (info@caltransit.org) and would be pleased to hear from interested communities writing to the CTA, 1414 K Street, Suite 320, Sacramento, CA 95814.

August 29, 2002

The Exclusionary Commission on Presidential Debates (CPD)

On the evening of October 3, 2000, the misnamed Commission on Presidential Debates (CPD) ignored my ticket-in-hand to go to an adjoin-ing auditorium on the campus of the University of Massachusetts to watch the Gore-Bush debate on closed-circuit television. With a state trooper by his side, the "security consultant" for the CPD made it very clear that I should leave the campus of a public university.

The CPD is not a governmental entity, despite its official sounding name. It is a private corporation, created in 1987 by the Republican and Democratic Parties to replace the League of Women Voters and control every iota of debate frequency, format, location, participation, selection of the questioner, etc. By securing the television networks coverage to the exclusion of all other potential sponsors, the CPD is a private corporate monopoly with access to tens of millions of voters in the crucial month of October.

The CPD's arrogance and misuse of the Massachusetts police to exclude me from the campus because of my political criticism of the CPD and my running on the Green Party ticket invited a response. On October 5, I sent a letter to the CPD demanding an official apology and a contribution of $25,000 to the nonprofit Appleseed Center for Electoral Reform at Harvard Law School. The CPD refused. On October 17, 2000, I filed suit in federal district court in Boston charging a violation of my civil rights.

After losing all court motions to dismiss the case, the CPD, having spent about $500,000, decided to settle just before trial. We requested the sum we had asked for in October 2000. The corporate lawyers for the commission agreed, on behalf of their client and cochairs, Republican Frank Fahrenkopf, Jr. and Democrat Paul Kirk, Jr., to send a letter of apology and $25,000.

Their attorney, for all those staggering legal fees, had to do something to reduce the CPD's embarrassment. So they insisted that the money go to pay our up-to-then pro bono attorneys, Howard Friedman and Jason Adkins. Which was what we were intending to do all along. And, of course, as is customary in a settlement agreement, the CPD denied all liability, as did their security consultant who also paid $26,000.

No sooner the ink was dry on the settlement agreement than the spin flaks for the CPD swung into their distortions. They found a *Boston Globe* columnist to say that the victory—receiving twice what we asked for in October 2000—was a defeat. The columnist called the settlement sums "chump change." He discounted the apology as just a formalism to get rid of the lawsuit, which, of course, arose out of a rejected demand by us for an apology.

The depositions and discovery during the pretrial period elicited some useful material for follow-up by reporters. The CPD's consultant produced a "face book" with photographs of the four third-party presidential and vice-presidential candidates as a guide to their enforcement personnel. If any of them showed up, such as Pat Buchanan of the Reform Party, they also were to be excluded from the campus—again based only on their contrary political views.

Exclusion is the CPD's main reason for being. It sets up a near impossible Catch-22—requiring for entry to the debate stage a third-party candidate achieving an average of 15 percent in five named polls by September. Low polls, little media, little media, low polls. It mattered not that it takes just 5 percent for a third party to receive federal matching funds in the next election cycle four years later. It mattered not to the CPD that several major national polls reported a majority of the responding Americans wanting me and Buchanan in the debates. One Fox poll reached 64 percent.

Looking ahead, the very bipartisan CPD needs to be decisively displaced by a broad-based peoples' presidential debate association that is nonpartisan and is not under the control of any party, parties, candidate, or candidates.

A decaying political system cannot regenerate itself unless it opens its doors on the ballot and on the debates to third parties. Historically, when given a chance, minor parties have done just that, especially in the nineteenth century before high ballot barriers and debate commissions arrived on the scene.

Third-party candidates could campaign in all fifty states, could be on the ballot in most or all states, could attract large audiences and still manage to reach less than 2 percent of the voters that being on just one televised debate could reach.

Nature allows seeds to sprout to regenerate itself. Without small business and innovators having a chance, the business world could not regenerate itself. It is time to open the highways and level the playing fields. It is also time for public funding of public elections and some free access to the electronic media—which uses our public airwaves—for ballot-qualified candidates.

Readers interested in joining the effort to start a new presidential debates organization can write to Debates, P.O. Box 19312, Washington, D.C. 20036 about how they are willing to help.

May 1, 2002

Soft Campaign Reforms

One of the hardest decisions for citizen reform groups to make when supporting legislation that has been pending for years is how much weakening they will tolerate before they break away in opposition.

Campaign finance reform in Congress, after years of struggle by coalition groups such as Common Cause and Public Citizen, passed and was unenthusiastically signed into law by President Bush last month. Popularly known as the McCain-Feingold bill (after Republican Senator John McCain and Democratic Senator Russ Feingold), this original reform of corrupt money in politics has been subjected to serious attrition. Originally, it provided for some free television and radio time for ballot-qualified candidates vying for federal office. That and other provisions were dropped in order to pick up support for passage—so much so that some observers began calling the legislation the "Cain-Gold" bill.

The core of the new law is banning "soft money"—those unlimited hundreds of millions of dollars mostly from business interests that flow only into the coffers of the political parties. But in return, McCain-Feingold had to agree to doubling "hard money" that any person could give directly to members of Congress or presidential candidates. Beginning after the 2002 elections, individuals can give $4,000 for an entire election cycle (primary and general election) instead of $2,000.

As congressional opponents and their outside patrons chipped away at the legislation during the past four years, the outside reform groups, which have been striving for reform of the auction system of elections for over two decades, continued to bite their lips and remained in support. First, it was "half a loaf is better than nothing;" then it was a quarter of a loaf. But then it became an unwillingness to turn against the legislation, given all those thousands of dedicated hours and a commitment to the idea of reform that had brought the process this far.

Well, one of the longtime citizen organizations concluded that the erosion of the legislation was too much to take. On March 20, the U.S. Public Interest Research Group (U.S. PIRG) denounced and opposed McCain-Feingold.

In its statement, U.S. PIRG said:

"In a climate of spiraling fundraising, and in the wake of the Enron debacle, Congress had the opportunity to pass real campaign finance reform that would have reduced the influence of money on American democracy. Unfortunately, politicians were not up to the task... the Senate passed a soft money 'ban' riddled with loopholes and actually increased the amount that the wealthiest individuals can contribute to candidates."

The partially student-funded PIRG predicted that "hard money will skyrocket, soft money will go to state and local parties and independent expenditures, candidates will not spend less time fundraising, and big donors will still buy election results to put their favored candidates in office."

The groups also predicted that President George W. Bush will become the first major-party candidate to refuse to accept voluntary spending limits in the 2004 general election. One Republican campaign manager has predicted that Bush could easily raise $500 million in hard dollars—an unheard of amount.

It was not easy for U.S. PIRG to oppose the bill.

April 3, 2002

Congress Feigns Shock over Enron

Enron, Enron, Enron—front page and center, top of the network television news, and the biggest criminally derived bankruptcy in U.S. history. A "gargantuan pyramid scheme," says Republican Senator Peter G. Fitzgerald.

Proposals for reform are gushing forth from congressional minds: tougher regulations to protect investors and pension holders from crooked self-dealing corporate executives and their compliant outside auditors.

No one is yet speaking of helping investors and pension holders organize themselves in order to defend themselves and provide the grassroots power to get the laws enforced. Last week the new chairman of the Securities and Exchange Commission, a former big-time attorney for the large accounting firms, Harvey L. Pitt, told a House of Representatives' investigating committee about his concern for ordinary defrauded people who trust their companies: "It is these Americans whose faith fuels our markets, who have no lobby and no trade associations, whose interests are, and must be, paramount. I am appalled at what happened to them as a result of Enron's collapse."

Ergo? Is Chairman Pitt implying that these ordinary people should continue to trust members of Congress to enact strong laws with enough funds for dutiful regulators to strongly enforce them? The lessons of history do not provide assurances for such trust. Does Chairman Pitt have a proposal to see that these faithful Americans have their own lobby? Not to my knowledge. Nor do members of Congress.

In his small, important book, *Here, the People Rule*, Harvard constitutional law professor, Richard Parker, argues that the federal government has an affirmative constitutional duty to facilitate the political and civic energies of the people. His point certainly finds resonance in Lincoln's words: "government of the people, by the people and for the people."

In 1974, I wrote my first article on the necessity to redress the imbalance between consumers and large companies—the latter being recipients of governmental privileges, such as legal monopolies or taxpayer subsidies—through mandatory inserts in company billing envelopes inviting consumers to band together in groups with full-time consumer advocates. The immediate occasion for this proposal was rising electricity rates, weak regulation, and powerless residential ratepayers.

But in the '80s, the savings and loans scandals started piling up. Corporate looters, mis-managers and their speculators put at risk or devoured tens of billions of dollars of ordinary peoples' savings. In September 1985, Representative Charles E. Schumer of New York, then perhaps more idealistic than today's Senator Schumer, introduced the Consumer Banking Act of 1985. A key provision of the legislation, Representative Schumer wrote, is establishing voluntary, membership-based, state-level Financial Consumers' Boards.

These self-funded, private boards "would act as an institutional watchdog for consumers' interests; representing citizens in financial services matters before regulatory agencies, legislatures, and the courts, and informing bank customers of these actions," he declared. These boards, the congressman added, would also conduct surveys, disseminate information such as shoppers' guides to financial services, as well as assist citizens in resolving consumer complaints.

Four years later, with an avalanche of collapsing S&Ls demanding a congressional bailout, Schumer's proposal was turned down in 1989, 1990, and 1991 by a large majority of the House Banking Committee members as they were passing massive taxpayer bailouts of these once-fiduciary institutions. And these boards would not have cost the taxpayer a penny, as the projected millions of members would become members after paying modest annual dues. An Illinois board, representing utility ratepayers, attracted over 150,000 members in that state within eighteen months of its establishment. In one negotiation nine years ago, this board persuaded Commonwealth Edison to refund $1.3 billion in overcharges to northern Illinois families.

Now comes Enron, capping a decade of casino capitalism and corporate crime, fraud, and abuse, chronicled in the *Wall Street Journal, Business Week, New York Times*, and other mainstream publications. How will investors and pension holders be able to protect their savings and retirement funds? By dusting off Representative Schumer's proposal and extending it across the entire financial industry to start Financial Consumer Associations in every state.

Let those who would be ripped off more easily organize themselves through facilities such as inserts in these companies' statements and bills that go out at least once a month to customers and beneficiaries.

For more information on this proposal during these momentous congressional hearings about what to do after Enron, contact Theresa Amato at Citizen Works, P.O. Box 18478, Washington, D.C. 20036, or visit www.Citizenworks.org or call 202-265-6164.

February 7, 2002

Congress Needs to Clamp Down on Future Enrons

Congress and the national media are feigning great shock and dismay over the revelations of accounting shenanigans in the collapse of Enron, the giant Texas-based energy corporation.

But the truth is that Congress and the financial media have long been aware of the accounting profession's shortcomings and its predilection to paint a rosy picture of their corporate clients—even when corporations were near collapse.

During the investigations of the savings and loan failures by the General Accounting Office (GAO), Congress, and the courts in the 1980s, questions were raised repeatedly about the failure of the accounting firms to find and report the problems that eventually led to the failure of hundreds of institutions and the loss of nearly one-half trillion dollars by taxpayers who were forced to bail out the industry. One GAO report, based on an analysis of eleven savings and loan failures, concluded that the auditors "didn't really try to determine what was going on." One congressional investigator suggested that "elephants were walking through the living room and the accountants missed them."

Despite the fact that Congress adopted a number of significant financial reforms in the wake of the savings and loan collapse, the practices of the accounting profession were largely left untouched. From 1995 through 1999, the Banking Committees of the House of Representatives and the Senate and the leadership of both Houses devoted great time and energy to what they described as "financial modernization." In reality, the exercise was simply old-fashioned corporate-driven deregulation of the financial industry, not "modernization."

Nonetheless, the hearings and the debate over the legislation provided a perfect opportunity for Congress to take another look at the accounting profession and its role in providing information for investors and regulators across key areas of the financial industry. In the end, Congress adopted legislation that allowed banks, insurance companies, and securities firms to merge under the umbrella of giant financial conglomerates. It certainly seemed that these new giants on the financial midway would need the maximum scrutiny if there was to be protection for consumers of financial products, investors and taxpayers who back the bank insurance funds.

It would be reasonable to assume that provisions for independent audits—truly independent audits—would be front and center in such far-reaching legislation. But, the two banking committees—and the bipartisan leadership of Congress—were not interested in consumer, investor, or taxpayer protections. They were interested only in meeting the demands of the financial industry and they refused to be bothered by regulatory and audit reforms.

Now, many of the same leaders who pushed the deregulation of the financial industry through Congress will be conducting investigations of what went wrong at Enron. And no one expects any mea culpas from members of Congress who failed to institute audit and other safeguards when the financial industry was salivating in its desire for the bank-insurance-securities conglomerates.

The Securities and Exchange Commission (SEC) needs to be given the assignment of licensing auditing firms. Leaving the licensing function with the fifty states means a crazy quilt of standards and oversight with the same shortcomings that plague the fifty separate state insurance departments in regulating multinational insurance companies. For large corporations, the SEC would assign qualified licensed firms at random to conduct audits, much as judges are assigned in federal courts. No company could select its own favorite auditor. Companies would continue to pay fees for the audits, but they would have no say in selecting their auditor.

In recent years, audit firms have become "consultants" to many companies in addition to carrying out audits. This practice has generated lucrative fees for the auditors and created a conflict of interest that destroys the independence so important to a credible audit. Legislation should prohibit accounting firms from accepting these consulting jobs for three years after they have conducted a financial audit of the company.

In addition to its licensing function, the SEC should establish a separate section that would monitor and supervise auditing firms much as the bank regulatory agencies supervise depository institutions. Congress needs to carry out full-scale investigations of Enron. But to leave the job as simply another splashy investigation for television would be a travesty. Congress needs to use this moment to atone for its failure to protect the public in the past by ensuring that there will be independent accurate information for investors, consumers, and regulatory bodies.

It is a tough job for a Congress riddled and compromised by large campaign contributions, not only from Enron but from the entire financial industry. But the job has to be done because there are other Enrons out there in the corporate world with variations on the scheme to deceive and dupe the public in their quest for easy profits. For more information on Enron visit the CitizenWorks.org web page.

January 24, 2002

Another Insurance Bailout

Last fall, the lobbyists for the insurance industry were swarming across Capitol Hill warning of dire consequences if Congress failed to enact federal assistance and guarantees to protect insurance companies from future losses from terrorist attacks.

In a transparent effort to stampede the legislators, the companies warned that credit for new construction would dry up unless there was taxpayer-backed reinsurance in place by the end of 2001.

The insurance lobbyists had hoped that Congress would respond to the fear tactics as they did so quickly in providing a $15 billion bailout for the airline industry within weeks of the September 11 attacks on the World Trade Center and the Pentagon. On second look, the need for the giveaway to the airlines seemed a lot less urgent and a lot more wasteful of taxpayers' money than the airline lobbyists had told Congress.

By the time the bailout for the insurance industry was being peddled on Capitol Hill, members of Congress were beginning to get complaints from back home and from consumer organizations about the unseemly rush to open up the Treasury vaults to the airlines. As a result, the pleas from the insurance industry faced a slightly more skeptical Congress that began to raise questions about the need for still another taxpayer subsidy.

The insurance bailout was still sitting there as unfinished business when Congress closed up shop and went home in late December. The issue will undoubtedly be revisited when Congress comes back in a few days, but now new information is beginning to surface that casts even more doubt on the tales of woe spun by the insurance lobbyists.

Surveys conducted by *The American Banker*, a daily newspaper published for the financial industry, reveals that few loans for construction projects are being rejected or called because of the lack of taxpayer-supported terror insurance.

"The banking industry is not going to immediately think every project is terror-prone and call-in loans or stop making new ones," reported the *American Banker*, quoting Maurice Hartigan, president of the RMA financial risk management association.

That is in contrast to the scare stories of last fall. Then Maurice Greenberg, chairman of the insurance giant AIG, was quoted as warning: "On January 1, you're going to see contractors and banks saying that all the loans they made may have had their covenants breached by not having full insurance."

But John Mastromarino, executive vice president for risk at Fleet Bank in Boston, scoffed at the idea that loans would be called. And another banker quoted in the *Banker* asked: "Why would a bank want to be stuck with a half-finished building by calling in a loan?"

There was also talk that federal bank regulators would put out guidance about curtailing credit because of insurance problems. But the *Banker* found no indication that the regulators had plans for such action.

Despite the lack of concern by bankers and regulators, the insurance industry isn't likely to give up using the September 11 attacks as a rationale for taxpayer subsidies. The lobbyists will be perched on the doorsteps of House and Senate as soon as Congress reconvenes.

But, if Congress does vote any aid, it may be in a more reasoned form than the outright giveaway ala the airline bailout package. And now that the insurance bailout train has been slowed, there may be time to convince Congress to include some safeguards that would help end the longtime problems of insurance redlining.

Inner-city neighborhoods still suffer from a lack of insurance at reasonable cost. Community groups, like ACORN and the Center for Community Change, pled with sponsors of the bailout legislation to at least include provisions that would require insurance companies to report where they make investments and write policies by census tract. This would give inner-city residents information with which to challenge the companies that turn their backs on entire neighborhoods in providing insurance.

Banks are required to report where they make loans under the Home Mortgage Disclosure Act (HMDA). And this data has proven to be tremendously valuable in halting discriminatory lending practices. Surely, the insurance companies can agree to provide the same kind of data on their operations, particularly if they are going to have their hands out for taxpayer bailouts.

January 16, 2002

Airline Giveaways

Never underestimate the flexibility of corporate executives who run the nation's major air carriers. Last week, they slammed file cabinet drawers shut on their favorite speeches about the glories of free markets and the horrors of government intervention, and marched to Capitol Hill, hats in hand, to ask Congress for multibillion dollar handouts of taxpayers' money. Suddenly, the federal government?so often demonized by the airlines' public relations machine had become a bosom buddy.

It was a well-timed move on the Treasury. In the wake of the suicide attacks on New York and Washington, the federal government had ordered a two-day halt to air traffic—a shutdown that admittedly hurt earnings of all airlines and the income of thousands of workers. But the bailout demands far exceeded anything that could be attributed to the brief stoppage of flights.

In fact, long before the first plane slammed into the World Trade Center, the airline industry had been in economic trouble. Business travel was down and airlines had run up huge debts in buying expensive jets and, like many other industries, faced high fuel costs.

Senator Ernest Hollings, Democrat of South Carolina, scoffed at the idea that the bailout was justified by the attacks on September 11. "The airlines told us they were going broke long before these attacks occurred while at the same time giving their executives $120 million in salaries and bonuses this year," Senator Hollings said.

But Senator Hollings' comments were pushed aside as Congress voted five billion dollars in grants to air carriers and provided for up to $10 billion in loan guarantees plus government payment of "terrorism-related" losses above $100 million and reimbursement for insurance premium increases that the airlines face.

As the bailout was voted, the layoffs of airline employees were approaching 100,000, but Congress refused to include benefits for these workers in the bailout package. Even an effort to have health insurance continued for the laid-off workers was rejected. There were some half-hearted suggestions that Congress would return to the problems of the workers later. (At least one airline—Southwest—which has consistently outperformed its bigger rivals, has managed so far to maintain its "no layoffs" record despite a big drop in passengers in the post-attack period.)

As the efforts to help laid-off airline workers were tossed aside, Representative Jay Inslee of Seattle shouted to his colleagues in the House of Representatives: "Why in this chamber do the big dogs always eat first?"

With the exception of some smaller and regional carriers, the corporate executives are taking the bailout money from the taxpayers without a thought of cutting their own salaries. A *Wall Street Journal* reporter, Susan Carey, who surveyed airline salaries came up with this report: "it is difficult to find a big carrier whose top executives are yet sharing the pain by cutting their own compensation, although such a move would have obvious symbolic value and actually could save some serious money."

The airline industry's swift and successful move for bailouts in the aftermath of the attacks is not the first, nor the last, time that the flag or a sagging economy will be used to prop up ailing corporations. If the economy continues to falter, look for other corporations to follow the example of the major air carriers. Already, there has been talk of insurance industry plans for tax breaks or similar benefits. The nation will be told that new tax cuts—like a reduction or elimination of the levy on capital gains—are necessary to spur the economy when their only real purpose would be to sweeten the financial pot for a handful of the most wealthy citizens. (The wealthiest 1 percent have financial wealth equal to the combined financial wealth of the bottom 95 percent of Americans.)

Similarly, economic downturns may become the rationale for assaults on the environment like a renewed push to drill for oil in the Arctic refuge. More corporate welfare, masked as an economic necessity, will be on a front burner. And, as in the airline bailout, the needs of workers employed by these corporations will at best be postponed or, more likely, never considered.

America can do better. Thousands of firemen, policemen, rescue workers, and ordinary citizens at the World Trade Center in New York and the Pentagon in Washington proved that on September 11. They rose to the occasion, took risks, some sacrificing their lives in reaching out to help others. Citizens helping citizens. It was a remarkable demonstration to the world of how great we can be as a people willing to sacrifice without thought of reward or personal safety.

Leaders, in both President Bush's administration and in Congress, have a responsibility to make certain that their political and economic decisions build on the spirit of these sacrifices. That may mean tougher tests for the demands of special interests—more rigorous tests than the bottom-line of corporate profits.

It means members of Congress have to stand up and take risks. Senator Peter G. Fitzgerald (R–IL) demonstrated some of that kind of courage when he cast the lone dissenting vote as the airline bailout passed the Senate, 98 to 1. Here is the way he defended his vote: "Congress should be wary of indiscriminately dishing out taxpayer dollars to prop up a failing industry without demanding something in return for taxpayers."

The corporate bailouts will keep coming, making Uncle Sam the guarantor of big business. Will the elected representatives from the White House to Capitol Hill have the courage to resist?

September 26, 2001

Time for New Reforms

Senator Jim Jeffords' party switch changed the Senate's power structure dramatically, but what hasn't changed in Washington is the increasing erosion of the public's right to know and the diminishing ability of citizens to have an impact on congressional actions.

In the reform atmosphere prevailing in the aftermath of the Watergate scandals, Congress adopted a number of rules and procedural changes in the 1970s designed to make the decision-making process of the legislative branch more open and accessible to citizens. Today, many of those reforms continue to be paid lip service, but are largely ignored as Congress increasingly returns to its old closed-door ways of doing business.

Conference committees, where differences between the House and Senate versions of legislation are reconciled, are fertile territory for backroom secret maneuvering and deal-making. Rules of both the House and Senate call for conference meetings and votes to be open to the public, but increasingly, final House-Senate conference decisions are put together in secret without formal meetings where the public and the media could observe the process.

In 1999, when the financial services legislation—involving hundreds of billions of dollars for insurance companies, banks, and securities firms—was at a critical point, Senator Phil Gramm adjourned a public session of the House-Senate conference and took a select group of conferees and Clinton administration officials into a small office to deal with the final critical details of the legislation. When a handful of representatives of consumer and community groups quietly followed the conferees into the office, they were summarily ordered out so that the negotiations could be carried out in secret.

When the president's big tax bill was in conference, the negotiations were so secret that some duly appointed conferees, who differed with the legislation, said they were not even informed of the time and place of the meetings where the legislative package was put together. So if conferees—the legislators, themselves—can be shut out, what can the public expect?

Both the House and Senate need to adopt binding rules that would prohibit the consideration of any legislation coming out of a conference committee that did not adhere strictly to the requirement for open deliberations.

Bills, particularly four- and five-hundred-page omnibus measures that come up in the last days of a congressional session when there is little time for debate, are often riddled with special-interest provisions, the authors of which frequently remain a mystery. Many times, these secret provisions and their impact are not discovered until long after Congress has departed.

Here a rule needs to be adopted that would flatly bar the consideration of any legislation on which there were no hearings and votes by the appropriate committees. A point of order would lie against any provision that did not meet this criteria.

Often, the witnesses called to testify before committees are carefully selected to stack the deck for or against particular pieces of legislation. Consumer and community groups that might raise embarrassing questions about the beneficiaries of special-interest legislation are sometimes refused a chance to testify, creating a distorted public record that deceives the public.

Major trade associations and law firms often pack hearing rooms by paying couriers to stand in line to hold all available space for the lobbyists, particularly when major legislation is being considered. When citizens arrive for the hearings, they are told that no seats are left.

This "buying" of seats in public buildings demeans the Congress. The leadership of the Senate and House should take action to end the practice.

Committee reports that accompany bills sent to the floor usually list the witnesses who have appeared before the committee. Rules should be adopted that require the committee report to also contain a list of witnesses who have formally requested an opportunity to testify, but have been refused by the committee. This would give the public some inkling of how the witness list was stacked. Such a disclosure would not only raise important questions when the legislation reaches the floor, but would serve to discourage the arbitrary rejection of witnesses.

Hearings on Senate confirmations of presidential nominations of officials for key federal offices are becoming insider games in the Senate. Some committees have adopted procedures that limit testimony to that of members of Congress and the nominee, excluding public witnesses. Some allow submission of written statements or questions, but not live testimony from public witnesses.

This means that many times representatives of citizen organizations are left without an adequate opportunity to present views on the qualifications and positions of nominees who will wield tremendous influence over wide sectors of the federal government, including offices involving health, safety, the environment, energy, civil rights, and consumer protections and rights. Rules should be adopted that would require Senate committees to demonstrate that they have sought opinions and testimony from the public.

In a shortsighted bit of economy during the 1980s, the Congress adopted rules that sharply limited the number of copies of hearing records that would be available for distribution to the public. These records are extremely valuable for citizens who want to track how legislation moves through the committees and how individual members of Congress perform on legislation that affects their daily lives. Congress needs to significantly increase the number of copies of committee hearings available and make certain that ample supplies reach libraries and schools.

Every member of Congress should be required to post his or her voting record—both on the floor and in committees—on the Internet in a form that would allow citizens to easily research votes in a database indexed by bill name, bill subject, bill title, and member name. The media do a pitifully poor job of publishing voting records. Major newspapers devote a significant number of their pages to long columns of stock prices, baseball box scores, and minute statistics on horse racing, but do not provide congressional voting records except on the most major pieces of legislation.

Senator Jeffords' party switch was described by some commentators as a "political earthquake." But what would really shake the Washington establishment—and both political parties—would be some new reforms (and enforcement of old reforms) that would open up the Congress to real scrutiny by citizens. Now is the moment to put some bipartisan muscle behind this effort.

May 30, 2001

The "Tough on Crime" Party

Sometimes, you can't tell the Washington players by the color of their jerseys. For decades, the Republicans have laid claim to the title as the "tough on crime" party. Now, a report issued by the Justice Policy Institute finds it's not the Republicans but the Democrats' recently departed President Clinton who has title to what the Institute labels as the "most punitive platform on crime" in the last two decades.

Noting that President Clinton consistently supported increased penalties and additional prison construction, the report said that 225,000 more prison inmates were added during Clinton's eight years than were added under President Reagan's watch. And President Clinton also topped President George Bush's incarceration score, adding 34,000 more during his first term (1992–1996) than were added to the prison population in the four years of Bush's single term (1988–1992).

The cost of these "tough on crime" policies is staggering. By 1997, the criminal justice system employed more than two million people at a cost of more than $70 billion annually. By the end of the Clinton administration, there were two million people in jails and prisons in the United States and 4.5 million others on probation and parole.

Sadly, today there are more people working in the criminal justice system than are working in community and social service occupations like employment, vocational, mental health, substance abuse counseling, and similar programs that might prevent crime and rehabilitate former prison inmates, according to the data analyzed by Justice Policy Institute.

African Americans, in particular, have felt the effects of the "tough on crime" politics of both major political parties. Between 1980 and 1999, the incarceration rate for African Americans more than tripled from 1,156 per 100,000 to 3,620 per 100,000.

Some of the growing prison population of African Americans is the result of tougher sentencing laws enacted in 1986 and 1988, which made the punishment for distributing crack cocaine one hundred times greater than the punishment for powdered cocaine. The result of these laws meant that persons convicted of crack cocaine offenses, who tend to be African Americans, received substantially harsher sentences than white citizens more likely to be users of the powdered form of the drug. For example, a person convicted in federal court for distributing five grams of crack cocaine receives a mandatory five-year minimum sentence while it takes five hundred grams of powdered cocaine to trigger a five-year mandatory sentence.

In 1994, the U.S. Sentencing Commission, which oversees federal sentencing guidelines, recommended that the sentencing be equalized so that the mandatory sentence would be triggered by the same amounts of cocaine whether in powdered or crack form. But Congress voted to reject the commission's recommendation and President Clinton signed the rejection into law.

Based on his record in Texas, President George W. Bush would seem to hold out little hope for reform of our criminal justice system. With Bush as governor, the state of Texas had the largest prison population among the fifty states, including California with 13 million more citizens than Texas. Last year, according to the National Coalition to End the Death Penalty, forty people were executed in Texas, twenty-nine more than Virginia, the second-place finisher in the death penalty sweepstakes.

Clearly, there needs to be a sane, fair, better administered, and less costly criminal justice system focused on treatment, rehabilitation, and prevention. Filling more expensive taxpayer-financed prisons with drug users and other nonviolent offenders serves no one but the politicians who want to posture as "tough on crime," while doing nothing to reduce root causes of crime.

President Bush has made great efforts to convince the nation that he is a "compassionate conservative." He has an opportunity to make that slogan come alive by demanding a better and fairer criminal justice system. He has his "crime fighter" badge from Texas. Now he has a chance to earn another badge as a true reformer of the criminal justice system in the United States.

March 15, 2001

Norquist-Reagan Legacy Project

Grover G. Norquist, chairman of the Reagan Legacy Project, is a man with a rapid mission. He and his colleagues want to place the former president's name on one location after another, while the ailing Gipper is still alive and accorded public sympathy for his condition. For once Reagan passes, he joins other deceased presidents on a more level playing field for such honorifics. Historically, places are named after presidents have left this world.

Norquist scored big in 1998 when he pushed through Congress the renaming, at some millions of dollars cost, of National Airport in Washington, D.C. to Reagan Washington National Airport. The hapless Democrats, beset by Clinton's Lewinsky scandal, never thought of countering with Franklin Delano Roosevelt, Lyndon B. Johnson, or a certain winner, Dwight D. Eisenhower. The four-star general was commanding the war in western Europe against Hitler, while Ronald Reagan was in Hollywood making wartime training films.

The next naming success by Norquist was the largest new government office building in town, an architectural blah with large cost overruns. Some conservatives were embarrassed by the building's excessive costs. But then Ronald

Reagan sent annual budgets with huge built-in deficits through Congress, according to the *Wall Street Journal*, which tripled the federal deficit during his eight years from about $900 billion in 1980 to over $3 trillion before he left office. He added more deficit dollars than all the previous presidents put together.

Most recently on March 4, an aircraft carrier, still under construction, was named USS Ronald Reagan. Now Mr. Norquist and allies are turning their attention to two new locations. One is the ten-dollar bill, presently printed with the picture of Alexander Hamilton. They want Reagan's smiling visage to replace Hamilton and are seeking a congressional enactment to get this done. They expect the Democrats to remain hapless.

The next project is more audacious—carving a likeness of Reagan on a piece of Mount Rushmore next to George Washington, Thomas Jefferson, Abraham Lincoln, and Theodore Roosevelt. On this move, geology comes to the rescue of the Democrats. No way, says Senator Tim Johnson (D–SD). This slab of pegmatitic granite, he is advised by Douglas A. Blankenship, a geomechanics consultant in South Dakota, is too veined with cracks and too crowded to take another sixty-foot-tall, thirty-foot-wide head. Oh well.

Ever glancing for another location, the Reagan Legacy Project has latched on to what is known as the 10th Street Overlook, a circle near L'Enfant Plaza in the nation's capital. Many millions of dollars have been raised by Reagan fans to build a monument at that location.

There is one hurdle, however. For thirty years, the retired District of Columbia historian, Louise Hutchinson, has been trying to place a monument there to America's first black man of science, the remarkable Benjamin Banneker, who was born free in 1731. Among his many achievements was the first surveying of the ten-mile square that would become Washington, D.C.

Ms. Hutchinson managed to get the overlook named Benjamin Banneker Overlook Park, but cannot get enough funds raised to implement her dream. Much of Washington, D.C.'s oldest government buildings, including the Congress, relied heavily on black slave construction workers. There are precious few monuments to African Americans in this predominantly black city.

The amazing aspect of these fervent Reagan namers is that their hero never had that kind of ego or hubris. Reagan may have been corporate-centric but he was not ego-centric. Rather, he was a jolly, shoulder shrugging amiable politician. He made people laugh about very serious matters.

In the classic book, *Reagan's Reign of Error*, by Mark Green and Gail MacColl (Pantheon, 1987), there is a collection of many of the Gipper's gaffes, such as:

• "We were told four years ago that 17 million people went to bed hungry every night. Well, that was probably true. They were all on a diet."

• "Fascism was really the basis for the New Deal."

• "A fearless mass waiting for handouts," referring to California's elderly on state Medicaid.

• In 1980 he said, "Our military is absolutely incapable of defending this country."

He once said that 80 percent of pollution comes from trees and other vegetation. Twice he publicly stated that a Trident nuclear missile once launched could be recalled.

None of this mattered to his supporters. Nor did his consistent record of supporting corporations over consumers, the environment, and workers, or tax dollars for corporate welfare over children's poverty programs.

Reagan's political legacy is that style, smile, and rhetoric prevail over substance and the actual record of things done and not done. Now if there was a monument to that triumph, it would be a great civics lesson for the country.

March 7, 2001

Bush's Tax Cut Proposal

President Bush may not realize it, but moderate and liberal members of Congress could save him a lot of grief if they voted down or sharply modified the administration's proposal for a massive tax cut.

Fueled by the excess of campaign promises, the president's $1.6 trillion tax cut threatens to return the nation to the dark days of growing deficits, higher interest rates and tight-fisted public investment policies that leave no room for dealing with the nation's most pressing social and economic problems.

Sadly, the president has put the plan forward with flimsy supporting data and with long-range, highly optimistic projections of budget surpluses that, if history is any guide, will fade under economic and political realities. The Congressional Budget Office (CBO), on whose projections the president hangs his tax cut hat, concedes that its projections are subject to wide-ranging variables that may or may not survive rising costs and unforeseen economic problems, for example, rising costs for health care or slower than anticipated economic growth.

CBO says that its projections could be off either up or down by as much as $52 billion this year, $120 billion in 2002, and $412 billion by 2006. Yet the administration and the tax cut proponents in Congress ignore the CBO's caveats, and sell the plan to the American public as if it were based on hard facts. In reality, the chance of coming up with accurate projections of budget surpluses over a ten-year period is more akin to hitting the numbers in a lottery game than it is to a mathematical science. It is the height of fiscal irresponsibility to cut taxes by $1.6 trillion on the basis of uncertain projections of surpluses that may never be achieved.

Fiscal irresponsibility may be an incurable Washington disease, but lurking under the cover of the tax cut is an attack on social and economic programs vital to the future of the nation. If budget surpluses are to be given away, the chances of dealing with long neglected core needs will be lost.

The proponents of the $1.6 trillion tax cut are essentially saying that they see no significant unmet needs in the nation now or over the next decade. It is a clear signal from the White House that the new administration has no plans to deal with serious problems of child poverty, health care, lack of affordable housing, the revival of our inner cities and depressed rural areas, public transit, and the decaying public works structure throughout the nation or other long-standing needs.

Members of Congress should wake up to the fact that the tax cut is locking the door on America's future. This lack of vision (or lack of caring) on the part of the administration will ultimately cost the nation many times the price of a $1.6 trillion tax cut.

Even if the proposal did not endanger social and economic programs, the tax cut should be rejected on the grounds that it is unfairly loaded in favor of wealthy citizens and provides no real relief for lower-income families.

More than 40 percent of the tax cut will go to the wealthiest 1 percent of the population, which is about double the share of federal taxes these citizens pay. The share of the tax cut for the top 1 percent of the income brackets will exceed the share of the tax cut received by the bottom 80 percent of the people combined.

Probably the biggest tilt in favor of the wealthy is the president's insistence that the inheritance or estate tax—levied only on the richest 2 percent of the population—be eliminated. Already, $650,000 of an estate is exempt from tax—$1.3 million for a husband and wife. Under existing law, the exemption will be raised to one million dollars in 2006 or two million for a couple.

Before falling for the propaganda about a "death tax," Congress should take a close look at the numbers. In 1998, 2.3 million persons died, but only 47,482 left estates subject to any federal estate tax. Only 1,418 of the estates that were taxable represented estates where the majority of the assets were family-owned businesses or farms. These estates paid less than 1 percent of all estate taxes.

Lobbyists for wealthy clients, nevertheless, are using the family farm and small-business issue as a smokescreen to promote the wipeout of the inheritance tax across the board at a cost of $27 billion annually to the Treasury. Obviously, the family-owned farms and businesses could be exempted from the tax without seriously reducing Treasury receipts and without giving the wealthy another loophole through which to avoid taxes.

The president has picked the wrong priority for his first real battle with the Congress. The immediate needs of the nation are not a massive tax cut that goes largely to the wealthiest citizens. The president, unfortunately, has introduced an unhealthy note of fiscal irresponsibility by proposing the giveaway of a "surplus" that is yet-to-be-achieved and that may never be achieved. Where is the old Republican tradition of fiscal responsibility? Has it been overtaken by the need to reward the corporate interests and the wealthy who finance political campaigns? And as an article in the February 7 editions of the *Wall Street Journal* points out, Mr. Bush would be rewarding himself, Vice President Dick Cheney, and other wealthy appointees in his administration.

February 14, 2001

Ashcroft and the Law

There are two questions that have not been asked about the post-election Clinton administration and the Bush nomination of John Ashcroft as attorney general.

First, why does Ashcroft want the job? In over twenty years, as Missouri state attorney general, Missouri governor, and U.S. senator, he has fought against numerous laws that, as U.S. attorney general, he would have to swear to enforce. At his Senate confirmation hearings, he declared that he accepted Roe v. Wade "as the settled law of the land," that he would aggressively enforce the civil rights laws and the ban on assault weapons. The *New York Times* noted: "Mr. Ashcroft's history of opposition and code-worded condemnation of those whose color, sexual preference, religious views and attitude toward abortions differ from his own."

The Justice Department has to enforce environmental, labor, antitrust, and corporate crime laws that the corporatist Ashcroft has little enthusiasm for, given his past record, remarks, and indifference.

Moreover, the Justice Department has kept hands off the state common law of torts, with few exceptions, while Ashcroft has been pushing for Congress to enact "tort deform" legislation that would federally preempt and weaken state laws that give wrongfully injured people rights to bring their perpetrators to civil justice.

Mr. Ashcroft separately told senators at his hearing that as a senator he was an advocate, while as attorney general he would be an enforcer to uphold all the laws, whether or not he disagreed with them. Some senators called his testimony "confirmation conversion." Ralph Neas, who is leading a coalition opposed to the Ashcroft nomination, said that the nominee was testifying as if he were a "Clinton Cabinet member." Representative Maxine Waters (D–CA) said, "I don't believe him and I don't trust him."

So, again, why does he want to be attorney general and swear to enforce laws his past record shows he abhors? The answer is what Professor Kenneth Culp Davis wrote about in his 1969 book, *Discretionary Justice*. Prosecutors and the attorney general have enormous discretion as to whether, when, how, and against whom to enforce the laws. A big country, limited budget, and policy decisions combine to give wide leeway. For example, there are ten law firms just in Washington, D.C. that have more lawyers than all the attorneys in the Justice Department Antitrust Division. This is why John Ashcroft will feel comfortable as attorney general and why he must wonder why he was not interrogated in detail about this pivotal issue of enforcement discretion.

Second, why did Clinton wait until after the election for his environmental and consumer protection agencies to do what they should have done many months ago? Medical privacy, food and job safety, truck diesel pollution control standards, public lands protection from commercial logging, drinking water controls on arsenic, labeling, and right to know (lead emissions). These and other regulations have been in the works for many months, even years. Why so late? They are very popular decisions for most Americans.

The answer: Issuing them before the election would imperil the raising of big campaign money from corporate fat cats and invite massive Republican television advertisements distorting these long overdue and proper police powers as big government. So now, these regulations appear rushed, suspect, and vulnerable because Gore did not run on them for validation when he won the popular vote.

Makes you wonder where the traditional values of forthrightness and fortitude are these days in politics.

January 30, 2001

Federal Inheritance Tax Giveaway

Never doubt the importance of language in politics.

In labeling as "death taxes" what should properly be understood as an Equality and Fairness Fee or an Anti-Dynasty Tax, corporate-funded think tanks and their congressional allies have launched a retrograde initiative to repeal the federal inheritance tax.

Earlier this month, the House of Representatives succumbed to the pressures of the corporate lobby and passed legislation to eliminate inheritance taxes by a deplorable 279 to 136 margin. The Senate is expected to take up the matter soon. President Clinton has, properly, promised to veto such legislation. But even if Clinton stands by his veto threat, the gathering momentum behind the call for elimination means expressed citizen outrage will be necessary to stop it from becoming law in the years ahead.

The logic of the inheritance tax is unassailable and deeply rooted in American history. As Citizens for Tax Justice points out, it "helps reduce concentrations of power and promotes equality of economic opportunity—to 'break up the swollen fortunes of the rich,' as Congress put it back in 1916 when the estate tax was first adopted."

The past two decades have seen a startling concentration of wealth in this country (and worldwide). To take one of the many staggering illustrations of the wealth accumulation at the top of the hierarchy, the wealth of the four hundred richest U.S. families grew by an average of $940 million each between 1997 and 1999—an average increase in wealth of $1,287,671 per day.

The role of the inheritance tax is to counterbalance, modestly, the ability of the very rich and superrich to create family dynasties in which family members by virtue of birth and birth alone have insuperable economic advantages over the rest of society. We live, or should live, in a land of equal opportunity, not a feudal regime in which life position is determined by hereditary birth.

Of course the inheritance tax only achieves this aim in small part, and is only one small part of the policy package needed as we strive to realize our democratic and egalitarian ambitions, but it is an important and necessary measure.

In practice, as is true with many taxes, there are escapes that enable the rich to avoid paying all or even most that they should—but that is a reason to fix it, not abolish it. The tax does successfully raise $27 billion a year.

And it is the most progressive of taxes. Estates under $675,000 (soon to rise to $1 million)—and effectively double that amount for spouses—are exempt from the tax. The tax is collected only from the richest 1.4 percent—and two-thirds of the inheritance tax revenues comes from the wealthiest .2 percent.

It is the very success and underlying logic of the inheritance tax that makes it such a concern for the corporate lobby. They want to preserve privilege, defend the concentration of wealth and delegitimize the government's role in promoting equality.

But no one wants to say that.

So the Heritage Foundation, the Cato Institute, Americans for Tax Reform, and other corporate-backed organizations spin fanciful tales of the immense burdens imposed by the inheritance tax on family-owned businesses and farmers.

Robert McIntyre's Citizens for Tax Justice (CTJ), one of the few reliable sources for credible information on tax policy, makes short shrift of these arguments. "The truth is that less than one in twenty farmers leaves a taxable estate," CTJ notes. "Even for the small number of farm estates that do pay any tax, the typical tax payment is only about $5,000. Only 0.5 percent of total estate taxes is attributable to farm assets. Nonfarm family businesses are also only a small part of the estate tax."

The story is similar for small businesses, CTJ explains. "Nonfarm family businesses are also a small part of the estate tax—less than 3 percent of total assets for estates worth less than $2.5 million. Only for the very largest estates does the business share of total assets become significant—and these businesses are hardly small." Moreover, the tax code already includes special breaks to keep family businesses going, including rules to permit family businesses to value assets at less than market value and to spread inheritance tax payments out over a long period of time.

Whether or not the progressive estate tax will remain in the tax code has virtually nothing to do with the viability of small businesses and family farmers. What is at stake are fundamental American norms of fairness and equality, and whether we as a society will continue to use one of our most direct and effective—if all-too-modest—tools to put a brake on the hyper-concentration of riches. Democracy or avaricious plutocracy, that is the question.

To get the real story on tax issues, contact Citizens for Tax Justice, 1311 L Street NW, Washington, D.C. 20005, www.ctj.org.

June 28, 2000

Dreary Campaigns

The major presidential candidates are grinding through the various television and radio press interviews and the town meetings with their three-minute, daily, redundant speeches and highly predictable replies to mostly predictable questions. That is what their advance people are supposed to accomplish.

But what is remarkable is that both the national and local television questioners give them this predictability without the candidates even asking. Every four years, campaigns revolve around half a dozen issues that are drably questioned and drearily answered. This year, some of the main issues are education, taxes, social security, Medicare, and health insurance.

Under education—the sub issues are class size, teachers' salaries, computer linkups, and vouchers. Notice the gap that envelopes what kind of education the children deserve. Wouldn't a question about the need for civic education to develop both the civic skills and motivation to participate in a democratic civil society advance the election year enlightenment? Never asked.

Under taxes—the sub issues are reducing tax rates and returning alleged surpluses back to the taxpayers. Wouldn't questions about a different kind of tax system, such as a wealth tax or a pollution tax be useful? And how about asking about the candidates' take on taxpayer assets—such as the public lands, government giveaways to big drug companies of taxpayer-funded and developed medicines, or the massive bonanzas known as corporate welfare?

Then there are the questions that could lead to some action. For example, the leaders of both parties in Congress have declined to place the voting records of each member of the House and the Senate on the Internet in clearly retrievable fashion. Asking whether the candidates favor this important voter access to their representatives' actual performance in Congress, in contrast to their propaganda and sugary slogans, might quickly get these voters online to invigorate and make concrete election year evaluations. Never asked.

Even the questions from the town meetings, apart from those that are planted, often reflect the narrow covey of "issues" that the candidates and the ditto media trumpet. There is some reluctance among citizens not to stray from the familiar subjects in the news when they stand to ask.

Yet there are numerous polls that show people want all kinds of changes from the existing status quo—for example, they want much stronger enforcement against environmental, consumer, and workplace crimes and frauds by corporations. In a phrase, people want the fairness that comes from basic corporate reform.

The media is supposed to be able to ask these fundamental questions about the concentration of power and wealth and its effect on people's everyday lives. But these "power questions" are never asked. Nor are questions offered about ways to give people more leverage in their roles as voters, workers, taxpayers, consumers, and small saver-investors.

Too much power in the hands of the few has further weakened our democracy in the past twenty years. People need stronger civic tools to band together, learn together, and act together to make the Big Boys behave.

One group, the Florence Fund, is trying to do something about raising fundamental issues about corporate power. It is placing notices in the *New York Times* and other newspapers that replace myths with facts and pose actual questions for the candidates.

One set of questions came from prize-winning, veteran reporter Morton Mintz who spent many years at the *Washington Post*. Mr. Mintz's sample questions and compelling observations by others about this year's campaigns and candidates can be accessed on the Internet at TomPaine.com: Money and Politics, Environment, Media Criticism, History.

At the least, the Florence Fund's efforts should make this election year more interesting and keep fewer citizens from sending the message "Wake Us Up When It's Over."

January 25, 2000

Limited Debates

On January 6, 2000, the Commission on Presidential Debates (CPD) announced that there would be three presidential debates and one vice presidential debate in October 2000 at different locations around the country.

The commission has an official-sounding name, but it is, in fact, a private organization run by the Republican and Democratic parties, led by co-chairmen Paul G. Kirk, Jr. (Democrat) and Frank J. Fahrenkopf, Jr. (Republican), and heavily funded by corporate money, which in 1996 included the tobacco and auto companies.

Both Mr. Kirk and Mr. Fahrenkopf represent corporate clients and the latter is well known as a chief lobbyist for the gambling industry.

The commission laid down three criteria for determining which candidates are invited to the debates, which are sure to be nationally televised on several networks.

These criteria are:

1) the candidate must meet the constitutional requirements of being at least thirty-five years of age, a natural-born citizen and resident of the United States for fourteen years, and otherwise eligible under the Constitution;

2) the candidate must be on enough state ballots to have "at least a mathematical chance of securing an Electoral College majority in the 2000 general election";

3) the candidate must have "a level of support of at least 15 percent of the national electorate as determined by five selected national public opinion polling organizations, using the average of those organizations' most recent publicly reported results at the time of the determination."

The five polling groups include the joint ventures between newspapers such as the *Washington Post, New York Times, Wall Street Journal,* and the television networks—NBC, CBS, ABC, and CNN.

Mr. Kirk and Mr. Fahrenkopf declared themselves satisfied that their "nonpartisan" commission has established an approach that "is both clear and predictable." Unfortunately, it is too clear and predictable for smaller party presidential candidates who will be excluded from the debates leaving only the two major-party candidates with the field to themselves. The commission is really not "nonpartisan;" it is "bipartisan" and designed to protect, as it did in 1996, the debates for its dominant Two-Party System.

These exclusionary rules are nothing new. For years the Republican and Democratic parties have conspired in one state legislature after another to enact laws that create huge barriers (often tens of thousands of signatures on petitions plus other harassments) to make sure that small political starts never have a chance to have a chance. These barriers are unique in comparison to the easy ballot access requirements in Canada and several other western nations.

So the two parties are acting in their grand exclusionary tradition—one which in the business world would subject them to antitrust prosecution.

There is yet another convoluted complication to the commission's year 2000 criteria—the reliance on polling organizations whose news and editorial bureaus can determine whether to report or not to report on third-party candidates. If a near news blackout prevails, then the polling arm can report that the candidate doesn't register much in the polls.

Why would the commercial news media agree to such an arrangement and expose themselves to legitimate charges that they are compromising their alleged detachment or objectivity? The commission's arrangement inexorably draws these media organizations into a partisan pit. Indeed, some of the moderators for the debates may come from these same news organizations. The matrix becomes more intricate.

When the commission was asked at a news conference "Why fifteen percent?," the reply was that was its fairest judgment in order to keep the debates manageable. No one representing the executive suites of the mass media was around to ask, "Why do these giant media corporations leave the number of nationally televised debates up to the two major parties?"

After all the time devoted to soap operas, sports, game shows, and advertisements, is there no time within these very profitable television and radio stations, which use our public airwaves free of charge, to air more accessible debates in the fall?

Hardly had Mr. Kirk and Mr. Fahrenkopf left their heavily attended news conference when Anheuser-Busch company announced that it had been selected by the commission as "a national sponsor of the four presidential debates. . . as well as the sole sponsor of the debate schedules for October 17 at Washington University in St. Louis." (The latter will be paid for with a contribution of $550,000.)

Imagine a beer company financing the presidential debates in the world's longest lasting, richest democracy. Will Anheuser-Busch haul out the free kegs at Saint Louis's bars in celebration?

January 11, 2000

Congress Pulls the Shades on the Net

The information age, we have been told repeatedly, is the signal characteristic of the modern political economy. Technology will liberate and advance the voices and impact of all people as it decentralizes power, say numerous books and essays.

Well, let's examine those articles of faith in two areas—congressional information and federal government contracting.

For years, less than 1 percent of U.S. Congress members would give the folks back home an annual summary of their voting records. Citizens had to research the cumbersome congressional record or other compilations for hours to come close to learning what the senator or representative could put inside one envelope every December.

Along comes the Internet and the proliferation of congressional web sites. Members of Congress filled them with their often self-serving messages. Yet something is missing: their voting records.

Voting records are key to the democratic process. Citizens must have ready and easy access to them as they are essential to understanding the record behind the political rhetoric and to holding politicians accountable.

The software and hardware technology is available. But, remarkably, Congress has not placed on the Internet a searchable database of congressional votes, indexed by bill name, bill subject, bill title, member name, etc. This database would be inexpensive to produce and simple to maintain.

Does technology have its own imperative? Not like concentrated congressional power does.

What about taxpayers trying to find out about the hundreds of billions of dollars in federal government contracts with business vendors? Here is the summary experience of one taxpayer, who wanted to conduct an exercise in self-education and started calling both contractors and government agencies that were on a list the *Washington Post* publishes every Monday in its business section.

First, he called the contractors, companies that provide products and services to government agencies. These include, among other things, landscaping, computer hardware, building construction, and publishing. He was quite surprised. Several of the government contractors had no listed telephone number, while others only had voice mail, and messages weren't returned.

When somebody did answer, the replies varied from "What business is it of yours?" to recommending that he call the contracting agency or file a freedom-of-information request from the agency. Some respondents said they couldn't locate a copy of the contract. Some said, "Sure, good-bye," or told him they would call him back, and never did.

The outcome of dozens of calls: Not one copy of a contract that taxpayers paid for and in many cases not even the courtesy of a telephone reply.

He next started calling the government agencies that received the products and services. Here he at least talked to human beings, many of whom said they could not even respond until he gave them the contract number. It was not sufficient that he gave them the description and date of the contract as it appeared in the *Washington Post.*

Some departments did not know which of their field offices or subdivisions did the contracting. Many of the departments—such as the Department of Justice, the Department of Labor, and the Army Corps of Engineers—said he would have to file a freedom-of-information request.

That advice doesn't guarantee a copy in a reasonable amount of time for a reasonable copying price. It just starts what often is a laborious, time-consuming process.

At least the Justice Department gave him the contract number and the name of the person to whom a formal information request should be directed, but there was no assurance that he would get a copy.

There is an obvious solution to difficulties in obtaining public contracts between government and business, whether they be corporate welfare; civilian and military services and products rendered; technology transfers; leases of public lands with oil, gas, coal, timber, and other natural resources; or even governmental functions themselves that are corporatized. The Clinton administration, which regularly boasts about the need to wire everything and everybody to the Internet, should place all contracts, grants, and other agreements over a minimum dollar sum on the Internet.

Then there would be massively greater public knowledge, scrutiny, and scholarship about these truly momentous agreements that make up much of what the federal government does every day. Citizens would be appraised much earlier through the media and through the Internet of excessive charges, unconscionable taxpayer assets being given away, and just bad policies.

As of now, the Clintonites have shown no interest in forging a comprehensive Internet disclosure policy in this area. It is not part of their reinventing government program.

Once again, available technology does not have its own imperative. Cliquish corporate/political power holds the reins. You may wish to write the president about this or e-mail him at President@whitehouse.gov.

December 13, 1999

Shaking the Money Tree

The brazen, bullying Senator Mitch McConnell (R–KY) is at it again. Only this time he is trying to intimidate a group of big business executives who are urging Congress to enact one important campaign finance reform—banning the unlimited "soft money" contributions to political parties.

In an ocean of election money corruption and deepening public cynicism, a group of corporate executives known as the Committee for Economic Development (CED) took a stand against a widening loophole that is being filled by a Niagara of money from corporations. Under existing law, corporations and unions cannot give money directly to candidates for public office, but they are not prohibited from giving money to their political parties.

This is a unique and commendable position by some leaders of major companies, especially since their lobbyists are always on Capitol Hill demanding various sorts of special privileges. These business leaders issued a report on the campaign finance laws in March deploring the corruptive impact on our democracy of the hundreds of millions of dollars pouring into political parties. While the report also recommended increasing the limits on individual contributions to $3,000 from $1,000, its authors did come down hard on "soft money" slush funds.

CED President Charles Kolb said: "We're tired of being hit up and shaken down. Politics ought to be about something besides hitting up companies for more and more money." The committee's report also concluded: "The suspicion of corruption deepens public cynicism and diminishes public confidence in Government. More important, these activities raise the likelihood of actual corruption."

The sleazy campaign fundraising game, as practiced by the major parties, is a marriage between the bribers (the givers) and the extorters (the takers). Senator McConnell, as chairman of the National Republican Senatorial Committee, is known in Washington circles as a very aggressive "demand" politician when it comes to shaking the money tree.

Through years of giving big business whatever it wants—be it tax holidays, immunity from lawsuits, corporate welfare handouts, or nonenforcement of the laws designed to rein in business abuses—he provided a mutually beneficial quid pro quo.

So it was not surprising to learn that Senator McConnell was upset. He wrote a threatening letter to ten business executives suggesting that they resign from the CED to delegitimate the CED's advocacy of what he called "antibusiness" speech controls. When business executives receive a letter like that, they sense a subtext that the author may take it out on them on matters dear to their interests on Capitol Hill.

Nonetheless, three leaders of the reform group replied to the senator, saying they had no intention of backing down "on an issue they believe threatens the vitality of our participatory democracy." Then they added acidly: "We find it ironic that you are such a fervent defender of First Amendment freedoms but seem intent to stifle our efforts to express publicly our concerns about a campaign finance system that many feel is out of control."

Well, well, well. This is a rare burst of business statesmanship from the private sector and one that intends to keep growing. "What we've been doing as a group of business leaders is obviously beginning to have an impact," declared Edward A. Kangas, chief executive of the giant accounting firm Deloitte and Touche. He told the *New York Times* that their goal was to have three hundred executives endorse their campaign finance proposal by late autumn.

Clearly, there is strength in numbers, and the larger the number, the less likely that the McConnells of the Senate and House of Representatives will seek retaliation.

The *Times* mentioned what many insiders knew—namely, that two billionaires, Warren E. Buffett and Jerome Kohlberg, have been talking up reform for a long time with their colleagues in the informal get-togethers where social becomes political.

Who knows? Maybe the American people will be witnessing the emergence of a dramatic collision between some political extorters and those who played the game of influencing politicians with showers of money and are now partially fed up. Maybe, just maybe, this struggle, if reported in more depth and with greater frequency, will tip the scales in favor of favorable votes on the campaign reform bills heading for a vote this month and next on the Senate and House floors. For more information on this battle, go to www.Citizen.org.

Related sites:

www.ced.org/—Committee for Economic Development

www.senate.gov/~mcconnell/—Senator Mitch McConnell's Senate home page.

September 3, 1999

Al Gore Sells Out

Few politicians have shrunken as fast, while rising in power, as Vice President Al Gore. In terms of standing up for what he believes, Gore is a shadow of his former self as Representative and Senator from Tennessee, although he never came close to the political courage of his father, also a senator. Gore senior, for example, spoke out for civil rights in the '60s when southern legislators were not supposed to do so.

Granted, the status of being vice president does turn many vice presidents into sycophants for presidents who seem to need, as does Bill Clinton, daily plaudits from his next in command. But Clinton chose Gore as his running mate in 1992 knowing that Gore had written a popular book on the environment filled with specific stands on one issue after another. Gore's clear expectation was that he was not going to be muzzled.

What Gore has done is to go one step lower—he muzzles himself, and does it with a forceful contradiction of his past political positions. For example, a few months ago, he journeyed to Detroit to prostrate himself before an audience of auto executives, assuring them that they need not worry about Al Gore. Indeed, he and Bill Clinton have largely abandoned law enforcement regarding safer vehicles, more fuel efficient engines, or lowering truck pollution.

Reagan did not do much worse, nor did Bush. The auto companies are making more profits than they did when those Republicans were in the White House and the engineering improvements are longer overdue for application to new vehicles.

Earlier this month, the *Washington Post* headlined a story—"Gore Woos Wall St. with the Help of Investment Insiders." He is wooing Wall Street, the article noted, because it is a "source of not only potential campaign contributions but also credibility in the corporate world...Wall Street executives and a Gore aide said the vice president in turn has reached out to Wall Street officials to solicit advice on economic issues and vet his speeches on business matters. Executives have encouraged him to tone down the environment rhetoric."

In a world of global warming, destroyed tropical forests, polluted air, water, and soil, enormous land erosion, the big business boys can't stand rhetoric, much less action. In the midst of making himself fully acceptable to the financiers and industrialists, Gore is even losing his rhetoric fast.

In six years, Gore has made no speeches or statements criticizing the nuclear power boondoggle. He has not pressed formidable programs in his speeches for solar energy or other renewable or efficient forms of power that are benign to the environment. Instead he has condoned huge taxpayer subsidies to the atomic power industry, including charging ratepayers for the "stranded costs" of bad and wasteful nuclear power plants owned by the electric utilities.

One would think that dramatic and long overdue policies for energy conservation applied to vehicles, appliances, lighting, heating, and air conditioning systems would not be moves too bold for a vice president observing huge oil import percentages and tens of billions of naval and air force tax dollars being spent over Middle East oil.

But then Gore cannot get himself to criticize corporations at all. Contrary to his former beliefs that international trade agreements should not jeopardize environmental health, Gore played the automatic role of defending NAFTA and GATT, which allow polluters to downgrade and erode environmental conditions and policies.

Gore may be called a Pavlovian politician. By displaying obeisance to corporate power, he and Clinton have been rewarded. They win special-interest, money-saturated elections and avoid having the varieties of corporate power arrayed against them as would occur if they were progressive political figures having what Professor James MacGregor Burns called "transforming leadership" qualities.

The plutocracy and the oligarchy condition Gore's responses and he acquires ever more political power. This explains why Gore loves to spend his time with business executives from Silicon Valley to Wall Street and, unlike Jimmy Carter, why he has declined for six years to address an audience of citizen groups, representing millions of citizen-members, in a hotel ballroom a few blocks from the White House.

January 12, 1999

Index

About the Author

Ralph Nader is a citizen advocate, lawyer and author. Born in Winsted, Connecticut on Febuary 27, 1934, Nader is the co-founder of numerous public interest groups including Public Citizen, Critical Mass, Commercial Alert, and the Center for Study of Responsive Law. In 2004 Nader is mounting his second bid for president of the United States, this time as an independent candidate, after running on the Green Party ticket in 2000. He continues to be a relentless force for grassroots activism and democratic change in the United States.